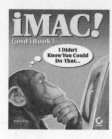

Internet Complete
Second Edition

SYBEX®

SAN FRANCISCO ▸ PARIS ▸ DÜSSELDORF ▸ SOEST ▸ LONDON

Associate Publisher: Cheryl Applewood
Contracts and Licensing Manager: Kristine O'Callaghan
Developmental Editor: Tracy Brown
Compilation Editor: Linda Orlando
Editors: Dann McDorman, Bronwyn Erickson, Jan Fisher, Ed Copony, Chad Mack, Laurie Stewart, Kim Wimpsett, Rebecca Rider, Brenda Frink, Malka Geffen, Anamary Ehlen
Compilation Technical Editor: Mark J. Kovach
Technical Editors: Tyler Regas, Rima Sonia Regas, Dana Jones, Gary Masters, Susan Glinert, Piroz Mohseni, Sheryl McKeown, Tom Maxwell
Book Designer: Maureen Forys, Happenstance Type-O Rama
Electronic Publishing Specialists: Judy Fung, Nila Nichols
Compilation Production Editor: Nathan Whiteside
Production Editors: Blythe Woolston, Shannon Murphy, Colleen Strand, David Zielonka, Lisa Reardon, Susan Berge, Charles Mathews, Catherine Morris, Jennifer Durning, Bronwyn Erickson, Michael Tom
Proofreaders: Camera Obscura, Nanette Duffy, Erika Donald, Andrea Fox, Laurie O'Connell, Lindy M. Clinton, Ho Lin, Suzanne Stein, Sarah Tannehill
Indexer: Nancy Guenther
Cover Designer: DesignSite

TRADEMARKS:

ACKNOWLEDGMENTS

This book represents the dedicated work of many people, both inside and outside Sybex. Developmental Editors Tracy Brown and Sherry Bonelli defined the book's overall structure and content. Nathan Whiteside, Production Editor, coordinated everyone's efforts, solved the many idiosyncratic problems a book like this poses, and kept the project in motion with a steady and cheerful hand. The Electronic Publishing Specialists, Judy Fung and Nila Nichols, deserve a loud round of applause for turning simple words and images into the pages you are now reading, and for being graceful even while under incredible pressure.

The Editor, Linda Orlando, kept everyone amused while also making sure that the text and illustrations were both consistent and correct, and Technical Editor Mark Kovach reviewed the book for technical accuracy with lightning speed and a gentle touch. A big thank-you goes out to Teresa Trego and Leslie Light for their patience and guidance in this project. Liz Paulus, Dan Schiff, and Malka Geffen also helped in various ways to keep the project moving.

Our most important thanks go to the contributors who agreed to have their work excerpted into *Internet Complete*: Christian Crumlish, Richard Sherman, Alan Neibauer, Alan Simpson, Bob LeVitus, Guy Hart-Davis and Rhonda Holmes, Gene Weisskopf, E. Stephen Mack and Jannan Platt Saylor, Deborah S. Ray and Eric J. Ray, Gayle Ehrenman and Michael Zulich, and Pat Coleman and Gene Weisskopf. A special thanks goes to Christian Crumlish, Chris Collins, and Laura Arendal, who wrote chapters specifically for this book.

Finally, thanks to the teams of editors, developmental editors, production editors, and technical editors who helped put together the various books from which *Internet Complete* was compiled. Without the efforts of all of these people, this book would not exist.

CONTENTS AT A GLANCE

CONTENTS

Part II ▶ Browsing and More   115

Part III ▸ Alternative Connection Methods   273

Chapter 12   Let AOL Rock Your World!   275

Chapter 13   WebTV   303

INTRODUCTION

Internet Complete is a unique and valuable reference tool for any Internet user—valuable both for the breadth of its content and for its low price. This compilation of information from a dozen other Sybex books provides comprehensive coverage of the Internet and related hardware topics. This book, unique in the computer book world, was created with several goals in mind:

▶ Offering a thorough guide that covers all the important user-level features of the Internet at an affordable price

▶ Helping you become familiar with essential Internet topics so that you can choose your next Internet book with confidence

▶ Acquainting you with some of our best authors—their writing styles and teaching skills, and the level of expertise they bring to their books—so you can easily find a match for your interests as you delve deeper into the Internet

Internet Complete is designed to provide all the essential information you'll need to get the most from the Internet, while at the same time inviting you to explore the even greater depths and wider coverage of material in the original books.

If you've read other computer "how-to" books, you've seen that there are many possible approaches to the task of showing how to use software and hardware effectively. The books from which Internet Complete was compiled represent a range of the approaches to teaching that Sybex and its authors have developed—from the quick, concise No Experience Required style to the exhaustively thorough Mastering style. As you read through various chapters of Internet Complete, you'll see which approach works best for you. You'll also see what these books have in common: a commitment to clarity, accuracy, and practicality.

You'll find in these pages ample evidence of the high quality of Sybex's authors. Unlike publishers who produce "books by committee," Sybex authors are encouraged to write in individual voices that reflect their own experience with the software at hand and with the evolution of today's personal computers. Every book represented here is the work of a single writer or a pair of close collaborators; when Christian Crumlish, for example, says, "Throughout this book I'll explain the jargon you hear when people start babbling about the Net...," you know you are getting the benefit of his direct experience. Likewise, all the chapters in this book are based on their authors' firsthand knowledge and experience about the Internet.

In adapting the various source materials for inclusion in *Internet Complete*, the compiler preserved these individual voices and perspectives. Chapters were edited only to minimize duplication, to omit coverage of non-Internet information, and to add new information so you're sure to get coverage of cutting-edge developments. A few sections were also edited for length so that other important Internet subjects could be included.

Who Can Benefit from This Book?

Internet Complete is designed to meet the needs of a wide range of computer users. Therefore, while you could read this book from beginning to end, you may not need to read every chapter. The Contents and the Index will guide you to the subjects you're looking for.

Beginners   Even if you have only a little familiarity with computers and their basic terminology, this book will get you up and running on the Internet.

Intermediate users   Chances are, you already know how to do routine tasks in e-mail or the Internet. You also know that there is always room to learn about working more effectively, and you want to get up to speed on new Internet features. Throughout this book you'll find instructions for just about anything you want to do. Nearly every chapter has nuggets of knowledge from which you can benefit.

How This Book Is Organized

Internet Complete has twenty five chapters and three appendixes:

Part I: Internet Basics   In the first five chapters of the book, we'll introduce you to basic Internet concepts, get you connected, and teach you how to use e-mail and useful e-mail tools. If you've never used the Internet before, Part I will help get you oriented before you start browsing.

Part II: Browsing and More   In Part II, you'll learn how to get around the Web. Chapters 6 and 7 will teach you the basic features of Internet Explorer and Netscape. In Chapter 8 you'll learn how to use search techniques to locate the information you need. Chapters 9, 10, and 11 will teach you about other useful Internet activities such as FTP, newsgroups, multimedia, and more.

Part III: Alternative Connection Methods   This section explores various ways to connect to the Internet other than through a standard ISP. Chapter 12 will show you some of the ways you can use AOL, such as searching for Web sites, playing games, chatting, and shopping. Chapter 13 introduces you to the wonders of WebTV, and Chapter 14 delves into accessing e-mail and the Web using your Palm VII palm organizer. Chapter 15 shows you how to browse using an iMac and iBook, and Chapter 16 talks about connecting from the road.

Part IV: Fun Stuff   The four chapters in this section give you all the information you need to get started shopping, buying, playing music, and playing games on the Web. (Tell the truth–this is the real reason you bought this book, isn't it?)

Part V: Creating a Web Page   Once you've spent some time surfing the Web, you may want to post your own Web site. No worries: the chapters in Part V give you a great introduction to all of the issues you'll need to consider. You'll learn about Web site planning and design; basic HTML tags; and Microsoft's easy-to use Web design tool, FrontPage 2000.

Part VI: Internet User's Reference   The appendixes are designed for quick lookup–or casual browsing. There's an alphabetical reference to some useful keywords in AOL, a comprehensive listing of HTML tags to use in your Web page design, and a glossary of Internet terminology that you may encounter.

A Few Typographical Conventions

When an operation requires a series of choices from menus or dialog boxes, the ➤ symbol is used to guide you through the instructions, like this: "Select Programs ➤ Accessories ➤ System Tools ➤ System Information." The items the ➤ symbol separates may be menu names, toolbar icons, check boxes, or other elements of the Windows interface—any place you can make a selection.

`This typeface` is used to identify Internet URLs and HTML code, and **boldface type** is used whenever you need to type something into a text box.

You'll find these types of special notes throughout the book:

TIP

You'll see a lot of these—quicker and smarter ways to accomplish a task, which the authors have based on their experience using the Internet.

NOTE

You'll see these Notes, too. They usually represent alternate ways to accomplish a task or some additional information that needs to be highlighted.

WARNING

In a very few places you'll see a Warning like this one. When you see a warning, pay attention to it!

YOU'LL ALSO SEE SIDEBAR BOXES LIKE THIS

These boxed sections provide added explanations of special topics that are noted briefly in the surrounding discussion, but that you may want to explore separately. Each sidebar has a heading that announces the topic so you can quickly decide whether it's something you need to know about.

For More Information...

See the Sybex Web site, `www.sybex.com`, to learn more about all the books that went into *Internet Complete*. On the site's Catalog page, you'll find links to any book you're interested in.

We hope you enjoy this book and find it useful. Happy surfing!

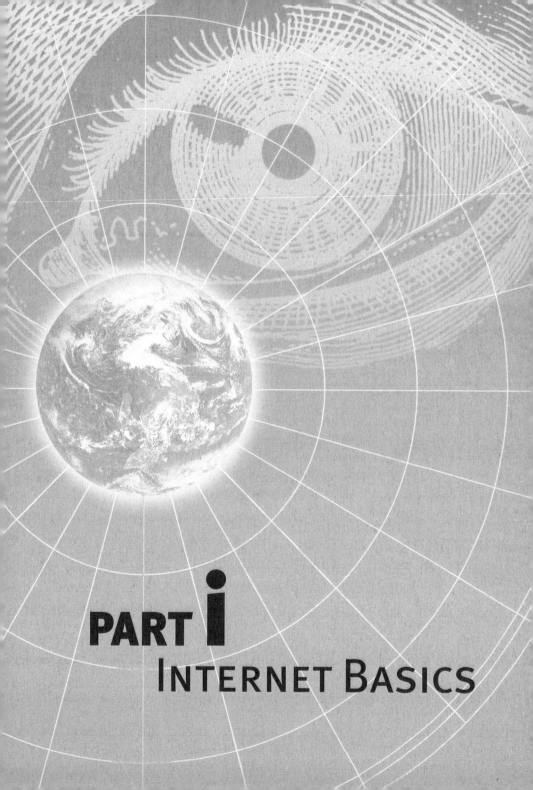

PART i
INTERNET BASICS

Chapter 1

UNDERSTANDING THE INTERNET

In this book there are no dumb questions. Everybody talks about the Internet and the World Wide Web, but most people don't really know what the Internet is or what the differences between the Internet and the Web are. One reason for this is that the Internet looks different depending on how you come across it and what you do with it. Another reason is that everyone talks about it as if it's actually a network, like a local network in someone's office or even a large global network such as America Online. The truth is, it's something different. A beast unto itself. The Internet is really a way for computers to communicate.

Throughout this book I'll explain the jargon you hear when people start babbling about the Net, so you can figure out for yourself what you want to learn about and what you'd like to ignore. Notice that I just used the word *Net* and not *Internet*.

Adapted from *The Internet: No experience required, Second Edition*, by Christian Crumlish
ISBN 0-7821-2385-6   470 pages $19.99

For the most part, the words are synonymous, although some people use the word Net to refer to just about any aspect of the global internetworking of computers. (Check out Appendix C—a glossary of Internet terms—to become more familiar with Internet jargon.)

As long as a computer or small network can "speak" the Internet lingo (or *protocols*, to be extra formal about it) to other machines, then it's "on the Internet." Of course, the computer also needs a modem or network connection and other hardware to make contact, too. But, regardless of the hardware needs, if the Internet were a language, it wouldn't be French or Farsi or Tagalog or even English. It would be Esperanto.

Having said that, I might backtrack and allow that there's nothing wrong with thinking of the Internet as if it were a single network. It certainly behaves like one in a lot of important ways. But this can be misleading. No one "owns" the Internet. No one even really runs it. And no one can turn it off.

COMMUNICATING THROUGH E-MAIL OR DISCUSSION GROUPS

In addition to being a network of interconnected computers, the Internet is also a collection of different tools and devices for communicating and storing information in a retrievable form.

Take e-mail, for example. If you work in an office with a local area network, then chances are you have an e-mail account and can communicate with people in your office by sending them messages through the company's internal system. (See Chapters 3, 4, and 5.) However, office e-mail is not the Internet.

Similarly, if you have an account at America Online and you send a message to someone else at AOL, you're still not using the Internet. But if your office network has a *gateway* to the Internet and you send e-mail to someone who does not work at your office, then you're sending that mail over the Internet. Likewise, if you send a message from your AOL account to someone at CompuServe, or elsewhere, then again you are sending messages over the Internet (see Figure 1.1).

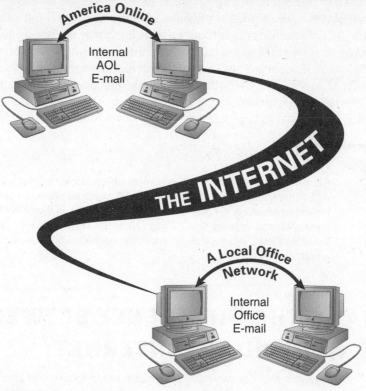

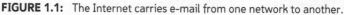

FIGURE 1.1: The Internet carries e-mail from one network to another.

NOTE

A *gateway* is a computer, or the program running on it, that transfers files (or e-mail messages, or commands) from one network to another.

But from your point of view, the Internet is not just a collection of networks all talking to each other. A single computer can also participate in the Internet by connecting to a network or service provider that's connected to the Internet. And while the local office network I described and the big commercial online services are not themselves the Internet, they can and often do provide access through their gateways to the Internet. (I cover online services in Chapter 2, "Choosing an ISP.")

All of this can be confusing to first-time Internet users (universally referred to as *newbies*). Say you have an AOL account and you join one of the AOL *discussion groups* (bulletin boards). It may not be obvious to you right away whether you're talking in an internal venue—one accessible only to AOL members—or in a public Internet newsgroup. One of the benefits of an online service is the way various functions, including e-mail, Internet access, and online content, are brought together seamlessly so that they appear to be part of the same program running on your computer.

NOTE

A *bulletin board* is a public discussion area where people can post messages—without sending them to anyone's individual e-mail address—that can be viewed by anyone who enters the area. Other people can then reply to posted messages, and ongoing discussions can ensue. On CompuServe, a bulletin board is called a *forum*. On the Internet, the equivalent areas are called *newsgroups*.

WHAT'S THE DIFFERENCE BETWEEN THE WEB AND THE INTERNET?

Nowadays, most of the hype about the Internet is focused on the World Wide Web. It has existed for less than ten years, but it has been the fastest growing and most popular part of the Net for many of those years (except, perhaps, for the voluminous flow of e-mail around the globe). But what is the Web (also called *WWW* or *w3*) and is it the same thing as the Internet? Well, to answer the second question first: yes and no. Technically, the Web is just part of the Internet—or, more properly, a way of getting around part of the Internet. But it's a big part because a lot of the Internet that's not (strictly speaking) part of the Web can still be reached with a Web browser.

So the Web, on one level, is an *interface*. A window on the Net. A way of getting to where you're going. Its appeal derives from three different benefits:

▶ It disguises the gobbledygook that passes for Internet addresses and commands.

▶ It wraps up most of the different features of the Internet into a single interface used by Web applications.

▶ It allows you to see pictures, and even hear sounds or watch movies (if your computer can handle it), along with your helpings of text.

TIP

To play sounds or movies, your computer needs a sound card, speakers, and some kind of software (such as Microsoft Media Player 7.0 or QuickTime 4.1 for Macintosh or Windows). For movies, you'll also want a lot of memory (or else the movies will play herky-jerky).

It helps to know a little bit about the history of the Net to understand why these three features of the Web have spurred the Internet boom. First of all, before the Web existed, doing anything beyond simple e-mailing (and even that could be difficult, depending on your type of access) required knowing weird and arcane Unix commands and understanding the Internet's system for numbering and naming all the computers connected to it. If you've ever wrestled with DOS and lost, then you can appreciate the effort required to surmount this type of barrier.

Imagine it's 1991 and you've gotten yourself an Internet account, solved the problems of logging in to a Unix computer somewhere (with a communications program and a handwritten script), and mastered the Unix programs needed to send and receive e-mail, read newsgroups, download files, and so on. You'd still be looking at lots of plain text, screens, and screens of words. No pictures. Well, if you were dying for pictures, you could download enormous text files that had begun their lives as pictures and then were encoded as plain text so they could be squeezed through the text-only pipelines that constituted the Net. Next you'd have to decode the files, download them onto your PC or Mac, and then run some special program to look at them. Not quite as easy as flipping through a magazine, is it?

The Web uses a coding method called *hypertext* to disguise the actual commands and addresses you use to navigate the Net. Instead of these commands and addresses, what you see in your *Web browser* (the program you use to travel the Web) are plain English keywords highlighted in some way. Simply select or click on the keywords, and your browser program talks the Internet talk, negotiates the transaction with the computer at the other end, and brings the picture, text, program, or activity you desire onto your computer screen. This is how all computer functions should work (and probably how they *will* work one day).

NOTE

You may have already encountered a form of hypertext on your desktop computer. Think about the Windows Help system or the MacOS Help, where clicking on highlighted words connects you to definitions or tangentially related help topics.

Early Unix-based Web browsers, such as WWW (developed at CERN, the European particle physics laboratory where the Web was invented) and Lynx (developed at the University of Kansas), were not especially attractive to look at, but they did offer the "one-step" technique for jumping to a specific location on the Net or for downloading a file or piece of software. Figure 1.2 shows Lynx running on a Unix machine in a terminal window and connected to a PC by a modem.

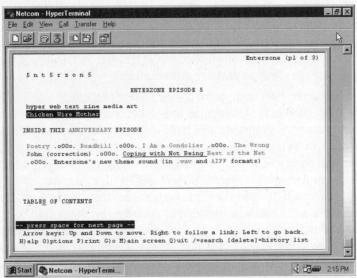

FIGURE 1.2: In Lynx, you can press Tab to get to and highlight a link, and then press Enter to execute the link and follow it to a file or another part of the Internet.

The next advance on the Web was the development of graphical Web browsers that could run on a desktop PC or Macintosh, permitting the user to employ the familiar point-and-click techniques of other software and incorporating text formatting and graphics into the browser screen. The first program of this type was NCSA Mosaic, which was developed at the National Center for Supercomputer Applications and distributed for free (see Figure 1.3).

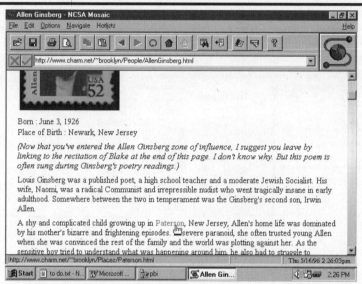

FIGURE 1.3: Mosaic made it possible to point to a link and click on it, making the Internet much more accessible to non-technical users. It also pioneered the use of in-line graphics (meaning illustrations mixed in with text).

Furthermore, the various Web browsers can more or less substitute for a plethora of little specialty programs (such as Gopher clients, newsreaders, FTP programs, and so on) that you had to assemble and set up yourself "in the old days." The browsers all have their own little idiosyncrasies, but they're still remarkably uniform and consistent compared to the maze of different programs and rules you had to work your way through just a few years ago. These days, the most popular browser is Internet Explorer, although Netscape's Navigator/Communicator browser (see Figure 1.4) is also well liked on all platforms.

NOTE

"Just a few years ago" is the old days on the Internet. Changes happen so rapidly in the online world that time on the Internet is like "dog years"—something like seven years go by for each one in the real world.

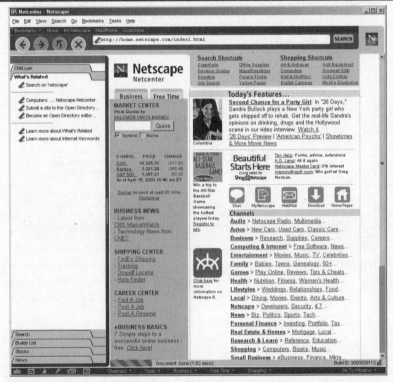

FIGURE 1.4: Netscape Navigator is a popular World Wide Web browser program. It works very much the way Mosaic did, but with a number of additional features and improvements.

The Web has made it possible for browsers to display pictures right there in the midst of text, eliminating the need to decode files. A picture's worth a lot of words, and pictures look better in newspaper articles and on TV than scads of typewritten text do. So this final ingredient made the Web seem both accessible and interesting to people who would never in a million years care to learn what a Unix "regular expression" is.

I have tried to briefly answer the question that heads up this section: What's the difference between the Web and the Internet? Technically, the Web and the Internet are not exactly the same, but for all intents and purposes, they have a lot in common. Web browsers are the must-have programs that have made the Internet what it is today.

NOTE
You can use the Internet and the Web to find new friends and uncover fun facts and interesting Web sites. Individuals and groups all over the planet have gotten together on the Internet to explore mutual interests. Environmental and political causes, entertainment, pets, sports, leisure activities, the arts, and the sciences are just some of the popular topics continually updated on the Internet.

DISCOVERING WHAT'S NEW ON THE NET

These days, the latest Internet developments are mostly driven by the access tools. Browser makers Netscape and Microsoft are each trying to develop all-in-one solutions that make their own products the "platform" for everything you do on the Net. New companies are offering free Internet accounts with a Web-based e-mail interface. The catch? You have to keep the ad window open on the screen. There are even Internet solutions that don't require you to have a computer, such as WebTV (your TV plus a modem plus a keyboard plus a remote). Some solutions eliminate the need for a modem, such as DirectPC (your computer plus a special satellite hookup).

The Web on Your Desktop

From the user's point of view, the biggest change in day-to-day Internet and World Wide Web use is that Internet access is now built directly into computer operating-system desktops (as well as directly into many new applications). Both Netscape and Microsoft are trying to turn their browsers into substitute desktops, more or less merging your view of the Internet (out there) with your own computer (in here).

NOTE

The Internet has also become a great source of career information. Companies frequently list jobs and freelance opportunities online, many of which you can also apply for online. You can research companies on the Internet and train yourself on a variety of topics that might come up in an interview. You can find business contacts and develop new ones through Internet e-mail, conferencing, and forums on particular subjects.

Applications with Internet Features

The growth of the Internet, coupled with the advent of smaller company or organization *intranets* (small, in-house networks running on Internet principles and technologies), has led users to expect their everyday business software to help them retrieve remote documents, collaborate with colleagues over network links, and save or publish documents to Web and intranet servers. To meet this demand, software publishers are adding Internet features to their programs left and right.

NOTE

Intranets are private networks running on Internet protocols so that, for example, an employee in one office may use an ordinary Web browser to seek access to sensitive files that are stored at another office.

You can expect your next upgrade of various programs to include the ability to transfer files (open them from and save them to remote computers) and probably to create documents and reports in HTML (hypertext Web format) as well. See Part V, "Creating a Web Page, for more on how to make Web documents.

NOTE

Knowing how to use Internet features in common business applications is a great job skill, even if you don't work in a high-technology field. All kinds of companies are depending more on the Internet and the World Wide Web to find information and promote their services and products. Companies and organizations are also developing in-house intranets to store policies, manuals, and other information. Having knowledge of the Internet is certainly a big plus in today's competitive job market.

WHAT YOU CAN DO ON THE NET

I've already touched on the most popular facilities on the Internet—e-mail and the World Wide Web—but now I'll run down some of the other useful features covered in this book. All of these things are interrelated, and you may notice me mentioning something before I cover it in detail. I don't want to leave you scratching your head when I'm forced to sputter terms of the trade, such as FTP, Telnet, and Gopher.

Once you start exploring the Web, you might get tired of its disorganization (imagine a library where every card-carrying member worked part-time as a librarian for one of the shelves, and each micro-librarian used their own system for organizing their section). Fortunately, there are a lot of useful *search engines* available on the Net, and I'll show you where to find them and how to use them.

NOTE

A *search engine* is a program or Web page that enables you to search an Internet site (or the entire Internet) for a specific keyword or words (see Chapter 8, "Internet Search Engines.").

The Web itself is becoming more of a whiz-bang medium with some of the bells and whistles we've come to expect in television advertisements and big budget movies. To take full advantage of some of the more dynamic Web offerings, though, you have to learn how to plug special tools into your browser. I'll show you where to find the tools and how to plug them in.

Those newsgroups I alluded to before, the Internet's public message boards, are organized (to use the term loosely) into a system called *Usenet*. I'll tell you how Usenet works, how to get and install a *newsreader*, and how to start participating in this public forum without getting called a jerk. If you plan to join the public discourse of the Net, you have to learn a thing or two about something called *netiquette*–the traditional rules of civilized behavior online. (Usenet and netiquette are explained in Chapter 10, "Newsgroups, Mailing Lists, and Chatting.")

If you prefer the idea of communicating with people "live" rather than posting messages and waiting for people to reply later, then you'll want to know about the various chat facilities available on the Internet–particularly *Instant Messaging* and *IRC* (*Internet relay chat*). These are also discussed in Chapter 10.

If you're willing to get your hands a little dirty and want to start tunneling your way around the Internet, connecting to computers all over the globe and moving files hither and yon, you might be able to do all of that from your Web browser. Or you may want to pick up the basics of *FTP* (*File Transfer Protocol*) and Telnet, systems that allow you to log in to remote computers over the Net. Read Chapter 9, "Getting Around with FTP and Telnet," to learn more about this technology.

Finally, if you want to join the ranks of people with their own home pages on the Web–to create a "presence" on the Net or to publicize your favorite Internet sites–I'll show you how to do that in Part V, "Creating a Web Page."

Downloading Files from the Internet

Another aspect of the Internet that you will especially enjoy is the ability to download files from a vast selection of sample applications, digital art and music, and many other offerings. Software companies promote their new products by maintaining sites where their customers can obtain samples, demos, updates, and related information. Entertainment conglomerates supply sound and video files for movies, bands, and video games. Some organizations just collect information relevant to their interests, such as schedules of upcoming activities, databases of similar organizations, and the like.

WARNING

You can access files from the Internet, but before you attempt this, you should protect your computer (or your company's network) with anti-virus software. Computers downloading Internet files are the principal point of entry for computer viruses.

Files obtained from the Internet can be quite large, so they often arrive compressed to a smaller size, and may also be coded for protection against unauthorized use or modifications. These files have to be decompressed and decoded before you can use them. Compression-decompression software and decoding applications are readily available, both as free Internet downloads (called freeware), and as commercial applications that you pay for.

Many Internet users are concerned about their privacy while using the Net, especially if they are filling out forms or making purchases with credit cards over the World Wide Web. Programming geniuses have given us applications that try to protect our good credit and our privacy. Some of these efforts are even given away free on the Internet.

Using Web Sites to Gather Information about the Internet and the Web

You can visit the Internet itself to glean more details about its history, policies, and users. Use the Web sites listed below to get various interpretations of how to use the Internet, how it evolved, and how it should be regulated. These sites all contain links to even more sites that will take you surfing farther afield in your quest for knowledge about the Web. (See Part II, "Browsing and More," for more info on how to get around the Web.)

The Internet Society
(http://info.isoc.org/)   A simple site that includes Internet history and a timeline, as well as links to other technical organizations dealing with the Web and communication in general.

Netscape Home Page
(http://www.netscape.com/)   The Web site of an extremely popular Web browser company. Click the Assistance button in the button bar right below the Netscape banner at the top of the home page. This will take you to the Assistance and Customer Service page. Scroll way down through Netscape's product and technical support listings to the Learning About the Internet section, where you can select links of interest.

Electronic Frontier Foundation
(http://www.eff.org/)   A mainly civil-rights oriented site with many pages on free speech, privacy, and policy. Also home of the (Extended) Guide to the Internet, a lengthy document containing everything you might ever want to know about the origins of the Internet.

World Wide Web Consortium
(http://www.w3.org/)   A site hosted by MIT, the European
Union, and DARPA (the defense agency that developed the
Internet). This site has everything from very technical and
lengthy documents to press releases and policy statements.

WHAT'S NEXT?

The first step in joining the online lifestyle is choosing an Internet Service
Provider (ISP). Chapter 2, "Choosing an Internet Service Provider," tells
you what issues to consider when selecting an ISP and how to establish
an Internet account. The 50 most important questions to ask before
selecting an ISP, discussed in the chapter, will help you to make the best
choice possible to ensure that your Internet experience is a good one.

Chapter 2

CHOOSING AN INTERNET SERVICE PROVIDER

For most of us, obtaining access to the Internet through an Internet service provider (ISP) is the most cost-effective and efficient way to join the online lifestyle.

Locating an ISP within your community or on a national level isn't difficult. Check your local newspaper's business section and chances are you will find a plethora of providers trolling for your Internet access dollars. You can also check the Yellow Pages or visit a bookstore and purchase a copy of just about any Internet magazine, which will include listings for national level Internet access providers as well.

Other ways to locate an ISP include asking for a recommendation at local software stores, asking friends, or calling an Internet consultant for a recommendation. Most "Internauts" are more than happy to share this information. If you belong to

Adapted from *Mr. Modem's Internet Guide for Seniors*, by Richard A. Sherman

ISBN 0-7821-2580-8   415 pages $19.99

a computer club, social group, high-tech religious cult or similar organization, be sure to check with other members. In increasing numbers, residential communities are being constructed already prewired for high-speed cable or other access to the Internet. Could there be more of an incentive to move in? I think not.

Readers of my "Ask Mr. Modem!" column frequently ask about the difference between an ISP and a service such as AOL (America Online). It's actually a very good question and fortunately, one that I can answer.

While an ISP provides access to a spectacular selection of informational resources on the Internet, the focus of an online service such as America Online or CompuServe is narrower. It provides information, or *content*, within its own perimeter. An ISP, on the other hand, exists primarily to provide access to the global Internet. Think of an ISP as a gatekeeper or toll collector at the on ramp to the Internet. Once you're connected, you're effectively pulling out into the high-speed lane.

Due to the enormous popularity of the Internet, information services such as AOL and others have been compelled to provide access to the Internet itself, as well as to their own content. Within that context, the service then becomes a *gateway* to the Internet. Think of AOL and other online services as taking a bus tour on the information superhighway. You're on the highway, but looking through the bus windows as your tour guide points out sights of interest. An Internet service provider doesn't typically provide content, other than perhaps a cheesy home page that you probably won't want to look at each time you log on.

If you already have access to the Internet via America Online or you know somebody who has access to the Internet, you can easily locate a local ISP using any of the following Web-based resources:

> **The List**   This Web site allows you to locate a provider that offers the access speed and related services that meet your needs and budget (see Figure 2.1). More than 6,500 ISPs are searchable by area code, country code, United States only, or exclusively Canada:
>
>   http://thelist.internet.com
>
> **isps.com**   Sponsored by Earthlink Network, this site provides searchable access to more than 4,000 ISPs. You can search by price, area code, and name, as well as national ISPs and toll-free ISPs:
>
>   http://www.isps.com

FIGURE 2.1: Use The List to locate an Internet service provider.
Excerpted with permission from Internet.com, May 1999.

The Ultimate Web ISP List   Use this site's "Simple Search" for a quick search of all matching ISPs within any area code. Use the "Power Search" to include variables such as modem or connection speed, then refine your search by selecting additional criteria.

```
http://webisplist.internetlist.com
```

There are other ways to obtain access to the Internet as well. For example, if you have an affiliation with a college or university, chances are that that institution provides Internet access to its students and faculty. Many corporations and businesses also provide access.

Most communities offer access via *freenets* or community-sponsored access available to residents of a given city or state, typically through the local library. A call to your state or municipal Chamber of Commerce will assist you in this regard.

So what does an Internet service provider actually do? An ISP maintains a full-time, high-speed connection to the Internet that is "subdivided" to provide you, me, and other individuals with an inexpensive connection.

There are several things to look for when selecting an ISP: location, stability, customer service, performance and price—or LSCPP, verbalized as *liskp* for mnemonic enthusiasts.

Location

It can actually be more expensive to dial an ISP within your state than to dial one out of state if you cannot locate an ISP in your local calling area. Many larger ISPs do offer 800 access numbers but typically charge for connect time on a per-minute basis, which tends to average around $6 per hour. While that might seem expensive at first, it is usually more cost-efficient than almost any long distance direct-dial price if you are required to dial outside of your local calling area. Whenever possible, select an ISP that is only a local phone call away.

Stability

It's always best if you can open an account with an ISP that has an established track record. The entire ISP industry is only a few years old, so be wary of any ISP that claims to have been "Serving the Internet Community since 1952." Stability is particularly important because once you are on the Internet you will be sharing your e-mail address as you begin corresponding with friends and family. Your e-mail address will become as important to you—and as widely distributed—as your telephone or fax number. If at some point in the future you have to change your e-mail address because your ISP takes a nosedive, at best, it can be inconvenient; at worst, it can ruin your life and kill your houseplants.

There are "lifetime" e-mail addresses available, though I'm not sure if they're referring to my lifetime, the company's lifetime, or the lifetime of the typical fruit fly. If it's my lifetime they're referring to, I'm not sure I like the sound of that. Perhaps they know something that I don't.

Customer Service

If you're new to the Internet, customer service or technical support is particularly important. The Internet is a wild and woolly grand adventure, and that means that you are blazing new cybertrails in the process of learning what it's all about. While that's poetic as all get out and sounds very adventuresome, what it actually means is that the technology of the Internet isn't at the plug-and-play level. Close, but not quite. Many would-be Internetters will have to install a modem, install software, and then configure the software to work with a particular ISP, so it might be comforting to know that you can call your friendly ISP's tech support people for a helping hand, if necessary.

The good news is that a new computer purchased today will be as close to Internet ready or plug-and-play as anything. So if you're teetering on the brink and can't decide whether to upgrade your trusty 486 to make it Internet capable or purchase a new computer, my advice is to go for what's behind curtain number two, Monty, and buy a new computer.

Most ISPs are acutely aware of the hurdles new users face while dipping a toe in the Internet pond for the first time. They are also aware that it's not always a walk in the park for newbies. Because of this heightened awareness, many ISPs offer wonderful technical support and ease of installation with very detailed instructions. Some ISPs will even make house calls (don't tell the AMA) and for a small fee ($50 to $75), will install and configure everything for you and get you up and surfing. While this service is not absolutely necessary, if you don't enjoy tinkering with your computer or cursing loudly in the privacy of your own home, you might want to explore the availability of on-site installation service. Look at it this way: Even if it costs you $75, it's still cheaper than Prozac.

Performance

The average ISP continues to grow at a rate of more than 50 percent per year. As in any business, that type of extraordinary growth can have an adverse effect on performance. It doesn't appear to be a function of large ISP versus small ISP (sometimes referred to as ISP-envy), nor a manifestation of performance anxiety—it's more a function of the ability of the ISP to manage its own growth. Inability to log on, repeated busy signals, heartburn, indigestion, and gastrointestinal distress are just a few of the most common indications of a lack of performance on the part of an ISP.

One question that is an absolute must to ask any prospective Internet service provider, and one that directly affects performance, is, "What is your user-to-modem ratio?" Anything less than 12:1 is acceptable. The higher the ratio (i.e. 15:1 or 20:1), the more likely it is that you will experience a busy signal when you attempt to log on. A user-to-modem ratio of 10:1 is ideal. We can dream, can't we? (See "50 Questions to Ask Before Selecting an ISP," later in this chapter.)

Pricing

Though it varies throughout the country, the average price range appears to be $15 to $25 per month for unlimited access to the Internet. I have also encountered some annual payment programs that provide unlimited Internet access for $99 to $150 per year. In some rural areas, monthly rates can be as high as $35 per month. A review of pricing information provided by over 3,700 Internet service providers revealed that the average 56K dial-up price is $19.95 per month for unlimited access.

Some ISPs are moving away from unlimited flat-rate service and heading toward a certain number of Internet access hours for x dollars per month. Additional hours are billed on a per-hour basis. Other ISPs offer unadvertised special pricing, so be sure to investigate pricing plans thoroughly.

You will discover that some ISPs offer two, three, and sometimes four different pricing programs. Most will offer a flat monthly price for unlimited access. Many ISPs also offer alternative programs with monthly minimums often as low as $4.95 per month, with slightly higher hourly charges and fewer hours included in the base charge. $4.95 per month with 10 hours included and $1 for each additional hour is fairly typical.

Speaking of time spent online each month, I recently conducted a quasi-scientific study among the readers of my "Ask Mr. Modem!" newspaper column. The column reaches more than two million households every month. What my exhaustive study revealed is remarkably consistent with bonafide studies conducted by researchers who know what they're doing. These studies reveal the following amount of time spent online per month, broken down by age group (or time spent online per month by broken-down age group, in my case):

55+	38 hours
45-54	34 hours
25-34	28 hours
18-24	22 hours

(**Source:** *Media Metrix Internet Research*)

The Internet is clearly a phenomenon within the seniors community. We use the Internet more frequently and for longer periods of time than any other segment of the population. And the best is yet to come.

ESTABLISHING AN INTERNET ACCOUNT

To obtain a dial-up connection to the Internet, you will need four things:

- ▶ Software for your computer to access e-mail, the World Wide Web, and other Internet resources

- ▶ A modem connected to your serial port (called a COM port or COMmunications port), or an internal modem

- ▶ A dial-up account with an Internet service provider

- ▶ A telephone line

If you are using Windows 95 or 98—and if you're not, you really should be—you already have the software you need to connect to the Internet. If your ISP requires something extra-spatial, as we say in Modemville, you will be provided with the appropriate software and instructions.

Establishing an account with an Internet service provider involves calling the ISP on the telephone (how archaic!) and providing them with some basic sign-up information and a credit card number—preferably your own. It may also involve configuring some software with some basic information provided by your ISP. In most cases, the ISP will send you a diskette or CD-ROM via the U.S. Postal Service (referred to in Internet parlance as *snail mail*) with the requisite software configured for you.

It typically takes five minutes or less to establish an Internet account with an ISP. During this process you will select and receive your own unique e-mail address. Your ISP will handle the registration process and will probably ask you to choose three alternate "usernames" to submit for registration, so be thinking of names before you sign up. A traditional naming convention used by many Internet users consists of the first letter of your first name along with your surname. For example, *rsherman* is followed by what is called the host and domain name, so the complete e-mail address would appear *rsherman@host.domain*. You are not limited to the traditional first letter and surname style by any means. Selecting a name for your e-mail account presents a wonderful opportunity to be creative, so have fun! For example, my e-mail address is MrModem@home.com. If you wish to contact me to tell me how much you're enjoying this book, this would be the appropriate e-mail address to use.

Every e-mail address is constructed in the same manner: Reading from left to right, first is the username, followed by the "at" sign, followed by the host and domain. That all sounds very technical, but it's really not. The username is you, the host is your ISP, and the domain will typically be .com indicating that your host is a commercial entity, .org if it's a non-profit organization, .net if it's part of a network, or .edu if it's an educational institution.

NOTE

BPWI (Bonus Piece of Worthless Information): The "at" sign or @ sign is formally known as a *streusel*. Next time you want to impress your friends or bore them to tears, just trot out this little gem and you'll be sure to be the talk of the neighborhood.

Your Internet username can be your real name, a pseudonym, or just about anything you would like to use. One caveat: You might want to avoid being too cutesy with your username selection. Nicknames or pet

names, for example, can come back to haunt you. Though you may start out using the Internet for fun and exploration just to see what all the Internet fuss is about, there are countless business, professional, and social opportunities that await your arrival. Just about the time you start discussing an opportunity with a prospective customer or client or you meet a very special person online, you may not want *Stinky* or *Muffin* to appear as your Internet identification.

On the other hand, if you're certain that you're primarily going to be using the Internet for staying in touch with family members or socializing with other individuals who share similar interests—a cyberspace pen pal or *e-pal*, for example—take it from Mr. Modem: just choose a username that you're comfortable with, then sit back, relax and have fun!

50 QUESTIONS TO ASK BEFORE SELECTING AN ISP

Selecting an ISP can be intimidating or downright scary for those new to the Internet community. Mr. Modem believes you should ask lots of questions so that your decision will be an informed one. Following are 50 suggested questions to ask a prospective ISP before establishing your account with them.

The Internet and Other Services

1. What Internet services do you provide? (Should include at a minimum: e-mail, World Wide Web, newsgroups.)

2. Is there a limit on the size of e-mail messages that can be sent or received? (This is important if you plan to send or receive e-mail attachments or files.)

3. Is there a limit on the number of e-mail messages that can be transmitted each month?

Modems and Connecting

4. What modem types (protocols) and modem speed connections do you support? (Hint: Be sure the V.90 protocol is supported.)

5. Is high-speed (above 56Kbps) access available? (Examples: ISDN, DSL, Cable, and Fractional T1.)

6. If high-speed access is available, what are its associated costs?

7. Do you provide toll-free number dial-in capability?

8. Is there a surcharge for connecting via your toll-free number?

9. How many local calling areas (telephone numbers) do you have throughout the country or internationally? (This is important if you travel or plan to connect to the Internet from different locations.)

10. Is there an additional fee for connecting to the Internet using any of your local calling areas other than the one I sign up with?

11. If so, what is that fee?

12. What is your user-to-modem ratio? (Hint: Ideally, it should be 12:1 or lower. Higher ratios—15:1 or 20:1—may result in a busy signal when attempting to establish your connection by dialing in.)

Automatic Disconnections

13. Do you have an automatic cut-off or disconnect feature? (Some ISPs will automatically drop your connection after a certain number of minutes have passed with no keyboard or mouse input.)

14. How many minutes of inactivity result in an automatic disconnect?

15. Is there an option (fee or free?) to disable the automatic disconnect or extend the length of time permitted before the automatic disconnect is invoked?

Home Pages and Data Storage

16. Do you provide a home page with each account?

17. If I have a home page, can I edit or modify it at any time?

18. What, if any, fees are charged for maintaining or editing a home page?

19. How much space (in megabytes) do you provide for each home page?

20. If additional space is required, what is the cost?

21. What are your minimum, maximum, or monthly flat fee data storage rates, if any?

Technical Support

22. Do you offer technical support?

23. Are there any fees associated with your technical support services?

24. What are the hours for your technical support or help desk?

25. Is there a toll-free number for technical support?

26. What is your average response time for technical support?

27. If I establish an account, will you send me an installation disk or CD-ROM containing the configured software I'll need?

28. What type of documentation or instruction manual will I receive with my account?

Account Cancellation and E-Mail Forwarding

29. How would I cancel my account?

30. Do you provide e-mail forwarding if I cancel my account?

31. Is there a fee associated with e-mail forwarding?

32. How long will you continue to forward my e-mail to a new e-mail address if I terminate my account?

33. Do you offer an e-mail forwarding service for a second or additional e-mail addresses?

34. If you do offer e-mail forwarding service for additional e-mail addresses, is there a fee for it?

Financial Matters

35. What types of accounts do you offer? (Examples: business, personal, family, and multi-user.)

36. What are your rates for each type of account offered?

37. What is your installation or account setup fee, if any?

38. Are any fees waived or can I receive a reduced rate or signup bonus if I am switching from another ISP?

39. What is your monthly fee for Internet access?

40. Is it for unlimited connect time?

41. If you do not provide unlimited connect time, how many hours of connect time are included each month?

42. What is the cost per minute or cost per hour for connect time above the number of hours included with my account?

43. Do you send a monthly invoice or is your monthly charge automatically billed to my credit card?

44. Is there a free trial period?

45. If there is a free trial period, how long is it?

46. If I pay for a year in advance, can I pay for 11 months and receive the 12th month free?

47. If I refer a friend, will I receive a free month of service or other incentive?

48. How much does an additional e-mail address cost?

49. What browser is included: Netscape or Internet Explorer? What version?

50. Do you provide a method for keeping customers current with new versions of your software or updates?

WHAT'S NEXT?

Now that you've gotten set up with an ISP, you'll probably want to let people know you're out there! Chapter 3, "E-Mail Basics," tells you everything you'll need to know to send, receive, read, reply to, and delete e-mail messages.

Chapter 3

E-MAIL BASICS

I f you have an internal network at your office and you're
already familiar with how to send and receive mail, you can
probably skip this lesson (although you might want to read
the parts about how to write an Internet e-mail address to send
mail beyond your network). If you don't yet have an e-mail
account or Internet access, go back and read Chapter 2, "Choosing an ISP," for how to get connected to the Internet and how to
get started once you are connected.

This lesson will cover the most basic e-mail concepts—mainly
how to send, read, reply to, and delete e-mail.

NOTE

When you get used to sending e-mail, you'll find that it's as useful
a form of communication as the telephone, and it doesn't require
the other person to drop whatever they're doing to answer your call.
You can include a huge amount of specific information, and the person you sent mail to can reply in full in their own good time. And
unlike the telephone, with e-mail you can edit your message before
you send it.

Adapted from *The Internet: No experience required,*
Second Edition, by Christian Crumlish
ISBN 0-7821-2385-6   470 pages $19.99

WORKING WITH E-MAIL

These are the things that you will do most often with e-mail:

- ▶ Run the mail program
- ▶ Send mail
- ▶ Read incoming mail
- ▶ Reply to mail
- ▶ Delete mail
- ▶ Exit the mail program

We'll discuss all of these topics in the following sections.

Running an E-mail Program

You start most e-mail programs the way you do any program, usually by double-clicking an icon or by choosing a program name from a menu (the Start menu in Windows 95/98, or the Apple menu or Launcher on a Mac). If your Internet connection is not already up and running, your e-mail program may be able to start that process for you.

TIP

If you have to log in to a Unix shell, then you'll start your mail program (probably Pine) by typing its name at the Unix prompt and pressing Enter. On the other hand, if you're using Linux or one of the more modern Unix versions (Solaris 8, FreeBSD) then you are likely booted directly into a graphical logon screen and X-window environment. From there you can click on an icon, launch it from a terminal, or even use a menu much like the Start menu on Windows (KDE, Gnome).

Your e-mail program will start and either show you the contents of your Inbox (the mailbox where your new messages arrive) or show you a list of all your mailboxes (in which case you'll want to open the Inbox).

NOTE

There are many, *many* free Internet e-mail account services (such as HotMail and Juno) that offer Web-based e-mail access. The accounts are paid for by advertising that appears on the Web pages that you access your account through or that you have to keep on your screen while you're connected. To find out more about them, see Chapter 5, "Free E-Mail and Useful E-Mail Tools."

In addition to an Inbox where new messages appear, and usually a deleted-messages or Trash mailbox where discarded messages are held until they are completely purged, you'll also have an Outbox where copies of your outgoing messages can be saved (some programs will do this automatically; with others you have to set it as an option). In the case of Juno Mail, there is a limit to how much you can store, after which the oldest stored mail is purged automatically. Figure 3.1 shows a Microsoft Outlook Inbox and an Inbox for Microsoft Outlook Express, which is part of Microsoft Internet Explorer.

Mailboxes generally list the sender's name and the subject line of the message (and often its date as well). When you double-click a message in any of your mailboxes, the message will open up in a window of its own.

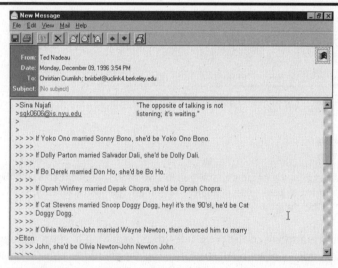

FIGURE 3.1: The first screen shows my Microsoft Outlook 97 Inbox with messages listed in the order they were sent, from the most recent to the oldest. Compare that Inbox to the one shown next for Microsoft Outlook Express, which comes with Microsoft Internet Explorer 4.

Sending Mail

All mail programs have a New Message or Compose E-mail command, often located on a message menu, and they usually have a keyboard shortcut for the command as well, such as Ctrl+N for New Message. When you start a new message, your program will open a new window. Figure 3.2 shows a new message window in Eudora, a popular e-mail program

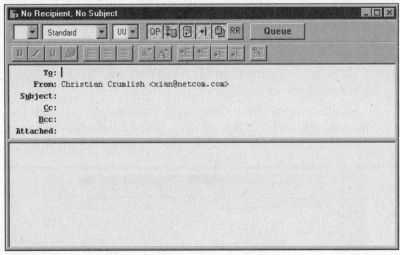

FIGURE 3.2: A blank new message window in Eudora

TIP

Most e-mail programs enable you to save addresses and then select them from an address book or list of names rather than type them in directly. See Chapter 4, "E-Mail Programs," for more on this.

Type the address of the person to whom you wish to send the mail. The person's address must be in the form *username@address.domain*, where *username* is the person's identifier (the name they log in with), and *address* is the identifier of the person's network or machine on the network (the address might consist of several words—the host and subdomain—separated by dots). The *domain* is the short code at the end indicating whether the address is a business (.com), a non-profit organization (.org), a university (.edu), a branch of the government (.gov), a part of the military (.mil), and so on. (Some e-mail programs require special text before or after the Internet e-mail address.)

Eudora allows you to use what it calls Nicknames, implying just what it says. When you create a new contact in Eudora's Address Book it will ask you to create a Nickname for that contact. Typically (or at least for me) I simply use the name of the person, group, or business, but there are a few that already have their own nicknames, like family members. "Mom" and "Dad" work just fine, as opposed to their full names (which might offend them if they happened to see it when they were on one of their inspections... er, visits). When you type the nickname for a contact into the TO:, Cc:, or BCc: fields, Eudora will automatically expand it into the real address as long as you have that option specified in your Preferences.

By the way, all the rules mentioned in the previous category apply only to sending mail over the Internet. Generally, if you're sending mail to someone on your own network (or another member of your online service or a subscriber of your service provider), you have to specify only the username, not any of the Internet information.

TIP

The easiest way to send mail to someone is to reply to mail that they've sent you. If you're not sure exactly how to form someone's e-mail address, ask them to send you some mail and then simply reply to it. That's what I always do.

One of my addresses is xian@netcom.com (you pronounce the "@" as "at" and the "." as "dot"). I log in as "xian," my service provider is Netcom, and Netcom is a commercial business.

Sending Mail to People on Other Networks

Many people have Internet addresses even though they are not, strictly speaking, on the Internet. Most other networks have gateways that send mail to and from the Internet. If you want to send mail to someone on another network, you'll need to know his or her identifier on that network and how their network address appears in Internet form. Here are examples of the most common Internet addresses:

Network	Username	Internet Address
America Online	Beebles	Beebles@aol.com
AT&T Mail	Beebles	beebles@attmail.com
AT&T WorldNet	Beebles	beebles@worldnet.att.net
CompuServe	75555,5555	75555.5555@compuserve.com
Fidonet BBS	1:2/3	f3.n2.z1@fidonet.org
MCI Mail	555-7777	555-7777@mcimail.com

As you can see, the only tricky ones are CompuServe, for which you have to change the comma in the CompuServe address to a dot in the Internet address; and Fidonet, for which you have to reverse the order of the three numbers and then put them after f, n, and z, respectively. (If you are given only two numbers, in the form a/b, then assume that they are the n and f numbers and that the z number is 1 (one).)

Creating an E-mail Message

Here's how to create an e-mail message:

1. After entering the recipient's address in the Address box, press Tab and then type a subject in the Subject box (keep it short). This will be the first thing the recipient of your mail sees. Providing a subject is optional.

TIP

The subject you type in the subject line should be fairly short, but should be a good description of the contents of your message. Good subject lines can help recipients categorize their mail and respond more quickly to your messages. If they are using Inbox filters, described in Chapter 4, "E-Mail Programs," they may be presorting their e-mail according to the contents of the subject line, making the subject even more important for getting your mail noticed.

2. If you want to send a copy of the e-mail message to more than one recipient, you can either:

    ▶ Type additional addresses on the Cc line.

WARNING

Keep in mind that your e-mail address should receive only limited exposure, something akin to a super hero protecting his secret identity. Sure, anyone that you correspond with will know it, but if you're careful you can protect it from the gathering techniques used by spammers. One of the ways that you can respect your recipients is, if you're sending the message to more than one address, to place all additional addresses in the Bcc: line and put only your own address in the To: line. No one among your recipients will be able to see the addresses of the other recipients of your message, and spammers won't have an easy list to add to their ill-gotten booty.

    ▶ Add addresses to the To line (usually separated by commas, although some programs, such as Outlook, use semicolons instead).

TIP

In almost all e-mail programs, you can press Tab to jump from box to box or from field to field when filling in an address and subject. You can also just click directly in the area you want to jump to in most programs.

3. Press Tab until the insertion point jumps into the blank message area, and then type your message.

4. When you are done, send the message or add it to a *queue*, a list of outgoing messages to be sent all at once. (A queue is useful if you have a lot of mail to write and send and you don't want to wait for each message to go out before drafting the next one.) Press the Send button, or select File ➤ Send.

TIP

Most e-mail programs can word-wrap your message, so you have to press Enter only when you want to start a new paragraph. I recommend leaving a blank line between paragraphs, to make them easier to read. Figure 3.3 shows a short e-mail message.

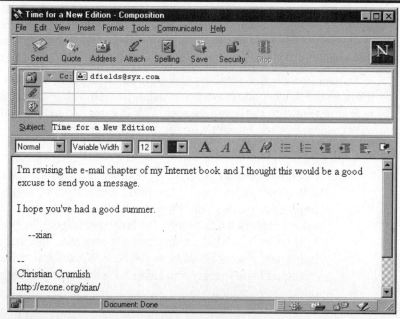

FIGURE 3.3: A short e-mail message to a friend

Some e-mail programs allow you to filter messages, meaning you sort them according to some criteria that need to be met as they come into your Inbox. The post office sorts regular mail according to zip code; similarly, you can use your e-mail program to automatically sort messages according to who sent them, the subject, the date they were sent or received, or any other category that is useful to you from an organizational standpoint. See Chapter 4 for more on message filters.

TIP

You can sort your messages in many e-mail applications according to categories and other criteria. Certain e-mail programs also allow you to flag messages according to the urgency of the response needed or other priorities. Check in your application's Help menu or under the File or Edit menus (in Windows programs) for commands such as Sort or Categorize. These options provide you with powerful organizational tools and transform your messages into valuable records that can be filed and retrieved for later reference. See Chapter 4 for more about sorting.

Reading Mail

Whenever I connect to the Net, the first thing I do is check my e-mail. It's like checking your mailbox when you get home, except the contents are generally more interesting—and usually don't contain bills! Some mail programs combine the process of sending queued messages with checking for new mail. Most also check for new mail when you first start them.

Unread (usually new) mail typically appears with some indicator that it's new: the Subject line may appear in bold, or a bullet or checkmark may appear next to the new messages. This is supposed to help you pick out the messages you haven't read yet, so you don't miss any.

Here are the steps for reading an e-mail message:

1. Open your e-mail program by double-clicking its shortcut icon or selecting it from the Start menu. Some programs begin by displaying your Inbox contents, but with others you will need to click a Get New Mail button or select File ➢ Get Mail or Get New Mail. Others have a special Mail menu selection where you choose Mail ➢ Get New Mail or Mail ➢ Read Incoming Mail. Display your Inbox with the command appropriate for your program.

2. To view the contents of a mail message, highlight it in the Inbox window and press Enter (or double-click it). The

message will appear in its own window, much like an out-going message. Figure 3.4 shows an example of an incoming message.

3. If the message continues beyond the bottom of the window, use the scroll bar to see the remaining text.

4. After reading the message, you can close or reply to the message.

TIP

I keep my mail around until I've replied to it. I could save it to a mailbox, but then I might forget about it. When my Inbox gets too cluttered, I bite the bullet, reply to all the mail I've been putting off dealing with, and then I delete most of it.

Replying to Mail

Somewhere near the New Message command (probably on the same menu or button bar), you'll find the Reply command. When you reply to an e-mail message, your new message is automatically addressed back to the sender, and depending on your e-mail program, you may be able to easily quote the message you received.

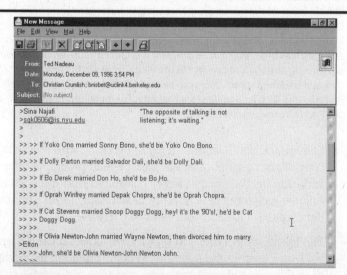

FIGURE 3.4: Here's an e-mail message I received.

TIP

If you start to reply by mistake, just close the message window and don't save the reply if prompted.

To reply to an e-mail message, follow these steps:

1. Highlight the received message in the Inbox or open the message, and then select the Reply command.

2. Your program will create a new message automatically addressed to the sender of the message you're replying to. Some mail programs will also automatically include the contents of the original message (or will give you the choice of including the contents or not). Often, especially with e-mail programs that were designed primarily for use on the Internet, the included message will appear with a ">" character at the beginning of each line to indicate that it is quoted text, although different mail programs have different ways of showing quoted messages. Some, for example, just indent the quoted material (see Figure 3.5).

TIP

Any Web addresses mentioned in e-mail messages can function as clickable links in many of the newer programs such as Netscape Messenger, Microsoft Outlook and Outlook Express, and Eudora. To use these links, click the highlighted address, which will probably be underlined or depicted in a different color, such as blue. Your e-mail program will launch your default browser if it's not running already and connect to the Web address in the link. Microsoft Outlook and Outlook Express users can also add Web shortcuts as file attachments. Just click the Web icon to head for that site. For more information on the Web, see Part II, "Browsing and More."

3. Sometimes, you'll want to reply to everyone who was sent a copy of the original message. Most e-mail programs offer a variation on the normal Reply command that includes all original recipients in your reply. Select Reply to All or a similar command to send your reply to everyone.

4. Tab to the subject line and type a new subject if the old one isn't very meaningful anymore. (People often fail to change the subject line of messages, even when the conversation has evolved its way onto a new topic.)

5. Add other recipients, if necessary. Tab your way into the message area to type your reply, and then choose the Send (or Queue) command when you are done.

TIP

E-mail tends to take on a life of its own, with people forwarding you messages from other people asking for help or information, or simply listing trivia, jokes, inspirational messages, you name it. Sometimes people send you long chains of related messages, often called *threads*. To avoid confusion when replying to a message forwarded to you, or when replying to many recipients, direct the mail program to "retain the original text," or however the command is worded, so that people reading the message will know what you are talking about and will know the history of the issue. However, if the thread starts getting too long, you can try to abbreviate it as described later in the section titled, "Using Proper E-mail Netiquette."

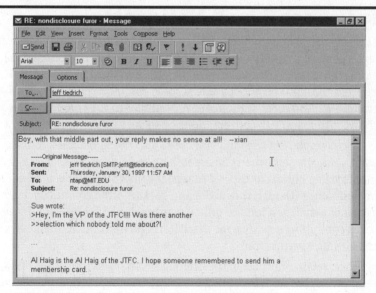

FIGURE 3.5:   A reply with the original message included

Deleting Mail

If you have read a piece of mail and you're positive that you have no need to save it, you should delete it so it doesn't clutter up your Inbox (and waste precious hard-disk storage space). To delete a message, you typically highlight it and press the Delete key on the keyboard (or click the Delete or Trash button, if there is one). In most programs, this moves the message to the Deleted Mail or Trash mailbox until you empty the trash (or quit the program).

WARNING

In some programs, you don't get a chance to undelete a message, so be sure you know how your program works before deleting messages willy-nilly.

If you change your mind, try opening the Trash mailbox (or Deleted Mail mailbox) and then looking for a command that allows you to transfer mail from one mailbox to another. It may even be called Transfer (as it is in Eudora). When you find it, transfer the mail back to your Inbox.

Using Proper E-mail Netiquette

Like any social system, the Internet has evolved to the point where its users observe a variety of informal rules for interacting politely. Collectively, these rules are known as *netiquette*, and most of them can be inferred through the application of some common sense to various social situations. And most of them are very similar to the common rules of conduct that apply to conversations or social interactions.

For example, it's generally not considered good manners to misquote what someone said when you are talking to someone else, to quote comments taken out of context, or to repeat something that was told to you in confidence (though the media and gossips often commit such acts!). Think of e-mail as a kind of online conversation. If people send you messages containing sensitive material, don't forward them to others without the author's permission.

If you retain only part of the original text of messages in your replies (to keep the replies from becoming too long), be sure it is not misleadingly taken out of its full context (and likely to be misinterpreted). And please do not intersperse your own comments with the retained pieces of other people's messages so that it's not clear to the recipients who wrote what.

Keep Your Messages Brief and Tactful

When you write messages to business associates and colleagues, stick to the point and be informative. Break up large blocks of text into smaller paragraphs. Reread your messages and run a spellcheck before sending them—this will give you a chance to minimize mistakes, fix poorly organized sentences, and reconsider bad word choices.

If you are writing to friends (or potential friends in usegroups or chat rooms), you can relax a little more, but still hold back on anything that could be considered offensive, even if you think it's funny and you are sure that your friends will, too. Seemingly innocuous statements spoken in conversation can take on a whole new meaning when written down. Figures of speech, jokes, and your own private way of referring to situations or people can seem a lot more serious or offensive when viewed in writing.

WARNING

The old adage about never saying or putting anything in writing that you would not want to see in a headline the next day also applies to e-mail and the Internet. Now you also have to worry about your words appearing on someone's Web page or showing up when someone searches the Web, a chat service, or a newsgroup. Journalists search the Web for juicy opinions every day. There's no law preventing potential employers from checking you out on the Web and uncovering some embarrassing thing you wrote or posted years ago.

When replying to messages, try to minimize the amount of quoted text that you keep in your return message. Leave enough so that it's clear what you're replying to (people don't always remember exactly what they wrote to you). However, as mentioned at the beginning of this section, don't send abbreviated message bits attributed to other people that could be taken out of context. Just use your good common sense, and do unto others as you'd have them do unto you!

Don't Fly off the Handle

In this book I'm trying not to give you too much advice about how to behave on the Net, for a couple of reasons. First, I assume you are an adult and can decide for yourself how to behave. Secondly, the Net has a strongly interactive culture, and you will receive plenty of advice and cues from others if you overstep the bounds of good behavior.

NOTE

Issues of netiquette arise even more frequently when you are communicating with large numbers of people on mailing lists or Usenet. See Chapter 10, "Newsgroups, Mailing Lists, and Chatting," for more details.

Nevertheless, I will point out that e-mail is a notoriously volatile medium. Because it is so easy to write out a reply and send it in the heat of the moment, and because text lacks many of the nuances of face-to-face communication—the expression and body cues that add emphasis, the tones of voice that indicate joking instead of insult, and so on—it has become a matter of course for many people to dash off ill-considered replies to perceived insults and, therefore, to fan the flames of invective.

This Internet habit, called *flaming*, is widespread and you will no doubt encounter it on one end or the other. All I can suggest is that you try to restrain yourself when you feel the urge to fly off the handle. (And I have discovered that apologies work wonders when people have misunderstood a friendly gibe or have mistaken sarcasm for idiocy.)

TIP

If you are the sort to flare up in an angry response, or if you find yourself getting emotional or agitated while composing a response to a message that upsets you, save your message as a draft rather than sending it right away. Most e-mail programs provide the option to save a draft message. You can review the draft message later when you have calmed down and decide then whether you want to send it, or you can send the draft to a more objective third party and ask them if it is too harsh before you send it out.

Exiting an E-mail Program

When you are finished sending, reading, and replying to mail, you can quit your program or leave it running to check your mail at regular intervals. You can quit most mail programs by selecting File ➢ Exit or File ➢ Quit.

WHAT'S NEXT?

Now that you know the basic ins and outs of e-mail, it's time to learn about some of the e-mail programs available and the features and options they offer. Chapter 4, "E-Mail Programs," discusses the most popular programs—Eudora, Outlook and Outlook Express, Netscape, Pegasus, and Pine.

Chapter 4

E-MAIL PROGRAMS

There are so many different e-mail programs available that I can't hope to cover each one in detail, which is why I discussed e-mail in generic terms in the last chapter. Nevertheless, it's quite likely that you'll end up using one of a handful of popular e-mail programs at one time or another. So that you can learn some specific skills, I'll discuss the most commonly used ones here: Eudora Pro, Microsoft Outlook Express, Netscape Messenger, Pegasus Mail, and Pine.

In the unlikely circumstance that you have none of the specific programs that I cover, the previous chapter will still give you a sense of what features to look for in the Help portion of your e-mail program or to discuss with your system (or network) administrator.

Adapted from *The Internet: No experience required*, *Second Edition*, by Christian Crumlish

ISBN 0-7821-2385-6   470 pages $19.99

EUDORA PRO

Eudora is one of the most popular and dependable Internet e-mail programs available. It can work on a network connection, with a PPP or SLIP dial-up account, or as an offline mail reader with a Unix shell account.

TIP

A free copy of Eudora can be downloaded from http://www.eudora.com/. See Chapter 9, "Getting Around FTP and Telnet," for instructions on how to download files from the Net. Qualcomm, the company that owns Eudora, makes improvements to the program all the time, for both Windows and Mac versions. Therefore, if you've been using Eudora for a while, you may have a slightly out-of-date copy of the program and some of your specific commands or menu names may differ from my instructions. Either upgrade to the latest version of Eudora or poke around the menus for similar commands.

Eudora has just about every state-of-the-art Internet e-mail feature you could wish for (in both the Windows and Macintosh versions, which are nearly identical with the exception of platform-specific differences). And for the first time, you can get and use the Pro version for as long as you like for free (or at least as long as you can stand the advertising). The Light version, which is simply a setting in Eudora Pro 4.7, offers most of the functionality of the ad-supported and paid versions, and is a bargain at the price.

To try out the features discussed in the following sections, start the Eudora program by double-clicking on its desktop icon.

Most of the useful Eudora commands are available on the Message menu shown here.

Creating Eudora Messages and Checking E-mail

Here's how to create and send an e-mail using Eudora:

1. Select Message ➢ New Message (or press Ctrl+N in Windows, Command+N on the Mac).

NOTE

If you have created a nickname for this recipient in your **Address Book** and checked the Put it on the recipient list checkbox, the nickname you specified will appear on the recipient list (a pop-up list that appears when you select **Message ➢ New Message To**). You can select the nickname from the recipient list and the note will be automatically addressed for you.

2. Type the address of the person to whom you wish to send the mail.

3. Press Tab to move the cursor down to the Subject line and type a subject for this note if you want one. Press Tab a few more times until the insertion point jumps to the area below the gray line. Figure 4.1 shows a short e-mail message.

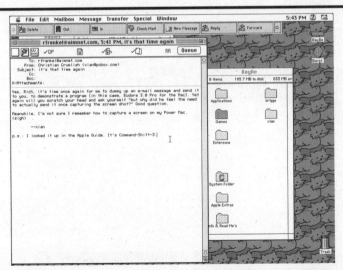

FIGURE 4.1: A new message window in Eudora for the Macintosh

4. When you are done, click the Send button in the upper-right corner of the message window. The button might read Queue instead of Send. This means that the message will be added to a list (a queue) of messages to be sent all at once when the program checks for new mail.

Eudora also makes it easy to check your Inbox for new mail:

1. Select File ➢ Check Mail or press Ctrl+M (F4 or Command+M on a Mac), or click the Check Mail icon on the toolbar. Eudora will connect to something called a *POP* or *IMAP server* (POP stands for *Post Office Protocol* and IMAP stands for *Internet Message Access Protocol*, but you can forget that) to pick up or display all of your mail.

2. Unread mail will appear with a large dot (or bullet) in the left column of the Inbox, unless you have changed your default mailbox preferences (see Figure 4.2). To view the contents of a mail message, highlight it in the window and press Enter (or double-click on it).

3. After reading the message, you can close its window or select Message ➢ Reply (or Ctrl+R) to reply to the message. If you start a reply by mistake, just close the message window. You will be prompted to save it only if you've made any changes.

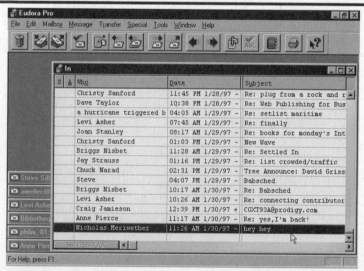

FIGURE 4.2: The Inbox of the Windows version of Eudora

TIP

If you want to reply to everyone who was also sent a copy of the message, press Ctrl+Shift+R instead of Ctrl+R (or select Message ≻ Reply to All).

Deleting Eudora Messages

After you have sent and received a number of messages, you may need to clean up your Eudora Inbox by deleting old messages. Use the following options to delete messages and undelete (restore) messages that you deleted by mistake.

▶ To delete a message, highlight it and click Delete, press the Delete key, or click the Trash icon at the top of the mailbox window. This moves the message to the Trash mailbox. It won't actually be deleted until you empty the trash (Special ≻ Trash).

▶ If you change your mind, select Mailbox ≻ Trash to open the Trash mailbox and look at the list of deleted messages. Highlight the message you want to rescue, and then select Transfer ≻ In to move the message back into the Inbox, or transfer it to any other mailbox.

TIP

If deleting the message was the last function you performed other than reading other messages or anything else that doesn't involve creating or deleting anything, you can simply hit CTRL+Z or select Undo from the Edit menu and the stray message or messages will be returned.

Sending, Forwarding, and Formatting Eudora Messages

Eudora's messaging features provide all of the basic e-mail functions, along with some extras that you may find useful. Here are some of the Eudora options:

▶ To send a message to additional recipients, type their e-mail addresses on the Cc or Bcc lines, separated by commas if there are more than one on any single line. You may also specify other recipients by selecting Insert Recipients from the Edit Menu.

NOTE

The Edit ➤ Insert Recipient, Message ➤ New Message To, and Special ➤ Remove Recipient menus all display the recipient list pop-up menu; they just perform different tasks with it.

▶ To forward a message you have open, select Message ➤ Forward. Then proceed as you would with a new message.

TIP

If you want to add some explanatory text before the forwarded message, but you don't want the forwarded message to have the ">" symbol before each line, select Message ➤ Redirect instead of Message ➤ Forward.

▶ If you wish to format your message, you can add MIME-encoded formatting. Use the formatting button just above the To line in the message window or select the formatting options from the Edit ➤ Text submenu.

NOTE

Eudora easily displays complete Web pages including pictures inside of its message windows. Even though it does not create HTML formatting for plain text messages, it does treat any URL (Web address) as a live hyperlink.

Filtering Incoming E-mail in Eudora

To set up a simple filter for keeping your messages neatly filed, follow these steps:

1. Select Tools ➤ Filters to open the Filters dialog box.

2. Click the New button.

3. The Incoming and Manual check boxes are checked by default. Checkmark the Outgoing check box as well, if you plan to sort your own outgoing mail with this same filter.

4. Click the Header drop-down list box and choose the header by which these e-mail messages can be recognized. Select Any Header for the broadest possible net. Headers can be any set of letters and numbers in the To line, any set of letters and numbers in the From line, or any topic in the Subject line.

TIP

If you have opted-in on a number of newsletters and would like to filter that whole mess in one fell swoop, configure a filter to send all items whose headers contain the word "newsletter" to a Newsletters mailbox. Be sure to check that mailbox periodically to make sure a friend didn't send you a message containing the word "newsletter" in a header.

5. Choose a criterion in the next drop-down list (usually Contains will work well, but there are many interesting choices), and then type the text to be found (or avoided or compared with) in the box to the right.

6. To further qualify the filter, add a second criterion by clicking the drop-down list box that currently reads Ignore and change it to And, Or, or Unless.

TIP

This is a good way to make dual-purpose filters. Say you get mail from News X and News Y. Create a filter that says "If the From field contains News X <OR> if the From field contains News Y ➢ Transfer to Mailbox Z".

7. Select an action in the first Action drop-down list box (you will probably want Transfer To, but, again, there are many interesting options).

8. If you choose Transfer To, click the button to the right and select a folder into which the filtered mail should be transferred automatically (see Figure 4.3).

9. Add up to four additional actions, if you are ruthless enough.

10. Close the window and save the changes when prompted.

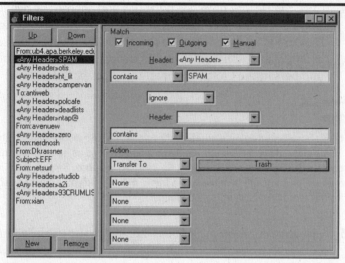

FIGURE 4.3: The simplest filter you can make with Eudora—straight to the circular file

For quick and dirty filtering, there's a simpler way, but it's less robust. Follow these instructions:

1. Go to your Inbox and select a message that you want to filter to a new mailbox.

2. Go to the Special menu and select Make Filter. This opens a dialog box that has the basic functions of the main Filters window.

3. Select the item from the offered headers that you want to filter messages by.

4. Now, select a place to filter it by accepting the offered automatic folder name or by clicking the None Chosen button and selecting from your existing folder set. There is also a trash item if you'd rather just get rid of it.

Checking Multiple E-mail Accounts with Eudora Personalities

You can set up Eudora to check multiple accounts with the Personalities feature.

1. To set up a new "personality," first find and select the Options or Settings command. (Its exact location on the menu differs in the various versions of the program, but it's over on the right somewhere!)

2. Choose the Personalities category in the dialog box. Now you can add additional addresses to your original, or "dominant," personality.

3. Click the New button to create a new personality. Enter the basic e-mail server and address information required for any account.

   ▶ Click Check Mail if you want Eudora to look for mail on this account any time that you tell it to check for mail.

   ▶ Click Leave Mail on Server if the mail will have to be accessible to some other e-mail program as well—one at home or work, perhaps.

Attaching Files to Eudora Messages

Eudora messages can also have files attached to them. Eudora's design lets you work intuitively with the drag-and-drop method, or you can use the keyboard or menu commands to add attachments, as explained here:

1. When you want to attach a file, first start a new message.

2. Then use one of these actions to attach the file:

   ▶ Drag the file from a folder window into the Eudora message window.

   ▶ Select Message ➤ Attach File.

   ▶ Press Ctrl+H or Command+H.

3. Choose a file from the Attach File dialog box (it's just like a normal Open dialog box).

4. Click OK to attach the file.

Depending on your version of Eudora, you might have the choice of several different formats for attached files, including MIME, *UUencode*, and *BinHex*—all different ways of translating files into a format that lets them travel across the Internet. Discuss the options with your intended recipient to find a format in common. The person you send the coded file to will need a program that decodes the file into a format usable in standard programs.

TIP

For the Mac version you can press F9 to display an Open dialog to add an attachment. For the Windows version, right-click the file you want to attach in Windows Explorer or on the desktop and select Eudora Pro from the Send To menu.

Adding a Name to Your Eudora Address Book

Eudora's address book feature is great for saving the e-mail addresses of people you correspond with frequently. It is not easy to remember e-mail addresses, so remember to enter the address in your address book as soon as you get a message from someone new. Here are the steps for adding addresses in Eudora:

1. Highlight a message from the person whose e-mail address you want to save and then select Special ≻ Make Address Book Entry (or press Ctrl+K).

2. Type a short, memorable "nickname" in the Make Address Book Entry dialog box that appears.

3. Click the Put it on the recipient list checkbox if you want to be able to select the address book entry from the pop-up recipient list menu (this is useful if you expect to send mail to this address regularly).

4. Click OK to add the new name to your address book.

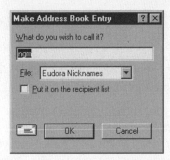

Now, whenever you want to use the address book entry, just type the nickname instead of the full Internet address. You can also use address book entries in a couple of other ways, as outlined here:

▶ If you add an address book entry to the recipient list, then you can send or forward mail to that address by selecting Message ➢ New Message To ➢ *Nickname* or Message ➢ Forward To ➢ *Nickname* (where *Nickname* is the name of the address you want). Eudora will do the rest.

▶ If you forget an address book entry, open the address book by selecting Tools ➢ Address Book (in earlier versions of Eudora, it was Window ➢ Nicknames—so poke around a little if you can't find the command), or by clicking the address book icon on the toolbar. Select the address book entry you want, and click the To button. Eudora will copy that address into a new message window.

Using Eudora's Spell Checker

To check the spelling in a message, select Edit ➢ Check Spelling. Eudora will scan the message for words that it doesn't recognize. If you've ever used the spell checker in any standard word processor, then you should be familiar with this drill:

▶ To skip a suspected word, click Ignore.

▶ To accept a suggested correction, click Change.

▶ To make your own correction, type it in the Change To box and then click Change.

▶ To add the word in question to the spell checker's dictionary, click Add.

Creating an E-mail Signature with Eudora

Eudora also has a signature feature. Here's how to use it:

1. Select Tools ➣ Signatures ➣ New (the free version of Eudora permits only one signature).

2. Type your signature and then close the window and agree to save it when prompted. If you create multiple signatures in Eudora Pro, you can set which one you want as the default in the Signatures category of the Options dialog box (the Settings dialog box on a Macintosh).

Eudora will automatically append this signature to all your outgoing mail unless you choose None in the Signature drop-down list box at the top of the new message window.

Quitting Eudora

When you are finished sending, reading, and replying to mail, you can quit Eudora or leave it running so you can quickly go back and check your mail. To quit Eudora, select File ➣ Exit (or File ➣ Quit in the Macintosh version of Eudora), or press Ctrl+Q (Command+Q for the Mac).

MICROSOFT OUTLOOK EXPRESS

Outlook Express (OE) has been available for some time now and has had ample time to prove itself. Pundits claim that many of Microsoft's products take until version 3.0 to become stable and contain the features they need to compete well, and OE seems to be one of them. Having reached its 5th birthday, OE has really matured into a very usable product. The most recent addition to the stable is the MacOS version 5.02, which brings a whole new interface and a full plate of new and improved features that can easily support multiple users and any number of e-mail accounts.

Long having superseded Internet Mail and Internet News, the application pair that accompanied Internet Explorer in its earlier days, OE has become a complete application capable of nearly everything Internet Explorer can do, short of actual web browsing. Without a doubt, it's also quite an accomplished e-mail client. One of the only shortcomings I note is that it's not very easy to set up filters, which OE calls Rules.

You can download Microsoft's latest e-mail software from the Microsoft Internet Explorer Web site: `http://www.microsoft.com/windows98/downloads/default.asp`, shown in Figure 4.4. Click on the Internet Explorer 5.01 link and follow the instructions. See Chapter 9 for an explanation of how to download files.

FIGURE 4.4: Microsoft's Internet Explorer Download Center site is the source of free trial versions of all Microsoft software, including Outlook Express.

OE can handle Internet mail, network mail, and mail from MSN (the Microsoft Network online service), as well as HotMail, Microsoft's free Web-based e-mail service. You can start OE by double-clicking the OE icon on your desktop, by selecting Start ➢ Programs ➢ Microsoft Outlook Express, or by clicking on the miniature Launch Outlook Express icon in the taskbar tray near the Start button.

Outlook starts you off in a window showing four panes. The pair on the left show the various mailboxes and newsgroup listings of the program that are available, with your Inbox first and foremost (see Figure 4.5) and your Address book below that. The pane on the right shows you the contents of your Inbox (but you can click the large Inbox button at the top of the list of messages to choose another mailbox and Outlook will show its contents below).

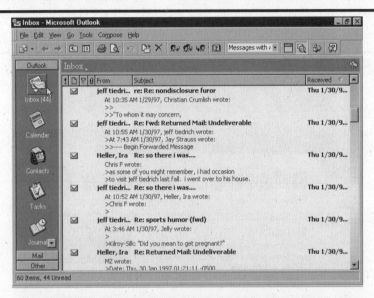

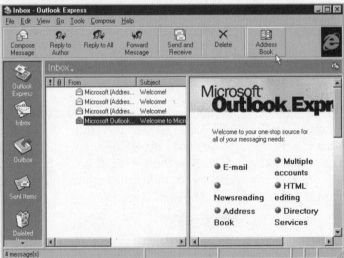

FIGURE 4.5: The opening window of Outlook Express

NOTE

Outlook Express has a big Preview pane that shows you the contents of the highlighted message. You can turn this Preview on or off and change its appearance and location with the View ➤ Layout menu selection.

Creating Outlook Messages and Checking E-mail

Here's how to create a new Outlook e-mail message:

1. Select Compose ➤ New Mail Message (Ctrl+N or Command+N for the Mac). This will open up a new message window.

2. Type an address (or click the To button, select a recipient, click the To or CC button, repeat for additional recipients, if any, and then click OK). Press Tab to get down to the Subject box where you can type a subject if you care to.

3. Tab down to the message area and type your message. Click the Send button and away it goes. If you are accumulating messages to send in bulk with Outlook Express, select File ➤ Send Later, then click the Send and Receive button in the main Outlook Express window when you are ready to send them all.

To read a message in your Inbox (see Figure 4.6), just double-click its subject line. The message will appear in its own window. To reply to the message, select Reply to Author or Reply to All in Outlook Express (Ctrl+R). Outlook will supply the recipient's address. Proceed as if you were sending a new message.

TIP

If you want to reply to everyone who was also sent a copy of the message, press Ctrl+Shift+R instead of Ctrl+R.

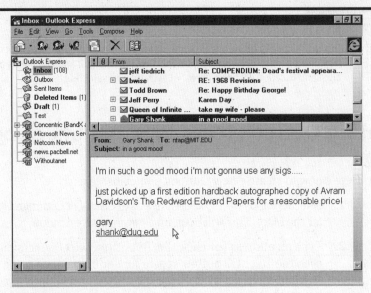

FIGURE 4.6:   My Inbox as shown by Microsoft Outlook Express

Deleting Outlook Messages

To delete a message, just highlight it and click the Delete button or press the Delete key on your keyboard. It will be moved to the Deleted Items folder until you specifically instruct Outlook Express to delete the folder's contents (even then, Outlook will warn you that you are permanently deleting the message).

TIP

To undelete a message, open the Deleted Items folder and select the message you want to restore. Then select File ➤ Move, choose the Inbox folder from the dialog box that appears, and click OK.

Sending and Forwarding Outlook Messages

Here are some commands you will probably use a lot:

▶ To forward a message in Outlook Express, click Forward Message. You can also press Ctrl+F and then proceed as you would with a new message

▶ To send mail to multiple recipients, type their addresses in the To box—separated by semicolons, not commas—or type additional addresses in the Cc box.

Creating More Message Folders

As you begin to accumulate messages, replies, and copies of original messages you sent to others, you will need additional folders to store them in for easy retrieval. It's quite easy to add new message folders to your set of personal folders:

1. Select File ➤ Folder ➤ New Folder.

2. In the New Folder dialog box that appears, type a name for the folder and click OK.

Once a folder is created in Outlook, moving a message into the folder is even easier; simply click on the message and drag it to the folder (in the left pane).

Sorting Outlook Express Messages with Filters

Microsoft Outlook Express has sophisticated, multiple-path filtering, just like the other guys. The general idea is to identify messages with certain values in them (those values being an e-mail address or some other in-message text) and move identified messages to different folders. Sort of like having an assistant to manage your filing cabinets.

These steps will get you started with the setup of an e-mail message filter in Outlook Express.

1. Select Tools ➤ Message Rules, and then click Mail.

NOTE

There are also News and Blocked Senders List, but they all work the same, so there's no need to cover them all. It would be like reading the same book three times and calling it a trilogy!

2. The Message Rules dialog box opens. Click the New button on the left side. The New Mail Rule dialog box appears. First, select the criteria you wish to use to filter the messages. Whatever you place a checkmark next to adds a line of text to the third box.

3. Next, define exactly what you want to happen to messages that meet the criteria. Most common is to move specific messages to specific folders so they can be sorted by sender, topic, or whatever organization you deem appropriate (see Figure 4.7).

4. In the third box, click on the hypertext items one at a time and enter the data that the messages are to be matched against. For example, if Clarabelle sends you weekly Chocolate Chip cookie recipe modifications, you'd want to file her messages in a separate mailbox, because they're easier to find when they're not all jumbled in with hundreds of other messages. In the rule you would set FROM to Clarabelle and send it to a Clarabelle folder.

5. Click OK to save the rule and then add more rules if you wish. Outlook Express lists your rules in the Message Rules dialog box (in plain English, such as "Move to 'Likely Spam' if Subject contains 'Money'").

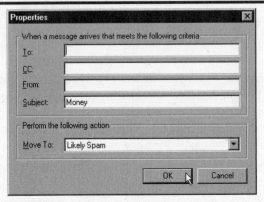

FIGURE 4.7: With Outlook Express you can sort your messages as they arrive.

Attaching Files to E-mail Messages in Outlook

Use one of these options to attach files to your messages:

▶ Use Explorer, My Computer, or File Manager to open the window the file is in, click on the file, and drag it into the new message window.

▶ Select Insert ➤ File Attachment, choose the file you want from the Insert File dialog box that appears, and then click OK. Figure 4.8 shows an attached file in an Outlook message.

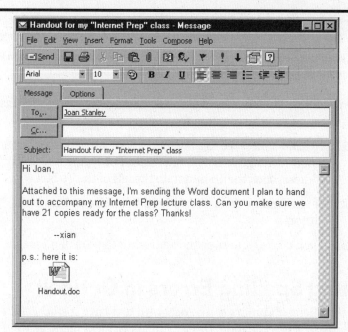

FIGURE 4.8: Outlook inserts an icon representing the attachment into your message at the insertion point. Your recipient double-clicks the icon to open the attached file.

Using the Outlook Address Book

Outlook's address book is useful for keeping track of all the e-mail addresses associated with your friends and business associates. Here's how to update the address book with new names:

1. To add a name to your address book, select Tools ➤ Address Book (or press Ctrl+Shift+B) and then select File ➤ New Entry (or press Ctrl+N).

2. In the New Entry dialog box that appears, choose Internet Mail Address and click OK.

3. Type a name for the address, press Tab, and type the e-mail address.

4. When you're done, click OK.

TIP

Right-click on a message from a person or group that you want to add to your Address Book and select Add Sender to Address Book. *Voilà!*

Using address book names in Outlook messages is even easier than adding them, as you can see from these steps:

1. To send a message to someone in your address book, create a new message as usual, but instead of typing a recipient's address, click the To button to the left of the To box.

2. Select a name from the address book list and click the To button.

3. Then click OK to copy the address to the e-mail message.

Correcting Spelling Errors in Outlook

All of the Microsoft products that deal with text have spell checkers. Outlook Express is no exception. In the Outlook Express message window, select Tools ➤ Spelling (or press F7) to check the spelling of a message.

Outlook will start scanning the message for words that it doesn't recognize. If you've ever used the spell checker in Word or any other standard word processor, then you should be familiar with this drill:

▶ To skip the word in question, click Ignore.

▶ To accept a suggested correction, click Change.

▶ To make your own correction, type the correct word in the Change To box and click Change.

▶ To add the word in question to the spell checker's dictionary, click Add.

Formatting an E-mail Message with HTML in Outlook Express

Outlook Express is set up by default to permit HTML formatting in your messages. If you don't see the HTML formatting toolbar in a new message window, you can add it by selecting Format ➤ HTML.

Then just select text to be formatted and use the buttons on the toolbar to apply HTML formatting, such as bold and italic, bulleted lists, alignment (center, flush left, or flush right), and text color.

WARNING

Bear in mind that not everyone will be able to see the formatting you apply, and some mail programs may even mangle your message trying to represent the formatting. Often the message is displayed as an attachment with nothing in the message window for the recipient to read. The message may even get displayed twice, once in plain text and once with HTML tags.

Using E-mail Signatures in Outlook

Microsoft Outlook Express supports signature files. These files retain your personal or professional information and add it to your messages according to your instructions.

Here are the steps for creating a standard e-mail signature in Outlook:

1. Select Tools ➤ Options and select the Signatures tab. This brings up the Signatures manager where all signatures (also called "sigs") are created, stored, and modified.

2. Click New and type your signature into the Edit Signature field. Add as many signatures as you feel you'll use.

3. When you're finished, you may add another signature or move on. I suggest that you first click Rename and give each signature a recognizable name that tells you what it contains or its intended purpose.

4. Use the check boxes at the top of the dialog box to determine whether or not Outlook Express will automatically add your default signature to all outgoing messages and whether it should use your signature when you reply to or forward a message.

Quitting Outlook

To exit Outlook Express, select File ➢ Exit.

NETSCAPE MESSENGER/MAIL

Netscape Communicator 4.7*x* sports a full-featured mail program called Netscape Messenger. Netscape 6's version is called simply Mail.

Basic Messenger Functions

NOTE

Because Messenger and Mail work essentially the same, I'll note only the places where Netscape 6 differs from Communicator. Otherwise, you can apply most aspects of Communicator to Netscape 6. I will, however, use screenshots from Netscape 6 so that you can see the difference.

Using Netscape Messenger for e-mail is a lot like using many of the other programs I've mentioned. Here's how to create and send an e-mail message:

1. Select File ➢ New ➢ Message (or press Ctrl+M or click the New Message button).

2. Type an address in the To box. Press Tab and type a subject.

3. Press Tab again to enter the message area and type your message.

4. When you're done, click the Send button.

If you receive mail while working in Netscape (the little envelope in the lower-right corner of the Netscape window will alert you), select Communicator ➢ Messenger. (The first time you do this, Netscape may require you to enter your password.) Just highlight a message in the upper-right pane to see its contents in the lower-right pane (see Figure 4.10).

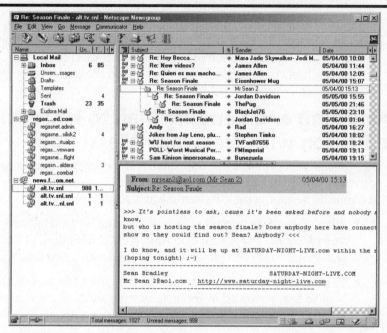

FIGURE 4.10: The Netscape Mail window lists messages in the upper-right pane and shows the contents of the current message in the hideable lower-right pane.

TIP

Remember that any Web addresses mentioned in Netscape Messenger e-mail messages you receive will function as clickable links. That means that when you finish reading, all you have to do is click on a highlighted word to go to that Web page and start surfing.

Here are some other Netscape Messenger commands you will find useful:

▶ To reply to a message, click the Reply button, press Ctrl+R (Command+R on the Mac), or select Message ➤ Reply ➤ To Sender Only.

▶ To delete a message, just highlight it and click the Delete button. Netscape will move the message to a Trash folder.

▶ To undelete a message, select the Trash folder in the drop-down folder list just above the top pane, select the message, and then choose Message ➤ Move Message ➤ Inbox.

You can close the mail window and keep Netscape running if you want. In Windows 95, click the close button in the upper-right corner (on the Mac, click the close button in the upper-left corner) or you can quit Netscape entirely by selecting File ➤ Exit (or, on the Mac, File ➤ Quit).

Forwarding and Sending Mail to More than One Person with Netscape Messenger

Netscape Messenger has a full complement of messaging features, including mail forwarding and the means to send mail to more than one person at a time. Here are the basic forwarding and sending options:

▶ When you want to forward a message, click the Forward button (or select Message ➤ Forward Quoted or press Ctrl+Shift+L or Command+Shift+L). Then proceed as you would with a new message.

▶ To send mail to multiple recipients, type the addresses in the Mail To box, separated by commas, or enter additional addresses in the Cc box.

Creating New Folders for Filing Messenger E-Mail

Messenger also allows you to create new folders for filing messages. Here's how you do it:

1. Select the folder in the left pane in which you want the new folder to appear (or select Local Mail to create an upper-level folder).

2. Then select File ➤ New ➤ Folder.

3. Type a name for the new folder in the dialog box that appears and then click OK.

Filing Netscape Messenger Messages in Folders

Netscape Messenger (and the rest of the Communicator suite) has a revamped menu structure that gives toolbar buttons mini-menus of their own. This means that it is even easier and faster to file messages in Messenger than it is in other e-mail programs, because you do not have to open a folder window or use a dialog box to find the folder where you want to put the message.

1. Highlight the message to be moved.

2. Click the File button on the toolbar (or select Message ➤ Move Message).

3. Choose the destination folder from the menu that pops up (subfolders appear on submenus).

Filtering Netscape Messenger E-mail

Netscape Messenger's rules for filtering e-mail are quite specific and give you more flexibility in organizing your mailbox than other mail filters. Most of the time you can use the existing rules provided by Netscape. If none of these rules are customized enough for you, you can construct unique rules for your own mail management needs.

Here's how to create a new filter for incoming messages:

1. Select Edit ➤ Message Filters.

2. Click the New button on the Message Filters dialog box.

3. In the top half of the Filter Rules dialog box that appears, enter a name for your filter (see Figure 4.11).

4. Choose one of the nine different aspects of the message to base your filter on (such as the subject, the priority, or who's on the Cc list).

5. Choose one of the six different comparison criteria (Contains, Doesn't Contain, Is, Isn't, Begins With, and Ends With) and then enter the text to look for or avoid in the third box.

6. Click the More button if you want to add additional criteria.

7. Below the More button, choose from six actions (usually you'll want Move to Folder—some of the instructions are more suited for discussion groups than for private e-mail), and then choose a folder (if applicable).

8. Finally, enter a description (if you wish), and click OK.

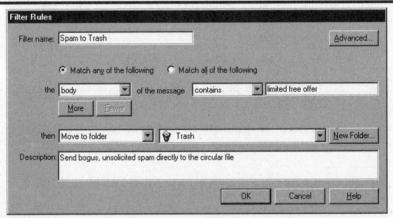

FIGURE 4.11: You can put together sophisticated filters easily with Netscape Messenger.

Attaching Files to Messenger E-mail

Netscape Messenger's provisions for attaching files to e-mail are quite simple. You can also attach Web page links to your messages with these commands:

1. Select Message ➤ New Message to open the Composition window. Or you can click the New Message button in the Messenger toolbar or press Ctrl+M.

2. Address your e-mail and type your message in the message body. To attach a file to the message, click the Attach button.

3. Choose File (as you can see, you can also attach Web pages, among other things).

4. In the dialog box that appears, choose the file you want to send, and then click Open.

5. Click the Save or the Send button to save a draft or to send your message on its way.

TIP

To check the spelling of your e-mail message in Netscape Messenger, choose Tools ➤ Check Spelling in the Composition window.

Using the Netscape Messenger Address Book

You can add names to Netscape Messenger's address book by following these steps:

1. Select Communicator ➤ Address Book from any of the Messenger windows.

2. In the Address Book window that appears, click the New Card button.

3. Enter the name, e-mail address, and nickname, and then click OK.

4. Select File ➤ Close to close the Address Book window.

To use the addresses in your new messages, do one of the following, depending on how good your memory is:

▶ In the Composition window, type the nickname on the To line.

▶ If you don't remember the nickname you made up, click the Address button, select the name, click To, and then click OK.

NOTE

You can add HTML formatting (or insert hyperlinks or even graphic images) to your message using the convenient toolbar in the Composition window. (Insert links and images with the Insert Object button furthest to the right.)

Adding a Signature File to Messenger E-mail

Messenger's signature file feature does not include much formatting support, but you can create basic signature files and add them to your messages with a minimum amount of fuss.

Here are the steps for creating and adding a signature file:

1. First, use a text editor or word processor to create and save a text file containing the signature you want to have at the end of your e-mail messages.

2. Then, in Netscape Messenger, select Edit ➤ Preferences. Double-click the Mail & Groups item in the Category list of the Preferences dialog box.

3. Click Identity in the Mail & Groups list item and type the full path and filename of your signature file in the Signature File box (or click the Browse button to find and select the file, and then click OK).

4. When you're done, click OK.

TIP

If your signature exceeds the recommended four lines (this rubric is a widely accepted netiquette standard, though many people violate it), Netscape will warn you, but all you have to do is click OK again to accept it.

PEGASUS MAIL

Pegasus is a popular, free e-mail program that can run on networks and over dial-up Internet connections. Pegasus employs all of the usual e-mail commands and features. Use the Pegasus buttons and menus as described in the following steps to do everything from forwarding mail to using your address book.

TIP

You can download Pegasus from its Web site at http://www.pegasus.usa.com/. See Chapter 9 for tips on downloading files from the Net.

Basic Pegasus Functions

When you are ready to send Pegasus messages, here's how to compose and send them:

1. Select File ➤ New Message (or press Ctrl+N).

2. Type the recipient's name, press Tab, and type a subject if you care to. Then press Tab two more times to get down to the message area and type your message.

3. When you're done, click the Send button to either send your message immediately or put it in a queue, depending on how your version of Pegasus is set up.

4. To send all queued messages, select File ➤ Send All Queued Mail.

To read new mail, select File ➤ Read New Mail (or press Ctrl+W). This opens the New Mail folder. (Once you've read a message, it will automatically be moved to the Main mail folder after you close the New Mail folder or exit Pegasus.)

The following commands will help you check for new Pegasus messages, read, reply, or delete messages you've received, and finally, exit Pegasus:

▶ To check for new messages, select File ➤ Check Host for New Mail.

▶ To read a message, double-click on it.

▶ To reply to an open message, click the Reply button.

▶ To delete a message, click the Delete button.

▶ To exit Pegasus, select File ➤ Exit.

Forwarding Pegasus Mail or Sending Messages to More than One Person

Your Pegasus Mail messages can be forwarded to other people and you can send forwarded messages or other types of messages to more than one person with the following options:

▶ To forward a message, just click the Forward button at the top of the message window. Then proceed as you would with any new message.

▶ To send an e-mail to multiple recipients, type the addresses in the To box, separated by commas, or enter additional addresses in the Cc box.

Managing Pegasus Mail with Folders

Like most of the other mail programs profiled in this lesson, Pegasus Mail has a folder feature for storing messages so that you can find them later when you want to refer back to them.

Here's how to create a new folder:

1. Select File ➤ Mail Folders to open the Folders dialog box.

2. Click the New button, type a name for the new folder, and click OK.

To move a message from one folder to another, double-click the folder currently containing the message, highlight the message you want to move, and drag it to the new folder.

Attaching Files to Pegasus Messages

File attachments are an important part of Pegasus Mail messages because the program supports many different Internet file types. When you start sending messages with attachments to many different people on many different systems, you might have to experiment with these file formats to see which one works best and gets the information to your recipients in a usable format. These steps will get you started:

1. Click the Attach button on the left side of the message window.

2. Select a file in the bottom part of the window that appears, and then click the Add button (top right).

3. Choose one of a wide variety of file-encoding formats from the Encoding drop-down list, or allow the mailer to choose one for you.

4. Click the Editor button (on the left side of the window) when you're ready to return to typing your message.

5. When you're done typing the message, you can just click Send.

TIP

If you use a PC—especially on a local area network—and you sometimes have trouble accessing the path the folder is in, you may have to move the file around with Windows Explorer.

Creating and Using a Pegasus Address Book

The address book feature in Pegasus Mail is a little different from other e-mail address books because you have to create the address book before you can add names to it. The advantage to this setup is that you can have more than one address book. For example, you could have Business and Personal address books to store the names and addresses of business associates and friends separately. (Some people might get listed in both books, however, if you are fortunate enough to have friends at work!)

1. To create an address book, select Addresses ➤ Address Books, and then click New in the Select an Address Book dialog box that appears.

2. Type a name for the address book and then click OK.

3. To open an address book, select Addresses ➤ Address Books and double-click on the name of the address book you want to open.

4. To add a name to the address book, click the Add button. Pegasus suggests the name and e-mail address from the currently selected message, but you can type in any name.

5. Press Tab seven times to get to the E-mail Address box and type a different e-mail address, if you like. Then click OK.

When you want to send e-mail to someone in one of your address books, you have two choices:

▶ Type their name in the To box.

▶ Open the address book (as just described), scroll down to select the person you want, and click the Paste button. Then click Close.

Correcting Misspelled Words in Pegasus Messages

You can access the spell-checking feature by selecting Edit ➤ Check Spelling. Pegasus will start scanning the message for words that it doesn't recognize. If you've ever used the spell checker in any standard word processing program, then you should be familiar with how it works:

▶ To skip the word in question, click Skip.

▶ To accept a suggested correction, click Change.

▶ To make your own correction, type the correct word over the suggestion and click Change.

▶ To add the word in question to the spell checker's dictionary, click Add.

Pegasus will tell you when you've reached the end of the message and ask if you want to start over from the top. Click No (unless you want to). Then click Close.

Creating and Adding Signatures to Pegasus Mail

Use the Pegasus Mail Signature feature to create signature blocks that you can use repeatedly in different messages. This is especially useful for business messages, because it saves you the time of retyping your name, title, company name, address, phone and fax numbers, e-mail address, and all the other contact information usually included on a business card. Just type it once and save it in a signature file, then reuse this file in all your messages.

Follow these steps to make your signature file:

1. Select File ➤ Preferences ➤ Signatures ➤ For Internet Messages.

2. Type your signature in the dialog box that appears and click the Save button.

PINE

If you're determined to get your hands dirty and log in directly to a Unix account to read mail with a Unix mail reader, then here's a quick run-down of the most useful commands in everybody's favorite Unix mail program, Pine. (Pine uses simple letter commands rather than menus and buttons to implement e-mail features, but the end results are the same as for the programs that run under Windows and the Mac OS, described earlier in this lesson.)

TIP

Another popular Unix e-mail program is Elm. For information about Elm, send mail to mail-server@cs.ruu.nl with no subject and type the two lines send NEWS.ANSWERS/elm/FAQ and end on separate lines as your message.

Basic Pine Functions

Here's how you create and send e-mail using Pine in the Unix environment:

1. Start Pine by typing **pine** (yes, all lowercase—it does matter) at the Unix command prompt and press Enter.

2. Pine starts you off at a main menu. To enter your Inbox, type **i** (and don't press Enter).

3. To send mail, type **c** (and don't press Enter). Pine will start a new message (see Figure 4.12).

4. Type the recipient's address, press Tab, and type a subject. Press Tab again until you're in the message area. Then type your message. Pine will handle word wrapping, so you have to press Enter only when you're starting a new paragraph.

5. When you're done, press Ctrl+X to send the message.

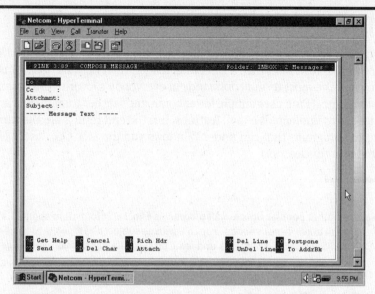

FIGURE 4.12: Pine is a full-screen editor, so it works something like a normal Windows or Mac program, even though it's text-only and runs in Unix.

AN INTERESTING CREATURE, PINE

Even if you're a diehard mouser and live and die by the GUI, Pine could work for you. The University of Washington (state, that is) has been maintaining Pine for many years and will likely go on doing so. In their ongoing efforts to make Pine the best possible mail client for Unix workstations, they have slowly added a few features here and there. One of those features is console mouse detection. In other words, you can run Pine in a console window in an X-window session, and use the mouse to click on things in Pine.

Pine also has a lot of display and message management options that other mailers don't have. Oh, and Pine can load and read newsgroups from news servers. The only other mailers I know that can do that are Microsoft Outlook Express and Netscape Messenger and Mail. Pine also makes it easy to manage your mail from pretty much any computer anywhere, as long as it has Internet access and your host computer offers Telnet access (see Chapter 9).

All in all, Pine is a very capable e-mail client and newsreader that is well worth the effort to look into.

The following list summarizes the commands for some specific Pine functions:

Function	Type
To run Pine	Type **pine** and press Enter
To move between listed messages	Press the up and down arrow keys
To read a message	Highlight it in your Inbox and press Enter
To send mail	Type **c**
To return to your message list	Type **i**
To reply to a message	Type **r**
To delete a message	Type **d**
To undelete a message	Type **u**
To quit Pine	Type **q**

Forwarding a Message in Pine

Although Pine may appear to be just a simple mail program, you can forward messages, and Pine even adds a reply separator between the message you type and the message you are forwarding. Use these steps to forward Pine messages to other Pine users:

1. When you receive a message you want to forward to another person, type **f.**

2. Pine will put you in the Forward Message screen, which is exactly the same as the Compose Message screen except that the message area includes the original message, preceded by:

   ```
   -----Forwarded Message-----
   ```

3. Proceed as you would with a normal message.

Sending Pine Messages to More than One Person

Pine also supports sending mail to many people at one time. You can add more than one address to either the To line or the Cc line in a Pine message using one of these options:

▶ Type each e-mail address on the To line, separated by commas.

▶ Type additional e-mail addresses on the Cc line, separated by commas.

TIP

You can always go back to your Inbox folder by typing g (for Go to) and then pressing Enter to accept the default.

If you want to save a piece of mail for future reference, press **s** either in the index or while reading the mail. Pine will suggest Saved-Messages as a folder name, but you can replace that name with anything you like.

Looking at Message Folders with Pine

Pine provides message folders for storing messages in an orderly manner. You can file messages in folders that reflect the message subject, sender, or other topics and revisit them later with these procedures:

1. To look at the contents of a folder, type l to see a folder list.

2. Press the Tab key to get to the folder list you want to see, and then press Enter.

3. When you are done and want to go back, type l to get back to the folder list and choose the Inbox folder.

Attaching Files to Pine Messages

You can also send a file with Pine. Here are the steps for adding file attachments to Pine messages:

1. In the Compose Mail screen, press Tab twice to get to the Attachment line.

2. Then press Ctrl+T. This will bring up a list of the files in your Unix directory.

3. Using the arrow keys, select a file and press Enter. Pine will send the file as a MIME attachment.

TIP

Okay, but how do I get the file to my Unix directory? You can use an FTP program, as explained in Chapter 9. Or check with your Unix system administrator to find out which modem protocol and commands to use on your system.

Creating and Using a Pine Address Book

To create an address book—a list of e-mail addresses you regularly send mail to—type **a** (from the Main Menu screen). This brings up the Address Book screen.

To add a new address to the Pine address book:

1. Type **a**. Pine will prompt you with:

    New full name (last, first):

2. Type the last name, a comma, and then the first name of the person whose Internet address you want to add to your address book. Then press Enter and Pine will prompt you with:

    Enter new nickname (one word and easy to remember):

3. Type a short nickname and press Enter. Then Pine will prompt you to:

    Enter new e-mail address:

4. Type the person's address and press Enter. The new address will be added to the address book.

5. Type i to return to the Inbox folder index, or type **m** to return to the Main Menu.

Now, whenever you want to use the nickname in the address book, just type it instead of the full Internet address. Pine will do the rest.

Adding Addresses to the Pine Address Book

Pine's address book supplies all of the usual address book functions and even has a nickname feature for storing address book entries. All you have to remember is the nickname and Pine will retrieve the person's e-mail address.

You can also take an e-mail address off a recent message and send it to the Pine address book with these steps:

1. To automatically add the sender of the current message to your address book from the Folder Index screen, type **t**.

2. Type an address book entry for the sender and press Enter.

3. Press Enter twice to accept the full name and address of the sender.

NOTE

Pine does not permit you to add formatting to message text (HTML or otherwise). Pine has no message filtering capabilities either.

Checking Message Spelling with Pine

Even though Pine may not have all the bells and whistles of its non-Unix counterparts, it does provide the essential spell-checking feature for proofing your messages before they "go public." Here are the steps involved:

1. To check the spelling of a message, press Ctrl+T (while in the message area itself).

2. Pine highlights any suspicious word and prompts you to correct it and press Enter—but Pine won't suggest any possible spellings. Press Enter to make the correction.

Adding Signature Files to Pine Messages

Pine's signature file function operates much like that of other e-mail programs. You can add all of your professional information to the signature file and it will be added at the end of all your Pine messages. The only disadvantage to the signature file is that it will appear on all your messages, not just the ones you select to have signatures.

1. Create a text file named .signature. To do so, type **pico**
   .signature at the Unix prompt and press Enter.

2. Type whatever you want to use for your signature (but keep it under four lines as traditional netiquette dictates).

3. Then press Ctrl+X, type **y**, and press Enter.

Your signature will appear at the end of your e-mail messages. When you reply to a message and quote the text in your reply, Pine will put your signature at the beginning of your new message, before the quoted text. The idea is for you to write your message before the signature and then delete as much of the quoted text as possible (while still letting it make sense).

TIP

The required location of the signature file might vary from one system to another, so if your signature file does not appear at the end of your messages, ask your system administrator where it should be stored.

WHAT'S NEXT?

Whew! You have just completed a very thorough examination of the e-mail capabilities of some of our most celebrated Internet programs. Now that you are an e-mail "expert," you're ready to learn about free e-mail programs and useful e-mail tools.

Chapter 5

FREE E-MAIL AND USEFUL E-MAIL TOOLS

Think one e-mail account is enough? No way! There are plenty of reasons to sign up for more free e-mail accounts.

Free e-mail offers are all over the Internet, and millions of folks are taking advantage of them. Why do companies offer e-mail for free? Repeat after me—ADVERTISING. The more hits, the more revenue, and the more likely you are to partake in some of the fee-based services that are available.

You'll need access to the Internet. You don't even need to have an ISP; you just need to be able to get into the Internet from any location.

Adapted from *Internet! I Didn' t Know You Could Do That..., Second Edition,* by Alan R. Neibauer

ISBN 0-7821-2844-0   282 pages $19.99

Sites and Features

Your first question may be, "Why do I need more than one e-mail address?" Oh, let me count the ways!

▶ Do you have an e-mail account at work and think (or know) your boss is reading your mail? Sign up for free e-mail to keep your personal mail just that—personal.

▶ Do you share an e-mail account with other members of your family and know that your spouse/children/significant other is reading your mail? Use free e-mail so every member of your family has their own address. (Some ISPs let you sign up for more than one e-mail address on one account anyway.)

▶ Do you have an ISP that you can access only from your home computer, or only from a computer where their special software is installed? Get free e-mail so you can get your mail from any computer connected to the Internet.

▶ Are you getting too much junk e-mail? Get a free e-mail account to use when filling out forms so junk mail is channeled there.

▶ Would you like an e-mail address with a snappy name, like the_boss@hotmail.com or clint@do.you.feel.lucky.punk.com? Yep, you can do that with free e-mail.

▶ Want to send an electronic complaint but not under your "real" address? Sign up for a free e-mail address and complain from there.

▶ Would you like to double-up on some free offers? You don't know whether the folks who give the offers would appreciate this, but many of them use your e-mail address to check whether you've already signed up. With a free e-mail account, you get another address to use.

If you answered YES! to any of those questions, then you are a perfect candidate for free e-mail. Here are some facts about free e-mail accounts.

All of the free e-mail programs are Web based. This means that you don't need any special software to get your e-mail, and you can get it from ANY location that has access to the Internet. You won't need any special e-mail program or special program provided by the ISP. You can get your mail from the library, the school, or the local Internet café—from anywhere that there is an Internet connection you can use.

The free e-mail programs are server based. This means that the e-mail is stored on their computer even after you read it. So if you check your mail at work, it will still be there for you to read again when you get home. You have to tell the system to delete it.

Some of the services also provide e-mail forwarding. This means that you can have mail from other accounts sent to their server. So all of your mail will be waiting for you in one location. The one drawback is that many of the services add a small ad to each message you send.

Who offers free e-mail? Just about everyone:

- ► www.v3mail.com
- ► www.excite.com
- ► www.homepageware.com
- ► www.lycos.com
- ► www.netscape.com
- ► www.visto.com
- ► www.yahoo.com
- ► www.iname.com
- ► www.mail.com

Hotmail

You almost can't browse anywhere on the Internet without tripping over a free e-mail program.

As an example, let's look at signing up for free mail on www.hotmail .com, a very popular free e-mail service. The process is about the same with the others; only the links are different.

1. Log on to www.hotmail.com.

2. Click Sign up now!

3. Enter the information requested. This includes entering a login name that will be your e-mail name, a password, your first and last name, your country, gender, and the year of your birth. You can also choose to have your name and location listed in the Hotmail directory and to have Hotmail add your name and e-mail address to general Internet directories.

4. When you're done, click Sign Up. A confirmation message appears showing your Hotmail login name.

5. Click Continue to Hotmail. You can now sign up for a free service to have news and other information automatically delivered to your Hotmail address.

6. Select the checkboxes for the types of information you want delivered and click Continue.

You can enter your login name and password to access your Hotmail e-mail and to send e-mail from the initial Hotmail screen.

A typical Hotmail inbox is shown in Figure 5.1. You can read or delete messages, move a message to another folder, and compose a new message.

The options on the left of the screen let you access other Hotmail features, such as a calendar and a notepad for storing reminders. If you click POP Mail, you can designate up to four mail servers that this e-mail will be linked to, such as your ISP or other free mail systems. Among other features, Hotmail and similar services let you create an online address book. Click Addresses from the list of options across the top to open your address book. Here you can add recipients and give them nicknames.

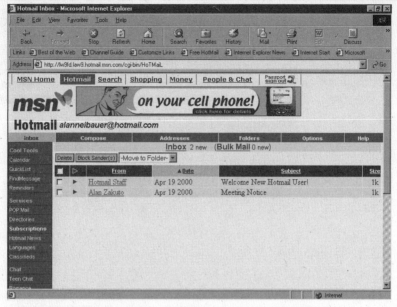

FIGURE 5.1: Hotmail inbox

To read a message, click its link in the From column. To delete mail, click to put a checkmark in the check box next to it and then click Delete. You can also move an e-mail to one of the other folders that Hotmail provides—Sent Messages, Drafts, the Trash Can, or a custom folder that you create.

To send a message, click Compose along the top of the screen. The mail composition window is shown in Figure 5.2. To access your address book, you can either type the recipient's e-mail address in the To line, or click To. The same goes for the cc and bcc lines. You can also click Directories to look up e-mail addresses.

Enter the subject of the message and then its text. Using the buttons, you can save the message in your Drafts folder, add an attachment, check your spelling, use the thesaurus, or look up a word in the dictionary. Click Egreetings to select and send an electronic greeting card. When you're done with the message, click Send.

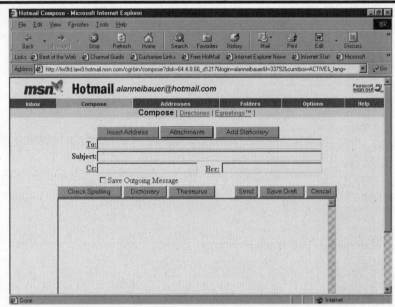

FIGURE 5.2: Composing mail with Hotmail

Also, the Add Stationery button lets you decorate your e-mail with a fancy graphic design. Click Add Stationery and, in the screen that appears, pull down the Background list to select from over 20 stationery designs. A preview of the design appears onscreen. Click Ok to add the design to your e-mail and return to the Compose form. Your design will be sent with the message, but it will not appear in the Compose form.

With all e-mail services, junk mail can be a problem. If you are getting mail from an annoying source, select the checkbox next to their message in the Inbox and click Block Sender(s). In the screen that appears, click OK to confirm blocking mail from that source so it will not appear in your inbox.

You can also turn on the Inbox Protector feature to channel mass marketing and other unwanted mail to a special Bulk Mail folder. Click Bulk Mail in the Inbox to open the Inbox Protector window, and then click the On option button to activate the feature.

Inbox Protector applies a set of rules to determine junk mail that will be sent to the Bulk Mail folder. In the Inbox Protector window you can choose to have these rules applied to mail from all Hotmail and Passport users, Microsoft and MSN, Passport partners, and specific addresses or domains that you enter. You can also choose to send the filtered mail to the Bulk Mail or Trash Can folder. Messages in the Trash Can are automatically deleted every night, while bulk mail is retained for 30 days.

TIP

Click Options on the top of a Hotmail window to change your profile information, customize blocked mail and Inbox Protector, create filters to channel mail, retrieve POP mail, create a signature for new mail, and set other Hotmail preferences.

NewCity

Most of the free e-mail services offer pretty much the same features, but NewCity provides a unique fun twist. With NewCity, you can create any number of *personalities*. A personality is a custom address for the sender of your e-mail, such as `alan@who.loves.you.baby.com`, or `bigboss@you.are.fired.com`.

If the recipient looks at the e-mail address for the sender, they will see the custom address of the personality, like this:

> E-Mail Address: alan@who.loves.you.baby.com

WARNING

Remember, though, that if you use a custom e-mail address instead of your regular NewCity address, the recipient will not be able to reply to your message unless they already know your regular NewCity address.

In addition to the custom address, you can also create any number of personal handles. A *handle* is a name that appears in the From line in place of an e-mail address. For example, here's the header of an e-mail that uses a NewCity handle:

> From: Love God

NewCity also lets you create a signature—text that is automatically inserted at the end of your e-mail.

Go to www.newcity.com and register for the free service. Then click Mail in the NewCity home page and enter your user name and password to access your Inbox. From the Inbox, you can read and compose new mail. Your NewCity e-mail address is your user name, as in alan@newcity.com.

To create a personality, however, click Preferences on the left of the inbox, and then click Personalities & Signatures. You will see the built-in personality called Me that uses your NewCity e-mail address, and a list of any personalities you have already created. Now follow these steps:

1. Click Create New.

2. Enter a name that will represent this personality in the list.

3. Enter the custom address.

4. Enter an optional handle. Do not enter a handle if you want the custom address to appear in the From portion of your e-mail.

5. Enter text up to 2000 characters to be used as a signature.

6. Click OK.

7. Click the Make Default button next to the personality you want NewCity to use for your e-mails by default.

To send an e-mail, click Write Mail to open the composition window. To choose a personality other than the default, pull down the From list and choose the personality to use for the message. Complete the e-mail and click Send.

MailStart

For a quick way to send e-mail using a custom non-returnable address, check out MailStart. MailStart offers a number of useful features, but its e-mail feature can be fun and ensure your privacy. You don't need to register with MailStart to send mail, and no special software is required.

To send mail, go to www.mailstart.com and click on the link Send E-Mail to Someone you Know to open the form shown in Figure 5.3.

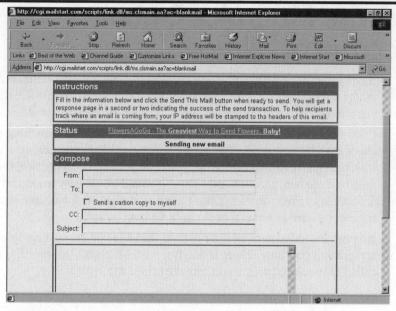

FIGURE 5.3:   Sending E-mail from MailStart

Enter your own e-mail address in the From line, or make something up for fun that looks like an e-mail address. Complete the form by entering the recipient's e-mail address, subject, and text of the message, and then click the Send This Mail button at the bottom of the form. The recipient will get the e-mail showing whatever address you entered in the From line as the sender.

NOTE

Your computer's IP address will be sent along with the message in the header. The IP address can be used to track you down, so be sure to use MailStart only for legitimate purposes.

Access Multiple E-Mail Accounts

Some Internet providers give you more than one e-mail account. You might use the accounts for each member of the family, or just use different names for various purposes, such as business and personal.

Once you have more than one e-mail account, you have to remember to check each for new mail. With all of the free e-mail offers available, and with multiple accounts at one ISP, you could end up checking two, three, four, or more mail accounts each time. It would be too easy to skip an account, and miss some important piece of mail. Having multiple accounts means you have to remember to check for mail on each.

No problem. All you need is a program that lets you access multiple accounts at one time. There is one free with Microsoft Internet Explorer, called Outlook Express, and there are others available.

Sites and Features

Checking more than one mail account at a time is easy. In fact, you can take advantage of free or inexpensive software to automatically check all of your accounts at the same time.

Before looking at these programs, however, you should understand about the two general types of e-mail systems—POP and Web-based.

Mail systems that use POP (Post Office Protocol) hold your mail on their computer until you access it. When you use a program to get your mail, your messages are downloaded to your computer and deleted from the service's computers.

Web-based mail is stored on the service's computer until you tell the service to delete a message. You access your mail by getting on the Internet and logging onto the service with your user name and password.

With that said, you should be aware that many systems use both POP and Web-based protocols. If you have an account with AT&T Worldnet, for example, you can use a program to download the mail using POP, or you can log onto the Internet and access your mail on the Web. While many Web-based mail services allow access to your mail only through your Web browser, some like Hotmail, Yahoo, and others also offer the option of POP access so you get the best of both worlds. If you have a free Web-based mail account, ask the provider if they also offer POP access.

Using Outlook Express

Outlook Express is a free e-mail program that comes with Microsoft Internet Explorer, which comes free with Microsoft Office and other programs. With Outlook Express, you set up one or more accounts that you want to use to send and receive POP-based mail. You can choose to send and receive from any or all accounts at the same time.

To set up an account in Outlook Express, start the program and then follow these steps:

1. Select Tools ➤ Accounts to open the Internet Accounts dialog box.

2. Click the Mail tab. Then click Add, and then select Mail. This starts the Internet Connection Wizard.

3. Enter the details of your account in the dialog boxes that follow. You will be asked for the name that you want displayed in messages, your e-mail address, the type of server, the name of the incoming and outgoing servers, and your account name and password.

4. Click Finish in the last Wizard dialog box.

NOTE

Outlook Express 5 also lets you sign up for a Hotmail account and send and receive Hotmail mail through POP. To sign up for a Hotmail account, choose Tools ➤ New Account Signup ➤ Hotmail. Follow the steps shown previously for adding a new account, but specify your Hotmail address in the second Wizard dialog box. You can also access your Hotmail account over the Internet using your Web browser.

When you click Finish in the last wizard dialog box, your accounts will be listed in the Accounts dialog box. The default account will be used automatically for all mail that you send. You can tell which account is the default by looking for the word "default" in the list of accounts. Use the Set as Default button to select another account as your default.

Before using the account, follow these steps:

1. Click the account in the Accounts dialog box.

2. Click Properties to see the dialog box shown in Figure 5.4.

3. In the text box at the top, enter the name that you want to appear for the mail account in Outlook Express boxes.

4. Notice the check box at the bottom labeled Include This Account When Receiving Mail or Synchronizing. Click to place a checkmark in the check box if you want Outlook Express to automatically include this account when you send and receive mail.

5. Click the Connection tab.

6. Click Always Connect Using, and then select the dial-up networking account.

7. Click OK.

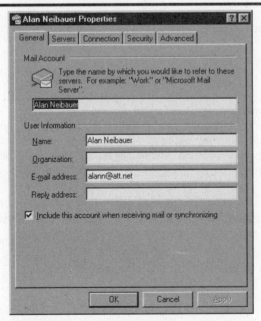

FIGURE 5.4: Account properties

Now when you are ready to send mail, you have to select the account to use. Click New Mail in the Outlook Express toolbar to open a mail window. Pull down the list at the end of the From box and select the mail account that you want to use. Complete the message and then click Send.

NOTE

The instructions for sending mail are for Outlook Express version 5. If you have an earlier version of the program, complete the mail messages, choose File ➤ Send Later Using, and then click the account to use.

When you click Send, Outlook Express adds the message to your Outbox. If Outlook Express isn't set up to send your mail immediately, click the Send/Rec button on the toolbar. Outlook Express dials your Internet provider, sends your mail from your Outbox, and checks for new mail. If you want to send mail without checking for new messages, pull down the list next to the Send/Rec button and choose Send All. You can also choose a specific account to use.

Changing Identities

When you check for mail with multiple accounts set up, all new mail appears in the same inbox. This means that you'll be able to read everyone's mail, and they'll be able to read yours. If you want to keep your mail separate and private, create an *identity* for each member of the family who has an e-mail account. The identity records the person's name and e-mail address, and creates an entirely new set of folders for each person.

To create an identity, choose File ➤ Identities ➤ Add New Identity to open the dialog box shown here:

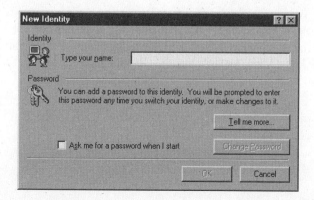

Type a name for the identity. If you want to password-protect the folders so that others cannot read the identity's e-mail, click Ask Me For a Password When I Start. Enter the password in both text boxes and click OK.

Now click OK in the New Identity dialog box. You'll be asked if you want to switch to that identity. If you select Yes, a whole new set of Outlook Express folders appears. If you select No, you can later change identities by selecting File ➤ Switch Identity. This will open the box shown in Figure 5.5. Click the identity in the box that appears, and then click OK.

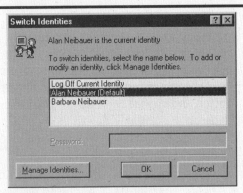

FIGURE 5.5: Switching identities

For each identity, you have to create an e-mail account. When you first create the identity, the Internet Connection Wizard starts. You'll first be asked if you want to use an existing account or create a new one. Click Create a New Internet Mail Account and then click Next. Complete the Wizard and then click Finish.

To choose which identity to use as the default when you start Outlook Express, select File ➤ Identities ➤ Manage Identities to see a list of defined identities. Choose the identity to use as the default and then click the Make Default button. Select Ask Me in this list if you want to choose the identity when you start Outlook Express.

Before creating or sending mail, make sure you are using your own identity. Choose File ➤ Switch Identity. Click the identity in the box that appears, and then click OK.

NOTE

The Netscape Navigator Web browser supports "profiles" that are totally separate environments for each user. Each user specifies their own e-mail configurations, and they get their own browser bookmarks and other settings. You get to choose a profile when you start up Netscape, if you have more than one.

MailAlert

As an alternative to setting up multiple accounts in Outlook Express, you can use the program MailAlert to check for e-mail and alert you when it has arrived. MailAlert is a highly customizable program that can not only tell when you have received mail, but can also beep your pager as well. You can download MailAlert from www.diamondridge.com.

The program works with most POP and IMAP mail systems, as well as with mail systems such as Microsoft Exchange and Windows Messaging. You can have MailAlert check for mail and, if any is received, automatically open your e-mail program and display the new messages. You can also use MailAlert as a mail program itself with which you can compose, reply to, forward, and delete mail.

MailAlert gets its initial settings from your current e-mail program. When you first install MailAlert, it will ask you to select from the e-mail programs on your computer, and then it will use the information from the first account it finds in that program, such as its names, mail servers, and connection type, and your member name and password.

You can then add additional accounts, determine when MailAlert checks for and alerts you about mail, and set other program options in the window shown in Figure 5.6.

Part I

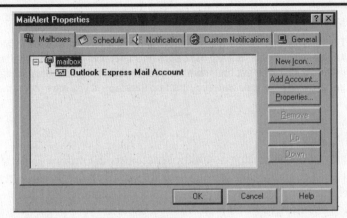

FIGURE 5.6: Setting up MailAlert

MailAlert will automatically check for mail at the times you specify in the Schedule tab of the window, and you can have it check at any other time using the MailAlert icon in the system tray of the Windows taskbar. When mail is received, the program opens its own mail window, shown in Figure 5.7.

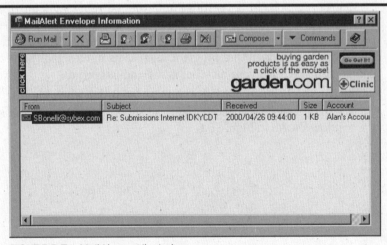

FIGURE 5.7: MailAlert mail window

Double-click a message to open it in its own window or click Run Mail to open your default e-mail program. Use the Run Mail list to select one of the e-mail programs on your system, or use these other MailAlert buttons to perform e-mail tasks:

- ▶ Close MailAlert

- ▶ Preview selected mail

- ▶ Reply to sender

- ▶ Reply to all

- ▶ Forward message

- ▶ Print message

- ▶ Delete message

- ▶ Compose new message

- ▶ Perform MailAlert commands

Using Ristra Mail Monitor

Although you can access multiple POP accounts using Outlook Express, it cannot download mail from services that offer only Web access. If you have several such free e-mail accounts, you can check them all for new mail using a program called Ristra Mail Monitor. You can download an evaluation copy of the program from `http://welcome.to/ristra`.

Installing the program adds it to the Start group, so that the program runs automatically each time that you start Windows. Installing the program also places an icon for it in the system tray on the Windows taskbar. Right-click the icon to display these options:

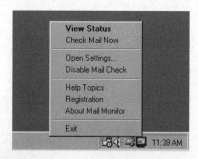

You first have to set up the program to access each of your Web-based e-mail accounts. To do this, follow these steps:

1. Select Open Settings from the shortcut menu to open the Ristra Mail Monitor Settings dialog box.

2. Click Add to see a list of accounts.

3. Enter your login name and the name of the service to complete your e-mail address. You can also pull down the list at the end of the Login Name box to select from supported services.

4. Next, enter your password and click Confirm. The e-mail address will be added to the List of Mail Accounts box.

5. Click the Preferences tab.

6. Enable the check box labeled Automatically Enter Login and Password when Logging In to the Mail Account. This setting will check for mail without you having to enter the login information to have Ristra check the mail.

When you want to check your mail at all of the accounts, just click Check Mail in the Settings dialog box, or choose Check Mail Now from the Ristra shortcut menu on the system tray. Ristra dials into your ISP and checks for new mail at each of the listed services, displaying the results in the Status dialog box.

To read mail, click the account and then click Log In to read your mail.

The Best of Both!

If you have both POP and Web-based mail systems, you might consider a program that accesses both types at one time.

Appload Notify, from www.appload.com, is an advertising-supported program that lets you check both types of mail. You can configure it for any number of POP and Web-based mail systems, and have it check them for mail all at one time. When Appload Notify finds mail, it displays this animated graphic:

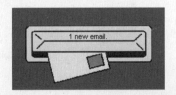

Appload Notify then opens a window listing all of your mail accounts, as well as advertisements from the program's sponsors. Select an account to see a list of messages that have been received, as in Figure 5.8.

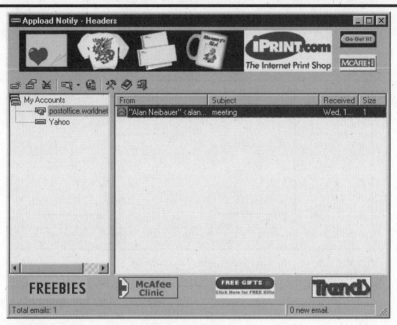

FIGURE 5.8: Getting mail with Appload Notify

Jo Mail, available at `www.download.com`, offers the same features. When you first install Jo Mail, you designate either one POP or one Web-based system that you want to check for mail. When you run the program, however, you can add other mail accounts of either type and then access your mail using the window shown in Figure 5.9.

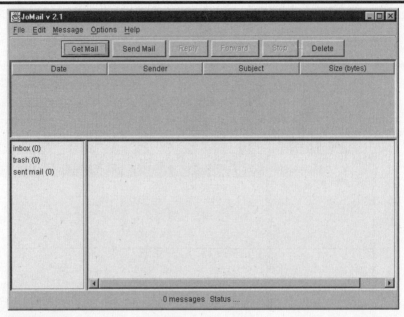

FIGURE 5.9: Getting mail with JoMail

Other programs for checking multiple mail accounts include Cyber-Info Webmail Notify for checking Web-based mail and Cyber-Info Email Notify for checking POP mail (both from www.cyber-info.com), and @nymail from www.tntsb.com/anymail.

TIP

Services such as Yahoo and Hotmail also let you access multiple POP mail accounts.

Active Names Email Tracker

Another alternative to checking mail at multiple accounts is to have mail redirected to your primary mail account. The program Active Names Email Tracker, for example, will automatically check your mail at various locations and send it to the email address of your choice. You can download a copy of Active Names Email Tracker from www.activenames.com.

Active Names Email Tracker has another great feature—it can confirm that e-mail addresses to which you send mail are still active. Before sending

mail, add the recipient's email address to your Active Names address book. The program will connect to the mail server at that address and confirm that the recipient's account is still active. You can also invite your recipients to register with Active Names so it can keep track of changes to their e-mail addresses.

Eating Spam

Spam is a meat-based product manufactured by Hormel Foods Corporation. But the Internet community has further immortalized Spam so that it has come to mean unsolicited e-mails sent to a large number of users on the Internet. No matter how you feel about the meat-based product (try it grilled like a hamburger), the Internet type of Spam is bad.

If you're getting tired of the junk mail that fills up your inbox, strike back! You can prevent junk mail from ever reaching your computer. You'll need an e-mail program with a junk mail filter, or download one of many programs available for dealing with spam, such as Spam Eater or SpamOff.

Sites and Features

An occasional piece of spam wouldn't be too bad, but have you been hit by five, ten, or more chunks of spam at the same time? If not, you probably will be. Here's the typical scenario—you see that 20 e-mails are coming in, get excited because you think you're so popular, and then you find out that it's the same spammer flooding your inbox with advertisements or other junk mail.

Fighting Back

Fighting back is not always easy, but there are steps you can take. First, you can try contacting your ISP to see if they can take some action by blocking known spammers. Many ISPs offer customer support advice for dealing with junk mail.

You can also try responding to the spam by asking to be removed from the list. Some spammers even tell you how to be removed from their list by returning the message with Remove as the subject, or by e-mailing another address. This doesn't work all of the time though. Some spammers send out their junk and close down the address so your reply is returned; some spammers welcome your reply because it confirms that your e-mail address is legitimate, and therefore they will continue to send you junk mail, or even rent your address to other spammers.

You could also try flooding the spammer's mailbox with your own junk mail and long file attachments, a technique called *bombing*. But this may not work, because often all of your junk mail to them will bounce right back.

You can also send an e-mail to the spammer's domain. If you get junk mail from someone at America Online, for example, send a complaint to abuse@aol.com. With other ISPs try postmaster@their_domain_name.

The fight against junk mail is far from hopeless, especially with a little help from the Internet and software developers. Some e-mail programs, for example, maintain junk mailer lists. You can add e-mail addresses to the list so that messages from those addresses can be deleted as soon as they come in. You don't actually avoid downloading their messages; you just don't see them.

In Microsoft's Outlook Express, for example, select a junk mail message in the Inbox, and then choose Block Sender from the Message menu. You'll see a message asking if you want to also delete all of the messages from that sender. Click Yes if you do. When any new mail arrives from the sender, it will automatically be moved to the Deleted Items folder.

If you change your mind about blocking mail from the sender, select Message Rules from the Tools menu and click Blocked Senders List. In the dialog box that appears, select the e-mail address of the person you no longer want to block and click Remove. Select Yes to confirm the deletion, and then close the Message Rules dialog box.

Spam-Eating Software

An even better solution to junk messages, however, is to delete them before they download onto your computer. If you get your mail over the Internet through a POP3 mail server, you can do just that. There are programs that dial into your ISP's post office and check the mail waiting for you. If the program finds an address or domain that you've identified as junk, it deletes the message without you having to download it.

SpamEater comes with a long list of known spammers, but you can add your own as well. There is a standard version that is distributed for free and a professional version with additional features available for a 30-day trial period. You can download the freeware version from www.hms.com/default.asp.

SpamEater can automatically check for spam and delete it, or it will let you view your messages' headers (the To, From, and Subject part of the message) to determine which ones you want to delete.

To see how SpamEater operates, choose Preferences from the File menu and create a profile, using the dialog box shown in Figure 5.10. You will see that the profile includes the address of your ISP's e-mail server and your logon name and password. You use the Spammers tab of the dialog box to view the list of known spammers and to add your own.

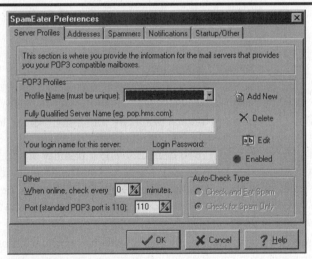

FIGURE 5.10: SpamEater

112   Chapter Five

You then use the Action menu in the SpamEater window to perform these actions:

Check and Eat Spam   Checks your waiting mail and deletes messages from people on the spammers list.

Check Only for Spam   Scans your mailbox for spam.

Check and View Headers   Displays the headers of messages so you can delete interactively.

Spam Off is another anti-spam program, and you can download it from lelsoft.hypermart.net/spamoff. It works in pretty much the same way that SpamEater does, by deleting messages from identified spammers. After installing the program, right-click its icon in the system tray, as shown here:

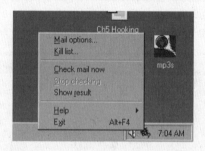

Use the Mail Options menu choice to specify your e-mail server, login name, and password. Use the Kill List command to designate the e-mail addresses of spammers or just their domains. The capability of adding domains to the list, rather than specific addresses on the domain, lets you capture spam from anyone using a spam-friendly mail server. Select Check Mail Now to dial into your e-mail server and delete messages from listed spammers.

Spam Buster is an advertiser-supported freeware program for filtering unwanted messages. You can download it from www.contactplus.com. When you install the Spam Buster, you can choose from areas of interest that will determine which sponsors' advertisements will be sent to you.

The program includes a list of identified spammers, but also uses keywords and other indicators to identify spam e-mails by their subject, header, and the sender's domain name.

A Spam-Fighting Server

A company called Brightmail (www.brightmail.com) offers a different approach to fighting spam. Rather than have the spam-fighting software and rules for filtering on your computer, Brightmail acts as an intermediary between you and your POP mail server.

To use the Brightmail service, you need to register for a free Brightmail account and download its setup program. You run the Brightmail program to reconfigure your e-mail program, such as Outlook Express, to connect to the mail servers at Brightmail instead of to your POP account. No Brightmail software is actually installed on your computer, except for an uninstaller that will reconfigure your e-mail program to connect directly to your POP account if you choose to stop using the Brightmail service.

Brightmail connects to your mail server, downloads your waiting mail, and examines it for spam. It stores the spam messages on its own computers and forwards the other mail to your computer so you can read it with your e-mail software. Spam is maintained on the Brightmail server for 30 days, so you can periodically scan the messages before they are deleted to insure that legitimate mail was not held by mistake.

For more information and programs about fighting spam, check out these sites:

▶ www.junkbusters.com/ht/en/index.html

▶ www.mindworkshop.com/alchemy/nospam.html

▶ www.cyber-info.com

▶ www.spamkiller.com

WHAT'S NEXT?

Now that you have a good working knowledge of e-mail programs and useful e-mail tools, we're going to shift gears in Part ii, "Browsing and More," and learn about some of the most popular Internet browser programs available. We'll start with Microsoft's offering in Chapter 6, "An Introduction to Internet Explorer 5."

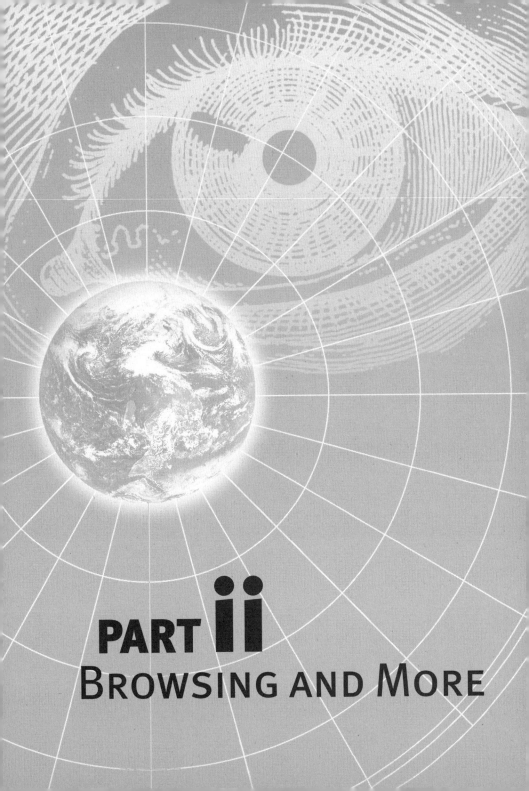

PART ii
BROWSING AND MORE

Chapter 6

An Introduction to Internet Explorer

This chapter will give you a broad overview of the way you work with Internet Explorer. We'll start at the beginning and show you the different ways you can start the program.

Later in the chapter, you'll learn about Internet Explorer's various tools, commands, and program features that help you navigate the Web. You'll also find extensive material on the types of files that Internet Explorer can display, and we'll tell you how you can specify the way it should handle the ones that it can't display. The chapter closes with a look at how you can open the underlying HTML code for a Web page—a neat way to learn the tricks of the Web-author trade!

Adapted from *Mastering Microsoft Internet Explorer 4*, by Gene Weisskopf and Pat Coleman

ISBN 0-7821-2133-0   923 pages $44.99

STARTING INTERNET EXPLORER

Like almost all Windows programs, Internet Explorer can be started in many ways. You can also have more than one window of Internet Explorer open at a time, which allows you to view multiple documents or different sections of the same Web page.

To start Internet Explorer at any time, simply choose it from the Windows Start menu. In a standard installation, it is located in Start ➤ Programs ➤ Internet Explorer ➤ Internet Explorer. The program will start and open its *start page*, which is the page Internet Explorer displays first whenever you start it this way.

If the start page is available on a local or networked drive on your computer or if you are already connected to the Internet, Internet Explorer opens that page immediately and displays it.

If you use a modem to connect to the Internet, however, and the start page resides there but you're not currently connected, Internet Explorer opens your Dial-Up Networking connector to make the connection to the Internet.

Dialing In to the Internet

If you normally use a network, DSL, or cable modem connection to access the Internet, any program can connect to the Internet as needed. That's not so when you link to the Internet through an analog modem (think of the difference between an analog and a digital watch) and a telephone line. In that case, whenever Internet Explorer (or any other Windows application) needs access to the Internet (such as to open its start page) but does not yet have it, something has to make that phone call to get connected.

That something is Dial-Up Networking, which makes the call and gets connected to your Internet service provider (ISP). For example, Figure 6.1 shows the Dial-Up Settings dialog box, in which you can revise or verify the user name and password and that will be needed to make the connection, and other information about your dial-up session.

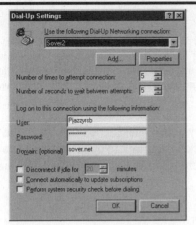

FIGURE 6.1:   When a program needs a connection to the Internet, the Windows
Dial-Up Networking connector makes the call over your modem.

Note that you'll see this dialog box only when you have enabled the
"Prompt for information before dialing" option, which you'll find when
you open the Dial-Up Networking folder and choose Connections ➤ Settings. If you have disabled this option, the call will be made as soon as
the dialog box opens.

Click the Connect button in the Connect To dialog box to make the
call. You'll see status messages as the call and connection are being
made. In about 20 or 30 seconds, the connection will be completed and
you'll see the Dial-Up Networking icon displayed on the status bar (as
shown here). Internet Explorer can now open its start page, and this connection to the Internet is also available to any Windows program that
needs access to it, such as your e-mail program, an FTP client, and so on.

Starting from Your Start Page

The start page serves as a "home base" while you are working in Internet
Explorer. You typically begin your leaps and bounds through the Web
from the links on your start page. If you ever want to return to your start
page (to return home, so to speak) during a session with Internet
Explorer, click the Home button on the toolbar.

Part ii

NOTE

You'll sometimes hear the start page referred to as the "home page." Even the button on the Internet Explorer toolbar that opens your start page is labeled "Home" and displays a picture of a house. Nonetheless, you should stick with "start page," the more commonly used term, to avoid any confusion with the *home page* of a Web site.

When your start page is open, you can navigate to any other page you choose. For example, you can click a hyperlink to open that link's target file, or you can choose an item from Internet Explorer's Favorites menu to go to that site.

TIP

You can specify any page to serve as the start page. You'll find this setting on the General tab in the Internet Options dialog box when you choose Tools ➤ Internet Options in Internet Explorer. You can also access the Internet Options dialog box by clicking the Internet Options icon in the Windows Control Panel.

If Internet Explorer cannot find your start page, such as when you cannot connect to the Internet, it displays a local page that offers a few tips for dealing with the problem. At this point, you can use your Favorites menu to go to a site, or you can enter a URL directly into the Address toolbar.

The start page is just like any other Web page you can open in Internet Explorer. The only thing special about it is that you see it each time you begin a session in Internet Explorer. A start page typically serves its purpose by containing one or both of the following types of content:

▶ Hyperlinks to one or more sites that you usually go to in each session with Internet Explorer

▶ Updated information that you want to see each time you start Internet Explorer, such as news, weather, stock market reports, sports scores, and so on

Starting Internet Explorer from a Hyperlink

Many programs besides Web browsers can display either text hyperlinks (which may be in a different color and underlined) or image hyperlinks; clicking the text or image opens the target file of that link. In a standard

Windows installation, when you click a link whose target is an HTML Web page, you'll find that the target will be opened in Internet Explorer.

TIP

A hyperlink, no matter what it appears as on the screen, will almost always be indicated in Windows by the mouse cursor turning into a pointing finger when it passes over it. The MacOS always shows URLs colored and underlined, but unless the application implements it, rarely shows the "finger" outside of the browser. Unix and Linux have their own esoteric rules that generally apply only to X-window, KDE, and Gnome sessions.

For example, suppose someone sends you an e-mail suggesting that you check out a site on the WWW, and the text of the message includes the URL of that site. In Outlook Express (and in most other e-mail programs), the text that makes up the URL is displayed in color and underlined, just as it would be in a browser. If you click the URL, Internet Explorer (or Netscape Navigator, for that matter) opens, and then it opens that site.

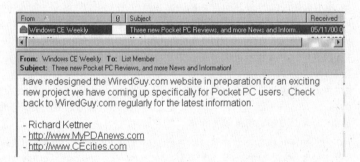

Opening an Existing Document

When you open an HTML file (one with an `htm` or `html` file name extension) in Windows Explorer, that file opens in Internet Explorer (assuming Internet Explorer is the default browser on your computer—if Navigator is your default browser, then Navigator will open).

NOTE

Quick reminder: When we refer to *Windows* Explorer, we're referring to the Explorer configuration you'll see when you're browsing your local disk drives or network drives. *Internet* Explorer is the browser used to view Web pages.

While you're in Internet Explorer, you can choose File ➢ Open to open a specific file, either by typing the path and name of the file or by clicking the Browse button to find the file on your local or networked disk. Once you've found the file, highlight it and choose OK to open it.

You can also open a file by simply dragging it from Windows Explorer or a folder window into Internet Explorer. Among the files you can open are HTML Web pages and GIF or JPEG image files (see *Viewing Various File Types* later in this chapter for more details).

MAKING INTERNET EXPLORER YOUR DEFAULT BROWSER

If you have installed another browser since installing Internet Explorer, Internet Explorer may not be set as your default browser, and that other browser will be called upon to open any Web pages you request. If you want to make Internet Explorer your default browser and keep it that way, here's how to do it.

In Internet Explorer, choose Tools ➢ Internet Options. On the Programs tab, you'll find an option called "Internet Explorer should check to see whether it is the default browser." Select this option, and close the Internet Options dialog box.

Now whenever you start Internet Explorer, it will check to see if it is still the default browser. If it finds that it isn't, it will ask if you want it to become the new default browser. If you choose Yes, it will change the Windows settings to make it the default. Now when you open an HTML file—for example, by clicking a hyperlink in a Word document that targets a Web page—Internet Explorer will be the program that opens it.

If you later install another browser that makes itself the default, the next time you start Internet Explorer it will check to see if it is the default and prompt you accordingly.

Closing Internet Explorer

To close Internet Explorer, choose File ➤ Close, or click the Close button on the far right side of its title bar. Remember, Web browsers such as Internet Explorer are used only for viewing documents, so you never need to save anything before exiting the program.

WARNING

Even though there are normally no documents to save in Internet Explorer, you might still lose data if you exit the program prematurely. For example, when you are filling out a form in a Web page, you must click that form's Submit (or similar) button to send your responses to the server. If you were to close Internet Explorer before doing so, any information you had entered into the form would be lost. Plus, if you open an OLE-compliant document, such as one created in Microsoft Word, and you have its associated program installed on your system, you'll actually be editing that document in Internet Explorer. In this case, closing Internet Explorer would have the same effect as closing Microsoft Word when a document is open.

Closing Your Dial-Up Networking Connection

When you started Internet Explorer, it may have caused Dial-Up Networking to make the telephone call over your modem to connect to the Internet. In that case, when you later exit Internet Explorer, you will be asked if you want to disconnect from the Internet.

You can choose to disconnect if you're through working on the Internet for now. Doing so will close the connection so that your telephone line can receive other calls. Otherwise, you can choose to stay online and maintain the connection. You could then open your e-mail program, for example, and send or receive mail on the Internet. Or you might open Internet Explorer again, and the connection would be waiting for it.

If you do leave the connection open, don't forget to disconnect later. To do so, double-click the Dial-Up Networking icon on the right side of the Windows taskbar, then click the Disconnect button in the dialog box. Or right-click the icon in the taskbar and choose Disconnect from the shortcut menu.

A Quick Tour with Internet Explorer

Now that you've read about starting and closing Internet Explorer, let's take it on a short test ride to experience the thrill of the wind in our hair as we travel to new lands on the World Wide Web.

1. From the Windows Start menu, choose Programs ➤ Internet Explorer.

2. If you connect to the Internet via a modem, Dial-Up Networking should open, dial your Internet service provider, give your user name and password, and complete the connection to the Internet.

3. Once connected, Internet Explorer opens its start page. If you installed Internet Explorer from a Microsoft source, for example, by downloading it from Microsoft's Web page, it opens the page at `home.microsoft.com`. The page you see in Internet Explorer will look something like the one shown in Figure 6.2.

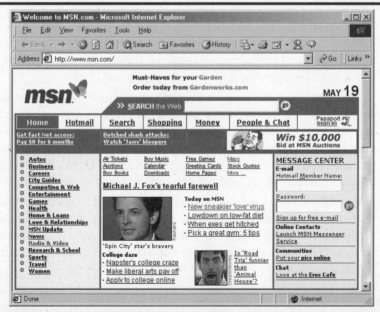

FIGURE 6.2: Internet Explorer opens your start page, where you can begin your travels on the World Wide Web.

4. At this point, you're free to click any of the hyperlinks in the current page to open a new page. Simply click a link, and off you go. Continue to click your way through several pages and see where you end up.

NOTE

When you point to a text or an image hyperlink, the mouse pointer changes to a small hand, and the address of the link's target is displayed on the status bar. Text hyperlinks are underlined and displayed in blue by default.

5. Now that you've traveled through several pages by following hyperlinks, go back through the pages you've followed by clicking the Back button on the toolbar. Each click takes you to the page you visited before the current one. Eventually you'll reach your start page.

6. Now let's go to a specific address on the Web, one of our own choosing. Either click within the Internet Explorer Address toolbar, or choose File ➤ Open. (If the Address toolbar isn't displayed, choose View ➤ Toolbar ➤ Address Bar.)

7. Type the following URL:

www.census.gov/datamap/www/

and press Enter to open that page.

8. In the blink of an eye (perhaps longer if it's a busy time of the day on the Web), we've opened the Map Stats page on the Web site of the U.S. Census Bureau, as shown in Figure 6.3.

9. Just in case you'd like to return to this page at another time, you should add it to your Favorites menu. Choose Favorites ➤ Add to Favorites, and then click OK.

NOTE

When you want to return to this site, simply select it from your Favorites menu, which you'll find not only in every Explorer window, but also on your Windows Start menu. You can also move this new item to another submenu on the Favorites menu.

Part ii

10. Click your home state, which will open a map of that state. Let's save this picture of your state to your local disk.

11. Right-click anywhere within the map, and choose Save Picture As from the shortcut menu.

12. Specify a location and name for the new file (the default will be your My Documents folder) and click OK to save it.

WARNING

Internet Explorer will not show the My Documents folder if you have used this feature before in this session and have selected another directory. Always be sure you know which folder you're saving an item in so you can find it later. When in doubt, put it on the desktop.

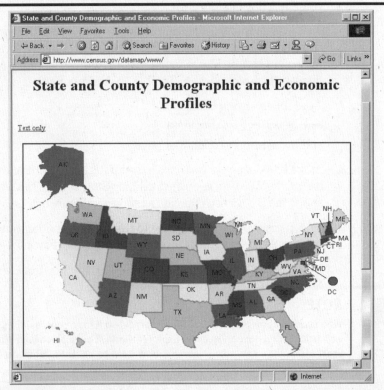

FIGURE 6.3: On the Map Stats page of the U.S. Census Bureau, you can access a wealth of information about any region in the country.

You now have a GIF image file of that map on your local disk, which you can later import into your word processor or any other program that handles GIF files. Just remember that most content you retrieve from the Web cannot be used for commercial purposes without specific permission from the owner of that content. When in doubt, drop a note asking whoever runs the Web site for permission to use the image or content.

13. Click a county within the state map, and then click the Tiger Map link, which opens an interactive map of that county.

14. Try magnifying the map by selecting the Zoom In option (or move the map to a new center as shown here) and then clicking within the map at the point you want at the center of the newly magnified map. In a few seconds, the new map will be displayed.

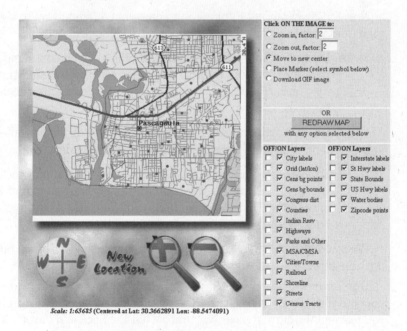

15. If you have a printer and you'd like to print this page, choose File ➢ Print, or click the Print button on the toolbar. In the Print dialog box, click the OK button.

SECURITY ALERT

When you click within the map to change its magnification, you may
see a Security Alert dialog box warning you that you are about to
send information over the Internet that could be seen by others.
This is simply a not-so-gentle reminder that the Internet is not a private network. When you make a choice on a Web page and then
click a Submit or Send Now button (or simply click within the map
to make your choice in this case), you are sending some information
over the Internet that could be viewed by others. Once you're familiar with these situations and no longer need the constant reminder,
you can turn off this message in the future by selecting its "In the
future, do not show this warning" option.

Now let's use Internet Explorer in a somewhat different way, to view a
page from your local disk.

16. Using the Address toolbar or the File ➤ Open command,
type the drive and path to the folder where you stored the
map image file you saved earlier in step 12. Press Enter when
finished.

17. Internet Explorer will open that folder and display its contents; you should see the GIF file you saved earlier.

18. To go back to the previous page you were viewing, simply click
the Back button on the toolbar. Or perhaps you might
choose the Map Stats site from your Favorites menu to go
back to that site.

We could play on this site for another dozen pages of this book, but
it's time to wrap up this tour.

Don't ever worry about getting lost, because that concept just doesn't
apply to your travels in Internet Explorer. Sure, you can easily forget how
you reached the current page, but that's what the Back and Favorites buttons are for.

Whatever happens, you can always jump back to your start page at any
time by clicking the Home button on the toolbar. Although there's nothing magical about your start page (it's just another page you can display
in Internet Explorer), it's a familiar place that will have familiar content
and links.

NOTE

There are vast numbers of services that provide custom Start pages free of charge. One in particular is Yahoo!, which not only provides you a customizable home page, but also a new e-mail address, a calendar, an online "briefcase" with lots of room, and a long list of other features, but also provides you with the Yahoo! Companion, a new toolbar for Windows-based browsers. Yahoo! still works with all other platforms, though.

Otherwise, you can simply close Internet Explorer by choosing File ➤ Close and call it a day. If you are connected to the Internet via a Dial-Up Networking connection, you should be asked whether you want to disconnect; choose Yes to hang up.

INSIDE INTERNET EXPLORER

Now we'll look at the components that make up Internet Explorer. You'll find that Internet Explorer has many similarities to other Windows programs you have used, especially to those in Microsoft Office (Word, Excel, Access, and so on). Figure 6.4 shows Internet Explorer displaying a Web page. As you can see, the Internet Explorer window contains many of the usual Windows components.

FIGURE 6.4: The Internet Explorer program window contains many components that are common to other Windows programs.

NOTE

A company or an Internet service provider (ISP) can customize Internet Explorer to make it look and act as though it were their own browser and then distribute it to employees or customers. So if your ISP or your employer gives you a copy of Internet Explorer, it may not look exactly like the one shown in Figure 6.4.

When you want to show as much of the Web page as possible, try the View ➢ Full Screen command, or click the Full Screen button on the toolbar. Internet Explorer will be maximized to occupy the entire screen; it will lose its title bar, status bar, two of its toolbars, and even its menu bar. (You can right-click a toolbar and choose Menu Bar to display it again.) You can switch back to the normal view by choosing the Full Screen command again or by pressing F11 on your keyboard.

The Components of Internet Explorer

Let's discuss the parts that make up the Internet Explorer window. Keep in mind that if a tool or an object looks similar to one you've seen in another Windows program, it most likely performs the same task in both.

Title Bar

At the top of the window is the usual title bar. It displays either the title of the Web page you are viewing (*Dave Central Shareware, Freeware, Demos and Betas - Microsoft Internet Explorer* in Figure 6.4) or the document's file name if it is not a Web page. On the right side of the title bar are the Minimize, Maximize/Restore, and Close buttons; on the left side is the System menu. As usual, you can double-click the title bar to maximize the window (or restore it to its previous size if it was already maximized), or you can drag Internet Explorer by its title bar to move the window on the screen (assuming the window is not maximized).

Program Window

Internet Explorer's program window is shown full-screen in Figure 6.4. If it is smaller than full-screen, you can resize it by dragging any of its corners or sides. You'll find that the paragraphs in a Web page generally adjust their width to the size of the browser window. As you change the dimensions of Internet Explorer, the page reformats to fit the new size.

Menu Bar

Beneath the title bar is the menu bar, which contains almost all the commands you'll need in Internet Explorer. If a command has a keyboard shortcut, you'll see the keystroke displayed next to the command on the menu. For example, you can use the shortcut Ctrl+O (hold down Ctrl and press O) instead of choosing the File ➤ Open command, or you can press function key F5 instead of choosing View ➤ Refresh.

Toolbars

By default, the toolbars appear beneath the menu bar in Internet Explorer and contain buttons and other tools that help you navigate the Web. The three toolbars are Standard, Links, and Address (top, middle, and bottom in Figure 6.4). We discuss these a little later in "Using the Toolbars." The Internet Explorer logo to the right of the toolbar is animated when the program is accessing data.

Document Window

Beneath the menu and toolbars is the main document window, which occupies the majority of your screen. The current document, such as a Web page or an image, is displayed here. You cannot display multiple document windows in Internet Explorer. Instead, you can view multiple documents by opening multiple instances of Internet Explorer (choose File ➤ New ➤ Window). Each instance of Internet Explorer is independent of the others.

Explorer Bar

When you click the Search, Favorites, or History, button on the Internet Explorer toolbar (or choose one of those commands from the View ➤ Explorer Bar menu), the Explorer bar will appear as a separate pane on the left side of the window. It displays the contents for the button you clicked, such as the search options shown in Figure 6.5.

Part ii

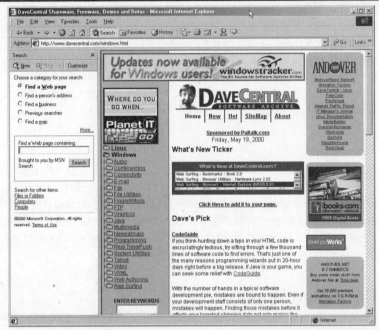

FIGURE 6.5: When you click the Search, Favorites, or History button on the tool-bar, the Explorer bar opens as a separate pane on the left side of the window, where you can make choices and see the results appear in the right pane.

With the window split into two separate panes, you can make choices in the Explorer bar on the left and watch the results appear in the pane on the right. For example, in Figure 6.5, you can specify what you want to search for in the Explorer bar, and the results of the search appear in that same pane as a list of links you can click. When you click one of the result links, the target of the link appears in the right pane, while leaving the Explorer bar unchanged. You can select another result link to try that target and continue through as many as you like.

To close the Explorer bar, choose the item you opened from View ➤ Explorer Bar, or click the appropriate button a second time, such as the Search button to close the Explorer bar in Figure 6.5. The Button you click will stay "pressed" while the item is open.

Scroll Bars

The horizontal scroll bar is at the bottom of the document window, and the vertical scroll bar is on the right side of the document window. When a document is too large to be displayed within the window, you can use the scroll bars to scroll the window over other parts of the document.

Watch that Status Bar

At the bottom of the Internet Explorer window is the status bar. It displays helpful information about the current state of Internet Explorer, so keep an eye on it.

▶ When you are selecting a command from the menu bar, a description of the currently highlighted command appears on the status bar.

> Searches the current window for text

▶ When you point to a hyperlink on the page (either text or an image), the mouse pointer changes to a hand, and the target URL of the hyperlink is displayed on the status bar.

> http://www.sybex.com/books.html

▶ When you click a hyperlink to open another page, the status bar indicates what is happening with a progression of messages. For example, if you click a hyperlink whose target is www .sample.com/somepage.htm you might see the following messages on the status bar, one after another:

```
Finding site: www.sample.com
Web site found. Waiting for reply
Opening page: somepage.htm
(7 items remaining) Downloading picture http://. . .
```

▶ Icons that appear on the right side of the status bar give you a status report at a glance. For example, you'll see an icon of a padlock when you have made a secure connection to a Web site, and you'll see a network wire with an X across it when you're working offline.

Part ii

TIP

You can use the Toolbar and Status Bar commands on the View menu to toggle on or off the display of the toolbars and status bar. You might want to hide these otherwise useful features to give yourself a little more screen real estate for displaying pages. If you want as much room as possible, try the View ➤ Full Screen command.

Getting Help

Internet Explorer offers the usual variety of program help, with a few touches of its own. When you choose Help ➤ Contents and Index, what you get is not quite the standard Windows help viewer. Internet Explorer uses a new help system that is built with HTML, just like a Web page. Nonetheless, it behaves very much like the more traditional help system. You can browse through the topics in the Contents tab, look up a specific word or phrase in the Index tab, or find all references to a word or phrase on the Search tab.

NOTE

To see if there is a newer version of any of the Internet Explorer software components, choose Tools ➤ Windows Update. This is the best way to keep your operating system current, including Internet Explorer—immediately and online.

The rest of the items are:

▶ Tip of the Day–Go here to get a quick usability or functionality tip on how to use Internet Explorer.

▶ For Netscape Users–Here's a collection of tips and a helping hand for those migrating from Netscape Navigator or Communicator so you can get up to speed quickly with Internet Explorer.

▶ Tour–Take a look at what Internet Explorer can do. Please keep your hands and legs inside the vehicle at all times.

▶ Online Support–This takes you to a page where you can head off in different directions to find answers to your Internet Explorer–related problems.

➤ Send Feedback–Have a yearning to tell Microsoft what you think about Internet Explorer? For good or bad, do so here.

➤ About Internet Explorer–Get version, author, and other information about Internet Explorer here.

Another source of assistance is ToolTips, which can greatly speed the learning process. You can often learn something about an object on screen from its ToolTip. Internet Explorer displays ToolTips when you point to some of its components, such as when you point to an icon on the status bar (shown here), a hyperlink within the page, or a button on the toolbar (when the button descriptions are not displayed). Here's what a ToolTip looks like:

Another way to find out about an object in the current document, such as a picture or video clip, is to right-click it and choose Properties from the shortcut menu.

At the Helm in Internet Explorer

The simplest way to navigate within Internet Explorer is to click a hyperlink to open another file (the target of the link). That's probably how you'll spend most of your time while browsing, but there are plenty of commands available that can help you explore the Web, save information to your local disk, and so on.

In Internet Explorer, you can perform an action in three main ways:

➤ Using the menus and shortcut menus

➤ Using the toolbars

➤ Using the keyboard and shortcut keys

Using the Menus and Shortcut Menus

In Internet Explorer, you can perform just about any action by choosing commands on its menus. Many components also have shortcut menus that you access with a right-click of the mouse.

Let's take a quick look at the commands on the menu bar (you can breeze over these just to familiarize yourself with them; you won't be tested on any of this):

File   Open the current page in a new Internet Explorer window; open a file by specifying a name and URL or location; save the current page to disk; print the current page; send the current page or its URL in an e-mail message or create a shortcut to it on your desktop; choose to go to a site that you've visited earlier in this session with Internet Explorer; view the properties of the current page; choose to browse without being online (data is opened from your Internet Explorer cache on your local disk).

Edit   Select the contents of the entire page; copy selected data from Internet Explorer to another program; edit the page in FrontPage Express; find characters on the current page.

View   Hide or display the toolbars and status bar; change the size of the fonts used in Internet Explorer; cancel the downloading of the current page; refresh the contents of the page by downloading it again; view the HTML source code for the current page in Notepad; switch to full-screen mode to show as much of the page as possible; view or change the options for Internet Explorer.

Favorites   Open a site that you have previously saved as a shortcut on the Favorites menu; add the current URL to the Favorites menu; open one of the channels you have subscribed to; open a URL from your Links toolbar; open the Favorites folder so you can rename, revise, delete, or otherwise organize its contents; create a subscription for the current page or any item already in the Favorites menu; manage your existing subscriptions.

Tools   Access Outlook mail and New; Synchronize the pages you've subscribed to; Update Windows and other Microsoft applications with Windows Update; Have Internet Explorer compile and display a list of sites related to the one you are currently visiting; Open the Internet Options control panel to have access to link settings, cache and cookie storage, security and server interaction policies, associated applications for external file viewing, and advanced settings.

Help   Access the help system for Internet Explorer; take the Internet Explorer Web tutorial; open a Microsoft site on the WWW to learn about Internet Explorer.

You can also invoke many of these commands from the toolbars or with shortcut keys, as well as with shortcut menus.

To access a shortcut menu for an object in Internet Explorer, point to the object and click the *right* mouse button. The choices on the shortcut menu depend on the object you click.

▶ Right-click anywhere on the page outside a hyperlink or an image, and the shortcut menu includes choices relevant to the page. You can open the next or previous page, add this page to your Favorites menu, show the properties dialog box for this page, print the page, and so on. If the page uses a background image, you can choose to save that image to a file or make it your Windows desktop wallpaper.

▶ Right-click a hyperlink, and the shortcut menu lets you open the target of that link, copy the link to the Windows Clipboard, or add the target of the link to your Favorites menu.

▶ Right-click an image, and the shortcut menu lets you save the image to a file, make that image your Windows desktop wallpaper, or copy the image to the Clipboard.

▶ Right-click selected text, and you can choose to print that text or copy it to the Clipboard.

Using the Toolbars

The toolbars in Internet Explorer (shown below) can appear in every Explorer window, whether you're viewing a Web page, folders and files on your disk, the Windows Control Panel, or anything else. They go by the names Standard, Links, and Address. You can rearrange the layout of the toolbars at any time, as discussed a little later in *Moving and Resizing the Toolbars*. Two of them are also available from the Windows taskbar.

TIP

Even the menu bar now behaves as a toolbar, in that you can place other toolbars on its row or move it to one of the other rows of toolbars. When you're working In Full Screen mode (choose View ➤ Full Screen), you can even hide the menu bar.

Standard Toolbar

You'll regularly use the buttons on the first row of the toolbar, as shown above. All are shortcuts for commands on the menus. As you'll see shortly, you can choose to hide the row of descriptive text below the buttons. Table 6.1 describes each button.

▶ Back—Takes you back one page. Note: The small button segment with the down arrow opens a pull-down list containing a history list of the last 10 pages you've been to.

▶ Forward—Takes you forward one page. This is available only if there is a page that you went to, returned from, and want to go back to. (I know, it can be a bit confusing.) Note: The small button segment with the down arrow opens a pull-down list containing a forward history list of up to 10 pages.

▶ Stop—Stops loading the current page. Sometimes it's not available and other times it doesn't seem to work. If you click the Stop button and it doesn't seem to work, click it again firmly once (the time you hold the mouse button down is more important than the amount of pressure you apply) and then wait.

▶ Refresh—Reloads the current page.

▶ Home—Returns to your defined Home page, the page that appears when you start your browser from the Internet Explorer icon.

▶ Search—Opens and closes the Search panel on the left side of window.

▶ Favorites—An alternative to the Favorites menu, this can come in handy when you want to jump to several pages in rapid succession.

▶ History—Quickly views all the pages you have visited. The pages can be sorted in many different ways. Try them until you find a method that works best for you.

▶ Mail—Opens a small menu displaying these options: Read Mail, New Message, Send Link, Send Page, and Read News.

▶ Print—Prints the current page.

▶ Edit—Opens the current page in NotePad, Word, FrontPage Express, FrontPage 2000, or a handful of non-Microsoft applications.

▶ Messenger—Activates MSN Messenger, Microsoft's instant messaging application, to see if your friends are online to chat with.

▶ Real Player—If you have installed RealPlayer 7 it will have asked you if you wanted to install the RealPlayer toolbar in Internet Exploder. If you did, this button toggles that window at the bottom of the screen on and off. The latest news and other interesting, multimedia-related information appears here.

▶ The IE Logo—This logo spins and gyrates when pages are loading. Click on it and you will be whisked to... well, nothing. If you were familiar with this before, it no longer works. Phooey.

Links Toolbar

Each of the buttons on the Links toolbar is a hyperlink to a URL (you can also access these links from the Links item on the Favorites menu). In the version we're using to write this chapter, by default, they all target Microsoft Web sites that serve as gateways to a wealth of information on the WWW (if you received a customized version of Internet Explorer, these hyperlinks may point to other locations). Microsoft updates these sites frequently, so their content will likely be fresh each time you visit.

Best of the Web   A useful collection of links to reference-related Web sites, where you might look up a company's phone number, find an e-mail address of a long-lost relative, or find sites that will help you with travel arrangements or personal finance.

Microsoft   The home page of Microsoft Corporation, where you'll find news about Microsoft and its products, a variety of support options for their products, press releases, and more.

Internet Explorer News   Valuable information about Microsoft Internet Explorer and its related applications (Mail and News, NetMeeting, and so on).

Today's Links   When you don't feel like poking around the Web on your own, you can go to the default start page for Internet Explorer, where you'll find links to what's "hot" on the Web today (at least, according to Microsoft).

Web Gallery   A good place to go when you're building your own Web pages. You'll find loads of content that you can download and incorporate into your pages. For example, you can grab images that you can use as lines, buttons, or bullets, sound files that can serve as a page's background sound, ActiveX controls and Java applets for making your pages come alive, and TrueType fonts that allow your Internet Explorer to display Web pages exactly as their authors intended when they specified those fonts.

Remember that the buttons on the Links toolbar are just hyperlinks to pages on the Web. Feel free to try them out and see what's there.

Once you've tried these buttons and have a feeling for the content on each of the sites, you may decide to revise the buttons so they point to other sites that you want to access with a click or to new buttons that point to other sites.

To add a new button, simply drag a link from a Web page onto the Links toolbar. To delete a button, right-click it and choose Delete from the shortcut menu. To move a button, drag it to another location on the Links toolbar.

TIP

The best way to know where you can "drop" an item on the toolbar is to watch for the black line that appears when you drag the shortcut over the toolbar.

The best way to revise a button's name or target URL is to right-click the button itself, select Rename, and enter the new name in the small dialog box that appears. You can rename a shortcut, and its new name will appear on the button. Right-click a shortcut, choose Properties from the shortcut menu, and you can revise the link's target URL. You can also right-click a button on the Links toolbar to access the Properties command on the shortcut menu.

Address Toolbar

This toolbar shows the address of the file currently displayed in Internet Explorer, which might be a URL on the Internet or a location on your local disk. You enter a URL or the path to a file and press Enter to open that file.

NOTE

When you are entering a URL that you have entered once before, Internet Explorer's AutoComplete feature recognizes the URL and finishes the typing for you. You can either accept the URL or continue to type a new one. Or right-click in the Address toolbar, choose Completions from the shortcut menu, and then select one of the possibilities from the menu.

To revise the URL, click within the Address toolbar and use the normal Windows editing keys. For example, press Home or End to go to the beginning or end of the address. Drag over any of its text to select it, or hold down the Shift key and use the keyboard arrow keys to select text. When you're finished entering the new address, press Enter to have Internet Explorer open the file.

The arrow on the right side of the Address toolbar opens a drop-down list of addresses. Select one, and Internet Explorer will open that site. You visited these sites before by entering the address in the Address toolbar and pressing Enter. They're listed in the order in which you visited them.

Moving and Resizing the Toolbars

The toolbars in Internet Explorer are quite flexible. You can change the size or position of each one in the trio, or you can choose not to display them at all. In fact, the menu bar is also quite flexible and can be moved below one or more toolbars, or share the same row with them.

▶ To hide a toolbar, choose View ➢ Toolbar and select one from the menu; to display that toolbar, choose that command again. Or right-click any of the toolbars or the menu bar and select a toolbar from the shortcut menu.

▶ To hide the descriptive text below the Standard toolbar buttons, right click on the blank space immediately following the buttons on the Standard toolbar (the one with the Back, Forward, and Stop buttons) and select Customize. Among a wide range of other things you can do to toolbars here, you will find the Text Options pulldown near the bottom. Select the No Text Labels item and that will take care of it.

▶ To change the number of rows that the toolbars use, point to the bottom edge of the bottom toolbar; the mouse pointer will change to a double-headed arrow. You can then drag the edge up to reduce the number of rows or drag it down to expand them.

▶ To move a toolbar, drag it by its left edge. For example, drag the Address toolbar onto the same row as the Links toolbar by clicking on the left edge of the Address toolbar and dragging it to the Links toolbar.

▶ When two or more toolbars or the menu bar share the same row, you can change the width of one (but not the left-most one) by dragging its left edge. In the arrangement shown below, the Address and Links toolbars are sharing the same row. You could drag the left edge of the Links toolbar to the right or left to make it narrower or wider.

▶ To expand a toolbar to display all of its buttons or to make the Address toolbar as wide as possible, double-click its name on the left side of the toolbar. Double-click the name again to shrink that toolbar.

NOTE

Remember that these three toolbars are common to both Windows Explorer and Internet Explorer; the Address and Links toolbars are also available on the Windows taskbar.

Using Your Keyboard

In a world of pure browsing, you would rarely need the keyboard. In the real world, however, you might be using the keyboard quite a bit. For example, you'll frequently encounter online forms in which you will want to enter information: for example, a feedback form for your comments, a survey form for your opinions, or a registration form that will give you access to an online newspaper.

As discussed earlier, you'll also be using the keyboard when you want to type a URL into the Address toolbar so you can open the file at that address. Many commands have keyboard shortcuts. Those that you may find useful on a regular basis are shown in Table 6.2.

TABLE 6.2: Useful Keyboard Shortcuts

KEY	COMMAND	DESCRIPTION
Esc	View ➤ Stop	Cancels the downloading of the content for the current page. (You can also click the Stop button on the toolbar.)
F5	View ➤ Refresh	Updates the content of the current page by downloading it again. (You can also click the Refresh button on the toolbar.)
F11	View ➤ Full Screen	Toggles the active window between normal and full screen.
Tab		Selects the next hyperlink on the page; press Shift+Tab to select the previous hyperlink.
Enter		Activates the selected hyperlink, as though you had clicked it with your mouse. Also, submits most form fields.
Home/End		Moves to the beginning or end of the document.
Space bar		Advances the page by one screenful. Useful for reading long documents.
Arrow keys		Use ↓ or ↑ to scroll toward the bottom or the top of the document. When the document is too wide for the Internet Explorer window (as evidenced by the display of a horizontal scroll bar beneath the document), use → or ←to scroll toward the right or left edge of the document.
PgDn/PgUp		Scrolls toward the bottom or top of the current document, moving approximately one screen at a time (the height of Internet Explorer's document window).
Alt+←	Go ➤ Back	Displays the page you were viewing before the current page. (The Back button on the toolbar also does this.)
Alt+→	Go ➤ Forward	Displays the page you were viewing before you went back to the current page. (The Forward button on the toolbar also does this.)

Accessing Outlook Express Mail and News

Internet Explorer and its software suite of components are an integrated package of Internet or intranet tools. While browsing in Internet Explorer, you can access Outlook Express directly from the toolbar.

NOTE

This discussion assumes that either Microsoft Outlook or Outlook Express is your primary e-mail and newsreader program. If you have not installed Outlook Express, you may not be able to perform these tasks in your own e-mail and newsreader programs.

You can send mail in several ways while working within Internet Explorer. You'll find the following commands by clicking the Mail button on Internet Explorer's toolbar:

Read Mail opens Outlook Express Mail and displays the contents of your Inbox (you can also choose Go ➤ Mail in Internet Explorer). You're free to continue working in Outlook Express as you normally would. You can return to Internet Explorer at any time in the usual ways, such as by pressing Alt+Tab.

New Message creates a new Outlook Express Mail message, as though you had clicked the Compose Message button in that program. You can also choose File ➤ New ➤ Message in Internet Explorer.

Send a Link creates a new Outlook Express Mail message that includes an attached file—a shortcut to the page that is currently displayed in Internet Explorer. The icon or the name of the attachment appears in the pane beneath the message pane. The recipient of the message can then treat the shortcut as any other shortcut, so that opening the icon will open the target page. You can also use Internet Explorer's equivalent command File ➤ Send ➤ Link by Email.

Send Page creates a new Outlook Express Mail message that consists only of the page that you're currently viewing in Internet Explorer. The recipient can view the page in Outlook Express

Part II

Mail or click a link to open its target in Internet Explorer. You can also use the command File ➢ Send ➢ Page by Email.

Read News opens Outlook Express News in the usual way (or you can choose Go ➢ News).

NOTE
You can access your Windows Address Book from within Internet Explorer with either the File ➢ New ➢ Contact or the Go ➢ Address Book command.

VIEWING VARIOUS FILE TYPES

Internet Explorer is a browser, which means that its primary purpose is to display files, not to edit or create them. Internet Explorer can display several types of files on its own, and it can display other files with the aid of other programs. When it encounters any other type of file, you can choose to save the file to disk or let Internet Explorer attempt to open the file by passing it to the appropriate program.

NOTE
Netscape users: The information in this section applies to Navigator/Communicator as well as to Internet Explorer, except where noted.

Viewing Standard Web Files

When you browse, you'll encounter several types of files at virtually every Web site you visit. Internet Explorer can display all of the following file types:

- ▶ .html
- ▶ .gif
- ▶ .jpeg
- ▶ .png
- ▶ .txt
- ▶ Active X files (not viewable in Netscape navigator)

Viewing Files with the Help of Other Programs

There are certainly plenty of other types of files in the world, but Internet Explorer can't display them on its own. With a little help from other programs, however, Internet Explorer can handle just about any file you might encounter. These ancillary programs can normally expand the file-handling abilities of Internet Explorer in two ways:

Helper or add-on   With a helper or an add-on program, Internet Explorer does not open the new file type directly; it hands the file over to the helper program. The helper may appear as a separate window of its own or as a new component within the Internet Explorer window.

Plug-in   A plug-in program allows Internet Explorer to open a new file type within the Internet Explorer window; the relationship between the two programs is almost seamless, as though the other program has been "plugged in" to Internet Explorer.

Any individual or company can create a helper or plug-in program to extend the capabilities of Internet Explorer. Most of these applications are available free for the downloading.

What happens if Internet Explorer encounters a file type that neither it nor any of its associated programs can open? That's when your Windows file associations come into play, as discussed next.

Dealing with Unknown File Types

When you click a link or otherwise open a file, Internet Explorer verifies that the file type is one it recognizes. It has two ways of recognizing files:

► By the file's MIME type

► By the file's file name extension

Before a server sends the file to Internet Explorer, the server first sends the file's MIME type. This acronym stands for Multipurpose Internet Mail Extensions and is a standard method on the Internet for identifying file types. If Internet Explorer recognizes the MIME type, it will know what to do with the file, such as displaying the file itself or passing it along to another program on your system.

Part ii

CRIPES! MIME TYPES YIPES!

Danger, Will Robinson! I wouldn't go looking for MIME types in Internet Explorer if I were you. Why? You won't find them there. In fact, you might just drive yourself nuts trying to. Let us hearken back to the days of Windows 3.1x and marvel at the thrill of associations, and we begin to see the light where MIME is concerned. If you are unfamiliar with earlier versions of Windows, then you'll need an explanation of MIME and associations. Try these:

association \ass-ohsh-ee-ay-shun\ *n* : A sort of roadmap that tells Windows which applications to use for which filename extensions. i.e., *document.doc* = Word 97, *picture.psd* = PhotoShop, *write.wri* = Windows Write, and so on and so forth

MIME \my-mm\ *n* **1** : An energetic individual uses familiar motions to mimic reality, **2** : also referred to as Multipurpose Internet Mail Extensions, MIME helps client applications, like e-mail or web browsers, determine which application to use for a file it cannot handle (i.e., RealAudio or RealVideo, QuickTime, or PDF...)

Do you feel as if you need to make some modifications to your MIME types or are just curious what they look like? Here, do this:

▶ Go to the Desktop, making the My Computer (or whatever you have changed the name to) icon visible.

▶ Open My Computer and go to View ➤ Folder Options. Or in Windows 2000 or Millennium Edition go to Start ➤ Settings ➤ Control Panel ➤ Folder Options and select the File Types tab.

▶ Click the File Types tab in the resultant dialog box to make the tab active.

▶ Wait.

▶ Wait some more.

You'll note that there is a large list of items, some familiar, some alien. Most of these items are not even related to the Internet at all, but there are some important ones. The key to the whole kit and kaboodle is the x-text/html MIME type that allows your browser to see Web pages in the first place. Nifty, huh?

WARNING

It's not nice to mess with Mother MIME! Unless you are very familiar with MIME or are tops at reading complex documentation, I do not suggest you modify MIME types. Doing so can cause you to lose the nifty gizmos you added in the first place. Just remember that the most qualified individual to properly install MIME types is the application installer itself. When in doubt, reinstall!

Many MIME types and file name extensions are already associated with the appropriate programs on your computer (as discussed in the next section). For example, an HTML document has the MIME type *text/html*, a GIF image file has the type *image/gif*, and a JPEG image file has the type *image/jpeg*. You can view or revise the MIME types and program associations for files on your system, which is discussed in the next section.

When you click a link to a file, several outcomes are possible, depending on the file's MIME type and file name extension:

▶ If Internet Explorer recognizes its MIME type as one that already has an association in Windows, it will automatically open that file from the server. Internet Explorer will display the file if it can (such as with an HTML or a text file) or pass it along to the program with which that MIME type is associated in Windows.

▶ If Internet Explorer does not recognize the file's MIME type, it will look at the file's file name extension. If a program in Windows is associated with that file type, Internet Explorer will then make the following determination.

▶ If the "Confirm open after download" option in the Edit File Type dialog box for this association (discussed in the next section) is not selected, Internet Explorer will open the file immediately, using the program defined for this file in the file's association.

▶ If the "Confirm after download" option is selected, Internet Explorer will display a dialog box, asking if you want to open the file or save it to disk. When in doubt, you're better off leaving that option selected so that you'll have the opportunity to decide what to do when you encounter that file type.

▶ If the file has no association in Windows, Internet Explorer will display the dialog box shown in Figure 6.6 and let you decide how to proceed. If you decide to open the file from the Internet, you'll then have to choose the program that should be used.

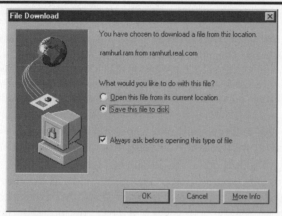

FIGURE 6.6: When Internet Explorer encounters a file that it cannot handle, you can either open the file in its associated program (if there is one) or save the file to disk.

▶ If the file is a viewable file for which you do not have the proper viewer software or plug-in (say, an Audio or Video file) Internet Explorer will try to fetch the missing plug-in from the company that makes it. The vast majority of plug-ins these days are what are called ActiveX Controls. (Don't bother with what, just know how.) Commonly a dialog box like the one in Figure 6.7 will appear telling you that software is being downloaded to your machine, and displaying authentication information.

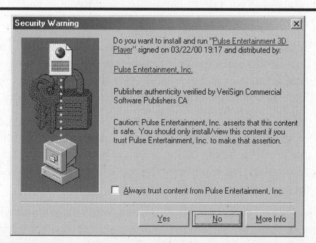

FIGURE 6.7: When Internet Explorer encounters a file for which you do not have the proper software or plugin to display it

WARNING

Here's where it can get a little tricky. Okay, if the page says that the media is provided by, say, Pulse (as in the figure) and the dialog box vouches that it is Pulse that's sending the application, you're okay. It would be extraordinarily coincidental if a bad guy (or gal) decided to intercept that and send you a virus or something equally destructive instead. If the same thing happens but you receive a warning that the certificate is not valid or signed, but you know the company or otherwise have a reason to trust the download, go ahead. Then again, it wouldn't hurt to just not get it and e-mail the company complaining of their lackadaisical practices.

When you are presented with the File Download dialog box, you can choose either to open the file in its associated program (if it has one) or simply save the file to disk. For several reasons, the latter choice is often the prudent one.

First, downloading a file from the Internet puts your computer at risk of being infected with a virus—who knows where that file has been lurking? When you save the file to disk, you can later run your virus-checking program on it to see if it gets a clean bill of health.

Another reason to save a file instead of opening it is to avoid the possible chaos of having too many things happening at the same time. While you're online browsing a Web site, an incoming program file that you opened might be setting up a new game on your computer, and the resulting clash might make a messy electronic battleground.

NOTE

You may often go to a Web site specifically to download a file, such as a program update for software you own. When you click on the link to the file, Internet Explorer displays the dialog box and asks you what you want to do with the file. Unless the site tells you to do otherwise, choose to save the file to disk.

Saving a file to disk is a neat trick because you can then deal with it later. You can still install that game or patch that software, but you'll do it when the time is right. Plus, with the file safely on disk, you can scan it for viruses, make a backup copy of it, if necessary, or pass it on to a friend or coworker.

As you can see, the way in which Internet Explorer handles a file depends on whether the file has an association under Windows and whether that association is by its MIME type or by its file name extension. The next section shows how you can view, create, revise, or delete a file association.

Setting File Associations

In Windows, when you choose to open a file outside the program that created it, such as by double-clicking the file in Windows Explorer, Windows must check to see which program is associated with that file type.

Windows makes the determination based on the file's file name extension (only Internet Explorer looks at a file's MIME type when you're connected to the Web or your intranet), which is the characters after the period in the file name (after the final period if there is more than one). Here are some common file name extensions that you may recognize and the file types that Windows associates with them:

BAT	MS-DOS Batch file
BMP	Bitmap image
EXE	Application
HLP	Help file
INI	Configuration settings
TTF	TrueType Font file
WRI	Write document

The extensions listed above are generic to Windows, in that those types are defined in a brand-new Windows installation. If you encounter one of these files in Internet Explorer and choose to open it, Windows takes over and performs the appropriate action.

For example, when you double-click a program file with a .bat or .exe file name extension, Windows simply runs the file. It opens an .hlp file in the standard help viewer in Windows, as though you chose a command from a program's Help menu. In Windows 98 and 95, a .wri file opens in WordPad, and in earlier versions of Windows it opens in Write.

When you install new programs under Windows, the installation routine may add new file-type definitions to Windows. For example, when you install Microsoft Office, the following file types are defined (and there are many more as well):

.doc	Microsoft Word document
.wkb	Microsoft Word Backup document
.xls	Microsoft Excel worksheet
.xlt	Microsoft Excel template

NOTE

In this case, with the help of its ActiveX abilities, Internet Explorer can view Word (.doc) and Excel (.xls) documents. Therefore, if you have Word and Excel installed on your computer, you won't even be offered the Open/Save dialog box when you click a link to one of these files. Internet Explorer will open it.

The point to remember is this: Any file that can't be viewed within Internet Explorer is handled by the program with which its file name extension is associated in Windows (unless it has a MIME type association, which will be used first). For example, when you attempt to open a file with a WKB file name extension, Windows tells Word to open that file.

You can also create your own file associations or revise existing ones. While viewing a folder (not a Web page) in any Explorer window, choose View ➤ Folder Options and select the File Types tab. You'll see a list of file types similar to the one shown in Figure 6.8.

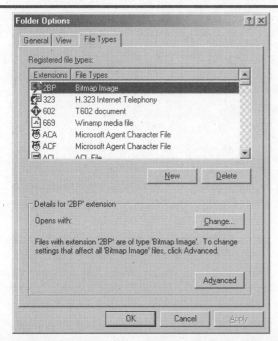

FIGURE 6.8:   You can view or revise file associations or create new ones in the File Types tab of the Folder Options dialog box.

DON'T ASK ME WHAT PROGRAM TO USE, JUST OPEN THE FILE!

How many times have you tried to open a file in Windows Explorer, only to be presented with the Open With dialog box (shown here), asking you to choose a program to use to open that file? The problem is that the file you want to open has no program associated with it under Windows, so Windows is stymied and now must wait for you to decide how to proceed. You'll also see this dialog box when you choose to open a file in Internet Explorer and that file has no association.

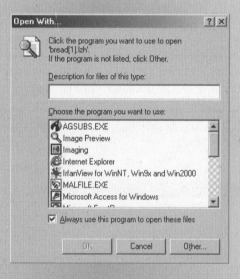

At this point, you can either choose a program from the list of associated programs already in Windows or click the Other button and select a program name from your disk drive.

For example, suppose in Internet Explorer you saved the file SOME-FILE.ABC, and in Windows Explorer you double-click the file to open it. Unless Windows on your computer has the file name extension .ABC already associated with some program, you'll get the Open With dialog box.

If you know that this .ABC file is, for example, a text file, you could choose Notepad from the list as the program to use to open it. If you're going to be working with more .ABC files in the future, you could also select the "Always use this program to open this file" option to establish an association between any .ABC files and Notepad.

If the item named Internet Document (HTML) is selected in the list of file types, then beneath the list of file types you can see that:

▶ The file name extension recognized for this type of file is .HTM or .HTML.

▶ The MIME type for this type of file is *text/html*.

The name of the associated program that will be used to open this type of file is Explorer. You can revise this definition by clicking the Edit button, which displays the Edit File Type dialog box (where you'll find the "Confirm open after download" option, which was discussed in the previous section). For example, you could specify that FrontPage Express be associated with the editing of this file type so that when you right-click the file name and choose Edit, the file would open in that program. To create a completely new file association, click the New Type button.

NOTE

There are no laws establishing sole rights to a file name extension! Therefore, the name and associated program for any given file type could vary on different computers. For example, the .doc extension might be used by some other program. In fact, if you were to install that program on a computer that already has Microsoft Word installed, a new association would be established for .doc files. When you later double-click a .doc file, the other program, not Word, would be the one to open it.

WHAT'S NEXT?

Gene Weisskopf and Pat Coleman took you on a whirlwind tour of Internet Explorer in this chapter and introduced you to the ways you can start the program; use its menus, toolbars, and keyboard shortcuts; and view different types of files. In the next chapter, Pat Coleman will offer similar information about Internet Explorer's main competitor, Netscape Navigator/Communicator.

Part II

Chapter 7

AN ALTERNATIVE TO INTERNET EXPLORER: NETSCAPE NAVIGATOR

Netscape Navigator is the Internet browser that is part of
Netscape Communicator, a suite of Internet tools.
Besides Navigator, these tools include an e-mail and
Internet newsgroups client (Messenger), instant messaging
software (AOL Instant Messenger Service, or AIM), a program
for creating Web pages (Composer), and Netscape Radio. In
this chapter, we'll primarily look at Navigator, but we'll also
take a look at some of the other features that are available
with Communicator.

Adapted from *PC Complete* by Sybex, Inc.

ISBN 0-7821-2778-9   1005 pages $19.99

Netscape vs. Internet Explorer

Unless you've been under a rock somewhere, you're aware of the browser battle that raged during the last few years. While it was the only browser on the market, Netscape Navigator was given away to educational institutions. Users in these institutions developed a keen loyalty to Navigator because of its stability and ease of use for intranet and Internet purposes. Navigator helped unify the variety of operating systems in use in classrooms and administrative offices.

Navigator is still the browser of choice in many of these institutions, as well as with other organizations and individuals, but it faced an uphill struggle in the marketplace when Microsoft integrated Internet Explorer with Windows. As you will see shortly, the easiest way to obtain Netscape Navigator now is to download it with Internet Explorer.

In several ways, a browser is a browser is a browser. Clicking an underlined term on a Web page takes you to that resource; clicking the Back button takes you to the page you were previously viewing; clicking the Stop button halts the loading of a resource, and so on. But there are differences between Navigator and Internet Explorer that lead some people to prefer one or the other.

If you're reading this chapter, you are probably trying to decide whether to install Navigator, or you have it and want to know how to use it more efficiently. Obviously, I can't tell you everything you'd ever want or need to know about Navigator within these few pages, but I can get you started and point you in the right direction for more information.

Let's get to it.

Finding and Installing Netscape Navigator

As I mentioned earlier, the easiest way to find and install Netscape Navigator is by using Internet Explorer, which you have if you are using Windows 98 or 98 SE. Assuming that Windows is up and running, that you have an account with an ISP (Internet Service Provider), and that you are connected to the Internet, follow these steps to locate Netscape Navigator:

WARNING

I know from personal experience that some ISPs don't support the latest version of Navigator. Before you go to the trouble of downloading, check with your ISP.

1. From the Desktop, click the Launch Internet Explorer Browser button on the Quick Launch toolbar.

2. In the Address bar, type the following URL:

    `http://home.netscape.com/download/index.html`

    You'll see the page shown in Figure 7.1.

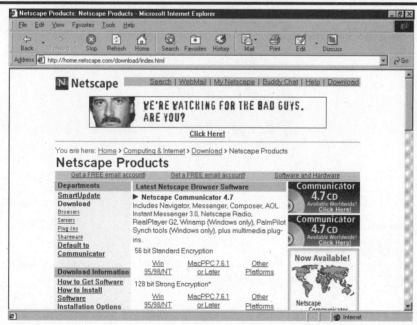

FIGURE 7.1: Select a version of Netscape to download from this page.

3. Click the version that you want to install. If you select to install the 128-bit encrypted version of the software, you'll need to accept the agreement that appears on the screen.

UNDERSTANDING ENCRYPTION

Whether you are downloading Netscape Communicator or Netscape Navigator, you can choose between Standard and Strong encryption. Encryption is the process of encoding information so that it is safe from prying eyes during transmission.

If you plan to engage in online banking or trading, you'll want to choose Strong encryption. For ordinary, everyday purposes, Standard encryption is sufficient.

4. On the next screen, select a location from which to download, and click Download. You'll then see the File Download dialog box:

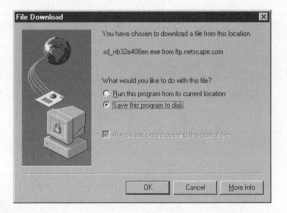

NOTE

By default, Netscape uses SmartDownload, which lets you pause the download, resume it, and surf the Web during the download process.

5. Select Save this program to disk, and click OK to open the Save As dialog box, as shown in Figure 7.2. By default, Netscape places the downloaded files in your Desktop folder and places an icon on the Desktop.

FIGURE 7.2: Select a folder in which to store the download.

6. Click Save to begin the download. Figure 7.3 shows the dialog box you'll see while the download is in progress.

FIGURE 7.3: A download of Netscape Navigator in progress

NOTE

The time to download varies with the speed of your Internet connection. With a 56Kbps modem, I downloaded the standalone version of Navigator in about an hour. Downloading Communicator took about twice that long.

Installing Netscape Navigator

When the download is complete, you'll see the following icon on your Desktop:

Click this icon to start the installation process, and follow the on-screen instructions. When you're finished, you'll see the Netscape Navigator shortcut on the Desktop:

Starting Netscape Navigator

To start Navigator, double-click the Netscape Navigator icon on your Desktop. You'll be asked if you want to make Navigator your default browser. Click Yes if you do; click No if you'd rather not. To avoid seeing this dialog box in the future, check the Do Not Perform This Check In The Future check box. You'll then see a page similar to that shown in Figure 7.4. You can also start Netscape by choosing Start ➤ Programs ➤ Netscape Navigator ➤ Netscape Navigator.

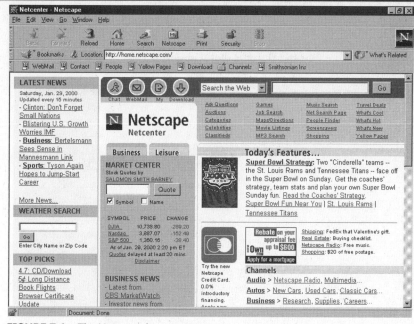

FIGURE 7.4: The Netscape home page

SELECTING YOUR DEFAULT BROWSER

When you install Windows 98 SE, it automatically makes Internet Explorer your default browser. The default browser is the one that opens when you, for example, click a hyperlink in a document or an e-mail message. To see which browser is set as the default, open

CONTINUED →

Internet Explorer, choose Tools ➤ Internet Options to open the Internet Options dialog box, and click the Programs tab:

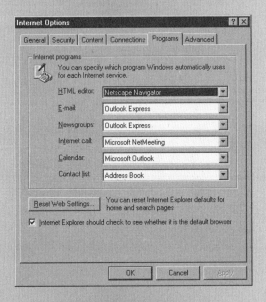

If you install Netscape Navigator after installing Internet Explorer, as we just did, some of the settings in this dialog box may have changed. To reestablish your original settings, click the Reset Web Settings button.

NAVIGATING THE NAVIGATOR

Netscape developers have made a concerted effort to keep you on the Netscape home page. As well as being a browser, Netscape is also a search engine, an entertainment center with multimedia links, and a starting point for finance and travel, among other things.

If you've used Internet Explorer or another browser, you can easily begin using Netscape. But you can also easily begin using Netscape even if you haven't used another browser. Simply click an underlined term or phrase to open that resource. If you've run across a Web address (URL) that interests you, simply select http://home.netscape.com/ in the box at the top of the page, type the URL you want to go to in place of that one, and press Enter to go to that site. It's just that easy.

To really use Netscape efficiently, however, you need to be familiar with some features of the interface, and in this section we'll look at several of those. If at any time you need help, you can get it. Click Help on the menu bar at the top of the screen (look back at Figure 7.4 if you need help finding the menu bar), and choose Help Contents to open NetHelp:

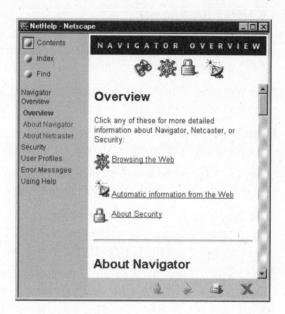

To search on a word or a phrase, you can click the Index or Find buttons. Contents provides an overview. I have to mention that NetHelp is not exactly up-to-date, so you may search in vain for information on some features. In such a case, the information found at http://help .netscape.com/products/client/pe/reflib/introcom.htm may be of value.

Using the Menu Bar

As is the case with Windows, in Navigator you can get where you want to be or do what you want to do in several ways. You'll pick up on this quickly as we explore the menu bar and the toolbars. Which method you use depends on your personal preferences, sometimes the task at hand, and myriad other considerations. Near the top of the screen is the menu bar, which contains some of the most familiar Windows commands. Let's start by looking at the File menu.

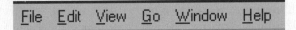

Using the File Menu

You'll probably use the commands on the File menu the most often, since it contains the commands for such tasks as opening, saving, and printing a file. Here's a brief explanation of what each does:

New Window   Opens a new browser window. To return to the previous window, click the Close button.

Open Page   Displays the Open Page dialog box, in which you can enter a URL or the name of local file to open.

Save As   Opens the standard Windows Save As dialog box that you can use to save the current page or selection as a file.

Save Frame As   If the page you're viewing is in frames, choose this command to save the page as a file. This command will be grayed out if the current page is not in frames.

Send Page   If you installed the Communicator suite, this command opens Netscape Messenger with an e-mail message ready to go. The Web address will be in the message, so you only need to address to the sender.

Page Setup   Opens the Page Setup dialog box, which you can use to choose how the current page will be laid out when it prints.

Print Preview   Opens the page in a print preview window so that you can see how it will look when printed.

Print   Opens the standard Windows Print dialog box.

Close   Exits Navigator.

Exit   Exits Navigator.

Using the Edit Menu

You use the Edit menu when you want to manipulate individual elements on a Web page, find something, or configure Navigator. The Cut, Copy, Paste, and Select All commands work just as they do in any Windows program. Here's a brief description of what each of the other commands does:

Find In Page   Opens the Find dialog box, which you can use to search for a specific word or term on the current page.

Find Again   Lets you search once more for the term or phrase you previously searched on.

Search Internet   Opens the Net Search page, which you can use to specify a search engine and look for specific information on the Internet. We'll look at this feature in detail in a later section of this chapter.

Preferences   Opens the Preferences dialog box in which you can customize Navigator so that it looks and works the way you want it to. We'll look at this feature in detail in a later section of this chapter.

Using the View Menu

Although you'll use the Preferences dialog box to make major changes to Navigator, you can use the commands on the View menu to customize what appears on the screen and to view the source behind what appears on the screen. To hide or display the Navigation, Location, and Personal toolbars, use the first three commands on the View menu. Here's a description of what each of the other commands does:

Increase Font   Increases the size of the font on the screen. You'll see a brief flicker, and then the current page will reappear with the type in a bigger size.

Decrease Font   Decreases the size of the font on the screen. You'll see a brief flicker, and then the current page will reappear with the type in a smaller size.

Reload   If a page is loading too slowly, choose Reload to start the loading process again.

Show Images   Displays images if you have previously turned them off.

Refresh   Refreshes the screen display.

Stop Page Loading   Halts the loading of a page. Handy if a page is taking forever to display.

Stop Animations   Calls a halt to those gyrating, pulsing, flickering images, banners, and so on.

Page Source   Displays the HTML source code for the current page, as shown in Figure 7.5.

Page Info   Displays the Document Info window, which provides information about the current page. Figure 7.6 shows information for the Netscape home page.

Encoding   Displays a list of languages for which you can specify a character set to use when you haven't specified page encoding or when page encoding is not available.

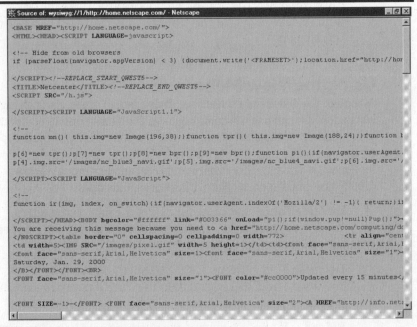

FIGURE 7.5: The HTML source code for a Web page

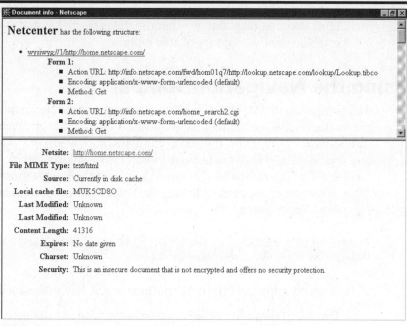

FIGURE 7.6: Information about the Netscape home page

Using the Go Menu

You probably won't use the Go menu frequently. It simply contains the Back, Forward, and Home commands, which are represented on the Navigation bar by icons that you can click much more quickly than choosing them from a menu. More useful is a list of previously viewed pages. Choose one of these to quickly retrace your steps.

Using the Window/Communicator Menu

If you installed the Communicator suite, you'll see a Communicator menu instead of a Window menu. If you installed only the Netscape browser, you'll see a Window menu. Here is a description of commands common to both:

Navigator   Opens a new browser window on your screen.

Bookmarks   Lets you add a favorite site to a list that you can use to quickly and easily access sites that you want to return to often. I'll discuss bookmarks in detail later in this chapter.

Security Info   Opens the Security Info dialog box, which contains information about whether the site is encrypted and establishes other security-related criteria.

Using the Navigation Toolbar

The Navigation toolbar contains buttons for some of the commands that are on the various menus, as well as buttons that have become common in Windows. For example, if you use Windows much at all, you've seen and used Back and Forward buttons in Windows Explorer and in Explorer-like folders. You've also most likely used the Print button in other Windows applications. Clicking the Reload button is the same as choosing View ≻ Reload.

Here's a description of the other buttons on the Navigation toolbar:

Home   Takes you to the Netscape home page or to a home page you have specified. We'll look at how to specify this later in this chapter.

Search   Opens the Net Search page. We'll look at searching in detail later in this chapter.

My Netscape   Takes you to a page designed to be used as a home page default in your browser. You can customize this page according to your interests and needs.

Security   Opens the Security Info window. Clicking this button is the same as choosing Window ≻ Security Info.

Stop   Stops the loading of a page. Clicking this button is the same as choosing View ≻ Stop Page Loading.

Using the Location Toolbar

If you did as I suggested earlier and entered a URL to replace the Netscape home page URL, you've already used the Location toolbar, which contains the Bookmarks button, the Netsite field, and the What's Related button:

Bookmarks   Netsite: http://home.netscape.com/   What's Related

You enter a URL in the Netsite field and press Enter to go to a specific site. If you click the down arrow at the right of the Netsite field, you'll see a list of previously visited sites. To go to one of these, select it and press Enter.

Clicking the What's Related button displays a list of other places that are similar in content to the current page. We'll look at Bookmarks in detail in a later section.

The Personal Toolbar

The contents of the Personal toolbar depend on whether you are using the Communicator suite or stand-alone Netscape Navigator, and on whether you have added any buttons to this toolbar.

Here's a description of the buttons common to both Communicator and Navigator. We'll look at how to add a button in the next section.

WebMail   Gives you access to a free Internet e-mail account. You'll be required to sign in with Netscape Center to use this feature, and if you aren't registered, you'll be required to register. Entering some of this information is tedious, but there's no charge.

People   Starts People Search, with which you can locate someone's phone number or e-mail address.

Yellow Pages   Starts the Netscape Yellow Pages, with which you can locate contact information for businesses and organizations.

Download   Opens the Download & Upgrade Page, from which you can download browsers, servers, shareware, updates, plug-ins, and so on.

Channels   Displays a list of bookmarked areas that exist on Netscape NetCenter.

KEEPING TRACK OF SITES WITH BOOKMARKS

The Netscape Navigator synonym for the Internet Explorer term *favorite* is *bookmark*. In Navigator, a bookmark is a link to a URL or some other

Web page that you store in a file to use later. When you happen onto a site that you know you'll want to return to in the future, you put it in your bookmark list. You can then simply click the site's link to open the page. You don't have to remember the URL or even the name of the site. A bookmark, then, is simply a shortcut to a Web site.

Bookmarks are stored in subfolders in the Bookmarks folder, which is shown in Figure 7.7. To open the Bookmarks folder, choose Bookmarks ➤ Edit Bookmarks.

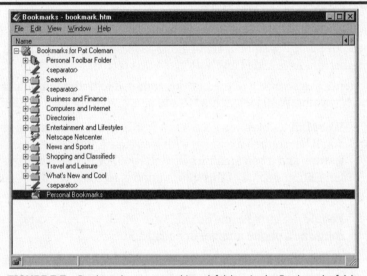

FIGURE 7.7:   Bookmarks are stored in subfolders in the Bookmarks folder.

The Bookmarks folder works much like Windows Explorer. You can store bookmarks in the subfolders that Netscape provides, or you can create your own subfolders. Click the plus (+) sign next to a folder name to display its subfolders.

TIP

If you aren't up to speed using Windows Explorer, you're depriving yourself of a skill that is really essential to using Windows and Windows applications.

Creating and Opening a Bookmark

With the page open that you want to bookmark, you can add a bookmark in several ways:

▶ Click Bookmarks, and then choose Add Bookmark. This places a link in your Personal Bookmarks folder.

▶ Right-click anywhere on a Web page, other than a link, and choose Add Bookmark from the shortcut menu. This places a link in your Personal Bookmarks folder.

▶ Click the down-pointing arrow to the left of the Bookmarks button to open the Bookmarks list, choose File Bookmark, and select a folder in which to store the link.

▶ Click the icon to the right of the Bookmarks button, and drag to a folder in the list of folders that is displayed in a shortcut menu.

Now, to use a bookmark you've created, click Bookmarks to open the Bookmarks list, click the folder where the bookmark is stored, and then click the bookmark.

Creating a Bookmark Folder

You create a new folder in the Bookmarks folder in much the same way that you create a new folder in Windows Explorer. Follow these steps:

1. Choose Bookmarks ➢ Edit Bookmarks to open the Bookmarks folder.

2. Select the folder in which to put your new folder. For example, if you want your new folder to be a primary folder, select Bookmarks For *Your Name* at the top of the list.

   3. Choose File ➤ New Folder to open the Bookmark Properties
   dialog box:

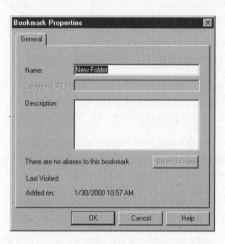

   4. Type a name for the new folder, enter a description if you
   want, and click OK.

Adding a Button to the Personal Toolbar

You can also use the Bookmarks command to add a button to your Personal toolbar. Perhaps often, even several times a day, you need to check
a particular site or sites. Create a button on the Personal toolbar. You can
do so in a couple of ways:

   ▶ Open the page, click the icon immediately to right of the Bookmarks button, and drag it to the Personal toolbar.

   ▶ Choose Bookmarks ➤ File Bookmark ➤ Personal Toolbar Folder
   ➤ Personal Toolbar Folder.

When you no longer need that button on your Personal toolbar, follow
these steps to delete it:

   1. Choose Bookmarks ➤ Edit Bookmarks to open the Bookmarks folder.

2. Click the plus sign next to the Personal Toolbar Folder folder to expand its contents, if necessary.

3. Press the Delete key, or right-click the entry for your button and choose Delete Bookmark from the shortcut menu.

Moving Bookmarks

Moving a bookmark from one folder to another is a bit tricky, though easy once you get the hang of it. Select the bookmark, drag it to just *beneath* the folder to which you want to move it, and then release the mouse button.

Deleting Bookmarks

You delete any bookmark in the same way that you delete a button from the Personal toolbar. Follow the steps in the previous section, "Adding a Button to the Personal Toolbar."

SEARCHING THE INTERNET

When you search for information on the Internet, you use a tool that has gathered lists of available files and documents and stored them in a database. This tool is known by various names, including search tool, search service, and search engine. Netscape Navigator uses the term *search engine.*

You access the Navigator search engine in various ways. Let's start with the easiest, using the text box next to the Search the Web drop-down list on the Netscape home page. Simply type a term or a phrase, and press Enter or click Go. Figure 7.8 shows the results I got when I searched on the phrase "Internet statistics." Click a link in the Search Results window to open that resource.

TIP

If you want to find an exact phrase, enclose it in quotation marks. If you don't do so and you enter multiple terms, your search results will include every resource that contains each of the words in your phrase.

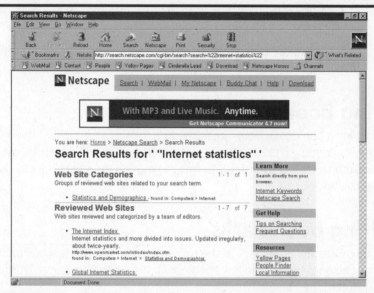

FIGURE 7.8: The results returned by searching the Internet for "Internet statistics"

To search using a search engine of your choice or to browse categories of information, (such as people, games, software, and so on), follow these steps:

1. Click the Search button on the Navigator toolbar to open the Net Search page:

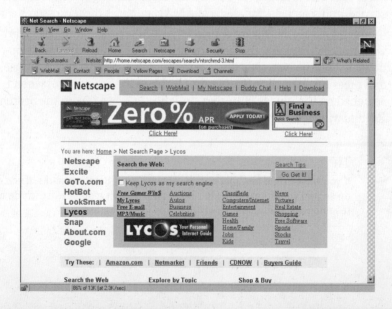

2. From the list on the left, select a search engine.

3. Type a term or phrase into the Search the Web text box.

4. Press Enter, or click Go Get It.

Your results will be returned on the Web site of the search engine you selected.

To search by browsing categories of topics, scroll down to the bottom of the Net Search page, and click a link.

TIP

For a list of tips that you can use to improve the results of your searches, click the Tips link near the bottom of the Net Search page. Chapter 8, "Internet Search Engines," talks about some of these search engines in more detail.

PERSONALIZING NETSCAPE

I promised earlier in this chapter that we would look in detail at the Preferences option on the Edit menu. When you choose Edit ≻ Preferences, the Preferences dialog box opens, as shown in Figure 7.9. You use the options in this dialog box to personalize Navigator. Here are just some of the ways that you can set up Navigator so that it works the way you want it to work:

▶ Change the appearance of toolbars to show pictures and text, pictures only, or text only.

▶ Change the font, font sizes, and colors in which Web pages and links appear.

▶ Specify that Navigator start with a page of your choosing rather than the Netscape home page.

▶ Specify the language in which you prefer to view Web pages.

▶ Specify helper applications for the various file types.

▶ Enable and disable the What's Related button.

▶ Specify your name, e-mail address, and signature file.

Part ii

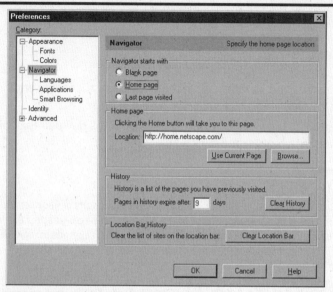

FIGURE 7.9: Personalize Navigator using the options in the Preferences dialog box.

To begin establishing your preferences, follow these steps:

1. Choose Edit ≻ Preferences to open the Preferences dialog box. By default, the Navigator category is selected in the list on the left, and the right part of this dialog box displays the options associated with Navigator.

2. Use the Navigator page to specify a start page and a home page, to specify the number of days that page will remain in the History list, and to clear the list of sites on the Location bar.

3. Click the Appearance category to display options that you can select to change the appearance of the display.

4. Click Fonts to display the dialog box shown in Figure 7.10. Use these options to change the font size on the screen.

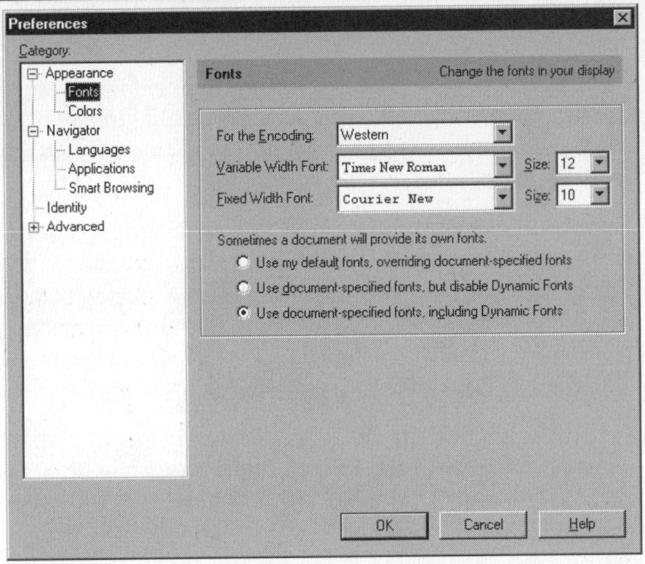

FIGURE 7.10: Changing the font size of the display on the screen

5. Continue to select categories from the Category list to get an idea of the available customizations.
6. When you have made all your changes, click OK to apply them and to close the Preferences dialog box.

TIPS FOR GETTING THE MOST OUT OF NETSCAPE NAVIGATOR

The purpose of this chapter is to give you an overview of Netscape Navigator. The best way to get to know a browser is simply to use it. Along the way, you'll discover all sorts of tips and tricks that will make you a more efficient user and let you find what you're looking for faster. Here are some tips to start with:

- In addition to the search methods described in the section "Searching the Internet," earlier in this chapter, you can also search by entering a term or a phrase in the Netsite field and pressing Enter.
- The What's Related button isn't always active even if it isn't disabled. You'll see it primarily for the more popular sites.

CONTINUED ➞

▶ If you visit a page you like but forget to bookmark it and you can't remember the URL, you may still be able to find it. Click the down arrow next to the Netsite field to display a list of recently visited sites.

▶ If you have a slow Internet connection or pages just seem to be unusually slow to load, turn off the display of graphics. Choose Edit ➣ Preferences to open the Preferences dialog box, click Advanced, and clear the check mark from the Automatically Load Images check box. Large images will now be replaced with small icons. If you want to view an image, click the icon.

▶ Experiment with right-clicking. Often right-clicking opens a shortcut menu with choices appropriate for the object you clicked. And even if right-clicking does nothing, it will never do any harm.

▶ Clicking the Security indicator in the lower-left corner of the screen displays the Security Info folder with security information about the current page.

▶ If you're really new to the Internet and browsing, don't always follow the first instruction you might see at a site. For example, you'll find advertisements at the top of many pages, with a link that says "Click Here!" If you want information about the advertiser, sure, go right ahead and click, but that's probably not what you were looking for when you navigated to the page.

▶ The activity indicator, which is the Netscape logo in the top-right corner of a page, will be active when Navigator is working— locating a resource, loading an image, searching, and so on.

▶ If you find an image, text, or other object that you want to insert in another document, select it and use the Cut, Copy, and Paste commands as you would in any Windows program.

▶ If you find an image you'd like to use as wallpaper, right-click it and choose Set as Wallpaper from the shortcut menu.

WHAT'S NEXT?

This chapter has given you a brief look at Internet Explorer's main competition, Netscape Navigator. In the next chapter, Richard Sherman provides an overview of the most popular search engines and how to use them.

Chapter 8

INTERNET SEARCH ENGINES

The World Wide Web need not be a tangled web. Information appears at first glance to exist in a seemingly elusive yet chaotic world of data. In reality, every bit and piece of information has its own unique address, based on no particular geographic location. When these bits of data are located and presented as a search result, they can appear on a computer screen anywhere in the world. It's amazing to me that the whole thing even works.

Accessing the Web is easy. Okay, "So much for his credibility," you may be muttering, but let's stop and think about it for a moment. All connections to the Web transport you to a screen within your Web browser software (usually Netscape or Internet Explorer). Each browser provides you with a blank field in

• •

Adapted from *Mr. Modem's Internet Guide for Seniors* by Richard A. Sherman
ISBN 0-7821-2580-8   415 pages $19.99

which to type a Web address or URL. Once you enter your first URL, the world is at your fingertips and life will never be the same.

Okay, that's all fine and dandy, but what if you don't know the URL or address of a particular Web page or Web site? How in the world do you find anything on the Web? First, stop whining. Nobody likes a whiner. Fortunately, the Web comes equipped with many specialty sites called search engines that are designed to help you find the information you're seeking. Bet you're feeling better already, aren't you? Well, this chapter will give you all the information you need to search the Web like a pro and find anything you want.

How Do Search Engines Work?

Most search engines prompt you to input keywords or words related in some way to the topic about which you are seeking information. When you enter a keyword, the search engine examines its database and presents to you a listing of sites that, in theory, match your search criteria.

The most common search technique deployed by millions of Internet users is the Single Keyword Search, or SKS for members of Acronyms Anonymous. This type of search casts a very wide net and will return lots of meaningless, irrelevant results. With a wee bit more sophistication, deploying a double keyword search with a "plus" sign (+) between the words will significantly improve your search results. The plus sign ties the two search terms together—for example, **tuna + melt**. Without the plus sign, a search engine would search for sites containing the word *tuna* and the word *melt* but not necessarily the scrumptious combination together as a phrase.

Surrounding search terms with quotation marks (**"tuna melt"**) will also result in search results that are an exact match. See "Boolean Searches" later in this chapter for a more in-depth look at the scintillating science of searching.

Search engines work best when you have a particular topic in mind that can be expressed in specific terms. But the downside to broad, keyword searches is that you'll sometimes be faced with hundreds or thousands of search results, referred to as *hits*, 90 percent of which will be meaningless for your purposes. The search results that contain your keywords are likely to be grouped at the top, and chances are you'll find what you're looking for among the first 25 to 50 hits returned.

There are actually hundreds of search engines residing on the Web and new ones make their cyber debut weekly. So how do you select a search engine? Many people ask me what my favorite search engine is and my answer is usually, "I'm using XYZ search engine right now, but check back with me in an hour." I continually experiment with and explore new search engines; my favorite at any given moment is the one that produced the most satisfactory results the last few times. If I use a particular search engine and the results aren't what I'm looking for, I'll usually try another one.

I would recommend creating a "Search Engines" Bookmarks or Favorites folder that contains an assortment of search engines so they're always just a mouse-click away. As you discover new search engines or lose interest in others that aren't particularly useful to you, you can add them to or remove them from this folder. Bear in mind, however, that search engines reinvent themselves periodically, so a search engine that's a dud today may be the latest and greatest six months from now. It's worth revisiting the duds periodically. Ultimately, you'll find two or three search engines that feel comfortable and are easy to use, and sticking with those few will probably serve your purposes beautifully.

NOTE
The Internet experiences a rush hour just like the average freeway. Peak hours of usage are from 7:00 to 11:00 p.m., local time.
    Source: StatMarket, Inc., http://www.statmarket.com

No matter what search engine you prefer, be sure to take the time to familiarize yourself with that program's capabilities. Most search engines include annoyingly detailed search tips documentation. It's time well spent getting up close and personal with a search engine's strengths, weaknesses, and search tip recommendations. You'll not only improve your short-term results, but you'll become a more skilled and sophisticated Web searcher in the process.

TYPES OF SEARCH ENGINES

There are three types of search engines: indexers or crawlers, directories, and metasearches or metacrawlers.

Indexers

These search engines use an automated or robotic method of collecting information. Sometimes they're referred to as *crawlers* because these programs crawl through the Internet 24 hours a day cataloging or indexing Web sites. It's best to use indexers when you want to cast a wide search net. An indexer will return lots of worthless sites and information, but once you separate the wheat from the chaff you may find some real gems—or perhaps some mixed metaphors. To further confuse things, some of these search programs straddle categories, and you know how uncomfortable that can be if it's not done correctly. Excite, for example, is both an indexer and a directory. My best advice: Try as many search programs as you wish, as frequently as you like. Nobody says you have to pledge undying loyalty to just one or two search engines.

Examples of Indexers:

Alta Vista: http://www.altavista.com

Excite: http://www.excite.com

HotBot: http://www.hotbot.com

Magellan: http://www.magellan.excite.com

WebCrawler: http://www.webcrawler.com

Directories

A close encounter of the directory kind will reveal a search engine that relies on living, breathing human beings to catalog Web sites that are often submitted by Internet users. Due to the human factor, these search engines tend to have a higher degree of accuracy, but generally return fewer hits. They are also typically updated less frequently. Think of directories as the card catalog of the Web.

Examples of Directories:

AskJeeves—technically an answer service, but definitely worth taking a look at: http://www.askjeeves.com

Galaxy: http://www.galaxy.com

LookSmart: http://www.looksmart.com

Lycos: http://www.lycos.com

Yahoo!: http://www.yahoo.com

Metacrawlers

Operating on the theory that if using one search engine is good, using multiple search programs at one time is even better, metacrawlers scour the databases of multiple search engines and deliver the results as one listing. Think of it as one-stop searching on the Web.

Examples of metacrawlers:

DogPile: `http://www.dogpile.com`

Go2Net (formerly MetaCrawler): `http://www.go2net.com`

Highway 61: `http://www.highway61.com`

Inference Find: `http://ifind.com`

BOOLEAN SEARCHES

If your Web searches are not returning the kind of information you're looking for, try not to take it personally, but it's probably the way you're conducting your searches. Refine your search query using special keywords called Boolean (pronounced "BOO-lee-an") operators. These nifty little words can narrow your search and reduce the amount of irrelevant material (referred to in geekspeak as *crappola*) that comes up as a result of overly broad searches. I don't like to brag, but when it comes to crappola, millions of people worldwide think first of Mr. Modem. I sincerely hope you're one of them.

The technical definition of Boolean is "of or relating to a logical combinatorial system treating variables, such as propositions and computer logic elements, through the operators AND, OR, NOT, IF, THEN, and EXCEPT." Try tossing that gem out at the next garden club meeting, and you're likely to be beaten to death with a shovel.

In simple Mr. ModemSpeak, Boolean searches include the words AND, OR, NOT, and NEAR. When used in conjunction with your search keywords, these operators help narrow or refine your searches.

▶ Use the word AND to search for information containing more than one keyword. For example, if you type **Internet AND legislation,** your query will give you only information containing both of these keywords.

CONTINUED ➡

▶ Use the word OR to search for results containing at least one of the keywords. For example: **munchkins OR leprechauns** would return any document that contained either of the words.

▶ The word NOT tells the search engine to look for results that do not contain the keyword, for example: **pets NOT anaconda**.

▶ The word NEAR shows results that contain the keywords only when they appear within approximately ten words of each other, for example: **Nixon NEAR resigned**.

A Boolean search can achieve better results faster and will save you time, NOT add to your frustration.

As a quasi-interesting side note, the word Boolean derives from George Boole, a British mathematician, 1815–1864, who, legend has it, kept misplacing his car keys. Under the influence of Mogen David wine, he developed a calculus of symbolic logic that permitted him to retrace his steps and find his keys: "I don't have my keys. Where do I last remember having them? I had them at the health club, NOT in the golf cart. I thought I had them in my Bermuda shorts EXCEPT today I was wearing my Dockers." Through this fascinating process of elimination and search refinement, Boolean logic emerged. Remarkably unchanged since the passing of Mr. Boole in 1864, Boolean logic is still in use today, which explains why most of us can't find anything on the Internet.

All seriousness aside, if you spend a lot of time using the Internet—and who doesn't—it's in your best interest to master the art of conducting efficient and effective searches. Understanding which search engine to use is the key to achieving the best results from your search queries. Toss in a few Boolean search operators to refine your searches and you'll soon be pestered unmercifully by friends and family members everywhere to find information for them on the Internet.

MR. MODEM'S TOP 31* SEARCH ENGINES

Millions of readers—well, maybe five or six people—have inquired why the top *31* search engines? Admittedly, it is an unusual number. Two reasons: First, every big-shot author uses an asterisk somewhere in his or her work to draw the reader's attention to a note or clarification of profound importance. I knew that *profound* and *importance* weren't adjectives likely to be associated with this chapter, so I seized upon this cheesy opportunity to include an asterisk. I could explain further, but inevitably I'd end up bursting into a chorus of *I Gotta Be Me*, and I wouldn't wish that on anybody. Some things are simply better left unsung.

Secondly, I began with the intention of writing "Mr. Modem's Top 10 Search Engines," but clearly lost my bearings somewhere along the way. There are just too darned many noteworthy search engines, so I expanded the Top 10 list to the Top 20, then the Top 25. Finally, demonstrating not even the slightest measure of self-control, I expanded it to 30. Done. Fini. I then remembered ZenSearch. So that's it, 31. No more, no less. At least so I thought. I then discovered that 31 search engines were too many for this book if I had any hopes of complying with the Surgeon General's recommendation that paperback books not exceed 47 pounds.

Because Mr. Modem is a law-abiding citizen, some adjustment was clearly in order. Accordingly, on the following pages you will find my top 10 favorite search engines. And that's just for starters!

In keeping with the great and wonderful spirit of cyberspace, I have added an Internet dimension to this book that is available to you right now, as you read these very words! Just point your browser to my Web site located at http://www.mrmodem.net and you will find more than 20 additional search engines profiled, along with hundreds of other links to my favorite Web sites, all frequently updated for your surfing pleasure!

What better opportunity to hone the skills you've been learning? So please stop by at your convenience, and be sure to use the e-mail link to say hello!

Part ii

Name That Tuna!

Mr. Modem's patented-yet-worthless TM testing protocol was used in order to assign a numeric value to the following search engines, where applicable. This rigorous testing involved searching for the term *tuna melt*. Depending upon the search engine used, the search query was launched using **"tuna melt"** (the search term surrounded by quotation marks) or **tuna+melt**. The Results notation reflects the number of hits each search engine returned.

NOTE

Testing was conducted by an Internet professional in a controlled laboratory environment with technical supervision. Trained medical personnel were standing by at all times. Do not attempt this testing protocol at home! Results under similar circumstances may vary. No animals were harmed during search engine testing, though the test administrator experienced inexplicable, episodic cravings for tuna. He was fed, treated, and released without further incident or complication.

So without further ado, here are Mr. Modem's Top 31 Search Engines (presented in alphabetical order).

1. AltaVista

More than 150 million indexed Web pages. AltaVista, shown in Figure 8.1, made its Web debut in December 1995, so its staying power is a tribute to its usefulness and popularity. It is modestly self-proclaimed as "The most useful and powerful guide to the Internet." The Simple Search permits you to input your keywords. A separate field invites you to Enter Boolean Expression. Not particularly helpful if you don't have a clue what a Boolean expression is. I had two years of high school Boolean and still have trouble speaking the language. The Advanced Search permits you to enter a question or use keywords. Comprehensive help is available, although it's more fun to fumble around searching than it is reading help pages. Results: 1,297.

    http://www.altavista.digital.com

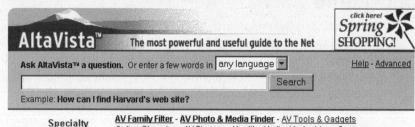

FIGURE 8.1:   AltaVista

2. Ask Jeeves

A relative newcomer to the search scene, Ask Jeeves invites you to type a question in plain English and click the **Ask!** button. For example, instead of using one or two search terms, Jeeves welcomes conversational questions such as "How do I make a tuna melt?" Ever the thoughtful host, Jeeves inquires if you would like to check your spelling before submitting your query. Jeeves, in true metasearch-engine format, displays results by search engine: 10 matches by AltaVista, 9 matches by InfoSeek, etc. The What People are Asking feature is similar to Webcrawler's Search Ticker and displays other ongoing searches in real time. Results: 37.

        http://www.askjeeves.com

3. DogPile

One of my favorite metasearch engines. DogPile (see Figure 8.2) is fast and easy to use, just the way I like 'em. Type in your search term, click the **Fetch** button, and results will be presented by search engine, 10 at a time. Searching can be restricted to the Web, Usenet (newsgroups), FTP archives, newswires, or business news resources. Results: the Web: 639; Usenet newsgroups: 3,302.

http://www.dogpile.com

FIGURE 8.2: DogPile

4. Excite

Is it just me, or are search engines trying to cram too much information on one page? Excite is a wonderfully robust search engine, but it's just too busy for my tastes. Call me a purist or just call me cranky. Searching is straightforward and easy to use: Type in a keyword. When search results appear, so does a Search Again button along with a variety of related search terms that you can select to further refine your search; a very nice feature. Additional search terms presented after the initial search for **tuna+melt** included casserole, grilled, tablespoons, lettuce, brine, grated, and wenzel. Results: 44,933. (What the heck is a wenzel?)

http://www.excite.com

5. Google

A newcomer on the search scene, and a model of simplicity. Enter a keyword and press either the **Google Search** or **I'm Feeling Lucky** button. Conducting a Google Search permits you to select 10, 30, or 100 search results. An I'm Feeling Lucky search actually takes you to the highest ranked result, rather than displaying a list of results, assuming you are, indeed, lucky. A red bar along with a percentage rating appears with each Google Search result. This reflects the PageRank, which is described as the "importance of a page; a result has high PageRank if lots of other pages with high PageRanks point to it." There you have it. So have a giggle and try the Google. Results: 2,965.

    http://www.google.com

6. GoTo

When it comes to searching, there is no simpler search tool on the Web. In fact, GoTo's tag line is "Search made simple." Even their tag line is simple. Type in a keyword, click the **Find It!** button, and you're done. No screaming banners, no weather reports, no stock tickers, horoscopes, farm reports, lottery numbers, or any of the other hoopla/clutter that adorns other search engines. Clean, crisp GoTo (see Figure 8.3) is one of the few search sites that doesn't appear to be suffering an identity crisis. It knows what it does, and it does it very well. Results: 240.

    http://www.goto.com

FIGURE 8.3: GoTo

7. Magellan

The Magellan Internet Guide is a refreshingly quiet search engine. No screaming headlines, no sensory overstimulation. If you're searching for sites that are appropriate for impressionable minds, select the Green Light Sites Only box. **Tuna+melt** returned 1,748 results from a generalized Web search, but only five from a Green Light sites search. So not only are children being protected from X-rated material, they're also being protected from fatty foods. Hats off to Magellan! Search results are presented ranked by relevance. As explained in the Search Tips and Hints section, "Relevance ratings are automatically generated by our search engine, which compares the information in the site against the information in your query." Makes sense to me. If you're searching for a simple yet comprehensive search engine, be sure to give Magellan a try.

        http://magellan.excite.com

8. Webcrawler

I'm not ashamed to admit it: I like Webcrawler. Oh, sure, it's not the most sophisticated search engine ever to appear on the Web, but as its tag line says, "It's that simple." It truly is. Webcrawler is one of the original Web search engines, and maybe because I'm one of the original Web inhabitants, perhaps we share a common bond.

Webcrawler, shown in Figure 8.4, is a model of simplicity and functionality. As soon as the site appears on your monitor, you will instantly observe a field for entering your search term(s) and a **Search** button. No dizzying array of animated figures, no happy little tunes. Just a **Search** button. It's that simple.

Critics of Webcrawler suggest that it returns too many results because it casts too wide a net. My **tuna+melt** query returned 2,333 results in the form of Web site titles. Using one of the oldest search techniques in the book and surrounding **tuna melt** in quotation marks—which restricts a search to precisely the search terms entered—returned 20 results. Try the old put-it-in-quotes trick next time you receive four million search results. After retrieving your results, click **Show Summaries for These Results** and review more descriptive information about each search result.

☐ books from **barnesandnoble.com**
☐ visit the **AT&T** Communication Center
☐ music from **CDNOW**

Don't Miss: Free trial issues: Worth, Newsweek, or Sports Illustrated!

Search and Channels

[_____] [Search]

yellow pages   maps   people finder   product finder   books
horoscopes   classifieds   stock quotes   weather   music   chat now!

Arts & Books
best reads, best buys...

Autos
new, used, classifieds...

Careers
write a resume, find a job...

Computers & Internet
software, hardware...

Education
colleges, k-12...

Entertainment
TV, movies, music...

Games
online games, downloads...

Local

Money & Investing
track stocks, invest...

My Page
personalize your page...

News - New!
today's top headlines...

People & Chat - New!
make friends, get advice...

Reference
maps, weather, tools...

Relationships
advice, personals...

Shopping

Today on WebCrawler
Cars & Trucks for Sale
WebCrawler Yellow Pages
Help! He's Lying to Me

Headline News
Updated: Apr 4 12:15AM ET

- Rights Group Reports Alleged Massacre In Kosovo
- Farrakhan Could Leave Hospital This Week: Post
- NATO Hits Belgrade, Kosovo Exodus Unabated

Daily Toolbox

Each day we bring you simple tools to save you time and money.

o How to Iron a Shirt
o Repair Pantyhose
o Shine Your Shoes
o Tie a Bow Tie

See our complete list of tools.

FIGURE 8.4: Webcrawler

WebCrawler is a trademark of Excite, Inc. and may be registered in various jurisdictions. WebCrawler screen display copyright ©1994-1999 Excite, Inc.

A fun feature for the little curious person who resides in each of us is the WebCrawler Search Voyeur. As other users type in searches, their text scrolls across your screen in ticker-tape fashion. Click on any of the scrolling search terms and you'll see the search results. Caution: The Webcrawler Search Voyeur is not for the easily offended. See the Webcrawler Search Voyeur at `http://webcrawler.com/SearchTicker.html`.

`http://www.webcrawler.com`

9. Yahoo!

Yahoo! is not technically a search engine. Instead of searching the Web at large, it searches its own database. But that's not to suggest that Yahoo! is limited! Au contraire, data dudes and dudettes. Yahoo! covers everything from heavy-duty technical and scientific research sites to health, news, sports, and entertainment. When it comes to searching, Yahoo! is the granddaddy of all search engines. Think "search," think Yahoo! (see Figure 8.5).

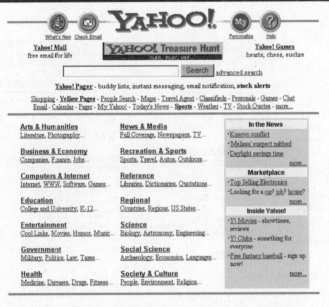

FIGURE 8.5: Yahoo!

Yahoo! has also created a number of handy geographical indices (World Yahoo!s and Yahoo! Get Local) that make it much easier to locate Internet resources with a local or international focus. There's also Yahooligans for the kiddos featuring a playground full of sites with a particular focus on the junior surfer.

Yahoo!'s People Search is legendary for its ability to help locate friends, relatives, colleagues, and people who owe you money. You can search by first name, last name, e-mail domain, hair color, eye color, birthmarks, physical dimensions, intrusive thoughts (by category), and proximity to the nearest Starbuck's. I'm not sure why that is.

Click the **My** button (short for My Yahoo!) at the top of the Yahoo! home page to create your own customized version of Yahoo!. You can personalize both the layout of your home page and its content. Elect to receive personalized stock quotes, sports scores, headline news, weather, city maps, and so much information, you could easily experience a cerebral hemorrhage.

You can refine any search by using the **Advanced Search** link located to the right of the **Search** button. While I highly recommend Yahoo!, there's a part of me that believes it has become too cluttered with lots of side offerings. I will continue to use it, however, until a Yahoo! Mime Locator appears that tracks mimes appearing anywhere in the world. The day that happens, I'll drop Yahoo! faster than you can say, "Look! It's an author walking against the wind!" Results: 467.

http://www.yahoo.com

10. ZenSearch

One of Mr. Modem's favorites because ZenSearch doesn't return 100,000 search results. Its focus is quality as opposed to quantity—a rare commodity, indeed. Sites presented are evaluated based on content, appearance and usability. Those that don't cut the mustard are not included in ZenSearch's searchable database. Sure, it's subjective, but these folks know what they're doing. I trust 'em. Results: None. Finally, a search engine that's gently suggesting to me that I'm wasting my time searching for **tuna+melt**. It's a nice way of saying, "Get a life, Mr. Modem!" Thanks, ZenSearch. I needed that.

http://www.zensearch.com

WHAT'S NEXT?

Time to sit back, relax and let the grand adventure begin! In the next chapter, "Getting Around FTP and Telnet," you'll learn about alternative ways to get around the net using file transfer and remote access.

Chapter 9

GETTING AROUND WITH FTP AND TELNET

Before the World Wide Web was invented, there were already ways to grab files from around the Net and connect to other computers. Nowadays, most people never look beyond e-mail and the Web, but there are still useful resources accessible via older technologies, such as FTP (*File Transfer Protocol*) and Telnet (a remote login, usually to Unix computers but available to any platform). Think of these methods as alternative ways of accessing the Net. Also, if you eventually set up an intranet or create a site on the Web, you may end up using FTP at least part of the time to get your files "out there," or to bring them back "in" to edit them. Telnet use is becoming a little more rare, but if you ever have to connect to Unix machines (and a lot of the computers that make the Internet work run a variant of Unix or Linux, not Windows or the

Adapted from *The Internet: No experience required,* *Second Edition,* by Christian Crumlish

ISBN 0-7821-2385-6   470 pages $19.99

MacOS), Telnet will come in handy. On the other hand, feel free to skip this chapter if you don't think these methods of file transfer and remote access will prove useful to you.

FTP—The File Transfer Protocol

You can send files attached to e-mail, but this is inefficient and wastes resources if the files are large. Instead, there's *FTP* (File Transfer Protocol), a method of retrieving files from (and sending files to) other computers on the Net.

Ideally, FTP will be built into the Windows and Mac operating systems some day (as it already is for Unix), so that managing files on the Internet will be as easy as managing files on your own computer. For now, though, you have to use FTP either with a special program designed for that purpose or with a Web browser.

NOTE

Keep in mind that when I say that FTP is built into Unix and its variants, I mean that in the sense that most people know Unix as a text-based environment, so Unix's FTP is also text-based. That, of course, is expected of Unix. On the other hand, Windows and MacOS users expect a graphical approach, and this is what is meant by "integrating."

You may also hear references to *anonymous FTP*. Most of the time when you'll use FTP, you'll use it anonymously at public FTP sites. This means you log in as *anonymous* and give your e-mail address as a password. If you use FTP to transfer files from a machine that you are authorized to access, then you won't do it anonymously. You'll log in as yourself and give your password.

What's New with FTP?

In just a few years, FTP has gone from a "techie" protocol you had to learn Unix to master to a file-transfer method as easy to manage as a Web browser. The next step in the evolution of FTP is its direct incorporation into programs and computer operating systems. Already, programs like Microsoft Office 2000 have the ability to open files from or save files to FTP sites (see Figure 9.1). Upcoming browser releases promise to turn FTP into a standard desktop operation. Windows 98SE and Windows Millennium Edition and MacOS 9, to a degree, incorporate FTP capabilities directly into their interface. Windows Internet Explorer integration and Web Folders turns simple folder windows into full-fledged FTP clients that attempt to seamlessly integrate local and remote file storage locations.

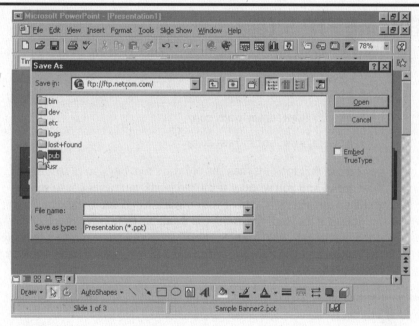

FIGURE 9.1:   You can transfer an Office document to an FTP site simply by saving it there.

It's also getting easier to find FTP sites on the Net. Since they're not technically part of the Web (although you *can* connect to FTP sites with a Web browser), FTP archives have not always been "findable" at Web search sites. The Archie legacy system was the only way to find sites and files. More recently, Web sites have appeared that specifically offer to search FTP sites for file names, as I'll explain in the next section.

NOTE

Even though you can download many files via the Web now, it is still a good idea to learn how to perform FTP downloads, because you may be asked to do just that in the workplace. Many companies store documents and other files on FTP sites, and you can often get access to these sites through reciprocal agreements with other businesses. Some FTP sites are used as repositories for Web content files, too.

Finding FTP Sites

If you're looking for files to download from FTP sites, try searching at any of these Web sites:

- ▶ http://www.shareware.com/
- ▶ http://www.download.com/
- ▶ http://www.hotfiles.com/

You can still look for files the old ways too. Say you're reading a Usenet newsgroup and you wonder if the old posts you never got to see are archived anywhere. You post your question and someone e-mails you to tell you that, indeed, the archive is available by anonymous FTP at archive.big-u.edu. You cut the address and paste it into a text file and then check out the FTP site with your FTP program. That's one way to find out about sites.

TIP

Archie is a special protocol for searching FTP sites, and there are programs designed to take advantage of it. I'll explain one of these, Anarchie (for the Mac), later in this chapter.

There's also an anonymous FTP FAQ and a huge, alphabetically orga-nized set of FTP site lists (16 in all) posted regularly to comp.answers, news.newusers.questions, and many other Usenet newsgroups.

To have any or all of these documents mailed to you, send an e-mail message (with no subject) to `mail-server@rtfm.mit.edu`. Include in it one (or both) of the following lines:

▶ send `usenet-by-group/news.answers/FTP-list/faq`

▶ send `usenet/news.answers/FTP-list/sitelist/part1` through send `usenet/news.answers/FTP-list/sitelist/part11`

These same files are also available via (what else?) anonymous FTP from `rtfm.mit.edu`. Look in the `/pub/usenet-by-group/news.answers/FTP-list/sitelist` directory for the 11 site list files, and the `/pub/usenet/news.answers/FTP-list/faq` directory for the FAQ.

TIP

More often than not, you'll find your way to an FTP site through your Web browser. Since you'll just be clicking on links, you may not even realize that you're connecting to an FTP site when you do this.

Many of the largest, most popular FTP archives have mirror sites, which are other FTP sites that maintain the exact same files (updated regularly) to reduce the load on the primary site. Use a relatively local mirror site whenever you can.

TIP

How do you tell if a server is near you or not? Good question. Often you can figure it out simply by looking at the address. Most general-purpose FTP sites that I know of are hosted by colleges and other institutions of higher learning. If you live in Virginia and have a choice between the ficticious `ftp.uva.edu` (University of Virginia) and ficticious `ftp.uha.edu` (University of Hawaii), then you would be better off selecting the UVA site.

Connecting with FTP

The typical FTP session starts when you run the FTP program and connect to an FTP site. Depending on the program you have, you'll either enter your login information before connecting or you'll be prompted to do it after you connect. If you're using a Web browser to connect to an anonymous site, the browser may prompt you to log in, though most send your e-mail address as the password automatically. These general steps illustrate a typical FTP session:

1. Start your FTP software or Web browser by double-clicking the program's desktop shortcut or by using the Start ➤ Programs menu.

2. Connect to an FTP site.

3. If you are asked for a username or user ID, type **anonymous** and press Enter. Then type your e-mail address when you are asked for a password, and press Enter. This will put you at an FTP prompt.

TIP

Popular sites such as RTFM at MIT are often busy. It's best to do your file transfers during off-peak hours, such as at night or on the weekends, to minimize the load on the FTP site.

WARNING

When logging into an FTP site as *anonymous*, never enter your real password. This is a security breach, as your password will appear in a log file that many people can read. If you do this by mistake, immediately change your password.

4. Now view the file lists and hunt through the directory structure for the files you want. If you're not sure where to start looking at the FTP site, start off by looking for a pub directory. If there is one, open it and work your way through the subdirectories.

5. If the files you want to transfer are not simple text files (if they're programs, for example), specify *binary* in the FTP program before doing the transfers. When you find the files you want, transfer them with the Get command, which is commonly indicated as *Download* in graphical FTP clients.

6. Quit the FTP program when you are done transferring files and browsing directories.

NOTE

When you are using FTP or Web software, you might connect to a Unix machine or to another type of computer on the Net in your quest for FTP sites. Fortunately, you won't have to know all the different commands they require. You need to know only the commands for your FTP program or Web browser. The program will then translate your requests into whatever format the host computer requires.

FTP with Your Web Browser

You've already seen how to download files from FTP sites with a Web browser (it usually involves just clicking on a link). If you want to go directly to an FTP site, you can type its address in the browser's address box, starting with `ftp://`, for example, `ftp://rtfm.mit.edu/pub/usenet-by-group`.

With older browsers, you could only connect anonymously, and you could only receive files, not upload them. However, with most new browsers, you can connect with a username by preceding the FTP address with the username and an @ sign. For example, to log in to the FTP site for my magazine, I connect to `ftp://xian@ezone.org`.

The commands for sending files to sites vary from program to program. I'll show you how to use FTP with the two main Web browsers: Microsoft Internet Explorer and Netscape Navigator.

FTP with Internet Explorer

Microsoft Internet Explorer's FTP interface is based on the ordinary Windows Explorer folders and windows, which makes remote file access as easy as poking around the folders on your own computer. Follow these simple steps to make an FTP connection with Internet Explorer:

1. Activate Internet Explorer by clicking its desktop shortcut or by selecting Start ➤ Programs ➤ Internet Explorer ➤ Internet Explorer.

2. Connect to a site directly by entering its address in the Address box (such as `ftp://ftp.microsoft.com` or `ftp://your-username:your-password@ftp.your-ISP.com`). (See Figure 9.2.)

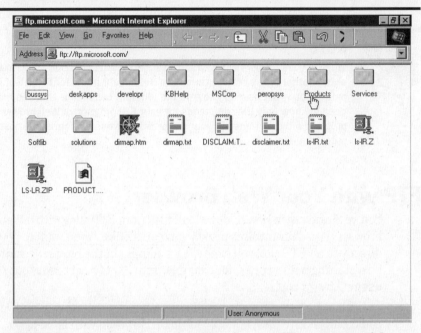

FIGURE 9.2: If you don't look in the address box, your FTP connection with Internet Explorer may seem like just another folder on your desktop.

3. To navigate the FTP site, click folder icons to open subdirectories.

4. Click on files to download them. (Internet Explorer will display files on your screen if it can; to prevent this, you can right-click or click-and-hold and select Save Target As.)

   ▶ To send files to a site where you have permission to upload, simply drag a file into the browser window and click Yes to upload it.

5. Exit Internet Explorer by selecting File ➤ Close. You will be prompted to disconnect from your Internet service provider.

FTP with Netscape Navigator

Netscape Navigator's FTP features are similar to Internet Explorer's. Access files and folders by double-clicking underlined text (indicating an active link) or file folder icons. The steps listed here will walk you through the process:

1. Launch Navigator by clicking the Communicator desktop shortcut or by selecting Start ≻ Programs ≻ Netscape Communicator ≻ Netscape Navigator.

2. Connect to a site directly by entering its address in the Location box (such as `ftp://ftp2.netscape.com` or `ftp://your-username@ftp.your-ISP.com`). For a private account, you'll also have to enter a password.

3. To navigate the FTP site, click folder icons to open subdirectories.

4. Click on files to download them. (Netscape will display files on your screen if it can; to prevent this, you can right-click, or click-and-hold, and select Save Link As.)

5. To send files to a site, use one of these procedures:

   ▶ Find your way to a folder where you have permission to upload files (usually your own account or one for which you have a private username). Then select File ≻ Upload File. Choose the file you want to send in the Open dialog box that appears and then click OK.

   ▶ You can also simply drag a file into the browser window and click Yes to upload it (see Figure 9.3).

WARNING

Netscape doesn't do a great job of uploading text files from one type of computer to another. Better FTP programs handle text (ASCII) and nontext (binary) files differently.

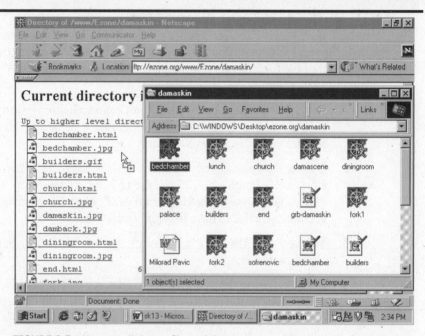

FIGURE 9.3:   You can click on a file and drag it onto an FTP directory for uploading with Netscape Navigator.

Specific FTP Programs

Before going on to discuss Telnet, I'll explain the details of a couple of
specific FTP programs. If you use a Macintosh, you'll want to use Fetch.
Fetch is an easy-to-use FTP client for the Mac. If you're stuck in a Unix
shell, you'll want to use Ftp or its slightly improved cousin Ncftp. If
you're using Windows, then WS_FTP is probably your best bet for FTP
(although those weaned on Unix FTP may prefer the DOS-style FTP program that comes with Windows these days).

TIP

Most online services, such as AOL and CompuServe, offer FTP, but they generally
also maintain their own archives of the most popular files and programs from the
Net, and you may find it faster and easier to download them directly from those
archives.

Fetch

On Macs, the standard file-transfer program is called Fetch. You can obtain Fetch from `http://www.dartmouth.edu/pages/softdev/fetch.html`. Fetch is simple to use and has a number of valuable features for getting around in FTP sites and obtaining files of different types. The procedures for using Fetch will be familiar to you if you have used other FTP programs for Macintosh or Windows environments. These steps will get you started:

Fetch

1. Double-click the Fetch icon, which brings up the Open Connection dialog box (see Figure 9.4).

2. If you don't want the default host, type a new one in the Host box.

3. Type your password in the password window and type a directory if you know the one you're headed for. (If you don't, just leave it blank.) Then click OK.

4. Once you're connected to the host, you can navigate to the directory structure by clicking the folder icons, just as with any Macintosh program.

NOTE

In Fetch 3, the Open Connection dialog box has become the New Connection box, but the FTP methods remain basically the same.

5. Click the Binary radio button to specify a binary file, or leave Automatic clicked to let the program figure it out.

6. Highlight the file or files you want and click the Get File button to get them (see Figure 9.5).

7. To send files, you can just drag and drop them into the Fetch window.

8. When you are done, select File ➤ Quit.

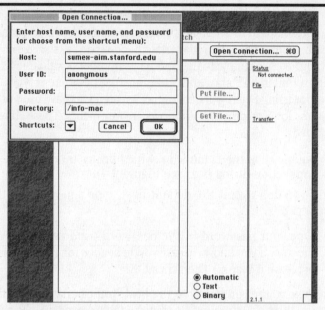

FIGURE 9.4: The Open Connection dialog box in Fetch

FIGURE 9.5: The Macintosh interface makes fetching files simple.

WS_FTP

A good FTP client for Windows is WS_FTP (ftp://129.29.64.246/pub/msdos/). WS_FTP is shareware and makes fair use of visual commands and point-and-click buttons to bring you the world of FTP. For guidance on using WS_FTP, work through the following steps:

1. Start WS_FTP by double-clicking the WS_FTP desktop shortcut.

2. The Connection dialog box pops up. If you don't want the default host, type a new one.

3. Enter the host address, your user ID, and password into the spaces provided in the Connection dialog box.

4. Enter a directory if you know the one you're headed for. Then click OK.

5. Once you've connected to the host, WS_FTP will show you the contents of your own computer in the left two panes and the contents of the remote host in the right two (see Figure 9.6). The top panes show directories and the bottom ones show files. Click the Binary radio button to specify a binary file.

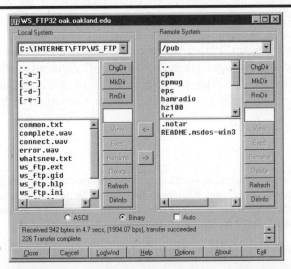

FIGURE 9.6: WS_FTP gives you an easy way to get around a remote computer and retrieve files from it.

6. Highlight the file or files you want and click the "<-" button between the Local System and Remote System areas to transfer the files.

7. To send files, you can just drag and drop them into the WS_FTP window, or highlight a file or group of files and click the "->" button between the Local System and Remote System areas. When you are done, click the Exit button on the far right at the bottom of the window to close WS_FTP.

PROBING THE INTERNET WITH TELNET

One aspect of the interconnectedness of the Net is that you can log in to other machines on the Internet directly from your own computer, no matter where you are. With Telnet, you can log in to any computer or network that supports Telnet access and for which you have a password, as well as thousands of public sites where passwords are not required. You would not be able to work on these Unix systems without Telnet, which turns your Windows or Macintosh computer into a remote terminal that is compatible with computers outside of the personal computer universe.

Many university and public libraries make their catalogs available by Telnet, as do countless other repositories of useful information. Of course, as with so many other Internet resources, you need to know where to go to take advantage of these public sites. Unfortunately, there's no comprehensive index or guide to available Telnet sites. In general, you have to ask around and collect remote login sites just as you do with FTP sites.

TIP

If you have a Unix account, you can Telnet to your own service provider and log in to your own account, even if you're already logged in there! This is actually more useful when you are borrowing someone else's computer and want to log in to your own account to, say, check your e-mail.

After you have started your Telnet program, you need to open an Internet connection and log in to the site with the steps described here:

1. Type **telnet** and press Enter at the Unix prompt.

2. This will put you at a `telnet>` prompt. Then type **open** *host-sitename* and press Enter.

3. Logging in with Telnet is the same as logging in to any computer system. You type your username and press Enter.

4. Then you type a password and press Enter.

TIP

For public sites, you might have to log in under some special name, and either you won't be asked for a password or you'll be able to just press Enter when asked for a password.

In Figure 9.7, I'm Telnetting from my Unix shell account to California State University's Advanced Technology Information Network to get information about California agriculture. The Telnet site is `caticsuf.cati.csufresno.edu`, and the username that I log in with is `public`.

```
{netcom2:4} telnet caticsuf.cati.csufresno.edu
Trying...
Connected to caticsuf.cati.csufresno.edu.
Escape character is '^]'.

SunOS UNIX (caticsuf)

login: public
```

FIGURE 9.7: Logging in to the Advanced Technology Information Network via Telnet

The site doesn't ask for a password. Instead, a screen full of welcoming information appears.

From this point on, you're on your own. Depending on where you've Telnetted to, you'll be either at a Unix prompt or, more likely, at the main menu of some information program. There are many such programs and each one works differently, but don't worry. They'll all prompt you, and they're designed for laypeople. Generally, you can press Enter to accept defaults until you're given a menu of information. Then you have to make some choices.

Logging out from a Telnet session is generally a matter of typing **bye** or **exit** or **logout** at a prompt, pressing **q** (for quit), or choosing the appropriate menu choice from within an information program. Telnet will sign you off with "Connection closed by foreign host."

Finding a Telnet Program

Windows 95/98, Windows NT, and Windows 3.11 for Workgroups come with a perfectly fine Telnet client program called, as you might expect, Telnet (the filename is Telnet.exe, and it is located in the Windows directory or folder on your hard drive). Unix also has a Telnet program builtin. To run it, just type **telnet** *sitename* at the Unix prompt and press Enter. For the Macintosh, you can download an excellent Telnet client program called NCSA Telnet (http://www.ncsa.uiuc.edu/SDG/Software/Brochure/MacDownSoft.html#MacTelnet).

Telnetting from Your Web Browser

Links to Telnet sites can be embedded into Web pages. When you select such a link, your browser will attempt to launch your Telnet program to connect to the site. It will fail, though, if you've never told your browser where your Telnet program is. Solving this problem involves going to the Options or Preferences dialog box, choosing the Apps tab or Apps area of the dialog box (or Applications, or Supporting Applications—not to be confused with Helper Applications), and then typing the path and file name of your Telnet program in the Telnet box.

In earlier versions of Netscape Navigator for Windows, for instance, you have to perform the fairly convoluted action of choosing Options ➢ General Preferences, choosing the Apps tab, clicking in the Telnet box, typing **telnet**, and then clicking OK. However, Netscape Communicator has bypassed this requirement and automatically launches the Telnet program when needed.

TIP

If you're not sure of the exact path or file name of your Telnet program, you can click the Browse button to hunt around on your hard disk for it.

WHAT'S NEXT?

This chapter has familiarized you with a couple of alternative ways to explore the Internet on your own. Now it's time to check into ways you can use the Internet to communicate with other people: Usenet newsgroups, chat rooms, and instant messaging. These topics are discussed in the next chapter, "Newsgroups, Mailing Lists, and Chatting."

Chapter 10

NEWSGROUPS, MAILING LISTS, AND CHATTING

Usenet newsgroups are another feature of the Internet. This particular feature gets the "most inappropriately named" award because despite the name, newsgroups have little or nothing to do with news. A more appropriate name would have been "discussion groups," because that's what people do in newsgroups. They discuss topics of mutual interest, newsworthy or not. Similar to newsgroups are *mailing lists*, which also provide a means of engaging in heated debates over whatever gets your goat. This chapter, as you may have guessed, will tell you all about participating in newsgroups and mailing lists.

Chatting is yet another way of communicating with people on the Internet. Unlike e-mail and newsgroups, which involve sending messages, chatting is more like a real-time back-and-forth conversation between two people. Only you don't talk: You type messages back and forth. Technically, the protocol for

Adapted from *Internet To Go* by Alan Simpson
ISBN 0-7821-2494-1   240 pages $6.99

chatting is called IRC, for Internet Relay Chat—which I mention only because you might stumble across that acronym from time to time. Normal people just call it "chatting."

Last, but by far not the least, is the ongoing craze called Instant Messaging. A mix between e-mail and chat, instant messaging's greatest appeal is its ability to notify you the "instant" one of your designated friends gets online. The only catch to this seemingly perfect communications solution is not cost, but exclusivity. Your pals need to use the same instant messaging service that you do in order to be detected as online. There are a number of these services available and we'll take a closer look at the more popular ones later in this chapter.

Why Mess with Newsgroups?

As mentioned, newsgroups are really more like discussion groups. Doing newsgroups is sort of like doing e-mail. In fact, you can use Outlook Express as your *newsreader* (a program that lets you participate in newsgroups). However, unlike e-mail, where your message gets sent to one person, the message you send to a newsgroup might be seen by thousands of people. Any one of those people can reply to your message, just as an individual can reply to the e-mail message you send them, and those potential thousands can also view their replies.

Probably the best, if not the most common, use of newsgroups is getting free answers to burning questions. For example, let's say you're thinking about buying a new car. You have a particular make and model of Toyota in mind. Before making your final decision you'd like to know whether existing owners of that car are satisfied.

First, you would want to find one or more newsgroups where people discuss Toyotas. Then, you could just send an e-mail message to that newsgroup saying you're thinking of buying this car and would like to know if current owners are happy with their purchase.

All the members of that newsgroup will see your message and some will certainly respond. Within a day or two, probably, you'll have a whole lot of honest answers from genuine owners, to further help you make your decision. Of course, there's a downside to the receipt of those "honest" answers. Like the global personality landscape, countless personalities are represented in newsgroups. Some are wacky, some funny, others rude, and still others actually helpful.

So, those 30 nice messages you might receive about how the owners liked their car could contain only 5–10 useful ones. The others could be just about anything, but you'd never know because the subject line (I'll explain soon) isn't changed, so it's hard to tell if the subject of *your* message was even paid any attention.

Newsgroup Jargon

Like all other things computer-ish, newsgroupies have their own language for describing things. Here's a quick rundown of the more common buzzwords:

▶ Each message in a newsgroup is officially called an *article* (though I've not heard that term actually used lately) or a *post*, though just about everyone refers to them as *messages* because, in a sense, they are like normal e-mail messages.

▶ A series of articles on the same subject is called a *thread*.

▶ Many newsgroups are *moderated* by volunteers who weed out posted messages that are irrelevant to the group or that are just plain obnoxious. Most newsgroups, however, are *unmoderated*, which means anything goes.

▶ *Lurking* is hanging around a newsgroup to see what's being discussed. But unlike lurking around public parks at night, which is generally not good and frowned upon by decent folk, lurking in a newsgroup is OK, particularly if you're new to the group. It gives you a chance to get a "feel" for the group and a better idea of what's acceptable when you finally do post your first message.

▶ *Spamming* is posting articles that are really advertisements. Don't do it, or you're likely to get *flamed*.

▶ *Flaming* is sending nasty messages to people in the group in retaliation for a real or perceived affront. Sometimes it might seem that a flame is exactly what's needed, but the passive approach typically wins in the end as the intended *flamee* gets continually ignored and eventually drifts off to bother another group.

▶ A *poster*, in newsgroup argot, isn't something you hang on a wall. It's a person who posts articles to the group.

▶ The *group charter* (although also someone that would chart lists) is, in this sense, the generally accepted underlying theme and ruleset for the group. Most groups have an implied charter, which generally follows that whatever the group is called is what gets talked about. Any other subjects (or threads) are labeled "off-topic" and the posters involved are typically asked to move the discussion "off-list."

Newsgroup Categories

There are tens of thousands of newsgroups on the Internet. The groups are divided into categories and subcategories. A single newsgroup's name generally follows the pattern:

    category.subcategory.sub-subcategory

For example, the newsgroup `alt.animals.dogs` is a newsgroup where people who are interested in dogs can gather. Even more specifically, `alt.animals.dogs.obedience` is where people who are interested in dog obedience can gather. There are thousands of categories out there. Some of the more widely used categories are listed in Table 10.1.

TABLE 10.1: Newsgroup Categories, Descriptions, and Names

Main Category	Description	Sample Newsgroup Names
Alt	Alternative lifestyles and topics	alt.astrology.metapsych
		alt.beer
Bionet	Biology	bionet.genome
		bionet.jobs.offered
Biz	Business	biz.marketplace
		biz.entreprenuers
Comp	Computers	comp.graphics
		comp.internet
Law	Legal matters	law.court.federal
		law.school.crim
Misc	Miscellaneous	misc.activism
		misc.computers.forsale

TABLE 10.1 continued: Newsgroup Categories, Descriptions, and Names

MAIN CATEGORY	DESCRIPTION	SAMPLE NEWSGROUP NAMES
News	Usenet news network	news.newusers
		news.newusers.questions
Rec	Recreation	rec.sport.football
		rec.photo.digital
Sci	Science	sci.bio.botany
		sci.med.midwifery
Soc	Social issues	soc.culture.hawaii
		soc.geneology
Talk	Debates and opinions	talk.bizarre
		talk.politics

Part ii

Setting Up Your News Reader

Outlook Express, that same program you may use for e-mail, can also act as your newsreader, provided that your ISP offers a news server, or NNTP server as it's also called (where NNTP stands for Network News Transfer Protocol). If your ISP does have a news server, you should have been provided that server's name with the information packet you received from your ISP. There are also a number of public NNTP servers that offer access to newsgroups of all flavors.

NOTE

I'm assuming that we will be using Outlook Express as a newsreader because it comes with every Windows-based computer we know of. All aspects of connecting to a news server are the same no matter what application you use to read it, but the options and configuration will not be the same.

ServerSeekers (http://www.serverseekers.com) is a service that lists news servers that are open to the public. To locate an address for a public server simply go to the ServerSeekers Web site, click on the Server List link and pick one from the list. If you click on the address (the first link on the left-most column that's either a number or a name that looks like a Web address) it should open your newsreader, but read on for more details on that.

If all else fails then you can skip all the way down to the section titled "Accessing Newsgroups via the Web" to learn how to use your Web browser (Microsoft Internet Explorer) to access newsgroups.

Assuming your ISP has given you the address of a local news server, here's how you go about setting up Outlook Express to access that server:

1. Open Outlook Express as you normally would.

2. Choose Tools ➤ Accounts from the Outlook Express menu bar. The Internet Accounts dialog box appears.

WARNING

The Internet Connection Wizard may have already set up a news account for you. To find out, click the News tab in the Internet Accounts dialog box. If you see an account listed, just click the Close button and skip to the section titled "Downloading Newsgroups."

3. Click the Add button in the Internet Accounts dialog box and then choose News from the menu that appears. The Internet Connection Wizard appears.

4. On the first Wizard page, type your name normally (it may already be there, from when you set up your e-mail account) and then click the Next button.

5. On the second Wizard page, type your e-mail address. Again, it may already be there from earlier. Click the Next button.

6. On the next Wizard page, type in the name of your news server as provided by your ISP.

NOTE

You may also type in the name or number of a free news server that you selected from elsewhere. This space is not limited to a server supplied by your ISP.

7. If your ISP requires that you log on to the server, and you have an NNTP account name and password, select (check) the My News Server Requires Me to Log On option. Then click the Next button and fill in your news account name and password.

8. In the next Wizard screen, choose *Connect using my phone line* (assuming you use a modem to access the Internet). Then click the Next button.

9. You should now be at the final congratulatory screen. Click the Finish button.

10. You're returned to the Internet Accounts dialog box. Click its Close button.

You will probably see a message asking if you'd like to download newsgroups from the news server that you just added. If so, go ahead and click the Yes button. If prompted to connect to your server, go ahead and do so. Then wait a few minutes for all the newsgroups to be downloaded to your PC. When the download is finished, you'll see a long list of newsgroups named in the Newsgroup Subscriptions dialog box. For now, you can just close the Newsgroup Subscriptions dialog box by clicking the OK button near the bottom of that dialog box.

NOTE

Though it's called "downloading newsgroups," all you're really doing at this time is downloading the names of newsgroups that are available on your ISP's news server. So don't worry about your hard disk being filled up with all the messages from all those newsgroups.

WARNING

Even though the newsgroup list doesn't take up much space on your hard disk it will take some time to download, depending on how many groups your server hosts. Even with a good 56K modem connection it can take up to 15 minutes to download 40,000 groups, so be prepared. It's a good idea to start this around lunchtime so you already have a break planned.

If, for whatever reason, you can't download newsgroups right now, don't worry about it. You can download them at any time, as discussed under "Downloading Newsgroups," later in this chapter.

When you return to Outlook Express, you'll see a new folder in your Folders list with the "friendly name" you gave to your news server. For example, in Figure 10.1 my news server name, news2.flashcom.net, appears at the bottom of the Folders list.

News server

FIGURE 10.1: News server added to my Folders list

Once the newsgroup name appears in your Folders list, you want to remember this important point: *Whenever you want to do anything involving newsgroups, you'll want to click that folder first* or choose Go ➢ News from the Outlook Express menu bar. The Outlook Express toolbar changes when you do, offering a new button titled Newsgroups. As you'll see in the sections that follow, that one little button gives you access to all the newsgroups on your ISP's news server.

Downloading Newsgroups

In most situations, Outlook Express will automatically download newsgroup names from your news server as soon as you establish the connection to that server. But if, for whatever reason, you were unable to download newsgroups or if you want to reload newsgroups to see if there are any new ones, follow these steps to update your list of newsgroups manually:

1. In the Outlook Express Folders list, click the name of your news server and then click the Newsgroups button on the

Outlook Express tool bar. The Newsgroup Subscriptions dialog box appears.

2. To update your list of newsgroups, click the Reset List button.

It might take several minutes to download all the newsgroup names, so be patient. When the download is complete, you should see the names of newsgroups listed in the large white area of the Newsgroups Subscriptions dialog box. For example, Figure 10.2 shows how my Newsgroups Subscriptions dialog box looks after downloading newsgroups from my ISP. There are over 40,000 newsgroups in the list—only the top few are visible, though. Use the scroll bar to the right of the newsgroup names, your mouse wheel, or the Page Up and Page Down keys to scroll through the entire list.

FIGURE 10.2:   My Newsgroups Subscriptions dialog box after downloading newsgroups from my ISP's news server

Finding Newsgroups that Interest You

Nobody has time to check out all the messages in 40,000 or so newsgroups. So the first thing you'll probably want to do is narrow the list down to a few newsgroups that discuss topics that are of interest to you. That's easy to do:

1. If you've left Outlook's Newsgroups Subscriptions dialog box, get back to it by clicking the Newsgroups button on the Outlook Express toolbar.

WARNING

Don't forget that the Newsgroups button on the Outlook Express toolbar is available *only* when the name of your news server is selected in the Folders list.

2. In the Display Newsgroups Which Contain box, type the word that best describes your interests. For example, if you play the banjo, you might type the word **banjo**.

The list of newsgroups in the dialog box shrinks to show only newsgroups whose name contains the word you typed. For example, in Figure 10.3, I typed the word **banjo**, and now only newsgroups that meet that criterion appear in the list.

FIGURE 10.3: The Newsgroups Subscriptions dialog box showing names of newsgroups that contain the word *banjo*

Beginner's Newsgroups

As a beginner, you might want to check out some of the groups that are designed for newbies. If you type the phrase *news.newusers* into the Display Newsgroups Which Contain box, you'll see the groups that are geared toward newbies, perhaps looking like the example in Figure 10.4. (Your news server might offer different groups.)

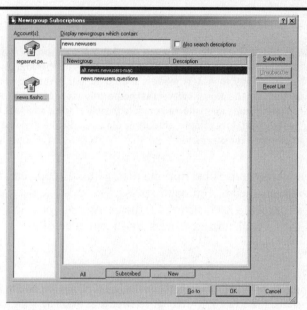

FIGURE 10.4: Groups geared toward newsgroup newbies

Previewing Newsgroup Messages

Before you decide whether you want to get involved in a newsgroup, you should lurk around and check out some of the articles within the newsgroup. Here's how to do that:

1. If you're not already in the Newsgroups Subscriptions dialog box, click the Newsgroups button on the Outlook Express toolbar to get back there.

2. Click the All tab near the bottom of the Newsgroups Subscriptions dialog box to make sure you're viewing the complete list of newsgroups.

3. If you haven't already done so, type some word in the Display Newsgroups Which Contain text box to narrow the list of newsgroup names to those that discuss a topic that interests you.

4. To see the messages in a newsgroup, click its name and then click the Go To button near the bottom of the Newsgroups dialog box.

NOTE

If the Go To button doesn't bring you any messages, you're probably working offline. Click the Connect button on the Outlook Express toolbar and connect to the Internet normally. Message headers should appear in the top pane after the connection is made. Note however that some groups *are* empty. Though not common, some groups go neglected or were merely started as a lark and the novelty has worn off (for example, alt.barney.dinosaur.die.die.die) and people no longer post new messages.

5. The Newsgroup Subscriptions dialog box disappears and you're returned to Outlook Express. The message list pane now contains a list of articles in the newsgroup you selected. As with e-mail, unread articles are shown in boldface.

NOTE

In newsgroups, the lines that appear in the top pane are referred to as message *headers*. The actual article is often referred to as the *body* of the message.

6. To read a message, click its header in the top pane. The bottom preview pane shows the content of the message.

7. If there are any responses to the message you're viewing, the message line in the top pane will have a + sign next to it. Click that + sign to expand the line and view a list of replies. Click any reply to view its message.

In Figure 10.4, I opted to view the news.newusers.questions newsgroup by clicking on it. A dialog box appears with message lines at the top. The indented messages beneath that message are replies—answers sent to the group in direct response to the groupie's question. You can always tell which questions have already been answered by the + sign just to left of that message line. Clicking the + sign displays the message lines for those replies.

TIP

You can adjust the width of any column in the list of message headers by dragging, left or right, the dark line that separates the column headings. You know you can drag when your mouse pointer changes into a vertical bar with arrows facing left and right. For example, to widen or narrow the Subject column, drag the dark line that's just to the right of the Subject column heading.

To read any message in the list of headers, just click the header of the message you want to read. Outlook Express will (probably) download the body of that message from the news server and display it in the lower preview pane (see Figure 10.5). I say "probably" because it depends on certain settings, which may have been adjusted by someone else that might have access to your PC. If that's not the case, I would investigate for traces of Gremlins, a common cause of inexplicable options modifications. (I'm kidding!!)

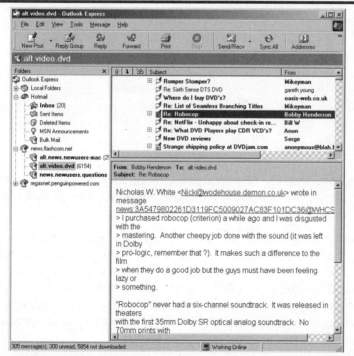

FIGURE 10.5: Viewing a newsgroup's message headers in Outlook Express

Instead of a message, you might see an instruction to "Press <Space> to display the selected message." You need to press the space bar on your keyboard to download that message. If pressing the space bar still doesn't bring the body of the message into the preview pane, you're probably no longer connected to your news server. Click the Connect button in Outlook Express to reconnect to your ISP's news server.

Spend a few minutes looking through the messages and replies in any newsgroup that you think might interest you. If you like what you see and you think that you might like to visit this newsgroup often, you can *subscribe* to the group to make future access easier.

Subscribing to Newsgroups

Subscribing to a newsgroup is simple and free. There are two ways to subscribe to a group. Use whichever is most convenient at the moment:

- ▶ If you've already previewed the group, and its name appears under your news server name in the folders list, right-click the newsgroup name and choose Subscribe from the menu that appears, as shown below.

- ▶ If you're in the Newsgroups Subscriptions dialog box, click the name of the newsgroup you're interested in and then click the Subscribe button.

Once you've subscribed to a newsgroup, its name appears beneath the newsgroup server name in the Folders list of Outlook Express. It's no longer "dimmed," as it may have looked after choosing the Go To button earlier. If you don't see subscribed newsgroups listed under the name of your news server in the Folders list, click the + sign next to the news server name to expand the list. Figure 10.6 shows an example where I've subscribed to four newsgroups.

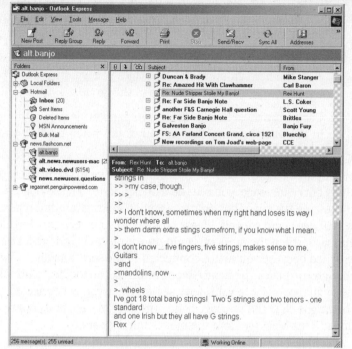

FIGURE 10.6: Four newsgroups I've subscribed to listed under
news.flashcom.net in the folders list

Be aware that if you "Go To" a newsgroup, but don't subscribe to it, its
icon in the folders list will be dimmed. When you exit Outlook Express,
the unsubscribed newsgroups will automatically be removed from the
Folders list.

TIP

To unsubscribe from a newsgroup, right-click its name in the Folders list and
choose Unsubscribe.

Browsing Newsgroup Articles

Once you've subscribed to one or more newsgroups, you'll probably want
to start digging a little deeper into its articles and conversation threads.
To get started:

1. Open Outlook Express (if it isn't open already).

2. If there is a + sign next to the name of your news server in the Folders list, click that + sign to view the newsgroups you've subscribed to.

3. Beneath the name of your news server in the Folders list, click the newsgroup whose messages you want to view. The top pane will list all the articles in the group.

4. Click any article header in the top pane to view its contents in the bottom pane, just as you would when reading your e-mail.

You can then read the body of the message down in the preview pane. If instead of the message, you see the instruction to "Press <Space>..." and if pressing the space bar only gets you an instruction that reads, "This message is not cached. Please connect to your server to download the message," then the message is not on your local PC and can't be downloaded because you're not connected to the server anymore. No biggie, though. Just click the Send/Recv button on the toolbar. Outlook Express will reconnect to your news server. Once you're connected, you can then right-click the message header in the top pane and choose Download This Message from the menu that appears.

TIP

A torn-page icon to the left of a header indicates that only the message header has been downloaded to your PC. A full-page icon to the left of the header means that both the header and message body have already been downloaded to your PC.

Replying to a Message

As you read messages, you may come across one or more that you want to reply to. For example, perhaps a person is asking the group a question, and you happen to know the answer to that question. There are two ways you can send a reply:

▶ To reply to the group, so that everyone in the newsgroup can see your reply, click the Reply To Group button on the Outlook Express toolbar.

▶ To reply privately to the author of the article, so that only he or she can see your response, click the Reply To Author button.

Either way, a window will pop up allowing you to type your response. This window is exactly the same one you use to compose e-mail messages. However, the To: and Subject: parts of the message are already filled in. Don't change them! Type your reply above the Original Message and click the Send button just above and to the left of the To: box. Simple.

Posting New Messages

As a beginner, you may spend more time asking questions than answering them. To ask the group a question, you need to post an article to the newsgroup. Here's how:

1. In the Folders list, click the newsgroup to which you want to send a message.

2. Click the New Post button on the Outlook Express toolbar. The New Message window opens, pre-addressed to the newsgroup you selected in Step 1.

3. In the Subject box, type a brief subject that describes your post.

 NEWSGROUP NETIQUETTE

The rules of etiquette that apply to e-mail also apply to newsgroups. When typing your message, don't use ALL UPPERCASE LETTERS. Don't post ads or anything that looks like an ad. Never leave the Subject line blank.

Furthermore, if you're replying to a post, don't change the Subject line at all. A conversation thread is really no more than a series of messages with the same Subject line. If you change the Subject line, your message will be treated as a new article and won't look like a reply to an existing message. On the other hand, if you are in the middle of a thread and want to start a new discussion, don't reply to a message to start it—start a new thread of your own.

4. In the larger area of the window, type your message. Figure 10.7 shows an example where I'm about to post some questions to the alt.banjo newsgroup.

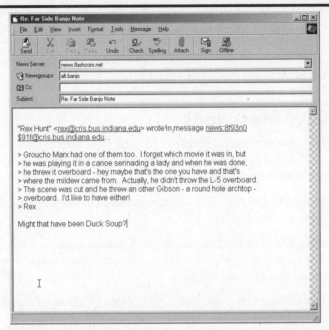

FIGURE 10.7: Sample newsgroup article I'm about to post to `alt.banjo`

5. When you've finished typing your message, click the Send button near the upper-left corner of the dialog box.

The message will either be posted to the newsgroup immediately or just sent to your Outbox. It all depends on whether your preferences are set to "Send messages immediately." If the message just goes to your Outbox, you'll need to choose Tools ➢ Send from the Outlook Express menu bar to actually post the message to the newsgroup.

You'll see a "Posting Messages..." dialog box and a progress indicator as the article is posted. (If you have any unsent e-mail messages in your Outbox, those will be sent before the newsgroup article is posted.) When the post is complete, you're done. Your article is now traveling around the world and landing in thousands of ISP's news servers.

View Your Own Post

It should take only a few minutes for your message to be posted to the newsgroup. However, it may not appear in your message list because your list of header messages represents items that were in that newsgroup the moment you performed the download. But if you just wait a couple of minutes you should be able to spot your own message by re-downloading new messages from the group. Here's how:

1. In the Outlook Express Folders list, click the name of the newsgroup to which you posted the message.

2. From the Outlook Express menu bar choose Tools ➤ Synchronize Newsgroup.

3. In the Download Newsgroup dialog box that appears, choose Get The Following Items.

4. Choose New Headers (if you just want to download message headers) or New Messages (headers and bodies) if you want new messages and the message bodies (which will take a little longer).

5. Click the OK button in the Download Newsgroup dialog box.

If you've waited long enough for your message to get to your news server, you should see it somewhere in the list of message headers. In Figure 10.8, I've located the message I posted back in the preceding section of this chapter.

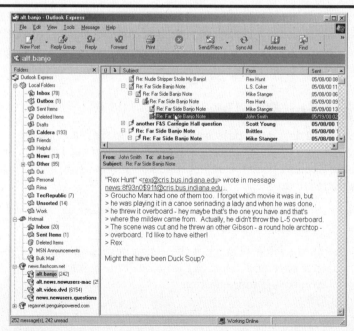

FIGURE 10.8: My message has been posted to the newsgroup.

If you can't find your message in the list of headers because the list is too long, sort the messages by date so they're in chronological order. To do that, just click the Sent column heading in the headers list.

NOTE

When you click a column heading in the headers list, all messages are sorted in ascending order by that column. The second time you click that same column head, the messages are sorted in descending order. So new messages will either be at the top or the bottom of the message list depending on whether they're currently sorted in ascending (oldest to newest) or descending (newest to oldest) order.

TIP

You can also search the message list for a name or subject. Click anywhere in the list of message headers and then choose Edit ➢ Find Message. In the dialog box that appears, type any part of your name or any part of the message subject. For example, I could type *Alan* to locate messages from myself. Then click the Find button. If the first matching message isn't the one you were looking for, choose Edit ➢ Find Next or press F3.

One way or another, you should be able to find your message. Don't expect any immediate replies though. It might take a day or two before someone who knows the answer to your question sees your message and sends a reply.

Checking for Replies

So let's say a day or two passes and you want to see if anyone has answered your profound question. Basically, all you need to do is fire up Outlook Express, go to the appropriate newsgroup again, and take a peek. Here are the steps:

1. Start Outlook Express in the usual manner. If prompted to connect, go ahead and do so.

2. In the folders list, click the + sign next to the name of your news server. Then click the name of the newsgroup to which you posted your question.

3. To bring your message list up to date, choose Tools ➤ Synchronize Newsgroup. Then choose Get The Following Items ➤ New Headers (or New Messages) and click the OK button.

4. When the new messages have been downloaded, choose View ➤ Current View ➤ Replies To My Post.

The list of message headers will shrink dramatically, displaying only messages that are direct replies to your post. (If there are no replies, the top panel will be empty.) To view the body of any reply, click its header in the top pane. In Figure 10.9, I'm viewing a reply to the message I posted earlier.

NOTE

OK, so I replied to my own post to create Figure 10.9. I know that wouldn't make sense in the real world, but I didn't want to wait around to see if anyone would really reply.

FIGURE 10.9: A reply to my message

After checking your replies, don't forget to choose View ➤ Current Replies ➤ All Messages to display all the message headers again.

And that, in a nutshell, is how newsgroups work. You post your message, then check back for replies once in a while.

Newsgroup Help

Don't forget that Outlook Express has its own built-in help, which you can use to supplement information provided in this chapter. As with most Windows programs, you just have to choose Help ➤ Contents And Index from the Outlook Express menu bar to get help. When the Outlook Express Help window appears, click the Contents tab and then click Viewing and Posting to Newsgroups. The tips and tricks and troubleshooting books also offer some solutions for newsgroupies.

ACCESSING NEWSGROUPS VIA THE WEB

There are a couple of services on the World Wide Web that allow you access to newsgroups via your Web browser. If your ISP doesn't offer a news server, the Web is really your only choice for accessing newsgroups. But even if you do have access to a news server, the Web sites for newsgroups can be a great way to scan multiple newsgroups for topics of interest to you and for answers to burning questions. The two main Web sites that offer access to newsgroups are:

▶ http://www.deja.com/usenet

▶ http://www.liszt.com/news

You can visit either newsgroup just by typing its URL in Internet Explorer's Address bar.

Here's how the newsgroup Web sites work. Let's say you go to www.dejanews.com. On the first page you should find a Search box that allows you to look up any word or phrase. Let's say you're thinking of adopting a pet chinchilla and you want to find newsgroups and articles dealing with chinchillas. You'd just type the appropriate phrase into the Search box, as shown in the following illustration, and then click the Find button.

After a brief delay, a list of messages dealing with that subject appears, as shown in Figure 10.10. If you use Outlook Express as your newsreader, you might just want to make note of the newsgroup names in the third column and then go back to Outlook Express and see if you can find that newsgroup on your ISP's news server.

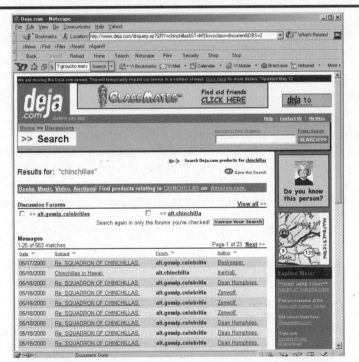

FIGURE 10.10: Newsgroup messages dealing with chinchillas

You can also access messages and even post replies right from your Web browser. To view a message, you can click any blue, underlined link to view any message in the list. When you're viewing a message, you'll see additional options such as View Thread and Post Reply, as shown in the example shown in Figure 10.11.

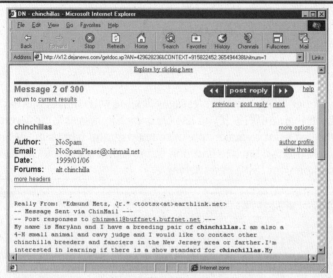

FIGURE 10.11:   Viewing a newsgroup message via dejanews.com

Keep in mind that the people who create Web pages can change those pages at any time. So the instructions I just gave you could be outdated when you get around to using the Web for newsgroups. I hope that won't happen. But if it does, and the new page has instructions that differ from the ones I just gave you, then by all means follow those newer instructions on the page.

Mailing Lists

Mailing lists are similar to newsgroups, only they use regular e-mail rather than a news server and newsreader. There are mailing lists on just about every topic imaginable—you just have to find ones that interest you. But that's not too hard to do because the Liszt Mailing List Directory keeps track of tens of thousands of mailing lists. To get to that Web site, point your Web browser to http://www.liszt.com.

The first page should provide a text box and "go" button that you can use to search for lists on your favorite topic. For example, if I search Liszt for mailing lists on *baseball*, I find that there are quite a few mailing lists out there having to do with baseball, as shown in Figure 10.12.

FIGURE 10.12: Mailing lists that discuss baseball

To learn more about a mailing list, click its link. The next page that appears will give you more information on that list. Most mailing lists originate from a Web site, and the information page that appears will provide a link to that site. Just click the link to go to the site, where you can learn how to subscribe to the mailing list. Others might just offer an e-mail address. You can click that link, type up a message saying you're interested in learning more about the mailing list, and send it off.

Once you've subscribed to a mailing list, you'll get e-mail messages daily or weekly (or whatever, depending on the mailing list) from that site. These will arrive in your regular e-mail Inbox, like any normal e-mail message. Just open the message as you would any regular e-mail.

Since different mailing lists have different rules and different ways of unsubscribing, I can't really tell you how to work a particular mailing list.

However, most lists will come with all the instructions you need to use that mailing list effectively.

INTRODUCING MICROSOFT CHAT

The freebie program that comes with Windows that you'll use to chat on the Internet is called Microsoft Chat. To open that program:

1. Click the Windows Start button.

2. Choose Programs ➤ Internet Explorer ➤ Microsoft Chat.

If Microsoft Chat isn't already installed on your PC, you can install it using the Windows Setup tab in Add/Remove Programs, or you can download a copy from Microsoft's Web site at

```
http://www.microsoft.com/msdownload/iebuild/chat25_win32/
EN/24592.htm
```

Define Yourself

When you first start Microsoft Chat, you'll be taken to the Connect tab of the Chat Connection dialog box. There you can choose a *chat server* and a *chat room*. As a newbie, you'll want to start at the suggested server and room shown below.

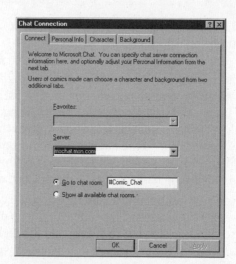

On the Personal Info tab, fill in as much, or as little, about yourself as you care to make public. All the fields are optional so you can leave them blank if you wish (or fill in the fields with false information if you just want to have some fun without telling anyone who you are).

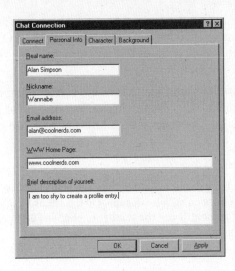

On the Character tab, choose a character to represent yourself. Just click each name until you find a character you like. Below, I chose Lance.

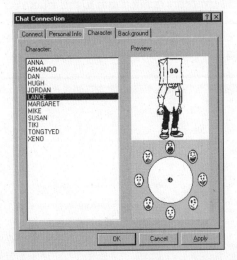

TIP

To change your identity at any time, choose View ➣ Options from Chat's menu bar and make selections from the Personal Info and Character tabs.

On the Background tab, choose whichever background you like. When you've finished making your selections, click the OK button. At that point your PC will connect to the Internet (or ask you to connect to the Internet). Go ahead and do so.

Once you're connected to the chat server, you might see a Message Of The Day dialog box. You can decide for yourself whether you want to read that message. Then click its OK button to get into the Chat program.

TIP

If nothing seems to work in Chat, you may be offline. In that case, the message *Now working offline* will appear in the status bar. To get back online, click the Connect button on the toolbar or choose File ➣ New Connection and then click OK.

FINDING A CHAT ROOM

Most chat servers are divided into *rooms* where people who share a similar interest meet and chat. To see what rooms are available on your chat server, choose Room ➣ Room List from Chat's menu bar. The Chat Room List dialog box shown in Figure 10.13 appears.

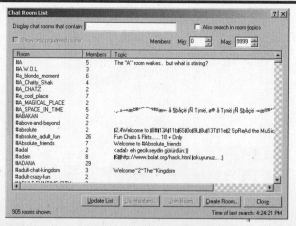

FIGURE 10.13: The Chat Room List dialog box

You can scroll through the list to see if you can find something that interests you or...

▶ To see which rooms are most/least crowded, click the Members column heading once to arrange them from least-crowded to most-crowded and click again to arrange from most-crowded to least-crowded.

▶ To search for a specific topic, type a word into the Display Chat Rooms That Contain text box and select the check box to the right of that option. The list will narrow to rooms that contain that word (if any). To return to the complete list, delete text from the Display Chat Rooms That Contain box.

To join a room:

1. Click the name of the room you want to join.

2. Click the Go To button.

You may see some automatic messages appear on the screen describing the rules of the chat room. Then you'll see ongoing conversations between room members appearing as comics. The members list in the top-right pane lists all the members of the current chat room. To see a list without the character faces, right-click that pane and choose List.

TIP

If you don't see comic frames in Chat, you're probably working in text view. To switch between comic and text views, choose View from the menu bar, then either Comic Strip or Plain Text. Alternatively, click the Comics View or Text View button on Chat's toolbar.

Each character in the comics represents one chatter. To see a character's nickname, just hover your mouse pointer over any character in any comic. The nickname appears in a tiny box near the mouse pointer. To see a chatter's profile, right-click the character and choose Get Profile. A series of frames appears, showing that person's personal information.

JOIN IN THE CONVERSATION

To join in the conversation, you need to start chatting. Here's how (although you can do steps 1–3 in any order you wish):

1. Type whatever you want to say in the strip near the bottom of the dialog box.

2. If you want your character to show an emotion, drag the little black ball in the emotion wheel, shown below, until your character shows the expression you want.

3. If you want to direct your message to a specific character, click that character in any comic frame or in the members list.

4. Click the Say button or any of the other buttons as summarized in Table 10.2. Alternatively, you can press the shortcut key listed in the third column if you don't want to take your hands off the keyboard.

TABLE 10.2: Chat Buttons for Displaying Your Text

BUTTON	NAME	WHAT IT DOES
	Say	Puts your message on the screen in a talk bubble (Ctrl+Y)
	Think	Puts your message on the screen in a thought bubble (Ctrl+T)
	Whisper	"Whispers" your message to only the character you selected in Step 2 above (Ctrl+W)
	Action	Displays your message as a caption rather than in a bubble (Ctrl+A)

That, in a nutshell, is what chatting is all about. You type a message and send it along. It appears on your screen and all the other room members' screens almost instantly (unless you whisper to someone, in which case your message appears only on that person's screen and your own).

As you may have guessed, though, there are plenty of options to play around with in Chat, as I'll discuss next.

CHAT ACRONYMS

Many of the acronyms that appear in your e-mail messages and newsgroup articles will show up in chats as well. Some favorites among chatters include:

A/S/L   Age / Sex / Location

AFK   Away from keyboard

BRB   Be right back

CYA   See ya

EAK   Eating at keyboard

K   Okay

LOL   Laughing out loud

NP   No problem

TY   Thank you

ROFL   Rolling on the floor laughing

WB   Welcome back

Whisper in my Ear

The Whisper button lets you send a single, private message to a member. If you'd like to have a lengthy private conversation with a member, you can sneak off to the Whisper Box. There, you and one or more other people can send messages back and forth without others seeing your messages. If you'd like to initiate a private conversation:

1. Type a message in the bottom line, as usual.

2. In the room members list, click the member you want to whisper to.

3. Alternatively, to whisper to several members, hold down the Ctrl key as you click their names in the members list.

4. Choose Member ➤ Whisper Box from Chat's menu bar. You're taken to the Whisper Box, which looks something like Figure 10.14.

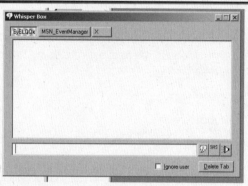

FIGURE 10.14: Chat's Whisper Box

5. Type your message in the long text box and click the Whisper button to send it.

If someone initiates a private conversation with you, you'll see the Whisper Box with that person's message in it. You can join in the private conversation simply by typing your reply in the bottom line and clicking the Whisper button to the right. If you don't want to join in, just close the Whisper Box. If the whisperer is insistent, and you want to get rid of them, you can click the Ignore User check box before you close the Whisper Box. You won't get any more whispers from that member.

Sending E-Mail to a Member

You can also communicate privately with a member by sending them e-mail—provided that the member has included his or her e-mail address in their personal information. To send an e-mail message:

1. Right-click the member's character in the comic pane or the member list.

2. Choose Send E-Mail. Outlook Express (or your default e-mail program) will open with a New Message window, with the chat member's e-mail address already filled in.

3. Type a subject and message and then click Send.

If Outlook Express is not set up to send messages immediately, the message will just go to your Outlook Express Outbox. To send the message, you'll need to open Outlook Express and choose Tools ➤ Send from its menu bar.

Sending and Receiving Files

You can also send any file on your PC to a member. In the members list, right-click the name of the member you want to send a file to and choose Send File. In the Send File dialog box that appears, browse to and click the file you want to send. Then click the Open button. You'll see a message indicating that Chat is waiting for the other person to accept the file. If they do, the file will be sent.

If someone sends you a file, you'll see a message asking if you want to accept the file. But be careful—some files can contain viruses and other unpleasant things that are not good for your PC. Don't accept the file unless you feel confident that you know what you're getting.

BROWSING ROOMS

You may want to hop around from room to room until you find one you really like. Here's how you can do that:

1. To leave the room you're in right now, choose Room ➤ Leave Room from Chat's menu bar (or click the Leave Room button on the toolbar).

2. To find a new room, choose Room ➤ Room List (or click the Chat Room List button on the toolbar).

You'll be returned to the room list where you can dig around for other rooms. To enter a new room, click whichever room you want to join and then click the Go To button.

LOGGING OFF

When you've finished your chat session, don't forget to disconnect from the server. If you want to announce your exit first, click the Leave Room button on the toolbar. To disconnect, click the Disconnect button on the toolbar. Then exit Chat by clicking its Close (X) button or by choosing File ➤ Exit from its menu bar.

MORE ON MICROSOFT CHAT

If you become a Chat fan, there are some more resources on the Internet you might want to check out. Here are a couple of Chat-related Web sites you can visit:

- ▶ Microsoft Chat's Page at `http://www.microsoft.com/catalog/display.asp?site=613&subid=22&pg=1&RLD=15`

- ▶ Code of Conduct at `http://communities.msn.com/chat/conduct.asp`

- ▶ Unofficial Chat Page `http://members.tripod.com/ComicChat`.

Chatting is a fun way to meet people online and share in some light banter. It's also the easiest Internet feature to use! Key points to remember:

- ▶ When you want to chat online, just fire up your Microsoft Chat program (Start ➤ Programs ➤ Internet Explorer ➤ Chat).

- ▶ While you're in Chat, choose View ➤ Options to choose your chat character or change your personal information.

- ▶ To see all the rooms available on the current chat server, choose Room ➤ Room List from Chat's menu bar. To enter a room, click its name and then click the Go To button.

- ▶ To chat, type your message in the bottom line.

- ▶ Use the emotion wheel to give your character an emotion.

- ▶ To send your message to a particular member, click that member's name in the name list or character in the comic panes.

- ▶ Click the Say, Think, or Whisper button to the right of where you typed your text.

- ▶ If you get disconnected from the chat server, choose File ➤ New Connection from Chat's menu bar.

INSTANT MESSAGING

Instant Messaging is one of the most popular technologies now available on the Web. As I mentioned at the beginning of this chapter, Instant Messaging (IM) allows people on the same IM system to notify others about their current online status. In other words, when Bobby starts using his AOL Instant Messenger (AIM) software it tells AOL's AIM servers that Bobby is online. Anyone who has Bobby in his or her Buddy List will then see that Bobby is online and available to chat or otherwise communicate.

This has made IM very, *very* popular. ICQ (http://www.icq.com), a pseudo-acronym for "I Seek You," is the second most popular the world over and can boast *20 million* users as of late 1998. PowWow (http://www.tribal.com) is one of the new entrants into the field and it already handles 3 million users. The hands-down winner, however, is AOL Instant Messenger (http://www.aol.com) with a claimed *49 million* users. There are also IM services from the Microsoft Network (http://www.msn.com) and Yahoo! (http://www.yahoo.com). All have different systems for instant messaging and all support millions of users.

Installing these utilities is simple and each one walks you through the details in a very clear fashion. What is important to understand, however, is the general functionality of these services. They all perform the same basic functions, but some are more comprehensive than others. Let's take a quick look by way of a features comparison chart (see Table 10.3).

TABLE 10.3: Comparing Instant Messengers

	ICQ	MSN Msngr.	AOL Instant Msngr.	Yahoo! Msngr.	Tribal Voice PowWow
Send & Receive Messages	*	*	*	*	*
URL Sharing	*		*	*	*
File Transfer	*				*
Text Chat	*	*	*	*	*
Voice Chat	*		*	*	*
Web Integration	*		*		*

TABLE 10.3 continued: Comparing Instant Messengers

	ICQ	MSN MSNGR.	AOL INSTANT MSNGR.	YAHOO! MSNGR.	TRIBAL VOICE POWWOW
Calendar	*			*	*
Address Book	*		*	*	*
POP/SMTP Mail Handling	*				*
POP3 Mailbox Checking	*	Hotmail only		Yahoo! Mail only	*
Search for Users	*		*	*	*
Search Internet	*		*	*	*
Enhanced Web Services	*		*		*

As you can see, each service offers a widely varying set of features. Of course, your choice depends ultimately on two things; what your friends are using, and what features you want. ICQ is tops in this set because it offers its services outside of any other service (i.e., AIM is also a part of AOL's proprietary software) and does not have a lowest common denominator to contend with. For these reasons ICQ has bloomed into a full-featured service that offers far more than any competitor. PowWow offers more features than ICQ, but because it is a new service, not many people are using it yet and that is something of a liability. Keep in mind that there is nothing to stop you from using more than one messaging service if too many people of the people you want to be in touch with user differering services.

One final note is that each service offers you the ability to control what you receive and most can also limit even who can place you on their Buddy List. For instance, in ICQ and AIM you can withhold all personal information and reject everything automatically except for any friends you specify. That way you receive the benefits of IM without having to put up with unwanted visitors. PowWow also has strong security features and promises to offer as many services as ICQ, but it is limited to Windows right now. ICQ and the others can work on the Macintosh as well. ICQ has clients for all platforms, even the Palm PDA!

WHAT'S NEXT?

This chapter has given you all the information you need to get started connecting with other users on the Internet via newsgroups, mailing lists, chat rooms, and instant messaging. Next up, we'll take a look at the tools you can use to work with multimedia on the Net.

Part ii

Chapter 11

WORKING WITH MULTIMEDIA

Part of the fun of the Internet and the Web is that there are a lot of different media out there to explore. That's the focus of this chapter.

What do I mean by media? Well, the most basic medium is text. The next most common medium is various forms of pictures. Beyond that, media available on the Internet include sounds, movie clips, animations, and even more elaborate formats combining the basic media in all sorts of different ways. We still haven't reached a point where your computer is going to be as flashy as a television, and I'm not sure we'll ever get to that point. For one thing, the snazzier the medium, the bigger the files. For example, even the smallest picture file is bigger than most text documents you find on the Internet. These bulky files can bring your system to a processing and playback standstill, unless you have a fast connection, a very powerful processor, and lots of free memory.

Adapted from *The Internet: No experience required, Second Edition*, by Christian Crumlish

ISBN 0-7821-2385-6   470 pages $19.99

Of course, all that's changing now. While it is true that we are *still* not at the point where TV and the Web are indistinguishable, the gap is closing. Streaming media—being able to play a file *as* it is being downloaded without having to wait until it is finished—has become more important these days as digital audio and video formats become more accessible via "broadband" connections, like DSL (Digital Subscriber Line) and cable modem service. These speedy access options are no longer available to just a trifling minority, but instead are available in most metropolitan areas. And as for that "...very powerful processor..." and "...lots of free memory...", it is now common for discount systems to ship with 500MHz CPUs, 64MB of RAM, and 10GB hard disks, all for around $500–700 (without a monitor, of course). But even the lowliest 150MHz Pentium with a good connection to the Internet through a 56K modem can access streaming media such as music, video, and a popular favorite, Shockwave. Oh, and then there's MP3, of course.

In general, to actually see, hear, or otherwise experience such media, you need a computer equipped with the right hardware—such as a sound card, enough memory to make movies play smoothly, a big enough hard drive to store large-format files (if you want to get in on the MP3 craze), and so on. You also need software installed on your computer, either as part of a Web browser (a plug-in) or as a stand-alone program (a helper) that can interpret and display—or just "play"—the various media file formats. Once you put together all the ingredients, then you can start to experience the Internet as the world's largest CD-ROM and video store, with new content appearing online daily.

There are dozens of media formats available but there are only a few that stand tall among the little guys struggling for a piece of the pie. At the top of the heap is Real Networks with their RealSystem software that is the very soul of expressive convergence, combining video, audio, and animation, and doing so with aplomb all the while. Close behind is Microsoft's Media Player, which, as of this writing, is getting a major overhaul to better fight with the big boys. Last, but by far not the least—and carrying the honor of being the application and format that started it all—is QuickTime. Apple brought QuickTime to the streaming game late, but has made up for it by snagging some very big partners, making the available content quite entertaining. With all that said, in this chapter I'll show you the various ways to handle this veritable blizzard of media by helping you to understand the tools that are available.

WHAT'S NEW WITH MULTIMEDIA?

The biggest handicap to multimedia development on the Web has been bandwidth limitations—people connecting to the Net via modems just can't be expected to wait long enough for huge media files to download. *Bandwidth* is the capacity of the communication lines transmitting data back and forth between the Internet and your computer. When you use a modem, your telephone line is transferring the data. This and the simple fact that there are limitations to what an analog (all that screeching when you dial up) modem can do can result in slow loading of Web pages or playback of video and audio clips. If you cruise the Internet from a network connection at work, your bandwidth capacity is likely greater, but network traffic can also be heavier because many people may be using the network simultaneously. Any of these factors (line capacity, traffic, modem speed) can interfere with smooth browsing.

Another problem has been that most multimedia extensions to the standard Web format (HTML) have required that the user install a special piece of software into the Web browser. In the past, this meant taking a side-trip from the site offering the media content to the Web site of the manufacturer of the plug-in. Any time someone leaves a site, there's some chance she'll never come back, as the siren call of tangential sites attracts her further and further from the original activity.

Fortunately, convergence has meant consolidation. Now there are several formats being represented by only a few "helper app" makers, namely the aforementioned Real Networks, Microsoft, and Apple. This means that with the included Media Player and a couple of 6MB downloads (free, of course) you are ready to receive generally any media format there is. There is an odd matter of overlap in which all three of the popular "helper apps" that I reference can handle certain file formats and depending on which one you installed last (invariably QuickTime or RealPlayer), it will be the default player for the formats that overlap. The others might get indignant and request that their formats be returned to their care, but there are ways to work through this.

As for Web browsers, the latest version of one major Web browser, Microsoft Internet Explorer, already incorporates a more automatic process for downloading and installing plug-ins called ActiveX (a proprietary format, of course). The other major browser, Netscape, recognizes when a plug-in or helper is asked for and asks if you would like to download it. As a matter of course, most popular Web browsers and other Internet tools update themselves from time to time automatically or per your request, by connecting to the software publisher's site, downloading patches or new setup files, and incorporating them into the existing package. Real Networks RealSystem 7 relies on this function for its subscription-based format where a $29.95 purchase gets you RealPlayer 7 Plus and unlimited updates for the next year.

DOWNLOADING AND INSTALLING APPLICATIONS

To experience almost any medium, you first have to either have access to a site that streams the media or, getting pretty rare these days, download a large file. Depending on what you have installed, the file will, at minimum, be stored on your computer where you can open it yourself using the right program. Alternatively, the browser will automatically start up a program that can display the file and it will appear outside the browser, or the file will be displayed inside the browser window.

The type of program that you launch separately to display a file is called a *viewer* or *player* program. If your browser can automatically start an external program whenever it needs to display certain types of files, then the program is referred to as a *helper application,* because it helps the browser with this extra job. The type of program that becomes part of the browser and enables the browser to display a file within the browser window is called a *plug-in.* I'll cover all three variations in the upcoming sections.

At Web sites that offer multimedia files, you will often find additional hypertext links to sites from which you can download the appropriate player software. Usually you can simply follow these links to the Web site housing the software, read the installation instructions, and download the correct program for your type of computer. You can often choose to automatically open and install the software as soon as it is downloaded (in fact, some programs can begin the installation process before the entire package is completely downloaded). Even others have you download a small installation host program that, when run, fetches the remainder of the software. Both QuickTime 4 and the new Netscape 6 work this way. Occasionally, you may still have to use a Setup or Install program to get the installation started.

NOTE

Your employment prospects will improve if you understand how sound, graphics, and video files work on the Web and how Web page design can accommodate system limitations while still looking good. Add a Web page to your portfolio—one that works whether the sound, graphics, or video features are turned on or off, so that people with any type of computer and connection can use it. (See Part V, "Creating a Web Page," for more information on how to make a Web page.)

DIFFERENT WAYS TO VIEW MEDIA

As I just suggested, there are different ways to view various media files depending on the type of browser you have, the media formats you're working with, and the additional software you install. Here's a quick rundown of the different approaches.

TIP

Don't be put off by the use of the word *viewer* to describe multimedia player applications. Because the first media (after text) to be widely distributed were picture (image) formats, the viewer terminology took hold and is now used even for media such as sounds that you can't actually see.

Viewers and Players

A viewer program is one that can be used to view or play a specific type of file. (Even the ones used to play sounds, for example, are still referred to as viewers in browser instructions, so viewers and players are different names for the same thing.) Even with a character-based browser like the Unix program Lynx, you can still download files. It's true that you'll then have to get the file from your Unix account to your desktop computer, but when that's done you can "play" the file you downloaded if you have the appropriate software (such as Windows Media Player) installed on your computer.

The trick, then, is finding the appropriate viewer program to display the media files you download. This is usually a matter of following the suggestions from the Web site where you found the original file. Other places you can look for files are mentioned in Chapter 8, "Internet Search Engines."

Part II

Helper Applications

Netscape Navigator and other browsers based on that graphical model
have the ability to launch external programs—called *helper applications*—
when a nonstandard file format is selected. Helper applications will let
your browser open files in formats it could not otherwise handle, such as
a Sun audio file. They do, however, have to be "taught" where to look for
the helper application. You can either do this in advance, by entering
the Options or Preferences area of the browser and looking for the
Helper Applications (or Helper Apps) section, or you can attempt to
download a media file and then, when the browser tells you it doesn't
recognize the file format, you can educate it about which viewer to use
with that type of file. You do this simply by typing in the path and file
name for the correct program, or by clicking a Browse button and rum-
maging around on your hard disk for the program you need. After that,
your browser will automatically launch the right helper application
whenever you select that type of media file again.

Plug-Ins

The most sophisticated way to work with multimedia files is to plug special add-on software directly into a browser. Such a program, usually
called a *plug-in*, is an application that works in tandem with a browser,
enhancing its features as if you had taken a piece of hardware and added
it to your computer to give it more features. Once a particular plug-in is
installed its capabilities are added to the browser so it is able to display a
media format that it could not before. In direct correlation to that convergence I mentioned before, both RealPlayer and QuickTime install plug-
ins so that their formats can also be viewed as *embedded* media, meaning
that it is displayed in the browser window and not in a separate helper
application or viewer.

Compressed Files and "Streaming Media"

One of the most common strategies used to address bandwidth limitations is to compress files as much as possible, most often using widely
accepted compression standards. This might mean converting media
files, such as images, to file formats that have data compression built
right in (pictures on the Web are all stored in compressed formats) or it
might mean compressing the original files with a zip or StuffIt type program, and requiring that the recipient decompress it himself. (The unzip

or StuffIt Expander programs are always available as freeware and share-ware. See Chapter 9, "Getting Around FTP and Telnet," for more on downloading and installing programs.)

NOTE

Despite all our efforts, competition for bandwidth may well always be a prob-lem—even when we someday have virtual-reality meeting rooms, we will probably be complaining about them being "jiggly" or something like that.

Today's most common approach to distributing long-format media (such as movies, radio, music, and the like) across limited bandwidths is to use a *streaming* format. Streaming format sends the information in a continuous stream (with some clever innovations to deal with the flux and discontinuities of the Internet), enabling the receiver or playback device to start playing the media content without waiting for the entire file to finish downloading.

Real Networks, as we've mentioned before, was first to the table with streaming media it called RealAudio. Now, Real commands the bulk of the streaming media market with their hybrid free/pay RealPlayer 7. RealPlayer 7 can understand many formats and can download more if it comes across something that it does not already understand. You can download the free version from Real (www.real.com) or you can pur-chase the enhanced and supported version for prices ranging from $19.95 to $39.95, the higher of which includes RealJukebox and a year of free updates and unlimited phone support.

Apple also offers a free/pay hybrid of their ridiculously popular Quick-Time 4 software. The free version is a viewer and plug-in that handles most of today's video and audio media formats while the Pro version (the one you pay for) contains many, many tools for multimedia viewing, manipulating, and even authoring. The Pro version is available for $29.95 direct from Apple (www.apple.com/quicktime).

One that you already have if you are using Microsoft Windows is Media Player, an all-around audio and video player solution. Media Player is able to play many different formats and uses a plug-in architecture (like RealPlayer) to add formats as fast as Microsoft can add them. Microsoft's Media Player, QuickTime, and RealPlayer are not the only streaming solu-tions available, but they're the most popular. There are other products and offerings from other companies, but the list would be huge.

Part ii

TYPES OF MEDIA

The multimedia world on the Internet is still in a sort of "Wild West" phase, with many competing formats for the various types of media, and even more appear every month despite the fact that the Real/Apple/Microsoft trio pretty much holds most of the cards. In this section, I'll describe some of the media you'll encounter and clarify how the different file formats are used to get those media onto your screen.

TIP

For more (or more up-to-date) information on multimedia file formats available on the Net, check out www.iics-sf.org/ (the San Francisco Bay Area chapter of the International Interactive Communications Society). This site has links to other multimedia resources.

Pictures

The first graphical Web browser, Mosaic, could display only one picture format when it first appeared—CompuServe's *GIF* (Graphic Interchange Format), which is a compressed file format. The other major picture format is called *JPEG* (named for the Joint Photographics Experts Group that designed the format). Mosaic, at first, could only display JPEG files in a helper application. When Netscape Navigator came along, it sported in-line JPEGs, which most browsers can now also handle. In-line JPEG files load right along with the Web page they are on without the need to launch an additional helper application.

Some GIFs are *interlaced*, which makes them appear to load faster on your screen. GIFs can also have transparent backgrounds, which accounts for the illusion of images with irregular (non-rectangular) edges. The images actually do have square edges, but their transparent background makes their content appear to float on the page.

NOTE

Using GIF files or the most current version of the JPEG format (progressive JPEGs) can be beneficial because, as they load on the page, the images appear to be gradually filled or drawn in. This activity may hold the attention of your average impatient Web browser who does not want to sit and stare at a static page, waiting for the graphics to appear. At least with GIF files, the viewer can watch the images slowly filling in and coming into focus. The older formats of JPEG files did not load in the same manner.

JPEGs can be compressed to much smaller file sizes than equivalent GIFs, but the more they are "squished," the worse the quality of the image becomes.

NOTE

The newest graphics format coming down the pike is *PNG* (which some say stands for "Png's Not Gif"). PNG combines some of the best features of GIF and JPEG formats in an open standard. MS Internet Explorer 4 and Netscape Communicator and its Navigator 4 browser can display PNGs.

Sounds and Music

There are many different sound file formats available on the Net. Of course, in line with the onward march of growth in the streaming media arena the most popular formats are MP3, short for MPEG Layer III, and Windows Media Audio (WMA), a Microsoft technology. Both of these compression technologies can get sound files down to as little as 1 MB per second and still retain CD-quality stereo sound characteristics. For example, the beautiful and haunting soundtrack to the Turner Broadcasting production of *The Native Americans*, written and performed by the talented Robbie Robertson and the Red Road Ensemble, is 54 minutes and 30 seconds in length. If it were to be encoded using typical MP3 encoding practices, all of the songs would comprise roughly 55 MB of space on a hard disk. This fact has made the MP3 format extremely popular—and not a little illegal, mind you.

THAT WICKED, WICKED MP3

If the RIAA (Recording Industry Association of America) had its way, you would think of MP3 files as nothing more than pure evil in the form of digital audio. Here's the trick; MPEG Layer III appeared in 1994, became popular on college campuses because it allowed students to trade music, logically moved to the Internet, caught fire, got poked at with a Law stick by the RIAA, and has never looked back since. Here's how it works. Get a computer, place an audio CD in the CD-ROM drive, launch what is called a *ripper*, convert the songs into MP3 files, and listen to the result with RealPlayer, Quick-Time, Windows Media Player, WinAMP, or any one of a few dozen

CONTINUED ➡

more programs that speak MP3. It's like copying a record to cassette tape, but worse. You can e-mail songs to your friends in minutes, and this is the problem the RIAA has with MP3.

Of course, this is where the law gets sticky because it is now up to the courts to decide whether or not it is legal to copy the music from a CD you purchased. The RIAA contends that you merely purchase the medium on which the music is distributed and therefore have no right to copy the music contained therein. MP3 proponents, like MP3.Com CEO Michael Robertson, claim that the music on the CDs belongs to the purchaser of the CD and they may listen to it in any format they choose, as long as *they* listen to it and do not redistribute it to others. Robertson's claim is that the purchase is a license. This may be why MP3.Com offers the MyMP3.Com service where you place a CD that you own in the CD-ROM drive of your computer, run a small program that identifies which CD it is, and then sends that information to a special Web site to which only you have access. What's the deal? Simple: the program tells the Web site what CD you put in the drive and the Web site makes that CD available to you over the Web to play anywhere with RealPlayer, but nary a song from *your* CD is ever copied. The CD that's used belongs to MP3.Com.

Nice service, eh? The RIAA thinks differently. The RIAA calls it piracy, obvious and blatant.

The complicating factor is the now vast number of software and hardware companies that are deeply vested in MP3. Diamond Multimedia sparked the hardware revolution with the introduction of the RIO, a portable, walkman-sized MP3 player. Again, you rip (copy and convert) your music to MP3 and move it to the RIO through a cable connected to your computer. You can then go outside, plug in your headphones and blast away to digital sound that never skips. Actually, there are a number of things that make the MP3 the perfect digital audio medium. The files are small yet sound great, and are often indistinguishable from CD audio when encoded at the optimal settings. MP3 files, like any other digital file format, can be encoded to protect them from being used by other people or on other equipment.

The most common of the traditional sound formats include Microsoft's *WAV* (wave) format, perhaps the most widespread; the Macintosh *AIFF* format; and the Unix (originally NeXT) *AU* format. Many Web sites that offer sounds do so in more than one format, in order to make it easier for each user to download a file format native to their type of computer. Other sound formats include *MIDI* (Musical Instrument Digital Interface), the Amiga *SND* format, and the *VOC* format for the SoundBlaster sound card.

After a while, you'll start to recognize what programs you'll need to view or play files by the (usually) three-letter extension following a file name. This will tell you whether it is a movie, a sound file, a picture, or something else, and what method of compression—if any—was used on it. Some of the more common file compression suffixes are `.zip`, `.hqz`, `.Z`, `.gz`, `.sit`, `.sea`, `.exe`, and `.tar`.

As I've mentioned before, there is also *streaming*. Streaming is when files are sent a little at a time and start playing almost immediately. This model differs from those in which an entire file is sent and then starts playing only after it has been completely downloaded. The most popular streaming format these days is *RealPlayer*. The tools needed to create and listen to such sounds are made by a company called Real Networks (`www.real.com`). This format allows sounds to be broadcast something like they are in radio. In fact, the National Public Radio Web site uses the RealAudio format to broadcast some of their reports over the Internet (see Figure 11.1).

NOTE

Microsoft Internet Explorer also plays *in-line* sounds, which will automatically start playing as soon as you arrive at a page, whether you like it or not!

Part II

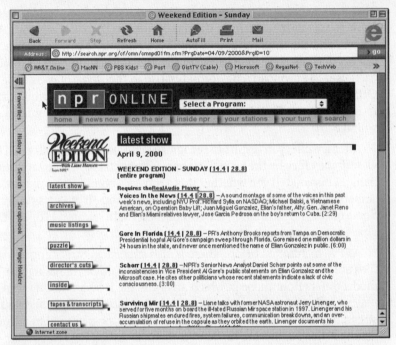

FIGURE 11.1: NPR's Web site offers current broadcasts in RealAudio format.

Movies and Animations

As with sounds and pictures, there are various competing movie and animation formats available on the Net. Technically, the difference between a movie and an animation is that movies use video or film images (variations on photographic technology), while animations use drawn illustrations. With computer art tools being what they are, this distinction will probably fade eventually. A lot of computer art these days starts off as photography and is then manipulated into something entirely different.

Probably the most widespread movie format is the MPEG (Motion Pictures Experts Group) format, a compressed format. Another popular format is *QuickTime*, which started off on the Macintosh platform but can now be displayed on both Macintosh and Windows-based systems. There are Unix/Linux players, such as Xanim, that can play *most* Quick-Time formats, but do not have the ability to playback files encoded with the popular Sorensen Codec, the compression format used to reduce the size of streaming QuickTime files. QuickTime files usually have a `.qt` or `.mov` extension.

A third common movie format, native to the Windows platform, is *AVI*. There are also streaming movie formats, such as Progressive Networks' RealPlayer. Webcasting's "push" model offers yet another alternative method for sending video-style content to a viewer's screen.

The next wave of special media formats for the Web will involve interactive programs or demonstrations, running either in separate applications or in the browser window. Macromedia makes a product called Director that enables artists to assemble movies, animations, pictures, sounds, and interactive elements (such as clickable buttons and other user-influenced choices) into a single, self-running application. The Director plug-in is known as Shockwave. Shockwave now has a Flash format designed specifically for the Web. Flash enables smooth interactive performance over an Internet connection in a streamable format using very compact vector graphics. Designers rave about Flash. See www.macromedia.com/software/flash/ for more about this format.

The other popular application-development format for the Web is Sun's Java programming language, a variant of C++. With a special Java-savvy browser such as HotJava, Netscape Navigator 4.7x and higher, or Microsoft Internet Explorer 4.x and higher, users can interact with fully operational programs inside of the browser window. But no longer is Java limited to the Web browser. An enterprising company, ThinkFree.Com, has created the ThinkFree Office, a Java-based office application suite that has a Microsoft Office 2000-compatible word processor, spreadsheet, and presentation application as well as a file manager that manages files both on your computer and those you store on the Internet. It's runs on Unix/Linux, Macintosh, and Windows-based machines. Oh, and it's free.

Document/Mixed-Media Formats

Aside from the familiar HTML format and plain text (.txt) files, which browsers can easily display, there are some document file formats intended to give designers and publishers more control over the precise look of a document. HTML is quite flexible, but HTML documents look different in every browser because they have to use whatever fonts are built into the user's computer, and they even change their shape and layout depending on the size and shape of the browser window and browsing preferences set by the user. For artists, publishers, and designers trained in the world of print publishing, most of these compromises are unacceptable.

Part ii

The most popular document format is Adobe's *PDF* (Portable Document Format). The external helper application for viewing PDF files is called Adobe Acrobat. The Netscape plug-in that performs the same function is called Adobe Amber. Visit www.adobe.com/ for more information on the PDF format.

Another document format that requires special viewers is Postscript, which can be used for both text and images. Postscript files usually have a .ps extension.

STAYING INFORMED ABOUT THE LATEST ADVANCES

There are new viewers and new file formats coming out on the Net all the time. It's literally impossible for me to make this discussion be fully up-to-date by the time you read it! As with any Internet software, you will have to do a little work if you want to stay up-to-date with the latest developments. Your best bet is to visit your browser's home page from time to time (most browsers have a logo button near the upper-right corner of the window to take you there automatically) and read the announcements to see if any new capabilities or plug-ins have been announced.

TIP

Netscape Navigator automatically provides you with a link to its Plug-In Finder page if you connect with a file format that Navigator does not support. You can also visit Netscape's Plug-In page by selecting Help ➢ About Plug-Ins in the Navigator or Communicator menu. The help document will show you which plug-ins are preinstalled in Communicator and Navigator. If you click on the "click here" link at the top of the document, you will be taken to the plug-in page (http://home.netscape.com/plugins/index.html at the time of this writing).

A FEW WORDS ABOUT SPECIALIZED BROWSERS

One way to experience some of the latest multimedia offerings on the Web, even without customizing your browser, is to obtain a specialized browser designed to display one or more of the multimedia formats. In the long run, as general-purpose browsers become more flexible, this may no longer be a useful option. But for now, if you have the type of access that allows you to install and run your own browser, you can download a program such as Sun's HotJava browser (www.javasoft.com/). There are actually quite a few stand-alone VRML browsers, such as Cosmo (http://cosmosoftware.com/), 3Space Assistant (ftp://ftp.sd.tgs.com/3SpaceAssistant/X86/), and Pueblo (ftp://ftp.chaco.com/pueblo/) to name a few.

MULTIMEDIA FOR SPECIFIC BROWSERS

I'll finish up by running through a quick discussion of many of the most popular Web browsers to tell you what alternatives you have (setting up helper applications or adding plug-ins) to increase the capabilities at your disposal, and what media can be viewed with them.

Microsoft Internet Explorer

Internet Explorer tries to automate the plug-in installation process by utilizing a technology called ActiveX. Like Java, ActiveX components, called *controls*, can be downloaded automatically and run immediately. Unlike Java, ActiveX controls are more like plug-ins and can remain resident in your computer to act whenever they are called upon. Of course, also unlike Java, ActiveX controls can present a major danger to your system and your files because once ActiveX is installed it has complete access to every function of your computer. Fortunately, trusted control vendors can have *certificates* applied to them by a trust provider like VeriSign or Thawte.

WARNING

Always look for a certificate from a known trust provider and (a personal opinion of mine) never, *never* accept automatic trust for *any* company. Doing so allows them to install software on your computer *at any time without asking you.*

If you visit a site with a media format that your browser does not yet "know," (such as the short Shockwave clip available via the "shocked house" link at (www.attraction.org/), Internet Explorer will automatically connect to the media-format maker's Web site and offer to download and install the appropriate add-in.

There is no way to manually install a plug-in to Internet Explorer. You may have to restart your computer once the plug-in has been installed.

Internet Explorer can display GIFs, JPEGs, and PNGs in-line. It can also play any of the standard Microsoft file formats (such as the AVI movie format, the WAV sound format, and so on), and it can be extended with a very, *very* wide range of plug-ins.

Netscape Navigator/Communicator

One way to tell Navigator about a helper application is to start downloading an "unknown" file type and then, when Navigator balks and the Unknown File Type dialog box pops up, tell it what program to view the file with by clicking on the Pick App button and following the instructions that appear.

You can also plan ahead by assigning file types to specific Helper applications with these steps:

1. Open Netscape Navigator and Communicator by double-clicking the Netscape Communicator desktop shortcut or by selecting Start ➤ Programs ➤ Netscape Communicator ➤ Netscape Navigator.

2. Select Edit ➤ Preferences, and click the Navigator ➤ Applications item in the Category box at the left (see Figure 11.2).

3. Select a file type in the large list box at the top of the dialog box and click the Edit button.

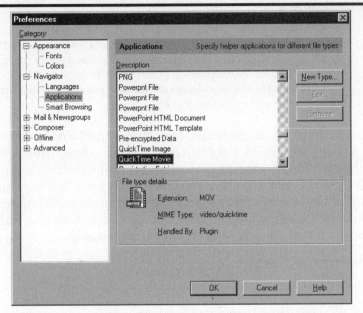

FIGURE 11.2:   Navigator's Preferences dialog box with Applications selected

4. In the Handled By area, choose the application you want to use when opening this type of file. Either type the path for the application in the Application text box, or click the Browse button and find the application and its path in your folders. Click Open to copy the path into the Application textbox.

5. Click OK to close the Edit Type dialog box, then click OK again to close Preferences.

NOTE

In Navigator, select Options ➢ General Preferences and click the Helpers tab in the Preferences dialog box. Select the Launch the Application button in the Action area near the bottom of the dialog box, and then either type the path and file name of the helper application that can display the file type or click the Browse button to hunt around on your hard disk for the program you want. Then click OK.

To set up a plug-in for Navigator, click the puzzle-piece "plug-in required" icon when you see it on a Web page. When the Plugin Not Loaded dialog box appears, click Get the Plugin. This takes you to Netscape's Plug-in Finder page, where you can download the plug-in you need.

WARNING

Plug-ins that you installed for Navigator 3 will not automatically work with 4.7x, nor will they be installed as far as Netscape Communicator is concerned. When you download plug-ins, save the setup files in a set-aside "Install" folder. Then, when you upgrade to a new version of Netscape, you can re-install the plug-ins, directing them to your new browser.

Install the plug-in as instructed. Navigator will do the rest. Navigator can display GIFs, JPEGs, and PNGs in-line (versions before Navigator 4 can't display PNGs), as well as animated GIFs—GIF files that contain multiple frames and instructions on how to show them. Navigator also has a built-in Java interpreter that can be set up to use an almost unlimited number of helper applications. There are already many plug-ins for Navigator on the Net, and more are always on the way.

NOTE

Netscape does not yet automatically download and install plug-ins the way Microsoft Internet Explorer tries to do.

Netscape 6: The Next Generation

As of this writing Netscape, owned by America Online, has released a preview version of Netscape 6. This new Web browser/mail client/news center/other pretty much takes the cake for browser releases for the year 2000. Netscape 6, despite the fact that it jumped from version 4.72 to 6.0, is a fine example of talented engineering. There's nothing really different in regard to plug-ins. In fact, most, if not all, of the plug-ins for Communicator 4.7x should work just fine.

WHAT'S NEXT?

This chapter has given you all the information you need to handle the vast array of media available on the Web by helping you to understand the tools that are available for working with media. The next chapter, "Let AOL Rock Your World," explores one of the Web's most popular browsers, America Online.

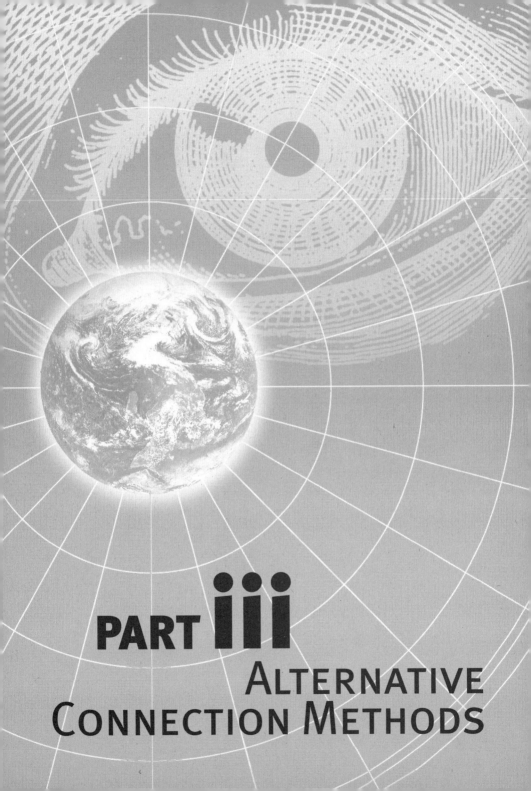

PART iii
ALTERNATIVE CONNECTION METHODS

Chapter 12

LET AOL ROCK YOUR WORLD!

AOL is the online arena of choice for a plethora of people, and it's obvious why. It's easy to use, it can be made safe for the youth of today, and yet there are nooks, crannies, tricks, and secrets that keep it interesting for the adventurers among us.

This chapter delves into the mysteries of AOL and beyond, from the banalities of cold cash to the fantastical programs you can use to augment your online experience. The only assumptions I'm making right off the bat are that you have AOL 5, and that you're somewhat comfortable with it. Otherwise, I'll let you in on all you need to know. From here on out, you're in AOL Land unless I say otherwise. Read on, and, above all, explore!

Adapted from *Internet! I Didn' t Know You Could Do That..., Second Edition*, by Alan R. Neibauer

ISBN 0-7821-2844-0   282 pages $19.99

NOTE
For more AOL tips and tricks, check out *America Online Amazing Secrets*, by Laura Arendal.

SAVE BIG BUCKS

You have five different price options when you sign up for AOL:

Unlimited monthly   What it sounds like.

One-year plan   Unlimited access for one year, entirely pre-paid, at what works out to be a slightly reduced monthly rate.

Limited plan   You pay a little bit less than half the regular monthly charge for a few free hours online per month. If you stay online past those few free hours (cumulatively, not per session), you will be charged a per-hour fee.

Light usage   The same idea as the limited plan, just *more* limited—and less expensive.

Bring your own access   Fondly referred to as BYOA, this plan allows you to use any other Internet Service Provider (ISP) to access the wonderful world of AOL; thus you pay slightly less than half of AOL's usual monthly fee, and if your ISP also charges less than the other half of AOL's monthly fee, you have unlimited access for cheap. Relatively, anyway.

Because you stand to save the most with BYOA, and because it's just slightly more obscure than the other options (being that you have to go outside the safe confines of AOL), I'll devote my discussion to this option.

NOTE
None of these plans will protect you from being charged for hanging out in AOL's premium areas, such as the supercool premium games offered through keyword games.

If you are unsure which plan will work best for you, check out your detailed bill at Help ➢ Accounts and Billing. In the AOL Billing Center window, click Display Your Detailed Bill (at bottom left). Choose Last Month's Bill from the Request Detailed Billing Information dialog box. You will be treated to a list of the times any of your screen names accessed AOL during the previous billing period. The minutes you spent on AOL per session are listed in the Paid column. Add them up and divide by 60 (minutes/hour). Did you spend more hours online than allowed under the light usage or limited access plans? If so—and if you're determined to spend less than the unlimited plan charges—BYOA might be for you.

NOTE

If you decide to go for one of the limited-access options, use Automatic AOL (found under the Mail Center menu) to keep your online hours low.

Bring Your Own Access!

The BYOA plan can be especially useful if you already have an account through school or work and wish to add AOL access on top of that; under these scenarios you will usually just be paying the BYOA fee. Plus, you won't have to deal with modem traffic, because your school or work will most likely use a network connection to the Internet. This connection will be more direct—and possibly faster.

If you choose BYOA, some caveats are in order: you must always connect to the Internet through your ISP *before* signing onto AOL; otherwise you will be charged extra per hour of use. In addition, if your ISP is slow or overloaded, you may find your online experience a frustrating one. That said, many people are as pleased as punch with BYOA.

WARNING

If you want to access AOL through your work account, you'd best discuss it with your Systems Administrator first; some companies' firewalls need to be modified to allow AOL access from within, and some companies may just plain prohibit such a move.

Part iii

Here's How It Works

First you need your own way to get on the Internet—either an ISP or a network that already has a way to connect to the Internet (such as you would find at work or school). If you don't have either, check out www.thelist.com for a comprehensive list of existing ISPs.

NOTE

Each ISP is different; follow the instructions provided by the ISP staff for installing the software and signing up.

You'll also need AOL software and a membership. Go to www.aol.com if you still need to sign up.

BYOA-ize Your Computer Setup

1. Open AOL (but don't sign on).

2. At the bottom of the Sign On window, click Setup.

3. Click Add Location.

4. First, glide down to the bottom of the Add Location dialog box and click the radio button next to Select a Custom Connection. Then, glide on back to the top of the dialog box. If you don't like the obvious but unexciting name AOL gives this connection, you can go for something more friendly, such as *Myrtle*. Finally, click Next.

5. AOL will confirm that you are set up to use an ISP or LAN to connect. Click OK.

Notice, in the Select Location field at the bottom of your Sign On window, that your new connection (Myrtle) is showing. You still have the option to connect from the Home connection—incurring the extra charges associated with using AOL's access numbers—if you want or need to.

NOTE

If your ISP or LAN is down and you *really* want to get your e-mail, you can minimize your cost by running an Automatic AOL session using an AOL access number to grab your mail. You'll be charged only for the scant few minutes that you're online fetching your mail, not for a full hour. Just remember to choose Home in the Select Location box before running Automatic AOL.

Now connect to the Internet via your ISP or network. After you have established this connection, go back to AOL's Sign On window and make sure your new ISP/LAN connection (Myrtle) is showing in the Select Location field. Enter your AOL password into the Enter Password field and click Sign On.

WARNING

If you hear the modem shrieking at this point, you're signing on through AOL, not through your ISP. Click Cancel and go back through Steps 1 through 5, above.

BYOA-ize Your Bill

Now you need to change your billing plan to the BYOA option.

NOTE

Your new BYOA billing price will take effect on the date that begins your next billing period. This monthly billing date is based on the date you signed up for AOL in the first place. To figure out your date, go to Help ➤ Accounts and Billing. In the AOL Billing Center window that appears, click Display Billing Date and Price Plan Info (at the bottom left of the screen under the View Your Bill heading). Your next billing date is the first line in the informative table displayed in the Billing Terms Explanation dialog box. This will be the date your BYOA charges will begin—as long as you sign up for BYOA 3 days before that date (72 hours prior to 10 a.m. of that date, to be precise).

Ready to make the switch? Get back to the AOL Billing Center window (Help ➤ Accounts and Billing) and click Change Your Billing Method or Price Plan.

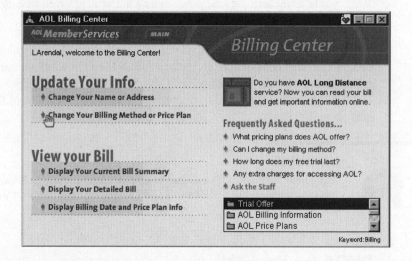

You'll be asked to enter your password, just to be on the safe side; do so and click Continue. Next choose Update Pricing Plan. At the bottom of the resulting Change Price Plan dialog box (under Price Plans), highlight the BYOA option and then click the Select Plan button.

You're done! Don't spend your savings all in one place, now, y'hear?

ACCESS AOL ANYTIME, ANYWHERE

Wouldn't it be great if e-mail were like phone mail? Pick up a phone anywhere in the world, and you can dial into your voicemail and retrieve your messages. What if you could turn on a computer anywhere in the world and get your e-mail messages?

Well, you can! AOL Mail is what makes it all possible. And it's yet another service available to you free—with your AOL membership.

Go Get 'Em with AOL Mail

With AOL Mail you can be anywhere in the world and receive and send your AOL mail from any computer that has Internet access. The interface looks almost exactly like your regular e-mail box, so actually, you already know how to use it! All you need is a computer that's hooked up to the Internet.

NOTE

Of course, there could be compatibility issues—no program runs on every single platform ever invented—but AOL Mail is pretty easygoing. As long as the computer you're using runs at least Internet Explorer 3 or Netscape 3.02 and has Windows 3.1, 95, 98, or NT—or is a Mac—you're in business.

Here's How It Works

You're in Finland meeting your boyfriend's parents for the first time, you need a break from the whole family thing, and you desperately want to read your e-mail because your best friend promised she'd write you every day.

Just sneak into his parents' den, turn on the computer, and connect to the Internet. Navigate to www.aol.com and click AOL Mail. At the AOL Mail Sign-On screen, which looks like a small AOL Sign-On window, enter your screen name and password. Click Enter AOL Mail.

Part III

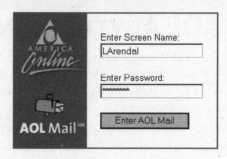

An interim sign-on screen assures you that the connection you are about to make is secure; click the Please Click Here to Complete the Sign-In Process button.

NOTE

You may or may not see a warning at this point. If you do, that's because you, conscientious netizen that you are, have asked your Web browser to tell you when you send private information (such as your password) over the Internet. Rest assured; your password has been secured, protected, and encrypted by AOL. Just click OK.

You're in! You can see your new mail, old mail, and sent mail; write a letter; delete an e-mail; and, after you've read your e-mail, choose to keep it as new.

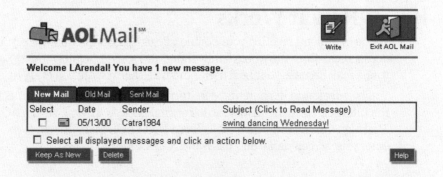

To read a message, just click once on the e-mail subject. From here you can move to the previous or following messages. After you are done reading, you could select any of the messages by clicking the check boxes in the Select column, and then you can either click Keep As New or Delete. Or you could just let the e-mail float to your Old Mail page.

The Old Mail and Sent Mail pages work just like they do in your AOL software; whatever time limit you've set for keeping old e-mails around will be honored by AOL Mail.

You can send e-mail from here, too, but if you don't have an e-mail to reply to, you'd better have your friends' e-mail addresses memorized or written on your Send Postcards To list. You can't access your Address Book, stored cozily on your hard drive, from here.

To return to reality, just click Exit AOL Mail.

WARNING

To keep your connection secure, AOL will boot you off AOL Mail if you dally in one place for more than 30 minutes, so don't plan on writing an e-novel this way.

NUISANCE-FREE AOL?

Yes, Virginia, there is an ad-free, shriek-free, ignoramus-free AOL in your future! This section will tell you how to pleasantize your online experience.

Of course, there are many annoyances—I mean, *features*—that can't be avoided. The AOL Welcome window's presence is one of them; trying to close it is especially annoying—because you can't. (I mean, really, why bother putting the Close button in the upper right corner if it's redundant with the minimize button?) But there are a surprising number of things you can do to rid yourself of pesky noises and people. All you need for these quick fixes is your AOL connection and these instructions!

Here's How It Works

After reading the rest of this section, you should be able to get rid of marketing ads, loud modems, and annoying chatters and IMers.

TIP

You *can* make that Welcome window go *poof* and so be completely nuisance-free—but you need an add-on program to do it. For the straight scoop, see "Power it Up," later in this chapter.

Put an End to Ads

Even US citizens, consumers that we are, enjoy an ad-free moment here and there. And we don't always want to know about the latest version of the automobile status symbol of the moment. Really, we don't.

Luckily, we can turn all advertising off in just a few fell swoops.

You'll have to be online to do this, so sign on now. Once you're on, go to My AOL ➢ Preferences. A dizzying array of options will swim before your eyes. Click Marketing, located on the bottom row.

Purple Sweet Tart–like buttons will tantalize you with the following options:

US Mail from other organizations   ("Select" organizations, that is, that AOL makes your name available to.) You too can receive offers for unwanted items from software to apparel!

US Mail from AOL   Here you can be tempted to shill for AOL or to buy AOL-sponsored material.

Telephone   Do you really want to get a call during dinner about the newest, hottest digital camera?

E-mail   All of the above, but through e-mail.

Pop-up   Very special product and service offers that appear immediately after sign-on.

Additional information   This useful write-up tells you how to avoid marketing campaigns *nationwide* by registering with the Mail Preference Service and Telephone Preference Service.

NOTE

Only master screen names see pop-ups. So if you want to see these but don't want your progeny to, rest easy; AOL has taken care of it already.

To sign up for or, more likely, to get rid of any of the above irritations, simply click the button next to the option you want to declare your preference on. A description of what you are about to prefer (one way or the other) appears; read it and click Continue. An even more detailed discussion about the ramifications of stating a preference can be scrolled through. Notice that your preferences will be respected for one year, after which time you will need to put your foot down again. After all, you could change your mind!

Click the radio button specifying which option you prefer (if you're reading this in eager anticipation, it will probably be the option beginning with *No*), and click OK.

After a dialog box that informs you that your preference has been sent, close out of the preference description, and you're back at the Marketing Preferences window. Go right down the list until you're satisfied with your choices, then close the window and move on to eradicating another annoyance from your life!

NOTE

Notice also that AOL reserves the right to send pop-ups, e-mails, and telephone calls your way, if the information is deemed essential for you to have. Like I said, you can't fix all the, uh, features.

Kill Modem Sounds

Little did you know, you can make your modem louder! Maybe the neighbors in the apartments next door, above you, and below you all need to know when you're signing onto AOL.

Alternatively, you can make your modem quieter—or just turn it off altogether.

If you're online, sign off. If you're on your computer but AOL isn't running, open it now (but don't sign on).

In the Sign On window, click Setup. Keep looking at the bottom of your screen; in the Setup window, click Expert Setup. In the Connection Setup dialog box, click the Devices tab to reveal the connection method(s) you've established. The modem you're using should have a check mark over its icon. Make sure it is highlighted (if it isn't, just click it) and click the Edit button in the lower-right corner. Speaker volume can be adjusted through the drop-down list at the bottom of the Expert Edit Modem dialog box; click the drop-down arrow and choose your poison; off, low, normal, or loud.

When you've made your choice, zoom over to the left side of the dialog box and click OK, then Close. You're home free!

Instant IM Rejection

There are three ways to deal with AOL members who bother you through IMs: report them, ignore them without actively shutting them out, or disallow IMs from them altogether.

To report the miscreant   When you receive an offensive IM, click the Notify AOL button at the bottom of your IM window immediately. Minimize any future IMs from the offender; the messages will stream in, but who can tell?

To ignore an irritant   If the IM isn't offensive and/or you don't feel like reporting the IMer, just minimize the IM window. Any other incoming IMs will appear in their own window(s) (one per screen name), and the IM messages you're ignoring will continue to disappear into your minimized IM window.

To block the bum   Go to My AOL ➤ Buddy List. In the Buddy List window, click the Privacy Preferences button. Here you can allow all IMs, select a few you'll allow through, or block them all. Notice at the bottom of the window that you can block either just Buddy Lists or both Buddy Lists and IMs. Blocking Buddy Lists will prevent your name from showing up on another person's Buddy List when you sign on. Blocking IMs, well, that's what we're here for, right?

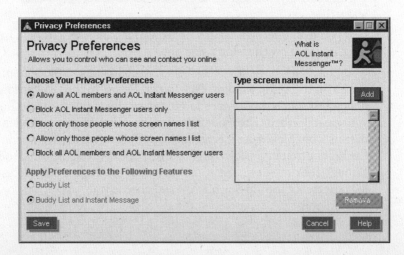

NOTE

You can also block IMs from AOL Instant Messenger users through Buddy List Preferences. Even if you don't block an AIM user outright, you will always have the option to decline incoming AIM messages.

Enjoy the Chat Room

You don't have to put up with other chatters just because they're in your space; chat rooms really can be a good way to dialog about what you're interested in. Following are some hints to help you do just that.

Use a Special Screen Name

If you're going to expose your screen name to the world of online wackos and wackas, some of whom do reside on AOL, don't use your master screen name. Create a second—maybe more playful—screen name so you can lurk and meander wherever your curiosity takes you. This way you won't need to worry about future e-mails and IMs from weirdos while you're conducting serious business with your master screen name. Speaking of which, don't forget to turn off all e-mail and IMs to your chat screen name, unless you enjoy witless and sophomoric exchanges.

To create your chat screen name   Go to My AOL ➤ Screen Names. Click Create a Screen Name and follow the easy instructions.

To block IMs   See *Instant IM Rejection*, earlier in this chapter.

To block e-mail   Go to Mail Center ➤ Mail Controls. Click Set Up Mail Controls, choose the screen name you want to control, and click Edit. Here you can choose from a variety of settings such as: receive and send all e-mails, allow only select people to send you e-mail, block all e-mail, and so on. When you have decided on your e-mail availability, click Save, and then click OK in the confirmation dialog box.

Ignore the Heck Out of 'Em

Even with e-mail and IMs disabled, you'll still run into AOL members who are, shall we say, still finding their place in the world—and in the chat rooms. Fortunately, you don't have to be part of their process of self-exploration and maturation. If you're in a chat room, and a chatter is becoming bothersome, you can shut them out with the Ignore feature. If you ignore them, you won't see their chatter on your screen (and if you've disabled e-mail and IMs to the screen name you're using, you have no worries about hearing from them).

WARNING

Ignore only works as long as the ignoree stays put. If they leave the chat room and then rejoin it, the Ignore spell you put on them will have lifted. Just Ignore them again.

To Ignore a chatter:

1. Notice to the right of the large chat box there is a list of the people currently enjoying the chat room. Double-click the screen name of the ignoree-to-be.

2. In the Information About dialog box, click the check box next to Ignore Member.

Blissful silence ensues. Satisfying, isn't it?

POWER IT UP!

Want more bang for your AOL buck? More oomph per second than you'll know what to do with? Then this is the section for you. Herein are described enhancements you can make to AOL by installing PowerTools, an AOL-approved program that will astonish and delight you, as well as PowerPlus or Power Vault, two similar AOL add-on programs.

PowerTools

There are two versions of this magnificent program, both of which will transform your AOL look and feel—and entire experience. To get a copy of PowerTools Light, go to www.bpssoft.com. Or you can download a copy of PowerTools Pro from keyword **BPS**.

> **PowerTools Pro**   Is super useful for power users who really want to soup up AOL, as well as for guides and hosts.
>
> **PowerTools Light Edition**   Is easier on hard disk space and will go a bit more trippingly than PowerTools Pro.

NOTE

BPS Software recommends that you have at least a Pentium 150 and 32MB RAM in order to run PowerTools Pro. It will function with less, but slowly. If you don't have quite this get-up-and-go in your computer, consider PowerTools Light.

Read on to find out whether PowerTools Pro or Light is for you.

PowerTools Pro

After you have installed PowerTools Pro, just double-click the PowerTools Pro icon on your desktop. It will launch and bring AOL with it.

Even before you sign on, your AOL window will be very different, as you can see in Figure 12.1!

Part iii

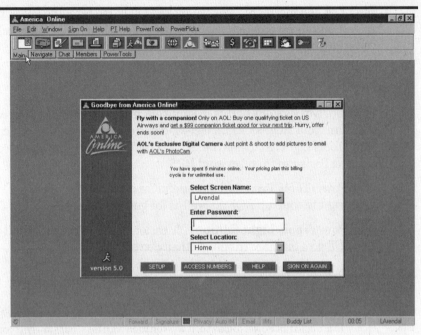

FIGURE 12.1: Egad! I'm surrounded by PowerStuff!

NOTE

You can always launch AOL without PowerTools by double-clicking your AOL desktop icon.

Notice the toolbar tabs; each toolbar page allows you to do extra stuff with your regular AOL functions. The Main toolbar is pretty much as usual, but not entirely:

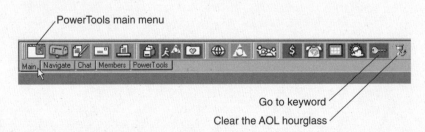

PowerTools main menu

Go to keyword

Clear the AOL hourglass

PowerTools main menu Includes PowerTools Help, customization options, and Sign-Off (no prompt). Sign-Off (no prompt) allows you to sign off AOL without having to deal with the "Are you sure you want to sign off?" dialog box.

Go to Keyword Gives you instant access to other keywords you've gone to as well as to the master keyword list found at keyword **keyword**.

Clear the AOL Hourglass Provides another extra-special PowerPerq; if AOL ever stops you in your tracks with the busy hourglass, just click this button and it'll clear. Whatever you were doing will quit executing, too, but it's usually worth it.

NOTE
You can change what your toolbar displays, so if you'd rather see the text descriptions for a button, you can add those (and you can choose where to add them!) or opt to replace the icons with text. Simply right-click a blank spot on the toolbar and choose Toolbar Options. The Icons Only option is the most compact—and colorful—so that's what you'll see in this chapter.

The Navigate toolbar is really no different from the regular AOL version, but it's prettier:

Enhanced keyword/Web address field

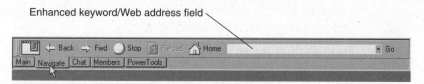

The big enhancement, other than the addition of the PowerTools main menu, is the Keyword/Web Address field drop-down list. Click this drop-down arrow to see precisely the areas and Web pages you've gone to recently (including addresses from earlier online sessions!). You can then navigate back to these places without having to search your memory for the path you took to get there.

The Chat toolbar is entirely fresh:

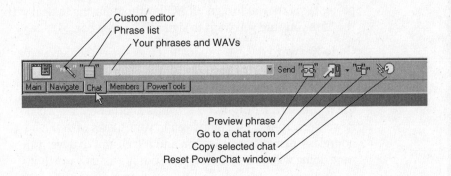

Custom Editor Lets you organize, edit, and add to those phrases in your phrase list. PowerTools supplies its own phrases—from stock chat phrases to quotable quotes.

Phrase List Shows you your list of phrases.

Your Phrases and WAVs Gives you a quick way to pick a phrase (like *be back shortly*) and send it before bolting from your computer to the refrigerator and back.

Preview Phrase Shows you exactly what the phrase you've selected in the Your Phrases and WAVs field looks like, and gives you some tools for modifying it.

Go to a Chat Room Click the drop-down arrow and select Create Your Own Chat to do just that. Realize the true power of this button by using the People Connection (on the Main toolbar) to find a chat room that is completely full. When AOL helpfully informs you that the room is full and offers to take you to a less-crowded alternative, just click the Go to a Chat Room button on the Chat toolbar. PowerTools will bombard this room with attempts to get in until someone leaves, and voilà! You're in!

Copy Selected Chat   Copies the chat you've highlighted; you can then alter it and add it to your list of phrases, send it to someone, or save it for posterity.

Reset PowerChat Window   Reconnects PowerTools to your chat window in case it disconnects.

Your chat window will look different, too; check out Figure 12.2. Most of the new features are handy and self-explanatory. The Options button at top left gives you all sorts of fancy options. You could spend days perfecting your welcome phrase, fonts, and colors; programming your bursts; or picking Hot Words so you can play the PeeWee Herman Word of the Day game (you know, when someone says The Word, everyone screams). The Options drop-down arrow gives you even more versatility, including the ability to switch back to plain ol' AOL chat. The Effects button, which brings up the extra Effects-related buttons you can see at the bottom of Figure 12.2, allows you to add gewgaws and color schemes to your droll sentences.

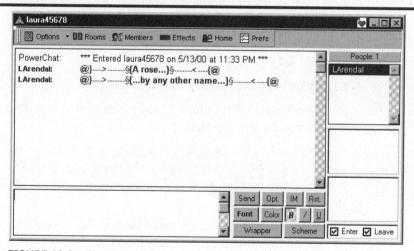

FIGURE 12.2: Chattin' in style

The Members toolbar encourages all sorts of interactive activities:

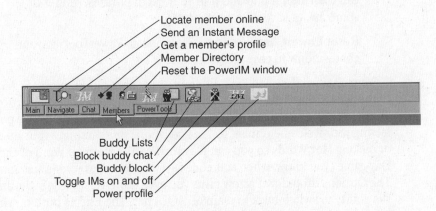

Locate member online
Send an Instant Message
Get a member's profile
Member Directory
Reset the PowerIM window

Buddy Lists
Block buddy chat
Buddy block
Toggle IMs on and off
Power profile

Locate Member Online   Provides a power-enhanced version of the usual Locate Member feature; you can locate someone, send them an IM, or add them to your Buddy List—all from here.

Send an Instant Message   Brings up the Send IM window, with some extra options like immediate access to your canned phrases.

Get a Member's Profile and Member Directory   Are standard.

Reset the PowerIM Window   Reconnects you to PowerTools if you become underpowered.

Buddy Lists   Is also fairly standard, but you do get to have some fun with your buddy names in the Buddy List window; you can assign nicknames, WAVs, and colors to them so they'll stand out in a crowd.

Block Buddy Chat   Is a toggle that blocks or allows chat invitations sent by other AOL members from their Buddy Lists.

Buddy Block   Pops up a colorful version of your Privacy Preferences window for Buddy Lists and IMs. The blocks you can set are the usual ones, but it's sure useful to get to them this easily.

Toggle IMs On and Off   Allows you to click this button to have PowerTools send the *IM off* or *IM on* code to IM central.

Power Profile   Connects you to BPS Software and lets you in on a little add-on that will manage the profiles you collect during your wandering chats.

When you receive an Instant Message, you'll notice immediately that the IM window is powered up now, too, as illustrated in Figure 12.3. If you had more than one incoming IM, each IM window would become accessible via a system of tabs.

Probably the Number One Cool Thing about PowerIMs is that you can type your message and just press Enter on your keyboard to send it. No more clicking Send, no more struggling to remember that the keyboard shortcut is Ctrl+Enter. Just Enter. Like any other normal program.

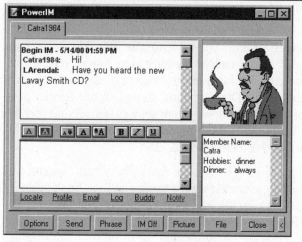

FIGURE 12.3:   PowerIMs show you pictures and profiles for any and all of your IM pals.

The PowerTools toolbar is the grooviest:

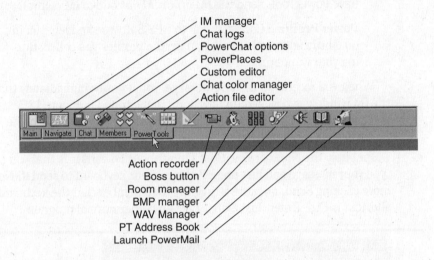

IM manager
Chat logs
PowerChat options
PowerPlaces
Custom editor
Chat color manager
Action file editor

Action recorder
Boss button
Room manager
BMP manager
WAV Manager
PT Address Book
Launch PowerMail

IM Manager   Allows you to customize your IMs. Besides the usual handy extras such as spellchecking, fonts'n'colors, and auto answering, IM Manager also makes it easy to autosave those IMs in logs. The best thing, though, is the priority password feature, which allows you to set a password that you then tell only Very Important AOL Members, who can use it to IM you even when you have IMs blocked.

Chat Logs   Shows you all the chats you've had. You can then transfer all those screen names to your address book or do things like log the time and room count every 15 minutes. I mean, who knew we needed to know that? Lucky for us, Chat Logs has corrected our ignorance.

PowerChat Options   Gets you to the chat options you can access from the Option button within a chat room window, which was described earlier in this section.

PowerPlaces   Is a souped-up Favorite Places, but it doesn't automatically load your faves into it. You can still access your pre-PowerTools favorites from the Main toolbar, but it is easier to just choose Tools ➢ Import AOL Favorite Places (or Tools ➢ Import Internet Explorer Favorites) and access your old friends right here. With PowerPlaces, you can group faves; quickly share faves with other AOLies via IM, chat, or e-mail; and even place fave groups on the menu bar for instant access.

Custom Editor   Is the same as on the Chat toolbar, discussed earlier in this section.

Chat Color Manager   Will make your chat and IM screens very colorful. You can assign fonts and colors to specific screen names, either permanently or for an online session only. This feature can really help a screen name stand out if, for instance, you're chatting with just one or two others in a crowded chat room.

Action File Editor   Lets you edit the actions you've recorded with the Action Recorder.

Action Recorder   Like Microsoft Word's macros, records your mouse movements and clicks so you can assign a shortcut key to an entire sequence of actions and have PowerAOL perform it for you. You can augment your sequence with the non-mouse-able actions (such as Wait) found on the Action Recorder's Custom Actions list.

Boss Button   First, open that spreadsheet you're working on, then open AOL on top of that. When your supervisor gets the urge to roam, just click the Boss Button and any trace of AOL will disappear from your screen—and even from your taskbar. Your boss will never notice the inconspicuous gray and black icon over by your clock, but that's how you'll reactivate AOL after your supervisor has disappeared around the corner. Heh heh.

Room Manager   Shows you all the active chat rooms available to you, as well as those you've grouped in your Favorite rooms list, and gives you the option to go—or knock until you get in. One-stop chatting, right here.

BMP Manager   Helps you track your BMP graphics files that are scattered all over your hard drive so you can access them quickly when you want to insert them into chats, e-mails, or IMs.

WAV Manager   Is like BMP Manager for WAV sound files. Especially cool is WAV Manager's AOL menu, which allows you to assign whatever sound you like to any of AOL's sound-triggering occurrences. "You've Got Mail" goes the way of the dinosaur (sorry, Elwood Edwards)!

Part iii

PT Address Book   Imports and expertly manages all the addresses, photos, nicknames, and e-mails you want to save and group. It also exports your address files to another address book (for instance, in the next version of AOL) or to WordPad for use in other programs and for printing.

Launch PowerMail   Like Launch PowerProfiles on the Chat toolbar, lets you in on the power you can add to your mailbox, for just a small add-on fee.

The PowerTools taskbar, sitting quietly at the bottom of your AOL window, adds some functionality and much one-click access:

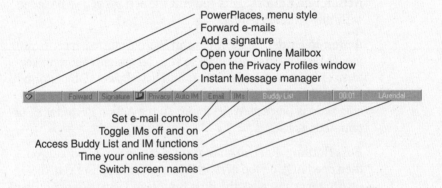

PowerPlaces, menu style
Forward e-mails
Add a signature
Open your Online Mailbox
Open the Privacy Profiles window
Instant Message manager

Set e-mail controls
Toggle IMs off and on
Access Buddy List and IM functions
Time your online sessions
Switch screen names

PowerPlaces   Grants you instant access to the areas and URLs you and PowerTools have added to your PowerPlaces.

Forward   Has three TOS addresses preset so you can effortlessly report harassing or junk e-mails to AOL's TOS folks. You can also add your own e-mail addresses to this list, like the group you often forward humorous e-mails to.

Signature   Adds a serious, funny, or custom-made signature to any e-mail, IM, or posting.

Open your Online Mailbox icon   Does what it says, even if you don't have any unread mail.

Privacy   Opens the Privacy Profiles window discussed earlier in this chapter.

AutoIM   Opens the Instant Message Manager window, discussed earlier in this chapter.

Email Allows you to quickly set who you allow or disallow e-mail from.

IMs Gives you one-click access to the IM on/off toggle, IM Manager, and other handy IM management functions (including Send IM).

Buddy List Accesses your Buddy List and also lets you send IMs. This button will show your buddies' names in blue when they sign on, and in red when they've signed off.

Clock Times your online sessions.

Screen Name Remembers who you are—and allows you to easily switch screen names.

Let me go on about just a few more great features, and then I'll let you go. In the menu bar, you'll notice that PowerTools has given you a few more menu items. Go to PowerTools ≻ Misc ≻ AOL Window List. This window will list way more than the usual nine open windows that fit on the AOL window menu. Merely click the window you want to bring to the top, and it does your bidding.

Now go to your Windows taskbar and click the PowerTools taskbar button. Here you can, among other things, minimize the Upload Status window that appears when you're downloading software, games, attachments, whatever. After this window is minimized, you can do whatever you want. Your AOL session will be a bit slower during downloading, so you may want to stick with simple things like reading and responding to e-mail, but it's still a giant improvement over finding something else to do for 15+ minutes.

Maybe the best thing about PowerTools is the most hidden. You can close the AOL Welcome window simply by going to AOL's Window menu and selecting Hide/Show AOL Welcome Window. Finally, the screen that never dies gets its due!

Well, that just about sums up PowerTools Pro. Your turn to play!

PowerTools Light Edition

PowerTools Light Edition brings with it the following basic features:

Buddy List Lists nicknames, features an always-visible buddy bar, buddy group colors, buddy history list, and special buddy WAVs.

Chat stuff   Organizes WAV files, WAV colors, WAV bursts, delayed WAV bursts, WAV wrappers, and canned phrases; allows multiline chat; and includes the IM window finder.

IMs   Contains priority passwords, features one-window IM management, sending with Enter, auto spellcheck, IM answering machine, IM logs, ignoring, and member searches.

Cool miscellanae   Includes signatures, fast-forwarding for e-mail, and a limited-function custom phrase editor.

If these are enough for you, and/or if your computer won't run Power-Tools Pro efficiently, PowerTools Light Edition is the power tool for you! You can download PowerTools Light Edition from keyword **BPS.**

PowerPlus

PowerPlus (power tools specifically for AOL Instant Messenger) is an AOL add-on program that is similar in many ways to PowerTools. Like any good add-on, PowerPlus adds more fun to your AIM frolic with the usual IM power-ups (spellcheck, multi-IM windows, etc.) as well as some features especially geared toward getting those AIMs across.

Table 12.1 illustrates the differences between IM, AIM, PowerIM, and PowerPlus.

TABLE 12.1: You Say IM, I Say AIM.

TYPE OF INSTANT MESSAGE	DESCRIPTION
IM (instant message)	You have IM capability with AOL, but only AOLies can send and receive IMs.
AIM (AOL Instant Messenger message)	Available free from AOL's Web site, AIM allows AOLies and non-AOLies alike to send and receive instant messages.
PowerIM	Take the plain ol' IM and add PowerTools, a BPS Software product.
PowerPlus	Take your basic AIM and add PowerPlus, another BPS Software product.

The special thing about PowerPlus, though, is that it gives you the ability to send and receive instant messages from your AIM buddies—even if they or you are offline. You can even opt for a WAV file to alert you when you have buddy mail waiting for you.

To wield the true power of PowerPlus (after you have installed AOL Instant Messenger), you can download the PowerPlus program from keyword **BPS**.

PowerVault

A close relative of PowerTools, the cleverly named PowerVault will get you leaping about AOL and the Internet with ease, plus give you a safe place to archive information.

With PowerVault, you can launch AOL and get onto any Web site (even those that require your login and password) with one command. In addition, you can back up and restore anything, as well as encrypt myriad AOL features, such as your Personal Filing Cabinet.

You can even remind yourself to change your password once every two weeks—and then not bother to remember your new one. In fact, you don't have to remember the passwords for any of your screen names, thanks to PowerVault's automatic screen name switching. Just remember your password to PowerVault, and it will take care of the rest.

You can download PowerVault from keyword **BPS**.

WHAT'S NEXT?

Now that you've learned how to get around the Web using AOL and its associated power tools, we're going to show you how to surf from the comfort of your favorite recliner, using WebTV.

Chapter 13
WEBTV

Have you ever dreamed about lounging in front of your television, comfy in your classic La-Z-Boy Dreamtime Reclina-Rocker, a profusion of high-fat/low-nutrition snacks and beverages within arm's reach, and simultaneously surfing the Internet? Me neither, but in this chapter, you'll discover how Microsoft's WebTV and WebTV Network Service are making those nondreams a virtual reality for more than 700,000 subscribers in the United States, Canada, and Japan.

With WebTV you can surf the World Wide Web using your television instead of a computer. You can also maintain up to six e-mail accounts and have access to thousands of discussion groups. In addition, you can monitor what your kids or grand-kids are doing on the Web.

Even if you know absolutely nothing about the Internet, computers, or the cost of microprocessor chips in Singapore, you can be accessing the Internet, receiving junk e-mail, get-rich-quick schemes, and virus hoaxes within minutes of using WebTV. Sounds like a dream come true, doesn't it?

∙ ∙

Adapted from *Mr. Modem's Internet Guide for Seniors* by Richard A. Sherman
ISBN 0-7821-2580-8   415 pages $19.99

WebTV is an excellent choice if you're not particularly interested in learning about computers. And if that's the way you feel, you're in very good company. But just because you may not be interested in computers doesn't mean you're out of the technological loop. Nor does it mean that you cannot communicate via e-mail with your children, grandchildren, friends, and former neighbors. The old neighborhood that physically may be thousands of miles away is always just around the corner on the Internet.

The process of setting up WebTV is as simple as plugging in the phone, hooking up the TV, and pressing the power button on the remote control unit. But first, you'll need to decide which WebTV service is right for you. Decisions, decisions, decisions.

CLASSIC OR PLUS?

WebTV is available in two popular flavors, WebTV Classic and WebTV Plus. WebTV Plus is a bit more expensive than WebTV Classic, but well worth the extra expense. Mr. Modem's rule of thumb when purchasing computers and related equipment is to purchase the best equipment— meaning newest, fastest, most-current-but-will-not-be-obsolete-next-Thursday—that your budget will comfortably permit. The important word here is *comfortably*.

Let's pause for a combination philosophical moment and reality check. Face it. Despite all the hoopla, accessing the Internet isn't a necessity of life. So let's be sure to keep this entire phenomenon in perspective. It's not worth taking out a second mortgage or selling the family kitty to obtain a computer or WebTV. In the overall scheme of things, it's just not that important. It's fun, it's convenient, and it's even kind of groovy, as we hipsters say, but it's not a necessity of life. Thus concludes today's Shermanette. Go in peace, my cyberfriend.

Okay, back to Classic versus Plus. Without going into mind-numbing detail, Plus is an upgrade from Classic—not that there's anything wrong with Classic—and the Plus user typically has a different focus than that of the Classic user.

WebTV Classic offers everything you need to get started. If you think of the differences between Classic and Plus in terms of buying a car, WebTV Classic is your basic transportation. It will transport you from Point A to Point B in comfort and safety. But wouldn't it be nice to have power seats, quadraphonic sound, maybe a little sunroof or perhaps more horsepower so you can rev the engine and impress/annoy the neighbors?

Of course it would! And that's why the good folks who offer WebTV include a number of upgrades in WebTV Plus.

Plus is really for those individuals who are interested in combining television and the Internet. For example, Plus features scrolling TV listings, a little TV window so you can watch TV while on the Web, and actual links or connections between TV shows and Web sites—"yo, Vanna!" The Plus processor provides more horsepower than the Classic, it has more memory, the modem is faster, and there's a larger hard drive.

AUTHOR'S LOOPHOLE

WebTV is continually evolving and improving, so be sure to check with your local consumer electronics store for the most current configurations available and/or additional differences between WebTV Classic and Plus. You can also visit http://www.webtv.com.

But if you can visit that Web site, that means you have access to the Internet, so perhaps you're just patronizing me by reading this chapter. Be honest, now. Are you reading this because you really want to or are you just doing it for me? Please, don't do it for me. I'll be fine. Go on, read ahead. Have fun. You have your whole book in front of you. I'll be fine. Really.

EQUIPMENT

WebTV-based Internet terminals and receivers are available from companies like Sony, Philips, and Mitsubishi at finer consumer electronics stores hither and yon, which is just a folksy way of saying "nationwide."

Only four pieces of equipment are needed to use WebTV: the WebTV terminal and remote control, a keyboard, and a few wires and cables so you can spend hours of quality time untangling them like most computer users do everyday. These cables, annoying as they may be, connect your WebTV terminal to your telephone line, your TV, and for you technical masochists, even your VCR. (You'll need WebTV Plus to be able to connect your VCR, though.)

When shopping for WebTV, you will learn that the keyboard is an optional item. Technically, it is an optional item, but trust me, it really isn't. You don't want to try to write e-mail using the on-screen keyboard.

That would be like trying to drive with three wheels on your car. Can you do it? Sure, you can. But it wouldn't be the most pleasurable driving experience of your life, so it would be best avoided if possible.

The Plus keyboard and the remote unit control TV functions, which will permit you to perform the always-popular WebTV "flip" between the Web and regular TV. If channel surfing drives your spouse or housemate crazy, just wait until the added dimension of flipping between television channels and the Web is within your grasp!

Cables, Wires, and Other Tangly Things

Let me state at the outset that I really don't like cables and wires. The good news is that connecting WebTV is about as foolproof as it gets.

There are only two types of cables and wires required: telephone and audio/video—or "A/V," as we who try in vain to impress our friends and neighbors call it. The telephone wire stretches from the WebTV terminal to the wall jack—or to the wall, Jack, as the case may be.

WARNING

Danger, geekspeak ahead!

To connect the WebTV system to your TV, your TV will need either an RCA jack (those are the round ones) or an S-Video input cable—the ones that have five or six pins.

The colorful cables—red and white for audio, yellow for video—are used for moving audio and video from your WebTV terminal to your TV. If you have a VCR, you'll be running the audio and video to the VCR first, then from the VCR to the TV. Everybody sing, "The headbone's connected to the neck bone; the neck bone's connected to the collarbone...."

WebTV Plus has a few additional cables and wires because the Plus terminal has a TV tuner lurking within it. You can hook cable directly into the antenna coax input thingy (technical term), which is cable-ready. Your cable-converter box can also plug into the coax input.

All this cable and wiring stuff sounds a lot worse than it is. WebTV, Classic or Plus, is about as close to plug-and-play as nickels in a slot machine.

For Whom the Ma Bell Tolls

Hooking up your WebTV to the telephone is easy. You do not need to have another telephone jack installed, so when the door-to-door telephone jack salesman comes calling, don't be intimidated. All you need to do is use the little splitter device thoughtfully included with your WebTV system to plug into your existing telephone jack. Plug the phone into one side and your WebTV into the other. Voilà!

The first time you power up and connect, your WebTV system will dial an 800 number to locate the closest access provider to your location. Configuring the system to use this number in the future is done automatically, so don't be concerned about it. For most folks, connecting to the Internet will be a local phone call. Documentation packaged with your WebTV will explain how to check first by using what's called the Phone Lookup Utility or PLU for TLA (Three-Letter Acronym) enthusiasts.

WebTV Networks also provides an optional service called OpenISP, which permits you to use the local or national Internet service provider (ISP) of your choice for access to the Internet. This comes in handy if Internet access would require a long-distance call using the access number provided by WebTV Networks. You don't want to be incurring long-distance charges every time you log on. The price of the OpenISP service is in addition to your ISP monthly charges.

Options and Accessories

It has often been said, that what distinguishes us humans from other members of the animal kingdom is our ability to accessorize. Nowhere is that truer than with WebTV. A plethora of accessories awaits your technology budget:

Wireless Keyboard   Though offered as an option, I would strongly recommend purchasing a WebTV-compatible wireless keyboard. The keyboard works by infrared, so you can hold it on your lap or use it just about anywhere without getting tangled up in cables.

RF Adapter   An RF adapter is available for WebTV Plus, which allows you to connect your WebTV Plus unit to older televisions without an RCA jack. An RCA jack is the type of jack found on most stereo speakers.

Printers   The WebTV Classic terminal requires a printer adapter, which is available only for the Philips Magnavox system and is compatible with the Hewlett-Packard DeskJet 400 and 600 Series. The receiver for WebTV Plus service has a built-in printer port, which is compatible with Hewlett-Packard DeskJet 400 and 600 Series, and the Canon BJC-80, 200, 600, and 4000 Series BubbleJet printers. The HP670TV color printer is specially designed for WebTV.

THE PRICE OF ADMISSION

WebTV is a very cost-effective method of joining your friends and family already frolicking in the Internet surf. But like all things in life, there is no free lunch, so you need to be aware of a few ongoing costs before deciding if WebTV is for you. The good news, however, is that WebTV is just a fraction of the price of a computer. A WebTV terminal is less than $200 and includes everything you need to cruise the Internet while sitting in your classic La-Z-Boy Dreamtime Reclina-Rocker.

WebTV Classic Pricing

Pricing (current at publication date) for WebTV Classic service on newer Internet receiver models (such as Philips Magnavox MAT965 and Sony INT-W150) is $21.95/month. WebTV Classic OpenISP service for these receivers is an additional $11.95/month. This charge is in addition to your ISP monthly charge.

WebTV Classic service on other Internet receiver models (such as Philips Magnavox MAT960 and Sony INT-W100) is $19.95/month. WebTV Classic OpenISP service for these receivers is an additional $9.95/month. This charge is in addition to your ISP monthly charge.

WebTV Plus Pricing

Pricing (current at publication date) for WebTV Plus service is $24.95/month. WebTV Plus OpenISP service is an additional $14.95/month. This charge is—let's say it together—in addition to your ISP monthly charge.

Billing

Every WebTV account requires a monthly subscription to WebTV Networks. A variety of subscriptions are available and average approximately $20/month. This service will be charged to a credit card—preferably your own—by the good folks at WebTV Networks. You will be requested to provide credit card information when setting up your WebTV equipment.

NOTE

Once you're online, please visit http://www.webtv.com for more information.

WHAT'S NEXT?

Now that you know all about the wonders of WebTV, we're going to completely forget you've got it! That's right, the next chapter will introduce you to the wonders of palm organizers, and how to use them to access e-mail and the Web.

Part III

Chapter 14

THE WIRELESS WONDER: ACCESSING E-MAIL AND THE WEB WITH YOUR PALM VII

You can set up any Palm organizer to send and receive e-mail and make an Internet connection, but it takes some doing. You need to get a modem, configure your Palm device to work with it, set up an account with an ISP, configure your Palm to work with the account, get e-mail and Internet software, and install that on your organizer. Then you're finally ready to link up with the outside world. Phew!

That approach is really your only alternative if you have any Palm organizer other than the VII. Fresh from the factory, your Palm VII has everything you need to send and receive e-mail and access the Internet.

Adapted from *Mastering Palm Organizers*
by Gayle Ehrenman/Michael Zulich
ISBN 0-7821-2569-7   676 pages $29.99

The Palm VII communicates through the Palm.Net service, which functions as an ISP devoted to the Palm VII. All you have to do is activate your Palm.Net service and you're ready to go.

MANAGING YOUR WIRELESS ACCOUNT

There are some things you can do through the Palm.Net application that comes installed on your Palm VII. But there are some Palm.Net account functions you can't control from your organizer. For those, you'll need to turn to the Palm.Net Web site (www.palm.net). Palm VII users should check in to this site regularly to find out what's new with their wireless service. We make it a regular stop on our surfing safaris.

The Palm.Net Web Site

If you haven't figured it out by now, the Palm.Net name covers multiple related applications. Palm.Net is the name of the network that provides wireless Internet service for the Palm VII; it's the name of the query application that lets you track your service usage from your Palm VII; and it's a Web site where you can manage your account, find new PQAs to download, and basically do anything you can do from the Palm.Net query application—plus a whole lot more.

You can find coverage maps on the Palm.Net Web site, which make it easy to figure out if wireless service is available in your area (see Figure 14.1). You can also check the status of your account from the site and even change your service plan and billing information. To perform these account management tasks, you'll need to log in with the username and password you created when activating your Palm.Net service. After that, making changes is easy.

There are also a couple of things you can do from the Palm.Net Web site that you can't do any other way—such as designating an address to receive copies of all your outgoing messages and deleting blocks of messages. You carry out both of these actions through the My Account area of the Web site. You can see this area in Figure 14.2.

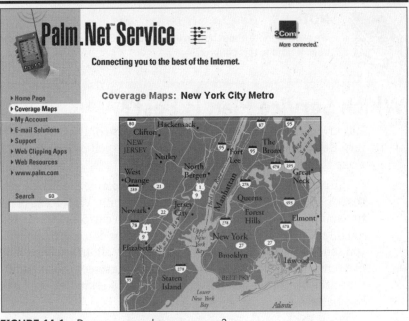

FIGURE 14.1: Does your area have coverage?

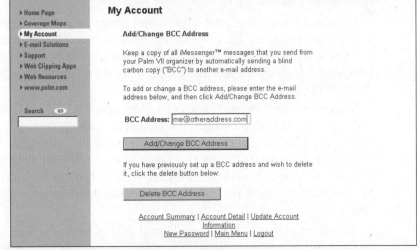

FIGURE 14.2: Specify a forwarding address.

Part iii

NOTE

We explain more about how to use the Blind Carbon Copy feature and why you need it later in this chapter.

Which Service Plan Is Best?

Palm.Net service is either incredibly expensive or the bargain of the century, depending on how you use it. We'll help you pick a service plan and make the most of your kilobytes.

Initially, there were two Palm.Net service plans: the Basic Plan, which costs $9.99 for 50KB or approximately 150 Palm VII screens of data transmission; and the Expanded Plan, which costs $24.99 for 150KB or roughly 450 Palm VII screens of data transmission. Each kilobyte of data you send or receive in excess of your monthly allotment costs $.30. So, five screens of information (at about 1KB per screen) costs $1.50. That's about the average number of screens you're likely to traverse just to check baseball scores.

These plans work just fine for light-to-moderate wireless communication use, but you'll spend big money with these plans if you send lots of e-mail, check the sports news daily, or execute more than a couple of stock trades a month.

If you plan to use your Palm VII as your primary communications tool, you'll want to look into the newly added Volume Plan. This one costs $39.99 per month for 300KB of usage, which works out to around 900 screens of information; you'll still pay $.30 per KB for every bit beyond the monthly allotment.

Most users would do well to start with the minimal level of service and see how much of their monthly transmission allotment they use. You'll need to do this for about two months before you'll get a clear picture of your wireless usage—it's the new toy factor at work. We blew almost a full month's worth of transmissions the first week we had our Palm VII, just because it was so much fun. After that, we tapered off to a more reasonable level.

Whichever plan you choose, you'll want to keep a couple of fundamental Palm.Net principles in mind. Remember that messages you send and receive count against your kilobyte allotments, as do Web clipping requests and the information that returns from those requests. Opening a Palm query application (PQA) doesn't usually incur you any charges, because those applications are stored locally. (See "Web Clipping with Your Palm VII" later in this chapter for more on how PQAs operate.)

So, you probably should be selective in who you give your Palm.Net address to and limit its usage for checking your mail from other e-mail addresses. If you do need to interact with your standard, non-Palm.Net e-mail account, be sure to use the filtering tools built into both your desktop software and third-party Palm-based mail tools to keep from downloading anything but the most important messages. If you're like us and receive about 50 messages per day at just one e-mail address (and we have several addresses), you can easily exhaust a full month's service allotment in just one day if you're not careful. We've taken to filtering out the advertisements, newsletters, and mailing list messages before downloading mail to our Palm VII. Sometimes, we'll filter out everything except mail originating from a particular user, such as our editor.

Beyond filtering your mail, you might want to consider using your Palm.Net account for sending messages, but redirect replies to an alternate, desktop PC–based mail address. We explain how to set this up in "The Inbox," later in this chapter.

SENDING AND RECEIVING MAIL WITH IMESSENGER

If you've ever used an e-mail application, whether on your desktop PC or even the Mail application on the Palm, you'll have no trouble using the iMessenger wireless e-mail application on the Palm VII. iMessenger follows the basic organizing principles of every e-mail application on the planet.

The biggest difference between sending and receiving e-mail on the Palm VII and on your desktop PC is that on the Palm VII, you have to raise the antenna to make a connection. Other than that, the differences are minimal.

iMessenger Basics

Like most desktop-based e-mail applications, iMessenger is organized into a series of folders. There's an Inbox, where your newly received messages go; an Outbox, where messages wait to be sent; a Deleted folder, where the messages you deleted from the other folders linger; a Filed folder, where the messages you save are stored; and a Draft folder, where messages in progress are held. Each of these folders appears as a list, like the list view of the Mail application.

By default, iMessenger opens to the Inbox. You access the other folders the same way you change categories in other Palm applications:

1. Tap the pull-down menu in the upper-right corner of the screen. You'll see a list of folders, as in Figure 14.3.

2. Tap the folder you want to open in the list.

FIGURE 14.3: They're folders, not categories.

The biggest difference between the folders in iMessenger and the categories used by other applications is that the iMessenger folders are uneditable. You can't rename them, delete them, or add new ones. And, you can't arbitrarily move messages from one folder to another—with the exception of moving messages from Inbox to Filed or from Draft to Outbox.

Like other Palm applications, iMessenger has a Menu Bar and some options you can set. The two menus available from the Inbox are Message and Options. Under the Message menu, which you can see in Figure 14.4, you have only one choice—Purge Deleted.

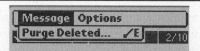

FIGURE 14.4: The Message menu

The Purge Deleted option comes in handy because deleting a message in iMessenger doesn't really make it go away. It just moves it into the Deleted folder. If you want to rid yourself of messages from the Deleted folder, you have to use Purge Deleted. Just choose it from the Message menu, and those useless messages will be gone for good.

TIP

The Deleted folder has a 50K maximum capacity. When Deleted reaches capacity, it automatically removes the oldest files in the folder from your system. This is the only time you don't have to purge files to get rid of them.

The Options menu offers more choices. Here, you can choose a font for displaying message lists (it works the same as in other Palm applications, so we won't explain it here), set Preferences, choose to Show Log, or find out About iMessenger. You can see the Options menu in Figure 14.5.

FIGURE 14.5: The Options menu

Preferences lets you decide how messages are displayed in the various message lists; any choices you make here will apply to all the iMessenger folders. You can see the Preferences dialog box in Figure 14.6.

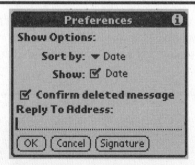

FIGURE 14.6: iMessenger Preferences

Preferences gives you the option to sort messages by:

▶ Date, which sorts messages by date in descending order, showing the most recent message at the top of the screen.

▶ Sender, which sorts messages by the sender's e-mail name, displaying messages in ascending alphabetical order based on the first word of the From field of a message.

▶ Subject, which sorts messages by subject in ascending alphabetical order.

By default, the message list includes a date column in its display (as in Figure 14.7). You can turn off this feature or reactivate it by tapping the Show Date check box in the Preferences dialog box.

iMessenger 3/6	▼ Inbox	
— gehrenman...	Fw: PMN New...	4:44p
— gehrenman...	Important m...	4:43p
— Mike.Zulich...	RE: Hello	10/5
✓ mzulich@wo...	Re: Hi from A...	9/13
✓ support@pal...	Welcome to...	7/20
✓ custcare@p...	Welcome	2/10

(New) (Check & Send ⟨)

FIGURE 14.7: Showing the date

Show Date displays the date for messages downloaded on a different day than the one they were sent, or the time for messages downloaded on the same day they were sent. You may want to turn off this option to leave more room for displaying the From and Subject fields.

From the Preferences dialog box, you can also choose to confirm all deletions. Tapping the Confirm Deleted Message box activates this option. You'll see a confirmation dialog box when you choose to delete a message, as in Figure 14.8.

Delete Message

(?) **Delete this message?**

(Yes)   (No)

FIGURE 14.8: Are you sure you want to delete that message?

You'll also notice a Reply To Address line in the Preferences dialog box. This option lets you reroute replies to your messages to any e-mail address that you specify. Any messages you send from iMessenger will list your Palm.Net address in the From field. People who choose to reply to your message will automatically be sending messages back to this address, unless you redirect your mail using the Reply To Address option. To specify another address for replies, from the iMessenger Preferences dialog box:

1. Tap the edit line under the words Reply To Address.

2. Use Graffiti or the on-screen keyboard to enter the address where you want to receive replies to your messages. For example, you would enter me@anotheraddress.com (see Figure 14.9).

FIGURE 14.9:   Redirect replies to save money.

3. Tap OK in the Preferences dialog box to accept this address and return to the message list.

There's one last option you can configure through the Preferences dialog box, though it's a bit hidden. Next to the OK and Cancel command buttons at the bottom of the screen, there's a third button labeled Signature. This button lets you specify a signature that you can add to messages you create. This signature can be different from the one you set in the Mail application. Also, your signature isn't automatically added to every message you create; you must choose to include it on a message-by-message basis. We explain how to add a signature to a message in the section on creating messages later in this chapter.

To create a signature, with the iMessenger Preferences dialog box open:

1. Tap the Signature button at the bottom of the screen. This will open up the Signature screen.

2. Enter the text of your signature using Graffiti or the on-screen keyboard. Your text can be as long or short as you like. You can see an example of a signature in Figure 14.10.

3. When you're satisfied with the text of your signature, tap Done to save the text. This will bring up the Signature dialog box, which explains how to add the signature you just created to your messages.

Signature

Gayle Ehrenman
Co-Author of Mastering The Palm
Organizer, Sybex Publishing

(Done) (Cancel)

FIGURE 14.10: Put your signature on the dotted line.

4. Tap OK to close this dialog box and return to the Preferences dialog box.

That covers everything you can do through the Preferences dialog box, but there are two other choices on the Options menu. These are Show Log, which displays a record of your most recent wireless transaction (see Figure 14.11) and About iMessenger, which displays the version number of the iMessenger application installed on your Palm VII.

FIGURE 14.11: What happened the last time you logged on?

The Inbox

By default, iMessenger opens to the Inbox message list screen. This screen displays a list of all the messages you've downloaded (except for those you've filed). It shows the e-mail address of the message sender, the subject of the message, and optionally, the date or time the message was sent. As you can see in Figure 14.12, messages you haven't read yet have a dash in the far-left column. Messages you have read are marked with a check. There is a third symbol you won't see in the Inbox—a diamond. This is used to indicate a message you created, so you'll see it only in the Outbox, Filed, Draft, and Deleted folders.

iMessenger 3/6		▼ Inbox
— gehrenman...	Fw: PMN New...	4:44p
— gehrenman...	Important m...	4:43p
— Mike.Zulich...	RE: Hello	10/5
✔ mzulich@wo...	Re: Hi from A...	9/13
✔ support@pal...	Welcome to...	7/20
✔ custcare@p...	Welcome	2/10

(New) (Check & Send ⫶)

FIGURE 14.12: The Inbox message list

From this screen, you can create new messages, open a message to read it, check for new messages, and set preferences for iMessenger (which we just finished explaining).

TIP

Tap on the checkmark or dash next to the sender column to see a pop-up menu of commands you can carry out on this message from within the Inbox message list. Your choices (which you can see in Figure 14.13) include File and Delete Message. Tapping on File will move the message from your Inbox to the Filed folder; tapping on Delete Message will move the message to the Deleted folder.

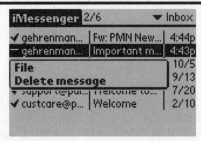

FIGURE 14.13: File that message the easy way.

Creating and Sending Messages

Creating and sending messages with iMessenger couldn't be easier. You don't need to raise the Palm VII's antenna to access iMessenger or to create a new message. But you must raise the antenna when you're ready to send your messages.

To create a new message, with the iMessenger application open to the Inbox message list:

1. Tap on the New command button at the bottom left of the screen. This will open the New Message screen. The To field will be highlighted.

2. You need to designate a recipient for your message. You can either enter their e-mail address using Graffiti or the on-screen keyboard, or you can look up a name from your Address Book.

3. To use the Look Up feature, tap on the Menu soft button to open the Menu Bar, then choose Options ➤ Look Up. This will take you to the Look Up screen, which you can see in Figure 14.14. Look Up will display only those entries from your Address Book that include an e-mail address.

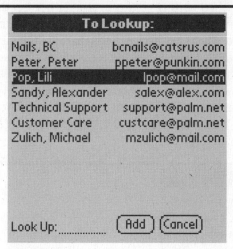

To Lookup:

Nails, BC	bcnails@catsrus.com
Peter, Peter	ppeter@punkin.com
Pop, Lili	lpop@mail.com
Sandy, Alexander	salex@alex.com
Technical Support	support@palm.net
Customer Care	custcare@palm.net
Zulich, Michael	mzulich@mail.com

Look Up: .... ⟨ Add ⟩ ⟨ Cancel ⟩

FIGURE 14.14: Look up an address.

4. Scroll though the Look Up list using the scroll button or the on-screen scroll arrows until you reach the name you want. Tap the name to select it (you'll see a black bar over it to show that it's selected).

5. Tap the Add button to add this e-mail address to your message. This will return you to the New Message screen, where the name you selected will appear on the To line.

TIP

To add multiple recipients, follow step 2 or steps 3 and 4. If you enter names manually, make sure to separate them with a comma. If you add names via Look Up, the commas will be added automatically.

6. Tap the line next to Subj to add a subject for your message, using Graffiti or the on-screen keyboard.

Part III

7. Tap the line next to Body to compose the body of your message. Again, you can use Graffiti or the on-screen keyboard to complete this task. You can edit your message using the standard cut, copy, and paste functions accessible from the Edit menu.

8. When you're finished writing your message, either tap the Check & Send button at the bottom left of the screen or tap the Outbox button (next to Check & Send) to move the message to your Outbox. From there, the message will be sent the next time that you log on to Palm.Net. If you choose Check & Send, the Palm VII will log on to Palm.Net, check for new messages, and send the message you just created. If you choose Outbox, you'll see the Send Later dialog box, as shown in Figure 14.15.

FIGURE 14.15: This message can wait.

9. If you'd rather forget about this message for a while, tap the Cancel command button. You'll see the Save Draft dialog box, as in Figure 14.16. If you tap Yes in this dialog box, your message will be moved to the Draft folder. If you tap No, the message will be deleted. Tapping Cancel will take you right back to the New Message screen, so you can work on your message some more.

FIGURE 14.16: Save it or trash it?

TIP

If you've moved a message to the Outbox, but changed your mind about it, don't panic. You can choose to delete the message, edit it some more, or move it back into the Draft folder for future consideration. Go to the Outbox message list by tapping the drop-down folder list in the upper-right corner of the screen, then tap the diamond shape at the left of the recipient's name for the message you want to alter. (The diamond shape is used to indicate a message you composed.) This will bring up a pop-up menu of choices. From that menu, tap Move to Draft, Edit, or Delete message, depending on what you want to do. If you choose Edit, the message will open in a New Message screen.

But wait, before you send off that message, don't forget to add your signature—the one you created through the Preferences dialog box. To add your signature, with the message you just created open:

1. Tap the screen at the point in the body of the message where you want your signature to appear. In general, this will be at the very end of the message.

2. Tap the Menu soft button to open the Menu Bar.

3. From the Menu Bar, choose Options ➤ Add Signature (see Figure 14.17). The signature text you specified will appear in the body of the message.

Part iii

FIGURE 14.17: Paste in your signature.

TIP

You can also add a signature by entering the Graffiti command stroke, followed by a Graffiti Z.

Checking for New Messages

The best part about e-mail is getting messages. With iMessenger, the process of downloading new messages is simple—it's hard to get it wrong, as long as you remember to raise the antenna of your Palm VII before you try to retrieve your mail.

The process works virtually the same way it does in any standard desktop e-mail package. But there are a few things you should know.

What You Can't Do with iMessenger

From an organizational perspective, iMessenger may look just like a desktop e-mail application, but it has some functional limitations those applications do not. These limitations are not oversights on the part of the Palm developers; rather, they've been put into place specifically to minimize the strain on iMessenger and the Palm VII's wireless communication capabilities. Here's a rundown on the limitations:

Message Length   iMessenger was designed to work with short messages. It can completely download messages with 500 or fewer readable characters. For messages with 500–50,000 characters, it downloads the first 500 characters and tells you how many characters are left to download. You can choose to download as much of the rest or the message as you like, or just ignore it. Messages with more than 50,000 characters are returned to sender as undeliverable—you will not receive any notification.

Download Capacity   iMessenger can download only a maximum of 60,000 characters in a single wireless transaction. If you have too many messages (or one that's too long) to download at once, you'll have to log back on to Palm.Net to retrieve the rest. You have 30 days from when you start downloading a long message to retrieve the remainder. After that, it's deleted from the Palm.Net network.

Distribution Lists   iMessenger offers only a To field; it does not support CC or BCC for messages you create or receive. If messages you receive use the unsupported fields, iMessenger tacks the names from those fields on to the end of the To list. Your address will always appear first in any distribution list. Sometimes, though, a distribution list may be truncated. This is because iMessenger allots a maximum of 300 of the first 500 characters to the distribution list. (A maximum of 100 characters of the first 500 goes toward the Subject field, and the remaining 100 characters are given over to the body of the message.) Any characters beyond the 300 allotted to the distribution list will be cut off; this is indicated by an ellipsis at the end of the distribution list.

Attachments   iMessenger doesn't do attachments. If someone sends you a message with a plain old ASCII text file attachment, iMessenger will append that text at the end of the body of the message. Other types of attachments just don't download; you'll get a warning that the message has a non-downloadable attachment when you open the message it belonged with.

Now that we've gotten all the technical stuff out of the way, let's start downloading mail.

To check for new messages, from the Inbox message list, just tap the Check & Send button at the bottom of the screen. This will download any messages waiting for you on the Palm.Net network, and send any messages you have queued up in the Outbox.

You'll see a Transaction Progress dialog box (as in Figure 14.18), which will let you know if your Palm VII succeeded in making a connection and whether it completed the Check & Send operation.

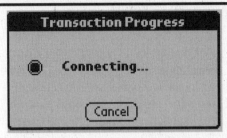

FIGURE 14.18: Progress in the making

Since iMessenger downloads no more than 10 messages at a time, the Transaction Progress dialog box will let you know if there are more messages waiting for you on the network.

You can tap the Cancel button at any time during a wireless transaction to end it. Keep in mind, though, that any messages downloaded before you cancel the connection will count against your monthly kilobyte allotment. So think before you check!

NOTE

You'll also see the Check & Send button in the list screen for all the other iMessenger folders. It works the same way all the time.

Reading Messages

When iMessenger finishes downloading messages, they go directly into your Inbox. All these messages are downloaded in compressed format to help them get to you a little bit quicker; the messages are automatically converted to an uncompressed format when you open them for reading.

To read a message, tap the message you want to read from the Inbox list screen. A full message screen will open. At the top of the message, you'll notice the header. By default, all you'll see is an abbreviated header displaying just the From and Subject lines.

Notice the two icons in the upper right corner of the screen—we're referring to the two small boxes with the horizontal lines on them (see Figure 14.19). These are the header icons.

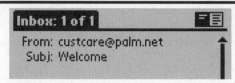

FIGURE 14.19: The long and short of it

The icon with just two lines on it, which will be highlighted when you first open a message, is the Abbreviated Header icon. The one filled with lines is the Complete Header icon. Tap this icon now to see the full header for the message you have open.

With the Complete Header option active, you'll see not just the From and Subject lines, but also the To line and the Date, as in Figure 14.20.

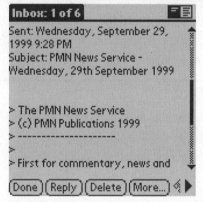

FIGURE 14.20: All the header info you could ask for

The Complete Header takes up a lot of screen real estate, but allows you to see everyone the message was sent to. However, in most cases, the Abbreviated Header will provide all the information you really need, and allow more of your message's body text to be displayed and read at a glance.

If your message is too long to fit on a single screen, you can scroll to see the rest by tapping the scroll bar along the right side of the screen or by using the Scroll button.

You can move to the previous message in the Inbox list by tapping on the leftmost of the two arrows in the bottom-right corner of the screen. Tapping the arrow to the right takes you to the next message in the list.

TIP

You can open and navigate through messages in the other folders using these same techniques.

When you read a message that's longer than 500 characters, you'll see a button labeled More at the bottom of the screen, next to the Previous and Next navigation arrows. You can see what we mean in Figure 14.20 above.

Tap the More button and you'll see the Retrieve More dialog box. What you see in this box will depend on how many more characters remain to be downloaded. For messages with fewer than 500 characters remaining, the Retrieve More dialog box will detail just how many more characters remain, and provide two buttons: Get Rest and Cancel. Tapping Get Rest will download the remainder of the message; tapping Cancel will leave the rest undownloaded and return you to the message screen.

If your message has more than 500 characters left to download, the Retrieve More dialog box will look more like the one in Figure 14.21.

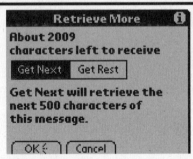

FIGURE 14.21: The text just keeps coming.

You'll still see how many characters are left to download, but you'll have the choice to Get Next, which retrieves the next 500 characters, or Get Rest, which downloads the remainder of the message. And, of course, you can choose to Cancel and forget the whole thing.

TIP

Unless you're absolutely certain that you need the full text of that long message, don't download it all. You're paying for every KB you download, one way or another.

No matter how long the message is that you're reading, you'll see Done, Reply, and Delete buttons at the bottom of every message screen.

Tap Done when you're finished reading the message. This will return you to the Inbox message list screen (or the list screen for whatever folder you're working in).

If you want to get rid of the message, tap Delete. Unless you turned off the Confirm Deleted Message option in the Preferences dialog box, you'll see a Delete Message confirmation box. From this box, tap Yes to move the message into the Deleted folder or tap No to leave the message where it is.

If you want to file the message, tap the Menu soft button to open the Menu Bar, then choose Message ➤ File. Alternately, you can enter the Graffiti command stroke followed by a Graffiti L. Either way, the message will move to the Filed folder.

Of course, you can also reply to that message. We'll tell you how next.

Replying to Messages

Replying to a message is as simple as tapping the Reply button that appears at the bottom of every message screen. That's oversimplifying things a bit, but it's a good place to start.

Here's what you do:

1. From the Inbox list, tap the message you want to reply to. This will open the message.

2. Tap the Reply button at the bottom of the screen. This will open the Reply Options dialog box, as in Figure 14.22.

FIGURE 14.22: The Reply Options dialog box

Part iii

3. To reply to the message, choose Sender next to Reply To, which will place the address of the person who originally sent you the message on the To line.

4. Tap to place a checkmark in the Include Original Text box to paste the text of the original message into the body of your reply.

5. Tap to place a checkmark in the Comment Original Text box if you want to have the original text marked in your reply. This option will place a > at the beginning of each line of the original text, as in Figure 14.23.

FIGURE 14.23: Fill in a forwarding address.

6. Tap OK when you're satisfied with your choices. The dialog box will close and the New Message screen will open, with the To line filled in.

7. Compose the body of your message using Graffiti or the on-screen keyboard, and edit the original text (if you chose to include it).

8. Tap Outbox to place the message in your Outbox folder from where you can send it the next time you log on to Palm.Net, or tap Check & Send to log on and send the message immediately.

If you'd rather forward the original message to a different party, follow steps 1 and 2. Then, choose Forward from the Reply Options dialog box. This will take you to the New Message screen, where the text of the original message will appear as the body and the To line will be blank, as in Figure 14.23. You can add an address the same way you would if you were creating a new message. Then, pick up from steps 7 and 8 above.

ALTERNATE E-MAIL SOLUTIONS

One of the early criticisms of the Palm VII was that it provided access only to the Palm.Net e-mail service. This meant that users needed to maintain yet another e-mail account, besides the one they already use at home and work.

Now that the Palm VII has gone national, that criticism is moot. There are a handful of third-party applications that let you download messages from Internet-based services, such as MindSpring and Worldnet, to your Palm VII. There are even applications that let you download Web-based e-mail, such as mail from Hotmail or Yahoo accounts. The one catch is that the e-mail system you're trying to hook up with must be either POP3 or IMAP compatible. This shouldn't pose too much of a problem, since virtually every e-mail service supports at least one of these Internet mail standards.

NOTE

POP3 (Post Office Protocol 3) and IMAP (Internet Message Access Protocol) are both protocols used for retrieving e-mail from a mail server. Most mail servers use the older POP3, but some that are based on the newer IMAP standard are starting to appear.

How E-Mail Works

Explaining how the whole e-mail process works is beyond the scope of this book, but we'll try to give you a quick understanding of how you can get your Internet mail onto your Palm VII.

When you sign up for Internet service with an ISP, you are paying for an Internet connection for a monthly fee. Typically, this fee includes an e-mail account. Your ISP maintains a mail server (think of it as the post office) that you dial into using client software, such as Eudora Pro, Microsoft Outlook, or Netscape Messenger. This client software resides on your desktop PC. It communicates to the mail server at your ISP through a series of communications protocols, including POP3 and IMAP. Because most mail servers understand these protocols, you can use any client that supports them to download and read your mail.

These same principles apply when accessing Internet e-mail on your Palm VII. You install a client application on your Palm VII, dial out to the Internet, and the client application communicates with the mail server at your ISP to locate and download your e-mail.

TIP

Not sure what protocols your mail system supports? Check out the E-Mail Solutions Help page on the Palm.Net Web site (www.palm.net/email_solutions/help/) for tips on finding out the answer.

Web-based e-mail, those free mail accounts that let you read your mail only in a Web browser, may not support either POP3 or IMAP. So, you'll need a different client to access these mailboxes. You can find clients for Yahoo! mail and Hotmail on the Palm.Net Web site.

The Tools for Getting Internet E-Mail onto Your Palm VII

There are two ways to get e-mail on your Palm VII organizer. You can access your mailbox directly using any third-party e-mail application on your Palm VII, or you can forward your messages to your Palm.Net iMessenger account. For accessing corporate e-mail systems such as Lotus Notes or Microsoft Exchange Server, you'll have to forward messages to your Palm. You'll need your network administrator's help and permission to get this set up.

There are two third-party applications you can use to access your POP3 and IMAP accounts: ThinAirMail and iPopper. Both of these applications are actually PQAs, and can be downloaded for free from the Palm.Net Web site (www.palm.net). Both applications leave the mail you download to your Palm VII on your mail server, so you can also download it on your desktop PC.

TIP

You will need to have an active Palm.Net account as well as an ISP account to use Internet e-mail tools. Mail that you download with these applications will be billed against your monthly transmission allotment.

ThinAirMail (ThinAirApps.com, www.thinairapps.com) offers access to both POP3 and IMAP mailboxes. You must download it, install it on your Palm VII, and then configure it for use with your Internet e-mail account. Rather than downloading entire messages, ThinAirMail retrieves the sender's name and subject of the e-mail, so you can preview your messages before downloading them. For long e-mail messages, ThinAirMail retrieves the first kilobyte and gives you the option to download the rest of the message. You can also filter your e-mail to retrieve only messages from a particular person, with a certain subject, or sent on a specific date.

The other mail application, iPopper (Corsoft, www.corsoft.net), works only with POP3-compatible mailboxes. Like ThinAirMail, you need to download, install, and configure this e-mail client on your Palm VII. After that, it's easy and intuitive to use, and provides complete e-mail functionality. Like ThinAirMail, iPopper downloads just the sender's name, the e-mail subject, and the date. You then decide which messages to download. You can also perform all the standard filtering to limit which messages get downloaded to your Palm VII.

If you would rather not install a mail application on your Palm VII, you'll want to look at Visto Assistant (Visto Corp., http://corp.visto .com/palm.html), which can forward your messages to your iMessenger Inbox. Visto Assistant (which is also free) runs on your Windows PC. It works with POP3 mail, as well as proprietary e-mail systems such as Lotus Notes and Microsoft Exchange Server.

Visto Assistant checks your e-mail periodically, and forwards any new messages that match your optional filtering criteria to your Palm VII. The big catch is that for this application to work, you must leave your PC turned on and connected to your e-mail account. If your ISP charges you by the hour, you're looking at one heck of a bill—not to mention what you'll rack up in telephone charges. For these reasons, this solution is better suited to accessing corporate e-mail than your personal account.

WEB CLIPPING WITH YOUR PALM VII

A Palm VII does not live by e-mail alone. Chances are, your Internet needs don't end there, either. This is precisely why the Palm VII provides Web access via Palm query applications (PQAs) and a technology it calls Web clipping. Web clipping isn't exactly like Web surfing, but it's the best approach we've seen for corralling the Internet and making it work in a small, limited environment like the Palm operating system and the Palm VII.

The Difference between Clipping and Browsing

Think about the typical Web page—it's big, loaded with colors, and slow to download. And that's on a desktop PC with a reasonably fast dial-up connection. Now think about your Palm VII—it's tiny, runs on batteries, offers a slower connection speed than the average modem, and gets billed for every kilobyte it downloads. When you look at it that way, the Internet doesn't seem like such a great thing. If you're surfing, that is.

Fortunately, Palm Computing came up with a way to access the Internet that makes sense for the Palm VII. It's called Web clipping, and it eliminates the need for lots of fast bandwidth and a big screen with color support. If you think of the Internet as a newspaper, and Web clipping as clipping an article out of the newspaper, you'll get the basic idea. With Web clipping, you get only the information you're interested in and you don't have to deal with all the extraneous stuff.

Here's how Web clipping works. Your interaction with the Internet is based on queries and responses, rather than a series of hyperlinks as in Web browsing. Essentially, you ask for a piece of information, and it's returned to your Palm VII. This interaction is controlled through a PQA, which is stored locally on your Palm VII. PQAs are request forms; there's a place where you enter data, such as a stock symbol to look up or a news topic. Since the PQA itself is stored on your Palm VII like any other application, only your data request gets sent out over the Internet. This keeps response time quick and the actual amount of data being transmitted to a minimum. In a typical application, the query you send out averages about 50 bytes; less than 500 bytes (compressed) are returned to your Palm VII. The process is so efficient that in most cases, the information you requested will be returned to your organizer in less than 10 seconds.

How to Use a PQA

Your Palm VII comes with a handful of PQAs installed and includes a bunch more on the Palm Software CD. We can't begin to describe how to use each and every PQA; that would be like trying to tell you how to navigate every site on the Internet. Instead, we'll walk you through using two of the pre-installed PQAs that use all the usual PQA functions.

For the purposes of this discussion, we'll primarily use the ESPN.com PQA because its design and operation are representative of what you'll encounter in most PQAs, and we're really big sports fans. (As we write this, basketball season has just gotten under way, and we have high hopes for the NY Knicks; but then, we are eternally optimistic about the hometown teams.) So now we have the perfect excuse to keep checking the box scores. We'll also briefly use the Weather Channel PQA to show one feature that's not included in ESPN.com.

Before we go any further, let's explain a few of the principles of a PQA :

- ▶ You tap to select an item or perform an action, the same way you would with any other Palm application.

- ▶ You enter text, when necessary, using Graffiti or the on-screen keyboard.

- ▶ Interface conventions, like scroll bars, pick lists, check boxes, command buttons, and menus, work the same way in a PQA as they do in any other Palm application.

- ▶ You access the Menu Bar in a PQA the same way you do in other Palm applications.

- ▶ You can cut, copy, and paste information to an edit line just as you usually do.

Now, let's look at some of the interface conventions that are unique to a PQA. Start by opening the ESPN.com PQA. You do this the same way you open any application: Tap the Applications soft button, then tap the icon for ESPN.com from within the Application Launcher screen. The ESPN.com PQA will open immediately, whether or not you've initiated a Palm.Net connection. You'll see the home page for this PQA, which is installed on your Palm VII. You can see it in Figure 14.24.

FIGURE 14.24:   What sport interests you?

First, notice that the different sports categories are underlined, just as a hot link would be in a standard Web application. The underlining indicates a link; tapping it will send out a request for information, and return a new page. This is the query part of a PQA. Take a good look at the line for Baseball. That little curved icon next to it is the over-the-air icon.

⬛ Baseball

This indicates that tapping on this option will initiate a wireless transaction. The minute you start a wireless transaction, you're incurring cost—either in the form of a deduction from your monthly kilobyte allotment or actual money, if you've run through that allotment.

At this point, you should raise the antenna on your Palm VII to connect to the Palm.Net service. Anything you tap from this home page will send a request out to the Internet; the information you requested will quickly be returned to your Palm VII. For the purposes of this demonstration, tap Baseball from the ESPN.com home page. Now tap Scores. You've just sent your first query to the Internet. As the information you requested is being located and downloaded to your organizer, the words

Connecting (or Sending) will appear at the top of the screen, followed by an icon like this one:

This circular icon is the Stop icon. You can tap it to stop the transaction you just initiated. For now, though, just let the request go through.

What you see on the screen now is the response to your query, otherwise known as a Web clipping. You'll notice an arrow at the top of the screen, about halfway across (see Figure 14.25). This is the Back arrow. It works just like the Back button in your Web browser. Tapping it will take you to the last page displayed in the query application. Tapping it repeatedly will take you all the way back to the Application Launcher.

FIGURE 14.25: Take one step back.

Let's send another query. Tap the line that says News. This will open the first news screen. In the top-right corner of the screen, where the category pull-down would appear in a regular Palm application, you'll notice the word History. Tapping this will drop down the History list, as in Figure 14.26.

FIGURE 14.26: Review your clippings.

This list works just like the History list in a Web browser. It displays all the clippings you've received for the PQA you're working in. It will show the name of the clipping and the time it was downloaded. You can tap any clipping in this list to return to that screen.

There's one last thing we'd like to point out on the Baseball News clipping screen. See the ESPN.com logo at the top left of the screen? This is the title area of the screen. You can tap it to find out how big the clipping you just received was, as in Figure 14.27.

FIGURE 14.27: Tapping on the title area of a PQA will show you how many bytes a clipping contains.

Sometimes, sending a query will involve more than just tapping a screen. For some interactions, you'll need to enter text or use a pick list to get more specific information. The ESPN.com PQA doesn't use these techniques, so we'll move over to the Weather Channel for this example.

Tap the Weather icon in the Application Launcher to open the Weather Channel PQA, and then tap Find A City. As you can see in Figure 14.28, the Weather Channel PQA requires you to either pick a state from the pick list, or enter a city name or zip code on the text line to get weather information for that region.

You work with these options the same way you would with any Palm application. Scroll through the pick list using the scroll arrow on the side of the box (or enter the first few letters of the state you want to automatically advance the list). When you get to the state you want, tap it to highlight it, then tap the Go State command button.

FIGURE 14.28: Either pick or write.

TIP

You can paste information from a standard Palm record into the text line of a Palm PQA. You do this the same way you copy and paste in any Palm application.

If you'd rather enter a city or zip code, just tap the text line to activate it, then use Graffiti or the on-screen keyboard to enter the city or zip code for which you want information. Tap Go to launch the query.

Pick lists and text lines are common elements in PQAs that let you search for specific information, such as a name, a movie listing, or a stock symbol. News and general interest PQAs will generally just offer options that you tap to access.

One option every PQA will offer is the ability to copy information from the application to paste into a memo, Address Book record, or any other basic Palm application. You can't select part of a PQA page or just some of the text from a clipping. You have to take the whole clipping.

To copy a clipping:

1. Make sure the clipping or page you want to copy is displayed on the screen.

2. Tap the Menu button to open the Menu Bar.

3. From the Menu Bar, choose Edit ➤ Copy Page (see Figure 14.29).

Part III

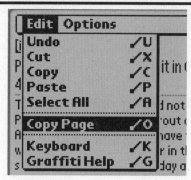

FIGURE 14.29: Copy a clipping.

4. Open the application you want to paste the clipping into.

5. Create a new record.

6. Tap the Menu button to open the Menu Bar.

7. From the Menu Bar, choose Edit ➤ Paste. The clipping will appear in this new record.

TIP

Copying a clipping always starts at the top of the current page, no matter what is displayed on the screen. Copy Page copies only tables and text; it doesn't pick up icons or other graphics.

That about sums up the basic functionality of PQAs. It's time to start exploring on your own.

Five Must-Have PQAs

The PQAs installed on the Palm VII and included on the Palm Software CD are great to start with, but there are thousands of other PQAs ripe for the downloading. The Palm.Net Web site is also a great resource for new PQAs. Once you've downloaded these PQAs to your desktop PC, you install them the same way you would any other Palm application. Here are five PQAs we consider must-haves, all of which can be downloaded from www.palm.net/apps:

Internet Movie Database   This listing of 6,500 movies is the perfect tool to have for those trips to the video store. You can search by title, actor, director, etc., and get detailed information.

Starbucks Coffee Store Locator   Keep yourself appropriately caffeinated with the Store Locator. It lists every Starbucks in the continental U.S., so you'll never have to go latte-less.

Amazon.com Anywhere   Shop from your Palm VII with this PQA that provides access to Amazon auctions and products. It even delivers Amazon.com reviews, product ratings, and prices, so you can make informed purchases.

PDA Dash Palm News   Keep up to date on the latest Palm news, rumors, and reports with this daily newsletter.

Vicinity BrandFinder   Looking for the nearest gas station, fast food restaurant, or hotel? BrandFinder can help you find the closest name-brand provider. Perfect for when a Big Mac attack strikes you in an unfamiliar city.

WHAT'S NEXT?

This chapter has introduced you to the wonders of the Palm VII and its Web surfing capabilities. If you're not lucky enough to have a Palm VII, turn to the next chapter to find out about "Seeing the Sites with Your iMac and iBook."

Part III

Chapter 15

SEEING THE SITES WITH YOUR IMAC AND IBOOK

The *i* in *iMac* or *iBook* allegedly stands for *Internet*. Every iMac or iBook is Internet ready, so this chapter should appeal to you. Whether you are a surfer or a Webmaster, this chapter is full of tips and hints for getting more out of the Internet with your iMac or iBook:

> **Your Dream Start Page**   Provides a tutorial showing how to tailor the default iMac or iBook home page on Excite to better suit your needs.

> **Seeing the Sites**   Offers a wealth of wonderful Web sites for keeping up with all things Macintosh and with the capabilities of your iMac or iBook.

Adapted from *iMac! (and iBook) I Didn't Know You Could Do That...*, by Bob LeVitus
ISBN 0-7821-2589-1   380 pages $19.99

Buy It on the Net   Shows you how to shop for iMac or iBook hardware and software (and more) without leaving the comfort of your home.

Getting the Most out of Sherlock   Shows you how to maximize the new Find File's functionality and use it to search the Internet.

Safety First on the Internet: Using the EdView Internet Safety Kit   Shows you how to protect your family (more or less) from smut on the Web.

Home Sweet Web Page with Adobe PageMill   Provides a quick look at the Web page builder included with "fruit-flavored" iMacs.

Publish or Perish on the Web   Talks about using your iMac or iBook as a Web server or using an ISP (Internet Service Provider) to serve up your Web pages. It also covers the advantages and disadvantages of each technique.

Fixing Pix for E-mail   Shows you how to prepare pictures so that you can send them by e-mail to Mac or PC users.

So log onto the Internet and get ready to rumble!

YOUR DREAM START PAGE

The first time you launch a browser—such as Netscape Communicator or Microsoft Internet Explorer—on your iMac or iBook, you will automatically be taken to a sign-up page for Excite's My Excite Start Page service, which is part of the iMac or iBook package. It's a great jumping off point for your Web-surfing adventures as it comes right out of the box; but as you'll discover in the coming pages, you can customize almost every aspect of it to suit your tastes and needs. If you haven't already done so, sign up for this service now and get ready to make this start page your own.

NOTE

If you've changed the start page in your browser preferences (if you don't see an Excite page when you launch your browser), you can surf to http://apple .excite.com/?cobrand=apple and follow along. If you like what you've done, be sure to bookmark the page or use your browser's preferences to choose it as your new start page.

Personalize Your Page

If you've not already done so, you need to register and choose a password. Click the Personalize Your Page link to go to a registration screen. After you've done this, a thank-you page will appear. Click Continue, and the Master Change Page appears, with icons showing all the options you have for personalizing your start page: Select Content, Move Content, Change Colors, and so on. You can customize each of these options to suit your personal tastes by simply clicking on the icon or the link beneath it.

Click the Select Content icon. The Personalize My Content window opens, presenting a list of content categories to choose from. When you click on a content category in the list on the left, it appears in the My Content list on the right. To remove a content category from the My Content list, highlight it and click the Remove button.

After you have selected the type of content you want to appear on your start page, you can change its placement in the My Layout window, which you can display in one of three ways. Click the Next button at the bottom of the Personalize My Content window, click the Layout tab at the top of that window, or click the Move Content icon on the Master Change Page. The My Layout window is simple; first select between 2-column or 3-column layout, and then arrange your content on the page by dragging and dropping the blue and green content boxes in the grid on the right. When you are satisfied with your selections, either click the Done button or close the window.

NOTE

Your stock portfolio will always appear at the top of the page if it includes seven or more columns, and the TV listings will always appear at the bottom of the page due to their size.

Content Is King

You can also choose the name your start page will use to address you by clicking on the Your Greeting icon. I changed mine from "Welcome, Bob" to "Hey, Good Lookin'," but that's not required. If you do not customize this option, the start page will call you by your first name, as you entered it during registration. You can choose password protection if you want to password-protect your start page so that nobody else can modify it; just click the Password icon.

Click the Time Zones icon to change the time zone setting of your start page, or to specify use of a 24-hour clock rather than the default 12-hour AM/PM clock. The Refresh Rate icon allows you to specify how often you want your start page to automatically refresh itself. The default is 10 minutes; other options available are No Refresh, 5 minutes, 15 minutes, 20 minutes, 30 minutes, 45 minutes, or 1 hour.

NOTE
If you see a dialog box that says something about transmitting insecure information, just click OK.

If you click on the Member Services icon, a window will open up showing you all the wonderful services you're now entitled to as an Excite member. Click the My Member Information link to change or update your password, contact, or profile information. Click the My Member Benefits link to learn about all of the free benefits and perks that come with Excite Membership. The My Excite Products link shows you all the products Excite has to offer to members. The Member Directory provides you with access to other Excite members who share your interests, and allows you to update your member profile so that other members can find you.

Colorize Your World (or at Least Your Start Page)

You can even specify the colors for your start page by clicking the Change Colors icon on the Master Change Page. On the Personalize My Colors page, you can specify your background, header, text, link, and other colors. Choose from one of the pre-designed color schemes on the left side of the window, and a preview of that scheme appears in the right side of the window. Click the Next button at the bottom or the Custom Colors tab at the top to design your own color scheme.

Making the News Your Own

Now that you've tuned up both the look and the content of your start page, you can choose the kind of news that will appear on it. There are two different adjustments you can make: You can decide exactly what types of news will appear on your start page, and you can set up a customized clipping service that will search the Internet for stories that match your criteria. This is one of my favorite features and I'm sure it'll become one of yours as well.

Tuning Up My News

Find the My News section on your start page and click the Edit link. The Personalize My News Categories page will open, and you'll see a massive list of topics that you can choose from. Select topics that appeal to you by holding down the Command key and clicking each one. Once all of the topics that you like are selected, click the Add button to add them to your start page. Click the Submit button to view your changes.

If you're feeling adventurous, go back to the Personalize My News Categories page and click the Advanced Personalization button. This lets you choose how many of each topic's headlines will appear on your start page, and what order they should appear in. It also lets you choose how old the oldest headline should be. When the news topics and number of headlines you see for each topic are just the way you like them, click the Submit button.

Your Own Clipping Service, Too

Now you can create a clipping service that searches the Internet for stories about topics that you specify. To set it up, find the news section called NewsTracker Clipping Service and click the Create Your Own Personalized News Topics link. (If you've created a topic before, it won't say that. Instead, click the NewsTracker Clipping Service link, then click the New Topic link on the next page you see.)

For each NewsTracker topic you create, you can choose keywords. For each keyword, you can decide whether it's a "must have," a "good to have," or a "must not have." Being an egomaniac, I have one NewsTracker topic set up that must contain *Bob* and *LeVitus*. And since I'm an avid Apple watcher, I have another search topic that must have *Apple Computer, Inc.* I have also created a search for news items containing the words *Steve Jobs*.

There are many uses for this feature. If you follow a stock, set up a topic for the company. If you are interested only in news about a company's stock (and not the company itself), include the word stock as a "must have." If you want all the news on your favorite singer or movie star, set up a topic just for that. It's fun, it's easy, and it's incredibly useful. (In other words, it rocks!)

Once you've set up a topic and filled in all its keywords, click the Create My Topic button. You'll see another page filled with suggestions that may be of use. Check any that apply (or none if you like) and click the Make Changes button. For instance, one of the words that was suggested

Part iii

for my Apple topic was *iMac*. I thought that was a good suggestion, so I accepted it. Now my NewsTracker Apple topic clips stories with iMac in them, too.

After you've created your topic(s), you can view a summary of articles that match your criteria by clicking a topic's name in the NewsTracker Clipping Service section of your start page.

Taking Stock of Your Portfolio

I love the fact that my start page can keep track of my stock portfolio and tell me at a glance how every stock I own is doing as of 15 minutes ago. (Stock quotes are delayed 15 minutes.) And unlike Quicken, this tracking is free.

To set up your own portfolio, find the My Stocks section on your start page and click the Edit button next to it. The Personalize My Stock Portfolio page appears. Start by giving your portfolio a name (the default name is your Excite user name). To choose which indices (Dow Jones, NASDAQ, etc.) you want to track, click the Indices tab and checkmark them in the list provided. In the Advanced section, enter the ticker symbol, shares owned, and price paid for each stock you want to track. In the Preferences section, customize your portfolio layout and choose which columns will appear in your full portfolio view. When you're satisfied with your entries, click the Done button to save your changes.

From now on, the My Stocks section will show all the stocks in your portfolio, their current price, and their price change (plus or minus) since the market opened that morning.

NOTE

For more details, click the Full Portfolio link. You'll see a large grid that shows items such as current price, the day's change in dollars and percent, share volume, number of shares owned, current value, gain/loss, and links to charts and stories about each stock. This is also where you can view the total value of your holdings.

Your total holdings—the only number that really matters at the end of the day—will appear at the bottom of the Current Value column. If you don't have a Current Value column, go back to the Personalize My Stock Portfolio page and choose Value from one of the pop-up menus in the last (Customize Your Portfolio Layout) section.

You can also choose to view additional data about stocks in your portfolio by choosing one of the following views at the bottom of the My Stocks section: Holdings, Fundamentals, Price Performance, or Day Trader. Each view uses different columns to show your portfolio.

NOTE

Don't forget, once you've customized your start page to your liking, you can set it to be the first thing that your browser brings up when you start it. To do so, use your browser's Preferences dialog box, Internet Config, or the Mac OS 8.5 Internet control panel—whichever appears on your particular iMac or iBook. Browser preferences can be found in the Edit menu of both browsers on all types of iMacs and iBooks. If you have an original Bondi Blue iMac, you can use the included Internet Config application. If you have one of the newer "fruit-flavored" iMacs or an iBook, use the Internet control panel. All three methods will achieve the same effect—making this the first page your browser displays when you launch it.

SEEING THE SITES

The World Wide Web is full of wonderful sites with a wealth of useful information about Macs in general and iMacs or iBooks in particular. In this section, I'll try to provide you with a list of the best and brightest, along with brief descriptions of what you will find at each site.

Keep in mind that sometimes Web sites move and leave no forwarding address. I checked every link in this book before it went to press, and every single one worked at that time. But that doesn't mean that they'll still work by the time you get this book home to read it. I hope they will; but as you know, stuff happens. Bottom line: If you encounter a dead or broken link, I apologize; but don't blame me. I did all I could.

NOTE

It's also a good idea to use your browser's bookmark feature to save sites you like and wish to return to in the future.

Great iMac-Specific Web Sites

The iMac has spawned hundreds of Web sites dedicated to every aspect of using our favorite computer. Here are a few of my favorites.

Ric Ford's iMacInTouch pages are great. 'Nuff said. This is one of the few iMac sites I visit every single day. You'll find it at www.macintouch.com/imac.html.

The iMac Channel, which the *San Diego Union-Tribune* referred to as "the most comprehensive set of [iMac] links and news," can be found at http://lowendmac.com/imac/index.shtml. If all you care about is the list of iMac Web site links, you'll find it at http://lowendmac.com/imac/links.shtml. This is another site worth visiting regularly.

Two more excellent places for news and iMac-related links are the iMac2day site at www.imac2day.com/ and the iMac.com site at www.theimac.com/. Both are updated frequently and filled with interesting information and late-breaking news about iMacs or iBooks.

There's also *Macworld* magazine's iMacworld site at www.imacworld.com/.

Finally, if you just can't get enough iMac Web sites, visit the iMac WebRing home page at www.webring.org/cgi-bin/webring?ring=1imac3;list. A WebRing is like a club for Web pages. This page is a list of more than 45 interesting sites that are members of the iMac WebRing.

NOTE

My favorite feature of WebRings is the Visit a Random Site link or button that you'll find on every member's pages. Click it and you'll be transported to a member site at random, which is kind of neat. Random ring surfing can be both fun and informative, so if you've never visited a WebRing, be sure to give it a try.

More Great Web Sites

Every morning after I read the morning local newspaper and the *Wall Street Journal*, I spend a few minutes surfing the Mac-related Web sites and seeing what's new in the Mac world. After all, iMacs and iBooks are also Macs. This section consists of six sites that cover the entire spectrum of things Macintosh (these are six great Mac sites that I read every day), followed by four other sites that are incredibly useful when you need them.

My Morning Reading (Web Sites I Visit Daily)

Just as iMacInTouch is a great resource for iMac owners, Ric's MacIn-Touch site is a great resource for all Mac users. A compelling blend of news, opinion, discussion, special reports, and product reviews, MacIn-Touch is a site I look forward to reading every single day. It's at www.macintouch.com/.

Conflict of interest alert: I write a column every Saturday for *MacCentral* and I'm about to recommend them as another site I visit daily. But I was a fan of *MacCentral* before I was a columnist there; and I still believe it's one of the best, with a great staff of writers, including yours truly. You'll find *MacCentral* Online at www.maccentral.com/.

Another great site for news and views is the Macintosh News Network at www.macnn.com/. This is primarily news about Apple and vendors of hardware and software for Macs; but it's updated twice a day or more and is often one of the first places I see a story.

There's nothing nutritious about MacOS Rumors. It's *the* National Enquirer of Mac Web sites, and I read it religiously the same way I read the Enquirer whenever I'm stuck in a grocery store line. You'll find it at www.macosrumors.com/.

Ted Landau, the proprietor of the MacFixIt Web site at www.macfixit .com/, is an old friend of mine. His book *Sad Macs, Bombs, and Other Disasters* is the classic Mac troubleshooting guide. His Web site continues the tradition with complete coverage of numerous ongoing issues about Macs, iMacs, and iBooks. It's published Monday, Wednesday, and Friday of every week, except during Macworld Expo.

The last place I stop for my daily fix of Mac news and information is MacSurfer's Headline News page at www.macsurfer.com/. This is a links page. It scans the Internet for stories about Apple and Macintoshes and offers you the headlines and links to select if you care to read more. It's updated several times a day, so it's a good place to find up-to-date information on a breaking story or issue.

Four More Great Mac Sites

The more pieces of software you use, the more useful you'll find MacUp-date and VersionTracker Online. Both sites offer up-to-date news on the latest versions of almost every Mac application, Control Panel, or extension. They also offer links to download any updates that you might need. They're at www.macupdate.com/ and www.versiontracker.com/, respectively.

Apple's Technical Information Library (TIL) is another great site to remember. It's Apple's keyword-searchable knowledge base of product information, technical specifications, and troubleshooting information. It's updated daily and contains more than 14,000 articles. You will find the TIL at http://til.info.apple.com/. If something is wrong with your iMac, this is a great place to begin your search for a solution.

The last site I want to tell you about is Apple's Macintosh Products Guide Web site, another searchable database with listings and descriptions of more than 14,000 Mac products.

NOTE

14,000 articles in the TIL. 14,000 products in the Macintosh Products Guide. Coincidence? You be the judge.

You'll find the Macintosh Products Guide at http://guide.apple.com/. It's a great place to find more information about software or hardware items for your iMac.

BUY IT ON THE NET

Basically, you have two ways to buy software and hardware for your iMac. You can get in your car, drive to the local CompUSA, park the car, go into the store, and find that they either don't carry what you're looking for or that they're out of stock on your desired item. Or, you can fire up your Web browser, find the best price on the item, order it with a few clicks of the mouse, and wait for it to be delivered to your door (which is often the next day).

As an iMac user, you've no doubt noticed that most of the computing world uses another operating system—Windows—and that the selection of Mac hardware and software in many local stores is downright meager. (But, to paraphrase my friend Peter Lewis of the *New York Times,* "Cockroaches also outnumber humans. That doesn't make them better.")

I rarely get in my car anymore for computer stuff because it's faster, easier, and usually cheaper to order it online. I know that I'll get exactly what I want at the best price and that it will be delivered to my door promptly.

NOTE
There are a handful of great Mac retail stores scattered around the world. The ComputerWare chain in Northern California is one. There are others in many cities. If you're fortunate enough to have a retailer who specializes in the Mac, give them whatever business you can. Unfortunately, no such thing exists in my neck of the woods.

Shopping on the Net is easy, it's safe, and it's fun. So let's go shopping!

Shopping on the Web

Being able to compare prices is probably the best thing about shopping on the Internet. When I want or need something for one of my Macs, I visit several online stores and see what they have to offer and how much they charge. Or I use a ShopBot, one of the comparison-shopping Web sites. After I've done my homework, I order from the vendor offering the best price or the most timely delivery, whichever is more important to me at that moment.

Good Mac Stores Online

If you want the most detailed information on a new Mac, visit The Apple Store (http://store.apple.com/). You can order a Mac from this site if you like, but the big four vendors listed next often have better prices.

If you want detailed information on third-party hardware and software for the Mac, visit the Macintosh Products Guide (http://guide.apple.com/). But when it comes time to buy, the MPG doesn't offer online shopping. Fortunately, there are at least four major online vendors with huge selections of both Apple hardware and third-party hardware and software.

The big four are Cyberian Outpost (www.outpost.com/), MacWare-house (www.warehouse.com/macwarehouse/), MacConnection (www.macconnection.com/), and MacZone (www.maczone.com/). Each is an authorized Apple reseller, so you can buy a new or refurbished Mac. Also, they all offer literally thousands of third-party Mac hardware and software products, accessories, and supplies.

It's easy to compare prices; just visit all four sites and use their search feature to find the item you're looking for. All four indicate whether a product is in stock, which is important if you need the item quickly.

Part iii

Finally, each vendor has a different policy and price for standard and overnight shipping, so don't forget to take those charges into account.

That's it. You have all the information you need. Choose a vendor, order your item, and wait for it to be delivered to your door. Each vendor's checkout procedure is a bit different, but all are easy to use.

NOTE

Having been totally fair so far, I want to say that I generally don't bother with most of the sites I just described. I usually just buy whatever I need from Cyberian Outpost. They usually have the lowest price; they offer free overnight delivery in the U.S. and a 30-day money-back guarantee on most items; and they have a great order-tracking system. Over the course of dozens of transactions, they've always been a pleasure to deal with; so I am a loyal Cyberian Outpost customer.

Shopping for Non-Computer Stuff

There are so many great places to buy things online, it's hard to know where to start. For books, look at the big three: Amazon.com (www.amazon.com/), Barnes & Noble (www.barnesandnoble.com/), and Borders (www.borders.com/). For technical and computer books, try FatBrain.Com (www.fatbrain.com), formerly known as Computer Literacy and home of one of the largest selections of computer book titles.

If music is your bag, all three big bookstores also sell music CDs. Or you can visit a site that specializes in music, such as CDNow (www.cdnow.com/), CD Universe (www.cduniverse.com), or Tower Records (www.towerrecords.com/).

NOTE

If you can't find the music CD you're looking for at one of those six sites, I suspect it's going to be very hard to find that CD anywhere on earth.

Truth is, you can buy almost anything online these days. Why, just last week, I ordered some shorts and swimsuits from Lands' End (www.landsend.com/) and sent a gift from Sharper Image (www.sharperimage.com/). The bottom line is that if you have a favorite printed catalog or store, chances are they also have a Web site with online shopping.

> **NOTE**
>
> Use your favorite search engine or Sherlock (discussed later in this chapter) to find your favorite catalog, store, name brand products, or whatever.

Online Auctions

Another great way to shop on the Internet is by frequenting online auctions. My family and I are big fans of eBay (www.ebay.com), which offers literally millions of items for sale on the world's largest online auction Web site. There are hundreds of auctions for Mac hardware, peripherals, and software—almost all used—going on at any given time. If it's collectable—Beanie Babies, coins, art, baseball cards, or whatever—you'll find auctions galore on eBay. Amazon.com (www.amazon.com/) also has an online auction, which you can link to from their Web site.

An all-Mac auction started up recently at www.auctionmac.com/. I haven't used it, but it looks promising. I plan to check this site every so often.

Buying and selling at online auctions is easy and fun. You might even get something at a bargain-basement price. I say online auctions are well worth checking out.

Online Shopping Tips

You may have reservations about shopping online. Perhaps you've heard that it's not safe to use your credit card on the Internet or that sometimes you get—and get charged for—things that you didn't order. Don't worry. Shopping on the Net is as safe as shopping at a mall, as long as you use good sense. Here are some tips.

Security and Safety Issues

You may have heard that your credit card number or other personal information can be stolen if you send it over the Internet. In some cases this is true, but it's not the threat that it's made out to be. Most reputable Web sites that offer online shopping offer a secure connection between your browser and the vendor. Your personal information, including your credit card number, is encoded and encrypted before it's sent over the Internet. It cannot be deciphered by anyone but the vendor at the other end of the secure connection.

NOTE

I believe all of the sites mentioned in this chapter offer secure connections. Sites that are secure usually display this information prominently. Still, before you submit credit card information over the Internet, it's a good idea to check that the connection is a secure one. Look for a link called Security, or About Our Secure Server (or something like that) on the vendor's pages. Both browsers that come with your iMac—Netscape Navigator and Microsoft Internet Explorer—support secure connections.

Your credit card is safer on a secure Internet connection than with a waitperson or salesperson who takes your card who-knows-where and does who-knows-what with it for five minutes, while it is completely out of your sight. So, if that's what has held you back from shopping on the Net, you have nothing to fear.

One other thing: Always use a credit card on the Internet. Never use your debit card or a check or money order. Why? Because using a credit card almost always provides you with rights if the product isn't up to snuff or if a dispute arises between you and the vendor.

If you use a credit card for a purchase and then have a dispute with a vendor, your credit card company may very well do battle for you. Write them a letter explaining the circumstances and request that the charge be disputed. They will try to work things out with the vendor for you. Having a 900-pound gorilla fight your battle for you usually gives you a better chance of having the situation resolved to your liking. If you use cash, check, or debit card, you don't get the benefits of the 900-pound primate.

Comparison Shopping Services

One last thing that bears discussion is the comparison shopping services (ShopBots), such as BottomDollar (www.bottomdollar.com/), Excite Search (www.jango.com/), Yahoo! Shopping (http://shopping.yahoo.com/), and PricePulse (www.pricepulse.com/). These Web sites purport to "search the Internet and find you the lowest prices." For the most part, they work.

There are some things to consider when you use a ShopBot. The first is that some vendors seem to be arbitrarily excluded from some Shop-Bots' searches. Don't think your ShopBot search is a sure thing; there still may be a lower price out there on the Net. The answer is to surf to your favorite sites after using a ShopBot and see if it really did find you the lowest price, because sometimes they don't.

The second thing is related to the first: The ShopBots often find a low price from a vendor I've never heard of and have never done business with. What they don't tell me is that my favorite online vendor offers the same item for a few cents more. And for a few cents (or even a few bucks), I'll order from Cyberian Outpost even if the ShopBot doesn't check their prices for me.

Finally, don't forget to check shipping prices and whether the product is in stock or back-ordered. Most ShopBots don't take these things into account, so check them out for yourself before you order.

The bottom line is that if you're the kind of person who likes to know you paid the absolute lowest price for something, the ShopBots are worth a try, as long as you remember that they're far from flawless.

GETTING THE MOST OUT OF SHERLOCK

If you have Mac OS 8.5 or higher, you have Sherlock, Apple's remarkable new search application.

NOTE

If you aren't sure which version of Mac OS you have, choose About This Computer from the Finder's Apple menu.

Like earlier versions of Find File, it can search your hard disk for files by name or attributes, such as creation date, size, and kind. But unlike earlier Find File incarnations, Sherlock has two hot new features:

▸ Sherlock can search for words within document files on your hard disk.

▸ Sherlock can search for words on selected Internet Web sites.

Since this is the Internet chapter, we're going to focus on that aspect of Sherlock for now.

NOTE

Suffice it to say that if the ability to search for words in documents on your hard disk appeals to you, click the question mark (?) in Sherlock to learn more about searching by content. Then click the Find by Content tab in Sherlock and index your hard disk. That's pretty much all there is to it.

If you don't have OS 8.5 (many early iMacs didn't come with it), consider upgrading your iMac to the latest version of Mac OS. You'll get Sherlock, plus much more. You can find information about operating system upgrades for your iMac at www.apple.com/macos/.

Search the Net with Sherlock

As far as I'm concerned, Sherlock's coolest ability is that it can search multiple Web sites simultaneously (and very quickly) and rank the results according to their relevancy. The relevancy ranking is occasionally quirky, but you'll probably find it helpful more often than not.

There is only one requirement before you can use Sherlock's Internet search: You must have an active Internet connection established. If you're not connected to the Internet, log on via AOL or your ISP. Once you're connected, launch Sherlock by doing one of the following:

▶ Choose Apple menu ➤ Sherlock.

▶ Choose File ➤ Find.

▶ Use the keyboard shortcut Command+F (for Find).

Searching the Internet for the First Time

Once Sherlock is running, click the Search Internet tab and you'll see a window that looks something like the one in Figure 15.1.

Type a word or phrase into the box at the top (where it says "iMac Bob LeVitus" in Figure 15.1) and click the Search button. Sherlock combs the Internet and returns its findings, as shown in Figure 15.2.

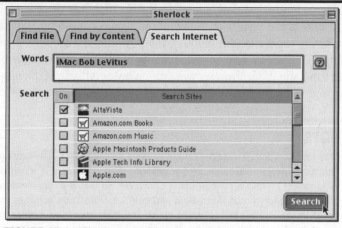

FIGURE 15.1: Sherlock, ready to search the Internet

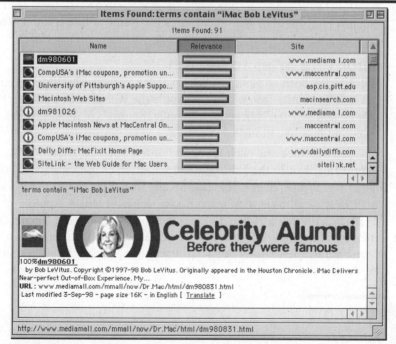

FIGURE 15.2: The results of my search, ranked by relevance

The Items Found window, shown in Figure 15.2, has two panes. The top pane shows the results of the search ranked by relevance. If you select an item in the top pane (dm980601), the bottom pane displays a synopsis, the item's URL, and an advertisement. To view an item, double-click it in the top pane. Your browser will launch automatically if it's not open already, and the item will be displayed.

NOTE

Let's see how the relevance ranking worked for my search. The most relevant link, according to Sherlock, was dm980601. This document is a review of the iMac article I wrote for the *Houston Chronicle*. So this is a very relevant document for the keywords *iMac*, *Bob*, and *LeVitus*. Unfortunately, the next three items in the list are not relevant at all. The fifth item is relevant. The sixth through tenth aren't. So don't depend heavily on the relevance ranking. It misses as often as it hits.

To sort your search results by name or Web site in the Items Found window (instead of by relevance), click the Name or Site column header.

Choosing Sites to Search

What you've seen so far is just the tip of the iceberg. Sherlock can search not only the entire Internet but also only the Web sites you want it to search; and you can choose from literally hundreds of different sites. (I'll show you how in a minute.)

Open Sherlock and click the Search Internet tab. It should look like Figure 15.1. Notice the list in the lower portion of the window, which is a list of search sites Sherlock knows about. Your iMac comes pre-loaded with 16 sites: AltaVista, Amazon Books, Amazon Music, Apple, AppleTIL, Barnes & Noble, CNN, DirectHit, Encyclopedia, Excite, GoTo, Infoseek, LookSmart, Lycos, MacGuide, and Yahoo. You can choose to have Sherlock search any or all of these sites by clicking the On checkbox beside the site's name.

NOTE

Sherlock knows which sites it can search by using plug-ins. A folder called Internet Search Sites in your System folder contains 16 plug-ins, one for each of the aforementioned sites. To have Sherlock search a site, download a plug-in for that site (see next section) and put it in this folder.

You can download hundreds of additional plug-ins for Sherlock. The official Apple Sherlock Plug-In Directory is at www.apple.com/sherlock/plugins.html. But it has only a handful of them. To get the good stuff, hit the Sherlock Internet Search Archives, the other official Apple Sherlock plug-in page, at www.appledonuts.com/sherlocksearch/index.html. This site has several hundred plug-ins for your downloading delight and has links to Sherlock add-ons and news, too. Finally, if you are a fan of Sherlock, check out the Sherlock Resource Site at www.macineurope.com/sherlocksite/. It is a great unofficial site with lots of interesting information about Sherlock and its add-ons and plug-ins.

NOTE

If you get the plug-in bug like me (I have more than one hundred of them so far), a program like Baker Street Assistant can help you manage things by letting you enable and disable plug-ins in sets. You can download a copy of Baker Street Assistant from www.casadyg.com/.

If Sherlock Crashes or Freezes

If you add a lot of plug-ins, Sherlock may crash or freeze when you launch it. This is simply Sherlock's way of telling you it needs more memory. To give it what it needs, follow these steps:

1. Click the Sherlock icon to select it. It's in the Apple Menu Items folder inside your System folder.

2. Choose File ➤ Get Info or use the keyboard shortcut Command+I.

3. Choose Memory from the Get Info window's pop-up menu and increase the Minimum Size to 2,000K and the Preferred Size to 3,500K.

4. Close the Get Info window.

If Sherlock still crashes, repeat these steps, but this time increase the Minimum Size to 3,000K and the Preferred Size to 6,000K.

SAFETY FIRST ON THE INTERNET: USING THE EDVIEW INTERNET SAFETY KIT

EdView Internet Safety Kit (EISK) blocks your browser from visiting any Web site that hasn't been authorized. Once it's installed and activated, you can access only pages that you have authorized yourself or that are in the EdView Smart Zone.

The Smart Zone contains a database of thousands of sites categorized by both subject and grade level that have been verified by a team of educators as being safe and having educational value. It works with most Internet connections, including ISPs and America Online. This is a heavy-handed approach; but it does block most, if not all, inappropriate content. When you request a site that is not authorized, you'll see the message shown in Figure 15.3.

FIGURE 15.3:   This is what you'll see if you try to access a site outside the Smart Zone.

The EdView Internet Safety Kit is bundled with all "flavored" iMacs and all iBooks, but you may not have even noticed that you have it. If your iMac came with it, you'll find its installer on the iMac or iBook Install CD-ROM in the Internet folder.

If you didn't get a copy with your iMac, you can download a 30-day demo from EdView at www.edview.com/download/fastdownload.asp. It'll cost you $40 if you decide to keep it after the 30 days expire.

NOTE

If you didn't get a copy of the EdView Internet Safety Kit with your iMac and you don't want to buy one, you may still use EdView's Smart Search for Kids search engine at http://school.edview.com/search/. It blocks out most age-inappropriate material, and it's free. However, it doesn't prevent kids from Note finding inappropriate sites on their own once they leave this site. That's what the Internet Safety Kit does.

Getting Started with EdView Internet Safety Kit

Once installed, EISK limits your browser to Web sites in the Smart Zone. You can also add pages manually. To get EISK up and running, follow these steps:

1. Insert your iMac Install CD-ROM.

2. Open the Internet folder or open the EdView Internet Safety Kit folder.

3. Double-click the Install EdView Family icon.

4. During the installation process, you'll be asked to enter a password. Do this and try not to forget the password.

5. Click the Set button and wait a few seconds. Another dialog box appears.

6. Click the Restart button.

When your iMac reboots, you'll notice a new item—the EV (EdView) menu on the right side of your menu bar. This tells you that your iMac is now protected. Notice how the *V* is red. If you use the menu to turn off protection, the *V* changes to gray. A red *V* means that the protection is on, and a gray *V* means that it's off.

Part III

Now let's see if it works. Make sure the EV is red, then connect to the Internet and launch your browser. Now type in any URL that should be blocked. Try your favorite search engine, for example, or try www.garbage .com. You should see a message telling you that this site is outside of the EdView Smart Zone.

NOTE

There are thousands of sites that are in the Smart Zone. So some innocuous sites—like Dell and Apple—come up properly, while others—like Gateway and Outpost—don't. Also notice that sites that you may not mind your kids visiting, such as Disney.com or Nationalgeographic.com, may be blocked by default.

Fortunately, there are two ways to view sites outside the Smart Zone.

Viewing Sites outside the Smart Zone

The easy way to view sites that aren't a part of the Smart Zone is to turn off EISK by choosing Disable Channel Lock from the EV menu. As long as you know the password, disabling EISK takes only a second and allows you to access anything on the Internet.

When you turn EISK back on (choose Enable Channel Lock from the EV menu), you'll see a dialog box that recommends that you clear your browser's cache immediately. If you've visited any sites you wouldn't want the kids to see, be sure to do that. The cache is in your browser's Preferences dialog box.

But this doesn't answer the bigger question: How do I allow my kids to see a site that isn't included in the Smart Zone without disabling EISK? Fortunately, this is also easy, although not quite as easy as shutting the thing off completely.

To add a site, choose Edit Preferences from the EV menu. In the Preferences dialog box, click the Sites tab. Now comes the hard part: This dialog box doesn't want to know the name of the site you want to enable; instead, it wants the site's IP address. No problem! Assuming you're already connected to the Internet, just click the little Go To NSLookUp link in the dialog box, as shown in Figure 15.4.

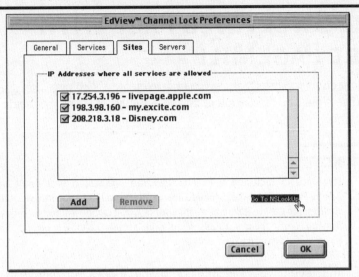

FIGURE 15.4: Clicking the Go To NSLookUp link in the EdView Channel Lock
Preferences dialog box lets you look up any site's IP address.

Your browser will launch and you can type in the name of any site you
want the IP address for. Type in a keyword, such as **Disney** or **National
Geographic**, and press Return. The IP address will appear. Write it down.
Now click the Add button in the EdView Channel Lock Preferences dialog box and type the IP address and domain name for this site. Click OK.
That's it. The site is now enabled and EISK will no longer block it. In Figure 15.4 you can see that I've added Disney.com as an approved site.

NOTE

Quite frankly, although this program worked fine in my limited testing, I feel
more comfortable being nearby when my kids, ages 6 and 10, surf the Internet.
On the other hand, this site is better than nothing, and the price (free if you
have one of the later-model, "flavored" iMacs or an iBook) can't be beat. I ultimately found it something of a hassle and eventually uninstalled it, but that
doesn't mean it's not worth a try.

HOME SWEET WEB PAGE WITH ADOBE PAGEMILL

This section will briefly show you how to create a Web page. Read the next section for a discussion of how to actually get pages you create onto the Web.

NOTE

PageMill is included with all "flavored" iMacs. If you don't have an Adobe PageMill CD-ROM (or you are an iBook user) and you still want to join in the fun and create a Web page for yourself, you can download a 30-day examination copy from Adobe's Web site at www.adobe.com/prodindex/pagemill/demodnld.html#mac.

To understand what PageMill is and what it does, you have to understand a little about how Web pages work. All Web pages are constructed using HTML (HyperText Markup Language). HTML looks like English, but it's a pain in the kiester for mere mortals to program. Since a picture is worth a thousand words, here's a quick demonstration. Figure 15.5 shows a simple Web page viewed with the Netscape browser.

FIGURE 15.5: A simple Web page viewed with a browser

Figure 15.6 shows the HTML code for the simple Web page shown in Figure 15.5.

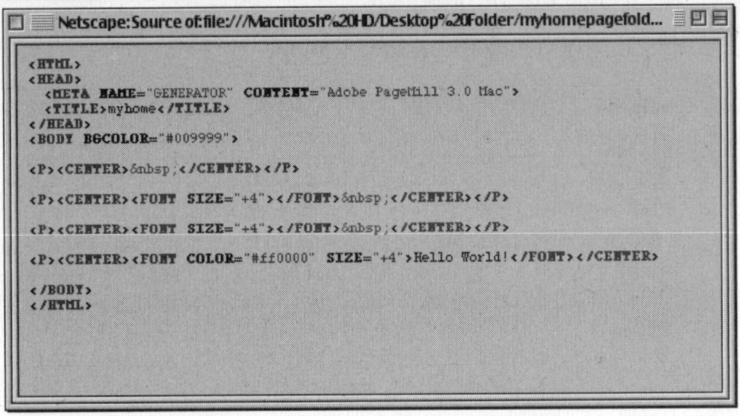

```
<HTML>
<HEAD>
   <META NAME="GENERATOR" CONTENT="Adobe PageMill 3.0 Mac">
   <TITLE>myhome</TITLE>
</HEAD>
<BODY BGCOLOR="#009999">

<P><CENTER> </CENTER></P>

<P><CENTER><FONT SIZE="+4"></FONT> </CENTER></P>

<P><CENTER><FONT SIZE="+4"></FONT> </CENTER></P>

<P><CENTER><FONT COLOR="#ff0000" SIZE="+4">Hello World!</FONT></CENTER>

</BODY>
</HTML>
```

FIGURE 15.6: The HTML code for the Hello World page

It's ugly, isn't it? Suffice it to say that creating Web pages by typing out HTML code isn't fun or easy for most people. That's what Adobe PageMill is all about. It lets you create Web pages, or even entire Web sites, without having to type a single line of HTML code. You don't really even need to know anything about HTML code (though you may want to if you're serious about creating Web pages).

Adobe PageMill is a visual Web page and Web site builder. It's a rich, complex program that lets you construct individual Web pages, as well as manage entire Web sites. Alas, I don't have the space to show you very much about PageMill. What I hope to do in our brief time is show you how easy it can be to construct a simple Web page using PageMill.

The Five-Minute Web Page

First, install PageMill if you haven't already done so. Now launch it. An untitled document will appear on your screen. This will become your Web page. Next, save the Web page. If I haven't mentioned it before, it's always a good idea to save important documents often. To save the page, follow these steps:

1. Choose File ➤ Save Page As.
2. Use the New Folder button to create a new folder for your Web site.
3. Name the folder Website.

4. Name the file homepage.

5. Save it inside the Website folder.

NOTE

Although we're going to create only a single page in this exercise, it's a good idea to dedicate a separate folder to each Web site you create. Most Web sites consist of numerous text and graphic files. It is a good habit to have one folder for all the text and graphics files that belong to a site. That way, as your site grows, it'll be much easier to keep track of its content if it's all saved in a single folder.

Now we're ready to create the five-minute Web page.

1. Near the top of the page, you'll find the Title field. Double-click the words *untitled document* and replace them with the words **My Home Page**.

2. Click in the gray area below the Title field. This is where you design your page. Press the Return key three or four times to move the cursor down toward the middle of the page. Type **Welcome to my home page** or something equally creative.

3. Choose Edit ➤ Select All or use the keyboard shortcut Command+A.

4. Click the Center Align Text button (Figure 15.7).

FIGURE 15.7: PageMill's Center Align Text button

5. Choose Largest Heading from the pop-up Style menu (Figure 15.8).

FIGURE 15.8: PageMill's pop-up Style menu

6. Choose Site ➤ Show Settings. In the Site Settings dialog box, click the Add button.

7. Type **My Home Page** for the Site Name.

8. In the upper section of the dialog box (Local Site Location), click the folder icon next to Local Site Location. Find your Website folder in the dialog box and click the Choose button.

9. In the lower section of the dialog box (Site Destination), click the Local Folder radio button at the bottom, click the icon of a folder next to it, and find your Website folder in the dialog box. Create a new folder and name it Webstuff. (You can't use your Website folder for this step; it requires a unique and separate folder.) Click the Choose button. The dialog box should look like Figure 15.9.

10. Click the OK button to dismiss the Edit My Home Page Settings dialog box. Choose File ➤ Upload ➤ Page. You'll see a brief flash as the file is created on your hard disk.

You have created a Web page and uploaded it to your hard disk! To check your handiwork, use your browser to open the homepage file inside the Webstuff folder.

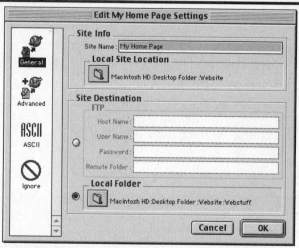

FIGURE 15.9:   Your Home Page Settings dialog box should look like this.

NOTE

If you want to see the HTML code for this page, choose View ≻ Page Source (in Netscape Navigator) or View ≻ Source (in Microsoft Internet Explorer).

This page is not yet live on the Internet. You'll have to read the next section to find out how to do that. But before we get to that, here is a quick look at some other stuff you can do to your Web page with PageMill.

Other Stuff You Can Do with PageMill

PageMill lets you do more than just put a few words on a Web page. For example, you can easily add a picture to spice up your page. Or, you can add a link to another Web page or another site.

Adding a Picture

You need a `.gif` or `.jpg` (GIF or JPEG) graphics file for this. If you don't have one of your own, there are some in the Tour folder in the PageMill folder on your hard disk. You'll find additional graphics files on the PageMill CD-ROM (if you have it) in the `Web Pages and Content folder`.

NOTE

AppleWorks and GraphicConverter can open many kinds of picture files and can save the picture as either a GIF or JPEG file. There's more about GIF and JPEG and what it all means in the last section of this chapter, which covers how to prepare pictures to send by e-mail.

To add a picture to your home page, follow these steps:

1. Open your homepage file in PageMill if it's not already open.

2. Click just above the text you typed earlier.

3. Choose Insert ➤ Object ➤ Image.

4. Choose your graphics (JPEG or GIF) file from the dialog box and click Insert.

The picture will appear in your page, as shown in Figure 15.10.

FIGURE 15.10:   Just like that, I added a picture to my home page.

Of course, there is much more that you can do with your picture now—resize it, reposition it, make it a link, and other stuff. But this is supposed to be a tantalizing look at creating your own Web pages. After I show you how to create a link, you're on your own.

Making a Link

Now you have a page with words and a picture. But how do you create a link to another page, which is the cornerstone of modern Web page design and implementation? To link to another Web page, follow these steps:

1. Type the words you want to make into your link anywhere on the page.

2. Select the words you want to make into your link.

3. Choose Edit ➢ Make Link or use the keyboard shortcut Command+M.

4. Type the URL of the page you want to link to in the Make WWW Link field.

5. Click the Make WWW Link button.

That's it—you've got a link, as shown in Figure 15.11.

There is much more that PageMill can do, but that's all we have space for. I hope I've, at the very least, shown you how very easy it can be to create a Web page from scratch.

NOTE
PageMill is a very capable and feature-rich program. If you are serious about building a Web page, be sure to check out the extensive PageMill help system.

FIGURE 15.11:   And just like that, a link is born.

PUBLISH OR PERISH ON THE WEB

The subject matter of this section—hosting a Web site or page—is broad enough to have its own book written about it. Therefore, this section will simply discuss the pros and cons of hosting a Web page or site locally on your iMac or iBook using Personal Web Sharing versus having an ISP or America Online host your page or site for you. Each approach has its advantages and disadvantages; we'll look at both approaches.

Using Your iMac or iBook As a Web Server

Mac OS 8.1 and above include the Web sharing control panel, which can turn your iMac or iBook into a personal Web server with just a few clicks. It's not designed to host a big, complex Web site; but it can host a simple home page. Moreover, Personal Web Sharing makes it extremely easy to share files with any Internet user.

The Advantages of Using Your iMac or iBook As a Web Server

Probably the biggest advantage of using your iMac or iBook as a Web server is that it's free (assuming you have an Internet connection already). Another plus is that it's very easy to set up a page that allows you to share files with others on the Internet, complete with password protection if you so desire. Finally, you can use your Mac to share files this way without having to create a Web page at all. Your Mac will automatically create a page listing files you have made available for others to download.

NOTE

If you want to try Personal Web Sharing yourself, open Mac OS Help and search for Web Sharing. There you'll find a bevy of articles and interactive guided tutorials that will have you up and running in minutes. Good luck.

The Disadvantages of Using Your iMac or iBook As a Web Server

First and foremost, your iMac or iBook Web server is available only when you are connected to the Internet. So, if you have a dial-up connection (you use a modem and not ISDN, cable modem, or DSL), you have to be connected for your page to appear on the Web. If you want a full-time site, you'll have to remain connected to the Internet 24 hours a day. A related drawback is that if you are connected by modem, your Web server will be fairly slow for users. Finally, Personal Web Sharing can handle only a single page or a list of files or both. But it can't handle a huge multi-page Web site, nor can it handle more advanced Web site features, such as guest-logging, e-commerce, and searching within your site.

NOTE

I could not get Personal Web Sharing to work using AOL as my Internet connection. I'm told that it can be done, but I couldn't make it work for me. (However, it worked fine when I used a local ISP to connect to the Internet.) If you use AOL for your Internet connection, you may not be able to use Personal Web Sharing.

Using an ISP or AOL to Host Your Web Site

If you want a full-time Web site or if your needs are greater than the single-page Personal Web Sharing offers, your best bet is to let someone else host your site. That way it will be faster; it will be available 24 hours a day, whether or not your iMac or iBook is turned on; and you'll have professional assistance if you need it.

The Advantages of Using an ISP or AOL to Host Your Web Site

First and foremost, an ISP or AOL host's connection to the Internet is guaranteed to be faster than yours; so your pages will be served up faster and can be seen by more users simultaneously. Another advantage is that your site will be available 24 hours a day. You can also add services like e-commerce, streaming audio or video, or secure transactions if you like (with an ISP but not with AOL). Finally, most ISPs (but not AOL) offer great technical support for your site.

The Disadvantages of Using an ISP or AOL to Host Your Web Site

The biggest disadvantage is that it's going to cost you something. If you use AOL and your needs are modest, you get 2MB of space for a Web page included with your monthly fee. But if your site exceeds 2MB, you'll have to find another host. AOL doesn't have an option for bigger sites. ISPs charge anywhere from $15 a month to hundreds of dollars a month, depending upon what services you require and the size of your site.

The only other disadvantage I can think of is that hosting a site remotely is somewhat more complicated than turning on Personal Web Sharing. Be prepared to invest substantial time if you want to set up and run a Web server hosted remotely.

Part III

The Bottom Line

If your needs are few and all you want is a simple home page or the ability to allow people to download files from your Mac via the Internet, Personal Web Sharing is for you. Don't forget that your iMac or iBook has to be connected to the Internet for your page to be available to others.

If you want a feature-rich, multi-page Web site that's fast, available 24 hours a day, and can include advanced features, your best bet is to find a good ISP and have them host it.

FIXING PIX FOR E-MAIL

This is a quick tutorial about how to prepare pictures—optimizing both the file size and quality—and send them via e-mail to Mac or PC users. If you don't work with pictures or don't e-mail pictures to others, you'll find this discussion totally irrelevant. Otherwise, read on.

The basic premise is that pictures sent via e-mail should almost always be converted to the JPEG file format before sending.

NOTE

JPEG is the Joint Photographic Experts Group file format. It creates smaller files than almost any other file format and preserves the integrity of your photos better than other compressed file formats, such as GIF.

There are two ways that you can accomplish this: the quick-and-dirty method using AppleWorks and the slightly more complicated (but more controllable) method using the shareware program GraphicConverter. Let's take a look.

Quick-and-Dirty Picture Fixing with Apple-Works

First, let's try the easy way to get your picture saved in the JPEG format:

1. Launch AppleWorks.

2. Open the picture file.

NOTE

This is the part that may throw you: AppleWorks cannot open all pictures. For example, if your picture is saved in the TIFF format, AppleWorks may or may not be able to open it. If you can't open your picture using AppleWorks, skip to the next section now.

3. Edit, resize, and otherwise manipulate the picture until you're satisfied.

4. Choose File ➤ Save As.

5. Choose JPEG from the pop-up Save As menu.

6. Name your file and click Save.

You're now ready to e-mail that file (see the final section of this chapter). Using this technique, I slimmed a 636K PICT file into a 40K JPEG file with almost no loss of quality.

While this method is easy and creates a JPEG file, which is what you want, you have no control over the quality or size of the JPEG file. This may well be all you want or need. But if you would like some additional control over the quality of your picture, you'll want to use Graphic-Converter instead of AppleWorks.

Picture Fixing with GraphicConverter

GraphicConverter is a great shareware program that can open almost every graphics file format ever invented and can save your file using almost any graphics file format ever invented. There are two reasons you might prefer GraphicConverter over AppleWorks. First, GraphicConverter can open many types of graphics files that AppleWorks can't open. Second, GraphicConverter lets you adjust the image quality of your picture, allowing you to tweak both the quality of your picture and the size of the resulting file.

NOTE

GraphicConverter is shareware. If you use it more than a few times, you are honor-bound to send its author, Thorsten Lemke, $35. Don't be a creep—if you use it, please pay for it.

Here's how to make a better JPEG file:

1. Install *GraphicConverter* if you haven't already done so.

2. Launch GraphicConverter.

3. Open the picture file.

4. Edit, resize, and otherwise manipulate the picture until you're satisfied.

5. Choose File ➣ Save As.

6. Choose JPEG/JFIF from the pop-up Format menu.

7. Click the Options button. This brings up the Options dialog box, where the real fun happens.

8. Click both the Preview and Calculate File Size check boxes. These two items make the Options dialog box much more useful.

NOTE

If you want to see a different part of your picture in the preview, click directly on the preview picture and drag. That will allow you to move it around.

9. Slide the Quality slider left or right. When you do so, keep an eye on the Preview so you can see how the quality setting affects the way your picture looks. While you're playing with the slider, keep your other eye on the file-size information so you know how big your file will be at this quality setting. See Figure 15.12 for an example. Ignore the Library section of this dialog box for now. Leave it set to JPEG 6.0 with the Progressive option unchecked.

NOTE

You'll achieve the best balance of file size and quality near the middle of the scale, where it says "Normal."

10. When you're happy with the quality and size, click OK.

11. Name your file and click Save.

That's it. You're ready to e-mail that file (see the final section).

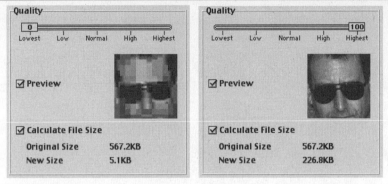

FIGURE 15.12:   Compare the quality and file size at the lowest setting (left) and highest setting (right).

Sending Your Picture via E-mail

The hard part is over. Now just launch your e-mail program, prepare a message to your recipient, then add the JPEG picture as an enclosure. Now send the message. Your recipient will receive the JPEG file; and, assuming they have a program that can open a JPEG file (which almost every computer user—Mac and PC—does), they'll be able to download and view your picture.

NOTE

If your e-mail program offers the option of compressing the file before sending, don't bother. When you saved the file in the JPEG format, you compressed it. Using your e-mail's compression won't make the file (much) smaller and may complicate things for the recipient.

WHAT'S NEXT?

This chapter provided a bounty of tips and hints for getting more out of the Internet with your iMac or iBook. Chapter 16, "Connecting from the Road," will tell you everything you need to know so you can connect to the Internet while traveling.

Part III

Chapter 16
CONNECTING FROM THE ROAD

The average mobile user appears bedecked with numerous electronic tools. Yesterday it was critical for the mobile user to have a laptop. Today, the mobile user needs a laptop, a PDA (that is, a handheld "personal digital assistant"), a cell phone, wireless access, two-way pagers, and a ton of other stuff they may not even really need for simple communications (when a decent cell phone will do), but that they consider critical nonetheless.

This chapter will take you through the aspects of being a mobile user in the Internet age, how to be prepared, and what to do when things go wrong (or at least ways to possibly prevent things from going wrong). In general, the technologies and functions of your computer(s) that are described in this chapter are more narrative than procedural.

You will find a great deal of help, pointers, and other tips that you, as the person "on the road," will find invaluable. Most of what makes up the mobile arsenal is taken from a wide array of tools that desktop users already have and what I've already covered in depth.

The Laptop

In general, any laptop can access the Internet. It may require some additional purchases, but if it can run Windows 95/98, the MacOS, or any flavor of Unix, and can physically accept a modem, it can access the Internet. Most modern laptops ship with a way to connect to some sort of network. Read on for details.

IBM PC-Compatible Laptops

Since the PC can host either Windows or Unix, the choice really comes down to hardware. The problem with PC hardware is the lack of any cohesive standards management. Subsequently, there are hundreds of possible combinations and their quality can range from excellent to practically non-existent based on how well the unit was engineered and whether the components used were of quality origin.

It's a lot easier than you might think to end up buying a junk laptop. Because of this simple fact, I can only suggest purchasing from major, well-known vendors that have a solid reputation. Examples of this are Compaq (www.compaq.com), IBM (www.ibm.com), Fujitsu (www.fujitsu.com), Toshiba (www.toshiba.com), Dell (www.dell.com), Quantex (www.quantex.com), Micron (www.micron.com), and Gateway (www.gateway.com). Each of these companies has an exemplary reputation and two of them, Quantex and Micron, have units good enough to stand up to the other members on this short list because they have guts and gusto and produce solid, reliable products.

All of the companies listed above develop laptop systems that are geared toward the mobile professional. All of them have lots of power, lots of memory, big, bright screens, and a lot of options. (They also weigh a ton—the average laptop bag can weigh up to 25 lbs!!) Most come with built-in 56K modems, but that's a point that needs to be watched for.

TIP

Look for S-video or NTSC/PAL/SECAM (depending on where you live, of course) out capabilities on your prospective laptop. This means you can connect your machine directly to a large-screen TV for your presentation, instead of having to lug a projector around.

The So-called WinModem

The PC is great, until you need to run something other than Windows on it. Sure, Windows is everywhere and used by everyone (not really, but it sure seems that way) so most computers are designed to meet Windows needs. That makes it tough for people who want or need to use Unix, Solaris, or Linux as their mobile x86 operating system. One of the chief complaints from non-Windows users is the so-called WinModem. It was discovered that with today's cheap processing power, manufacturers could build modems that aren't really modems, but more akin to a sound card, thus the WinModem was born.

These "faux" modems work just fine. In fact you'd never know you were using one unless you asked . . . or unless you use a non-Windows OS. These modems, though they work in Windows with special drivers, will not work without these special drivers on systems *other* than Windows. Very few WinModem drivers are available for non-Windows OS's. There is one group of programmers that is working on writing drivers for such modems. They call themselves LinModem (www.linmodem.org). They have working drivers for a smattering of WinModems so you might want to check them out before you run off with a modem that won't work and are then forced to buy a new one. There are several companies that now pre-install Linux on their laptops. There's even one that is dedicated to building and supporting Linux-based laptops, appropriately called TuxTops (Tux, the little penguin, is the Linux mascot). They can be found at www.tuxtops.com.

The next item to look for is an Ethernet connection. Very few PC laptops have built-in Ethernet ports. This is mostly because there's much to fear from a competitor who avoids the cost of built-in Ethernet and forms a partnership with a card vendor and ends up getting a 56K modem and a 10Base-T Ethernet connection in one card for less. In the end, this is pretty much why all of them do it, so keep an eye out for that bundled combination Modem/Ethernet card, as it will save you *lots* of time and effort.

The nice thing is that your Ethernet port may come in handy *away* from the office. Later in the chapter, you will see that there are a growing number of hotels that are installing Ethernet access into their buildings. If you can get this, it means fast access to files and services right from your room. Miraculously, most hotels do *not* charge much of a premium for these new services, though you should watch out for excessive billing on "pamper" services such as hand-delivered color copies.

Apple PowerBook

These latest PowerBooks are completely "there." You need nothing extra. Whatever you add is just icing on an already very rich cake. There's a built-in 56k modem and 10/100Base-T Ethernet. There are some things still left to consider, however. Not all things are peachy in Laptop Land, even in Macdom. Older models of the PowerBook line do not have Ethernet, but do have one or more serial ports so an external modem can be added.

NOTE

From the PowerBook 100 to the PowerBook 180 and all in between you will require a special AppleTalk-to-Ethernet adapter from Asante (www.asante.com).

Identifying these models is difficult indeed, as Apple has removed all model-identifying insignia on all of their machines. To give you an example, there's only one iMac. Yet did you know that there have been four revisions of the iMac since it was introduced? Now, you have three different models to choose from, but none of them are marked, you just have to pick the right box! The only thing that has changed for the buyer is a small case redesign, some updated internal components, and ever-speedier CPUs.

Well, Apple did the same with their G3 laptops. They made some internal adjustments and improved performance, upping the ante for their PC counterparts. The most recent visual changes were the updates codenamed "Wallstreet" which changed the keyboard from the traditional solid plastic to a nice amber translucent tone. It was also thinned at the waist and lightened.

ALTERNATIVES TO THE LAPTOP

Wireless is just now starting to explode into the mainstream. Sure, we've had cellular phones and pagers for some time and it's unlikely that we'll see the end of them. In fact, we're likely to see a lot more of them very soon. There are a number of companies that are releasing a wide range of new devices and updated versions of old friends.

The best known these days, it seems, is 3Com's Palm device line. Just before this was written, Palm was spun off into its own company and announced new products, including a color version of its popular Palm III. A Palm is a simple device, but they are popular because of equal shares of simplicity and customizability. Either you can use it as it ships and have a fine little organizer, or you can add all sorts of applications to it, including the new AOL Everywhere. Interesting! We'll get there in just a second.

It would be unfair not to mention Microsoft's Pocket PC line of PDAs. As of this writing, Microsoft, Casio, Hewlett-Packard, and Compaq have announced the third version of Windows CE, a slick new look, new devices, and a new campaign: "Can your palm do that? Not unless it's holding a Pocket PC." Ouch! Microsoft wants you to use their OS and buy devices from their partners, not Palm or Visor. Visor? Haven't heard about that one yet, have you? Let's take a quick look at what these devices can do, and a few other alternatives.

Palm

Palm devices are small and fit nicely in the palm of your hand. There are several models of Palm devices (note Table 16.1), each having a slightly different appearance and configuration, and varying capabilities. Although this will likely be inaccurate by the time you read it, prices for Palm devices range from $150 to $450, the most expensive of which is Palm's claim to fame, the world's first self-contained wireless PDA, the Palm VII.

TABLE 16.1: Palm devices and their Internet connectivity capabilities

	MEMORY	CONNECTIVITY SOLUTION	OS	EST. PRICE
Palm IIIe	2MB		3.0	$150*
Palm IIIc	8MB		3.5	$450**
Palm IIIxe	8MB		3.0	$250
Palm V	2MB	Palm V Modem ($169) 33.6 snap-on modem for remote HotSync (from 3Com)	3.0	$330
Palm Vx	8MB		3.5	$400
Palm VII	8MB	Built-in PalmNet access	3.2	$450

*also includes the Special Edition version with a clear case ; **first Palm device with a color screen

Now, as far as I can tell, there is no presentation solution for the Palm device line. Technically, this would leave a hole open for a laptop, but a large number of mobile professionals who use Palms would likely tell you that without it they would be mindless automatons (or perhaps that with their Palm they are permitted to be mindless automatons when need be!).

Pocket PC and Windows CE Devices

Again, this offering from Microsoft's hardware partners is out to prove that it can out-Palm Palm. The numbers have not shown that they have succeeded, however. Palm still holds approximately 70% of the PDA market over all other competitors. The Pocket PC isn't out of the game, though. There are things that a Pocket PC and its older Windows CE (WinCE) cousins can do that Palm devices wish they could do, or at least that's what Microsoft expects consumers to think. Bigger, after all, is better.

TIP

Something else the Pocket PC and Windows CE devices can do that Palms can't—they can use Compact Flash (CF) and PCMCIA cards (sometimes called PC Cards or mistakenly, CardBus). All Pocket PCs, previously known as Palmtop PCs, have built-in CF slots.

There are generally two forms that Windows CE devices take, the Handheld and the Clamshell. The handheld, or P/PC, is roughly the same in appearance as a Palm device, just somewhat bulkier. There are buttons arrayed about the various units, but they do not have keyboards. All input is via handwriting recognition, tapping on the screen with a stylus, or tapping little digital keys of an on-screen keyboard. There is a smattering of external keyboards for P/PCs.

The clamshell design, also called an H/PC, is somewhat like a laptop in function, just smaller. The lower half contains a keyboard of varying functionality dependant upon its manufacturer, and the upper half contains the screen. Input is generally by keyboard and using the stylus to approximate the functions of a mouse. There is a larger format called the Jupiter-class that looks suspiciously like a full-size laptop.

One ability in particular is delivering presentations *without* a laptop. Step back in time to last year (or 1999, depending on when you are reading this) and witness the NEC MobilePro 780. This unit can slide into a coat pocket and the keyboard is still big enough to touch type on. It has a VGA out port to connect it to a projector or, with an adapter, connect it to a TV. Pocket PowerPoint is part of the package, so you're ready to give presentations without lugging a 9-pound laptop around.

WARNING

There are limitations. These devices are not particularly speedy and there are space constraints that disallow large presentation files.

TIP

Iomega (www.iomega.com) makes a great little peripheral called Clik!, a tiny 40MB cartridge drive for digital cameras and PDAs. The drive comes in various form factors to fit your needs. Possibly the coolest version is the PC Card drive.

They are, however, great for remote data retrieval and viewing as you can see in Figure 16.1, which shows the AvantGo service displaying HTML-based content from various vendors. AvantGo also sells a version of their server so your IT division can make the absolute latest data available to you in the field. It's just a cell phone call away.

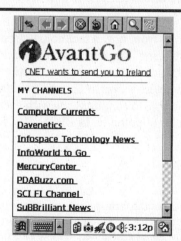

FIGURE 16.1: AvantGo (www.avantgo.com) displaying its personal home page with links to pages stored on the device and downloaded from pretty much anywhere you have access to the Internet.

The latest from Microsoft, Pocket PC (PPC), does not exactly have these capabilities, as it is in direct competition with the Palm devices. Oddly, for a company that wants its devices to be taken seriously, it comes packed with entertainment features such as an MP3 player and a Web browser. Though there are no versions to compete directly with the Palm VII, there are wireless and remote solutions for these devices. There are a lot, so here are a few (for pointers to more, there are a few links a bit later):

▶ CDPD Modems–(Cellular Digital Packet Data) These are essentially cellular phones in a modem card that can be inserted into the CF or PCMCIA slots that are part and parcel of all WinCE and PPC devices.

▶ IrDA–Though it's not as cool as a cellular modem card, there are a few cell phones that have modem capabilities and can communicate with PDAs through the ever-present IrDA port. It's slow, but what other wireless Internet access isn't?

▶ The RJ-11 Kludge–Pronounced KLOOGE, this one is a bit complicated, but it works. Get a PCMCIA or CF analog modem and an RJ-11 adapter for $150. This device allows you to connect a plain-vanilla phone jack (RJ-11) cable into a cell phone and use it to dial out.

▶ The Future Gambit–Not too long from now a technology from IBM called BlueTooth will start being integrated into more and more devices. Palm has already made announcements that their entire line will be able to offer wireless access by the end of 2000 and that these devices would be able to communicate with each other via BlueTooth. There's a lot of potential in BlueTooth, so keep an eye out.

NOTE

BlueTooth? Okay, the name is weird, but the technology is sound *and* is gaining ground fast. IBM said, why not place a small radio transceiver in every device and teach them how to know about each other? It's like kids passing notes in school. When they're close together it's easy to pass a note. BlueTooth works something like that; you just don't have to hide it from Mrs. Cratchelberry from 3rd grade.

In general, the idea is to install a modem or modem connectivity device to the PDA and dial-up to your provider or a Remote Access Services number hosted by your company (make sure they either pay the long distance or get an 800 number).

PREPARING TO HIT THE ROAD

Nobody knows or can predict everything, especially road-weary mobile professionals harried by impossible schedules.

7:00am awake

7:15am breakfast

7:30am rental car to conference center

7:45am unpack equipment, find that you forgot the projector

7:55am rush back to the hotel to get missing link

8:10am back at conference center, deal with squabble over allocated floor space

8:15am you lose squabble *and* time

8:25am find 150' bright orange extension cable for 20' problem

8:30am not ready but zoom by announced presentation time; several dozen potential customers sit waiting

8:40am almost finish setting up PowerPoint, spill coffee on shirt

8:45am remove most of stain thanks to someone's Shout™ Brand instant spot remover sheets

8:55am complete setting up PowerPoint presentation with *correct* slide order

9:05am technical staff finds missing microphone

9:10am begin presentation 40 minutes late

In the span of just short of two hours one can manage to have an aneurysm based simply on the fact that too many things can go wrong in such a short period of time. The name for this is Murphy's Law, which states that anything that *can* go wrong *will*. There is, however, a way to beat Murphy, and that is to be prepared. Let's look at another list that's more helpful. Here is a basic checklist that gets you out the door with room to spare:

- ▶ Shirts/Blouses
- ▶ Slacks/Skirts

- ▶ Ties/Accessories
- ▶ Sundry personal items
- ▶ Shoes
- ▶ Casual clothing
- ▶ Travel kit (shampoo, soap, toothbrush, etc.)
- ▶ Laptop/Electronic devices
- ▶ Diskettes

TIP

If you have a PC laptop or older PowerBook, get a Zip drive. If you have a new PowerBook, get the LS SuperDisk option (120MB cartridge). Place all important files and related material on these disks. Do *NOT* put them on the hard drive. You *will* lose them when you need them most.

- ▶ Extra battery
- ▶ Battery charger
- ▶ System disk

TIP

Since you have all of your important files on removable media, you can format and reinstall your system software without a care in the world. What!!?? You didn't have your important files on a removable disk??

- ▶ Extension cord
- ▶ Digital-Analog converter

TIP

Most hotels use digital phone equipment, which happily consumes analog modems for breakfast. In other words, you cannot use an analog modem on a digital line, even if the plug fits in the jack. For $150 you can get a converter that keeps your trusty 56K modem from frying. Get one.

- ▶ Power converters (if traveling abroad)

Here's a list of optional items that could come in handy:

- ▶ Extra batteries (more than one extra battery is always better; however, they aren't cheap)
- ▶ Portable CD-R/RW drive & media
- ▶ Extra external modem
- ▶ Serial and Parallel cables
- ▶ Portable printer
- ▶ Acoustic coupler

TIP

What? Yes, an acoustic coupler is absolutely critical if you happen to be somewhere that prevents you from using anything else to get connected. Plug it into your modem, strap it to the handset, and dial. Not pretty, and quite ancient looking, but it works. Period.

ON THE ROAD AGAIN

Most texts that attempt to assist a mobile pro like you often skip over one of the most important aspects of being mobile, *the actual travel*. Let's face it, if you work for someone they likely expect you to work anytime you get the chance. Why else would they buy you that shiny new laptop for many thousands of dollars? Then again, if you work for yourself you have to hustle 110% of the time to stay ahead of the game.

One of the ways to stay up to speed is to know when and where you can connect or just plug in. Let's look at the big three: car, rail, and air.

Car

The car is great because you always have a ready power source. Just make sure you have the right adapters and other cables for your equipment. There is also an in-car desk that mounts over the passenger seat if you are a really hardcore mobile pro.

Part III

Rail

Trains may be slow, but they have normal plugs. You can plug your equipment in without adapters and save your batteries all in one go. There are also large tables in the dining cars that you can simply take over, plug in, and start working.

Air

Planes are cramped unless you spend the outrageous fees on first class and there's still not enough room to spread out. Fortunately, with exception to international flights, the flights tend to be significantly shorter than the other modes of travel. Most planes, however, do have a plug here and there.

WARNING

If you've never heard, watch out. The FAA has banned the use of electronic devices on airliners during take-off and landing and you can never, *ever* use a cell phone.

BEING THERE

A critical capability these days is to have access to the Internet. Sure, you could hook that snazzy $150 adapter and cable up to your cell phone, but you'd be limited to a measly 14.4Kb/s data transfer rate. Phooey! You need some raw, unadulterated power. Most places can't give you that, but a few can.

Most places offer simple dial-up connectivity through what is commonly called a dataport. The dataport is simply a built-in Digital-to-Analog converter (also called a DAC) that you can connect your analog modem to without frying it. Not all hotels offer this, though, so you need to call and check out the services offered at the actual hotel you intend to stay at. Otherwise, you'll need a DAC that you can take with you. Also around US$150, there are a few such devices, but then again, I happen to think $150 is worth protecting multimillion dollar contracts.

North American Hotel Chains

Table 16.2 is a compilation of what I've found by my own experience, check-ing out respective Web sites, and actually communicating with company staffers regarding the level of service that is provided. This is by no means a comprehensive overview, but there's enough here to give you an idea of where to start. Make sure to read the notes after each hotel and especially the notes after the table. Note this key when referring to the table:

- I = Internet access
- R = In-room access or features
- C = Computer Center on premises

TABLE 16.2: Comparison of North American Hotel Chains

	I	R	C	NOTES	URL & NUMBER
Best Western	Y	Y	N	Not all locations have access, as it's up to each hotel owner to add such a feature.	http://www.bestwestern.com 800-780-7234
Hilton*	Y	Y	Y	Hilton reports that they have already wired over 100 Hilton brand locations with in-room DSL access. It's quite a feat and they are expanding to even more locations.	http://www.hilton.com 800-774-1500
Howard Johnson	Y	Y	Y	Surprisingly, HoJo has special rooms in all of their locations. Cendant, the parent company, also owns Days Inn and Wingate Inns, the former of which has business traveler rooms in 200 of their locations. The latter boasts high-speed access in every location, and has the noted Business Centers.	http://www.hojo.com 800-406-1411
Hyatt	Y	Y	Y	Data ports are located in most rooms and there is access to enhanced business services when traveling abroad. I was informed that Hyatt is begin-ning a chain-wide move to upgrade all rooms at all sites. Business Traveler rooms will have high-speed access and in-room fax machines. Nice.	http://www.hyatt.com 800-633-7313

Part iii

TABLE 16.2 continued: Comparison of North American Hotel Chains

	I	R	C	NOTES	URL & NUMBER
Marriott**	Y	Y	N	Marriott International is quite the hospitality organization. They have a *very* wide range of business-related services, including conference centers.	http://www.marriott.com 800-228-9290
Starwood***	Y	Y	Y	With Sheraton and Westin being the best-known names in Starwood's collection, it's easy to expect excellence. Most of their locations include the expected components, but not all. Starwood's Luxury Collection of hotels is more oriented toward the pricey get-away.	http://www.starwood.com 800-325-3535
Ramada	Y	Y	N	Most locations include Business Class rooms that have in-room data ports.	http://www.ramada.com 888-298-2054
Accor	Y	Y	N	Accor, a French company, owns both the Red Roof Inn and Motel 6 chains, the leaders in low-priced hospitality. Why are they listed here? You will be surprised to find out that every single Motel 6 (808 locations) and Studio 6, their new long-term stay brand, has data ports in the rooms.	http://www.redroof.com 800-733-7663 http://www.motel6.com 800-466-8356

* Hilton Hotels owns several brands such as DoubleTree, Embassy Suites, Harrison Conference Centers, Homewood Suites, Hampton Inn, Red Lion, Conrad International, and (of course) Hilton and Hilton Garden hotels. Connectivity information refers to all Hilton brands.
** Marriott includes the following brands: Renaissance, Courtyard, Residence Inn, Fairfield Inn, ExecuStay, TownePlace Suites, and SpringHill Suites; also, Marriott is a partner with Ritz-Carlton.
*** Starwood owns several brands as well: Westin, Four Points, St. Regis, and W Hotels.

International Chains

There are really far too many hotel chains to make listing them here easy. Twenty-seven different chains are recognized in the previous table, and that covers a small percentage of hotel chains in North America. Of course, most of the brands listed in the table also have many, *many* sites located around the world. If you would prefer to stay with a familiar name, call their toll-free number and ask if they have a property at or near your destination. At the very least, they may have a partner they freely suggest, and some can even book rooms for you.

The best resource I have found is the Accommodation Search Engine at www.ase.net where you can select a country, choose your price range and features (make sure you select the Business Facilities option), and, once you find one you want, instantly book a room.

OPTIONS FOR CONNECTING

To be honest, there are few. There are wireless solutions, but they are slow. I'll go over those solutions, however, because sometimes that's all there is. The most common remote and mobile access point is dial-up, the modem—the *analog* modem. In this day of cheap "Fat Pipe" access, the analog modem seems to be limiting, but there are only rare exceptions. In general, you're going to use your modem or an Ethernet port.

In this section I'll hit on a few topics. First, I'll touch on the few options there are for getting connected when you're in the States but have no convenient facilities. Next up I'll talk about some of the more esoteric and exotic options. That section is short and sweet. Finally, I'll note some aspects of getting connected in the mobile sense. Not so much setting up your portable device to connect to the Internet, as you likely already have that set up, but more options, tricks, tips, and utilities that make the whole thing easier.

Part iii

External Options

One external option is Kinko's. It may seem strange, but Kinko's, if you are unaware, has high-speed access at all of their locations, and most of them are open 24 hours a day. Unfortunately, you cannot use their Laptop Station, which provides Ethernet LAN connectivity to their in-store printers. However, you can use their systems (both MacOS and Windows flavors; sorry, Linux users) to quickly retrieve large presentation files and other material from remote locations and then move them to your laptop with Zip disks.

Of course, therein lies the problem. You need a Zip drive to copy those files and if you don't have one, you'll be saddled with having to copy to 1.44MB floppy diskettes. Floppies can take a very long time, depending on how large your files are, but what else can you do? Do you spend $250 to "same-day" FedEx a CD-R containing your missing presentation files or do you spend a couple of hours downloading them from your servers at $12/hour?

Another option is the hotel itself. There are Kinko's stores everywhere, but there is an ever growing number of hotel chains that are adding business centers with computers, Internet connection, fax, copiers, and other business-related services. Some are even going as far as to stock individual rooms with a PC, Internet connection through Ethernet, an analog telephone jack (I'll get to that), and remote access to color print jobs that get delivered by room service.

This sounds better than any Kinko's with floppy swapping, but not all hotels have this. In fact, this type of service is still in the minority. It will be easier to locate a hotel that meets your needs in a major metropolitan area, but if you ask for these things in places where the population is less than 10,000, you will likely get looked at funny. Examine the table in the previous section to determine whether the hotel chain you are planning on using can supply you with what you need. Some are quite a bit better than others, but the mass majority do, at the very least, offer analog dialup capabilities in the room or in special rooms. Be sure to ask when you make your reservations.

TIP

If you've never visited your selected hotel chain, do not make a reservation over the Internet first. Always call and ask questions.

The Unconventional

I've mentioned it before, but I was actually somewhat serious when I mentioned that there is a roughly $150 way to connect your cell phone to an incompatible laptop modem card. Some modem cards simply don't have the special cable jack that they need to communicate with the phone. Then you might be one of the unlucky individuals that acquired your laptop and cell phone separately and with no preconception that you'd ever connect them together.

Apple PowerBook IrDA ‡ Cellular Phone

The new G3 PowerBooks from Apple offer three ways to connect: built-in modem, Ethernet port, or Infrared (IrDA). The modem and Ethernet are easy, but the IrDA port is a new one. Some cellular phones have the ability to offer connectivity services to various devices, one of which is the G3 PowerBook. It's easy to get hooked up. Try this:

1. Get an IrDA-compliant phone (Ericsson SH888 or Nokia 7110 are two that Apple notes support for).

2. Point the PowerBook's IrDA port and the phone's IrDA port at each other. Keep them within reasonable range.

3. Go to the Apple menu and open Control Panels > Modem. Select Infrared Port from the Connect Via pulldown.

4. Test.

5. Be disappointed with the speed.

6. Disconnect.

So it's not a speed demon compared to your cable/DSL/T1 connection at home/the office but in a pinch it can get the job done.

NOTE

Some Windows CE devices are also capable of using this method, also with certain phones. At the time of this writing I was unable to locate any information on how to do this with any Windows-based systems other than WinCE.

Part III

The Actual Connection

If you are not connected or do not know how to setup your machine to connect to the Internet, Chapter 1, "Understanding the Internet," details everything. Read that chapter first, then this material will be more comprehensible. I do include the raw steps to define various required parameters in the MacOS and Windows, but it's not complete if you haven't already been through the real material. The following sections detail some notes to remember.

Any Platform

Access numbers are crucial, no matter what you're dialing into. If you don't have a number, you can't call. Taping them to the bottom of your laptop or keeping a list near your pocket cash stash is always smart.

If you're dialing into your ISP, make sure they have access numbers in the rest of the country or that they have other means to connect. If your ISP doesn't have a remote access policy, or access numbers from where you're going, it may be time to find another provider.

Major ISPs are MindSpring/EarthLink, Prodigy Internet, WebPathway, PISN.net, Global Internet Solutions, and Aireus Internet Solutions. AT&T WorldNet service is pretty much everywhere. You'll be hard pressed to find an ISP that offers global access, though. Microsoft Network (MSN) is, not surprisingly, available only to Windows users.

That leaves AOL and CompuServe; both offer access overseas with local dialups in many countries and regions. Though AOL is considered unpopular due to its undeserved "newbies only" status, it is the largest non-Internet ISP in the world (AOL provides its own superstructure, from which users can, if they wish, access the Internet). CompuServe (incidentally, AOL owns CompuServe) also has global dialup services.

MacOS

For regular ISP access, make sure you have the IP numbers for the Primary and Secondary DNS servers. If the ISP requires that you use a *gateway*, make sure to get that number as well. All of these numbers are in the format *xxx.xxx.xxx.xxx*. An example would be 216.59.48.3, which is the address of a site on the Web. Those numbers are entered in the TCP/IP control panel, which you can find in the Apple menu under Control Panels.

WARNING

If you ever have to remove the battery from the case to shut down a stiff Power-Book, check all of the OT/PPP control panels. This includes TCP/IP, Modem, AppleTalk, and PPP control panels. If you use FreePPP or Gearbox (both from Rockstar.com; one free, one not), then you don't have to worry about these settings. They are stored in preferences files located in Macintosh HDD:System Folder:Preferences.

Try to use the correct ARA modem script for your unit. If you have an older PowerBook then you might have a third party modem installed, like a Global Village. The external TelePort modems and the internal replacement modems, the PowerPorts, came in many different models and all have slightly different init strings. Finding the correct ARA script will allow the modem to perform at its peak ability.

TIP

Init strings are great and all, but if you really need to get going and don't have time to fiddle with things, try AT&F1. It's not much, but it'll likely get you the best speed out of your modem.

OpenTransport Setup

Although there are other PPP packages that I've mentioned here, the official one is direct from Apple and it's called OpenTransport (OT). OT began shipping with System 7.6, but is available for System versions 7.1.2 through 7.5.5. Older versions of the MacOS need to use MacTCP and its related files.

If you didn't install it already, you can find a copy on the MacOS CD-ROM that came with your PowerBook. Look in the Installers folder, which will be below the edge of the window that appears when you insert the CD into the drive. You can also download the most recent version (ironic, isn't it) from the following address:

```
ftp://ftp.apple.com/apple_support_area/apple_software_up
dates/english-north_american/macintosh/networking-communi-
cations/open_transport.
```

WARNING

Make sure there are no spaces in this address when you type it in. If there are, it won't work. Everything that looks like a space is really an underscore character (_ or Shift Dash).

Installation is easy:

1. First, go to the Apple menu and point to Control Panels, then select the TCP/IP control panel item. Figure 16.2 shows the TCP/IP control panel.

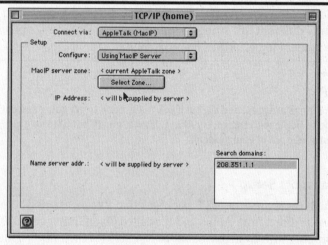

FIGURE 16.2: The TCP/IP control panel in the MacOS

2. Set the Connect via pulldown to PPP. The lower section of the dialog will change if it wasn't already set correctly. At the top of the new section is a pulldown called Configure. Set this to PPP Server.

3. The remaining fields should be filled in using the information you wrote down about your ISP, including DNS and Search Domains. If your ISP allocates you a gateway, they will also instruct you on how to set up TCP/IP. Close TCP/IP and choose Save when prompted.

4. Go back to the Apple menu, select Control Panels, and open the PPP item. Select the Registered User radio button and enter your Username and Password in the spaces provided below. If your ISP allows Guest access, select that radio button, but it's unlikely that they do.

5. You may optionally click on the Options button and select the Connection tab to set how PPP will show you that it's connected to the Internet. Click OK to save your changes and close the dialog box.

6. Click the Connect button and PPP will attempt to connect to your modem, open the line, dial the number you supplied, and handshake with whatever answers on the other end. There are some circumstances under which you will not connect. Those are:

   ▶ No dial tone

   ▶ No answer

   ▶ No modem on the other end

   ▶ Wrong number

   ▶ Bad init string (try AT&F1)

   ▶ Bad login or password

7. Once your connection has been established, the Apple menu will flash the PPP connection icon and the PPP control panel will change to display your connection status. When you are finished, you may terminate your PPP connection by clicking the Disconnect button.

When you're all done, you can make a wide range of changes and modifications to your overall Internet connection scheme by using Apple's superior Internet control panel (Figure 16.3). Most Mac Internet applications are Internet Config-savvy and Apple rolls that into this release.

Part III

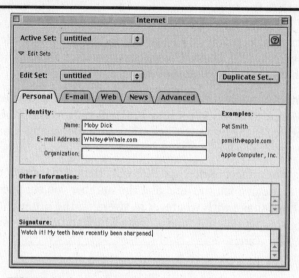

FIGURE 16.3: The Internet control panel

Windows

As always, keep your connectivity numbers near at hand at all times. Important numbers are your Primary and Secondary DNS numbers. These numbers are entered into the Network control panel located in Start ≻ Settings ≻ Control Panel ≻ Network. Click on the DNS tab, enable DNS, and type the DNS numbers into the spaces provided. When you are done with each number, click the Add button.

If you are lucky enough to have a static IP address, make sure you have that. (Imagine how annoying it would be if your house were allocated a new address every time you returned home from the office or the grocery store. A static IP address is the opposite.) It must be entered into the Network .

Dial-up Networking Setup

To set up dial-up networking in Win95/98:

1. To use PPP with Win95/98 you must have the TCP/IP network protocol installed. Verify that TCP/IP is installed by checking the Network Control Panel folder. Your network configurations must include a Dial-up adapter (your modem) and TCP/IP. Consult Windows online help to add a network protocol.

NOTE

Windows that is already installed for you already has Dial-up Networking (DUN) ready to go, with rare exceptions. If you do *not* have DUN installed (in other words, if there is no Dial-up Networking item in the Control Panel), you can install it pretty quickly. Start by inserting your Windows CD in the drive. Unless you have disabled AutoRun a menu will appear with the familiar Windows startup sound. Click the Add/Remove Programs item in the window and a dialog box will appear. Go to the Internet Tools item and double-click it. Another dialog box will open, and near the top of the item list will be an item called Dial-up Networking. Check this box and click OK. Click OK again and Windows will ask you to restart. Do so. Now you can follow the instructions.

2. Go to Start ➢ Settings ➢ Control Panel and open the Network item. Locate and double-click the item in the list called TCP/IP to display the TCP/IP Properties dialog box, shown in Figure 16.4. There are several tabs here. If you have standard ISP service, go directly to the DNS Configuration tab and click Enable DNS.

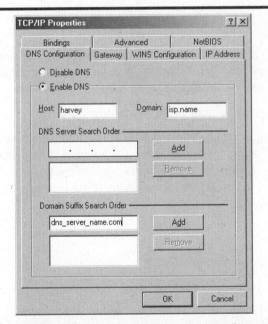

FIGURE 16.4: The TCP/IP Properties dialog box with the DNS Configuration tab selected

3. Time to enter a few things. Host means the name of *your* computer, as you want it to be seen on the network. This really applies only to local networking, but fill it anyway. Next, the Domain Name will be the name of your ISP. For example, if you use MindSpring, then you would enter **mindspring.com**, omitting the "www" at the front.

4. Next, enter the Primary DNS number supplied to you in the field marked DNS Server, and then click Add. The number will appear at the top of the list below. Enter the Secondary DNS number the same way and then click Add. That number will be added below the Primary DNS number. Although it's not important, this is the order in which an address will be searched.

5. Finally, enter the domain suffix, as above with your domain name, and click Add. If they are needed, then your ISP will have given them to you. Otherwise, ignore it.

Now we can move on to the dial-up configuration:

1. Go to Start ➤ Settings ➤ Control Panel ➤ Dial-up Networking and double-click the Make New Connection item.

2. On the first screen you'll be asked to enter a name for this connection. Name it something "mobile" sounding. Your modem device should appear below. Click Next.

3. Enter the access number you will be using. Click Next.

4. If everything is set up properly, then you will be shown the settings and asked to confirm them. Click Finish. A new icon will appear in the Dial-up Networking window with your named connection. It should look something (not exactly) like Figure 16.5.

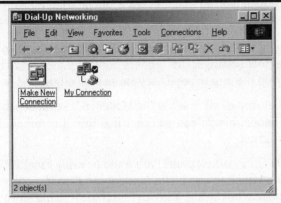

FIGURE 16.5: The Dial-up Networking window open and showing a new connection icon

Now you can make a connection by simply double-clicking on the new icon. A status window will appear and give you feedback on how the connection is going. When and if it does connect, the dialog box will minimize to the System Tray (next to the clock) and appear as a pair of little monitors with randomly flashing green screens. Right-clicking this icon opens a menu. Double-clicking it gets you the status window. You can disconnect from either of these.

TROUBLESHOOTING

Okay, I can talk endlessly or I can get to the point. Most likely you're in a hurry if you're looking at this section, and extra chit-chat won't help. So check these items first.

No Dial Tone–MacOS

If you are using a MacOS and you have no dial tone, here are some things you can check:

> ▶ First, check to see if the phone cable is properly inserted into the wall and the modem port. The Modem/Ethernet ports on G3 PowerBooks are combination ports, so the smaller RJ-11 jack fits inside where the larger RJ-45 jack for an Ethernet cable end fits.

▶ Check the Modem control panel to see if the internal modem is selected.

▶ If you are using an external modem, check the Serial cable connection, the port settings, the Modem control panel, and the power switch on the unit to see if they are all correctly seated/set.

▶ Make sure that AppleTalk is set to the Modem port and, depending on what model Macintosh you're using, that it is not set to Printer or Ethernet.

▶ Open your OT/PPP control panel (you could be using FreePPP or GearBox) and check to see if the modem is set to the correct model and modem init string. You can find the init string for your modem in either the documentation that came with your system or at the system maker's Web site.

▶ Voicemail systems typically notify users of new messages by pausing the dial tone a few times when you first pick up. This confuses the modem into thinking there's no dial tone. Add a "*70,," in front of the access number you are using. Alternately, you may turn off dial tone detection in the Modem control panel.

▶ If you are calling from your hotel room, you may need to add an "8" or a "9" in front of the number you are dialing.

No Dial Tone–Windows

If you are using a Windows OS and you have no dial tone, here are some things you can check:

▶ Check the wall end of the phone cable to make sure it's seated properly. On the modem card end, check to see that the end of the cable is properly seated in the jack adapter. Typically the adapter is a version of the X-Jack jumper from 3Com. The black tab pops out from the end of the card and provides a square area where you can place the RJ-11 jack head. Make sure the copper wire brushes inside the square are making contact with the copper pads on the jack head.

TIP

Some cards have full-size ports and most others have a special cable that plugs into the card and has a full-size jack on the other end. Avoid these, as it's very easy to lose the cable and very difficult to find a replacement.

▶ In Windows, go to Start ➤ Settings ➤ Control Panel and open the Modems item. Check to make sure a modem is even listed. If not, follow the manufacturer's instructions on how to properly install the modem drivers. Otherwise, select the Diagnostics tab.

▶ Click on the Com port that the modem is listed as being installed on and click the Driver button. A small dialog box should appear listing a driver size and a date installed. If the name of the driver is Comm.drv then it is the driver supplied by Microsoft. You may want to locate drivers specific to your model of modem, either from the maker of your laptop or from the maker of the modem, if you purchased it after the laptop.

▶ Click OK to close the Driver information dialog box and click on More Info. After a moment of probing the modem, the port, and the phone line, a new dialog box should appear. If there are any noted errors, reinstall the modem drivers according to the manufacturer's instructions. If all is well, close the dialog box.

▶ Go to Start ➤ Settings ➤ Control Panel ➤ Dial-up Networking and open the item that you set up as your travel set or remote access set, whichever approach you're using. Check the number. Make sure the area code is present and correct, if one is needed.

▶ Voicemail systems typically notify users of new messages by pausing the dial tone a few times when you first pick up. This confuses the modem into thinking there's no dial tone. Type *70,, in front of the access number you are using. Alternately, you may turn off dial tone detection in the Advanced properties sheet for the modem you are using. You can find that in Start ➤ Settings ➤ Control Panel ➤ Modems; then select the modem and click the Properties button.

▶ If you are calling from your hotel room or from an office, you may need to type an **8** or a **9** in front of the number you are dialing.

Part III

WHAT'S NEXT?

Now that you know everything about connecting to the Internet while you travel, Chapter 17, "Buying Online," will tell you everything you need to know in order to shop successfully on the Internet.

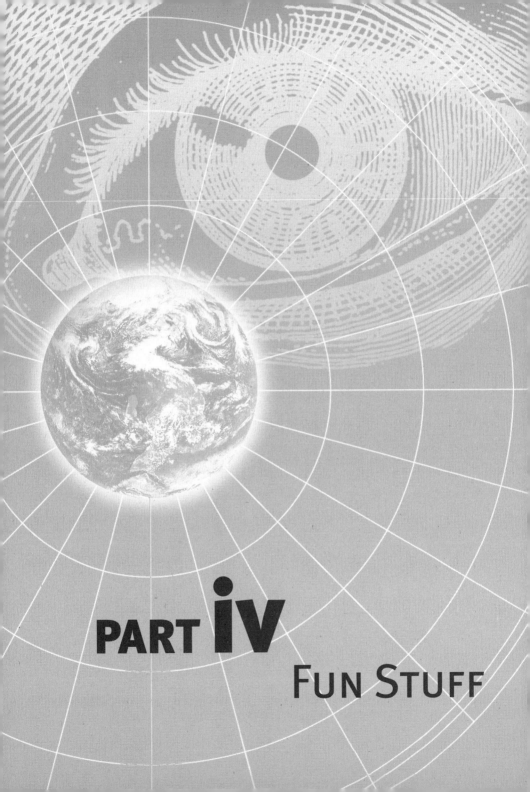

PART iV

FUN STUFF

CHAPTER 17

BUYING AND SELLING ONLINE

There are a lot of free things available on the Internet, but there are a lot of good things to buy as well. You can find all sorts of items that can be delivered right to your door, and at great prices. The Internet is also a great place to sell things, whether you have your own business or just want to clear out that old junk from the attic.

THE WORLD'S LARGEST BOOKSTORES

Without ever leaving your home, you can access the world's largest selection of books for sale. "So? Everybody already knows that," you say. But did you know that you can get hard-to-find, out-of-print, and antique books as well?

Adapted from *Internet! I Didn't Know You Could Do That..., Second Edition*, by Alan R. Neibauer
ISBN 0-7821-2844-0   282 pages $19.99

Remember that great book you had when you were a child? Do you collect books and paraphernalia about the Civil War or some other subject? Because of the global nature of the Internet, you can locate hard-to-find books on virtually every subject.

All you need is access to the Internet and a credit card that hasn't expired or exceeded its limit.

Sites and Features

First, to buy current books, check out one of these sites:

► www.amazon.com

► www.fatbrain.com

► www.barnesandnoble.com

► www.borders.com

Each of these sites has an easy search function for finding the book you want, and each features current best sellers right on their home page. You can also try the home pages of most publishers for book and ordering information. You just might be able to purchase directly from the publisher at a discount.

Searching Many Stores with AddALL

Rather than search through individual stores, you can search several stores at one time. By navigating to www.addall.com, for example, you can enter search criteria into a form and search 40 bookstores at the same time.

NOTE

You can also use AddALL to search for music and to sign up for free, Web-based e-mail.

Here's how to use the form:

1. Pull down the Shipping Destination list and choose the country or region where you want to send the book.

2. If shipping in the United States, select the state from the State list.

3. Choose the currency in which you want the prices displayed.

4. Pull down the Search By list, and select how you want to search the bookstores. The options are Title, ISBN, Author, and Keyword.

5. In the text box to the right of the Click to Find button, enter the search text—a title, ISBN number, author name, or keyword.

6. Click the Click to Find button.

You'll see a list of the available books that meet your search criteria. Click a book title to compare the pricing and availability at various online bookshops. To order the book, click Buy It to the right of your selected source.

To look for used, rare, and out-of-print books, click the Click Here link next to the Searching for Used Books? prompt that's below the addall .com form. In the form that appears, enter your search criteria. You can also designate the binding (all, hardcover, or paperback), whether you want a first edition or a signed copy, and the price range. Click Find the Book to get a listing of the online sites that have that book listed in their catalogs, along with their asking prices.

Searching with BookFinder.com and Bibliofind

The Web site at www.bookfinder.com also lets you search for new, used, rare, and out-of-print books using a similar form. The results appear in a separate table for each online store.

Many of the search sites such as the two already discussed include www.bibliofind.com as one of their search sites for used and out-of-print books. You can also go to that site directly to look for books. At Bibliofind, you can maintain a personal "want list" of books you are looking for.

Bibliofind maintains a database of books in a large number of bookstores. The results of your search are displayed as a list of books, each preceded by a check box. Click to place a checkmark in the check box next to the listing for each book you want to order, or click the Seller's link to read more about the seller. Click the price of a book to display the price in many of the world's currencies. If there are more books than can be listed in one page, click the More Titles button at the bottom of the list.

If the book you are looking for is not listed, you can scroll to the end to display the Personal Want List form. Enter information about a book you're looking for and click the Place on Want List button. The list is available to Bibliofind's member stores, and you'll be notified if the book is located.

Once you've checked the boxes for the books you want to purchase, click the Add to Shopping Basket button at the bottom of the list. You'll see a screen summarizing your order. Click the button labeled Place Order to enter your address, provide credit card information, and process the order. At this screen you'll also have a chance to empty your shopping basket if you change your mind.

Buying at Internet Auctions

Auctions such as eBay and Amazon can give you the same thrill as a real live auction house, from the comfort of your home or office. The auctions at eBay alone may have over 1.5 million items up for grab at any one time. You'll find something for every collection, both old and new merchandise, as well as some real bargains.

Making Sure You Win

The trick to getting what you want is to win the bid at a price you think is fair, and then actually get what you paid for. Some folks get carried away with the spirit of competition and end up paying more than they want—and often more than the object is worth.

All you will need to get started is access to the Internet and an e-mail address. Of course, when you start bidding, you will also need to dig for your checkbook.

Sites and Features

There are plenty of online auctions, but the granddaddy of them all is at www.ebay.com. Amazon and other companies have their own auctions, but eBay seems to have the greatest number and variety of items for sale.

If you're not familiar with online auctions, here's how they work. People with stuff to sell and people who want to buy things register with the auction by giving their e-mail address and usually their name and mailing address. Registration is almost always free. The sellers list items for sale. The listing includes a short description of the item, a minimum bid, and often a photograph of the item for sale. The description also states who pays the shipping charges—usually the buyer. The seller pays a small listing fee, usually under a dollar. Usually the seller's e-mail address is included in the description, in case prospective buyers have questions about the item for sale.

The auction usually runs for a set number of days—7 to 10 is about the average. Some auctions even let the seller select the number of days. Many auctions send a daily e-mail to the seller listing the current high bids on their items.

If you want to buy an item, you bid on it simply by filling out a form. You can check back regularly to see how the auction is going, and who has the current high bid. You may be notified if someone outbids you on an item, giving you a chance to submit a higher bid.

Many auctions, including eBay, use a *proxy bidding* system. This means that you can specify the highest amount that you are willing to pay for the item. The auction house will post your bid as either the minimum bid or one bid increment above the current winner. (Bid increments vary depending on the value of the item up for sale—they can be as little as 25 cents or as high as $10.) If someone bids higher than you do, the auction house automatically raises your bid, but only up to the maximum bid that you set.

For example, suppose you see an antique that you are interested in. It has a $10.00 minimum bid with a $1.00 bid increment, and you decide to post a maximum offer of $20.00. If no one else has bid on the item yet, your bid is recorded for just $10.00 (the minimum bid amount). If someone else has already bid at $10.00, your offer is shown as $11.00 ($10.00 plus a bid increment of $1.00).

Each time someone outbids you, the auction raises your bid to make it the highest until it reaches $20.00 (your maximum bid). Of course, you can always go back and change your maximum bid to make a larger offer, if you really want the item.

When you win a bid, you and the seller get in touch with each other via e-mail. The seller will tell you the shipping charges and how to make payment; you then send the seller a check or money order (according to whatever payment arrangement you have made), and they send you the item. There are also escrow services available. These usually charge a small fee to the buyer but allow them to pay by credit card. Until the merchandise is received, the funds are not released to the seller, who must agree to use the escrow service. See www.iescrow.com for more information on escrow services.

All in all, online auctions are a great way to buy interesting items that you may not be able to find locally.

Pick Your Items Wisely

Before bidding on an item, make sure it is what you want to spend your
money on and that the seller is reputable.

Read the description carefully, and if there is a picture, look at it
closely. If you have any questions, send an e-mail to the seller. Most auctions give you the e-mail address of the seller along with the item. If it is
not listed, you can get it easily. With eBay, for example, every item shows
the seller's eBay registration name. Sometimes the name is their e-mail
address, so all you need to do is just click it to send them an e-mail. Other
times, you'll need to click their eBay name and enter your own eBay name
and password to obtain the seller's e-mail. If the seller does not respond
at all to your inquiry, think twice about making a bid.

Look for similar items by other sellers. Auctions let you search in many
different ways—by keyword, category, price, or seller, to name a few. With
millions of items for sale, it may take some time, but you'll get a clearer
picture of an item's worth if you can find similar items to compare it to.

While you are in eBay's own search utility, you can open eBay Crawler
on your screen. The eBay Crawler screen is shown here:

To search using eBay Crawler, first enter a keyword for the item. Then
select the way the list is sorted, the auction type, and what you want to
search; then click GO. The program will connect to eBay by launching
your Web browser, if it is not already online; it will then display your
search results in the eBay window.

NOTE

Search for completed auctions to see what comparable items actually sold for in previous auctions. This gives you a better gauge of an item's value than the asking price.

Also, it's very important to check the feedback rating of the seller. The feedback rating is the way the auction site keeps everyone honest. After completing a transaction, the buyer and seller can leave a comment about each other—either positive or negative. In the screen that describes an item for auction, you will see a number following the seller's name. This number represents the feedback rating, which is roughly the number of positive comments minus the number of negative comments. A large feedback number indicates that the seller is active and has completed a number of transactions successfully.

Click the feedback number to read all of the comments, looking for negative remarks from unhappy buyers. Just bear in mind that it is impossible to please everyone all of the time, and some folks just can't be pleased at all. So a couple of negative comments shouldn't necessarily deter you from bidding on an item, if there are plenty of positive comments to balance them out.

Winning Strategies

When you find an item you want to bid on, don't jump into the auction right away with your maximum bid. Use some of these techniques to help get the item at the right price.

Check the date and time that the auction ends.   It will be shown along with the auction listing. If you will be available at that time, you'll be able to get online and follow the bidding so you can make a last-minute high bid before anyone else can outbid you.

Don't be the first to bid on an item.   There are some folks who just love competition. They may not bid on an item if they don't think anyone else is interested in it. So wait until the last possible moment to show any interest with your first bid, or with raising a previous bid on the item. If you wait until the end, you might get in when everyone else is offline.

Don't be the only bidder on an item.   If you see the item going off auction without a bid, don't be the only bidder. Wait

until the auction is done, then contact the seller by e-mail and ask if they are still interested in selling it. You may be able to purchase the item for the minimum bid, or even less, directly from the seller.

If someone else wins the auction, send a note to the seller asking whether they have any additional or similar items.   They just might, and you can then negotiate with the seller yourself.

HARD-TO-FIND COLLECTIBLES

Online auction houses such as eBay aren't the only places to locate antiques and collectibles. There are plenty of online sources, both commercial and private.

It's All in the Search

Locating items is really an exercise in searching the Internet. It can be time-consuming, but it is usually well worth the effort. As your search abilities improve, you'll be able to locate items more quickly, and you'll build up a Favorites or Bookmarks list.

You'll need access to the Internet and some time to search in order to use the tips provided here.

Sites and Features

When you're searching for a hard-to-find item, use all of the techniques that you learned about in Chapter 8, "Internet Search Engines." Unfortunately, even the best search techniques can result in thousands of items being listed, especially if you use multiple search engines.

Collectibles Organizer Deluxe

The best place to start is by using the program Collectibles Organizer Deluxe. You can download it from www.primasoft.com.

Collectibles Organizer Deluxe is a database management program that you can use to organize information of all types. It comes with two built-in databases, CollectData and WebResources. The CollectData database, illustarted in Figure 17.1 is ideal for storing information about items in your own collection.

The WebResources database is designed for listing online sources of antiques and collectibles, and it includes a number of built-in listings, as shown in Figure 17.2. To select the database to display, click the Load button at the bottom of the Collectibles Organizer Deluxe window, choose the database from the dialog box that appears and click Load.

Use the tabs on the top of the form to open additional pages of information. You can also click the Browser tab to access the Internet, displaying Websites directly on the Collectibles Organizer deluxe window.

NOTE

Before purchasing an item online, look up the prices of similar items on eBay and other auctions to judge its value.

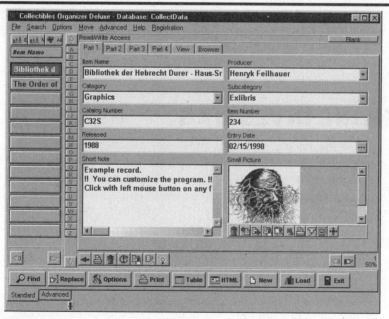

FIGURE 17.1: Collectibles Organizer Deluxe item database

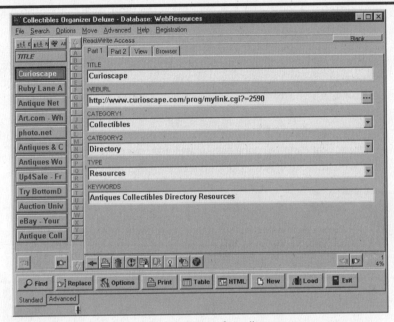

FIGURE 17.2: Database of Web resources for collectors

ONLINE INVESTING

While the market has its ups and downs, there's money to be made in stocks and mutual funds. Certainly there's some risk involved, but the rewards can be substantial. Use your computer and the Internet to buy and sell stocks, and to track your investments.

Buying and Selling Online

The Internet has put a lot of pressure on the traditional stockbroker. Trading through the Internet is fast and easy, and much less expensive than using a traditional broker. On the Internet, you can buy and sell stocks for as little as $5.00 per trade. Try getting that kind of deal from your broker!

Here's What You Need

You'll need access to the Internet, and you'll need to register with an online brokerage. You may have to provide a credit card number, send a check as a deposit for your trades, or establish credit through your bank or current broker, if you have one.

Sites and Features

If you are just looking for stock quotes—before you place an order or just to check your portfolio—look on the home pages of most ISPs. Usually they offer an investing link, and this is a good place to start. Many ISPs, such as AOL, CompuServe, and AT&T WorldNet, let you maintain a database of your stocks for instant tracking. When you log onto the investing area, you'll see the updated values of your stocks. At AT&T WorldNet, for example, your portfolio is maintained free by the Thomson Investors Network, which offers these features:

- ▶ Real Time Quotes
- ▶ Portfolio Tracker/Flash Mail
- ▶ First Call Center
- ▶ Stock Center
- ▶ Mutual Fund Center
- ▶ Investor Education Center
- ▶ Help

All of the major search engines have links to investing information. Over at Yahoo!, click the Stock Quotes link to search for a quote using this form:

NOTE

You can go directly to the Yahoo! stock quotes site at http://finance.yahoo.com.

Enter the symbol for the stock in the first text box, and choose the extent of information you want in the drop-down list. The options are Basic, DayWatch, Performance, Fundamentals, Detailed, Chart, and Research. Then click Get Quotes.

If you don't know the symbol, click Symbol Lookup or go to http://finance.yahoo.com/l. In the box that appears, enter the name of the company and click Lookup. You can also click Alphabetical Listing for a list of companies.

From the www.excite.com home page, enter the symbol in the Get Quotes box in the My Stocks section, and click Go. Click Find Symbol to find the stock's symbol.

At Lycos, go directly to its stock quotes and information page at http://investing.lycos.com.

Most of the major stock brokerages have their own sites for getting account information and for placing buy or sell orders. You can get the lowest commissions, however, from firms that specialize in online trading. For example, at Brown and Company (www.brownco.com), you can purchase stocks for as little as $5.00 per trade, and options as low as $10.00 per trade.

To place orders at deep discounts on commission, try these sites:

A. B. Watley, Inc., www.abwatley.com

Accutrade, www.accutrade.com

Ameritrade, www.ameritrade.com

Brown and Company, www.brownco.com

E*trade, www.etrade.com

The Net Investor, www.netinvestor.com

TradeOptions, www.tradeoptions.com

Vanguard, www.vanguard.com

If you are concerned about the dependability of online trading, check out www.sonic.net/donaldj. At this site, you'll find ratings for online discount brokers based on customer feedback. The ratings are updated twice a month.

There are a lot of other investing and financial sites on the Internet. For investment advice, for example, check out The Motley Fool (www.fool.com). You can apply to get a free credit report online from www.consumerinfo.com. You should also check with your bank for online banking information. Many banks let you transfer funds and pay bills over the Internet or by using programs such as Microsoft Money, Managing Your Money, and Quicken.

WHAT'S NEXT?

In this chapter we've talked about how to buy and sell things successfully using the Internet. In the next chapter, "E-Commerce: Shopping Online," we'll discuss and debunk the common perception that it is unsafe to use a credit card for online shopping transactions.

Chapter 18

E-Commerce: Shopping Online

Purchasing goods, services, and tchotchkes online is a growth industry. According to the experts at http://emarketer.com, $3.7 billion was spent on consumer goods purchased online in 1998; $6.1 billion in 1999; and a budget-bustin' $10 billion will be spent in 2000. Why do you think that is? Can't we spend our money fast enough offline? And what happens if your credit card gets stuck in the floppy drive when attempting to make a purchase via computer? In this chapter, we'll explore the phenomenon of online shopping from the consumer's perspective—your side of the credit card. Not only do you need to know if it's safe, but you also need to know what you can do to protect yourself from the e-slime who are just waiting to tap into your hard-earned dollars.

Adapted from *Mr. Modem's Internet Guide for Seniors*, by Richard A. Sherman

ISBN 0-7821-2580-8   415 pages $19.99

First, let's understand what the term *e-commerce* means. E-commerce is simply a high falutin', high-tech way of saying "buying things online." E-words are very popular on the Internet. Too popular, if you ask me. So any time you see e-something, be sure to roll your e-eyes and know in your e-heart that it's the result of another marketer's less-than-fertile e-magination at work.

Few thoughts strike more terror into the hearts of Internetters than the notion of purchasing something online using a credit card. While common sense is never out of style and always appropriate, the reality is that it's generally very safe to use a credit card—preferably your own—online. But if you have a concern about transmitting your credit card information via the Internet, relax, take a deep breath, and know that you're not alone.

Truth: There is not a single documented case of a credit card ever having been stolen or misappropriated while being transmitted over the Internet. If you know of one such incident that is, indeed, documented and authenticated by the credit card company or a law enforcement agency, please e-mail me at MrModem@home.com. In the following sections we'll explore why and how some people have developed the perception that using a credit card online is unsafe. If we can understand the basis of these fears, we'll be well on our way toward eliminating any unfounded anxiety—and we'll do it all without Prozac. (Mr. Modem...Nobel Peace Prize...it's all coming together.)

To Fear or Not to Fear?

Let's begin by thinking about how we use our credit cards in the offline world. How many of us wouldn't think twice about using a credit card in a restaurant? After presenting our credit card to a person we don't know, we sign the charge slip, remove our copy of the receipt, leave the other copies on the table, and walk away. Let's pause for a dramatic moment and reflect: *We leave the other copies on the table and walk away.* Hello? What's wrong with this picture?

Does it make any sense at all to leave your credit card information on the table, unattended, unsupervised, unmonitored, and walk away? Of course not. In theory, anybody could pick up the receipt and have access to your name, credit card number, and expiration date. And armed with that information, at least for a short period of time, that person has access to more fabulous merchandise than what awaits behind Door Number 2.

Yet somehow, in some strange and amazingly complacent way, we don't worry about things like that because we're comfortable using a credit card in this manner. It's the norm for most of us. We just assume the credit card will be processed in an appropriate manner and the charge will appear on our monthly statement. How that happens is a mystery to most of us, but our history and experience tells us that it works, so why be concerned?

NOTE

The 50+ age group leads the way when it comes to online spending, according to a study conducted by Zona Research, Inc. of Redwood City, California (www.zonaresearch.com). More than 1,000 Internet users were surveyed after the 1998 holiday buying season. Results show online holiday spending by Internet users rose from an average of $216 in 1997 to $629 in 1998, nearly a 200 percent increase. Spending for respondents age 50 to 54 grew 545 percent, while spending by those 55-plus rose 547 percent. Online holiday shopping spending by the under-25 set grew by just 36 percent, compared to the previous year. More than half of the sample said their primary reason for shopping online was to save time or money. Source: Arizona/Nevada Senior World Newsletter, Feb 1999 (www.seniormedia.com).

So why the fears about using a credit card online? Several reasons. First, fear of the unknown is a basic human characteristic. For many individuals, using a credit card online is a new and therefore unfamiliar experience. It may even be a little intimidating, just like using a credit card, debit card, fax machine, microwave oven, cell phone, computer, or CD-ROM for the first time.

Confronting Our Fears

The perception of risk about credit cards being stolen online originates with the media. But this is one time when it's really not the media's fault. We listen to stories, we hear the buzzwords and then we often form our own inaccurate conclusions.

For example, on occasion *hackers* (cyberscoundrels who break into computer databases) have gained unauthorized access to credit card databases at large banking institutions. These break-ins result in the breaker-inners having access to millions of credit card numbers and related information. So these criminals used the Internet as their vehicle for breaking into the databases, but what they had access to was your credit card information, my credit card information, and the card information of millions of other individuals who may or may not have used their credit cards online. Oh, the irony of it all. These modem marauders may or may not have used the purloined credit card information to make purchases from respectable merchants.

When the media presents stories like these, the public is generally left with buzzword impressions. These buzzwords include *Internet*, *hacker*, *credit cards,* and *purchases*. Misperceptions arise when we blur these terms together and come to the erroneous conclusion that using credit cards online is very dangerous. The truth is, it is not.

The hackers in our example did not steal credit card information from good folks like you and me while we were transmitting our credit card information over the Internet. Reaching that conclusion is as appropriate as believing that because you can fly to Las Vegas and lose all your money, that airplanes are therefore dangerous to your financial health. In these instances, both the Internet and the airplane are simply vehicles. Some people use vehicles for good purposes, others don't.

Hysterical Precedent

For many years, whenever you presented your credit card to a retail merchant, it was swiped through a little terminal. You then waited anxiously for authorization or approval from somebody unknown. Now comes the big surprise: That data transfer and authorization, in most instances, occurred via the Internet. So for many of us, our credit card information has been careening around cyberspace for digital eons, yet we've never really known about it. How do you like them apples? Who says ignorance isn't bliss?

Also, as opposed to perceived risk, consider your actual risk. If, and it's a big IF, your credit card information is the first in Internet history to be stolen while being transmitted, your liability is generally limited to $50. It's been my experience that if you notify the credit card company as soon as you discover an unauthorized charge, chances are excellent that you won't even have to pay the $50. The bottom line is that it's simply worth the convenience to use a credit card for online purchases, software registrations, and a host of other financial transactions.

Faxing and Phoning Credit Card Information

Through the years I have encountered many individuals who had the desire to purchase something online, but expressed concern about using a credit card. They chose to fax their credit card information to an Internet-based merchant instead of transmitting it online. Faxing information is frequently viewed as an acceptable alternative, but let's talk about that. Exactly how safe is it?

When you fax information, you typically have no idea who is on the receiving end—and that's assuming you dial the fax number correctly. Unlike an online, form-based financial transaction that is routed to one specific e-mail address, a faxed document usually winds up in hard-copy format, languishing in the tray of a distant fax machine. It will remain in that location, accessible by anybody with access to the fax machine, until somebody comes along, removes the document, and processes the information in an appropriate manner—you hope.

Faxing credit card information is a risky process at best, yet most people are comfortable with the concept of faxing, so it is not perceived as being particularly insecure. Many of the same people who refuse to transmit credit card information online are infinitely more receptive to the idea of transmitting that same information by fax. I have no idea why, other than it's comfortable and familiar.

The same thing holds true when providing credit card information by telephone. Think about the process: You're providing your credit card information to somebody you don't know, in an unknown location, and if you call the same number back immediately, it's highly unlikely that you'll ever reach the same person again. There's no paper trail, it's all verbal, and chances are you won't even know the name of the person you're speaking with. If you do obtain the name of the person you're speaking with, which is always a good idea, it's going to be Jennifer, Heather, or Jason. It's always Jennifer, Heather, or Jason.

E-mail addresses used for the online routing of credit card and other personal information are typically embedded hyperlinks within a Web page or order form. That means you need only click the link to retrieve a form, enter your information, and transmit it to a predetermined e-mail address. The chances of entering an incorrect address are minimal, and certainly far less likely than manually dialing a 10-digit fax number. Transpose two digits of a fax number and you'll be sending your credit card or other personal information to a complete stranger. And unless you're Blanche DuBois relying on the kindness of strangers, you're not likely to know you faxed your information to an incorrect location. Talk about anxiety!

NOTE

Bank's cost to process an in-person transaction: $1.07 Bank's cost to process an Internet-based transaction: $0.01 **Source: Wells Fargo Bank,** www.wellsfargo.com **cited in ComputerWorld,** www.computerworld.com

A Calculated Risk

So what is the risk or danger associated with using your credit card online? Reality check: Insurance experts tell us that you're more likely to have your credit card stolen offline than have your information misappropriated on the Internet. Okay, maybe not insurance experts, but I do have a neighbor who has an insurance policy and that's what he thinks. As increasing numbers of people use the Internet (some 600,000 new users every month), the probability of your credit card information being intercepted during transmission decreases from nil to what we in the biz call *IAGH* or "It ain't gonna happen."

Is it possible for somebody to intercept the transmission of your credit card information over the Internet? Technically, yes, it is. But let's not toss common sense out the window here. Ask yourself why anyone with the level of skill necessary to intercept the transmission of your credit card information would want to go to all the trouble? Wouldn't it make more sense for that person to simply get a job as a clerk in a store and have access to credit card information all day long? If one really wants to have access to credit card information, there are infinitely more opportunities available that require a heck of a lot less computing skill and knowledge than waiting for you to decide to purchase something online.

12 STEPS TO SAFE ONLINE SHOPPING

E-commerce and shopping online are here to stay. As we've discussed in this chapter, transmitting credit card information on the Internet is at least as safe, if not safer, than telephoning or faxing the same information. When considering purchasing anything online, there are a few things you should keep in mind at all times. Follow Mr. Modem's 12 Steps to Safe Online Shopping and you'll be well on your way toward ensuring that your online shopping experiences will be both enjoyable and safe.

1. Start Conservatively

If you have never shopped online before, start by purchasing a small, inexpensive item just to get a feel for the process. Many people fear online shopping because it's unknown to them. Online shopping is a wonderful convenience, but like anything new, it may take a few times before your comfort level reaches the point where it's—er, um, well, comfortable. Remember the first time you pulled into a self-service gas station and had to pump your own gas? I sure do. It was very intimidating to me to be pumping ethyl right out there in front of everybody. But once I became familiar with the process, it was no big deal and I quickly mastered the art of spilling gas on my car just like the pros do.

2. Be Patient

Shopping online will require you to fill out one or more forms to process your order. On occasion your connection to the Internet may be slow or the site you're visiting may be very busy, and it may take a few minutes for information you provide to be processed. Be patient. Don't provide your credit card information and then throw a hissy fit about waiting for a few extra minutes. No matter how long it takes to process your order online, it's still infinitely faster than driving to a store (in the case of software) or waiting on hold and having to listen to Boxcar Willie's Greatest Hits. Just think back to the days when "online ordering" meant calling Sears on the telephone line. You would provide a product number from their 400-pound catalog, then wait three weeks. (Good news: The Sears catalog is now online at www.sears.com.)

3. Comparison Shop

Just because you're comfortable with the price of an item found at one site doesn't mean there aren't better values available elsewhere on the Web. Prices vary widely on the Internet, just as they do in the offline world, so be a savvy shopper and do some comparison shopping. And while you're comparison shopping, don't compromise on quality, size, color, or model. If you can't find exactly what you want at one site, just keep looking. The world is at your fingertips. Comparison shopping is effective only when it's applied apples-to-apples, tchotchke-to-tchotchke.

4. Don't Forget Shipping and Handling Charges

Many online merchants don't tell you how much the shipping and handling charges will be until you're almost finished checking out. If the shipping is too high, don't complete your order just because you're in the checkout line. Simply click the Cancel or Reset Form button to bail out, or click the Back button and start all over again. Sometimes the default shipping method is a more expensive overnight or second-day shipping service. Always select a slower and less expensive method of shipping, if possible.

5. Check Out the Company

One of the highest and best uses of the Internet is its ability to place vast amounts of information at your fingertips. Use this ability to do a little investigating on your own about the company or merchant with whom you're doing business. Several e-commerce e-sources are presented at the end of this chapter.

6. Look for Additional Contact Information

Try to shop with merchants who include a toll-free number on their Web site so you can place a customer service call if you have a problem or question. Sometimes just knowing that there is another way to contact a merchant can be comforting. It wouldn't hurt to look for a street address, as well. Who knows? They might be located right down the street. If that's the case, just get up and walk there. The exercise will be good for you.

7. Understand the Offer

Read all the information presented about the item you're contemplating purchasing. If you would like more information, request it by e-mail. If you don't receive a response, you have your answer about dealing with that company. Make sure you know and understand what you're purchasing, the total price, the delivery date, the return and cancellation policy, and the terms of any guarantee. Merchandise purchased must be delivered by the promised time or, if none was noted, within 30 days.

8. Protect Your Personal Information

Some sites sell the personal information they collect from shoppers, which usually results in junk e-mail or even junk snail-mail cluttering up your mailbox. If you're not comfortable with that—and many people are not—look for a privacy policy statement posted on the Web site of any company with whom you're considering doing business. If you're not satisfied with the policy as posted, don't make any purchases.

9. Pay by Credit Card

As we discussed earlier in this chapter, nothing is more misunderstood in the wild and wacky world of e-commerce than using a credit card to make purchases. Purchasing by credit card is the safest method of shopping online. Not only do you have all the safeguards and protections afforded by the credit card company, but also you can often earn frequent flyer miles or bonus points towards the purchase of aluminum siding for your house, as well. If you don't have a credit card or the thought of using a credit card online makes you drop before you shop, try to find a seller who will place your money in escrow until the merchandise arrives in satisfactory condition. Due to the increasing popularity of online shopping, third-party escrow services are popping up on the Internet to perform this very service. Service availability will be noted by participating merchants.

10. Use a Secure Web Site

Look for a message on screen that informs you that your transaction is being transferred to a secure server or system. A *secure server* is one that encrypts or scrambles your personal information during transmission over the Internet. A secure site will display a little key icon, a picture of a closed padlock, or a Web address that begins with https (see Figure 18.1). For more information about encryption, visit www.mrmodem.net.

11. Stay Informed

Information about shopping online abounds on the Web, so do your homework! See the "Additional E-Commerce Resources" box at the end of this chapter for a list of Web sites that provide helpful online consumer protection information. The more you know and understand about shopping online, the more comfortable you will be with the process. Stay informed and stay safe.

Part iv

FIGURE 18.1: Secure Server Indicators

12. Use Common Sense

You've accumulated a lifetime of common sense that you use every day in the offline world, so why should you set that aside when functioning in the online world? The answer, of course, is that you should not. Be skeptical of offers that sound too good to be true because they probably are. Listen to the voice of your inner modem. If that little voice is telling you to be on your guard about a certain merchant, don't do business with that company. Chances are, that little voice isn't going to steer you wrong.

LOOKING AHEAD

Purchasing goods and services via the Internet will soon be as commonplace and comfortable as using the telephone or microwave oven. Today, students register for classes and purchase their books online; parents register their children for day care online; physicians make virtual house calls by e-mail; and you can even pay your taxes online and receive your refund (we can dream, can't we?) electronically by direct deposit.

As technology continues to evolve and further integrates with society, and as our collective comfort level with the Internet grows, we will continue to see online communication and commerce converge to the point where they will simply be a part of our everyday e-life.

ADDITIONAL E-COMMERCE RESOURCES

Better Business Bureau Online—News alerts, searchable business report databases.

   www.bbb.org

Better Web Business Bureau—Free consumer access to the BWBB complaint and history database.

   http://brbc.net/www.bwbb.com

Consumer Reports Online

   www.consumerreports.com

Internet Scambusters—Mr. Modem's favorite!

   www.scambusters.org

U.S. Consumer Gateway—A one-stop link to federal information about online scams and fraud.

   www.consumer.gov/Tech.htm

WHAT'S NEXT?

In this chapter, I've gone out on a limb and predicted the convergence of online communication and e-commerce, in the hopes of reassuring you that online shopping is safe and convenient. In the next chapter, we'll take a look at MP3, a file format you can use to store digital audio much more compactly than was possible with previously available formats.

Part iv

Chapter 19

GETTING STARTED WITH MP3

In this chapter, we'll show you how to get started with MP3. You'll learn the following:

- ▶ What MP3 does
- ▶ What you can do with MP3
- ▶ What hardware and software you'll need to take advantage of MP3
- ▶ The legalities of downloading, creating, and distributing MP3 files
- ▶ How to use Winamp to play MP3 files
- ▶ How to use MusicMatch Jukebox to rip, play, and enjoy MP3

Adapted from *MP3! I Didn' t Know You Could Do That...*, *Second Edition*, by Guy Hart-Davis and Rhonda Holmes
ISBN 0-7821-2791-6   464 pages $19.99

Understanding What MP3 Is and What It Does

Put simply, MP3 is a highly compressed file format for storing digital audio in computer memory. MP3 takes up only a tenth of the space that was needed to store high-quality audio in previously available formats. The audio can be anything from the spoken word to soothing ocean sounds to the latest speed metal. If you can hear it, you can create an MP3 version of it.

Once you've recorded an MP3 file, you can store it on a computer—a laptop, a desktop, or a server—and play it back whenever you want, using MP3 player software such as the applications included on the CD that comes with the book from which this chapter was adapted. You can also download an MP3 file to a portable MP3 hardware player (such as a digital Walkman) or a handheld computer or a palm-sized PC and listen to it wherever you roam. In addition, you can get hardware MP3 jukeboxes that function more like stereo components than computers, and you can get MP3 players for your car—so with a little effort and a lot more money, you can have MP3 audio with you more or less wherever you go.

MP3 Turns Your Computer into a Jukebox

Computers have been able to record high-fidelity sound for many years now. But the resulting audio files have been far too large to handle easily—from 35MB to 50MB for a typical music track of three to five minutes. So, as recently as 1997, you could fit only a few hours of high-quality audio onto the largest hard drive that the average wallet could provide, which meant that it wasn't worth using a computer to store music unless you had a compelling reason.

Many recording studios have been using computers to record, process, and enhance audio, because computers let them record and manipulate the sound more easily, more accurately, and more cheaply than analog recording equipment. But once they'd finished processing the files, they stored them on tape and then duplicated them onto noncomputer technologies—cassettes, records, and CDs—that could easily be distributed to, and played by, the target audience.

The development of the MP3 format has changed all that. Compressed as MP3 files, high-quality audio takes up much less space than it used to. And because hard disks have grown dramatically over the last few years, you can fit several months' worth of music—playing 24/7—on a single hard disk.

Using a computer to record, store, and play music has become not only feasible but also advisable. With a little effort, you can put your entire CD collection on your computer and manage it effortlessly, turning your computer into an MP3 jukebox. From the computer, you can download MP3 tracks into your portable player or car player, burn them onto CDs, or simply pipe them to speakers in the various rooms of your house until your family or roommates have fled with their ears ringing.

Why Is MP3 Such a Breakthrough?

MP3 is a major breakthrough because it retains high audio quality while maintaining a small file size. MP3 works very well for both music and voice recordings such as radio shows, speeches, or audio books.

Before the MP3 standard was developed, downloading a single track of CD-quality audio over a modem took hours. For example, in the early 1990s, Aerosmith broke new ground by releasing a single as a WAV file on CompuServe, which at the time was an influential online service rather than a struggling subdivision of America Online. Because the file was so huge (something like 35MB) and the highest modem speed being used then was 28.8Kbps, downloading took the best part of four hours. Few people bothered: it simply wasn't worth the time (or the money—in those days, CompuServe charged by the minute).

MP3 files are far more compressed than WAV or other sound files. They consume only about 1MB of disk space per minute of music. Spoken-word audio, which typically doesn't need such high fidelity to sound okay, can fit several minutes into each megabyte of an MP3 file.

Not only have modem speeds increased, but also an increasing number of people have better-than-modem access to the Internet. To start with, many homes in North America now have access to cable modems or digital subscriber lines (DSLs), which provide download speeds of several megabytes a minute—50 to 100 times faster than a modem. These high-speed connections give you the power to download an MP3-compressed track of average length in a minute or less. Some tech-heavy communities are now hooking up new residences with fiber-optic lines so fast that you'll be able to download a whole track in the time it takes to have a couple of good sneezes. And many colleges are way ahead of those tech communities in the bandwidth stakes, with dorms wired at blazingly fast speeds.

Part iv

You can also play tracks directly off the Web without downloading them to your hard drive. This can come in handy when you're sampling new music and don't want to commit drive space to music you aren't sure of. When you do find something you like, just download it and it will be available to you until your music tastes change or your hard drive dies.

A WORD ABOUT TERMINOLOGY

Unless we're missing it, there's really no appropriate word in English for "chunk of audio." For example, a "song" is usually understood to have words, and a "track" is usually understood as meaning one piece of music (or speech) from a CD, a cassette, or one of those black-vinyl Frisbees that nostalgic people call "records." In the absence of a better word, we'll refer to a chunk of audio as a "track," except when one of the applications chooses to refer to it as a "song."

While we're on the subject, the words "folder" and "directory" mean the same thing for Windows-based computers. We've used them interchangeably, trying to follow the terminology that the application being discussed uses.

Where Did MP3 Come From?

The MP3 format gets its name from having been created under the auspices of the Moving Pictures Experts Group (MPEG for short, pronounced *em-peg*). Dr. Karlheinz Brandenburg at the Fraunhofer Institute for Integrated Circuits IIS-A in Germany developed the coding method, thus ensuring himself a listing in the digital music hall of fame.

MP is a shortened form of MPEG. But why 3? MP3 is the third compression method Fraunhofer developed. As you'd imagine, the first two methods were MP1 and MP2. They offered less compression than MP3 and didn't catch on widely, though a number of people did get kinda excited at the time.

How Does MP3 Work?

We mentioned that MP3 files are compressed, making them about 10 times smaller than equivalent CD audio files or WAV files. Let's look quickly at how this works. We won't get too technical here, but you need to understand a couple of points in order to create high-quality MP3 files that you'll enjoy hearing.

The key to the compression that MP3 uses is *sampling*. This isn't the same kind of sampling that techno artists use to achieve their musical effects—grabbing pieces of other artists' works and inserting mutated forms of them in their own creations. As far as MP3 is concerned, sampling is the process of examining the patterns of a sound to determine its characteristics and to record it from an analog format into a digital format.

NOTE

Tech moment: *Analog* is continuously variable, and *digital* is binary with two positions only—on or off. To create a digital version of an analog sound, you examine it at a sampling rate and a sampling precision and digitize the resulting data points. The higher the sampling rate and the sampling precision, the more accurate the sound is, the more data has to be stored, and the bigger the file is.

The *sampling rate* is the frequency with which the sound is examined, and the *sampling precision* (also called the *sampling resolution*) is the amount of information about the individual sample that is saved to the audio file.

CDs sample audio at a sampling rate of 44.1 kilohertz (kHz)—44,100 times a second—with a sampling precision of 16 bits (2 bytes) per sample. This high sampling rate is considered perfect as far as the human ear goes—the sampling is frequent enough, and the sampling precision stores enough information about the sound, that the human ear can't detect anything missing.

Is CD-quality audio perfect? Not really, but it's more than good enough for most people. If you look around hard enough, you can find a few people who claim to hear defects in CD-quality sound. Such people can probably hear dog whistles and see in the dark too.

Scientists call the study of what people can and can't hear *psychoacoustics*. In this case, *hear* doesn't refer to the ear's capacity to pick up a sound, but rather to the brain's capacity to identify it as a separate sound. You hear many things every day that your brain filters out, and there are whole sections of the spectrum of sound that you don't hear at all. (Ask dogs and bats.) An MP3 encoder trashes the frequencies and sounds that you won't be able to hear and saves only those that you will be able to hear. When a loud sound occurs at the same time as a quieter sound

Part iv

around the same frequencies, the encoder keeps only the loud sound because the loud sound masks the quieter sound.

Technically, MP3 is a *lossy* method of compression—it actually removes information from the source rather than just squashing the source down to its smallest possible size. (The opposite of lossy compression is *lossless* compression.) Because it's lossy, MP3 can compress audio to different degrees: the more you compress it, the more information is removed, and the worse the result sounds.

If you've ever listened to a CD on decent equipment, you know that CD-quality audio can—and should—sound great. But if you listen to CD-quality audio on poor equipment, you'll hear the defects in every measure.

So, CD-quality audio is basically excellent or at least good enough for 99.5 percent of the population. The only problem with it is that the files it produces are huge. If you sample at 44.1kHz and 16 bits, the files will run between 9MB and 11MB a minute. Because you can get about 650MB on a regular CD, most CDs can hold up to about 74 minutes of music. (Extended-capacity CDs, new at this writing, can hold 700MB and 80 minutes—a relatively trivial increase in capacity.) Not so coincidentally, most artists these days judge 50–70 minutes to be a CD's worth of music. (If you're old enough to have enjoyed vinyl before it became outmoded, you'll remember that most albums in those days were more like 30–45 minutes long—the amount that would comfortably fit on a vinyl LP.)

CD-quality audio is fine for CDs. But when a 4-minute track weighs in at a hefty 40MB, you don't want to try to transfer it over the Internet. At that size, you can put a couple of tracks on a 100MB Zip disk, but not enough music to entertain you for longer than a 40-ounce soda. Ten minutes of music isn't going to get you very far. These huge file sizes are great for the record companies, because they amount to *de facto* copy protection—the files are too big for anyone to distribute easily. But for the audio fan, something smaller is needed.

Enter MP3. Providing almost CD-quality audio together with a decent rate of compression, MP3 solves both the quality problem and the file-size problem. Recorded at a decent sampling rate (as you'll see in a bit, you can use various sampling rates when recording MP3 files), MP3 provides the high-quality sound that audiophiles demand. And it also provides enough compression that the resulting files can easily be transferred from one computer to another and from a computer onto palm-size PCs and dedicated hardware MP3 players. That's the key feature of MP3—quality with portability. But wait, there's more.

In addition to the audio information stored in an MP3 file, there's also a *tag*—a container with various slots to hold key pieces of information about the MP3 files. A typical tag contains the artist's name, the title of the piece or audio item, the title of the album (if applicable), the genre, the year, and an optional comment.

Tags are great because they give you the power to sort your MP3 files by any of the pieces of information in the tags. So you can easily pull up everything in your Techno-Industrial, Nippon Pop, or Christian Metal collection.

Compare that to WAV files. WAVs have a filename and nothing else. You can sort them by filename, but you haven't a hope in hell of sorting them by genre or artist. And WAV files of a quality comparable to MP3 files are the same size as CD tracks. MP3 wins hands down.

What Can You Do with MP3?

Briefly put, you can easily create MP3 files from already-recorded music or audio (for example, from CDs) or audio you create yourself. You can save the files on your computer or play them back either on the computer or on portable players. You can sort them into collections or databases, and distribute them easily via the Internet (or other computer networks) or on conventional portable media such as CDs or removable disks (Zip, Jaz, Orb, and others). In essence, you can become a music creator *and* publisher. David Geffen, move over.

What Are the Advantages of MP3?

MP3 has massive advantages over conventional methods of distributing and listening to music. (Most of these advantages apply to other audio as well—for example, poetry or other spoken-word audio—but in this section, we'll assume you're mostly interested in music.)

For the Music Lover

The advantages of MP3 are clearest for the music lover. Now you can do the following:

Take your music with you   MP3 provides portable audio that you can play back on small players that don't skip, don't break, and are small enough to hide from view.

Store files on your electronic pal   You can store the files on computers.

Download and upload files easily   You can download or upload files without difficulty, even over a lame modem connection.

Create your own customized CDs   You can convert MP3 files to WAV format and burn them onto CDs. Better yet, if you use the MP3 format, you can fit between *100 and 200 tracks* onto one CD—up to a full night's worth of music, from seduction to regrets.

For the Artist

MP3 offers compelling advantages to artists too. Here's what you can do:

Publish and distribute your own music over the Internet   You no longer need to find a record company prepared to spend many thousands of dollars recording, packaging, and promoting you and your music. You can simply record the music, convert some tracks to MP3 format, and post them on the Web so that people can download them instantly and listen to them.

Promote your work by releasing samples of it   You can do this in any or all of several ways, including placing MP3 files on Web sites for distribution, posting them to MP3 newsgroups, distributing them as e-mail attachments, or sharing them via Napster.

Easily release different versions of a track rather than agonizing over which version to include on an album   You can even release work in progress and let your fans vote on which direction you should pursue.

Keep control of your destiny   No record company need be involved, whether you're releasing one track every decade or a couple of albums' worth of music every year.

As you might imagine, the point about the record company is where friction starts to set in. Until the mid-1990s, record companies decided which artists would be unleashed on the public, when the music would appear, and how it would be produced, packaged, presented, and priced.

Recording and producing an album took weeks or months—even years, if you were the Human League. The album then had to be manufactured (at great expense) and distributed in quantity to radio stations and record stores, preferably accompanied by an expensive promotional campaign and Bolivian Marching Powder to persuade the DJs to play the record and the stores to carry it.

Now an artist or a band can record high-fidelity sound with an affordable computer, mix it to professional quality, and then distribute it immediately and painlessly using MP3 files. If anyone likes the music, they can pay to download further songs or buy a CD directly from the band.

You can see why the record companies weren't pleased when MP3 took off.

For the Record Company

MP3 seemed to pose a severe threat to record companies by bypassing first their control of the selection and recording process and then their expensively built production and distribution systems.

But MP3 cuts both ways: if it wants to, a record company can use MP3 to promote its songs and artists to customers—just as independent artists can, only more so. By using cross-promotion and the economies of scale, a record company can reap great benefits from MP3.

Here are the basic advantages for a record company using MP3:

> **Reduced production and distribution costs—*way* reduced**   If a record company no longer needs to manufacture 100,000 CDs by its great new hope, print 100,000 inlay cards, buy 100,000 jewel cases, assemble them, and truck them around the world, it will save a huge amount of money.

> **Simple promotion**   By offering a good selection of freely downloadable MP3 files, a record company can make its Web site a major destination for music fans. It can then move on to the next advantage—direct sales.

> **Direct sales to customers via the Web**   What could be sweeter? The record company produces the music as usual and then sells it directly via the Web to the customer. Better yet, the record company can sell dozens of different mixes of any track—they've found out by now that people will pay for the Ultra Boonga-Chonka Techno remix as well as the Extended Boonga remix and the Techno remix. As a distribution mechanism, the

Web allows far greater customer choice than physical stores can. The record company can also sell CDs—regular CDs and custom-made CDs—via mail order.

Simple cross-promotion   The record company can present information about related bands to customers, offering them free tracks to try. Customers can sign up for news (via, say, e-mail newsletters) on bands they're interested in, upcoming releases, concerts, and so on.

Seeding the market with low-fi tracks   The music company can release low-fidelity MP3 files of music they want to promote and then wait for people to buy the high-fidelity versions.

The advantages of MP3 for record companies are almost enough to make you want to start a record company yourself. And with MP3, there's little to stop you.

What Are the Disadvantages of MP3?

To compare with its advantages, there are several disadvantages associated with MP3. For most people, they're not too severe.

For the Music Lover

For the music lover, only a few disadvantages are associated with MP3. First of all, in most cases you must have a computer to download, record, and play MP3 files. You can now get portable MP3 players and MP3 players for cars, but you still need a computer to get and store the files. (There are hardware MP3 players that resemble stereo components but inside, they're computers.)

Second, the music quality isn't quite as high as CD quality. Most people find the music quality good enough, and for most spoken-word recordings, quality isn't an issue. You can adjust the quality of MP3 files by choosing a higher or lower sampling rate when you create them.

And third, you may receive illegal MP3 recordings unwittingly. We'll examine the legal issues later in this chapter, but you need to know from the beginning that it's illegal to distribute someone else's MP3 files, and it's illegal to have illegally distributed MP3 files in your possession.

For the Artist

For the artist, the main disadvantage of MP3 is that any CDs they have released can be *ripped* (extracted and compressed) to MP3 files and distributed illegally, either directly (on CDs or other removable media) or via the Internet. In this way, an artist can lose money through piracy. Because MP3 files are digital, each copy retains the same quality of the original—unlike, say, audio tapes, for which each generation of duplication loses sound quality. New software such as Napster, which provides instant sharing of tracks by all members logged into a loose online community, can achieve savage levels of piracy within a period of hours.

At this writing, various artists groups, from the Recording Industry Association of America (RIAA) and downward, are working on ways to keep MP3 piracy to a tolerable level. *Tolerable* is hard to define in this context, but you'd think a good target would be a level analogous to the level of piracy tacitly accepted when people taped LPs and duped cassettes for their friends. Suggested "solutions" range from banning the MP3 format (which, even if it were not stupid and impractical, would be ineffective) to vigorously policing Web sites and newsgroups for illegal content, which is already happening to some extent.

For the Record Company

For the record company, the main disadvantage of MP3 is the same as that for the artist: the record company can lose money through piracy of released material.

When it comes to MP3, some record companies are in a more peculiar situation than others are. For example, Sony Corp. is a top record label, with big-name artists such as Celine Dion and Fiona Apple—but it's also a major manufacturer of audio equipment. Sony's hardware division spent late 1998 and most of 1999 chafing at the bit to release a killer MP3 player and lock up a market that could be even more lucrative than the Walkman market it created in the 1970s. But Sony's music side has been scared spitless by the thought of its massive revenue stream from music dragging its mauled carcass into the desert to die after a cataclysmic showdown with MP3 hardware.

Toward the end of 1999, Sony finally released the VAIO Music Clip—externally exactly the kind of innovative MP3 player that you'd have expected to see from them about a year earlier. Longer and much thinner than most portable hardware MP3 players, the VAIO Music Clip handles MP3 and ATRAC3 formats, is SDMI (Secure Digital Music Initiative)

compliant, and is designed to be hung on a neck strap around the user's neck rather than clipping to the belt like most portable players. Unfortunately, the stringencies presumably exercised by Sony's music side have resulted in a truly grotesque software implementation that forces you to convert each MP3 file into a secure format before you can upload it to the Music Clip—a severe pain in the anatomy.

Where Is MP3 Heading?

Toward MP4—of course. An MP4 Structured Audio format is currently under development, but it's far from mainstream deployment.

At this point, it's hard to say with any certainty what's going to happen with MP3 in the long term. The dramatic spread of MP3 has already started a tectonic shift in how music is distributed, at least among people who have computers. The three key groups involved with music—fans, artists, and record companies—can benefit greatly from MP3. Artists and record companies can also benefit from other audio-compression technologies that are less friendly to the consumer than MP3.

It should be no surprise to learn that—after a couple of years of denial—the music business and technology companies are working hard to neutralize the threats that MP3 presents to them. Initial efforts included a suit by the RIAA to prevent the release of the Diamond Rio hardware MP3 player. (It failed.) There has also been talk of trying to "ban" the MP3 format. Subsequent efforts have—more realistically—centered on securing the files so that you cannot play them at all or play them more than a few sample times without paying for them. And copying them without paying (more) is out of the question.

At this writing, several technologies have been developed for distributing music securely online, including a2b, ATRAC3, Liquid Audio, MS Audio, Mjuice, and VQF. We'll give you a short overview of each in the following sections, after these prefatory words of wisdom.

Reduced to the essentials, there are two problems for music formats competing with MP3. Neither problem is insurmountable, but each is huge, and together, they make a formidable roadblock.

▶ The first problem is that, from the consumer's point of view, none of the wannabe music formats has any compelling appeal. Each format is designed for secure distribution of music, which almost invariably means that consumers (a) get to pay for the music, preferably through the nose, and (b) are restricted from using the music as they want. (For example, some technologies can lock a particular track to the computer on which you first play it, so that you cannot then play it on another computer without paying more. Imagine how you'd react if your portable CD player prevented you from playing a CD on your car CD player.) The only advantages the wannabe music formats can claim for the consumer are a smaller file size (which is nice, but MP3 files are already plenty portable) and better audio quality (which is even nicer, but MP3 quality is more than good enough for most people).

▶ The second problem is that MP3 has such a massive lock on the market right now—because it's free, easy to use, and delivers more than acceptable audio quality—that it's hard for any other format to build any momentum behind it.

The wannabe formats are essentially aimed at commercializing the online distribution of music (or, to put it another way, enabling commercial online distribution of music). Because MP3 has such a head start over the other formats, is widespread if not rampant at this time, is open to everyone, is essentially free, and is easy to use, it's likely that MP3 will remain the dominant audio-compression technology for several years.

OK, enough general blather. Let's get into the formats.

a2b

The *a2b* format from AT&T stores audio in compressed and encrypted files. a2b claims better compression (2.25MB for a 3-minute song) and sound quality than MP3 and has the advantage of being able to store text and art with the audio. Therefore, a track can bring with it its lyrics, its credits, a brief enjoinder to save the whales, and a picture of the CD cover (or of a friendly whale). But these advantages are more than offset by a2b's minimal distribution so far—at this writing, a2b is more a curiosity than a valuable way of playing digital audio.

ATRAC3

ATRAC3 is a sound compression format developed by Sony for use with its OpenMG copyright-protection technology. Together, ATRAC3 and OpenMG enable secure distribution of digital music. At this writing, ATRAC3 has been implemented only in Sony hardware and software, making it a marginal player so far—but RealNetworks is currently integrating ATRAC3 into its RealJukebox ripper/player/jukebox, which will help bring ATRAC3 into the mainstream.

Part iv

Liquid Audio

Liquid Audio (www.liquidaudio.com) makes a player that can play secured files and can also burn CDs. Liquid Audio has been used for several years on the Internet Underground Musical Archive (IUMA), which describes itself as "the granddaddy of all music Web sites." Liquid Audio is almost a major player in the digital music market, but it has yet to achieve widespread distribution. Not that it isn't trying—Liquid Audio made a splash in late 1999 by persuading Alanis Morissette to use Liquid Audio in the Internet marketing campaign for her CD *MTV Unplugged*.

MS Audio

Microsoft's Windows Media Technologies 4.0 has a secure compression scheme called *MS Audio* that claims to surpass MP3 in both compression and music quality. Problem is, Microsoft has been struggling to get enough music available in the MS Audio format for consumers to start taking them seriously. Several MP3 players, including Winamp and Sonique, can play MS Audio files, as can later versions of Windows Media Player.

Mjuice

Mjuice is a secure digital format that includes features such as an expiration date, allowing artists and record companies to release promotional files that will expire at a suitable point. For example, an artist promoting her forthcoming CD might release Mjuice versions of several tracks online, using an expiration date that coincided with the CD's release, a tactic used recently by bands such as Third Eye Blind (or, to be more precise, their record company, Elektra). A number of MP3 players (including Winamp) and jukeboxes (including RealJukebox) can play Mjuice files, so if you get them, you'll have no problem listening to them.

VQF

The *VQF* format (Transform-domain Weighted Interleave Vector Quantization, if you must ask) boasts better compression and higher sound quality than MP3, but almost nobody's using it as of this writing. If you do decide to try VQF, you can download a Winamp plug-in to play the tracks, or you can use the MP3 player K-jofol. For information on the VQF format, visit www.vqf.com.

GET THE RIGHT HARDWARE

To record and play MP3 files, you need a moderately powerful computer. It doesn't matter if it's a PC, a Mac, or a Unix or Linux box—even a Be box is fine. What does matter is that it must have enough horsepower to process the MP3 files and play them back without faltering.

What does "moderately powerful" mean? Well, the computer doesn't have to be the latest screamer, although the faster chips with multimedia features will rip selections faster than older chips. For example, computers based on Pentium II, Pentium III, Celeron, K6-2, and Athlon chips rip at a goodly speed, as do PowerPC-based Macs. A 486 won't cut it. But if you're currently using your computer to play games involving sound and motion, and you haven't yet put a brick through your monitor in frustration at the lack of speed, you're probably in pretty good shape for playing MP3 music. If you have a CD-ROM as well, you'll also be able to rip MP3 files from CDs you own.

Let's look at the specifics of what you need in a computer to play, rip, and enjoy MP3 music.

NOTE

If your computer is generally underpowered, you'll probably do better to buy a new one rather than upgrade multiple components. Because computer prices have fallen dramatically in the last two years, and continue to fall, you can now buy a reasonably full-featured PC (not including a monitor, printer, and other accessories) for about $500—only a little more than it would cost to upgrade the processor, RAM, and hard drive of an older computer. Weigh your options carefully before putting any money down.

The Chip: Pentium 200MMX or Better; Mac G3

For most ripping programs, you need at least a Pentium 200MMX, although for older rippers you may be able to get by with an ancient Pentium 133 (that's the "classic" Pentium without the MMX extensions). But as you'd imagine, a faster chip will give you better performance.

For playing back MP3 files, you may be able to stagger along with a Pentium 75 or so (or even a 486DX4 with a high clock speed), depending on the program you're using. Be warned that if the computer is around

this level, you may hear interruptions in the audio as it struggles to keep up, and you may not be able to run other applications without interrupting playback.

For the Macintosh, you'll want a PowerPC chip—preferably a G3. You'll get plenty of performance at 233MHz or above.

RAM: 32MB or More (Preferably Much More)

For ripping, you need 32MB of RAM—absolute minimum. For playback, you need 16MB of RAM—absolute absolute minimum. As with almost any program, more RAM will make rippers and players run better. At this writing, RAM is once again nearing the historic low price it reached it mid-1999 (before an earthquake in Taiwan temporarily doubled prices). An extra 32MB or 64MB of RAM is a bargain that will give your computer a decent boost in performance. If you're buying a new PC, get 128MB to start with; you won't regret it.

CD or DVD Drive

For ripping CDs, you need a CD drive or a DVD drive. Most any CD speed above 2X will work, but one of today's drives (say 40X or better) will give far better performance. A SCSI (Small Computer Systems Interface) drive minimizes the load on the processor, whereas ripping with an IDE (Integrated Drive Electronics) drive imposes a significant load. If your chip is lame, a SCSI drive might help you out, but it'll be more expensive than an IDE drive.

The CD drive needs to support digital audio extraction in order to rip tracks digitally. (Most rippers offer an analog ripping option for CD drives that don't support digital audio extraction, but the results typically aren't as good as digital ripping.) If your CD drive isn't up to ripping, get another; it'll cost you anywhere from $35 on up.

WARNING

DVD speeds refer to the speed at which the DVD drive works with DVDs, not with CDs, which they read at a faster rate. For example, a 6x DVD drive typically delivers more like 24x performance for CDs—enough to rip at a goodly speed.

Sound Card

To produce any sound worth hearing, you need a decent sound card. All other things being equal, the better your sound card, the better the music will sound.

Choosing a sound card is about as personal as choosing underwear. But we'll give you a few pointers to help you avoid buying the digital equivalent of nylon briefs that are one size too small:

► Make sure the sound card will work with your computer and operating system. If your PC doesn't have a PCI (Peripheral Component Interconnect) slot free, a PCI sound card won't do you much good. If you *do* have PCI slots free, you probably don't want to get an ISA (Industry Standard Architecture) sound card. ISA cards draw much more heavily on the computer's processor than PCI cards do, so go with PCI if it's an option. Many modern ATX motherboards have 16-bit SoundBlaster chips built into the motherboard, which may be enough to get you started with MP3. If you find yourself listening to a lot of music, you'll probably want to get something better pretty soon.

► Choose the number of *voices*—individually mixed tracks—that you'll need the sound card to produce. You'll need at least 64 voices to make music sound good, because most music is mixed with 64 separate tracks. Advanced sound cards support several hundred voices. That'll probably be overkill—until you get seriously into MP3 and want your music to sound as good as it possibly can.

► Make sure you have the appropriate connectors for connecting your sound card to your speakers or your stereo. You'll think this is dumb advice until you find that you don't have the right connectors. If you want to connect your PC to your stereo, you'll usually need different connectors than if you're just going to plug a pair of speakers into the sound card. If you're buying connectors, make sure they're of an appropriate quality for your sound card—there's no sense in using Radio Shack's cheapest connectors with an advanced and expensive sound card, because chances are they'll lower the quality of the output.

► If you're making your own music, make sure that the sound card provides the MIDI (Musical Instrument Digital Interface) connections you need.

Part iv

The following list mentions some sound cards you may want to consider, with approximate prices as of this writing. But because hardware companies are constantly bringing out new models, you'll probably want to do some research of your own.

▶ The SoundBlaster Live! from Creative Labs is a PCI card that can play as many as 512 voices at the same time—enough for professional-quality music playback. The SoundBlaster Live! MP3 costs $99, comes with a bundle of MP3-oriented software, and is a good value. If you want bells and whistles, the SoundBlaster Live! Platinum costs $199 and includes a Live! Drive—a drive bay that fits into the front of your computer like a CD-ROM drive and provides input and output jacks for S/PDIF (Sony/Phillips Digital Interface Format), headphones, line or microphone, and MIDI. Having the jacks right there is much handier than having them at the back of the PC, but you may not need to spend the extra money.

▶ The SoundBlaster AWE from Creative Labs is a 64-voice ISA card that costs about $199. It's also available in a Value Edition that costs $99.

▶ The Turtle Beach Montego II Quadzilla, which costs $79, is a 320-voice card that supports four-speaker output for quadraphonic audio. If you want digital I/O, Voyetra Turtle Beach Inc. also makes the Montego II Plus, a $149 board that provides lossless digital signal transfer and four-channel positional audio.

▶ The Diamond Monster Sound MX400 supports a maximum of 1024 voices and costs about $79.

WARNING

Before you buy a sound card for a Linux box, make sure that drivers are available for it—otherwise, its voices will be silent. A good place to start looking for information on drivers is the sound card vendor's Web site, followed by the Linux distributor's site. For example, Red Hat Software keeps a list of supported hardware on its Web site at www.redhat.com. At this writing, leading sound cards such as the SoundBlaster Live! and Montego II Quadzilla do not have solid Linux drivers—though the folks at Creative are working hard to deliver them for the SoundBlaster Live!.

Now you need speakers (discussed in the next section) or headphones (discussed in the section after that). Alternatively you can direct the output from your computer into your stereo system and use its speakers instead.

Speakers

Speakers come in a wide range of sizes, prices, and capabilities. This section discusses the key points that you need to keep in mind before opening your wallet.

Good Speakers Don't Come Free

Most every PC sold these days proudly advertises that it comes with "multimedia speakers." Most of these speakers aren't worth their weight in landfill. You can listen to spoken audio or to low-fi radio through them without annoyance, but music will suffer, along with your ears and your brain. Plan to invest some money in better speakers right from the start. Anywhere from $60 to $400 will get you what you need, though you can easily spend more than that.

Tweeters, Woofers, and Subwoofers

Each speaker contains two or more *cones* or *drivers*. In a two-cone speaker, the *tweeter* plays the treble (high-frequency) sounds, and the *woofer* plays bass sounds. In a subwoofer system, the *subwoofer* plays the bass and very low-frequency sounds—those bass rumbles you feel reverberate in your body more than you hear in your ears. A subwoofer typically provides more bass sounds than a non-subwoofer setup and is considered a must by most gamers and many audiophiles. (Bear in mind that subwoofers have also been considered grounds for arrest, divorce, and eviction, not necessarily in that sequence.)

Passive or Amplified?

You need to choose between passive speakers—unpowered speakers—and amplified speakers. *Passive speakers* are typically used with an amplifier (which is often integrated into a receiver), as in a "normal" stereo system: The output from the CD, cassette deck, and radio goes into the amplifier into which you plug the speakers. The amplifier runs on AC and provides the heavy-duty lifting; the speakers just reproduce the sound. When you plug passive speakers into a sound card that's designed to work with amplified speakers, you get minimal volume.

Amplified speakers, as their name suggests, contain their own amplifier or amplifiers. Usually there's one amplifier in one of the speakers, which makes it much heavier than the other one. That speaker is the one that receives the power—usually from AC, because batteries won't get you

Part iv

far—and provides the boosting. In a subwoofer set, the subwoofer typically contains the amplifier and lives on the floor so that it doesn't break your furniture.

How Loud Are They?

Speaker volume is measured in watts, but the way manufacturers measure the wattage of speakers varies wildly. You'll see measurements in RMS watts (*root mean square* watts), which measures the wattage that the amplifier or speaker can deliver continuously rather than the wattage volume at which it maxes out. The peak wattage is sometimes referred to as *peak output* or *peak power*. The peak is basically the point beyond which the speaker blows up.

Unless you live for distortion and feedback or are the reincarnation of Jimi Hendrix, you'll seldom want to listen to music anywhere near your speakers' peak power, because it'll sound horrible. But many manufacturers of, uh, less expensive speakers list the peak wattage rather than RMS wattage so that the figure looks more impressive. So if you see inexpensive speakers advertised as delivering 100 watts, be on your guard: They probably can't sustain that volume, and if they can, you won't want to listen to it. At 100 watts RMS, the volume is enough to shake your house on its foundations and make the neighbors call the cops. Believe us, we *know*.

Passive speakers of 5 or 10 watts may be about right for discretion in an office cubicle; amplified speakers of the same power will give the feeling of a bit more punch, even if you keep the volume turned down.

If you want to rock out, you'll need a speaker system that delivers more like 20–50 watts. For example, the Altec Lansing ADA880R subwoofer system ($299) delivers 40 watts RMS through its satellites and 40 watts RMS through the subwoofer, giving a total of 80 watts RMS. The Creative Labs MicroWorks subwoofer system (built by Cambridge SoundWorks), which was one of the systems we used for everything from Morphine to the Chemical Brothers while writing this book, delivers 13 watts per channel on the satellites and 45 watts on the subwoofers. This is enough to disturb the rest of the household. A nice feature of the MicroWorks system is that it accepts twin inputs, so you can hook in two computers at the same time and play them simultaneously for bizarre mixing effects when the urge strikes you.

Choose Your Poison

Different speakers are designed for different types of uses: Some speakers are specifically designed for gamers, so they're better at reproducing shotgun blasts and roars of monstrous rage than delivering delicate violin passages. Some speakers are built for rock music; others, for classical music. Make sure the speakers you get are suited to your needs.

Some speakers succeed in being, if not all-purpose, at least multipurpose. For example, the MidiLand S2/4030 subwoofer set (about $200— you don't pay more for the catchy and memorable name) can comfortably both detonate the earth on *Armageddon* and deliver the details of your favorite Van Halen guitar solo. (We won't vouch for their fidelity on Chopin, though—our ears are still ringing.) The 4030s provide 30 watts; there's also an S4/4060 set that delivers 60 watts (30 from the subwoofer and 15 from each of the twin satellites).

Surround Sound and Home Theater

Surround sound uses four or five speakers to produce the effect of being surrounded by the sound source. For example, when a car zips by in the background, you'll hear it go from left to right as you would with a normal stereo system, but you'll also hear that it's behind you rather than in front of you (or going straight through your head). Surround sound systems typically cost more than regular subwoofer systems, but if you like the effect, you may well find the expense justified.

If you have a DVD drive or a sound card that supports positional audio, you may want to consider a *home theater system*. Home theater systems typically use *5.1* setups—five satellite speakers with a powered subwoofer—to deliver realistic sound effects; some even use 7.1 setups. One example of a 5.1 setup is the DeskTop Theater 5.1 from Cambridge SoundWorks, which costs $299. DeskTop Theater is rated at 5 watts RMS to the main speakers and the surround speakers, 15 watts RMS to the center speaker, and 15 watts RMS to the subwoofer. The numbers may not seem impressive, but the sound is room-filling. Other home theater systems cost upward of $1000 and are designed to hook into your TV and stereo system—into which you can hook your PC.

Listen to Them

It's an obvious suggestion—but if you can, listen to speakers before you buy them. Many stores display demonstration sets of speakers pulling from a common control panel that delivers samples of different types of audio so that you can test-drive the speakers with rock, classical, soothing sounds, or games to see if they meet your needs.

Known Brands

We've mentioned a couple of PC speaker brands: Altec Lansing and Creative Labs, which also distributes speakers made by Cambridge Sound-Works. Other well-known speaker brands include Bose (stunningly good, shatteringly expensive), Boston Acoustics, JBL, Yamaha, and Philips. Even Microsoft is getting in on the act, offering a speaker/subwoofer set that plugs into your computer's USB (Universal Serial Bus) port.

Headphones

If anything, headphones are even harder to choose than speakers: one person's dream set is another person's instrument of torture. So it's hard to give specific recommendations. But we can tell you this much: rather than buying headphones as an accessory to your stereo based largely on looks and price, you need to establish what you need in a pair of headphones and then find it.

Several styles of headphones are available:

Circumnaural (or over-the-ear) headphones   These are the headphones that completely enclose your ears. You can get either *open headphones*, which expose the back of the diaphragm to the air, providing better sound, or *sealed headphones*, which look and act more like a pair of ear defenders, insulating you somewhat from outside sound. As you'd guess, sealed headphones are good for noisy environments such as music studios or busy family rooms. If you've worn them, you'll know they're heavy enough for Ah-nold to use for neck presses. If you're looking for a recommendation, we can give you a couple to try. The Beyerdynamic DT831 headphones (about $200) deliver music pure enough to fry your brains if your ears don't melt from being clamped in. The Sennheiser HD565 Ovations (about $220 street) are super comfortable, open circumnaural headphones that give a very civilized feel to all but the most raucous music while delivering exceptional punch and clarity.

Supra-aural (or on-the-ear) headphones These are the ones that sit on your ears. They're lighter and smaller than circumnaural headphones, so they can be more comfortable to wear provided they don't press too hard against your ears. Like circumnaural headphones, most supra-aural headphones use a headband to keep them in place, but Koss makes a style of supra-aural headphones that use ear-clips to attach to your ears. This style frees you from a headband but makes you look like you're Spock using two old-fashioned hearing aids. A recommendation for standard supra-aurals? Check out the Grado 225s (about $200), which provide a good kick throughout rock ranges and whose leather headband snuggles sexily against your shaven skull.

Ear-bud headphones These come in two styles: with a headband (buds that poke into your ears but don't wedge there) and without a headband (buds designed to wedge into your ear and stay there). Ear buds deliver an intense music experience but typically lower music quality and serve up less bass than circumnaural or supra-aural headphones. They're considered by some to carry a higher threat of hearing damage than circumnaural or supra-aural headphones. No recommendation here, because it will depend on the shape of your ears and the state of your brain—but anything real cheap is probably a bad idea. Because ear-bud headphones actually sit in your ear, you need to be especially alert for discomfort—it can indicate imminent damage.

You don't have to pay a huge amount for headphones. A $20 set of ear buds can sound great, and a $75 set of supra-aural or circumnaural headphones can sound better than a $300 set of speakers. But if you want to, you can drop the best part of a grand on headphones.

When buying headphones, don't overlook mundane concerns in your quest for the perfect sound for you. First, make sure that the headphone cord is long enough for your needs so that you can bop your head to the music without yanking the player off your belt or the stereo stand. (If the cord's not long enough, get an extension.) Second, make sure the headphones come with the right kind of plug for the output jack you're planning to use. Many headphones use the ¼-inch plug that slides into the ¼-inch jacks on stereo equipment rather than the mini-plug that most portable audio items use. You may need to get a ¼-inch-plug–to–mini-plug adapter. (The better headphones usually come with one.)

Big names in headphones include AKG, Beyerdynamic, Grado, Koss, and Sennheiser. (That's alphabetic order, not an order of recommendation.)

TIP

If you'll always be using headphones rather than speakers, you may want to invest in a headphone amplifier to help power your headphones. For home use, you may also want to get wireless headphones that will let you roam further from your sound source. *Try these out before you buy them.* Cheaper sets can seriously clip the top and bottom end of the frequencies, and even better sets tend to suffer in comparison to wired headphones.

As with speakers, you'll want to listen to headphones before buying them. Besides the obvious—to hear the sound quality—you should make sure they fit your ears and are comfortable enough to wear for your typical listening session.

Plenty of Storage

If you're going to store MP3 files (and we'll bet you are), you'll need plenty of storage space. Typically, this means space on your hard disk or disks, though you may also choose to use removable media as well. We'll discuss each in turn.

Hard Disk Storage

With MP3 providing roughly a 10:1 compression rate at almost CD quality, each minute of music takes up about 1MB of storage space. So a 4-minute piece of music consumes about 4MB in MP3 format, and each gigabyte (GB) of disk space can store about 250 pieces. As of this writing, the biggest affordable hard drives are in the 40GB range and cost about $300. (The biggest *unaffordable* hard drives are in the 73GB range and cost more like $1700.) You don't even need to do the math to know that this translates to a serious boatload of music.

All IDE-controlled motherboards can take at least two drives; many can hold four; and if you have SCSI, you can chain a small horde of devices. Consult your friendly computer store for upgrade possibilities. Or, if you're prepared to roll up your shirt sleeves and get your hands dirty, grab the *Complete PC Upgrade and Maintenance Guide* or *PC Upgrading and Maintenance: No Experience Required* (both from Sybex, both good, the former three times the size of the latter).

Removable Media Storage

If you're all maxed out for hard disk storage space, or if you need portable storage, you may want to fall back on removable media. These are the main candidates at this writing:

- ▶ Zip drives (made by Iomega Corp.) should need no introduction, because they've been around for a number of years. Zip drives come in IDE, SCSI, parallel port, and USB versions. The basic Zip—the Zip Classic, if you think in marketing-speak—holds a marketer's 100MB, which translates to 95.7MB in the real world. (You'll recall that a megabyte is 1024 by 1024 bytes—1,048,576 bytes—rather than a million bytes clean.) The Zip 250 holds two-and-a-half times as much—250 marketing megabytes.

- ▶ The Jaz drive, as you probably know, is the bigger brother of the Zip, with the original Jaz holding 1GB and the Jaz 2GB packing twice that. (Again, these measurements are *billions* of bytes rather than true gigabytes.)

- ▶ The Orb from Castlewood Technologies is a 2.2GB drive—a little bigger than the Jaz, and at a better price.

- ▶ CD-R and CD-RW media hold 650MB each (or 700MB for extended-capacity CDs).

- ▶ DVD-RAM discs hold 2.3GB per side. You can get single-sided or double-sided discs; as you'd guess, double-sided are more expensive. At this writing, DVD-RAM is too expensive for most people to use as a regular storage medium—but if you've got the bucks, it sure is fast and convenient.

Last, if you're hurting for disk space, consider external hard drives such as those made by LaCie. Various sizes of drives are available, from parallel port to USB, Firewire, and PC Card.

Port City: Parallel, Serial, USB, or Firewire?

If you'll be using a portable hardware MP3 player, you'll want to make sure that your computer has the right port or ports for it.

The first generation of hardware MP3 players relied on the parallel port, whereas the second generation tends toward USB. The main advantage of the humble parallel port is that it is almost as ubiquitous as the even more humble serial port (though not quite as slow). Almost every computer built since about 1990 has a parallel port.

The main disadvantage of the parallel port (apart from its lack of speed) is that the parallel port on many computers is already in use, usually for a printer (the main beneficiary of the parallel port). Or it might be used by one of several technologies—scanners, removable drives (such as external Zip drives, CD drives, and DVD drives), network adapters, and even some cameras—that have glommed onto the parallel port as the easiest way of connecting to a computer without adding hardware and expense. If you've got a device using your parallel port, you'd do well to look for an MP3 player with a better connection.

NOTE

Some MP3 players come with pass-through ports that theoretically pass through any data intended for devices other than the MP3 player. In practice, pass-through ports make many printers and scanners unhappy. Another possibility for attaching an MP3 player via a parallel port when your parallel port is already used is to add a PCI card that provides one or more additional parallel ports.

More recent MP3 players use the USB port to provide decent speed— USB can (and should) provide much faster throughput than the parallel port. If your computer already has USB and an operating system that can handle it, you're all set; if not, you can add USB to a computer with a PCI card easily enough. It'll cost a few bucks, but the installation procedure is straightforward.

For a desktop computer, get a PCI card with two or more USB ports. Siig makes an interesting PCI card that has five USB ports, but it's hard to find as of this writing. In general, you'll probably do better to get a two-port USB card and plug into it a hub that has the number of ports you require. Unless you keep your computer front and center on your desk, a hub will usually be easier to plug USB devices into.

What lies in the future for hardware MP3 devices? For some, internal hard drives—the direction in which portable players such as the eGo are moving. For most, Firewire connections will provide savagely fast download speeds. Firewire—or IE1394, if you go for the technical number; or iLink, if you have a Sony machine—looks to be the wave of the future, offering bandwidth almost enough to meet the dreams of Croesus.

Also in the near future is USB 2, which promises far higher speeds than the 12Mbps of current USB devices. USB 2 will provide either 400Mbps or

800Mbps, depending on whom you listen to, and will be *totally free* of all the problems that have dogged the first generation of USB.

Will USB beat out Firewire for dominance of the next generation of local-machine connectivity, or will Firewire manage an end-around and take the prize? The contest will be academically interesting, but as a consumer, you don't have too much to worry at this point about the result of this battle. If you're one of the minority who now has Firewire available, you'll probably want to use it—at least until USB 2 makes its presence felt. And if you don't have Firewire, make the most of USB—it's your best bet.

Internet Connection: As Fast As Possible

Last, you'll want an Internet connection in order to be able to download MP3 files—and possibly to publish your own MP3 files as well.

Many books have been written about how and why to get on the Internet, so you probably know the basics. We'll confine ourselves to the key points:

- ▶ If cable modem access is available where you live, go for it. Cable provides the fastest affordable residential access—up to several megabits (millions of bits) a second—with some drawbacks, such as upload speed caps and some security concerns that you can deal with.

- ▶ If digital subscriber line (DSL) access is available and affordable where you live, get that. DSL typically offers between 384Kbps and 1.5Mbps downstream (to the consumer) and slower upstream (to the ISP) speeds. At this writing, the Baby Bells are vying with the cable companies for high-speed customers, so the cost of DSL is reasonable—from $35 to $50 a month for good service, including an account with their ISP.

- ▶ If you can't get cable or a DSL, try for ISDN (Integrated Services Digital Network)—a digital line that's not as fast as a DSL but is more widely available, especially for people outside major metropolitan areas. ISDN's *basic rate interface,* or *BRI,* provides two bearer channels that deliver 64Kbps each, plus a 16Kbps signaling channel, so it delivers decent speeds when both bearer channels are open. Check the prices before you order ISDN: it's traditionally been a business service, and it can be expensive (can you say *per-minute charges*?).

▶ If you're too rural to get ISDN, or if ISDN is too slow for you, consider one of the satellite solutions available, such as DirecPC. Satellite solutions have one major drawback: The satellite provides only downlink capabilities, so you have to use your phone line to send data to your ISP to tell them which information to deliver by satellite. But given that your only alternative is likely to be a modem connection, you may find this flaw quite sufferable. DirecPC currently offers plans starting at $19.99 a month for a truly measly number of hours; make sure the plan you choose provides enough hours each month that you don't start incurring expensive extra-hour charges.

▶ If you're stuck with modem access, try to get 56Kbps-modem access—the fastest possible. Consider getting a *dual-line modem* (also known as a *shotgun modem*) that bonds together two conventional modems (on two separate phone lines) to increase your speed. You need an ISP that supports modem bonding for this to succeed—and two phone lines, of course.

▶ Whatever speed modem you have, make sure you're getting maximum performance out of it. Use a utility such as TweakDUN (DUN is the acronym for *dial-up networking*) or MTU Speed Pro (MTU is the abbreviation for *maximum transfer unit*). Both TweakDUN and MTU Speed Pro tune your TCP/IP settings to make sure that your connection is as efficient as possible. TweakDUN and MTU Speed are shareware and are available from many shareware archives. They're not infallible, but they're worth a try.

▶ If your connection is less speedy than you'd like, get a download-scheduling utility such as GetRight from Headlight Software (www.getright.com) or AutoFTP from PrimaSoft (www.prima-soft.com) that will let you line up your downloads to perform at a time when you don't need to do other things on your computer. For example, you can arrange to download a hundred megs of music at an antisocial hour in the early morning, when your corner of the Internet is likely to be less busy.

GET THE RIGHT SOFTWARE

To record and play MP3 files, you need two types of applications: a *ripper* to record MP3 files from existing sound sources, and a *player* to play them back. As you'll see, some applications combine rippers and players.

To organize your collection of MP3 files, you may want some form of jukebox software that enables you to catalog the tracks, arrange them by category, and so on. Some applications combine a jukebox with a ripper.

Some of the main MP3 players have add-on features, including plug-ins that create special audio and visual effects and *skins* (not drums but alternative graphical interfaces for the player) that change the player's appearance.

GO TO JAIL FOR DISTRIBUTING MP3 FILES

WARNING
You need to read this section. It could save your ass. We'll keep it brief.

There's a lot of confusion about what's legal and what's illegal when creating, playing, and distributing MP3 files. The truth is really simple, but you need to know what you're doing before you start creating and distributing MP3 files.

There's nothing inherently legal or illegal in MP3. It's just a file format for compressed audio. MP3 is an ISO (International Organization for Standardization) standard, so it's not controlled by any one company in the way Microsoft controls, say, the Word document file format.

For an MP3 file to be distributed legally, the copyright holder for the music or other material in question needs to have granted permission for the music or material to be downloaded or played. The copyright holder might be the artist, their record company, or a distributor.

The Politically Correct Version

If you're downloading MP3 files from the Internet, make sure that the files you're downloading are being distributed legally.

Sites such as Riffage.com, MP3.com, and EMusic.com post only MP3 files that they have permission to distribute. Other sites, including many of those that blast you with porn banners and almost all of those that use the words "pirate" and "warez," are (how shall we put this?) less discriminating about the provenance of the files they make available for download.

The only way you'll be able to tell if a file is legal or not is from the source supplying it. You'll find plenty of files that look like someone has ripped them illegally but that are fully legal although incompetently labeled and delivered. (Some of the worst perpetrators of badly labeled MP3 files are the garage bands who stand to benefit most immediately from MP3.)

Most people agree that you can rip MP3 copies of music (or other material) for your personal use. That's legal, in much the same way that recording a CD onto a cassette tape for personal use is legal. What's not legal is distributing MP3 files that you make from your CD collection, records, or whatever—or selling MP3 files created from such sources. In other words, you can't distribute or sell MP3 files without the explicit written permission of the copyright holder.

That's the theory—the politically correct version. But we'd be doing you a disservice—read: *lying*—if we pretended that legal MP3 distribution is the only thing that's going on in the real world.

The Politically Incorrect Version

So what's *really* happening? *Weeeelll*, some people are ripping everything in sight to MP3 tracks, permission or no (that'd be mostly no), and either posting them to pirate MP3 sites on the Web for the world to download or just sharing them on-the-fly via Napster. Other people are chopping MP3 files up into manageable segments that can be sewn together again easily and posting them to MP3 newsgroups on the Internet for the world to download. Other people are e-mailing MP3 files directly to one another, much to the distress of their ISPs and of AOL, whose servers don't appreciate 5MB files piling through like semis hogging the carpool lane of the New Jersey turnpike.

So—where do *you* come into this? Are you a decent, moral, upstanding citizen, or are you going to be bending the copyright laws into a pretzel the moment you pick up your mouse?

Don't answer that—but know that the penalties for copyright infringement are savage. Under the No Electronic Theft Act (NET Act for short—a nice acronym) passed in 1997, you're committing a felony when you infringe a copyright by creating or distributing unauthorized copies of copyrighted work, *even if you're not doing it for commercial advantage or private financial gain.* The penalties include up to three years in jail for the first offense and six for the second—and fines, of course.

If you *are* infringing a copyright for commercial advantage or private financial gain, the penalties include up to five years in jail for the first offense. The definition of "financial gain" includes your receiving anything "of value" in return, specifically other copyrighted works. So trading or swapping MP3 files is not a good idea from a legal point of view.

If you're feeling cynical, the copyright laws are a bit like the speeding laws. The highway patrol tends to tolerate most people cruising a few miles per hour above the speed limit, only pulling over vehicles that blow past them at grossly illegal speeds, weave, or whose drivers flip them the bird. They're also only looking at a tiny minority of cars on the road at any given time.

Similarly, the forces of the law seem to seldom bother swinging the heavy hammer of copyright infringement law at relatively discreet individuals. In practical terms, the copyright police expend most of their effort on the gross violators, shutting down as soon as they can such pirate MP3 sites as they find. But Jane and Joe Sixpack with their 40GB hard drive stuffed with MP3 files, some legal and some perhaps not, are unlikely to find the feds busting down their front door. (Still, it could happen.)

Morally, the situation is clear: ripping off music is theft, and you know the seventh commandment (yeah, the one about not stealing). But because morality bends with the wind these days (ask Linda Tripp), you may be motivated more by practical concerns than morality.

The reason you shouldn't steal too much music is that if everyone steals music, nobody will be able to make a living creating it. All the artists (debate the word if you must) will be reduced to assembling Grande Meals and Big Macs for a living, and your only sources of music will be advertising jingles and such recycled '90s riffs as you can cobble together yourself.

Part iv

Frightened enough to abide by most of the laws? Okay, good. Let's move into the Twilight Zone of Temptation and look at how you can find MP3 files—legal and illegal—online.

PLAYING MUSIC WITH WINAMP

In this section, we'll show you how to use Winamp, one of the most popular and versatile MP3 players for Windows.

At this writing, Winamp is freeware and even comes distributed with recent versions of Netscape Navigator, so you shouldn't have any trouble getting hold of it.

Get and Install Winamp

To get Winamp, visit www.winamp.com and download the latest version. To install Winamp, follow these steps:

1. Double-click the Winamp distribution file. This is an executable file, so double-clicking it runs it. You'll see the Winamp Setup: License Agreement dialog box.

2. Read the license and click the Next button if you can handle the terms. You'll see the Winamp Setup: Installation Options dialog box, shown in Figure 19.1.

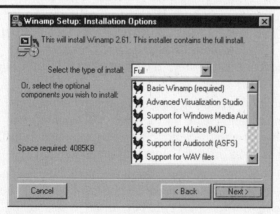

FIGURE 19.1: Winamp Setup: Installation Options dialog box

3. In the Select The Type Of Install drop-down list, choose Full, Lite, Minimal, or Custom to select a predefined package of the options shown in the list box:

    ▶ Full selects all options. We recommend this option unless you're severely short of disk space (at this writing, the full package takes a little less than 4MB), sure you won't want advanced visualizations, or are prejudiced against certain sound formats.

    ▶ Minimal selects only the Basic Winamp option.

    ▶ Lite adds to Basic Winamp support for the key music file types.

    ▶ Custom lets you select whatever you want by clicking its entry in the list box. When you select an item, the llama to its left turns from gray to black and dons a checkmark.

TIP

You can also choose a custom setup by selecting and clearing llamas as you see fit—the Select The Type Of Install drop-down list will select Custom automatically when you select any group of options other than Minimal, Lite, or Full.

Select your install option, and click Next to proceed. Setup will display the Winamp Setup: Installation Directory dialog box.

4. If you don't like the directory that Winamp has chosen to install itself into, select a different directory. You can either type the directory's name into the text box or click the Browse button and use the resulting Select Install Directory dialog box to navigate to and select the folder you want to use. Click Next when you're ready to proceed.

5. Winamp will go ahead and install itself in the specified directory. You'll then see the Winamp Setup: Settings dialog box, shown in Figure 19.2.

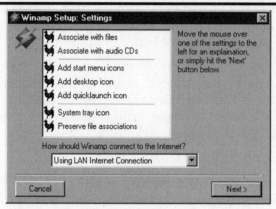

FIGURE 19.2: Winamp Setup: Settings dialog box

Here's what the items in this dialog box do. (If you've got a later version of Winamp, there may be additional features.) Again, select and clear the llamas as you see fit, and then click Next:

Associate With Files   Selecting this check box makes Winamp the default audio player for all files in formats that Winamp considers to be audio. This list of formats includes MP3 (of course) and most audio file formats. If you prefer to play some forms of audio through a different player, you can deselect them later. Alternatively, you can specify Winamp as the default audio player for specific formats after installation.

Associate With Audio CDs   Selecting this check box causes Winamp to spring to life when you insert an audio CD into your computer's CD drive. If you don't like autoplay, clear this check box. Note that this setting does not change the Auto Insert Notification setting on your PC. If Auto Insert Notification is off (in the CD drive's Properties dialog box), Winamp will not automatically play CDs even if you select the Autoplay Audio CDs option.

Add Start Menu Icons   Selecting this check box adds a Winamp group to the Start menu. Unless you prefer to have a Winamp icon on the Desktop or the Quick Launch bar and nowhere else, keep this check box selected.

Add Desktop Icon   Selecting this check box adds a Winamp icon to the desktop. Having the icon there is often handy.

Add Quicklaunch Icon   This option is available only if your computer is running Windows 98/98 SE or Internet Explorer 4 or 5. Because the Quick Launch bar is always accessible, it's usually the quickest way to get to Winamp.

System Tray Icon   This option adds a Winamp icon to the system tray, so that you can quickly access Winamp and its bookmarks.

How Should Winamp Connect To The Internet drop-down list   This drop-down list lets you choose the way that Winamp will use the Internet. If the computer you're using doesn't have an Internet connection, or if you don't want to use Winamp's Internet features, choose No Internet Connection Available. If your computer has a modem connection, choose Using Dial-Up Modem Internet Connection. If your computer connects to the Internet through a network (for example, a company's local area network or a home network, or a cable modem or DSL), choose Using LAN Internet Connection.

6. Winamp will install the icons and groups you chose and will display the Winamp Setup: User Information dialog box. Enter information here if you want to—there's no obligation.

Never Ask Me Again   Select this check box if you don't want to be invited to register again.

Please Send Me Winamp Announcements   Select this check box if you want Winamp announcements mailed to you. You may find it easier to visit the Winamp Web site periodically at your convenience to scan for new information rather than having it pushed out to you.

Allow Winamp To Report Simple, Anonymous Usage Statistics   If you don't want Winamp to send back to Winamp.com anonymous statistics on how much you're using Winamp, clear this check box.

Part iv

If you fill in the user information, click the Next button to send it. Winamp will connect to the Internet using the connection you specified in the previous dialog box and will send the information to Nullsoft Winamp. If you don't fill in the user information, click the Later button.

7. You'll then see the Winamp Setup: Winamp Successfully Installed dialog box. Click the Run Winamp button to run Winamp.

Use the Winamp Interface

In this section, we'll examine the Winamp interface. If you're feeling impatient and have some MP3 files already, click the Open button, select a track or three, and listen to some tunes while you're playing with the interface.

Exploring the Winamp Windows

The illustration below shows Winamp's basic look. As you can see, it consists of four windows: the Main window, the Graphical Equalizer window, the Playlist Editor window, and the Browser window (see Figure 19.3). Here's a brief overview of each window:

Main window   This window displays information about the track that's currently playing and provides CD player-style controls. The Main window also provides quick access to the Playlist Editor window and the Graphical Equalizer window.

Graphical Equalizer window   This window provides a software graphical equalizer that you can use to tweak the sound that Winamp produces.

Playlist Editor window   This window contains the current playlist, buttons for creating and manipulating playlists, and a minimal set of play controls (so that you can dispense with the Main window if you want).

Browser window   This window provides a quick way of inputting information into your main Browser window for searching Amazon.com for music by the current artist. Whether you find the Browser window useful depends on your interests.

We tend to find it annoying and recommend turning it off straightaway.

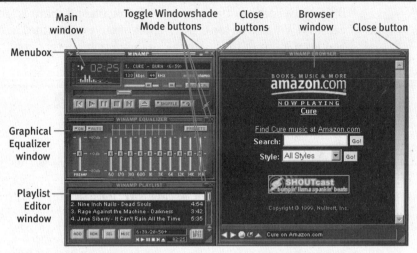

FIGURE 19.3: Winamp windows

Arranging the Winamp Windows

Here's what you need to know about arranging the Winamp windows on screen. You can do the following:

▶ Close any Winamp window by clicking its Close button—the X button in its upper-right corner. Clicking the Close button on the Main window closes Winamp.

▶ Rearrange the Winamp windows any way you want by clicking the title bar of a window and dragging it to where you want it to appear.

▶ Move each Winamp window independently. When you move the edge of one of the satellite windows so that it touches any edge of the Main window, the satellite window sticks to the Main window. When you then move the Main window, any windows stuck to it will move along with it.

▶ Minimize all displayed Winamp windows by clicking the Minimize button on the Main window.

▶ Reduce any of the windows except the Browser window to a windowshade strip by clicking its Toggle Windowshade Mode button. In Windowshade mode (see Figure 19.4), Winamp takes up very little space and provides only key information and controls. You can keep Winamp on top of other applications (as described next) and keep it out of the way by positioning it in another application's title bar.

FIGURE 19.4: Winamp in Windowshade mode

▶ Keep Winamp on top of all other running applications so that it's always at hand. Press Ctrl+A to toggle the Always on Top feature for all Winamp windows except the Playlist Editor. Press Ctrl+Alt+A to toggle the Always on Top feature for the Playlist Editor.

▶ Toggle the display of the Winamp windows with keyboard shortcuts: press Alt+W to toggle the main Winamp window; press Alt+E to toggle the Playlist Editor window; press Alt+G to toggle the Graphical Equalizer window; and press Alt+T to toggle the Browser window. Alternatively, click the menu box in the upper-left corner of the Main window and select the entry for the window from the menu to toggle it on and off, as shown in Figure 19.5.

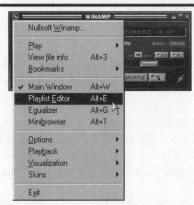

FIGURE 19.5: Winamp Main window and upper-left corner menu, selecting Playlist Editor with mouse pointer

NOTE

When you've hidden all the Winamp windows, make sure that the Winamp item is selected in the Taskbar when you try to restore a Winamp window by using the keyboard shortcut. If another application is selected, you can press these keyboard shortcuts all you want, but Winamp won't react. You may find it easier to right-click the Winamp item in the Taskbar, select the Winamp Menu item from the shortcut menu, and choose the window you want to restore from the submenu that appears.

▶ Display Winamp at double size by pressing Ctrl+D to make it easier to see what you're doing. When you need to reclaim your screen real estate, press Ctrl+D again to restore Winamp to its usual discreet size.

To exit Winamp, click the Control menu on the Main window (or press Alt+F), and choose Exit from the menu. Alternatively, click the Close button on the Main window.

TIP

If you chose during installation to add the Winamp icon to your system tray, you can also control Winamp from there when it's minimized. For example, right-click the system tray icon and choose Exit from the shortcut menu to close Winamp.

Play Tracks and SHOUTcast Streams with the Winamp Main Window

The Main window is dead easy to operate with the mouse, but it has many keyboard access features that you'll want to know as well. Figure 19.6 shows the components of the Main window.

Part iv

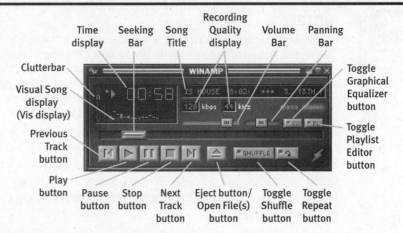

FIGURE 19.6: Winamp's Main window

To open one or more tracks, click the Open File(s) button to display the Open File(s) dialog box. Navigate to the track or tracks you want, and select them. To select a contiguous list of tracks, click the first track; then hold down Shift, and click the last track. To select multiple individual tracks or to add them to a Shift-click–selected list, hold down Ctrl and click each track in succession. Click the Open button to open the files in Winamp. Winamp will add them to the current playlist and will start playing the first track. Usually Winamp decides that the last track you selected is the first track, so you may want to try selecting the tracks in reverse order.

Most of the buttons and displays in the Main window are easy to recognize because they look like those on a CD player or a cassette player. You click the Play button to play the current track, the Stop button to stop play, and so on. But you should know about a couple of mouse techniques for the Main window:

- ▶ Click the time in the Time display to toggle between time elapsed and time remaining on the track.

- ▶ Click the Visual Song display (the Vis display) to switch between visualization modes.

- ▶ Click the letters in the Clutterbar at the left side of the Time display window to perform common maneuvers. O displays the Options menu; I displays the File Info dialog box; A toggles the Always On Top feature; D toggles the double-size feature; and V displays the Visualization menu, which contains options for the visualization feature below the Time display.

► Right-click the Song Title to display a shortcut menu for moving around the current track and current playlist. (More on these in a moment.)

► Click the lightning-flash logo in the lower-right corner to display the About Winamp dialog box.

As well as listening to music you've downloaded, you can play music straight off the Web with Winamp—either MP3 files from a server or a SHOUTcast server stream. *SHOUTcast* is streaming software created by Nullsoft (the makers of Winamp) that allows you to broadcast music over the Web.

To play music straight off the Web, follow these steps:

1. Press Ctrl+L, or choose Play Location from the main menu to display the Open Location dialog box, as shown in Figure 19.7.

FIGURE 19.7: Open Location dialog box with a valid URL for music entered

2. Enter the URL of a file or of a SHOUTcast stream.

3. Click the Open button. Winamp will start playing the file or the stream.

You can also add Web tracks or SHOUTcast streams to the Playlist Editor as follows:

1. Display the Playlist Editor if it's not already displayed.

2. Click the Add button to display the menu of buttons, and then choose the Add URL button to display the Open Location dialog box.

3. Enter the URL of a file or of a SHOUTcast stream.

4. Click the Open button. Winamp will add the file or stream to the playlist. You can then play the file or stream by using the Winamp controls as usual.

NOTE

You won't always need to use this technique to play music directly off the Web because sites such as MP3.com include links that automatically start your MP3 player or browser plug-in playing the track.

Create and Use Winamp Playlists

Like most MP3 players, Winamp lets you build playlists—lists of tracks in the order in which you want to play them.

To work with playlists, you use the Playlist Editor. To display the Playlist Editor, click the Toggle Playlist Editor button in the Main window, or press Alt+E. Figure 19.8 shows the Playlist Editor with a playlist loaded in it.

FIGURE 19.8: Playlist Editor with playlist loaded

NOTE

Because you can control play by using the controls in the Playlist Editor, you may want to close the Main window to save space on screen. To toggle the Main window on and off, press Alt+W.

Creating a Playlist

To create a playlist, add tracks to it and arrange them in the order you want. You can add tracks to the playlist in several ways:

▶ Drag tracks from an Explorer window to the Playlist Editor.

▶ Double-click the Add button in the Playlist Editor to display the Add File(s) to Playlist dialog box, select the tracks, and click the Open button. (The first click of the Add button displays the menu of buttons, and the second selects the Add File button, which appears in place of the Add button—but you can perform the action as a double-click.)

▶ To add a whole directory to the playlist, click the Add button to display the menu of buttons, and then choose the Add Dir button. Winamp will display the Open Directory dialog box (Figure 19.9). Navigate to and select the directory you want to add. If you want to add all the subdirectories under the directory you're selecting, make sure the Recurse Subdirectories check box is selected; if you don't, make sure it's cleared. Then click the OK button.

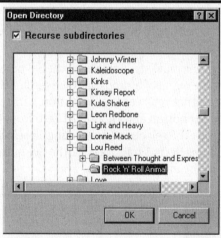

FIGURE 19.9:   Open Directory dialog box

NOTE

To play a track more than once in a playlist, add two or more instances of it to the playlist.

Part iv

Arranging and Sorting a Playlist

You can then rearrange or remove the tracks as follows:

▶ To remove a track from the playlist, select it and press the Delete key or click the Rem button. (The first click displays the button menu, and the second selects the Rem Sel button—Remove Selection—that replaces the Rem button.)

▶ To rearrange the tracks in the playlist easily, select tracks with the mouse and drag them up or down to where you want it or them to appear.

▶ To sort the playlist, click the Misc button, and choose Sort List from the menu of buttons (see Figure 19.10). You can sort a list by title, by filename, or by path and filename. You can also reverse the current order of the playlist—which can be good for variety— or randomize the playlist to produce something unexpected. There's nothing quite like the mind-jarring juxtaposition of Bach and Nine Inch Nails.

▶ To select all the tracks in the playlist, double-click the Sel button. (The first click displays the menu of buttons, and the second click selects the Sel All button that replaces the Sel button.) To deselect all tracks, click the Sel button and choose Sel Zero from the menu of buttons. To invert the selection (deselecting all selected tracks and selecting all unselected tracks), click the Sel button, and choose Inv Sel from the menu of buttons.

FIGURE 19.10: Misc. Opts button and Sorting submenu

Saving a Playlist

To save a playlist, click the List Opts button, and choose Save List from the menu of buttons. Winamp will display the Save Playlist dialog box. Enter a name for the playlist—**Full Metal Morning**, **Dance into Bed**, whatever—and specify a different location if necessary. Then click the Save button to save the list. The default file format is M3U Playlist, but you can choose PLS Playlist in the Save As Type drop-down list if you want to save your playlists in the PLS format.

Opening a Saved Playlist

To open a playlist you've previously saved, double-click the List Opts button to display the Load Playlist dialog box. (The first click will display the menu of buttons, and the second will select the Load List button that replaces the List Opts button.) Navigate to the playlist, select it, and click the Open button.

Tips for Working with Playlists

Here's how to get around the current track and playlist quickly:

▶ To jump to a specific time in the track that is currently playing, press Ctrl+J, or right-click the Song Title display and choose Jump To Time from the shortcut menu to display the Jump To Time dialog box. Enter the time to which to jump in the Jump To text box in *minutes:seconds* format (for example, **2:15**), and click the Jump button. This is the precise way to skip lame intros.

▶ To move less precisely through a track, drag the Seeking Bar to the left or right.

▶ To jump to another track in the current playlist, press **J**, or right-click the Song Title display and choose Jump To File from the shortcut menu to display the Jump To File dialog box (Figure 19.11). The Jump To File dialog box lists the tracks in alphabetic order. Double-click the track to which you want to jump. To search for text in a track's name, you can enter the letters in the Search for Text text box. As you type, Winamp will reduce the list to tracks that have that sequence of letters in the title.

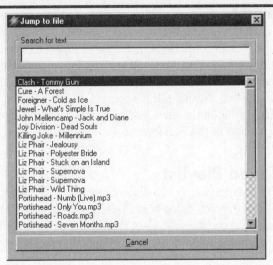

FIGURE 19.11: Jump To File dialog box

▶ You can also navigate the playlist by using the Playback submenu on the main Winamp menu (accessed by clicking the menu box in the upper-left corner of the Main window). This submenu offers navigation items including Stop W/ Fadeout, Back 5 Seconds, Fwd 5 Seconds, Start Of List, 10 Tracks Back, and 10 Tracks Fwd.

▶ You can control play by using the keyboard shortcuts listed below. These shortcuts aren't mnemonically obvious (though you can certainly make up some innovative mnemonics for them), but you'll notice that they're all on the bottom-left row of the keyboard, just where you can reach them most easily when you're lying wasted on the floor. (That's assuming you're using the QWERTY keyboard layout—if you're using a Dvorak keyboard layout, you'll need to get up off the floor to use the shortcuts.)

Keyboard Shortcut	Action
Z	Previous track
X	Play
C	Pause
V	Stop
B	Next

Use Winamp Bookmarks to Access Tracks Quickly

To enable you to quickly access a track or a SHOUTcast stream in your current playlist, Winamp provides *bookmarks*, virtual markers that you can use to tag a track or stream.

To bookmark the current track or stream, press Alt+I, or choose Bookmarks ➤ Add Current as Bookmark from the main menu. You can also add a bookmark to one or more selected tracks or streams in the Playlist Editor window by right clicking and choosing Bookmark Item(s) from the shortcut menu.

Once you've added a bookmark, you can go to it by choosing its name from the Bookmarks submenu from the main menu, as shown in Figure 19.12.

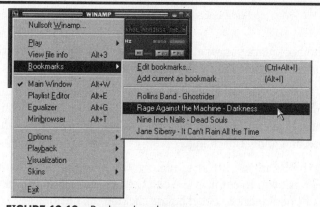

FIGURE 19.12: Bookmarks submenu

To edit a bookmark, press Ctrl+Alt+I with the Main window active, or choose Bookmarks ➤ Edit Bookmarks from the main menu. Winamp will display the Winamp Preferences dialog box with the Bookmarks page displayed, as shown in Figure 19.13.

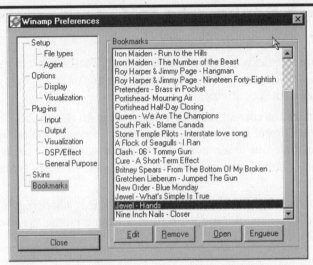

FIGURE 19.13:   Winamp Preferences dialog box, Bookmarks page

Select the bookmark you want to affect in the Bookmarks list box, and then take one of the following actions:

▶ Click the Edit button to display the Edit Bookmark dialog box (Figure 19.14). Change either the title of the bookmark or the file to which it refers, and then click the OK button to close the dialog box and apply the change.

▶ Click the Remove button to remove the bookmark. Winamp doesn't ask you to confirm the deletion, so make sure you have the right bookmark selected before clicking the button.

▶ Click the Open button to open the bookmarked track in Winamp and start playing it.

▶ Click the Enqueue button to add the bookmarked track to your current playlist.

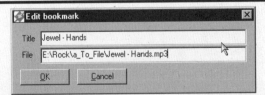

FIGURE 19.14:   Edit Bookmark dialog box

TIP

To go quickly to a bookmark, right-click the Winamp icon in the system tray, and then choose the bookmark from the Bookmarks shortcut menu.

Make Music Sound Good with the Winamp Graphical Equalizer

Winamp provides a full-featured graphical equalizer for adjusting the balance of the music. The graphical equalizer lets you increase or decrease 10 different frequencies in the sound spectrum to boost the parts of the music you want to hear more of and reduce those you don't.

Graphical Equalizer Basics

To display the Graphical Equalizer window (Figure 19.15), click the Toggle Graphical Equalizer button in the Main window or press Alt+G. The frequencies are measured in hertz (Hz) and kilohertz (kHz)—the number of cycles per second. As you can see, the left end of the graphical equalizer controls the lower frequencies—from 60Hz booms and rumbles upward—and the right end controls the higher frequencies—up to 16kHz. You can increase or decrease each frequency up to 20 decibels (dB), enough to make a huge difference in the sound. (For example, boost all the bass frequencies and crank up Hole to knock all the ice off your bedroom window on snowy winter mornings.)

FIGURE 19.15: Graphical Equalizer window

First, make sure the graphical equalizer is on. (It's off by default.) Click the On button to toggle the graphical equalizer on and off. When it's on, the On button will display a bright green light; when it's off, the light is a darker green. (Guess we're lucky the Winamp guys didn't design traffic signals.)

The PreAmp slider on the left side of the Graphical Equalizer window raises or lowers the preamplification of the graphical equalizer all at once. Usually you won't need to mess with the PreAmp slider because you can control the Winamp volume output through the Main window, through the Windows Volume Control (usually in the Taskbar's tray), or through the volume control on your amplifier or speakers. If you do adjust the Pre-Amp level, don't set it too high because that will distort the sound.

To adjust the sound, drag the sliders up and down. Winamp takes a second or two to implement the changes, so be patient. You'll notice that the equalizer display at the top of the Graphical Equalizer window changes shape to match the slider settings (as shown in Figure 19.16, with settings you might try for playing rap in a '65 Impala). This display helps you see when you've got a setting out of whack with the others.

FIGURE 19.16:   Graphical Equalizer window with sliders moved enough to show big changes in the equalizer display

Keep in mind that the graphical equalizer works with (or in some cases against) your sound card and your speakers. If your speakers are tinny and deliver too much treble, you can reduce the high frequencies on the graphical equalizer to help balance the music. And if your speakers are bass-heavy, you can use the graphical equalizer to minimize the bass late at night when the folks next door start complaining—or crank it up if they tick you off.

NOTE

Don't expect the graphical equalizer to act as a panacea for a poor stereo system. If your audio hardware sucks, clever use of the graphical equalizer may make it suck less. But it won't make it sound like a $5000 Bang & Olufsen system.

Saving and Loading Preset Equalizations

The graphical equalizer's killer feature is its ability to save and auto-load preset equalizations. This means that you can create a custom equalization profile for any particular track and have Winamp automatically use it each time you play the track.

To create an auto-load preset equalization for a track, play the track and set the graphical equalizer sliders appropriately. Then click the Presets button to display its menu, highlight the Save menu to display its submenu, and choose Auto-Load Preset to display the Save Auto-Load Preset dialog box (Figure 19.17). The dialog box will suggest the title of the song as the name for the equalization; edit the name if necessary, and click the Save button to save the preset.

FIGURE 19.17:   Save Auto-Load Preset dialog box full of auto-load presets

Then enable the auto-load presets by clicking the Auto button in the Graphical Equalizer window so that it displays a light-green light. (It's off by default.) From here on, Winamp will use your customized equalization whenever you play the track.

NOTE

When auto-load preset equalizations are enabled and Winamp finishes playing a track with a preset equalization, it will continue to use that equalization for the following track if that track does not have its own equalization.

Winamp comes with preset equalizations that you can load at will by clicking the Presets button, highlighting Load to display its submenu, and choosing Preset to display the Load EQ Preset dialog box, as shown in Figure 19.18.

FIGURE 19.18:   Load EQ Preset dialog box

Select the equalization you want from the list box. Wait a couple of seconds and see how it sounds. To apply it, click the Load button. For example, you might select the Large Hall equalization to make Winamp sound as if it's playing in a large hall. Winamp's preset equalizations are well put together and demonstrate how different a graphical equalizer can make music sound. When you look at the slider positions for some of the equalizations, you may expect minimal changes in the sound—but your ears will tell you otherwise.

To add to the list of preset equalizations, set the sliders for the equalization, click the Presets button, and choose Save ➣ Preset to display the Save EQ Preset dialog box. Enter the name for the new preset, and click the Save button.

To delete a preset, click the Presets button, and choose Delete ➣ Preset or Delete ➣ Auto-Load Preset to display the Delete Preset dialog box or Delete Auto-Load Preset dialog box. Select the preset, and click the Delete button to delete it.

Check and Set Track Information with Winamp

Winamp lets you quickly view and change the track information, called *tag information*, that each MP3 file can store.

In the Playlist Editor, right-click a track, and choose File Info from the shortcut menu to display the MPEG File Info Box + ID3 Tag Editor dialog box (see Figure 19.19) with the information for the track. (From the Main window, you can display this dialog box by double-clicking the track title.) Change the information as appropriate, and then click the Save button to save it to the MP3 file. You can also click the Remove ID3 button to remove the tag information from the MP3 file.

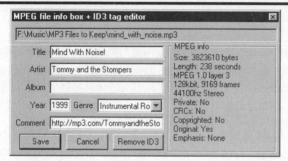

FIGURE 19.19: MPEG File Info + ID3 Tag Editor dialog box

RIPPING AND PLAYING WITH MUSICMATCH JUKEBOX

In this section, we'll show you how to use MusicMatch Jukebox, one of the most popular ripper-jukeboxes. MusicMatch Jukebox offers a Standard version that you can download for free, but it is limited to recording at 96kbps (kilobits per second) or below—sampling rates that most people find unacceptable for sustained music listening. (It's a bit like listening to AM radio when you're used to FM.) MusicMatch is betting that, after listening to low-quality audio for a short while, you'll be prepared to register and cough up $29.99 for the full version of MusicMatch Jukebox that can record at 128kbps (the standard for "CD-quality" MP3 files) and higher speeds to make music sound good again.

Before we get started on MusicMatch Jukebox's features, we'll discuss quickly how to choose the right sampling rate for the MP3 files you'll create.

Choose the Right Sampling Rate

Minor alert: This section gets mildly technical. But as with the legal stuff earlier in this book, this is information you need to know—and we'll keep it short.

As we discussed earlier in this chapter, MP3 rocks because it compresses audio into a small file *and* it retains near-CD quality. To compress the audio, it uses sampling.

Before you start recording MP3 files, you need to set the sampling rate you'll use. To put it simply, the higher the sampling rate (within reason), the better the music will sound, and the larger the file size will be.

For example, a ripper such as MusicMatch Jukebox offers preset sampling rates of 64kbps, 96kbps, 128kbps, and 160kbps, together with custom sampling rates that you can choose for yourself. A rate of 64kbps is somewhat euphemistically termed "FM Radio Quality" (we reckon it's much worse), 96kbps is described as "near CD quality" (we'd say it's not within easy commuting distance of CD quality), and 128kbps and 160kbps are described as "CD quality" (which is almost true). Most people find music sampled at a rate below 128kbps to be unacceptable to listen to, but for spoken audio this high-capacity option is a good choice.

When recording music, you'll usually do best to use a sampling rate of 128kpbs. Using a higher sampling rate generally produces little improvement in sound quality, and the file sizes will of course be larger. Some people swear by 160kbps, and others by 192kbps, so try them yourself and see which suits you the best.

If you want to cram as much music as possible onto a device and are prepared to settle for poorer sound quality, experiment with lower bit rates, and establish what you find tolerable for listening. But if you're looking to digitize any serious chunk of your music collection, be sure to do it at a sampling rate high enough that you'll enjoy the music for years rather than weeks.

Keep in mind that you won't be able to increase the sampling rate of any tracks you've already recorded. Though with certain specialized programs, you can decrease the sampling rate if you really want to do so.

NOTE

It doesn't take any more time to rip tracks at a higher sampling rate than at a lower sampling rate. (In fact, with most ripping programs, ripping at a higher sampling rate takes less time because it requires less compression and less processing power.)

Get, Install, and Configure MusicMatch Jukebox

To install MusicMatch Jukebox, double-click the distribution file. Install-Shield will walk you through a standard installation routine in which you accept a license agreement, are encouraged to register the software, and specify an installation folder, music folder, and Start menu group. We'll mention just the highlights here and leave you to handle the routine decisions.

The first thing to note is the Software Registration dialog box, in which you have to enter at least one character in the Name text box, the Email text box, and the Postal Code text box in order to enable the Next button, which is disabled by default. These entries are unavoidable, though they don't have to be honest; but think twice before you leave the Notify Me Of Software Upgrades check box selected, as it is by default.

Next, you get the Personalize Net Music dialog box, which invites you to let MusicMatch Jukebox upload to a MusicMatch server information on the music you listen to, save, and download. MusicMatch uses this information to deliver personalized recommendations to you, and assures you that "your personal music preferences... will never be sold or shared"—but the idea of MusicMatch Jukebox automatically uploading information about our listening habits creeps us out too much for us to recommend using this feature. However, your mileage will vary, so select the Yes (Recommended) option button rather than the No option button if you like. The option buttons are implemented a little strangely, and to access the No button via the keyboard, you'll need to press one of the arrow keys (for example, ➔) rather than the Tab key.

After you choose the destination location, your music folder, the program folder, and whether you want MusicMatch Jukebox icons on your Desktop, on your Quick Launch toolbar, and in your system tray, you get to a more serious decision. In the Filetype Registration dialog box (Figure 19.20), you must decide: For which file types do you want to use MusicMatch Jukebox?

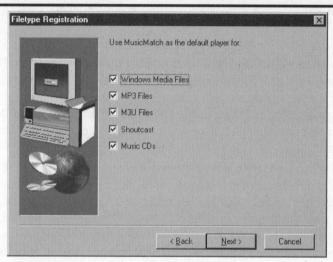

FIGURE 19.20: Filetype Registration dialog box

If you're using another MP3 player (such as Winamp, Sonique, or XingMP3 Player), you'll probably want to clear some or all of these check boxes. If you'll be using MusicMatch Jukebox primarily or exclusively, leave them selected.

If you do choose to make MusicMatch Jukebox your default MP3 player, it will monitor your file associations aggressively, even when you're not running it, to see if any have been stolen by another application. (Typically, this will happen when you install another MP3 player or jukebox after installing MusicMatch Jukebox; it may also happen when you run another player or jukebox that reclaims file associations it finds MusicMatch Jukebox has stolen.) If MusicMatch Jukebox detects that it no longer has its associations, it will display the MusicMatch Jukebox File Associations dialog box shown in Figure 19.21.

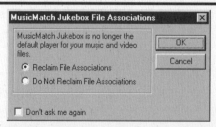

FIGURE 19.21: MusicMatch Jukebox File Associations dialog box

To restore the associations, leave the Reclaim File Associations option button selected (it's selected by default), and click the OK button. To leave the file associations with whichever application has stolen them, select the Do Not Reclaim File Associations option button, and click the OK button. You can prevent MusicMatch Jukebox from bugging you about this by selecting the Don't Ask Me Again check box before closing the MusicMatch Jukebox File Associations dialog box.

Once you're done with the file types, MusicMatch Jukebox will complete the installation and will display the Setup Complete dialog box. Click the Finish button to close this dialog box. You're just about ready to rock. Double-click the MusicMatch Jukebox icon on your Desktop or in your system tray, or click the icon on your Quick Launch toolbar, to get going.

The first time you run it, MusicMatch Jukebox will display the Search for Music dialog box, shown in Figure 19.22. In the Look In drop-down list, select the drive or drives you want MusicMatch Jukebox to search. To limit the search to a particular folder, click the Browse button to display the Browse for Folder dialog box, navigate to and select the drive, and click the OK button.

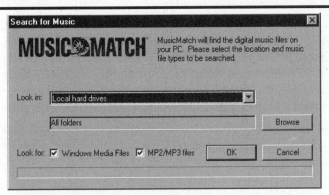

FIGURE 19.22: Search for Music dialog box

MusicMatch Jukebox will automatically enter the appropriate drive in the Look In drop-down list. Make sure the Windows Media Files check box and the MP2/MP3 Files check box are selected or cleared as suits you, and then click the OK button. MusicMatch Jukebox will search for music and will display the Adding Songs to Music Library dialog box (Figure 19.23) until it has finished adding all the songs to its music database.

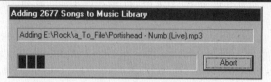

FIGURE 19.23: Adding Songs to Music Library dialog box

Next, you may see the Confirm Association dialog box (Figure 19.24), in which MusicMatch Jukebox is trying to grab some unspecified file associations from another application. You probably want to choose the Yes button in this dialog box, though it's tedious not to know which file associations MusicMatch Jukebox is after.

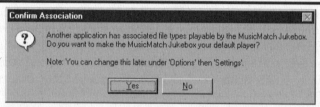

FIGURE 19.24: Confirm Association dialog box

Figures 19.25 and 19.26 show the Main window and the Music Library window. You'll probably be seeing them joined together, but we've pulled them apart so that we could label them better. You'll also be seeing the Recorder window, which we'll show you how to use in a few pages' time, and a Welcome Tips window, which we'll let you explore on your own.

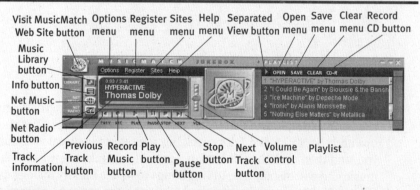

FIGURE 19.25: MusicMatch Jukebox Main window

Add button   Delete button   Tag button   Find button   Auto DJ button

FIGURE 19.26: MusicMatch Jukebox Music Library

The MusicMatch Jukebox windows are easy to handle:

▶ You can drag the windows around as you want.

▶ You can click the Separated View button on the Main window to separate the Playlist window (on the right side of the Main window in the illustration above) from the Main window. Click the resulting Integrated View button on the Playlist window to reunite the two.

▶ To make the Music Library window move with the Main window, drag the Music Library window so that one of its sides sticks to a side of the Main window.

▶ You can resize the Music Library window by clicking its border and dragging.

NOTE

To register your copy of MusicMatch Jukebox, choose Register ➤ Enter Key to display the MusicMatch Enter Key dialog box. Enter the key in the Enter The Key (Include Hyphens) text box, and click the OK button.

Configuring CDDB

If your computer has an Internet connection, make sure CDDB is configured correctly. You need to configure CDDB only once, and, as you'll see, it offers compelling benefits for most people.

CDDB is an online database of CD information from which PC CD-player applications (including MP3 players that play CDs) and rippers can download CD information—the artist's name, the CD title, track titles, and even lyrics for some tracks.

To configure CDDB, follow these steps:

1. Choose Options ➤ Settings to display the Settings dialog box, and then click the CDDB Preferences tab (see Figure 19.27).

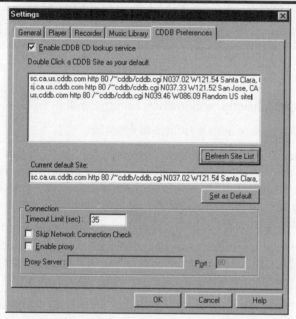

FIGURE 19.27: CDDB Preferences page of the Settings dialog box

2. Make sure the Enable CDDB CD Lookup Service check box is selected. (If you don't want to use CDDB, clear this check box.)

3. Click the Refresh Site List button to get the latest CDDB sites available.

4. In the Double-Click A CDDB Site As Your Default list box, double-click the CDDB site that you want to use. All other things being equal, you'll probably do best with one that's geographically close to you. But if your choice turns out to be slow or too busy, try another. Your selection will appear in the Current Default Site text box.

5. Click the Set as Default button to set the site as your default.

6. If you need to use a proxy server, select the Enable Proxy check box in the Connection group box, and enter the server's details in the Proxy Server text box and the Port text box. (Consult your network administrator for this information if you don't know it.) You can also select the Skip Network Connection Check check box to prevent MusicMatch Jukebox from checking your network connection before contacting CDDB, and you can change the timeout limit from its default setting in the Timeout Limit text box.

7. Click the OK button to close the Settings dialog box.

Choosing the Sampling Rate

Next, choose the sampling rate to use for your recordings. Like CDDB, this is something you'll typically want to set and forget. Here's what to do:

1. Choose Options ≻ Recorder ≻ Settings to display the Recorder tab of the Settings dialog box (see Figure 19.28).

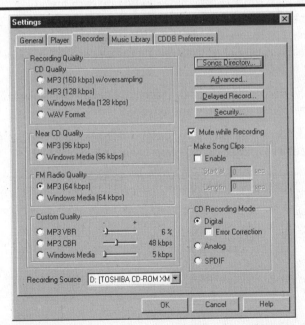

FIGURE 19.28: Recorder page of Settings dialog box

2. In the Recording Quality group box, select the sampling rate at which to record. For most music, you'll want to start with the MP3 (128kbps) setting, the default setting for the full version of MusicMatch Jukebox. (If you have the free version of MusicMatch Jukebox, you'll be able to record only at 96kbps or 64kbps.) If you find the quality not high enough, try the MP3 (160kbps) W/ Oversampling setting. For spoken audio, experiment with the MP3 (96kbps) and MP3 (64kbps) settings found in the Near CD Quality and FM Radio Quality group boxes, respectively. For special purposes, you can use the VBR and CBR options found in the Custom Quality group box. Here's what you can do with them:

VBR   VBR stands for *variable bit rate* and lets you emphasize the quality of the audio; the amount of information recorded (the *bit rate*) varies according to the complexity of the music. Be warned that VBR can produce large files, and some MP3 players cannot play back VBR files successfully.

CBR   To squeeze even more audio into each megabyte of storage, select the CBR option button, and drag its slider to the left to reduce the bit rate. CBR stands for *constant bit rate* and is best used for reducing the size of the MP3 files you're recording.

3. In the Recording Source drop-down list, select the CD or DVD drive from which you want to record.

4. Click the Songs Directory button to display the New Songs Directory Options dialog box, shown in Figure 19.29.

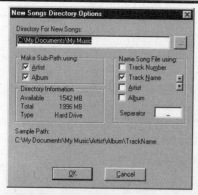

FIGURE 19.29: New Songs Directory Options dialog box

5. In the Directory for New Songs text box, enter the name of the folder in which to store the folders and tracks you rip. Click the ... button to display the Browse For Folder dialog box, navigate to the folder you want to use, and click the OK button.

6. In the Make Sub-Path Using group box, select the Artist check box and Album check box as appropriate to include them in the name of the subfolders that'll be created. For example, if you're ripping the album *Exile On Coldharbour Lane* by A3, selecting the Artist and Album check boxes produces the subfolder \A3\Exile On Coldharbour Lane\. The Sample Path label at the bottom of the New Songs Directory Options dialog box will show a generic path reflecting your choices.

7. In the Name Song File Using group box, select the information to include in the track file by selecting the check boxes for Track Number, Track Name, Artist, and Album as appropriate. You can change the order of these items by selecting one of them and using the up and down arrow buttons to move it. In the Separator text box, enter the separator character to use between these components. The default is an underscore, but you can use a different character (or several characters) if you prefer. For example, you might prefer to use two or three hyphens or a space, a hyphen, and a space (for readability).

8. Click the OK button to close the New Songs Directory Options dialog box.

9. Select the Mute While Recording check box to specify that MusicMatch Jukebox rip the tracks without playing them back at the same time. Using this option lets MusicMatch Jukebox record much faster—at least, on a fast computer.

10. Make sure that the Enable check box in the Make Song Clips group box is cleared. (This feature lets you make a clip from a song: you select the check box and specify a start second and a length—for example, a 29-second clip starting at second 10. The main reason for creating clips is to provide a quick sample that will allow the recipient to identify or judge the song—for example, for sharing a small part of a copyrighted song without transgressing too horribly against the law.)

Part iv

11. In the Recording Mode group box, make sure that the Digital option button is selected. If you want to use error correction in your recordings, select the Error Correction check box. (Error correction helps reduce clicks and pops that occur when a CD disagrees with your CD drive's read head during the recording. Using error correction slows down the recording, so you probably won't want to use it unless you're experiencing quality problems with your MP3 files.)

12. Click the OK button to close the Settings dialog box.

NOTE

You can also quickly change the sampling rate by choosing Options ➤ Recorder ➤ Quality and choosing the appropriate setting on the Quality submenu.

Rip Tracks with MusicMatch Jukebox

Now that you've got CDDB and your recording options set up, you're ready to rip tracks with MusicMatch Jukebox. Here's how to proceed:

1. Slot a CD into your CD drive (or DVD drive), and close it. MusicMatch Jukebox will read the CD. If you're using CDDB, MusicMatch Jukebox will retrieve the information for the CD from CDDB and will display the album's name, the artist's name, and the track titles. If CDDB can't decide between a couple of possible listings for the CD, it will display a dialog box, such as the one shown in Figure 19.30, to let you decide. Do so.

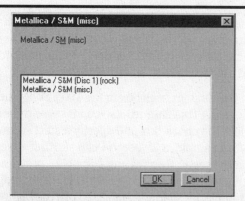

FIGURE 19.30: Metallica/S&M (misc.) dialog box

2. Click the Record Music CDs Into Digital Tracks button to display the Recorder window (Figure 19.31).

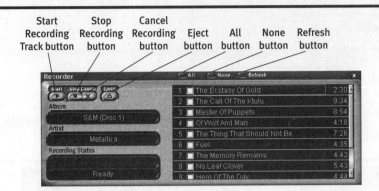

Start Recording Track button / Stop Recording button / Cancel Recording button / Eject button / All button / None button / Refresh button

FIGURE 19.31: Recorder window

3. Select one or more tracks to record by selecting the check boxes for the tracks or by clicking the All button.

   ▶ Click the None button to deselect all currently selected tracks.

   ▶ Click the Refresh button if you want MusicMatch Jukebox to reread the CD's contents. (This button is mainly useful if you have auto-insert notification disabled for your CD drive and manage to insert a fresh CD without MusicMatch Jukebox's noticing.)

4. Click the Start Recording Track button to start ripping.

   ▶ The first time you go to rip tracks from a CD to MP3 files, MusicMatch Jukebox will configure your CD drive or drives. You'll see the CD-ROM Preparation dialog box (Figure 19.32). Make sure that each of your CD drives and DVD drives that you'll ever want to use for recording contains an audio CD, and then click the OK button. MusicMatch Jukebox will configure the drive for you and will then start recording.

Part iv

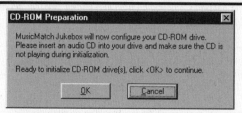

FIGURE 19.32:   CD-ROM Preparation dialog box

5.   As MusicMatch Jukebox records the track, it displays a readout of its progress (Figure 19.33).

FIGURE 19.33:   Recorder window with some tracks recorded and another in
progress

6.   When MusicMatch Jukebox has finished recording a track, it
automatically adds the track to the music library.

Keeping Everything You Need to Know in a Track's Tag

MusicMatch Jukebox makes it easy to add tag information to all the
tracks from the same album:

1.   With a track selected in the Music Library, choose Options ➢
Music Library ➢ Edit Track Tag, or right-click the track
in the Music Library window and choose Edit Track Tag from
the shortcut menu, to display the Tag Song File dialog box
(Figure 19.34).

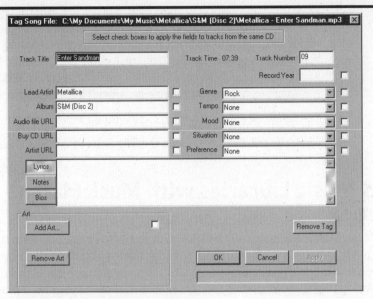

FIGURE 19.34: Tag Song File dialog box

2. Enter information for the track by typing in the text boxes and by choosing items in the drop-down list boxes. If you want to apply the same information to all the tracks from the same CD, select the check box to the right of the text box or drop-down list box.

3. To add lyrics, notes, or bios to the track, click the Lyrics, Notes, or Bios button, and enter the information in the text box.

4. To add a bitmap or JPEG picture to the track, click the Add Art button to display the Open dialog box. Navigate to and select the picture file, and then click the Open button. The picture will appear to the right of the Remove button. Select the check box to the right of the picture if you want to apply the picture to all the tracks from the CD. So if you gotta have pix of Shania or Ricky on all your MP3 files, it won't cost you much effort. (To remove a picture from a track, click the Remove Art button. To remove a picture from all the CD's tracks, select the check box to the right of the picture before clicking the Remove Art button.)

5. Click the Apply button to apply your changes to the tag or tags. The readout at the bottom of the dialog box will show you which file's tag MusicMatch Jukebox is currently updating. If you're applying tag info to all the tracks from the CD, it'll take a little while, and MusicMatch Jukebox will display an MMJB message box telling you the results when it has finished.

6. To remove a tag from the track, click the Remove Tag button.

7. Click the OK button to close the Tag Song File dialog box.

Build Music Libraries with MusicMatch Jukebox

MusicMatch Jukebox's key feature is its ability to create music libraries that you can use to store, organize, and retrieve your music files. By using music libraries, you can manage your music much more easily than schlepping thousands of individual files in and out of your MP3 player.

You can create as many music libraries as you want. If you prefer to have all your music in a single music library, that's fine, but be warned that it may become unmanageably large. We suggest segmenting your music into the different themes, moods, or occasions by which you'll want to play it. You can put any individual track into multiple music libraries, so creating music libraries isn't exactly difficult.

If you don't have the Music Library window displayed, click the Music Library button in the Main window to display it.

Planning Your Music Libraries

Before you create a music library, choose options for the music libraries you'll create. (You can choose options for a music library after creating it, but you'll save time by setting things up right before creating any music libraries.) Here's what to do:

1. Choose Options ➤ Music Library ➤ Music Library Settings to display the Music Library tab of the Settings dialog box (Figure 19.35).

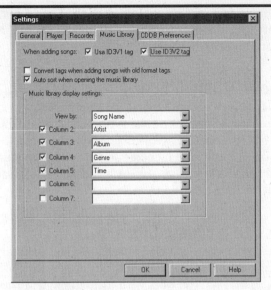

FIGURE 19.35: Music Library tab of the Settings dialog box

2. Make sure the Use ID3V1 Tag check box and the Use ID3V2 Tag check box are selected so that MusicMatch Jukebox adds all available tag information to the music library. (ID3V1 tags can contain title, artist, album, year, comment, and genre data; ID3V2 tags can add information, lyrics, and a picture.)

3. Select the Convert Tags When Adding Songs With Old Format Tags check box if you want to convert tags from older tag formats to new ones when you add them.

4. Select the Auto Sort When Opening The Music Library check box if you want MusicMatch Jukebox to automatically sort the tracks in the library each time you open it.

5. In the Music Library Display Settings group box, select the columns that you want to appear in the Music Library window. For each column, select the appropriate contents in the list box.

6. Click the OK button to close the Settings dialog box.

Now drag the dividers on the column headings in the Music Library window left or right to resize the columns to display the information you want to see. For example, you might want to narrow the Time column so that it takes the minimum amount of space possible and leaves more room for the track title and album names.

Creating a New Music Library

To create a new music library, choose Options ➤ Music Library ➤ New Music Library. In the Please Specify The Name And Location Of Your New Library dialog box (which is a Save As dialog box after a quick name-change operation), specify the filename and folder for the music library, and then click the Save button. MusicMatch Jukebox will save the music library with a .ddf extension.

Adding Tracks to a Music Library

MusicMatch Jukebox automatically adds to the current music library any new MP3 files you rip with it. But you'll need to add any existing MP3 files to the database so that you can work with them through Music-Match Jukebox. The same goes for any MP3 files that you download.

Here's how to add files to the current music library:

1.   Click the Add button in the Music Library window to display the Add Songs To Music Library dialog box (Figure 19.36).

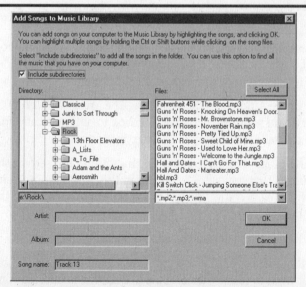

FIGURE 19.36:   Add Songs to Music Library dialog box

2. In the Directory list box, select the directory from which you want to add the MP3 files to the database.

3. If the directory contains subdirectories, select the Include Subdirectories check box.

4. In the Files list box, select the MP3 files you want to add to the database.

   ▶ To select all the files shown, click the Select All button.

   ▶ To view the information about a particular track (for example, to identify it more precisely), select it in the Files list box. The Artist, Album, and Song Name text boxes will display the information included for those categories in the file's tag.

5. Click the OK button to add the selected MP3 files to the database.

Deleting Tracks from a Music Library

To delete a track from a music library, select the track, and click the Delete button (or press the Delete key). MusicMatch Jukebox will display the MusicMatch Jukebox dialog box (Figure 19.37).

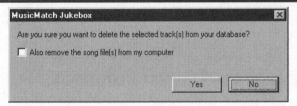

FIGURE 19.37: MusicMatch Jukebox delete dialog box

If you want to delete the file from your computer's hard disk, select the Also Remove The Song File(s) From My Computer check box. Then click the OK button.

Part iv

WARNING

To nuke the contents of a music library, choose Options ➤ Music Library ➤ Clear Music Library. You won't usually want to do this, so MusicMatch Jukebox displays a confirmation dialog box to make sure you know what you're doing before it wipes out your carefully built library. Of course, if a well-meaning relative ripped the *Titanic* soundtrack into your music library, go right ahead and tear it out root and branch.

Opening a Music Library

To open a music library, choose Options ➤ Music Library ➤ Open Music Library to display the Open dialog box. Navigate to and select the music library; then click the Open button. MusicMatch Jukebox will open the music library, closing any music library that is currently open.

Dropping a Music Library on a Friend

To inflict a music library on friends, export it to a text file by choosing Options ➤ Music Library ➤ Export Music Library, entering a filename in the Save As dialog box, and clicking the Save button. You can then e-mail the text file to your friends, and they can import it by choosing Options ➤ Music Library ➤ Import Music Library.

Sharing a music library like this gives your friends only the list of tracks in the library. They need to have the MP3 files that the music library references in order to play them back—but you knew that already.

Rock Out with MusicMatch Jukebox

Once you've got your music organized into music libraries, you can create playlists, save them, and play them back. You can also use the Auto DJ feature to create automatic playlists for you.

Creating, Saving, and Opening Playlists

The Playlist window initially appears docked to the Main window. When you're working with it, you'll usually want to display it separately so that you can expand it to see more of its contents.

Click the Separated View button to display the Playlist window as a separate window. Click the Integrated View button to attach the Playlist window to the Main window again.

Creating a Playlist

Here's how to create a playlist:

▶ If you have tracks in the Playlist window that you don't want to include in the new playlist, click the Clear button to remove them all.

▶ Add tracks to the Playlist window by dragging them from the Music Library window or by selecting them in the Music Library window, right-clicking, and choosing Add Track(s) To Playlist from the shortcut menu.

▶ To preview a track, select it in the Music Library window, and choose Options ➤ Music Library ➤ Preview Track. MusicMatch Jukebox will start playing the track without adding it to the playlist.

▶ To rearrange the tracks in the playlist, drag them to where you want them. This is your opportunity to correct the crimes of the music publisher—now you can put all the best tunes up front and kill the abysmal tracks they included only to pump up the CD's total running time.

▶ To delete a track from the playlist, select it and click the Delete button.

Saving a Playlist   When you've assembled your playlist, save it by clicking the Save button to display the Save Playlist dialog box, entering a name, and clicking the Save button.

MusicMatch Jukebox supports really long names for playlists, but anything over about 40 characters tends to be hard to work with. Best types of titles: Guitars That Killed Cleveland; Psychedelic Psongs; Lame Ballads Babes Love. Keep it short but descriptive so you don't confuse yourself.

Opening a Playlist   To open a playlist, display the Playlist window in Separated View. In the Saved Playlists list, click the playlist to display its contents in the panel to the right, or double-click the playlist to add its contents to the Current Tracks list.

Having MusicMatch Jukebox DJ for You

MusicMatch Jukebox's AutoDJ feature lets you specify vague guidelines
by which MusicMatch Jukebox should put together automatic playlists
for you. The AutoDJ feature isn't for everyone. If you've ever sat out a
dozen songs in a row at a party waiting for the one track to which you *can*
dance, you'd do better to give MusicMatch Jukebox more specific instructions on how to please you.

If you want to chance your luck at the AutoDJ feature, here's how to
start:

1. Click the AutoDJ button on the Main window to display the
   AutoDJ dialog box (Figure 19.38).

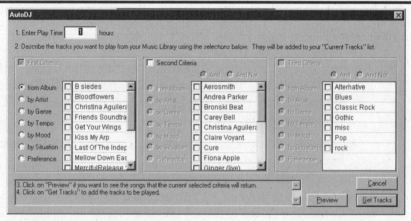

FIGURE 19.38: AutoDJ dialog box

2. In the Enter Play Time text box, enter the number of hours
   that you want MusicMatch Jukebox to play. Keep this number low until you see what kind of effect AutoDJ produces
   with your pet music collection.

3. In the First Criteria group box, select the first set of criteria
   by which MusicMatch Jukebox should select the music.
   Choose From Album, By Artist, By Genre, By Tempo, By
   Mood, By Situation, or Preference, as appropriate. The first
   list box will display check boxes for the category. Select the
   check boxes for the items you want to include. For example,
   you might select the By Genre option button and the Techno,
   Trance, and Trip-Hop check boxes.

4. Define a second set of criteria if you want to by selecting the Second Criteria check box, selecting the And option button or the And Not option button as applicable, and making a choice from the same list. Select check boxes as appropriate. For example, you might select the And option button, select the By Artist option button, and select the check boxes for artists such as Massive Attack, the Chemical Brothers, and The Orb.

5. Define a third set of criteria if you want to by selecting the Third Criteria check box, selecting the And option button or the And Not option button, making another choice, and selecting from the resulting check boxes. For example, you might select the And option button, select the By Tempo option button, and select the Pretty Slow check box to find mellow music to get wasted by.

6. Click the Preview button to display information about how many tracks MusicMatch Jukebox has found matching those criteria (up to the play time you specified in step 2).

7. Adapt your criteria as necessary to produce the play time you want.

8. Click the Get Tracks button to close the AutoDJ dialog box. MusicMatch Jukebox will display a message box telling you how many tracks it has found and the total playing time.

9. Click the OK button. MusicMatch Jukebox will add the tracks to the current playlist, from which you can play them as usual.

What's Next?

Now that we've rocked through MP3, we are going to take a look at another hot topic—computer games. Chapter 20, "Games on the Internet," will tell you a little about the different categories of games available on the Internet, as well as where to find them.

Chapter 20

GAMES ON THE INTERNET

Games are good. Games give you an active (non-TV) diversion from real-life stressors; plus, they hone your skills, from problem-solving puzzle skills to quick-reflex shoot-em-up skills. Games on the Internet are especially good—there are many games you can play that you don't have to go out and buy, and on the Internet you don't have to worry about finding friends to play with. Or, God forbid, shuffling and dealing with your own two hands.

From the plethora of freebies to games you pay for, the Internet offers all the fun of an arcade and a old-time game parlor with much action-packed adventure thrown in for good measure. And the choice of beverage is yours. What more could you want?

Well, maybe you'd like some details. Here is a smattering of games from various categories to get you going. May the best netizen win!

WARNING

You must register for many free games, which means that your name and gaming proclivities are Out There in the floating cybergame world. Usually during the registration process, you'll see a screen that asks you whether it's okay to share your name with other cyberthings that might want to send you "select information." (Advertisements.) And, usually, Yes will already be checked for you by the kind and thoughtful online gaming company. Click No—or uncheck Yes—for a saner cyberlife.

FREE WEB GAMES

Whoever said "the best things in life are free" was undoubtedly predicting online games that anyone could play for free, either solo or against an opponent. Though this category overflows with traditional parlor games, you can find some heart-pounding action and brain-intensive strategy games here and there. Happy clicking!

Action

On your marks, get set...

Absolute Zero
www.won.net/channels/quickgames/absolutezero
Finally, the perfect mix of environmental concern and shoot-the-h-e-double-toothpicks-out-of-everything-in-sight. You're in space, but so are asteroids, satellites, black holes, and space junk. Save us from being overrun by space detritus!

Adrenaline
www.zone.com/adrenaline
By Toyota. It just screams racing, doesn't it?

Burning Metal
www.won.net/channels/quickgames/burningmetal
Race through dirt, ice, and bombs faster than the other drivers (or just blow them into the hereafter). Just don't start having flashbacks when someone cuts you off during your afternoon commute!

Defense of the Squid Man
http://multiverse.com/~jvgeier/Defense.html
It's Mr. Squidman against the space pirates. Help him defend his
home and family by making the pirate ships go ka-blooey!

HP JetSpeed
http://193.129.255.102/jetspeed/
Race up to three other players and get ready to hit Esc when the
boss comes knocking!

Panumbra
www.shareplay.com/panumbra/index.htm
Monster-killing, multiplayer, fantasy, role-playing, and free!

Roach Invaders
www.won.net/channels/quickgames/roachinvaders
Save the cupcake from the roaches—is it just me, or is this game a
little too reality-based?

SnowCraft
www.won.net/channels/quickgames/snowcraft
Snowballs and forts in the coziness of your room or office. What is
winter coming to?

Board

All sites accommodate beginners, casual competition, and the big
leagues.

Abalone
www.clickhere.nl/cgi-bin2/abalone
Sumo wrestling en masse, on board.

Backgammon
www.mplayer.com/cardgames/games/backgammon
www.playsite.com
www.pogo.com
www.won.net/channels/hoyle/backgammon
http://games.yahoo.com
www.zone.com/backgammon
A deceptively simple-looking board game involving getting your 15
pieces off the board before your opponent gets the competing 15 off.

Part IV

Bingo
www.mplayer.com/cardgames/games/bingo
www.pogo.com
htttp://games.yahoo.com
An Emcee-moderated Tic-Tac-Toe for grownups, winning bingo is pure luck.

Checkers
www.mplayer.com/cardgames/games/checkers
www.playsite.com
www.pogo.com
www.won.net/channels/hoyle/checkers
http://games.yahoo.com
www.zone.com/checkers
The usual: jump and capture your opponent's pieces, king yourself, gather all your opponent's pieces.

Chess
www.interligence.com
www.mplayer.com/cardgames/games/chess
www.playsite.com
www.pogo.com
www.won.net/channels/hoyle/chess
http://games.yahoo.com
www.zone.com/chess
Move each type of piece according to its allotted path, capture your opponent's pieces, and corner the king.

Go
www.interligence.com
http://games.yahoo.com
www.zone.com/go
Surround territory or your opponent's pieces and win points, but be careful of being surrounded. A classic.

Othello
www.htmlgames.com
Trap and flip in an online game that won't crash as long as your ISP doesn't.

Pachisi
www.won.net/channels/hoyle/pachisi
Move your piece around the track and then head for home before anyone else gets there. Bumps, blockades, and passes rule.

Reversi
www.interligence.com
www.mplayer.com/cardgames/games/reversi
www.playsite.com
www.won.net/channels/hoyle/reversi
http://games.yahoo.com
www.zone.com/reversi
Also known as Othello, you'll be trapping and flipping your opponent's pieces over to your color in no time.

Yahoo! Towers
http://games.yahoo.com
Clear your blocks faster than your opponents can add 'em. May the best un-architect win!

GAMES BY TURN

Games by turn allow you to play turn-based games (like checkers or poker) at your convenience. Log on, move your piece, play your card, then go to dinner. In the morning, check whether your opponent has made the next move.

ItsYourTurn
www.itsyourturn.com
Yes, they know there should be an apostrophe in their name—tell it to the URL czar. ItsYourTurn brings you a graphical interface (all HTML, nothing to install) and turn-based moves for absolutely free. Play variations of backgammon, reversi, chess (shown in Figure 20.1), and others.

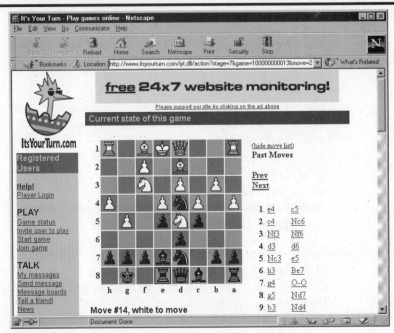

FIGURE 20.1: Waiting patiently for Move #14....

Card: Parlor & Casino

Whether you're looking to re-create the kitchen table or the casino floor, you can find almost any card game you can think of somewhere on the Internet.

Blackjack   www.won.net/channels/hoyle/blackjack
http://games.yahoo.com
www.zone.com/blackjack
The old get-as-close-to-21-as-is-comfortable card game with fake money—but real rules.

Bridge
www.playsite.com
www.pogo.com
www.won.net/channels/hoyle/bridge
http://games.yahoo.com
www.zone.com/bridge
If your grammie and gramps didn't teach you, a paragraph can't do this game justice. There are detailed instructions online.

Canasta

`http://games.yahoo.com`

You and your partner want to be the first to gather seven or more of the same card (possibly with the help of several wild cards) and go out.

Cribbage

`www.playsite.com`

`www.won.net/channels/hoyle/cribbage`

`http://games.yahoo.com`

`www.zone.com/cribbage`

A complicated card game that's so challenging, it uses a board to keep track of everything. I could go on, but I won't. Try it. (Figure 20.2 gives you a taste of PlaySite's version.)

Euchre

`www.playsite.com`

`www.pogo.com`

`www.won.net/channels/hoyle/euchre`

`http://games.yahoo.com`

`www.zone.com/euchre`

Win three of five tricks in each hand with the goal of winning 10 points before your opponent(s). More old-fashioned madness.

Gin

`www.won.net/channels/hoyle/gin`

`http://games.yahoo.com`

Draw and discard to create sets, then go gin when you can lay them all down and have nothing left over.

Go Fish

`http://games.yahoo.com`

Ask the other players for the cards you need to complete your set of four, but be careful; now they know what you're looking for!

Hearts

`www.mplayer.com/cardgames/games/hearts`

`www.playsite.com`

`www.pogo.com`

`www.won.net/channels/hoyle/hearts`

`http://games.yahoo.com`

`www.zone.com/hearts`

An old favorite; take all the Hearts plus the Queen of Spades and win. Just remember: points are bad.

Napoleon
www.boxerjam.com/nap
Draw Poker *á la Française.*

Pinochle
www.won.net/channels/hoyle/pinochle
http://games.yahoo.com
Your grannies and great-uncles would be beside themselves with pride if you took up online Pinochle. Kind of like Spades, Pinochle is not for the get-the-game-over-with, go-to-bed-early set.

Poker
www.mplayer.com/cardgames/games/poker
www.pogo.com
www.won.net/channels/hoyle/poker
http://games.yahoo.com
Virtual poker takes care of the pokerface problem, but you still gotta know when to hold them and so on.... Play anything from seven-card stud to myopic monkey.

Sheepshead
http://games.yahoo.com
If you've ever played Schafkopf, you know how to play Sheepshead. You haven't? Well, check out the rules. All I can say is, be prepared for trumps and tricks, Schneiders, and Schwarzes.

Spades
www.mplayer.com/cardgames/games/spades
www.playsite.com
www.pogo.com
www.won.net/channels/hoyle/spades
http://games.yahoo.com
www.zone.com/spades
Bids, trumps, tricks, contracts—oh my aching head. If you like competitive trickery, you'll love Spades.

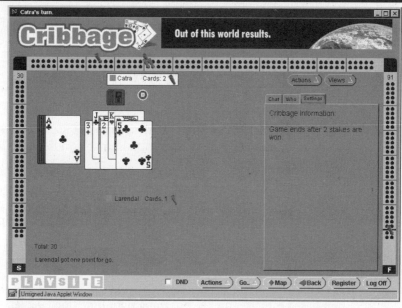

FIGURE 20.2: Catra and Larendal face off over the Cribbage board, er, cards.

Dice and other Objects

You won't be surprised to find casino games and little goofy games online, but Mah-Jong? That's a winner!

Craps
www.won.net/channels/hoyle/craps
Bet your dice against the casino. The rules are many and the reward potential is large—in your favor, for once.

Dominoes
www.won.net/channels/hoyle/dominoes
Connect a maze of pieces by matching the numbers. Fun for the whole family!

MahJong
http://games.yahoo.com
A fast-paced rummy with cool tiles, MahJong is played by 4 players, no partners.

Roulette
www.pogo.com
www.won.net/channels/hoyle/roulette
Bet on a number and watch the wheel spin past it. What could be more entertaining?

Speed Waster
www.zone.com/speedwaster
Stack colored disks in their piles as the clock ticks and the disks pile up. Not for carpal tunnel syndrome sufferers.

Yacht
www.won.net/channels/hoyle/yacht
Take 5 dice, take 12 turns, take 3 rolls, and score points in as many of the 12 categories as you can for some pokerish fun sans cards.

Puzzle

Brain-based exercises are *the* hot thing right now: don't get left behind!

Animal Ark
www.pogo.com
Just like Shanghai, Animal Ark offers a pile of tiles. Click the matching pairs—as long as one side of each tile is free—to bring them safely off the ark. Complete with groans and squeaks.

Blender
www.zone.com/blender
Memorize the picture before it gets jumbled up, and then reposition the pieces back into a picture.

Dingbats!
www.boxerjam.com/puzzles/dingbats_gw.html
It's Wheel of Fortune sans Vanna White! Click a letter to see it appear in the three words or phrases below, and rack up points.

Double Trouble
www.zone.com/doubletrouble
Click matching and adjoining symbols to clear the board
before your time runs out.

Mancala
http://imagiware.com/mancala/mancala.cgi
www.lookoutnow.com/game/man.htm
This classic game from Africa, illustrated in Figure 20.3,
involves moving your pieces, gathering new ones, strategy,
addition, and subtraction.

Mastermind
www.math.berkeley.edu/~bdavis/Mastermind/
www.mit.edu/people/mnoel/mastermind.htm
Which colorful pieces does the computer have hidden—and
in which order? A Twenty Questions for logicians.

Maze
http://games.yahoo.com
A maze, of course. Drag the blue ball to mark your recursive
path to the exit.

Overflow
www.pogo.com
You get one straw piece at a time, no guarantees which way
it will bend; use them to connect the straws before the vis-
cous drink runs all over everything. Hint: start connecting
from the top straw.

Roof Rats
www.won.net/channels/quickgames/roofrats
Click similar, adjacent rooms to lower the tenants to safety
and hopefully clear the board. There's no clock and no
opponent; it's all in the planning.

Poppit!
www.pogo.com
Release the prize balloon by popping 2 or more balloons of
the same color. Roof Rat-like, but in the other direction.

Symbolic Link
www.zone.com/symboliclink
A Roof Rats of pretty pieces. Highlight as many similar symbols as are connected to remove the bunch and create a new pattern, with the end goal of removing the whole shebang.

Trax
www.zone.com/trax
Using the three different types of connection pieces, close a loop of your color before your opponent closes a loop of the competing color. More fun than a map of the London Underground!

Twenty Questions
www.20q.net/index.html
Turning the tables for a minute, play 20 Questions against an artificial intelligence program and try to pick something obscure but generic enough to keep it guessing. You'll get some suggestions of objects that the program needs practice in, such as a gas grill, a pry bar, or a knitting machine. In this version of 20 Questions, Yes and No are supplemented by such grey-area answers as: Unknown, Irrelevant, Probably, Doubtful, Sometimes, Usually, and Rarely. Seems like cheating to me...

Twistitz
www.puzzlepage.com/ppage/play.php3?puzzle=tw
Between the clue at the bottom and the twisting pieces that untwist as you watch (and then twist right back up again), you can ably if slowly move the pieces into their proper positions and get the whole picture.

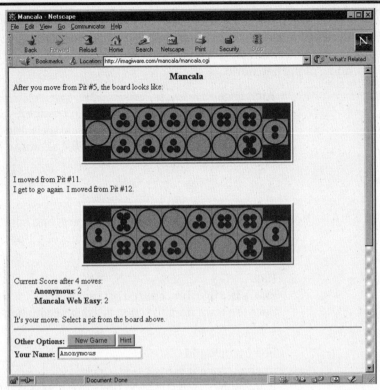

FIGURE 20.3: Brian Casey's Mancala, only at imagiware.com.

Sports

Not surprisingly, virtual sports are somewhat rare. Why do something virtually when it's more fun to do really?

> Fantasy Sports
> www.smallworld.com
> Create a team of real players from auto racing, baseball, basketball, golf, hockey, or soccer and run them through a season based on their real-season scores. And you thought the weather couldn't affect virtual reality!
>
> Basketball
> www.shockwave.com
> Use the arrow keys and spacebar to fake out the blocker and score as many baskets as you can in 2 minutes.

Strategy

More action for the brain, these strategy games cover financial matters, insects, and spirituality, as well as the usual squelching and subsequent ruling of the free world.

Archmage
http://archmage.magewar.com/archmage/
Guild or no guild, your object is to rule the world in this role-playing strategy game. Figure 20.4 shows an example of the main screen.

Ants
www.zone.com/ants
It's your colony against everyone else's; find and collect as much food as you can before time runs out. Upgrade your ants, steal food, or start a microwar.

Cult
www.studio-blum.com/cult/index.html
Save the town from the cultists using negotiation and trade.

Forgotten World
http://forgotten.acs-isp.com/
Nongraphical but complex, this game allows you to use magic, trickery, and outright war to become the most powerful player.

Monarchy
http://monarchy.shareplay.com
This turn-based strategy game features the high goals of both becoming the most powerful kingdom *and* bringing honor to your faith.

Space Merchant
www.shareplay.com/spacemerchant/index.htm
Sick of being the good guy? Choose between being a trader, pirate, or bounty hunter, then conquer, conquer, conquer!

SpiritWars
www.won.net/channels/strategy/spiritwars
Move your weapons into place and unleash magic spells to try to destroy your opponent's castle—but remember to wait for your turn!

Stellar Crisis
http://stellar.gamestats.com/SC.html
A turn-based, real-time fight for galactic dominance.

Stock Market Challenge
http://games.yahoo.com
Play the stock market for a month with fake money, and
win prizes for 1st, 2nd, and 3rd place. Be careful out there!

Virtual Combat
www.virtualcombat.com
Maintain your factories and other possessions by diplo-
macy and strategic alliances.

FIGURE 20.4: Catra begins her personal mage war at Archmage.

Trivia

Ah, trivia. It's so wonderful to have an outlet for the little pieces of junk that clutter the mind and refuse to allow facts like your new colleague's name to even gain a foothold in the memory.

2 Minute Trivia
www.mplayer.com/cardgames/games/2mintrivia
Answer 10 questions in 2 minutes to win a shot at the weekly $25 prize! Choose from these trivia categories: general, movie, games, Star Wars, Star Trek, sports, Beanie Babies, current events, and music bands Korn and Eminem.

5 Alarm Trivia
www.pogo.com
You know: trivia. The clocked kind where there are questions and you have answers, right or wrong!

Any Given Sunday
www.won.net/channels/quickgames/sunday
Football trivia to whet your movie-going appetite.

Austin Powers—Operation: Trivia
www.won.net/channels/quickgames/operationtrivia
Answer trivia questions from the '60s, '70s, '80s, and '90s—oh be*have*!

Cosmic Consensus
www.won.net/channels/bezerk/cosmic/
cosmic-play.html
Guess how the majority of people answer these questions, win points, and climb the Ziggurat.

CrossWire
www.puzzlepage.com/ppage/play.php3?puzzle=cw
Ready to cross your wires? Match a fact from the left with a fact on the right according to the connection that you deduce from the title of the round. Start with your worst category to save your knowledge for the higher-scoring rounds.

Encarta Challenge Trivia
www.zone.com/ encarta/
Pick from three random categories, then pick your answer. Get ready, get set, click!

Pocket Quiz
www.pogo.com
Answer the daily question—from the Periodic Table of Elements to Burger King—and be entered to win $50.

Strike a Match
www.boxerjam.com/sam
Click the three answers that satisfy the given clue.

Take 5
www.boxerjam.com/take5 (sports)
www.boxerjam.com/take5e (entertainment)
Kind of a trivia game, kind of a sentence-forming game; use the clue to create a five-word sentence from the various words.

Triviatron
www.pogo.com
Not just one trivia game, but four! Four trivia games, ah ah ah ah!

You Don't Know Jack
www.won.net/channels/bezerk/jack/jack-play.html
Feeling too knowledgeable and superior? Get taken down a notch or two with this irreverent trivia game that'll throw pop-culture, current events, and classic trivia questions at you until you scream I DON'T KNOW JACK!

Word

Think you're a word wizard? These games are for you!

Acrophobia
www.won.net/channels/bezerk/acro/acro-play.html
Witty phrases born of witty fingers and wittily displayed letters will win the day.

Anagrams

http://games.yahoo.com

Unscramble all the words in the given puzzle and then unscramble the solution. Puzzles are refreshed daily and archived for 2 weeks.

Crossword

www.puzzlepage.com/ppage/play.php3?puzzle=xw
www.mplayer.com/classics/crossword/
www.pogo.com
http://games.yahoo.com
www.zone.com/crossword

You know this one; find it in your paper, or play it online for grins. Or see Figure 20.5.

Cryptogram

http://games.yahoo.com

Decode the encrypted message. I'll give you a hint: 'e' is the letter used most in the English language. You're on your own from here.

DoubleCross

www.won.net/channels/hoyle/doublecross

If you've liked Scrabble well enough but feel ultimately dissatisfied by your inability to destroy your opponents' attempts to create words, DoubleCross will more than meet your needs.

FakeOut!

www.eduplace.com/dictionary/

Choose a word from the lists, categorized by age, and guess the definition. (Is *glebe* really a second-grade-level word?)

Get the Picture

www.won.net/channels/bezerk/picture/
picture-play.html

Create the best captions for pictures from cartoons to photographs. Loads of fun!

Hangman

www.won.net/channels/hoyle/hangman

You can play this fill-in-the-blank-or-hang game by yourself or against another person.

Jumble
www.pogo.com
Just like in the papers; the cartoon, the clue, the scrambled clues and the solution to fill in.

Magnet-O
www.puzzlepage.com/ppage/play.php3?puzzle=mg
It's Scrabble with word magnets! Form phrases, then link the phrases (peppermint patty, hamburger patty—get it?).

Out of Order
www.boxerjam.com/ooo
Unscramble the jumbled word.

Wordox
www.won.net/channels/hoyle/wordox
Two to four players place tiles on the game board to make words. Scrabble-like, yet not Scrabble.

Word Racer
http://games.yahoo.com
Hoo boy! Hold onto your hats and get your typing fingers ready. Race your opponents to form words from the connected letters. Adrenaline rushes for English majors.

Word Search
www.playsite.com (here they call it Tangleword)
www.pogo.com
www.won.net/channels/hoyle/wordsearch
http://games.yahoo.com
Neatly stacked, seemingly random letters with hidden words upside down, diagonal, any which way they'll go.

Word Yacht
www.won.net/channels/hoyle/wordyacht
Like Yacht the dice game, in Word Yacht you roll a bunch of dice and try to fill as many categories as you can, but the dice are lettered and you form words, not runs of numbers.

Wordzap
www.mplayer.com/cardgames/games/wordzap
Compete to form more words than your opponent from a soup of 12 letters.

Part IV

Y.A.R.N.

www.mplayer.com/cardgames/games/yarn

Tall tales are just a part of life, and you can't get much taller than yarns that are spun a sentence at a time by multiple players. Complete with separate clean and adult-language lobbies, Y.A.R.N. grants points to sentences based on number of votes.

FIGURE 20.5: Pogo's crossword puzzles call on knowledge of current and very ancient culture alike.

GET YOUR FRESH JAVA APPLETS HERE!

Java applet games are all over. They're free, they're simple, they range from goofy to goofily goofy, and you could lose yourself in them for minutes. Here are a few choice sites for tons of games:

Ability.org
www.ability.org.uk/ongames.html
Puzzles, asteroids, pong—these little applets are your gateway into fun.

ArcadePod.com
www.arcadepod.com/java
You know you've found a huge listing when the games are divided into categories like *Indoor Sports* and *Outdoor Sports*.

Archie Comics Fun'n Games
www.archiecomics.com/funngames
From action-packed burger-flipping to negotiating the maze in time for your movie date, Archie Comics Fun'n Games has everything you need to remind you of simpler times.

Enchanted Mind
http://enchantedmind.com/newjava.htm
Featuring Java puzzles for both sides of the brain, you can find such simple yet addicting puzzles as tangrams (as in Figure 20.6), mastermind, and Rubik's cube at this site, as well as thought-provoking puzzles and other sorts of creativity enhancers.

Happy Puppy
www.happypuppy.com/web
Pick from such funky oddities as DJ Boyardee Battle, where you match your spins against the DJs, or sodaconstructor, which is not a game but a Tinkertoys-meets-Kinefex animation creator, and much more. Happy Puppy sports a huge archive that lists the most recent games first.

Part iv

ShockWave

www.shockwave.com

Get your action highs, your conundrum jollies, your rollicking adventure, and new takes on classic games like Mancala and Mastermind.

!WorldVillage Games

www.worldvillage.com/cat/games.html

Have you ever wanted to be Amadeus for the day? This site is for you.

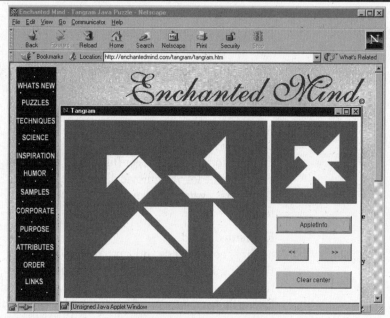

FIGURE 20.6:   My soaring bird is just not going to take off...

GAMES YOU BUY

Your cubie neighbor has joined the Peace Corps and flown off to Thailand, leaving you his heirloom Quake software. Your computer is in tiptop shape, your workday is over, and you're fingerloose and fancy free. What better thing to do than fire up the old multiplayer game and join in the fray?!

But how?

There are two ways to play games you buy (like Quake) with your friends and neighbors: one is to set up a multiplayer game and let your opponents in on your TCP/IP address, which will allow them to join you directly. The other way is to go through a program like Game Ranger (for Macs) or GameSpy (for PCs) or Kali (for just about everything) and find strangers far and near who are already playing your game.

NOTE

Of course, the game itself has to support the multiplayer option. Much as you try, SimCity 3000 just will not run in multiplayer mode.

Setting up a Multiplayer Game

So you wanna play Quake with Ralphie, do you? Just follow me:

1. Launch Quake.

2. Select Multiplayer ➢ New Game. The Host Game box, shown in Figure 20.7, will appear. In the Connection box (on the left), look at the number next to Your Address.

3. Call Ralphie up. Say: "Ralphie! Write this down! 171.211.218.7! Buh-bye!"

4. Click OK.

This is the number your opponents need to know in order to join you.

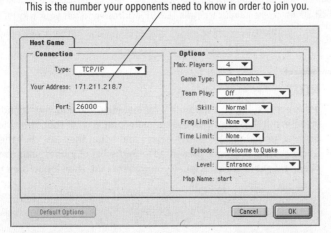

FIGURE 20.7: Set your multiplayer game options on the right.

Ralphie now needs to open *his* copy of *Internet Complete* and follow these steps:

1. Launch Quake.

2. Select Multiplayer ➤ Join a Game.

3. In the Join Game box, shown in Figure 20.8, you'll see a Join Game At/Address text box. Type in the TCP/IP address your friend gave you. (Ralphie, that's 171.211.218.7.)

4. Click OK.

5. Blow your friends up.

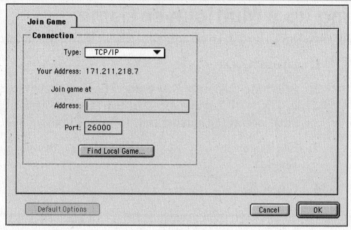

FIGURE 20.8:   Type in your friend's TCP/IP address and get your trigger finger ready.

NOTE

If you are playing on a network—for instance, you and your friends are working late (not that you'd ever use company property for your own entertainment, but just for instance)—follow steps 1 and 2, but then just click the Find Local Game button and, once presented with the list of games your coworkers are playing, double-click the game you want to join. Then follow step 5.

Joining a Game Online

So Ralphie's sleepy but you're just getting revved up. All is not lost! You can save your friendship *and* gun down strangers by following these simple steps. First, download Game Ranger, GameSpy, Kali, or any other server-finding software you can find. (For the purposes of this example, I'm going to use Game Ranger.) Then do the following:

1. Launch Game Ranger.

2. On the Chat tab, choose a room from the Room list. As you check out the rooms, glance at the Games box in the lower-left corner to see what people are playing, if anything.

    a. If you see a game you're interested in, hover your mouse over the game's name to see your ping rate (see the sidebar titled, "Ping? I Beg Your Pardon?," for details).

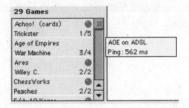

    b. If it's a ping rate you can live with (literally), and you own the game, double-click the game name to join in.

3. Click the Servers tab to look at the plethora of registered and running servers for the games you already own.

4. Go to the menu bar and click Servers ➤ Return New Servers. You'll see the list of servers currently up and running, as in Figure 20.9.

5. Check the Resp (ms) column for your ping rate.

6. Next double-click the server name (from the Name column in the right pane). You'll see each player's current score and ping rate. (Hint: If your ping rate is 309 and everyone else's is 52 or less, you're DOA. See the sidebar titled, "Ping? I Beg Your Pardon?" for more information.)

Part iv

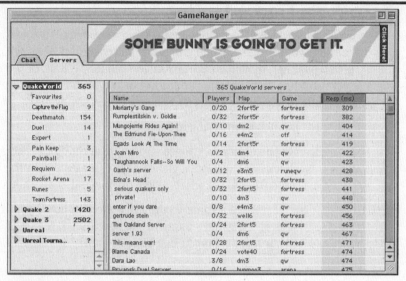

FIGURE 20.9:   Many choices, many pings. What's a modemer to do?

7.   To join, go to the menu bar and click Servers ➤ Join.

8.   Blow strangers up.

PING? I BEG YOUR PARDON?

Pings are measured in milliseconds, so a ping rate of 500 means that that information starts on the server (the computer hosting the game) and travels over your modem to your computer in 1/2 of a second. When you're trying to dodge fire and shoot darting targets, this is not fast. In the ideal world, you'd be the host, which would net you a ping rate of zero. In the real world, you'd be fine if you were on a network and sporting a ping rate of around 50. From home, you'll probably be hurting a bit.

To even out high-ping-rate pain, try to find a server where other players are also suffering through high ping rates. Barring that, select a game server that shows more than one player playing. That way they'll be too busy shooting each other to notice you—at first, anyway.

MUD!

Or should I say Moo. The progenitor of this kind of game, a MUD is a traditionally free, text-based *multi-user domain* that allows many gamers to join any of the somewhat cerebral games online. Classic MUDs, MOOs, MUCKs, MUXes, and so on rely solely on text, requiring that you bring only imagination, patience, and a willingness to familiarize yourself with Telnet (and with the game). With graphics and other wonders of the modern world, some MUDs now use avatars and even 3D graphics, Everquest being one example (it and its software fee *and* its per-month fee).

MUDs, etc. are most often seriously fantasy-oriented; it's like Alice-in-Wonderlanding it into The Hobbit. Telnet itself is a cinch compared to the rules and magic and possibilities in some of these games.

To get started, check out the MUD/MUSH/MOO Catalog of Catalogs at www.educ.kent.edu/mu/catofcat.html. Another good resource for a list of MUDs is the Mud Connector at www.mudconnect.com.

TELNET TIPS

You use Telnet to connect to another computer, usually called the remote computer. The result is text-based, and will give you a taste of yesteryear, back when mainframes were cutting edge. You then need to figure out which commands will make the remote computer do what you want it to do. Because every computer is different, there is no List of Telnet Commands. But here are some general guidelines:

> ▶ The easiest way to get into MUD, MUSH, MOO, MUX, M-whatever! is to find an interesting one on a site such as the Mud Connector and link to it. Your Telnet application will pop forth, and usually you'll see instructions on how to log on to the MUD, as in Figure 20.10. If you don't see an obvious connection and your Telnet app shows a menu bar, go to the Telnet menu bar and click Connect ➤ Remote System. The dialog box that appears should already contain the necessary info; just click Connect.

CONTINUED ➡

Part iv

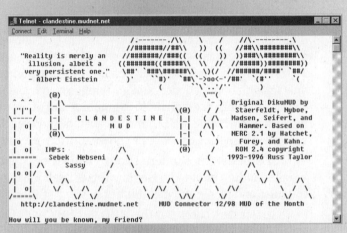

FIGURE 20.10: A taste of MUD.

▶ Once you're in, type **help** or **?** and write down the commands you need—or print them out. Pay special attention to the logoff command; you'll need it eventually. Note also that the remote computer will not always recognize fancy keyboard gizmos like Backspace and Delete.

▶ To disconnect from the game, go to the Telnet menu bar and click Connect ➢ Disconnect. If your Telnet app doesn't have a menu bar, type in whatever you gleaned from the list of commands you looked at. If that list didn't happen for you, try LOGOFF or LOGOUT, QUIT, END, EXIT, STOP, or any other termination-type word that springs to your fingers.

If you don't like the Telnet application you currently have—or you don't have one—try the Java Telnet Application/Applet, which is public domain freeware you can download from www.mud.de/se/jta/.

GAMES BY MAIL

What's the point, you may ask, of playing a game by mail when there's the Internet right there. Well, you may not have hours to play Quake online, or you may want to play with a select group of friends, but not all have the same schedules or live in the same time zone or both. Playing games by e- or snail mail allows you to play with others without whipping out your schedulers each time you're ready to play. Plus, it won't be quite so obvious when you're writing an e-mail at work that you're just a graveyard away from Necropolises and beginning the final battle for complete control of the underworld...

Lists of PBM games
ftp://ftp.pbm.com/pub/pbm/PBM.list.gz
www.pbm.com/~lindahl/pbm_list

PBM homepage
www.pbm.com/~lindahl/pbm.html

Dice rolls
http://dice@pbm.com.
Give this dice roller your opponent's e-mail address, and both of you will receive an e-mail of the dice roll. For complete instructions, e-mail dice@pbm.com with **help** in the body of the message.

Java dice rolls
www.irony.com/java/igedb

PBEM Magazine
www.pbm.com/~lindahl/pbem_magazine.html

The PBEM News
www.pbem.com

Sites

Game sites throw new games into the mix all the time. Just so's you can keep track, here's a list of sites that are worth keeping your eye (and bookmarks) on.

Game House
www.ncbuy.com/entertainment/gamehouse
Game House has action and arcade games, brain and board games, chat rooms and message boards, and play-for-prizes games.

Part iv

Games Kids Play

www.gameskidsplay.net/

Not really Internet-based, but a neat resource anyway, this site lists the games children play—rhyming games, clapping games, and so on.

Global100 PC Games

www.global100.com/chart.asp?Chart=1

What's hot? Check out official ratings of current games. (Ratings are gathered by visitor vote, but Global100 gets a lot of visitors.) Updated every Sunday.

Just for Girlz

www.gamegirlz.com

The game downloads available here aren't free, but they have been reviewed and played, so you can get an idea of what you're getting into before you buy. Fun, obscure stuff!

MPLAYER

www.mplayer.com

MPLAYER features direct play lobbies where others can use your copy of the game to play with you, downloads, demos, a retail center, and the usual community area. There is also a Swap center where you can swap or buy and sell stuff, plus the Java games gallery, a collection of simple arcade-like games that are great fun after a busy, complex day.

MSN Gaming Zone

www.zone.com

Besides many free games and a plethora of games that involve some exchange of cash, this site has chat rooms, tournaments, competitions with prizes, a software shop, a newsletter with online entertainment news, and gaming partner search capability.

PlaySite

www.playsite.com

This Go2Net site features free board, card, and word games. You can also download an installable client that allows you to go straight to the games rather than waiting to log in to PlaySite.

Pogo

www.pogo.com

This c|net site offers classic arcade games like Tank Hunter and Tube runner, as well as games with cash prizes.

WON.net
www.won.net
Here you can find many free games, free home pages, demos, a store, a newsletter, game channels, a game searcher and a game detector, a trade center for maps and skins, as well as strategies and hints from Hoyle's rules for classic games and Prima's strategy guide for Quake III. WON.net also hosts a bunch of games where you can win reality-based prizes like DVDs and Gameboys.

Yahoo!
http://games.yahoo.com
Besides a search engine and free e-mail, Yahoo! offers board and card games.

Tools

In your quest for the perfect gaming experience, you will want more than your favorite carbonated beverage and a locked door between you and the citizens of the nonvirtual world. Here are some tools that'll help you get closer to online Nirvana.

FilePlanet

FilePlanet is a source for ping tools (which show you how quickly your connection is running), control panels and front ends for your games (which allow you to customize various aspects of your games). FilePlanet also provides game launchers and server finders (which help you find and join the online game of your choosing), as well as many miscellaneous files that allow you to configure your games.

www.fileplanet.com (click on Front Ends & Launchers)

GameRanger

GameRanger will find all the Mac servers playing games like Quake and Unreal so you can choose an ongoing game to join. GameRanger is free.

www.gameranger.com

Part iv

NOTE

Although sites that specialize in tools like server-searching software will often offer free demo versions of games, server-searching software is for people who have bought a game—like Baldur's Gate—and want to play it with strangers over the Internet.

GameSpy

GameSpy will find the quickest servers playing the following games: Baldur's Gate, Half-Life, Hexen II, Quake, Quake II, Quake 3: Arena, Shogo, Sin, Starsiege TRIBES, Turok II, and Unreal. GameSpy costs $20 for lifetime use.

www.gamespy.com

Gator

Gator stores your personal information (secretly and securely) so when you want to check out a game site, it registers for you. Fast and free!

www.gator.com

Kali

Kali is game-searching software with some extra goodies. Not only does Kali support all major platforms—making them compatible with one another, so you PCers can finally deathmatch your DOS and OS/2 (and Mac) gaming buddies. But also, Kali provides Internet support to games that don't have it. Kali costs $20 for lifetime use.

www.kali.net

WHAT'S NEXT?

Now that you're all relaxed and stress-free after playing a few games on the Internet, let's take a look at how to create an Internet presence of your own. Chapter 21, "Getting Acquainted with HTML, Its Tools, and Its Resources," will discuss the basic components required to start building a Web page.

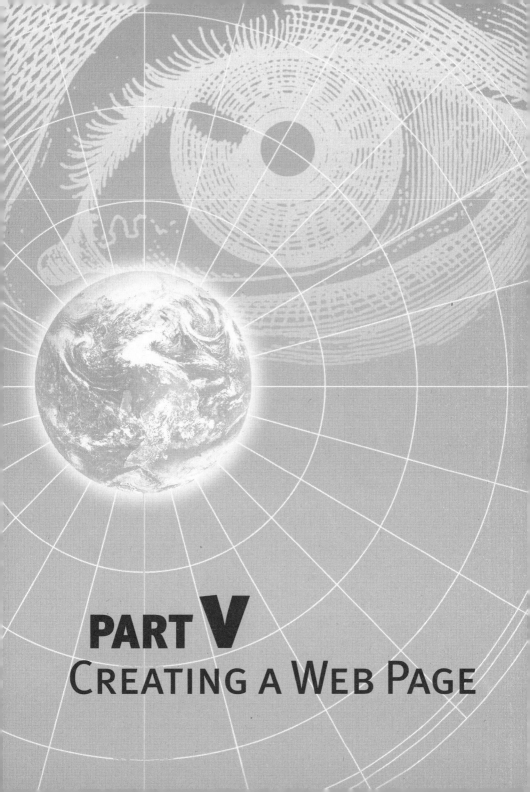

PART V
CREATING A WEB PAGE

Chapter 21

GETTING ACQUAINTED WITH HTML, ITS TOOLS, AND ITS RESOURCES

Hypertext Markup Language, or HTML, is a system of codes that you use to create interactive, online pages. You're probably familiar with the most common HTML application—World Wide Web pages. Visitors can jump from topic to topic, fill out forms, submit information, and search databases, among other things, rather than slogging through information in a linear fashion. HTML, though, is not what you see onscreen as a Web page. Instead, HTML is the behind-the-scenes code that tells browsers what to display.

Adapted from *Mastering HTML 4*, by Deborah S. Ray/Eric J. Ray
ISBN 0-7821-2523-9   1010 pages $49.99

NOTE

Throughout this book, we use the term "visitors" to describe the people who use the HTML documents you develop.

In this chapter, we'll introduce you to HTML—what it looks like, what you use it to accomplish, and what tools you need to get started—and we'll give you a foundation for learning to use HTML throughout the remainder of Part V of this book.

WHAT IS HTML?

HTML is a system of codes that identify the parts and characteristics of documents. As Figure 21.1 shows, HTML documents are plain text files. They contain no images, no sounds, no videos, and no animations; however, they can include "pointers," or links, to these file types, which is how Web pages end up looking like they contain nontext elements.

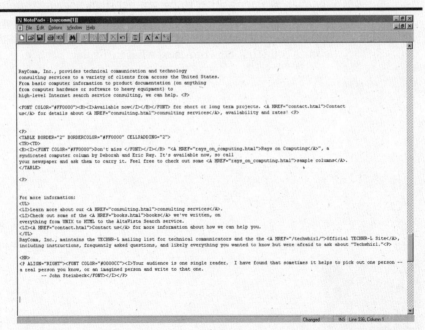

FIGURE 21.1: HTML documents are just text files, containing the code and content you provide.

As you can see, HTML documents look nothing like the Web pages you have likely seen before. Instead, HTML is made up of *tags* and *attributes* that work together to identify document parts and tell browsers how to display them. Figure 21.2 shows how the tags and attributes of Figure 21.1 work together to create a Web page.

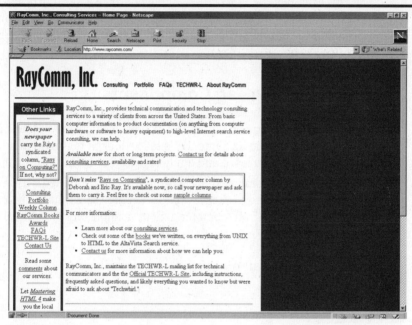

FIGURE 21.2: Browsers interpret the code to determine how to display HTML documents.

Understanding Tags

HTML tags actually serve two purposes. First, they identify logical document parts—that is, the major structural components in documents such as headings (<H1>, for example), numbered lists (<OL>, for ordered list), and paragraphs (that is, <P>). So, for example, if you want to include a heading, a paragraph, and a list in your document, you type the text and apply the appropriate tags to it (we'll show you how in the following sections). And that's it.

Second, tags in HTML documents also reference other elements—that is, tags can include pointers and links to other documents, images, sound files, video files, multimedia applications, animations, applets, and so on.

For example, if you want to include an image of your company's product in your HTML document, rather than pasting in an image (as you might in a word processing document), you simply include a tag that points to the image filename, as shown here:

```
<IMG SRC="logo.gif">
```

In this example, the <IMG> (image) tag points to a logo file (`logo.gif`) that the browser should display. So, here again, the browser relies on the information contained within an HTML document to tell it what to display as well as how to display it.

Understanding Tag Components

As you can see from these examples, HTML tags are fairly intuitive. Although tags are occasionally cryptic, you can usually get an idea of a tag's function just from its name. Let's take a look at tag components, which should help you learn and apply tags to your HTML documents.

First, all tags are composed of *elements* that are contained within *angle brackets* (< >). The angle brackets simply tell browsers that the text between them is an HTML command. Some sample tags look like these:

- ▶ <H2> (for heading level 2)

- ▶ <BODY> (for document body)

- ▶ <B> (for bold)

NOTE
You'll learn more about these tags and their uses in Chapter 22, "Creating Your First HTML Document."

Second, most tags are paired, with an opening tag (for example, <H1>) and a closing tag (</H1>). Both tags look alike, except the closing tag also starts with a forward slash (/). To apply tags to information in your document, place the opening tag before the information, and place the closing tag after the information, like this:

```
<H1>information that the tags apply to</H1>
```

It's a good idea to type both the opening and closing tag at the same time so that you don't forget the closing tag. If you happen to forget it, most paired tags will run on and on until the browser finds a matching closing tag.

NOTE

Less commonly, you'll use nonpaired tags, which do not include the closing tag. We'll point those out throughout this section and show you how to use them appropriately.

To apply more than one tag to a chunk of information, you nest the tags. *Nesting* means placing one set of tags inside another set. For example, to apply italic to a heading, you nest the tags, like this:

```
<H1><I>information that the tags apply to</I></H1>
```

or like this:

```
<I><H1>information that the tags apply to</H1></I>
```

When you nest tags, the first tag should be paired with the last tag, and the second tag should be paired with the next to last tag, and so on.

Typing Tags Correctly

When typing tags, be particularly careful not to include extra spaces. If you do so, a browser may not recognize the tag and will not display the information correctly. Or, the browser might display the tag itself. For example, a title should look like this:

```
<TITLE>Correctly Formed Title</TITLE>
```

Do *not* include spaces within the tags, like this:

```
< TITLE >Incorrectly Formed Title< /TITLE >
```

Improving Readability

You'll find it easier to read and use tags in your HTML code if you follow a few conventions. In particular, we suggest that you type tags using all caps and that you use hard returns to create shorter lines. These conventions do not affect how browsers display code—they just make it easier for you to read the HTML.

The following two examples show you how using caps and hard returns can improve readability of the HTML code. The code in the examples is identical.

```
<!doctype HTML public "-//w3c//dtd HTML 4.0//en"><html><head>
<title>Mastering HTML Document
Title</title></head><body>Mastering HTML Document
Body</body></html>
```

or

```
<!DOCTYPE HTML PUBLIC "-//W3C//DTD HTML 4.0//EN">
<HTML>
 <HEAD>
  <TITLE>Mastering HTML Document Title</TITLE>
 </HEAD>
 <BODY>
   Mastering HTML Document Body
 </BODY>
</HTML>
```

No question which is easier to read, right? Typing your HTML code in this manner also makes it easier to be sure that you haven't forgotten to type any end tags.

Understanding Attributes

Some tags work in conjunction with attributes, which provide additional information about an element, such as how elements should align, what other files should be accessed, or even the color of an element. For example, an attribute might indicate that a heading should appear centered in the browser window, that the browser should load an image file from the Web, or that the Web page background should appear sky blue.

So, suppose you want to center a heading in the browser window. You start with your heading and tags, like this:

```
<H1>A heading goes here</H1>
```

and then add the ALIGN= attribute to the opening tag, like this:

```
<H1 ALIGN="center">A centered heading goes here</H1>
```

All attributes go in the opening tag and are separated from other attributes and the tag itself by a space. Some attributes require quotes; some don't. As a general rule, most attributes—those that include only letters, digits, hyphens, or periods—work fine without quotes. For example, you can type ALIGN=CENTER or ALIGN="CENTER"; all browsers should display these in the same way.

Attributes that have other characters, such as spaces, % signs, or # signs, however, *always* require quotes. For example, if you use the WIDTH= attribute to indicate a percentage of the document window, type WIDTH="75%".

TIP

When in doubt, use quotes with attributes. Although they aren't always necessary, they never hurt. Throughout this book, we've included the quotes—for good practice and good example.

You can include multiple attributes in a tag by using one space between each attribute, like this:

```
<H1 ALIGN="center" SIZE="+2" COLOR="#FF0000">A wildly format-
ted heading goes here</H1>
```

NOTE

In HTML, the attributes can go in any order after the tag, but the tag must always go first.

WHAT CAN YOU DO WITH HTML?

You're likely most familiar with HTML as it's used to create Web pages; however, HTML has expanded to include many other uses:

Developing intranet or extranet sites   HTML is commonly used to develop intranet and extranet sites, which are company-wide Web sites that are accessed by people within the company from one or more locations.

Developing help files   HTML is also used to develop online help files, allowing developers to inexpensively produce documentation that is accessible on any platform.

Developing network applications   HTML is particularly suitable for creating entire applications, such as training programs, interactive chats, or databases that are available through Web pages.

Developing kiosk applications   Finally, HTML can also be used to create kiosk applications—those stand-alone computers with the neat touch-screen capabilities.

What Tools Do You Need?

For your first documents, you need only two basic tools:

▶ An HTML editor, to create and save your HTML documents

▶ A Web browser, to view and test your HTML documents

HTML Editors

In general, HTML editors fall into two categories:

▶ Text- or code-based, which allow you to see the HTML code as you're creating documents

▶ WYSIWYG (What You See Is What You Get), which show the results of code, similar to the way it will appear in a browser, as you're formatting your document

Although dozens of excellent WYSIWYG editors are available, you should learn to code HTML using a standard text editor. Text editors force you to *hand-code* HTML, meaning that you, not the software, enter tags and attributes. Hand-coding helps you learn HTML tags and structure and lets you see where you've made mistakes. Also, with hand coding, you can easily include the newest HTML enhancements in your documents. Notepad for all Windows versions, vi or Pico for Unix, and TeachText or SimpleText for Macintosh are good choices.

TIP

Learning to hand-code is essential for using the latest-and-greatest HTML effects—whether it's the current HTML 4 or a future version. Most new HTML versions are not immediately supported by WYSIWYG editors, so you would need to hand-code those tags and attributes in your documents.

Part V

> **WARNING**
>
> Using a word-processing program such as Word, WordPerfect, or even Word-Pad to create HTML documents can often introduce extra formatting and control characters, which will cause problems. HTML requires plain text with no formatting at all, so either make a special effort to save all documents as plain text, or just use a text editor.

Simple WYSIWYG editors, such as Netscape Composer and Microsoft FrontPage Express (included with Internet Explorer 4 and 5), are good for quickly generating HTML documents. These editors give you only a close approximation of page layout, design, and colors, but are good for viewing the general arrangement of features. They do not, however, give you, the author, as much control over the final appearance of your document as code-based editors do.

After you've developed a few HTML documents and understand basic HTML principles, you may choose to use both a WYSIWYG editor and a code-based editor. For example, you can get a good start on your document using a WYSIWYG editor and then polish it (or fix it) using a code-based HTML editor. For now, though, we recommend that you hand-code HTML using a standard text editor.

Web Browsers

If you've ever surfed the Web, you've used a Web browser to view HTML documents. The most common browsers are Netscape Navigator/Communicator and Microsoft Internet Explorer, although a variety of browsers are available for virtually all computer platforms and online services.

Exactly how your documents appear, though, will vary from browser to browser and from computer to computer. For example, most browsers in use today are *graphical browsers*: They can display elements other than text. A *text-only* browser can display—you guessed it—only text. How your HTML documents appear in each of these types of browsers differs significantly, as shown in Figures 21.3 and 21.4.

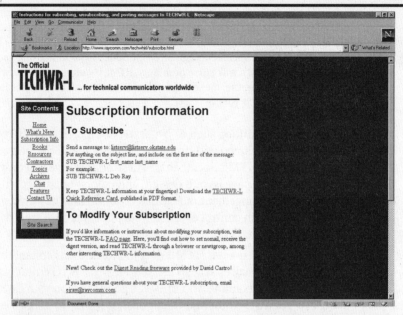

FIGURE 21.3: An HTML document displayed in Netscape Navigator

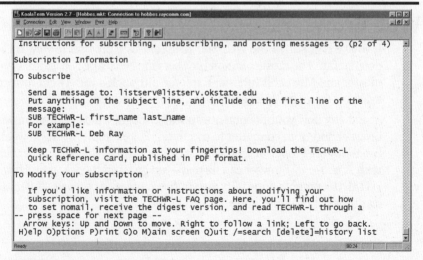

FIGURE 21.4: The same HTML document viewed in Lynx, a text-only browser

Additionally, even graphical browsers tend to display things a bit differently. For example, one browser might display a first-level heading as 15-point Times New Roman bold, whereas another browser might display the same heading as 14-point Arial italic. In both cases, the browser displays the heading as bigger and more emphasized than regular text, but the specific text characteristics vary. Figures 21.5 and 21.6 show how two other browsers display the same HTML document.

Finally, your visitor's computer settings can also make a big difference in how your HTML documents appear. For example, the computer's resolution and specific browser settings can alter a document's appearance, as shown in Figure 21.7.

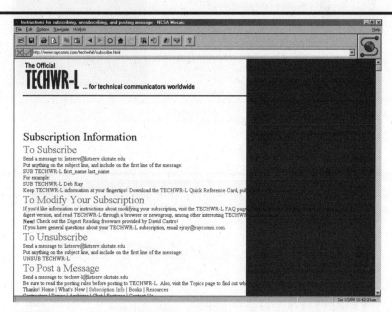

FIGURE 21.5: The old NCSA Mosaic browser displays the HTML document with a few problems.

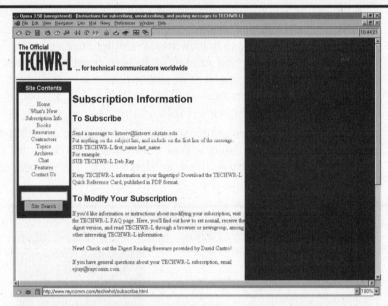

FIGURE 21.6: The Opera browser shows the same document with slightly different formatting.

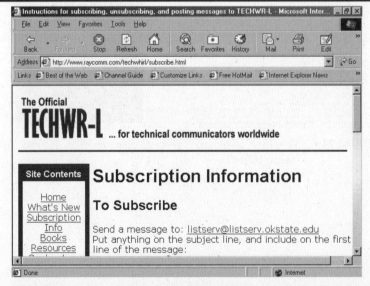

FIGURE 21.7: Internet Explorer and a very low resolution combine to make the document look completely different.

So, as you're developing and viewing your HTML documents, remember that your pages will likely look a bit different for your visitors. If possible, test your documents in as many different browsers at as many different resolutions and color settings on as many different computers as possible. You won't be able to test for all possible variations, but you will be able to get a good idea of what your visitors might see.

What Other Resources Can Help?

In addition to this book, you can find a wealth of information, resources, and specifications on the Web. In particular, the World Wide Web Consortium site, as well as several product-specific Web sites, will help you learn, use, and keep up with changes in HTML.

Visit the W3C

The *World Wide Web Consortium (W3C)* was founded in 1994 at the Massachusetts Institute of Technology (MIT) to oversee the development of Web standards, including HTML standards. This consortium defines and publishes HTML standards, including the tags and attributes within HTML documents. So an excellent way to monitor HTML changes is to visit the W3C site:

www.w3.org/

Here, you'll find new releases of HTML standards, proposed standards, and other developments in Web-related specifications, such as Cascading Style Sheets (CSS) and eXtensible Markup Language (XML) specifications.

Can you use new tags and attributes as they become available? For the most part, yes. By the time many popular tags and attributes become part of the standard, they already have browsers' support. Some tags and attributes, however, including some that were introduced with HTML 4, did not have wide or stable browser support when that specification was released and do not to this day have nearly the breadth of support that other tags do. We'll point these out throughout this section and show you how they differ from the previous versions of HTML.

Part V

Monitor Netscape and Microsoft Sites

Each time that Netscape and Microsoft release a new browser version, look for new HTML *extensions*, which are browser-specific tags and attributes. Some of these extensions are useful, and some less so, but as a whole any nonstandard tags introduced into HTML cause problems both for Web developers and for visitors. Fortunately, fewer extensions seem to be introduced with each new release, but you should still be aware of what's added with each release.

If you're considering using extensions in your HTML documents, keep in mind that they're not standard HTML. That is, an extension specific to a particular browser (say, Netscape) will likely not work in other browsers (say, Internet Explorer, Opera, or others). For this reason, we generally recommend that you don't use extensions and, instead, use only HTML standard tags and attributes so that all your visitors can access the information you provide.

TIP

At the time of this writing, about 50 percent of Net surfers used Netscape Navigator, about 40 percent used Internet Explorer, and the remaining 10 percent used a variety of other browsers. Realistically, about 80 to 90 percent of all Web users can access the majority of sites incorporating the latest HTML tags and recent enhancements.

You can find Netscape's extensions at:

`developer.netscape.com/index.html`

And you will find Microsoft's extensions at:

`www.microsoft.com/windows/ie/`

Monitor Other Sites

Although definitive information comes from the W3C, Microsoft, and Netscape sites, you can reference other reliable resources too. Table 21.1 gives you a list of some to check regularly.

TABLE 21.1: Some Sites That Provide Up-to-Date HTML Information

ORGANIZATION	URL
Web Design Group	www.htmlhelp.com/
Web Developer's Virtual Library	www.stars.com/
HTML Writer's Guild	www.hwg.org/
ClNet's Builder.com	www.builder.com/

WHAT'S NEXT?

This chapter gave you a brief overview of HTML—what it is, what it's used for, and how it came about. Although you haven't yet done any HTML coding, you should have a good foundation for getting started with it in Chapter 22, "Creating Your First HTML Document."

Chapter 22

CREATING YOUR FIRST HTML DOCUMENT

I f you're ready to create your first HTML document, you're in the right chapter! Here, we'll help you start a new HTML document and save it using the appropriate file formats, show you how to add structure tags (which help browsers identify your HTML document), and show you how to apply some common formatting tags.

If you're new to HTML (or rusty at hand coding!), you might want to review the tag and attribute information in Chapter 21, "Getting Acquainted with HTML, Its Tools, and Its Resources." Before starting this chapter, you should be familiar with tags and attributes, as well as how to apply them to the content you include.

Throughout this chapter, we provide lots of figures and code samples to help guide you and to show you what your results

• •

Adapted from *Mastering HTML 4,*
by Deborah S. Ray/Eric J. Ray
ISBN 0-7821-2523-9   1010 pages $49.99

should look like. You can substitute your own text and images if you prefer, or you can duplicate the examples in the chapter. The step-by-step instructions will work regardless of the specific content you use. After you work through this chapter, you'll have developed your first HTML document, complete with text, headings, horizontal rules, and even some character-level formatting.

TIP

We recommend that you practice using HTML by doing the examples throughout this and other chapters.

CREATING, SAVING, AND VIEWING HTML DOCUMENTS

Exactly how you start a new HTML document depends on which operating system and editor you're using. In general, though, you'll find that starting a new HTML document is similar to starting other documents you've created. With Windows or Macintosh, you'll choose File ➤ New. Or, if you're using Unix, you'll type **vi**, **pico**, or **emacs**, and use the appropriate commands. You'll make your new document an official HTML document by saving it as such, which is discussed next.

Before you begin hand-coding HTML, be aware that you should frequently save and view your work so that you can see your progress. By doing so, you can make sure that things appear as you expect them to and you can catch mistakes within a few new lines of code. For example, we typically add a few new lines of code, save the HTML document, then view it...then add a few more lines of code, save the document, then view it...and so on. Exactly how often you save and view your documents depends on your preference, but—at least initially—you'll probably be doing it frequently.

You create an HTML document in much same way that you create any plain text document. Here's the general process:

1. Open your text editor.

2. Start a new document. If you're using Windows or Macintosh, choose File ➤ New. If you're using Unix, type **vi** or **pico** to start the editor.

3. Enter the HTML code and text you want to include. (You'll have plenty of practice in this chapter.)

4. Save your document. If you're using Windows or Macintosh, choose File ➢ Save or File ➢ Save As.

GUIDELINES FOR SAVING FILES

As you work your way through this chapter, keep these saving and viewing guidelines in mind:

▶ Name the file with an htm or html extension. Windows 3.1 doesn't recognize four-character extensions, so you are limited to htm on that platform.

▶ If you aren't using a text-only editor such as Notepad or Teach-Text, verify that the file type is set to Text or ASCII (or HTML, if that's an available menu option). If you use word-processing programs to create HTML documents (and remember our earlier caveat about this), save your documents as HTML, Text Only, ASCII, DOS Text, or Text with Line Breaks (the specific options will vary with your word processor).

▶ Use only letters, numbers, hyphens (-), underscores (_), and periods (.) in your filename. Most browsers also accept spaces in filenames; however, spaces often make creating links difficult.

▶ Save the document (and the rest of the documents and files associated with a particular project) in one folder. You'll find that this makes using links, images, and other advanced effects easier.

Viewing the HTML documents that you develop is as simple as opening them from your local hard drive in your browser. If you're working with an open HTML document in your editor, remember to save your latest changes, and then follow these steps in your browser:

1. Choose File ➢ Open and type the local filename or browse your hard drive until you find the file you want to open. Your particular menu commands might be File ➢ Open Page or File ➢ Open File, but it's all the same thing.

2. Select the file, and click OK to open it in your browser.

ALTERNATIVE WAYS TO OPEN FILES

Most browsers provide some clever features that can make developing HTML files easier.

You can easily see your editing changes in a file by *reloading* it. For example, after you view a document and then save some editing changes, you can reload the document and see the latest changes. You'll probably find that clicking a Reload button is much easier than going back through the File ➤ Open and browse sequence. Generally, you reload documents by clicking a Refresh or Reload button or by choosing options from the View menu.

In addition, you can open a file by selecting it from a *bookmarked list* (or from a Favorites list, in Microsoft parlance). Bookmarking a file means adding a pointer to the file so that you can open the file quickly, just as a bookmark makes it easier to open a book to a specific page. Creating bookmarks (or Favorites) is as easy as clicking a menu option while viewing a page. Whenever you want to go back to that page, simply click the bookmark rather than choosing File ➤ Open and opening the file as you usually would. Most browsers have bookmark options; just look for a button or a menu command.

APPLYING STRUCTURE TAGS

After you create a new document, your first task is to include structure tags, which provide browsers with information about document characteristics. For example, structure tags identify the version of HTML used, provide introductory information about the document, and include the title, among other similar things. Most structure tags, although part of the HTML document, do not appear in the browser window. Instead, structure tags work "behind the scenes" and essentially tell the browser which elements to include and how to display them. Although these tags do not produce the snazzy results you see in Web pages or help files, they are essential for telling browsers how to interpret the document.

NOTE

Most browsers, including Netscape Navigator and Microsoft Internet Explorer, correctly display documents that do not include structure tags. However, there is no guarantee that future versions will continue to do so or that your results will be consistent. We strongly advise using structure tags.

All HTML documents should include five structure tags, nested and ordered as in the following example code:

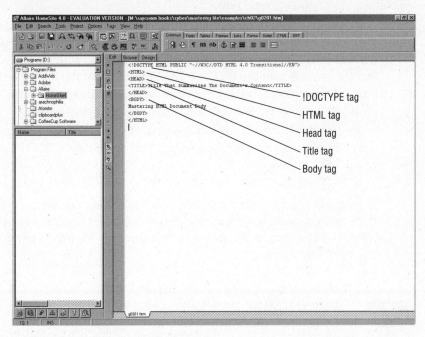

The following sections describe these tags and how to use them.

TIP

You can save time when creating future HTML documents by saving structure tags in a master document. That way, you can easily reuse them in other HTML documents, rather than retyping them time after time.

The <!DOCTYPE ...> Tag

The <!DOCTYPE...> tag tells browsers (and validation services) the HTML version with which the document complies. The HTML 3.2 and 4 specifications require this nonpaired tag (it has no ending tag), and, therefore, you should use it in all your documents. Enter it at the top of your document, like this:

```
<!DOCTYPE HTML PUBLIC "-//W3C//DTD HTML 3.2 Final//EN">
```

or, like this:

```
<!DOCTYPE HTML PUBLIC "-//W3C//DTD HTML 4.0
Transitional//EN">
```

The key part of the `<!DOCTYPE...>` tag is the DTD element (*Document Type Definition*), which tells browsers that the document complies with a particular HTML version—the first example complies with HTML 3.2, and the second, with the HTML 4 Transitional (most flexible) specification. A DTD specifies the organization that issues the specification (W3C, in these cases) and the exact version of the specification.

As new HTML standards evolve, you can expect this tag to change to indicate new versions. For example, in a year or so, the `<!DOCTYPE...>` tag might look like this:

```
<!DOCTYPE HTML PUBLIC "-//W3C//DTD HTML 5.23 Final//EN">
```

Even after new standards appear, you don't need to revise the `<!DOC-TYPE...>` tag in existing documents. If your document conforms to the HTML 3.2 standard, it'll conform to that standard, regardless of more recent HTML versions.

WHICH HTML 4 DTD SHOULD I USE?

The HTML 4 specification comes in three varieties: strict, transitional (loose), and frameset. The strict version prohibits everything except "pure" HTML, and you're unlikely to use it unless you're writing HTML documents that use no formatting tags and are relying on Style Sheets to make them look good. To indicate that your document complies with the strict specification, use:

```
<!DOCTYPE HTML PUBLIC "-//W3C//DTD HTML 4.0//EN">
```

The transitional version is the most flexible for accommodating deprecated but still useful tags and attributes, including nearly every formatting tag. To indicate that your document complies with the transitional specification, use:

```
<!DOCTYPE HTML PUBLIC "-//W3C//DTD HTML 4.0
Transitional//EN">
```

The frameset specification is similar to the transitional specification, but also supports the tags needed to use frames.

To indicate that your document complies with the frameset specification, use:

```
<!DOCTYPE HTML PUBLIC "-//W3C//DTD HTML 4.0
Frameset//EN">
```

The <HTML> Tags

The <HTML> tags identify the document as an HTML document. Technically, these tags are superfluous after the <!DOCTYPE> tag, but they are necessary for older browsers that do not support the <!DOCTYPE...> tag. They are also helpful to people who read the HTML code. To use the <HTML> tags, enter them in your document below the <!DOCTYPE...> tag, like this:

```
<!DOCTYPE HTML PUBLIC "-//W3C//DTD HTML 4.0
Transitional//EN">
<HTML>
</HTML>
```

NOTE

You don't have to type tags and attributes in uppercase. However, as we mentioned in Chapter 21, "Getting Acquainted with HTML, Its Tools, and Its Resources," you'll find it easier to read and use tags in your HTML code if you follow a few conventions. In particular, we suggest that you type tags using all caps and that you use hard returns to create shorter lines. These conventions do not affect how browsers display code—they just make it easier for you to read the HTML.

The <HEAD> Tags

The <HEAD> tags contain information about the document, including its title, scripts used, style definitions, and document descriptions. Not all browsers require these tags, but most browsers expect to find any available additional information about the document within the <HEAD> tags. Additionally, the <HEAD> tags can contain other tags that have information for search engines and indexing programs. To use the <HEAD> tags, enter them between the <HTML> tags, like this:

```
<!DOCTYPE HTML PUBLIC "-//W3C//DTD HTML 4.0
Transitional//EN">
<HTML>
<HEAD>
</HEAD>
</HTML>
```

TIP

Don't confuse this document head tag, which is a structure tag, with heading formatting tags such as <H1> that create heading text in a document body. We discuss heading tags later in this chapter in the "Headings" section.

The <TITLE> Tags

The <TITLE> tags, which the HTML 3.2 and 4 specifications require, contain the document title. The title does not appear within the browser window, although it is usually visible in the browser's title bar. Between the opening and closing tags, include a title that briefly summarizes your document's content. To use the <TITLE> tags, enter them between the opening and closing <HEAD> tags, like this:

```
<!DOCTYPE HTML PUBLIC "-//W3C//DTD HTML 4.0
Transitional//EN">
<HTML>
<HEAD>
<TITLE>
Title That Summarizes the Document's Content
</TITLE>
</HEAD>
</HTML>
```

Titles should represent the document, even if the document is taken out of context. Here are some examples of good titles:

- ► Sample HTML Code

- ► Learning to Ride a Bicycle

- ► Television Viewing for Fun and Profit

Here are some examples of less useful titles, particularly taken out of context:

- ► Examples

- ► Chapter 2

- ► Continued

The <BODY> Tags

The <BODY> tags enclose all the tags, attributes, and information that you want a visitor's browser to display. Almost everything else in this entire chapter takes place between the <BODY> tags. To use the <BODY> tags, enter them below the closing </HEAD> tag and above the closing </HTML> tag, like this:

```
<!DOCTYPE HTML PUBLIC "-//W3C//DTD HTML 4.0
Transitional//EN">
<HTML>
<HEAD>
<TITLE>
Title That Summarizes the Document's Content
</TITLE>
</HEAD>
<BODY>
All the tags, attributes, and information in the document
body go here.
</BODY>
</HTML>
```

If you've been following along and creating your own HTML document, save your document, view it in a browser, and compare it with Figure 22.1 to confirm that you're on the right track. The title appears in the title bar, and some text appears in the document window.

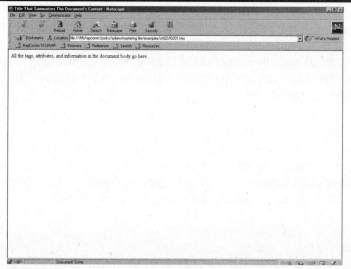

FIGURE 22.1: Your first HTML document, including all structure tags

MINIMAL COMPLIANCE FOR STRUCTURE TAGS

As shown in the previous sections, the HTML 4 specification does not require all structure tags. In fact, only two are required: the `<!DOCTYPE...>` tag and the `<TITLE>` tag. If you choose to use only these two tags, the code would look like this:

```
<!DOCTYPE HTML PUBLIC "-//W3C//DTD HTML 4.0
Transitional//EN">
<TITLE>The name of a minimal and content free
document</TITLE>
```

Of course, there's no purpose in creating a document with nothing but the minimal tags—the document doesn't say anything and doesn't present any information. If you use these two tags as a starting point, however, you can create a standard, compliant document to use as a template and save yourself a few keystrokes on each new document you create.

APPLYING COMMON TAGS AND ATTRIBUTES

After you include the structure tags, you're ready to start placing basic content in the document body. The following sections show you how to include headings, paragraphs, lists, and rules (horizontal lines). These elements constitute the basic HTML document components and, unlike the structure tags, do appear in the browser window. Learning to apply these basic tags and attributes will prepare you to apply practically any HTML tag or attribute.

As you create your content, keep in mind that its exact appearance will vary from browser to browser. For example, a first-level heading in one browser might appear as approximately 16-point Times New Roman Bold, whereas another browser might display it as 14-point Arial Bold Italic. Both browsers display the heading bigger and bolder than other headings and body text, but the specific font, size, and emphasis will vary.

Creating Paragraphs

One of the most common tags you'll use is the paragraph tag, <P>, which is appropriate for regular body text. The paragraph tag absolutely does not have to be paired—you can simply use the opening tag, <P>, where you want to start a new paragraph. As with many tags, however, it's easier to identify where the tag begins and ends if you use both opening and closing tags.

To use the paragraph tags, put them around the text you want to format as a paragraph, like this:

```
<P>
A whole paragraph goes right here.
</P>
```

Figure 22.2 shows a sample paragraph.

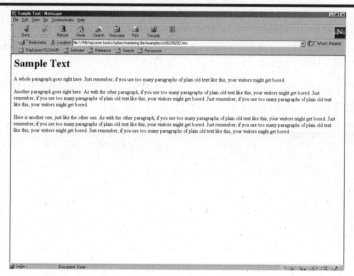

FIGURE 22.2: Paragraph text is the most common text in HTML documents.

You can also apply other paragraph formats instead of the <P> tag to achieve some slightly different paragraph formats, as explained in Table 22.1.

Alignment attributes are often used with these paragraph formatting tags, including ALIGN=LEFT, ALIGN=CENTER, and ALIGN=RIGHT. To apply these attributes, include them in any of the opening paragraph tags, like this:

```
<P ALIGN=CENTER>
Paragraph of information goes here.
</P>
```

TABLE 22.1: Other Paragraph Formatting Tags

PARAGRAPH FORMAT	EFFECT
<ADDRESS>	Used for address and contact information. Often appears in italics.
<BLOCKQUOTE>	Used for formatting a quotation. Usually appears indented from both sides and with less space between lines than a regular paragraph.
<PRE>	Effective for formatting program code or similar information. Usually appears in a fixed-width font with ample space between words and lines.

Figure 22.3 shows how the <PRE> and <ADDRESS> tags appear in Internet Explorer.

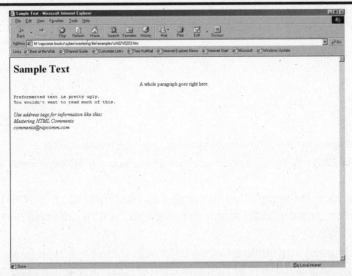

FIGURE 22.3: Special paragraph-level tags make information stand out.

Creating Headings

Headings break up large areas of text, announce topics to follow, and arrange information according to a logical hierarchy. HTML provides six levels of headings; <H1> is the largest of the headings, and <H6> is the smallest:

```
<H1> ... </H1>
<H2> ... </H2>
<H3> ... </H3>
<H4> ... </H4>
<H5> ... </H5>
<H6> ... </H6>
```

TIP

For most documents, limit yourself to two or three heading levels. After three heading levels, many visitors begin to lose track of your hierarchy. If you find that you're using several heading levels, consider reorganizing your document—too many heading levels often indicate a larger organizational problem.

To use heading tags, enter them around the heading text, like this:

```
<!DOCTYPE HTML PUBLIC "-//W3C//DTD HTML 4.0
Transitional//EN">
<HTML>
<HEAD>
<TITLE>Sample Headings</TITLE>
</HEAD>
<BODY>
<H1>First Level Heading</H1>
<H2>Second Level Heading</H2>
<H3>Third Level Heading</H3>
</BODY>
</HTML>
```

Figure 22.4 shows how Netscape Navigator displays a few heading levels.

In general, you should use heading tags only for document headings—that is, don't use heading tags for figure captions or to emphasize information within text. Why? First, you don't always know how a browser will display the heading. It might not create the visual effect you intend. Second, some indexing and editing programs use headings to generate tables of contents and other information about your document. These programs won't exclude headings from the table of contents or other information just because you used them as, say, figure captions.

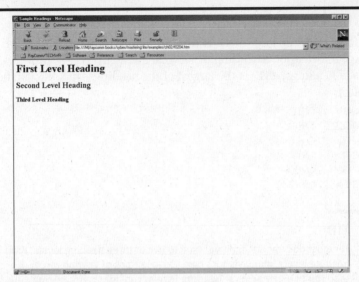

FIGURE 22.4:   Heading levels provide visitors with a hierarchy of information.

By default, all browsers align headings on the left. Most browsers, however, support alignment attributes, which also let you right-align and center headings. Table 22.2 shows the alignment attributes.

TABLE 22.2: Alignment Attributes

HEADING ATTRIBUTE	EFFECT
ALIGN=LEFT	Aligns the heading on the left (default).
ALIGN=CENTER	Aligns the heading in the center.
ALIGN=RIGHT	Aligns the heading on the right.

To use the alignment attributes, include them in the initial heading tag, like this:

```
<H1 ALIGN=LEFT>Left-aligned Heading</H1>
<H1 ALIGN=CENTER>Centered Heading</H1>
<H1 ALIGN=RIGHT>Right-aligned Heading</H1>
```

Figure 22.5 shows headings aligned left, center, and right.

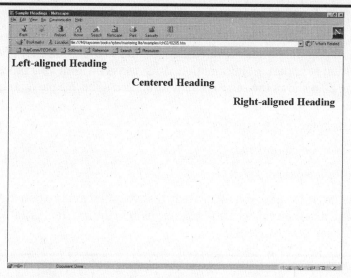

FIGURE 22.5: Headings can be aligned left, center, or right.

HTML 4 OPPORTUNITY

Although most browsers support the ALIGN= attribute, consider using Style Sheets to create the same effect. The HTML 4 specification strongly discourages using the ALIGN= attribute, in favor of using Style Sheets. So, although this attribute has wide support, if your visitors will be using very new browsers, you might consider moving toward Style Sheets for your formatting needs. For comprehensive information about creating Style Sheets, see *Mastering HTML 4* by Deborah S. Ray/Eric J. Ray, also by Sybex.

NOTE

If you're writing for a wide audience, some of whom might be using older browsers, surround any <H1> tags containing ALIGN=CENTER attributes with <CENTER> tags to ensure that the text actually appears centered, yielding something like this: <CENTER><H1 ALIGN=CENTER>Centered Heading</H1></CENTER>.

Creating Lists

Lists are a great way to provide information in a structured, easy-to-read format. They help your visitor easily spot information, and they draw attention to important information. A list is a good form for a procedure. Figure 22.6 shows the same content formatted as both a paragraph and a list.

Lists come in two varieties:

▶ Numbered (*ordered*)

▶ Bulleted (*unordered*)

To create either kind, you first specify that you want information to appear as a list, and then you identify each line item in the list. Table 22.3 shows the list and line item tags.

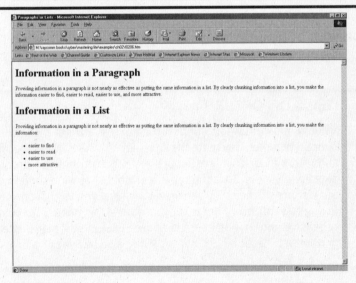

FIGURE 22.6: Lists are often easier to read than paragraphs.

TABLE 22.3: List and Line Item Tags

LIST TAG	EFFECT
<OL>	Specifies that the information should appear as an ordered (numbered) list.
<UL>	Specifies that the information should appear as an unordered (bulleted) list.
<LI>	Specifies a line item in either ordered or unordered lists.

The following steps show you how to create a bulleted list; use the same steps to create a numbered list, except use the <OL> tags instead.

1. Start with text you want to format as a list:

```
Lions
Tigers
Bears
Oh, My!
```

2. Insert the <UL>tags around the list text:

```
<UL>
Lions
Tigers
Bears
Oh, My!
</UL>
```

3. Type the <LI> tag for each list item:

```
<UL>
<LI>Lions
<LI>Tigers
<LI>Bears
<LI>Oh, My!
</UL>
```

The resulting list, viewed in a browser, looks like the list shown in Figure 22.7.

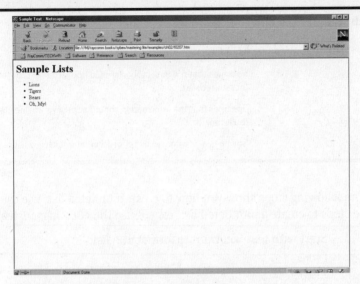

FIGURE 22.7: Bulleted lists make information easy to spot on the page and can
draw attention to important points.

To change your list from unordered (bulleted) to ordered (numbered),
change the <UL> to <OL> (and </UL> to </OL>). The resulting numbered
list is shown in Figure 22.8.

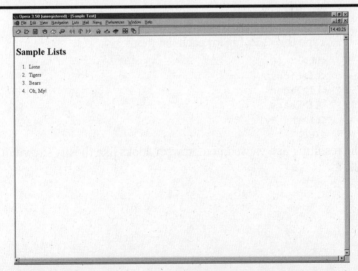

FIGURE 22.8: Numbered lists provide sequential information.

TIP

Other less commonly used list tags include <DIR>, to create a directory list, and <MENU>, to create a menu list. You use these tags just as you use the <UL> and <OL> tags. For more information about these tags and their uses, see Appendix B, "HTML Quick Reference."

Specifying List Appearance

By default, numbered lists use Arabic numerals, and bulleted lists use small, round bullets. You can change the appearance of these by using the attributes listed in Table 22.4.

TABLE 22.4: List Attributes

List Tag	Effect
For numbered lists:	
TYPE=A	Specifies the number (or letter) with which the list should start: A, a, I, i, or 1 (default).
TYPE=a	
TYPE=i	
TYPE=i	
TYPE=1	
For bulleted lists:	
TYPE=DISC	Specifies the bullet shape.
TYPE=SQUARE	
TYPE=CIRCLE	

To use any of these attributes, include them in the beginning <OL> or <UL> tag or in the <LI> tag, like this:

```
<OL TYPE=A>
<LI>Outlines use sequential lists with letters.
<LI>So do some (unpopular) numbering schemes for documentation.
</OL>
```

or like this:

```
<UL TYPE=SQUARE>
```

```
<LI>Use bullets for non-sequential items.
<LI>Use numbers for sequential items.
</UL>
```

or like this:

```
<UL>
<LI TYPE=CIRCLE> Use bullets for non-sequential items.
<LI TYPE=SQUARE> Use different bullets for visual interest.
</UL>
```

Figure 22.9 shows how these attributes appear in a browser.

TIP

You can add the COMPACT attribute to beginning <OL> or <UL> tags to tell browsers to display the list as compactly as possible. Generally, this setting will make little difference, as most browsers render lists this way by default.

NOTE

Type attributes for unordered lists are currently supported by many browsers, but by no means all of them; however, support is expected to continue to grow.

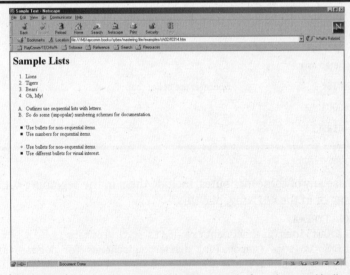

FIGURE 22.9:   You can change the appearance of numbers and bullets using list attributes.

More Options for Ordered Lists

Ordered lists have additional attributes that you can use to specify the first number in the list, as well as to create hierarchical information.

First, you can start a numbered list with a value other than 1 (or A, a, I, or i). Simply include the START= attribute in the initial <OL> tag, as in <OL START=51>. Or, you can even change specific numbers within a list by using the VALUE= attribute in the <LI> tag, as in <LI VALUE=7>. To use these attributes, include them in the <OL> tag, like this:

```
<OL START=51>
<LI>This is the fifty-first item.
<LI>This is the fifty-second.
<LI TYPE=i VALUE=7>This item was renumbered to be the
seventh, using lowercase roman numerals, just because we can.
</OL>
```

Figure 22.10 shows how this code appears in a browser.

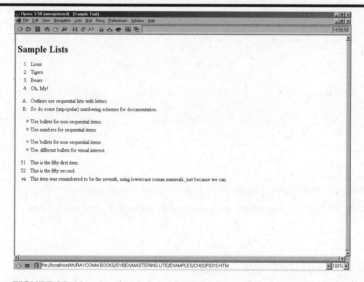

FIGURE 22.10:   Attributes let you customize ordered lists in a number of ways.

Second, you can use nested ordered lists and different TYPE= attributes to create outlines. The numbering continues past each lower-level section without the need to manually renumber with a VALUE= attribute. The results are shown in Figure 22.11.

```
<OL TYPE=I>
<LI>Top Level Item
```

```
<LI>Another Top Level Item
<OL TYPE=A>
   <LI>A Second Level Item
   <LI>Another Second Level Item
   <OL TYPE=1>
      <LI>A Third Level Item
      <LI>Another Third Level Item
   </OL>
   <LI>Another Second Level Item
</OL>
<LI>A Top Level Item
</OL>
```

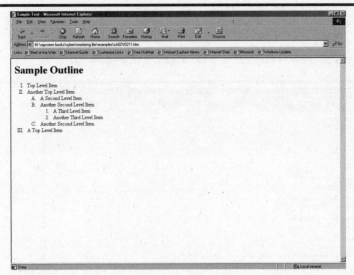

FIGURE 22.11:   Ordered lists are even flexible enough to format outlines.

Using Definition Lists

Finally, one special list variant, *definition lists*, can be useful for providing two levels of information. You can think of definition lists as dictionary entries—you have two levels of information: the entry, followed by a definition. You can use these lists to provide glossary-type information, or you can use them to provide two-level lists. Table 22.5 details the tags and their effects.

TABLE 22.5: Definition List and Item Tags

List Tag	Effect
<DL>	Specifies that the information should appear as a definition list.
<DT>	Identifies definition terms.
<DD>	Identifies definitions.

Part V

To create a definition list, as shown in Figure 22.12, follow these steps:

1. Enter the <DL> tags to start the definition list.

   ```
   <DL>
   </DL>
   ```

2. Add a <DT> tag to identify each definition term.

   ```
   <DL>
   <DT>HTML
   <DT>Maestro
   </DL>
   ```

3. Add a <DD> tag to identify an individual definition.

   ```
   <DL>
   <DT>HTML
   <DD>Hypertext Markup Language is used to create Web
   pages.
   <DT>Maestro
   <DD>An expert in some field. See "Readers of
   <I>Mastering HTML</I>" for examples.
   </DL>
   ```

TIP

A great way to apply definition lists is in a "What's New" list—a special page that tells people what's new and exciting on your site or at your organization. Try putting the dates in the <DT> tag (maybe with boldface and italics) and the information in the <DD> tag.

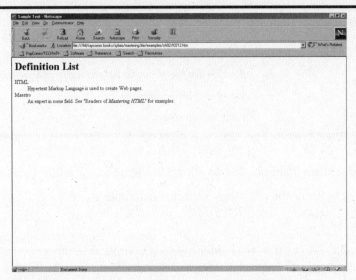

FIGURE 22.12:   Definition lists are a formatting option that is useful when presenting dictionary-like information.

Applying Bold, Italic, and Other Emphases

In addition to creating paragraphs, headings, and lists, you can also apply formatting to individual letters and words. For example, you can make a word appear *italic,* **bold**, <u>underlined</u>, or superscript (as in e$^{2)}$). You use these character-level formatting tags only within paragraph-level tags—that is, you can't put a <P> tag within a character-level tag such as <B>. You have to close the character-level formatting before you close the paragraph-level formatting.

Correct:

```
<P><B>This is the end of a paragraph that also uses
boldface.</B></P>
<P>This is the beginning of the following paragraph.
```

Incorrect:

```
This text <B>is boldface.</P>
<P>As is this </B></P>
```

Although many character-formatting tags are available, you'll probably use <B> (for **boldface**) and <I> (for *italics*) most often. Table 22.6 shows a list of the most common character-formatting tags.

TABLE 22.6: Common Character-Formatting Tags

CHARACTER TAG	EFFECT
`<B>`	Applies boldface.
`<BLINK>`	Makes text blink (usually considered somewhat unprofessional in Web page design).
`<CITE>`	Indicates citations or references.
`<CODE>`	Displays program code. Similar to the `<PRE>` tag.
`<EM>`	Applies emphasis; usually displayed as italic.
`<I>`	Applies italics.
`<S>`, `<STRIKE>`	Applies strikethrough to text. Use of these tags is discouraged in the HTML 4 specification.
`<STRONG>`	Applies stronger emphasis; usually displayed as bold.
`<SUB>`	Formats text as subscript.
`<SUP>`	Formats text as superscript.
`<TT>`	Applies a fixed-width font.
`<U>`	Applies underline. Use of this tag is discouraged in the HTML 4 specification.
`<VAR>`	Displays variables or arguments.

To use these tags, put them around the individual letters or words you want to emphasize, like this:

```
Making some text <B>bold</B> or <I>italic</I> is
a useful technique, more so than
<STRIKE>strikethrough</STRIKE> or
<BLINK>blinking</BLINK>.
```

Figure 22.13 shows some sample character formatting. (Obviously the blinking word can't appear in this figure, but you can see that it disappears.)

TIP

Spend a few minutes trying out these character-formatting tags to see how they work and how they look in your favorite browser.

HTML 4 OPPORTUNITY

The HTML 4 specification strongly encourages using Style Sheets for your formatting needs. Although the specification still supports many individual-formatting tags, it is moving toward Style Sheets as the recommended way to include formatting in your HTML documents. Using Style Sheets, you can apply the following:

▶ Character-level formatting such as strikethrough and underline

▶ Paragraph-level formatting such as indents and margins

▶ Other formatting such as background colors and images

FIGURE 22.13:   Character formatting helps you emphasize words or letters.

Using Horizontal Rules

Horizontal rules are lines that break up long sections of text, indicate a shift in information, or help improve the overall document design. The <HR> tag is a nonpaired tag; it has no ending tag. To use a horizontal rule, put the <HR> tag where you want the rule to appear, like this:

```
<P>Long passages of text should often be broken into sections
with headings and, optionally, horizontal rules.</P>
```

```
<HR>
<H3>A Heading Also Breaks Up Text</H3>
<P>A new long passage can continue here. </P>
```

By default, horizontal rules appear shaded, span the width of the browser window, and are a few pixels high. You can change a rule's shading, width, height, and alignment by including the appropriate attributes. Table 22.7 shows horizontal rule attributes.

NOTE

Pixels are the little dots on your screen that, taken together, produce an image. The word "pixel" is actually an abbreviation for "picture element." If your display is set to 800 × 600, you have 800 pixels horizontally and 600 pixels vertically.

TABLE 22.7: Horizontal Rule Attributes

RULE ATTRIBUTE	EFFECT
SIZE=n	Specifies rule height; measured in pixels.
WIDTH=n	Specifies rule width (length); measured in pixels.
WIDTH="n%"	Specifies rule width (length); measured as a percentage of the document width.
ALIGN=LEFT	Specifies left alignment.
ALIGN=CENTER	Specifies center alignment.
ALIGN=RIGHT	Specifies right alignment.
NOSHADE	Specifies that the rule has no shading.

To use any of these attributes, include them in the <HR> tag, like this:

```
<HR WIDTH="80%" SIZE=8>
<HR WIDTH="50%">
<HR WIDTH=400 ALIGN=RIGHT>
<HR NOSHADE ALIGN=CENTER WIDTH=200>
```

Figure 22.14 shows some sample horizontal rules, with height, width, alignment, and shading attributes added.

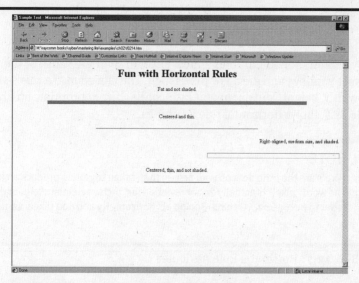

FIGURE 22.14: Horizontal rules can help separate information, improve page design, and simply add visual interest to the page.

Inserting Line Breaks

Sometimes you need to break a line in a specific place, but you don't want to start a new paragraph and insert the associated empty vertical space that comes with a paragraph break. For example, you might not want lines of poetry text to go all the way across the document; instead, you might want to break them into several shorter lines with no space between them. You can easily break paragraph lines by inserting the <BR> tag where you want the lines to break, like this:

```
<P>
There once was an HTML writer,<BR>
Who tried to make paragraphs wider.<BR>
He found with a shock<BR>
All the tags did mock<BR>
The attempt to move that text outside-r.<BR>
Mercifully Anonymous</P>
```

USING FANCIER FORMATTING

Now that you have a firm grip on using the basic HTML formatting options, you can dive into some of the fancier formatting effects. In the following sections, we'll show you how to add colors and specify fonts and sizes. Although most newer browsers support these effects, not all browsers do; your fancier effects might not reach all visitors. Also, the HTML 4 specification discourages many of these effects in favor of Style Sheets. If your visitors use Style Sheet-capable browsers, you might consider using Style Sheets instead of the tags and attributes mentioned here.

Adding Colors

One of the easiest ways to jazz up your documents is to add colors to the background or text. You can enliven an otherwise dull Web page with a splash of color or an entire color scheme. For example, add a background color and change the text colors to coordinate with the background. Or highlight a word or two with color to make the words leap off the page. Or, if you're developing a corporate site, adhere to the company's color scheme to ensure a consistent look.

TIP

As you'll see in Chapter 25, "Wowing Them with Design," developing a color scheme is a great way to help unite your pages into a cohesive Web site.

The drawback to setting colors is that you really don't have control over what your visitors see. Visitors might set their browsers to display colors they like, or they might be using a text-only browser, which generally displays only black, white, and gray.

You specify colors using hexadecimal numbers, which combine proportions of Red, Green, and Blue—called RGB numbers. RGB numbers use six digits, two for each proportion of red, green, and blue. As you're choosing colors, remember that not all RGB numbers display well in browsers; some colors *dither*, meaning that they appear spotty or splotchy. We recommend that you select RGB values that are appropriate for Web page use, as listed in Table 22.8. Although you'll never go wrong with these "safe" colors, it's most important to use these colors in page backgrounds or in places with large patches of color, where dithering will occur if you don't use these number combinations.

TABLE 22.8: Recommended RGB Values

R	G	B
00	00	00
33	33	33
66	66	66
99	99	99
CC	CC	CC
FF	FF	FF

To create an RGB number from the values in this table, simply select one number from each column. For example, choose FF from the Red column, 00 from the Green column, and 00 from the Blue column to create the RGB number FF0000, which has the largest possible red component but no blue and no green, therefore appearing as a pure, bright red. You'll find a complete list of appropriate RGB numbers and corresponding descriptions in Appendix B.

Setting Background Colors

Using a *background color*, which is simply a color that fills the entire browser window, is a great way to add flair to your Web pages. By default, browsers display a white or gray background color, which may be adequate if you're developing pages for an intranet site or a pure reference site, where flashy elements aren't essential. If you're developing a public or personal site, however, you'll probably want to make your site more interesting and visually appealing. For example, if you're developing a public corporate Web site, you might want to use your company's standard colors—ones that appear on letterhead, logos, or marketing materials. Or, you might want to use your favorite color if you're developing a personal site. In either case, using a background color can improve the overall page appearance and help develop a theme among pages.

TIP

Check out Chapter 25 for tips and information about developing coherent, well-designed Web sites.

As you'll see in the next section, pay careful attention to how text contrasts with the background color. If you specify a dark background color, use a light text color. Likewise, if you specify a light background color, use a dark text color. Contrast is key for ensuring that visitors can read the information on your pages.

To specify a background color for your documents, include the BGCOLOR="#..." attribute in the opening <BODY> tag, like this:

```
<BODY BGCOLOR="#FFFFFF">
```

Specifying Text Colors

Like background colors, text colors can enhance your Web pages. In particular, you can specify the color of the following:

- ▶ Body text, which appears throughout the document body
- ▶ Unvisited links, which are links not yet followed
- ▶ Active links, which are links as they're being selected
- ▶ Visited links, which are links previously followed

Changing body text is sometimes essential—for example, if you've added a background color or an image. If you've added a dark background color, the default black body text color won't adequately contrast with the background, making the text difficult or impossible to read. In this case, you'd want to change the text color to one that's lighter so that it contrasts with the background sufficiently.

Changing link colors helps keep your color scheme intact—for unvisited as well as visited links. Set the visited and unvisited links to different colors to help visitors know which links they've followed and which ones they haven't.

To change body text and link colors, simply add the attributes listed in Table 22.9 to the opening <BODY> tag.

TABLE 22.9: Text and Link Color Attributes

ATTRIBUTE	DESCRIPTION
TEXT="…"	Sets the color for all text within the document with a color name or a #RRGGBB value.
ALINK="…"	Sets the color for active links, which are the links at the time the visitor clicks on them, with a color name or a #RRGGBB value.
VLINK="…"	Sets the color for links the visitor has recently followed with a color name or a #RRGGBB value (how recently depends on browser settings).
LINK="…"	Sets the color for unvisited links with a color name or a #RRGGBB value.

TIP

We recommend setting all Web page colors at one time—that way you can see how background, text, and link colors appear as a unit.

To change text and link colors, follow these steps:

1. Within the <BODY> tag, add the TEXT= attribute to set the color of text within the document. The example presented here makes the text black.

   <BODY TEXT="#FFFFFF">

NOTE

When setting text colors, using a "safe" color is less important for text than it is for backgrounds. Dithering is less apparent in small areas, such as text.

2. Add the LINK= attribute to set the link color. This example uses blue (#0000FF) for the links.

   <BODY TEXT="#FFFFFF" **LINK="#0000FF"**>

3. Add the VLINK= attribute to set the color for visited links. If you set the VLINK= to the same as the color for links, links will not change colors even after visitors follow them. This could be confusing, but also serves to make it look like there

is always new material available. This example sets the visited link to a different shade of blue.

```
<BODY TEXT="#FFFFFF" LINK="#0000FF" VLINK="#000099">
```

4. Finally, set the ALINK= to specify the active link color. This is the color of a link while visitors are clicking on it; this color will not necessarily be visible in Internet Explorer 4, depending on visitor settings. This example sets ALINK= to red.

```
<BODY TEXT="#FFFFFF" LINK="#0000FF" VLINK="#000099"
ALINK="#FF0000">
```

TIP

Specify fonts and increase font sizes to improve readability with dark backgrounds and light colored text.

Specifying Fonts and Font Sizes

If your visitors will be using fairly new browsers, you can use the <FONT> tag to specify font characteristics for your document, including color, size, and typeface. Table 22.10 describes the tag and attributes you'll use to set font characteristics.

TABLE 22.10: Font Characteristics

TAG/ATTRIBUTE	DESCRIPTION
<FONT>	Sets font characteristics for text.
SIZE="..."	Specifies relative font size using a scale of 1 through 7. Three (3) is the default or normal size. You can also specify the relative size by using + or – (for example, SIZE="+2").
COLOR="..."	Specifies font color in #RRGGBB numbers or with color names. This color applies only to the text surrounded by the <FONT> tags.
FACE="..."	Specifies typefaces as a list of possible typefaces, in order of preference, separated by commas—(for example, FACE="Verdana, Arial, Helvetica").
<BASEFONT>	Sets the text characteristics for the document.

As you're determining which font face to use, keep in mind that the font must be available on your visitors' computers for them to view the fonts you specify. For example, if you specify Technical as the font to use and your visitors do not have Technical, their computers will substitute a font that might not be a font you'd consider acceptable. As a partial way of overcoming this problem, you can list multiple faces in order of preference; the machine then displays the first available. For example, a list of "Comic Sans MS, Technical, Tekton, Times, Arial" will display Comic Sans MS if available, then try Technical, then Tekton, and so forth.

So, which fonts should you choose? Table 22.11 lists fonts that are commonly available on PC, Mac, and Unix platforms.

TABLE 22.11: Fonts Commonly Available on PC, Mac, and Unix

WINDOWS	MACINTOSH	UNIX
Arial	Helvetica	Helvetica
Times New Roman	Times	Times
Courier New	Courier	Courier

TIP

You might check out Microsoft's selection of fonts, which you can easily download (go to www.microsoft.com). These fonts are cool, and are available to visitors who have specifically downloaded the fonts to their computers, who are using Internet Explorer 4 or newer, or who are using Windows 98.

To specify font characteristics, follow these steps. You can set some or all of the characteristics used in this example.

1. Identify the text to format with the <FONT> tag.
   `<FONT>Look at this!</FONT>`

2. Select a specific font using the FACE= attribute. See Table 22.11 for a list of commonly available fonts.
   `<FONT FACE="Verdana, Times New Roman, Times">Look at this!</FONT>`

3. Change the font size using the SIZE= attribute. You set the size of text on a relative scale—from 1 to 7, with the default size being 3. Either set the size absolutely (with a number from 1 to 7) or

relatively (with + or–to change the size). Almost all newer browsers, and all HTML 3.2 and 4–compliant browsers, support SIZE= to set font size. The only significant downside to setting the font size is that your visitor might already have increased or decreased the default font size, so your size change might have more of an effect than you expected.

```
<FONT FACE="Technical, Times New Roman, Times"
SIZE="+2">Look at this!</FONT>
```

4. Add a COLOR= attribute to set the color, using a color name or a #RRGGBB value.

```
<FONT FACE="Technical, Times New Roman, Times" SIZE="+2"
COLOR="#FF0000">Look at this!</FONT>
```

Figure 22.15 shows the resulting appearance.

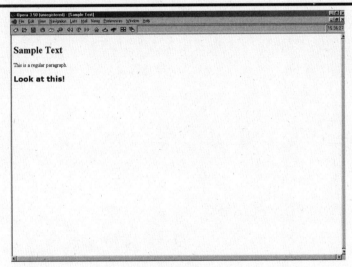

FIGURE 22.15: Setting font characteristics can spiff up your pages and help you achieve the visual effect you want.

WHAT'S NEXT?

Congratulations! You've just learned to apply HTML code, and you even learned some of the most common tags and attributes. Now you can put this knowledge to good use in Chapter 23, "Creating a Web Site and Web Pages."

Chapter 23

CREATING A WEB AND WEB PAGES WITH FRONTPAGE

F rontPage is a Web site navigation center, the place where you start and finish your work on a Web page. This chapter shows you how to create a FrontPage web and use the Page view to create exciting Web pages. In FrontPage, a *web* is something like a directory, in that it is a means of organizing the files that you use to create a Web page. In the chapters that follow, you'll learn about other useful products for building Web pages and how to use them to design a terrific Web site.

Adapted from *Microsoft Front Page 2000: No experience required*, by Gene Weisskopf

ISBN 0-7821-2482-8   409 pages $19.99

The Standard toolbar (shown below) contains many of the tools you'll use to manage and edit your web.

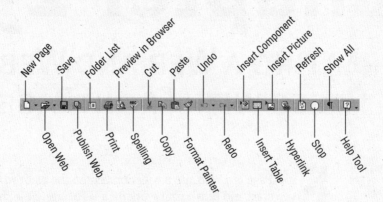

CREATING A NEW WEB

We'll call the web you are viewing or modifying in FrontPage the *current* or *active* web. When you create and save individual pages for that web using FrontPage's built-in editor, they become part of the active web unless you specify otherwise.

Because creating or revising Web pages is probably the job you'll perform most often in FrontPage, when you start the program you'll normally see just two panes: the Views bar and the Page view with a blank Web page, ready for editing. You can instead open an existing page or an entire FrontPage web, or create a brand new FrontPage web.

TIP

You can also choose to have the last web you worked on open automatically when you start FrontPage. Choose Tools ➢ Options, and select Open Last Web Automatically from the General tab in the Options dialog box.

There are two primary steps required to create a new web: select the type of web you want to create, and specify a location for it. First choose File ➢ New ➢ Web, or select Web from the drop-down list in the New Page button (on the Standard toolbar). This opens the New dialog box, which is shown in Figure 23.1.

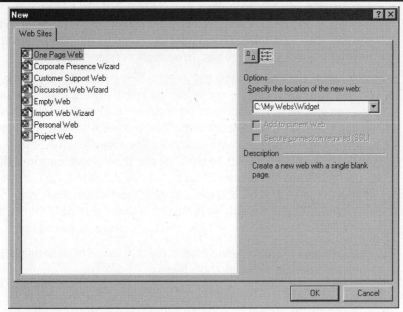

FIGURE 23.1:   The New dialog box lets you create a new FrontPage web from a web template or wizard.

In this dialog box, select one of the web templates or wizards listed on the Web Sites tab. For example, if you are new to FrontPage, you may want to start out by creating just a one-page web from the template of that name. This way you can get comfortable working with web pages before moving on to more complex projects.

You also specify a name and location for the new web in the New dialog box. You can give your web any name you want using spaces, upper- and lowercase letters, numbers, and any other characters that are acceptable in filenames.

WARNING

You may want to avoid spaces in your web names, because some Web servers won't accept them. You should also stick with just lowercase letters, because some servers are case-sensitive and will distinguish between the file or folder name "my web site" and "My Web Site." It's easier for visitors to enter all lowercase letters in their browsers to access your site, and not have to remember the case of the name exactly.

When you are creating a local web (as opposed to a web on a server), the default location for your web is generally the My Webs folder. When you are ready to publish your web for the entire world to see, you can transfer the web from your local drive to its permanent location.

A FrontPage web contains not only the files you create, but several other folders and files that are created by FrontPage and used to manage and run your web. The names of these folders begin with an underscore, such as _borders, and are not normally displayed within the Folders List in FrontPage because they are strictly for FrontPage's own use. You can, however, view these folders by enabling the Show Documents in Hidden Directories option, which you'll find on the Advanced tab for the Tools ➤ Web Settings command. You can also view them within Windows Explorer, although you definitely should not change or delete them. There are two FrontPage folders that you are free to use, as you need them:

images   This is a convenient folder in which to store image files, such as GIF and JPEG files.

_private   This folder is not visible to browsers when your FrontPage web is hosted by a FrontPage-aware server, so any files in it are invisible as well. Once your site is up and running under a server for the public to see, this might be a place to keep pages that are under construction, reference files, and other documents that you want to be available for your use only. Unlike the other FrontPage folders that begin with the underscore character, the contents of this folder are visible to you while you're working in FrontPage.

When you create a new web, it is ready for you to enhance and expand it.

NOTE

One bonus of FrontPage is that you don't have to worry about periodically saving your web. When you make changes, such as renaming pages or importing new files, those changes are saved automatically. When you are editing pages, however, there is a File ➤ Save command for you to use, just as you would in a word processor.

OPENING AN EXISTING WEB

 To open an existing FrontPage web that you've recently worked on, use the File ➤ Recent Webs command, which lists the webs you've opened in the recent past. Otherwise, use File ➤ Open Web, or click the Open Web button on the Standard toolbar. If that button is displayed as the Open button for opening a file (not a web), click the down arrow next to it and select Open Web.

The Open Web dialog box is similar to a typical files dialog box, except that in this case you are not selecting a file but an entire folder—the folder that contains a FrontPage web. Select the one you want and click OK to open that web. If you already had a web open in FrontPage, a new FrontPage program window will be started for the web you're opening. You will then have two FrontPage windows open, each displaying a different web. If the web you open has security controls placed on it, you may have to enter your username and password before you can open the web.

To open a different web in the same window, choose File ➤ Close Web first. You can choose File ➤ Exit at any time to close FrontPage. If you have been editing one or more web pages and have not saved your work, you will first be asked if you wish to do so. Note that if you have multiple FrontPage windows running, each displaying a separate web, you can close any of them while leaving the others open.

CREATING, OPENING, AND SAVING WEB PAGES

You normally use the Page view's built-in HTML editor to create and revise web pages. If you are familiar with an earlier version of FrontPage, you'll most likely be pleased that the HTML editor is now an integral part of FrontPage, and not a separate application. You don't need to switch back and forth between the page you are editing and your web in FrontPage.

Creating a New Page

 To create a new blank web page, simply click the New Page button on the Standard toolbar, and the new page will appear in the right-hand pane. You can have multiple pages open at the same time, switching among them as needed by choosing one from the Windows menu.

You can also create a new page from a FrontPage template, which is a ready-built page that serves as the basis for the new page. You choose a template when you use the File ➤ New ➤ Page command (Ctrl+N), or you can right-click a folder in the Folders List and choose New Page from the shortcut menu. The Normal Page template is the standard blank page that opens when you click the New Page button.

To close the active document, choose File ➤ Close. If you have not saved the document since making changes to it, you will be prompted to save it to avoid losing that work.

Opening an Existing Page

There are several ways to open an existing page for editing in FrontPage. You can use File ➤ Open (Ctrl+O) and choose a file from the Open File dialog box, or click the Open button on the Standard toolbar. You can also double-click a page name or icon from the Folder List or the Hyperlinks view, or right-click the filename or icon and choose Open from the shortcut menu.

Saving Your Work

Just as in your word processor, you must save your work to keep it. Normally, you will save a Web page within the active web in FrontPage, but you can choose to save it elsewhere as a separate file, independent of your web. Use the File ➤ Save command (Ctrl+S), or click the Save button on the Standard toolbar. If the page is a new one that you have not yet saved, you will see the Save As dialog box, shown in Figure 23.2, which will always be displayed when you choose File ➤ Save As.

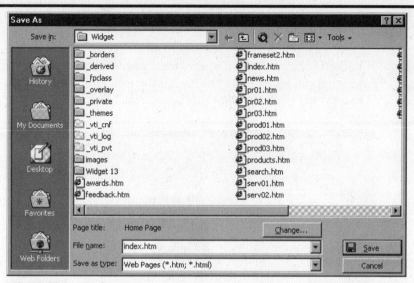

FIGURE 23.2: The first time you save a web page, or when you choose File ➢ Save As, you specify the filename, location, and page title in the Save As dialog box.

In the Save As dialog box, you pick a location for the file (normally one of the folders in your web), enter a name for the file, and, optionally, click the Change button and specify a page title (you can also specify a title while editing the page).

TIP

You can create folders in your FrontPage web to organize its files. For example, you can save or move files to them, just as you do with the normal folders and documents you create on your computer. When you insert a hyperlink into a page in your web, the location of its target is automatically specified in the link.

ENTERING AND EDITING TEXT

Editing a page in the Page view is very much like working in a typical WYSIWYG word processor, where "what you see is what you get." In this case, what you see is pretty much what the rest of the world sees in their Web browsers when they view that page on your Web site (see Figure 23.3).

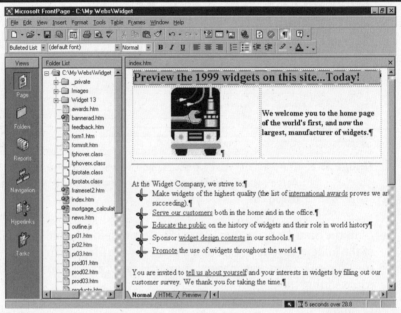

FIGURE 23.3: You create Web pages in FrontPage in much the same way that you create documents in a word processor.

If you are a Microsoft Word user, you may notice that the process of editing an HTML document in FrontPage looks suspiciously similar to Word. The similarities are not accidental. Microsoft has worked very hard to have all of its Office products—Word, Excel, PowerPoint, and Front-Page—share the same look and even the same program resources. For example, you'll find the same toolbar buttons for commands such as New, Open, Save, Cut, and Paste. Those commands also appear in the same menus, so if you're already familiar with Microsoft Word, you won't have any trouble getting started in FrontPage.

TIP

Paste Special is also available, so you can insert text with or without formatting, copied from within FrontPage or from other applications. For example, when you copy a paragraph from a Word document, FrontPage will convert the formatting into an equivalent look in HTML (as best it can). If you want the text without any formatting, choose Paste Special ➤ Normal Paragraphs.

Let's take a quick look at some of the features of the Page view shown in Figure 23.3:

▶ At the top of the screen beneath the title bar are the menu bar, the Standard toolbar, and the Formatting toolbar. Several other toolbars are available as well. You can turn the display of a toolbar on or off by selecting it from the View ➤ Toolbars menu.

▶ At the bottom of the screen is the status bar, which displays useful information as you work on your Web page. For example, the left side of the status bar displays the target address of a hyperlink when you point to that link in the page.

▶ Just above the status bar are three tabs that let you switch between views of your document: Normal, HTML, and Preview (more about those later).

▶ The web page you're editing appears in the window beneath the toolbars and to the right of the Views bar and Folder List (unless you have closed those panes to provide more room for the page you're editing). You can open multiple Web pages and switch between them with the Windows menu.

▶ The horizontal and vertical scroll bars offer one way to scroll through your document; you can also use the usual keyboard keys, such as PgUp and PgDn. If your mouse has a scrolling wheel, such as Microsoft's IntelliMouse, you can use the wheel to scroll up or down through the page.

Basic Editing Procedures

The best way to familiarize yourself with the process of editing pages in the Page view is to start typing. Most of the basic procedures you've already learned in your word processor are applicable in FrontPage:

▶ You can have multiple documents open at the same time, but only one is active. The active page receives the text you enter and is the target of any commands you issue.

▶ In the active document, you enter text just as you would in your word processor; FrontPage wraps text automatically, so you press Enter only to create a new paragraph.

▶ Press Del to delete the character to the right of the insertion point; press Backspace to delete the character to its left. Press Ctrl+Del to delete the word to the right of the insertion point, and press Ctrl+Backspace to delete the word to its left.

▶ Press Home to go to the beginning of the current line and press End to go to its end. Press Ctrl+Home to go to the top of the document and press Ctrl+End to go to the bottom.

▶ When you have opened multiple documents, their windows are stacked one on top of the other in the Page view pane; you can't reduce their size or minimize them.

▶ Select text by dragging over it with your mouse or by pressing the Shift key while you use a keyboard arrow key to select the material.

▶ Once you select a portion of the document, you can act on the selection by making choices from the menu, a toolbar, or a shortcut menu. For example, choose Edit ➢ Cut from the menu, click the Cut button on the toolbar, or right-click and choose Cut from the shortcut menu to remove a selection from the document and send it to the Windows Clipboard.

▶ You can transfer text or images between FrontPage and other programs in the usual ways by using Copy or Cut and Paste with the Clipboard.

▶ To undo your most recent action in a document, choose Edit ➢ Undo from the menu, click the Undo button on the Standard toolbar, or press Ctrl+Z. You can "undo an undo" by choosing Edit ➢ Redo or by clicking the Redo button.

You can add comments in a page by selecting Insert ➤ Comment from the menu. The text you enter is displayed in the page you're editing, but does not appear when the page is viewed in a browser. A comment can explain an area in the page or serve as a reminder to you or another author.

Inserting Paragraphs and Line Breaks

When you want to create a new paragraph in a document, simply press Enter, just as you would in your word processor. Behind the scenes, this inserts new <P> and </P> opening and closing tags in the underlying HTML code, defining the beginning and end of the new paragraph.

A new paragraph not only begins on a new line, it also has its own formatting, just as in Word. For example, if you press Enter at the end of a left-aligned paragraph (the default alignment), you can center the new paragraph, right align it, or add other paragraph formatting without changing the left-aligned formatting of the previous paragraph.

NOTE

When you press Enter but do not enter any text in the new paragraph before pressing Enter again, FrontPage places the HTML code for a non-breaking space (Ctrl+Shift+Space) between the two paragraph tags, so the code created looks like this: <P> </P>. The non-breaking space on a line by itself forces a browser to display a blank line, where it might otherwise ignore the "empty" paragraph.

You can force a line to break without creating a new paragraph by pressing Shift+Enter instead of Enter. This inserts the line break tag,
 (you can also choose Normal Line Break from the dialog box of the Insert ➤ Break command). The text that follows the line break appears on a new line, but is otherwise still a part of the current paragraph and carries all of its formatting.

Most browsers automatically insert some extra space between two paragraphs of text, so there are instances when you'd rather use the <BR> tag than the <P> tag to create a new line. For example, when you display your name and address in a page, you don't want extra space between each line of the address.

The next graphic shows two addresses in a table in a page being edited in FrontPage. In the address on the left, Enter was pressed at the end of each line to insert a line break. In the address on the right, Shift+Enter was pressed.

¶ Notice that FrontPage displays a right-angle arrow for the line break and a paragraph mark between regular paragraphs. You can turn the display of line breaks and other on-screen formatting marks on or off by clicking the Show All button on the Standard toolbar.

Inserting Special Characters

Your computer's keyboard is limited to a standard set of letters, numbers, and punctuation. But there are a lot of other characters that simply are not included on your keyboard. For example, there's the degree symbol (100°), the copyright symbol (©1999), and the fraction symbol for one-half (½).

In FrontPage, you insert symbols into your page just as you do in Word, with the Insert ➤ Symbol command, which displays the Symbol dialog box (see Figure 23.4). Select the symbol you want and click the Insert button to place that symbol into your document at the insertion point. You can continue to select other symbols in the dialog box and click the Insert button. When you are finished, click the Close button.

FIGURE 23.4: The Insert ➤ Symbol command lets you pick a symbol to include in your page.

HTML and Browsers—The Start and End of Your Work

All of the pages that you edit are built from HTML code. However, Front-Page does such a good job of displaying the page and letting you manipulate it that you often just work along without even thinking about the underlying code that is being created.

Nonetheless, HTML is there and waiting if you need it, and the more you work with Web pages, the more often you may want to take a peek at the HTML code. The Page view gives you several ways to interact with a page's HTML code:

- ▶ You can view the code at any time, making changes to it as though you're working on the page in a text editor.

- ▶ You can display the HTML tags within your document while still viewing your document in the WYSIWYG format.

- ▶ You can insert HTML tags that FrontPage doesn't support.

- ▶ You can view your page in any available Web browser, so you can see exactly how the HTML in the page will be interpreted by various browsers.

Seeing the HTML Source Code

When you want to see the HTML code behind the active page, click the HTML tab on the bottom left of the editing pane. The display switches to show the actual HTML code for your page—the same code that is saved to disk when you save your page.

Figure 23.5 shows the HTML view for the page that was displayed in Figure 23.3. If you're just viewing the code and do not want to make any changes to it, you can return to the page by clicking the Normal tab.

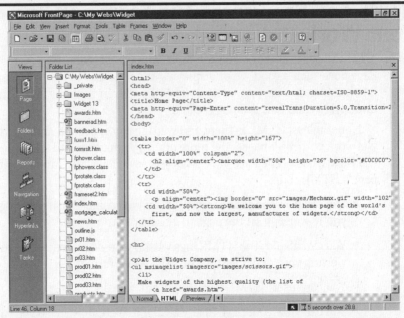

FIGURE 23.5: Clicking the HTML tab lets you view or edit the underlying HTML
code for a page.

The HTML view is just another way to display your Web page. Use caution when making changes to the HTML code, as they're reflected in the
page when you return to Normal view. If, for example, you accidentally
delete one of the angle brackets for an HTML tag, you'll see the result
reflected on the page when you switch back to Normal view.

NOTE

Many, but not all, of the menu choices are available while you are in HTML view.
For example, you can use Cut, Copy, and Paste to move or copy text, insert a
horizontal line or graphic image, and create a data-entry form.

HTML view not only displays the underlying HTML for the active
page, it also helps you interpret it by color-coding it. For example, text
you enter is shown in normal black, while HTML tags are shown in blue.
To adjust the colors that are used, choose Tools ➤ Page Options and the
Color Coding tab in the dialog box.

The different colors make it a lot easier to make sense of the code as you scroll through it. Viewing the underlying code is always a good exercise to help you get a feel for the ins and outs of HTML.

Displaying HTML Tags in Your Document

Another way to get a sense of the HTML code that makes up a page is to display just the tags—choose View ➤ Reveal Tags (choose it again to turn off the display of the tags). Your page will still be shown in the Normal view, but the HTML tags for paragraphs and text will be displayed as well. Figure 23.6 shows the same page from Figure 23.3 after the Reveal Tags option was turned on.

The tags can help you differentiate among the various codes, and you can delete a tag to eliminate that code from your document. Point to a tag and its definition will be displayed in a pop-up screen tip. On the other hand, the tags tend to clutter the screen and slow down screen scrolling, so you will generally want to leave them turned off.

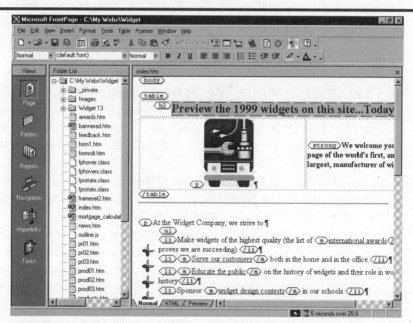

FIGURE 23.6: Choosing View ➤ Reveal Tags displays the basic HTML paragraph and text formatting tags within your WYSIWYG page.

Inserting Unsupported HTML Code

The fast-paced development of HTML means that there will always be some tags that some browsers accept even though those tags have not been incorporated into the official HTML specification.

Even if it is not supported by FrontPage, you can still add HTML code to your Web pages by using the Insert ➤ Advanced ➤ HTML command. This displays the HTML Markup dialog box, in which you enter the HTML code you want to include in the page.

WARNING

FrontPage basically ignores the HTML code you enter in the HTML Markup dialog box, and does not check it for accuracy. So it's up to you to enter the code with no mistakes and ensure that it will be interpreted correctly by a browser.

 When you click OK to close the HTML Markup dialog box, you'll see a small icon in your page (as shown here) that represents the code you added. Even though you won't be able to see how the page lays out around this new material in Page view, the code you added will be interpreted and displayed (assuming you entered it correctly) when you preview the page in a browser, as discussed in the next section.

Previewing Your Work in a Browser

The ultimate outcome for a page is to be viewed within a Web browser. Although FrontPage does a very good job of showing you how a page will appear within a browser, it can never offer the final and absolutely definitive view of a page. No editor can.

The primary reason for this is that HTML is designed to be very flexible in the way its pages are formatted. The same HTML code can be interpreted somewhat differently in different browsers.

On top of that inherent flexibility is the fact there are just too many variables that affect the ultimate appearance of a page within a browser. For example, a browser running within a screen resolution of 800 × 600 pixels displays over 50 percent more of a page than a browser running within a screen resolution of 640 × 480.

The only way to be sure how your web looks is to view it within a browser or, preferably, in several of the more popular browsers. You can also view a single Web page right from within FrontPage, to see how that page looks in Internet Explorer. Click the Preview tab at the bottom of the editing pane to view the page. (This requires that you have Microsoft

Internet Explorer 3.0 or higher installed on your system. If you do not, you won't have a Preview tab.)

To open an actual browser such as Microsoft Internet Explorer or Netscape Navigator, choose File ➣ Preview in Browser. The Preview in Browser dialog box, shown in Figure 23.7, opens so you can choose which browser you want to use.

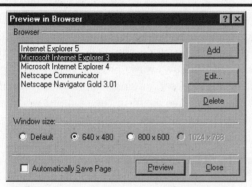

FIGURE 23.7:   The Preview in Browser dialog box lets you choose a browser to open to view your page.

When you initially install FrontPage, it searches for browsers on your computer and automatically adds installed browsers to the list in the Preview in Browser dialog box. If you add other browsers after you install Front-Page, you can add them to the list by clicking the Add button. You enter a name for the browser, which appears in the list of browsers, then enter the command that opens that browser. Use the Browse button to select the program from a typical Windows files dialog box.

Once the new browser appears in the list, you can select it to preview the page you're editing. Use the Edit or Delete buttons in the Preview in Browser dialog box to revise the settings for a browser or to remove a browser from the list.

If you have not saved the page you want to view, click the Automatically Save Page check box. (If you don't, you'll be told that you can't view the page until you save it.) FrontPage opens a Save As dialog box if you haven't saved the page. If you've previously saved the page, it just goes ahead and saves it again before displaying it in the browser.

Before clicking the Preview button, select a size for the browser's window in the Window Size group of options. For example, if your monitor's resolution is 800×600 or higher, you can choose the 640×480 option to see how the page looks in a browser that has been maximized to full-screen size on a monitor whose screen resolution is only 640×480. Choose the Default option to open the browser without specifying a size.

Now you're ready to click the Preview button. If you've already saved your page, this action takes you directly to the browser you selected.

 When the page opens in the designated browser, you can see how your page actually looks when others view it on the Web. Review how the page looks when displayed within the specified window size and how the features within the page compare to the way they appear in FrontPage. When you're ready to go back to work on the page, switch back to FrontPage in one of the usual Windows ways: press Alt+Tab, click its icon on the Taskbar, minimize the browser, or close the browser completely. When you are ready to view the page again in the same browser, all you have to do is click the Preview in Browser button on the toolbar.

Printing Your Page

You can print the active page of the Page view in the same way you print a document in your word processor. Of course, the need to print rarely arises, since a page is meant to reside on a Web site and be viewed by a browser. Nonetheless, you may wish to print pages to proof them for accuracy, hang them on your refrigerator, or show them to others when you can't access a computer.

 To print the active page using the current print settings, choose File ➤ Print or click the Print button on the toolbar. This displays the standard Print dialog box, in which you can specify the number of copies to print, the range of pages to print, and the printer to which the job should be sent.

Previewing the Printout

Before you print a page, take a few seconds to preview what your printout will look like on paper by choosing File ➤ Print Preview. The buttons on the Preview toolbar perform the following tasks:

Print   Closes the preview but opens the Print dialog box, where you can print as usual to a printer.

Next Page   Displays the next page of a multi-page printout; you can also press the PgDn key. The left side of the status bar shows the current page number.

Previous Page   Displays the previous page; you can also press the PgUp key.

Two Page/One Page   Toggles between displaying a single page or two pages of the printout.

Zoom In   Magnifies the preview so you can see more detail on the page, but less of the entire page.

Zoom Out   Shows you more of the page but shrinks the size of the characters on it.

TIP

Here's a fast way to zoom in on a specific portion of the page without having to hunt for it after the screen is magnified. Just point to the portion of the preview you want to see and click. Click again to zoom out again.

Close   Closes the preview and returns to the active page; you can also press the Esc key.

Again, your pages are meant to be viewed within your Web site by a browser, so you'll probably print pages only if you're developing the web and want input from others, or if you want to lay it all out and see how the pages fit together.

SPELL CHECKING

When you create a web, you should make sure that all the text is spelled correctly in each page. After you publish the web, you still need to provide periodic maintenance as new pages are added and existing pages require editing. It's all too easy to introduce a misspelling, even if you only spend 30 seconds on a page.

You probably use the spell checker in your word processor every day as a quick and easy way to check the spelling of all the words in a document. FrontPage offers you the same tool, and it's even more powerful than you might suspect, because you can check the spelling in every page of your entire web in one operation. This is yet another example of how FrontPage condenses huge Web site management tasks into simple, one-step operations.

NOTE

FrontPage checks only the spelling of text that you can edit from the Normal tab of the Page view. Generally, that's the text that a visitor to your site will see. FrontPage doesn't check the underlying HTML code, such as the page title or hyperlink target names, nor the text in any included pages in the active page. These are pages that appear as the result of the Include Page component. You must open these pages separately to check their spelling.

Checking the Spelling of the Active Page

 To check the spelling of the active page in the Page view, choose Tools ➤ Spelling (F7), or click the Spelling button on the Standard toolbar. If you have experience with any of the applications in Microsoft Office, this routine is quite familiar.

If the spell checker finds no misspelled words in the page, a dialog box notifies you of the success. If it finds a misspelled word (or rather, a word not in the spelling dictionary), you see the Spelling dialog box (shown in Figure 23.8) with the suspect word displayed in the Not in Dictionary field.

TIP

FrontPage can check your spelling as you work and underline those words that it can't find in the spelling dictionary. To turn this feature off or on, choose Tools ➤ Page Options, select the Spelling tab, and select or deselect the Check Spelling As You Type option.

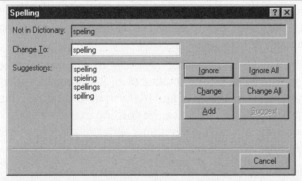

FIGURE 23.8:   The Spelling dialog box displays a suspected misspelled word and offers a list of suggested replacements.

If the Word Is Spelled Correctly

The spell checker flags many words that are actually correct, especially proper names, acronyms, and technical or medical terms. When the suspect word is correct, you can do any of the following:

- ▶ Click the Ignore button to bypass this word and continue to check the spelling; if the suspect word appears again, it's flagged again.

- ▶ Click the Ignore All button, bypassing all occurrences of the suspect word during this spell-checking session.

- ▶ Click the Add button to add this word to the custom dictionary. In the future, FrontPage will recognize that the word is spelled correctly.

If the Word Is Misspelled

If the word in question is not correct, you can either type the correct spelling into the Change To field or select one of the words from the Suggestions list (which then appears in the Change To field). At this point you have some options:

- ▶ Click the Change button to replace the misspelled word with the word in the Change To field.

- ▶ Click Change All to change all occurrences of the misspelled word in the active page.

You can also click the Cancel button at any time to end the spell-checking session.

Checking Spelling in an Entire Web

To check the spelling of all or selected pages in the active web, first save all open Web pages in the Page view to ensure that they are up to date on disk. Then display your web in Folders view, Navigation view, or Hyperlinks view. If you want to check the spelling of only some files, select those files in the Folders view. Then choose Tools ➤ Spelling (F7), or click the Spelling button. This displays the web-wide Spelling dialog box, shown in Figure 23.9, which offers two options for web-wide spell checking:

- ▶ Choose to check all pages in the web or just those you have selected.

▶ Choose whether to fix misspellings immediately, or simply to add a task to the Tasks view for each filename that contains misspelled words so you can return at your convenience to correct the misspellings.

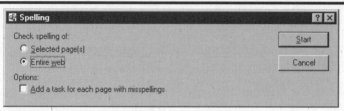

FIGURE 23.9:   The web-wide Spelling dialog box allows you to check the spelling in selected pages or the entire web.

When you click the Start button to begin checking spelling, the dialog box expands to list all the pages in which misspelled words have been found, as shown in Figure 23.10. You can click the Cancel button at any time to stop the checking spelling.

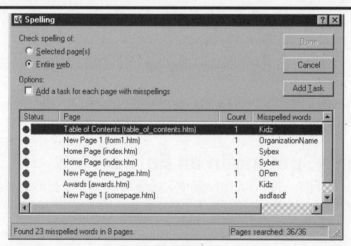

FIGURE 23.10:   Each page that contains a suspected misspelling is listed in the web-wide Spelling dialog box; you can either fix each one immediately or add a task so you can fix it later on.

When the process is finished, you can double-click a page to open it, at which point the spell checker continues as described earlier for a single page. When you're finished with one page, you're given the option to open the next one and continue.

You can also choose to return to a page later by selecting the page in the list and clicking the Add Task button. A new task will be added to the Tasks list that reminds you to check the spelling on that page.

FINDING OR REPLACING TEXT

Suppose the Widget Company decides to change its business focus and create a new image, including changing its name to the Technical Tools Company. Even though you redesign the Web site to reflect the company's new image, you also want to make sure that the company's online presence is maintained through the transition so that visitors to the site aren't disappointed. You need to find every occurrence of *Widget* in every page in the web, and replace it with *Technical Tools*.

Once again, FrontPage can come to your assistance by providing another set of tools that you undoubtedly already use on a regular basis in your word processor—the Find and Replace commands. You use these commands to seek out a word, sentence, or just a few characters in the document, and to replace text with other text. Like the spell checker in FrontPage, the Find and Replace commands can act on the active page of the Page view or on every page in your entire web.

Finding or Replacing Text in the Active Page

Select Edit ➢ Find to find all occurrences of text you specify in either the active page or in all pages in your web (that procedure will be discussed a little later). Enter the characters you want to find in the Find What field of the Find dialog box (shown in Figure 23.11). There are several options you can use to refine your search:

▶ You can find the specified characters in the current page or in all pages in the web.

▶ You can select the Find Whole Word Only option to specify that the characters should be found only when they are a complete word.

▶ You can select the Match Case option to specify that the case (UPPER or lower) exactly matches the case of the text you entered.

► You can also choose to search up or down the page, starting from the current cursor location.

► When you're displaying a page in the HTML view, you can use the Find in HTML option to search through all the HTML code that underlies your page, allowing you to find, for example, all occurrences of a <B> or <HR> tag.

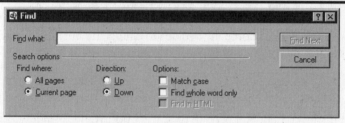

FIGURE 23.11: While in Page view, the Find dialog box lets you search for text in the current page or in all pages in the web.

To begin the search in the active page, click the Find Next button. The first occurrence of the specified text is selected in the page. At this point you can:

► Click Find Next to find the next occurrence.

► Click Cancel to close the Find dialog box.

► Click on the page so you can continue to work in it, perhaps to edit the text that was found. The Find dialog box remains open.

Select Edit ➣ Replace to specify the text to search for as well as the text with which to replace it. If you leave the Replace With field empty, the text that is found is deleted. You perform the Replace operation using three buttons in the Replace dialog box:

► Click Find Next to find the next occurrence of the specified text.

► Click Replace to replace the current occurrence, then move on to find the next occurrence.

► Click Replace All to replace every occurrence of the text.

TIP

Practice safe computing by saving the page before using the Replace All command on the entire page.

When you're finished finding and replacing text, you can click on the page to leave the dialog box open and continue working on the page, or click the Cancel button to close the dialog box and return to the page.

Finding or Replacing Text in the Entire Web

The process of finding or replacing text in all or selected pages is very much like the spell-checking process described earlier in "Checking spelling in an Entire Web." If you want to check just a few pages, first select them in Folders view. Then choose Edit ➤ Find or Edit ➤ Replace, and choose either the Selected Pages or All Pages option.

This time, instead of seeing the matching text that is found, you'll see a list of all the pages that contain that text. As with the web-wide spell checking (look back at Figure 23.10), you have two options. You can double-click a page to open it and then decide whether or not to replace each occurrence of the text in that file, or click the Add Task button to create a reminder task for a page so you can return to it later on.

NOTE

When you double-click a page to replace text within it, the Replace command does not automatically replace the text it finds; you can verify each change within the page itself so you can confirm the changes.

WHAT'S NEXT?

Now that you have a basic knowledge of FrontPage under your belt, let's take a look at some inexpensive but powerful tools you can use for designing your Web site. Chapter 24, "Other Web Page Building Products," will introduce you to a wealth of Web-design products that are available as freeware and shareware.

Chapter 24

OTHER WEB PAGE BUILDING PRODUCTS

This chapter takes an introductory look at the wide array of products available for you to start building Web pages quickly and cheaply. As you explore the vast inventories of Web page creation tools available online, you should begin to develop a good idea about what's worth downloading and what's not. You'll also learn who's behind the ratings guides and what they should mean to you.

This chapter concentrates on cheap alternatives to some of the more expensive Web page creation software packages. It is important to note that any shareware that you download and use should be purchased (usually very inexpensively), but freeware is always free.

As you'll discover, creating and managing a Web site can be a surprisingly inexpensive and easy process. And just because a tool is cheap, that doesn't mean that it's not powerful. You'll also find that a number of Web page creation tools function similarly; once you learn the basics of one, there's a good chance that others may use some of the same functionality concepts.

Note that many software designers offer "previews" of their products (sometimes called beta versions), so don't be afraid to try out something you might otherwise hold off on purchasing.

You may find that a unique animation tool or page-counter offers something specific to your site that even the more expensive software packages can't. Happy hunting!

YOUR FIRST SHAREWARE SEARCH

The old saying goes that there are two kinds of information: the kind you know and the kind you know how to find. Navigating the Internet in order to find the most effective yet inexpensive Web page creation tools can be a daunting task. But, luckily, most search engines now are designed to actually make some sense of what's out there. Yahoo!, Excite, HotBot, and many more all maintain hierarchical lists of the kinds of shareware that will have you designing and posting your Web page in no time. Table 24.1 lists some popular shareware sites.

Be sure to check out the "top 10" kinds of lists, too, which generally list the most popular (and, likely, most reliable) shareware and freeware that others have been downloading.

TABLE 24.1: Some Popular Shareware Sites

ADDRESS	DESCRIPTION
Shareware.com www.shareware.com	A searchable shareware database of software files from the computer network CINET.
Download.com www.download.com	Another good shareware directory from CINET.
Jumbo! www.jumbo.com	A searchable database that includes freeware and shareware for Windows, DOS, Mac, OS/2, and Unix.
SoftSeek www.softseek.com	Shareware, freeware, software reviews, and more.
Super Shareware www.supershareware.com	A directory of shareware applications.
Dave Central Shareware Archive www.davecentral.com	A highly navigable collection of Internet software for Windows and Linux users.
Rocket Download www.rocketdownload.com	

Many of the programs have screenshots, reviews, author information, and a threaded discussion area. All programs are on servers that assure fast, complete download.

As previously mentioned, if you end up using some of the programs you've downloaded, be sure to pay the usually modest fee the authors charge (often between $5 and $25). This encourages them to keep creating better versions of the shareware you'll come to use and love.

RELYING ON RATINGS GUIDES

The ratings guides you'll find can be very useful in your attempts at weeding through the multitudes of available software out there. Remember that almost all are not affiliated with the software they're reviewing, so you can, for the most part, be assured of receiving unbiased information (whether or not you agree with them is another matter). Also remember that the guides have a vested interest in you visiting their site, not in the success of the shareware they're reviewing.

It's usually a safe bet to try out some guides that are affiliated with computer magazines. ZDNet, for example, is the online publishing arm of magazines like *PC Week, PC Magazine,* and *Macworld,* among others. ZDNet maintains a testing lab that inspects freeware and shareware and publishes its results for you before you download (www.zdnet.com).

FREEWARE THAT'S REALLY FREE

Aside from the computer you're working on—unless you create your Web pages from one of those 24-hour copy places that have computers—it is possible to create a Web page for almost nothing. Every Web designer should probably get at least one freeware HTML editor, such as HoT-MetaL Pro (Windows) or BBEdit Lite (Macintosh). Both of these wildly popular freeware programs are available at www.download.com.

HTML editors make the repetition that accompanies HTML markup a much less tedious task. You can add tags via keyboard shortcuts, pull-down menus, or buttons, all of which help to cut down on mistakes.

For a truly incredible selection of wallpaper, buttons, clip art, templates, animations, Java applets, and even more freeware, be sure to check out awg.virtualave.net/topsites2/index.shtml. Here, you'll find the Freebies Top 99 freeware list (see Figure 24.1) that updates every 30 minutes and resets every seven days.

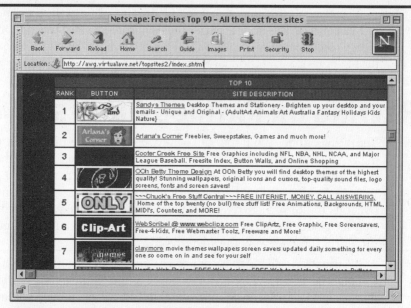

FIGURE 24.1: The exhaustive Freebies Top 99

RCEdit

Although created for more advanced users, RCEdit provides a wide assortment of wizards to help out burgeoning Web page designers. Features like toolbars and browser windows also make this approach to HTML editing relatively easy.

Beginners, though, should really benefit from the wizards, which cover image links, scripts, and tables. There is also an extended find/replace feature, a special character palette, and the ability to create a template from your current file. Particularly helpful is easy access to three components that you may find yourself using quite often: Notepad, Calculator, and your Web browser.

The documentation is very helpful, too. Oh yeah, and it's free. Go to www.zdnet.com/downloads/, and type **RCEdit** into the search engine.

Web Page Creation Shareware and Inexpensive-ware

The following section discuss shareware and other reasonably priced products that are currently downloadable and should help you get started on creating a Web page quickly and cheaply. This list should be considered a good starting point, but is by no means a complete index of what the wide world of downloads has to offer.

8Legs Web Studio

Web Studio is a Web publishing application that doesn't require that you know anything about HTML to get started on your site. This program uses a simple drag-and-drop format that lets you easily work between the Web site you're working on and the elements on your hard drive or other areas where you might store graphics, like CD-ROMs or Zip disks. The HTML tags are hidden, so you won't be confused by complicated syntax that sometimes makes creating Web pages more difficult than it should be.

Web Studio also includes a feature that lets you add reusable components from other Web sites simply by dragging a block of text from a Web page directly into the work area. It's also easy to preview the site as you work by using either Microsoft's Internet Explorer or Netscape Navigator. Best of all, a very helpful tutorial gets you up and running quickly.

Version 1.0 of the full shareware release is from Foghorn Software, its file size is 2.84 MB, and it requires Windows 95. Go to www.zdnet.com/downloads/internet/publishing_tools.html and type "Web Studio" into the search engine.

HomeSite

A mainstay for serious HTML Web authors everywhere, HomeSite has forged a reputation for providing one of the best HTML editors available, and has now successfully made the leap into WYSIWYG (what you see is what you get) territory. Its list of tools and wizards alone is nearly worth the download and rivals some of the best editors available.

Support for nearly every HTML tag imaginable is built into HomeSite, as is a link verifier, a tag validator, and one-click integration with Macromedia's Dreamweaver. The wizards also cover style sheets, image maps, JavaScript, tables, frames, and more. The support documentation is extremely useful and includes sections on HTML tags and general Web page design.

One of HomeSite's most interesting features, though, is something called a Tag Insight button. This innovation tells the editor to take an educated guess at what tag or attribute you'll want next. For example, after each paragraph, you might want to insert a new heading or paragraph tag.

The demo version of the latest HomeSite is free, but the retail version costs $89.99—which is still relatively cheap in comparison to other HTML editors that don't do nearly as much. Check out HomeSite at www.zdnet.com/downloads/internet/publishing_tools.html. Type **HomeSite** into the search engine for the most recent version.

WEBalley

WEBalley is a Web site that includes a comprehensive array of Web publishing tools, tutorials, design tips, and numerous resources to help start your pages out on the right foot.

The site, run by Gerben Hoekstra, also includes a feature called "Web Announcer," which submits your Web site to about 72 search engines with a few easy steps. Hoekstra also provides a thorough guide to downloading Internet software and even a page wizard that creates a sample homepage for you instantly. Check out WEBalley (Figure 24.2) at www.weballey.net.

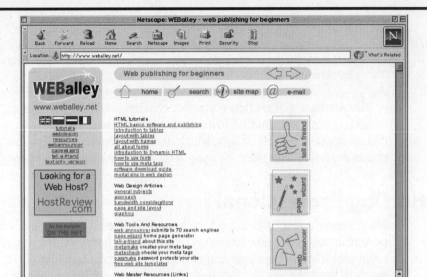

FIGURE 24.2: WEBalley, a comprehensive site for beginning Web page builders

Adobe LiveMotion Beta

If you really want to take your Web site to the next level quickly, you may want to try out Adobe's LiveMotion, which enables you to create interactive graphics and even introduce animation and sound into your Web pages.

LiveMotion allows you to create everything from individual graphic elements to complete Web pages, and lets you export graphics in a wide range of formats, including GIF, JPEG, PNG, and SWF. Although it may be somewhat advanced for beginners, the program is still worth taking a look at, if only to demonstrate the potential for Web graphics. You'll also have access to a comprehensive tutorial, which you can download or follow along with online.

The product is now available as a public beta for Macintosh and Windows, and it will carry an estimated street price of $399 when it is released later in 2000. Fill out the short form at www.adobe.com, go to the "Download" area, and get started adding dynamic, live graphics to your Web creations.

NOTE

Many software manufacturers offer free beta or demo versions of their products — the cheapest of the cheap ways to take advantage of opportunities to try before you buy.

The Adobe site also offers a number of other useful Web resources. At its Web Center, you can find features, articles, tutorials, advice columns, and an impressive Web Gallery, which demonstrates the creative things others are doing with their Web pages (using Adobe products, of course).

HotDog Professional

Many people swear by HotDog Pro. As an HTML editor, it is an incredibly powerful tool, and it now has many new features that make the program more user-friendly than ever. Since Web pages can contain literally thousands of lines of code, HotDog has a feature that enables you to open large text documents and quickly locate the code you need to edit.

HTML is now no longer just line after line of complex text. With HotDog's HTML Navigation View, you can work with your page's elements within a simply structured tree view. An easy to use set of wizards is one of the best new features of this latest version, which lets you design entire site structures with a simple point and click. You can also import style sheets and apply them to your original work.

Check out some of the current users' testimonials at www.sausage .com and it will be hard not to investigate this product further, especially if you want to approach Web page design from an HTML perspective. You can download HotDog Professional 6.0 (see Figure 24.3) for a free 30-day trial. After that, the U.S. version is $99.95, available on the Web.

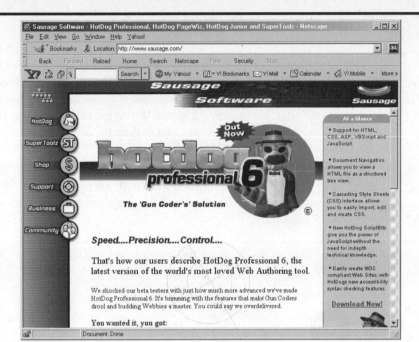

FIGURE 24.3:   You'll find a serious HTML editor in HotDog Professional.

HotDog Junior

How about one for the kids? HotDog Junior is a very simple, kid-friendly Web design tool that helps youngsters age 6 and up build their first Web page in minutes.

Junior guides kids through a four-step process and at the same time, educates them about basic Web page creation. Neat sound effects make HotDog Junior a great introduction to cyberspace for kids. The 30-day trial is free; after that, registration is $39.95 (www.sausage.com).

Cool Page

If simple dragging-and-dropping is the way you want to go, check out Cool Page (see Figure 24.4). In terms of technical know-how required to get a Web page up and running, this product is at the other end of the spectrum from HotDog. Cool Page has a WYSIWYG format that allows you to drag and drop almost anything into the layout area. And then by simply pushing a Publish button, you can automatically upload your site to the Internet.

The program also contains unlimited undo and redo functions, which allows you to go back to how your page looked at any point during the design process. With the latest version (2.1), you also get expanded image control capability.

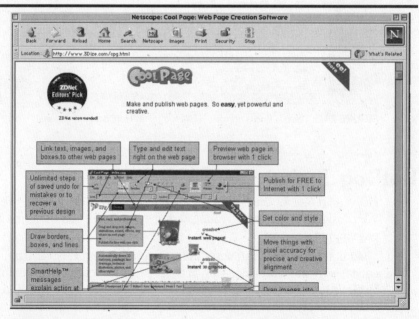

FIGURE 24.4:   Cool Page emphasizes its highly flexible drag-and-drop features.

You can download a free, fully functional version of Cool Page at www.3Dize.com/cpg.html. But for just $28, you can get the full standard version of the program, which includes full technical support, the ability to use all the typefaces in your computer, and free future upgrades.

CoffeeCup HTML Editor

Even though this product is considered a non drag-and-drop HTML editor, you don't have to know one line of code to get started on your Web page using CoffeeCup.

This enormously popular editor seems to be designed for beginning site designers who may desire suggestions regarding text color, background color, heading sizes, and so on. It's also relatively simple to start using animated GIFs, Java, and interesting backgrounds. The Hot Stuff menu is a group of preformatted HTML tricks that add frames, image maps, and page formatting—again, all without having to learn any code whatsoever.

You'll likely want to add some images, and with the latest release, you're able to choose from a library of around 100 animated GIFs and 30 backgrounds. CoffeeCup also contains a built-in Web page viewer, so you can monitor your work as you go.

Registering your download of CoffeeCup gets you an additional 10 JavaScripts and another five VBScripts, reason enough alone to pay the $30 shareware fee. Check it out at www.coffeecup.com.

The one component that CoffeeCup HTML Editor lacks is an FTP client, so that's where CoffeeCup Direct FTP comes in. This bit of shareware allows you to edit HTML directly on the server you're using to host your Web site, and you can even back up your site with a click of the button. Previewing images directly on the server is a neat bonus, as are some other unique features for an FTP client, like find-and-replace, a built-in list of HTML tags, and even page wizards.

The shareware version is fully functional and is good for 30 days; after that, registration costs $30.

Alchemica WebSite

This Web site development tool is interesting because the company wants to make sure you know that this is *not* just an HTML editor. Alchemica lets you use the graphics creation tools you already own to build and publish your Web pages.

The folks at Alchemica maintain that their product does two things that make managing a Web site the most time-consuming and nerve-wracking: managing your files and getting them to the server. The latest version keeps track of what files you've changed (sending only those to the server, if you want), uploads files, and sets access permissions.

Although this product contains what could be considered a "suite" of Web development utilities, it is actually a seamless, single application that also lets you publish content to CD-ROM. The full version includes the HTML Editor, Image Map Editor, FTP Session, and Telnet. But the great thing is that if you've really gotten to like HotDog's editing capabilities, for instance, you can just plug that in to Alchemica's interface.

You can try Alchemica WebSite (http://24.93.29.58/Alchemica/) for 15 days for free. After that, you can purchase it online, over the phone, or through the mail for $29.95.

USING WEB GRAPHICS TOOLS

There are lots of tools available on the Web that you can use to spice up your Web pages with interesting and useful graphics. The products listed in Table 24.2 will give you a good start, but there are many more products out there to be discovered.

TABLE 24.2: Some Web Graphics Tools to Get You Started

PRODUCT	DESCRIPTION	ADDRESS
1 Cool Button	Create a diverse array of button styles.	www.buttontool.com/
CuteMap	Create image maps for your Web site.	www.globalscape.com/
Image Converters	Incorporate JPEG, GIF, PCX, PNG, and BMP into your Java Applets.	www.iba.com.by/
Advanced GIF Optimizer	Make your GIF files smaller without losing quality.	www.gold-software.com/
Advanced Batch Converter	Convert graphic files one-by-one, or in batches.	www.gold-software.com/
Ulead SmartSaver Pro	Optimize graphics and animation for the Web.	www.webutilities.com/
Ulead PhotoImpact Viewer	View and convert between image types.	www.webutilities.com
CompuPic	Do just about everything with just about every graphic format.	www.photodex.com/
LView Pro	View and edit images in a variety of formats.	www.lview.com

WHAT'S NEXT?

This chapter has given you a quick overview of the many Web page building products available as shareware or freeware. Chapter 25, "Wowing Them with Design," will give you some pointers for using the tools and products we've been talking about to design a killer Web page.

Chapter 25
WOWING THEM WITH DESIGN

N ow that we've spent the last few chapters teaching you the HTML elements, features, and tools you'll use to create Web pages, we'll give you perspective on the overall design process. The most successful approach to designing Web pages encompasses four key principles: Keep it logical, simple, compatible, and accessible.

You'll want to set your Web site apart from the pack and make it attractive, but you'll probably have to make some compromises along the way. HTML can't do everything, and there are some sensible reasons for keeping Web pages fairly simple. A good design places content above flashiness. The best Web sites have achieved a balance between attractiveness and simplicity.

Adapted from *HTML 4.0: No experience required,*
by E. Stephen Mack, Jannan Platt Saylor
ISBN 0-7821-2143-8   677 pages $29.99

USING LOGICAL DESIGN

One of HTML's weaknesses is that it will do exactly what you tell it to do. For example, if you accidentally omit a necessary portion of HTML, your page may not display at all, even if your text is perfectly ordered on the page. (At the end of this chapter, we'll talk about how to validate your pages in order to prevent errors like this from undermining all of your hard work.)

You can also easily create a Web site with pages that illogically connect to pages and pages and yet more pages, until your readers are lost in a confusing maze.

The simplest method for a first go-round with Web page design is to work with a logical structure. For most sites, this means using a top-down approach with clear subpages and then topic-level pages not more than four levels deep from your main page. Designing by these rules allows you and your visitors more navigational control—a good trick to master from the outset. As you explore more complexity in your designs later on, you'll have mastered the skill of creating pages that appear simple but are actually rather complex.

Planning Your Web Site

Many excellent Web sites started as just a sketch on a napkin. The creators had a flash of inspiration and drew out their ideas for different pages and design elements. From there, they developed an outline of their site. Then they tied it all together by creating test pages and building the site from the top down.

You should do the same. Start by spending some time exploring the Web. Pay attention to what designs you like, which ones don't work, and why you think they fall short. The only way to know what's possible is to spend a lot of time surfing the Web.

TIP

If a flashy design technique is common on the Web, consider avoiding it, because it's probably become a cliché. Far too many sites, for example, use a border of color on the left side containing a list of links—a practical design popularized by CINet (www.cnet.com/) and imitated by many.

Once you have some design ideas, you should set some objectives for your Web site by answering these questions: What do you want to accomplish? Who is your target audience? What elements are critical to include? Where do you foresee problems? How will you express your ideas clearly to your audience? What will be the scope of your Web site? Your design can, and should, evolve as you go along, but it's helpful to make some decisions before you type a single HTML tag. To get started on your outline, try to answer this series of questions:

- ▶ Will your site have a consistent design for every page?

- ▶ If so, does this design include a background image?

- ▶ Does it involve a consistent color theme that's attractive, unique, and (most importantly) easy to read?

- ▶ What kind of navigation device will be used to help visitors move around your Web site (frames, a button bar, a textual list of links, a menu, a sidebar, or some combination of these)?

- ▶ How often will you update your site?

- ▶ How can you make visitors feel welcome?

- ▶ How will your design include interactivity (for example, forms, e-mail, chat rooms, scripting)?

- ▶ How will you generate design ideas to get your message across?

- ▶ Will your site have a consistent writing style?

You can achieve consistent formatting on your Web site by choosing a common theme in your backgrounds, menus, writing style, and other design elements. If you use the same background theme for all of your pages, for example, your readers will feel comfortable with the boundaries of your pages. Choosing an external link will lead to a different background image or theme—so your audience will immediately sense that they've surfed beyond your pages. A consistent writing style is another way to make your readers feel more comfortable with your content.

These consistent elements don't need to be complex or time-consuming to create. You can gain control over your readers' comfort factor with a few simple and consistent formatting techniques. The Literary Kicks site (www.charm .net/~brooklyn/) uses a traditional and clean style with hyperlinks embedded in the text. Literary Kick's editor, Levi Asher, uses one simple bottom-of-the-page menu link that takes you back to the home page.

In contrast, HotWired (www.hotwired.com/) uses fresh, simple, and brightly monocolored backgrounds and text links along with simple graphics. Both sites value content over flashiness, and the choice of format is sympathetic to their content.

TIP

For information on how to create an interesting page that's not annoying, try Jay's Crafting A Nifty Personal Web Site (www2.hawaii.edu/jay/styleguide/). For what you *really* shouldn't do, check out Web Pages That Suck (www.webpagesthatsuck.com/). Some graphic design tutorials, like Lance Arthur's Design Tank (www.glassdog.com/design-o-rama/designtank.html) and the Yale Web Page Guide (info.med.yale.edu/caim/manual/), offer excellent page design techniques but neglect accessibility to a wide audience.

Drawing a Map

Your next step is to create an organizational map of some sort. This can be in the form of a list or a sketch that shows all of the levels and major sections of your Web site (see Figure 25.1).

For each type of page you plan to include, sketch it out on paper. When inspiration strikes, be sure to write your ideas down right away (a napkin will do fine).

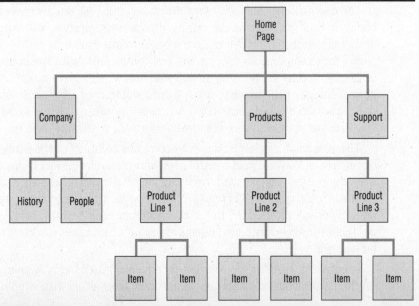

FIGURE 25.1: Drawing a map of your site

Starting Simply

Starting simply keeps the process fun. After you've developed some basic objectives, created an outline, and sketched out a map, you may want to start with some of the ideas included in this book.

TIP

Keep in mind that commercial Web design is work, but personal Web design is often play. As Howard Rheingold of Electric Minds (www.minds.com/) wrote, "After a false start at HotWired, I went home and got sucked into updating my home page on a daily basis. It's hard to have more fun than that!"

Your design should favor the top-down approach, where the more general pages lead you to the more specific (see the next section). You can also view the HTML source while you're Web surfing and try out someone else's Web page as if it were a template. If you use this technique, you'll have to resist the temptation to plagiarize.

You can always make your pages more complex after your site is up and running. A simple page can be redesigned with less effort later. Our favorite thing about simple page design is that it can usually handle browser upgrades and technology changes easily.

In many cases, a simple white background is much more attractive than a more complicated background image. Not only is a plain, white background faster, but it usually shows off your images more cleanly. People are used to reading black text on a white background.

Also, a simple page is often quick to load. Web surfers are extremely impatient; if they have to wait more than a few seconds to see your page, then you run the risk of them surfing on to the next site.

Using a Top-Down Approach

Most Web sites have a single *home page* that acts as an index to the rest of the site. You can think of this page as the front door or cover page that lets visitors in. Once inside, they can decide where to go next by choosing from the list of options. Each subpage has more choices, which lead to more and more specific pages. As each page is chosen, the surfer has gone from the top-level page of the Web site, which is general, down to lower and lower subpages, which are more specific.

As you can imagine, creating a complete Web site this way is a lot of work. You'll have to create one top-level page (and since it's the first page that most visitors will see, you'll want to give it the best design you can), and several level-two *subject pages*. For each subject page, you may need to subdivide into several specific level-three *topic pages*. And each topic page may have several level-four *item pages*.

There's no way to automate the creation of each of these four designs—you'll have to create the design yourself. Once you've created a sample page for each of the four designs, you should spend some time testing the design in several browsers; with trial and error you'll finalize your design.

Suppose you have four subjects, each with three topics, and each topic with five items. This means you'll create one home page, four subject pages, 12 topic pages, and 60 item pages, for a total of 77 pages. Bearing that in mind, you'll want to create a design that's simple enough to prevent you from spending too long on each page, yet complete enough that you have a compelling result, as well as all of the information that each page needs to contain. Now you need to create the 77 pages...which can be extremely time-consuming.

TIP

To avoid frustration, set a time limit, or a session goal, when you start to work on your pages. Remember to try to have some fun—that way, you'll be motivated to come back to revise your pages when your readers need you.

You can investigate using one of the HTML-creation tools to automate some of the work of creating the pages (see Chapter 21, "Getting Acquainted with HTML, Its Tools, and Its Resources." Alternately, you'll want to create a template (which we'll discuss later in this chapter).

Keeping It Flexible

After you've begun your basic design, it's a good idea to start to think about how you'll expand on this design so your pages will easily adapt to changes and new situations. Keeping your pages flexible will save you a lot of time when you update and redesign them. This also means using a basic design that is readable in different browsers.

You can also start to think about ways to generate new ideas to get your message across. Searching through a stack of magazines is a great way to get a feel for text styles, sizes, colors, and page formatting. Or you might find inspiration in nature. While taking a hike, you can get ideas for shapes and colors that appeal to your senses. You can experiment on your napkin sketch as you continue to develop your design. You can also find inspiration from some idea or process in your daily life. An office party discussion might give you new ideas for starting a chat area. Or maybe you'll create a new page design by reinterpreting the way the grocer stacks the cereal box display. Try breaking your idea down into its components so you can apply it to your design logically and effectively.

TIP

One example of flexibility involves using the same background image for every page. That way, you can give your site an instant facelift later by changing the image but keeping the basic information the same.

Creating Attractive Pages

Everyone has different ideas about Web page design, and it's easy to become intimidated by the work of professional designers. However, there are a few simple ideas to keep in mind that will help make your pages attractive:

- ▶ **Employ white space**   Empty space is a vital feature of every page. Don't crowd too much text or too many images into a small area. Instead, space everything out (use the </P> tag after each paragraph to make sure there's enough vertical space between elements; make sure to use CELLPADDING and CELLSPACING attributes in your tables with a generous value, as well as HSPACE and VSPACE attributes in your floating images). A style sheet that adds margins to a page will benefit a page's attractiveness and legibility tremendously.

- ▶ **Create balance**   Too much white space in one part of the page, or using huge fonts in one area but small fonts elsewhere, will create a page that looks unbalanced.

- ▶ **Use color sparingly**   Too many colors on a single page can look garish. Instead of using many different colors, try to use only a few colors that harmonize well together.

- ▶ **Use different fonts frugally**   Most pages need only two different fonts: one for headings, and another for body text. Perhaps a third font can be used in a logo, as long as it doesn't overwhelm the page. Use more fonts than this and your page risks looking like a ransom note.

▶ **Resist gratuitous decoration**   Avoid any decorative horizontal rule or icon unless it adds real content to a page. Be particularly wary of pointless animation, unnecessary Java applets, irrelevant badges or logos, and other clutter. Some Web designers refer to page decorations like spinning globes and animated mailboxes as "dancing baloney."

Considering Other Web Design Metaphors

Some famous HTML designers advocate "third-generation HTML sites" that use different metaphors for navigation (circles within circles, multi-dimensional hubs, rings, and other new concepts that avoid the standard book-like metaphors often used for Web pages). Some approaches to Web design endorse the concept of tailoring your content to the audience so that a potential client sees a different set of choices and facts on your home page than, say, a relative or friend.

The Web rewards experimentation. But all of these considerations need to be tempered by practical considerations: Is your site comprehensible? Do the metaphors make sense? Will you lose part of your audience if they're confused by your site's ultra-modern design?

WARNING

Some of the new approaches to Web design are impersonal and sterile, as if the site had been designed by a committee instead of by a unique personality. One of the attractions of the Web is its personal face—for example, after reading a technical paper or marketing report, you can usually find the author's home page and learn about his family, hobbies, and interests.

CREATING TEMPLATES

A *template* is simply a file you use as a basis for creating pages. Templates can be mostly complete pages (where only a few words, paragraphs, or images need to change to reflect what the page is about)—such as the personal home page template or the résumé we present in the next two sections. Or a template can be just a basic skeleton of the requirements of a page. (Templates are sometimes called *stub files*.)

TIP

On a Macintosh, you can specify that a document is a template by viewing the template's document information (Command+i) and checking the Stationery box located at the bottom of the info window. On a PC, just make sure to have a backup copy of your template, and save each page that's based on the template with a different filename (using the File ➢ Save As command).

Here's a minimum template that uses the recommended HTML elements for every page:

template.html

```
<!DOCTYPE HTML PUBLIC "-//W3C//DTD HTML 4.0//EN">
<HTML LANG="EN">
<HEAD>
 <TITLE>[Title of Page Here]</TITLE>
 <LINK REV="made" HREF="mailto:[Your E-Mail Address Here]">
 <META NAME="DESCRIPTION" CONTENT="[Describe this page]">
 <META NAME="KEYWORDS" CONTENT="[List keywords, separated by
commas, to ease searching]">
</HEAD>
<BODY BGCOLOR="#FFFFFF" TEXT="#000000">

<H1 ALIGN="CENTER">[Level One Heading of Page Here]</H1>

<P>
[Content of Page Here]
</P>

<HR>
<ADDRESS>
[Your Name Here]<BR>
[Date of Last Change Here]<BR>
<A HREF="mailto:[Your E-Mail Address Here]">[Your E-Mail
Address Here]</A>
</ADDRESS>
</BODY>
</HTML>
```

You'll want to modify this basic template by customizing your name and e-mail address, then save it in your web directory. Once you've gotten the basic template working, try creating a color scheme, adding a logo image, or using a navigation bar. After you've created a basic template for your Web site, start any new page by opening the template and customizing it for the individual page you want to create.

Using a Personal Home Page Template

Here's a typical template for a personal home page that you can use as a basis for your own page:

personal.html

```
<!DOCTYPE HTML PUBLIC "-//W3C//DTD HTML 4.0//EN">
<HTML LANG="EN">
<HEAD>
 <TITLE>[Your Name]'s Home Page</title>
 <LINK REV="made" HREF="mailto:[Your E-Mail Address Here]">
 <META NAME="DESCRIPTION" CONTENT="[Describe your page]">
 <META NAME="KEYWORDS" CONTENT="[List your name and variants,
as well as any nicknames]">
</HEAD>
<BODY>

<P>
<FONT ALIGN="LEFT" FACE="ARIAL" SIZE="+1">Your Name Goes
Here</FONT>

<IMG HSPACE="20" ALIGN="RIGHT" WIDTH="150" HEIGHT="200"
SRC="photo.jpg"
ALT="[complete description here]">

<P>
You can put some text here about yourself. You can write a
few paragraphs about your <A HREF="bio.html">personal</A> and
your <A HREF="professional.html">professional</A> life with
lower-level links to more detailed pages. This design is
structured to be printable so it has the same look as the on-
screen document.
</P>

<P>
A few of your favorite Web sites:

<UL>
<LI><A HREF="www.xxx.com/xxx.html">First favorite site</A>
<LI><A HREF="www.xxx.com/xxx.html">Second favorite site</A>
</UL>
```

```
<P>
Send mail to: <A HREF="mailto:[Your E-Mail Address
Here]">Your name</A>
<BR>
Copyright &copy; 1998, Your name
</BODY>
</HTML>
```

WARNING

This template is intentionally boring. Jazz it up with whatever makes you unique and will interest your friends, family, co-workers, and random surfers.

Using a Résumé Template

Similarly, here's a template for a résumé, which you can customize for your own needs.

resume.html

```
<!DOCTYPE HTML PUBLIC "-//W3C//DTD HTML 4.0//EN">
<HTML LANG="EN">
<HEAD>
 <TITLE>[Your Name]'s R&eacute;sum&eacute;</TITLE>
 <LINK REV="made" HREF="mailto:[Your E-Mail Address Here]">
 <META NAME="DESCRIPTION" CONTENT="[Describe your page]">
 <META NAME="KEYWORDS" CONTENT="[List your name and its vari-
ants, as  well as any nicknames, separated by commas]">
</HEAD>
<BODY>

<CENTER>
<TABLE ALIGN="CENTER" WIDTH="600" CELLSPACING="10">

 <TR>
  <TD WIDTH="100"><IMG ALIGN="LEFT"
  SRC="photo.jpg" HEIGHT="75" WIDTH="100" ALT="[Your photo]">

  <TD ALIGN="CENTER" WIDTH="500"><FONT SIZE="+2">Your
Name</FONT>

 <TR>
  <TD ALIGN="RIGHT"><P><BIG>Objective:<BIG></P>

  <TD><P>To work as a Web page designer.</P>
```

```
<TR>
  <TD ALIGN="RIGHT" VALIGN="TOP"><P><BIG>Education:</BIG></P>

  <TD><P><EM>Bachelor of Science</EM>, <STRONG>University of
  California at Berkeley</STRONG>, Berkeley, CA, 1992.<BR>
  Business Administration, Human Resources.</P>

<TR>
  <TD ALIGN="RIGHT"
VALIGN="TOP"><P><BIG>Experience:</BIG></P>

  <TD><P><EM>City of Redding</EM>, <STRONG>Director of
  Administration &amp; Human Resources</STRONG>, 1992 to
  present.<BR>
  Involved in policy and procedure development, strategic
  planning, training and personnel relations.</P>

<TR>
  <TD ALIGN="RIGHT" VALIGN="TOP"><P><BIG>Contact<BR>
  Information:</BIG></P>

  <TD><P>1594 Court Street<BR>
  Redding, CA 96001<BR>
  Phone: (916) 555-9768<BR>
  Fax: (916) 555-9767<BR>
  E-mail: <A HREF="mailto:[Your E-Mail Address]">[Your E-Mail
  Address]</A></P>

</TABLE>

<P>
<SMALL>References available upon request</SMALL>
</P>

</CENTER>

<HR NOSHADE SIZE="1">

<ADDRESS>
Your Name<BR>
Last updated: April 23rd, 1999
</ADDRESS>
</BODY>
</HTML>
```

NOTE

This résumé uses a table for layout, which is sort of cheating (although you could argue that a résumé is really a type of table). Unfortunately, until style sheets are more widely implemented, the use of tables for layout purposes will continue.

The unaltered résumé template is shown in Figure 17.2.

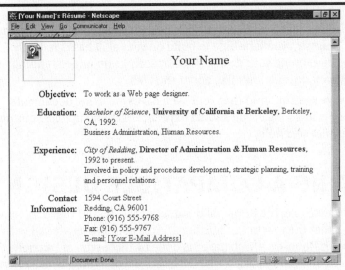

FIGURE 25.2:   The résumé template as displayed by Netscape Navigator (make sure to put your photo in place to avoid this missing image icon)

Revising, Testing, Reading

Now that you've gotten a good start on your basic design, it's time to take a more objective look at your writing and typing. Your readers will appreciate your pages more if all of your links are fresh (no dead-end links) and entered correctly. It's amazing how many good sites have typing errors in their linked URLs. It's a good idea to always double-check your links; link problems are a good way to drive away visitors.

Try to find another set of human eyes to check your grammar and spelling (spell checkers can't catch everything). After you've finished testing your pages, you can always set them aside for a day or two, and then take a fresh look. Try to honestly eyeball your pages for a word, phrase, graphic, or other design element you personally love, but you know isn't effective. Try taking off the first element that catches your eye. Sometimes this trick works to get rid of that last stubborn "little lovely." In this manner, you are able to stay true to your writing without any element overshadowing your content.

Before you publish your pages on the Web, it's important to test the pages under different hardware and software conditions. Try to view your pages in many different browsers and on many different types of computer platforms.

We've found it really helps to "idea surf" the Internet on a regular basis. This way, you'll be able to build on your skill base gradually. You'll also be developing your design voice by seeing and understanding more of what you do and don't like about the Web.

Always keep in mind that your Web pages are living documents. Unlike a printed page, you should expect to visit and update your pages on a regular schedule.

CREATING A COMPATIBLE DESIGN

Tim Berners-Lee, the principal designer of HTML and the Web, remarked in 1996 that the practice of putting a "This page is best viewed with browser X" label on a Web page "is done by those who are anxious to take the community back to the dark ages of computing when a floppy from a PC wouldn't read on a Mac, and a WordStar document wouldn't read in WordPerfect, or an EBCDIC file wouldn't read on an ASCII machine. It's fine for individuals whose work is going to be transient and who aren't worried about being read by anyone." The beauty of the Web is its widespread interoperability. A valid HTML document is truly cross-platform. (*Cross-platform* means the ability to work on many different types of computers and operating systems.)

While most people using the Web currently use either Navigator or IE, there are still many other browsers in use, on many different types of computers. Older computers, such as a Commodore Amiga, and powerful workstations, like an SGI Indy, all use a wide range of different browsers. Millions of people still use Lynx, a text-only browser. Other popular browsers still in use include Mosaic and various browsers included with America Online's software. Any of these browsers will display a standard HTML document just fine. There are even browsers that work on tiny handheld computers or using a telephone touch-tone pad.

Because so many designers use Navigator or IE, they tend to forget about all the other browsers. If you follow their bad example and rely on platform-specific tricks or the proprietary extensions to HTML, you may be excluding a significant portion of your audience. That's why it's important to consider all of the different ways in which your page may be viewed. There are four main areas that are important to consider: color depth, screen resolution, browser features, and bandwidth.

Designing for Different Color Depths

Color depth refers to how many different colors can be displayed on screen at one time (see Table 25.1).

TABLE 25.1: Popular Computer Color Depths

NUMBER OF DIFFERENT COLORS	USES
2	A black and white system
16	4-bit color—in use on the majority of Windows 3.1 systems and older Macintosh systems
256	8-bit color—the default for Windows 95 and older Macintosh systems (for technical reasons, only 216 different colors may be available to the browser)
65,536	16-bit color (also known on Mac systems as "thousands of colors," and on PC systems as "High Color")
16,777,216	24-bit color (also known on Mac systems as "millions of colors," and on PC systems as "True Color")

The two most commonly used formats for images on the Web are GIF and JPEG. GIFs can have a maximum of 256 different colors, while JPEGs are always 24-bit. Color depth can make a huge difference in how a page appears.

So what can you do to accommodate the varying color depths that your audience will be using to read your page? Here are some suggestions:

▶ First of all, you have to have some faith in the browser. Navigator and IE will do quite a lot of dithering automatically, and they do a fair job at making every image viewable. As long as you have enough contrast in your images to support black-and-white systems, you shouldn't have to worry too much.

NOTE

Dithering is the process of adjusting an image to be displayed on a screen with fewer colors than the image contains. Dithering works by substituting the closest available colors and by mixing pixels of different colors to make up an approximation of the original color.

▶ Second, consider making any navigation buttons and logos using GIF files. That way, they're already 256 colors. When you're designing a GIF image from scratch, always use a browser-safe 216-color palette.

▶ Third, always have a text alternative to navigation images somewhere on the page, or as an ALT attribute to the image itself.

▶ Fourth, and most important, it's essential to test your design on black-and-white and 16-color systems *before* you create every page on your entire site. Make sure the essential features of your page still come across. It doesn't matter that the image doesn't look *as* good with fewer colors—as long as the images are comprehensible at 16 colors, you should be fine.

▶ Fifth, try printing out your page. The majority of printers in use around the world are black and white, so your images should be designed accordingly. Since printing out important information is a common activity, this is one practical application of designing enough contrast into your images.

Another point to bear in mind is that graphics usually appear brighter and better on Macintosh screens than on PC screens. So if you use one platform but not the other, make sure to at least borrow a friend's or co-worker's computer (or try to find a library or copy store where they have both PCs and Macs). Monitors vary widely, so the bottom line to consider is that you'll never be able to exactly reproduce the way your Web site appears on your screen on anyone else's computer.

Designing for Different Resolutions

Windows users and Macintosh users can set their monitors to display any of a number of different screen resolutions. If your design is for a specific browser on a screen of a particular resolution with a certain number of colors, then the vast majority of surfers (or potential customers) who visit your page will not see what you may have intended. Table 25.2 lists four commonly used resolutions.

TABLE 25.2: Common Screen Resolutions for PCs and Macs

RESOLUTION	COMMENTS
640 by 480	The default resolution for Windows and Macintosh users; on a PC, this resolution is known as "VGA."
800 by 600	A very common resolution; on a PC, this resolution and the higher resolutions below are sometimes called "SuperVGA" or "SVGA."
1024 by 768	The highest resolution in common use on a PC.
1280 by 1024	Possible with newer monitors and graphic cards; popular with designers who are using very large monitors. Many UNIX work-stations use resolutions far higher than this.

WARNING

If you don't take resolution into account, your audience may not be able to view your page properly.

Just as different color depths alter the appearance of images, different screen resolutions can vastly affect the layout of your page. That's why it's so important to have a flexible design and to test your design at different resolutions.

TIP

On the smaller end, a laptop may have a lower resolution than a desktop PC, and a handheld computer such as the Newton or the Palm Pilot has a resolution of only a few hundred pixels.

The best way to design to accommodate different resolutions is to always specify sizes for horizontal rules, frames, table cells, and style sheet units using percentages. That way, the browser will scale the page appropriately for the resolution of the screen.

Considering Browser Differences

Not only do Navigator and IE have different strengths and approaches to laying out a page, but you also have to consider different versions of Navigator and IE. Some HTML 4.0 features are new and not widely accommodated by earlier versions of Navigator and IE.

Don't get us wrong—there is definitely a good reason to learn about the latest additions to HTML and to use them when you need them. If everyone designed for the lowest common denominator, the Web would never advance. But if your page is rich in graphics, applets, frames, and proprietary HTML, you should be aware that a significant part of your audience won't be able to view your page. For these types of pages, you should strongly consider having text-only pages as an alternative.

TIP

You can use JavaScript or meta refresh to automatically take users of newer browsers to a page that's designed specially for them, while leaving the older browsers looking at the current page. For more information about these tools, see *HTML 4.0 NER* by E. Stephen Mack/Jannan Platt, also by Sybex.

Accommodating Limited Bandwidth

For at least the next few years, the Internet will probably be too slow to render the big images of print magazines, the full-motion video of TV, and the dynamic sounds that we're used to enjoying from a stereo, television, or radio.

A surfer's typical *bandwidth* (a measure of how much data can be transferred through an ISP's connection) isn't always able to transfer its full capacity of data because the load on most ISP's computers is heavy. Also, most modems are too slow to receive the bigger data files quickly, even if the ISP's bandwidth is fast enough to support full-motion, full-screen video.

Because servers are often busy, they can be slow to respond. These response time problems can cause delays that affect the viewing quality of your pages. The most crucial aspect of adding graphics to your page design is addressing the bandwidth problem. You'll need to learn how to keep your image's file sizes to a minimum while keeping the viewing quality to a maximum. Most surfers who use 28.8 modems won't want to wait for more than a total of 50–75K of images per page.

Designing for Full Accessibility

Most Web designers assume that their audience can read—but should they? The newest proposals for Cascading Style Sheets discuss auditory properties for text-to-speech browsers. These types of browsers are useful for all sorts of people in all sorts of situations:

- ▶ People who are blind or visually impaired

- ▶ People whose hands and eyes are occupied but still need to get data from the Web (for example, someone driving a car who wants to hear directions to your location, or a surgeon who's operating on you and needs your medical records)

- ▶ People who are illiterate

- ▶ Anyone who prefers to have information read aloud for any reason

TIP

On the other hand, another important consideration is making sure that people who are deaf or hearing-impaired can still access any information in your multimedia files. Consider having text transcriptions of any speeches or interviews that are available from your site only as audio files.

How can you design your pages to be accessible to all people, to the greatest extent possible, without the need for adaptation or specialized design? To design for full accessibility, try applying the following universal principles:

- ▶ Maximize legibility (avoid color schemes with poor contrast, don't rely on shades of red and green for contrast, and don't use small fonts or extreme font size changes)

- ► Adapt to your reader's pace: Split long sections off into separate pages and offer a choice of length (summary, basic information, full information)

- ► Use a simple, intuitive, consistent design

- ► Don't abuse HTML elements or use proprietary extensions just to get a particular visual effect

- ► Validate pages to minimize errors (see the next section)

- ► Minimize repetitive actions (for example, don't make a visitor always return to a table of contents to move to the next section in a long document; instead, be sure to allow navigation from each section of your document, even if it's three simple buttons for next, previous, and introduction)

You must always trust browsers to do the right thing. If you use valid HTML, then a good text-to-speech browser should be able to render your page properly. But if you rely on a lot of tricks or extensions, then you may start receiving complaints from surfers.

VALIDATING YOUR WORK

The best HTML design is a legal HTML page, since most browsers will be able to deal with it. An invalid page will be treated differently by every browser. You can use a few simple tools to *validate* your pages (that is, check to make sure your pages use valid HTML).

There are two ways to check pages. The first is to go to an online validation site that checks your Web pages (after they've been published on the Web). The second method is to use a local software program that can check the HTML documents on your computer.

We'll look at the online validation tools first. They're simple to use: Go to the tool's URL and simply fill in the form, indicating what the URL of your page is—the tool will do the work from there. There are two popular and useful online validators.

- ► WebTech's Validation Service (`www.webtechs.com/html-val-svc/ index.html`)

- ► A Kinder, Gentler HTML Validator (`ugweb.cs.ualberta.ca/ ~gerald/validate/`)

As its name indicates, the Kinder, Gentler Validator (KGV) has error reports that are a little more helpful, but WebTech's service is a little more flexible (for example, it can check more than one page at once and check fragments of HTML).

In addition, Doctor HTML (www2.`imagiware.com/RxHTML/`) can offer all sorts of useful advice, but it isn't as sophisticated at catching HTML mistakes as the other two validators (since they use an advanced SGML-based tool called `sgmls` to catch mistakes). Doctor HTML is similar in concept to WebLint (`www.cre.canon.co.uk/~neilb/weblint/lintform.html`), which can also point out problems and HTML errors.

There are several useful lists of validation tools, such as the Chicago Computer Society's Suite of Validation Suites (`www.ccs.org/validate/`).

NOTE

A fairly new service for validation is NetMechanic (`www.netmechanic.com/`), which offers a background error check service for your entire Web site's HTML files. Just leave your e-mail address and NetMechanic will send you a report when it's finished.

A few shareware or freeware programs can check the HTML files on your computer. One option is to use the HTML tools discussed in Chapter 21, and another option is to view the source in Navigator (it highlights invalid code by making it blink, although it doesn't catch everything). A more comprehensive tool is the Spyglass HTML Validator (`www.spyglass.com/products/validator/`), available for Windows systems.

TIP

Validate your HTML files religiously. These tools will catch mistakes that might otherwise make your page completely invisible.

In this chapter, we've learned several important approaches to Web page design. We've seen how to create simple, flexible, and attractive pages that are also compatible and accessible. The more you create pages, the better your eye will be for design.

What's Next?

Well, that's it! We've introduced you to the main concepts, tools, and processes of the Internet, and told you about some fun stuff along the way. You should have enough information to connect and explore the Web, as well as publish your own Web site. The appendixes that follow will provide you with reference information to make your browsing and creating more productive.

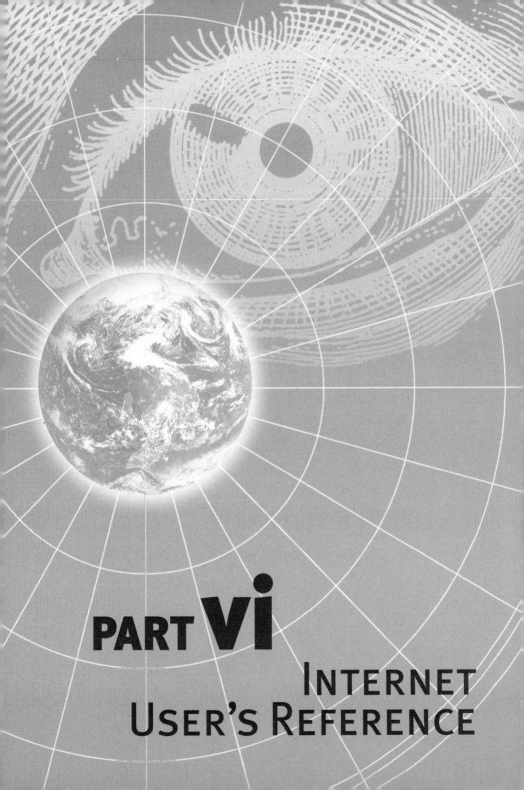

PART **vi**

INTERNET
USER'S REFERENCE

Appendix A

KEYWORDING IT THROUGH AOL

The most challenging thing about keywords is training yourself to type up to three words without letting your thumb hit the spacebar. Okay, there are *two* most challenging things: the first is typing them, the second is finding good ones that'll give you the info you need without spending a half hour just figuring out what search words will work best. Oh, okay, three! ***Three*** most challenging things about keywords: one, the typing. Two, the quality of the end result. Three, finding cool and obscure keywords that will open portals you never knew existed, that will transport you to areas you can enjoy, learn something from, or that just lead you to shake your head at the diversity of quirky things people do.

The keywords I've selected for your browsing pleasure try to meet all of these challenges head on. You'll find some really unusual and interesting areas represented here, as well as some terribly practical areas that you'll turn to again and again. However, I'm not a miracle worker; you will sometimes have to type two or three words without spaces.

Among the serious and useful areas and sites that can help you diagnose a condition, decide how to invest your money, and give you e-access to your political reps, you'll find weird and wonderful sites like these:

steaks Am I the only one that thinks ordering meat online is a weird idea? Omaha Steaks International sure doesn't. Hmm, that sirloin does look pretty juicy...

i cant believe its not butter Who is really going to type this entire keyword in? If you didn't know it existed, would you, on a whim, try out a 6-word advertising slogan just for the heck of it? And you know what's even stranger? This keyword doesn't even connect to a margarine page; it connects you to The Romance Page, which has a small I Can't Believe It's Not Butter advertisement on it. A 50-cent coupon is your pot of gold at the end of this odd rainbow.

Although you may wonder about some of the keywords discussed here, you have to admit that **:)** (Grateful Dead Forum) and **;)** (Hecklers Online) make a whole lot of sense.

orangecurtain Is this Orange County, CA's version of the Iron Curtain?

Free Stuff!

The best thing about the Internet is that there's so much stuff you can get for free. Interactive get-well cards, music, coupons, newsletters, and above all, information. The following keywords offer some of the more tangible freebies and you can score.

Sort-of Free Stuff

AV free gas

free oil change

free credit report

Really Free Stuff

lemon check Get almost any car's title history with CarFax's free Vehicle History Report.

free greeting card The American Greetings online store (where you can also find **free postcards**, **free Christmas cards**, and **free slideshows**)

free love Don't get too excited; the '00s version of free love just involves Love@AOL's free newsletter.

free love personals Here the "free" part describes Love@AOL's Photo Personals and the act of viewing them, nothing more.

free reminder service Be the first one on your block to remember all-important dates.

free webart Banners and bullets and buttons, oh my!

freechristmasscreensavers Deck your PC with merriness from Holiday Downloads.

freegames AOL's online game shows are free of the premium charges tacked on to many excellent online games.

love at AOL coupons Out of romantic ideas? Download or print a Love@AOL coupon to give to that special somebody.

GOOD USES OF ONLINE-NESS

The following sections are what being online is all about. Saving time—and wasting it. Er, I mean, *entertaining* yourself.

For Efficiency's Sake

Who has time to run all of life's little errands? Especially when you're busy online! Here are a few real time savers:

white pages

yellow pages

phonebook Much phone directory help lurks behind this innocent keyword.

find an address Lost your pal? Find their screen name or their Internet e-mail address—even place a personal ad.

bank

estamp Stamps the e-way.

directions Maps and directions for the US and Canada.

personalogic The PersonaLogic interactive guides can help you make decisions on careers, dates, fashion, gifts, mutual funds, presidents, toys, and everything in between.

Of course, you can always try the brand name you're looking for—there may be a keyword for it. Or try **ebay**. If all else fails, try **buy+** or **shop+** the object of your consumption (examples: **shopgolf**, **shop for toys**, even **shoppbs**, PBS.org's store!).

Whiling Away the E-Hours

Here's a collection of sites and areas that are just plain fun. Take the perfect break from your job, your homework, and your housework, with any and all of these keywords. Before we get started, how about some **popsicles** to fortify yourself for some arduous whiling?

Fun and Informative

madwrld Weird news from a weird world (yes, *ours*).

dailyfact A fact a day.

urbanlegend Read all about the circulating tall tales.

truetales Or peruse heartwarming stories of how the Internet has changed some people's lives.

cartalk It's Click & Click, dose cah tawk guys from Bahst'n!

Comic Strips

funnies

backpage

close to home

oliphant

foxtrot

doonesbury

tonyauth

stone soup

bizzaro

dilbert

Mini Contests

qotd Sports trivia question of the day.

graffiti How creative is your digital graffiti?

guesstheyear Guess the year...

guessanimal Guess the animal...

guesstheperson Guess the person...

namethatflag The international channel's Name That Flag contest.

intlwordgame The international language challenge.

Other Ways to Goof Off

daily horoscope

top10 Last night's Late Show Top Ten List.

puzzle Interactive daily puzzles.

amazing Amazing board games, trivia games, bingo, and more.

mindgames Online personality tests can be a bit hokey (I mean, really; I have a hard time believing I'm a borderline lip balm addict...) but they are amusing.

don't worry be happy This is tongue-flappingly silly.

Hangin'

ho Hecklers Online: funny stuff, games, or just plain ol' chat.

hot chats Chat lists.

Games

Time to play! This list includes game portals and other useful areas. Wherever you go, there's always someone ready to challenge you:

game faqs Learn how to play games on AOL.

games Tune into the Games Channel.

ant It's you against the Antagonist Games Network...

paradise Join the many games and trivia contests played in chat rooms and on message boards.

newgames Play free game demos.

premium The guide to AOL's premium games, from bargain family style to spendy Xtreme games. Read all about 'em before running up the bill.

worldplay Play old-time parlor games at no extra cost.

brainbuster Real-time trivia quiz. Aaack!

Still stumped? Try **cheat codes** for video game hints and tips.

Computers and Techie Stuff

Can't live with 'em, can't live without 'em. At least there are some helpful areas (and sites) that will ease your computing traumas.

Around, on, and in AOL

How can you cut your AOL bill? What are those weird acronyms you've seen tossed around in the chat rooms? Do you really have to hear that chipper "You've Got Mail" message every time you log on? The answers to these questions and much, much more can be found in this list of keywords:

annual plans Research AOL's annual pricing plans.

clock Get the time, date, and your estimated time online.

billing Keep tabs on your tally.

byoa Lower your AOL fee by switching to the bring-your-own-access plan.

upgrade Download the latest AOL software.

BPS You have to pay a little for BPS software, but there's much here to enhance AOL!

aol fast facts Get basic information on using AOL.

postmaster Get help and information about your e-mail—AOL *and* Internet—without fear of e-Uzis.

aolglossary Learn the secret meanings behind the acronyms and jargon you've seen thrown around the chat rooms.

tips Get AOL insider tips.

shh Uncover some AOL secrets.

aol sounds Had enough of Elwood Edwards? Customize your Welcome greeting and other AOL sounds with celebrity voices from Rosie O'Donnell to Dennis Rodman.

gpf Find out what those error messages really mean.

buddy Onward to your buddy list!

change password Do it regularly and often.

suggestions Make a suggestion.

tos Bone up on the Terms of Service agreement.

hyperlink scams Read all about current hyperlink scams.

notify aol Alert AOL to a Terms of Service violation.

bien communiquer sur aol If you speak French and you wish to communicate well on AOL *and* you think to type in this entire string, you will be well rewarded.

And if all else fails, **ask the staff**.

As Techie as You Wanna Be

From computer-purchasing tips to virus information to Gopher (the Web still hasn't *completely* taken over...), this list helps you get the most out of your online experience:

cnet Looking to buy? Check **cnet top picks, cnet news, cnet software**...

techie toys Wallow in gadgets for sale at Shop@AOL's Tech Store.

computing new Find out what's new in the world of computing.

netscape Escape the tyranny of Internet Explorer.

gopher Fast, simple, and text-based, gopher isn't as pretty as the Web, but it's great.

virus AOL's Anti-Virus Center gives out the latest in virus and anti-virus information.

And don't forget to try **computer+** or **computing+** the topic you're searching for. Works like a charm!

RELATIONSHIPS ET CETERA

Online romance is here to stay. If you don't know someone who has met his or her sweet thing through the Internet, you will. However, that's not all: you also get the community to support your joys and heartbreak.

Dating

With seven possible screen names, you've got plenty of masks to choose from before entering the ballroom. Just keep those glass slippers on!

flirt! The Love@AOL Flirt! game: need I say more?

score! The Love@AOL Virtual Dating game, not to be confused with **score**, which will give you just the latest sports scores.

instarose Show your hunnybun you're thinking of her or him without blowing your lunch money. Better yet, **sendakiss**!

flowerstore Order all the candy, flowers, and cards money can buy.

holiday dating Simple preparations can help you avoid relationship ruin in the coming holiday season.

weddings Keep up with weekly wedding-related developments at The Knot.

lovelettergenerator Is your sweetie on AOL? Woo him or her with such sentiments as "I know only one word—your name." Guaranteed to bring tears (of some sort or another) to the eyes.

break up letter generator Need to let a former flame down gently? The breakup letter generator would not be the way to do it. (But it sure is fun!!)

Mark your calendars, O seekers of luv; every Wednesday you can **meet mr right** or **meet ms right**, a fellow love-seeker personally picked and highlighted by the lovin' staff at AOL. (If you want to see all the personals, try **love**.)

For Women

In the age of information sickness, no woman can keep up with all the demands family, friends, and work make on her time. Get support and tips for simplifying your crazed life at **de-clutter**. Or expand your network of friends and neighbors at **women talk**. For more ideas, read on:

girls Hey teengurl! Do you need style tips? Or some new tunes? Are you obsessing about why you wore That Outfit in last night's dream? You've come to the right place!

ivillage The Women's Network. Info about news, stocks, diets, dating... what more could a modern woman want?

oxygen A huge, superfun gathering of links for all women.

tapestryofwomen Gifted but unrecognized? Express yourself and your talents on this Online Psych area.

guide to men Yeah, men's minds can be scary, but wouldn't you rather find out what's in them before facing one in real time?

lovestinks Single? Love Stinks will help you make it through the reddest, candiedest, floweriest so-called holiday of the year.

she monster Your "friends" getting you down? Confront them or ditch them.

For Men

for men only Dude! Finally, an area just for men that has everything you need to know about that ancient art of seduction, "feng schwing"; how to decode women; and other manly, manly topics.

men's health Thank goodness there's finally a way to avoid calling the doctor for another 24 hours. Here you can get information about eating disorders, how dads can make a difference, and on all those gnarly things you don't want to admit to worrying about.

bathing suit The Sports Illustrated swimsuit issue. With back issues! Hooee!

Being Who You Are

ages&stages From young adults to the Third Age, there's support and companionship out there for you.

netnoir Everything a black netizen could want for in community.

gay Gay, lesbian, bi, trans: find all the news, chats, personals, and message boards fit to print on this AOL area.

planetout Explore being out on the Web.

break bad habits Remember, M&M's might be better than money (You can't eat a pound of money, can you? Case closed.), but they're still not the answer.

hobbies Plug in to events and news about your favorite hobbies, from aviation to martial arts to scrapbooking.

living large Need someone to tell you again that Rubenesque is beautiful? You've come to the right place.

Advice

First we'll get the sharks out of the way. Legal advice is not free, but lawyers *are* online and keyword-accessible:

lawyer Need a lawyer? The AOL.com legal center is one way to find one.

attorney Join others of your legal ilk here—or eavesdrop (heh heh).

But, oh, there's plenty of free advice online. Plen-ty! Just remember, you get what you pay for:

astrology.net iVillage astrology goes the distance. Free reports, horoscopes, your choice of full-length personalized astrological report; `astrology.net` has it all.

astrology If you need more star-encoded help, try the Astrology & Divination area.

horoscope Get your daily fix here or just figure out how to get through those trouble spots.

netgirl Love advice! Get your love advice here! Then try **dear-suz** for advice for the new age. And then try **drkate**, the resident Love@AOL advice giver.

askdelilah Sex, relationships, kissing, and jealousy: Delilah answers all.

askpeggy Having an extramarital affair? Solicit Peggy's advice.

ask cindy Ask Cindy a yes or no question; she's the magic 8-ball with breasts.

asktodd Those of you trying to juggle real art and that stuff you draw to pay the rent will find a veritable font of information here.

ask a teacher Get the best online homework advice available.

dear addy With advice on selling and advice on buying, Dear Addy has the classified-ad racket down.

dear myrtle Be the life of your family reunion with DearMYRTLE's daily column and genealogy research advice!

ask mom Ask mom a yes or no question; she's the magic 8-ball with cookies.

PRACTICAL STUFF

Whether you're growing up, already a grownup, or both, you need to be practical once in a while. And sometimes it's not too bad, if you have a little help in the form of a keyword to unlock the information you need.

Job Stuff

Not sure where you want to spend your precious 40+ hours per week? Try the interactive **career guide**. Need some extra motivation today? How about some advice on common office predators? Try **careeradvancement**. To play with the big boys and girls, check out **career link**, an executive recruiting service. And take a look at these:

> **monster** Monster.com has hunkered down, in a monstrous sort of way, on AOL. You benefit from nationwide job listings and other online career services. You can also opt for a **job alert** by e-mail every time a new job in your field of interest is posted.

> **dull resume** Before you send yours out, take a gander at these dos and don'ts.

> **post a resume** Learn all about e-izing your resume and splashing its pixels across the net.

> **research a company** What it sounds like, but cooler; not only can you get quotes and newsfeeds, but you can find out what actual employees think!

> **ipo** Latest filings, latest pricings, IPO scorecards, and more; if you know what this all means, this site is for you.

> **industry** More business info.

And if that's not enough for you, try **business+** the topic of your choice: **business chat**, **business know-how**...

Money Money Money Mo-ney!

Just plain **finance** will get you to the AOL Personal Finance area, not a bad jumping-off point—ahem! so to speak—but you'll want to explore the keywords below for the nitty-gritty:

> **ires** If you're not quite sure where to start, try everything on the AOL Investment Research page. If you're the type that can't get enough analysis, you'll love this area.

> **lingo** This encyclopedia of investment terms is perfect for anyone trying to make heads and tails of the whole money-in, money-out scheme.

stock Get your stock quotes, your charts, and the market news; but remember to confirm everything with your financial advisor before investing.

newsbyticker Search very recent company news by ticker symbol.

mktw Do you know what stocks to keep your eye on come Monday? CBS Market Watch does!

downturn Everything you need to know about the downside of market volatility.

fund The Mutual Fund Center offers the best that conservative investing has to offer.

oli The Online Investor gives you the skinny on the market today, the ins and outs of online investing, what's hot and what's not, and even invites your inquiries.

fool The Motley Fools offer pecuniary security in the foolishness of disregarding the "wisdom" of Wall Street. Those boys and girls on Wall Street are still working, aren't they?!

taxlogic Tax Logic presents actual experienced accountants to complete your returns for you as well as give you free expert advice. Not too shabby!

bankrate Thinking of buying one of those big-ticket items—like a house? Check out today's average fixed mortgage rate. Or get some small biz advice, or scrutinize your bank! Could managing your money online get more exciting?

Family

If you're in the process of creating your family, I'm sure you'll be wondering whether there's **sex after baby**. Or maybe you'll be worried about how to help your **octuplets** develop their own identities. And if you don't have a family, you may be feeling **baby lust**—or devoting your attentions to getting little Fluffybuff recognized as the **aol pet of the day**. Whatever your family quest, these keywords may come in handy:

genealogy If the family history bug has bitten you, start searching through the zillions of databases here.

adoption Adopted? Raising a foster child? Thinking about adopting? Books, newsletters, and chatty folks await.

baby names Need ideas? Just want to check whether the name that you're about to saddle another living creature with is hot—or wacky? For your baby's sake, check out this area.

moms online Take a sanity break and see what other moms are doing for fun, relaxation, and for their families.

single parent Step right up to these resources, community, and government benefits for the single parent.

stepfamily Raising her kids? Sharing your room with his son? Learn how to out-Brady the Bradys.

fen From Stuart Little to the SATs, `familyeducation.com` has what you need to encourage your children's learning.

ftn Traveling with kids doesn't have to be a nightmare—not every day, anyway. At Family Travel Network you'll find tips, bargains, baby resorts, and more.

spooky soup Right this way, dearie; the secrets of surviving Halloween can be yours! (Tee hee hee hee hee hee!)

Grrls and guys! Once you've kicked mom and dad offline, check out **tp+** (like **tpfun**, **tpstyle**, **tpbuzz**) for some teen people action or check out **otl**, OnTheLine teen talk from SATs to teen diaries.

Parents! For more wisdom and that valuable community feeling, try **ps+** for Parent Soup areas like **psfun**, **psnewsflash**, **psteens**.... Of course, **child+** and **childrens+** (such as **childrenshealth**, **childrens software**, **childrens books**, **child safety online**) will net you even more of what you seek.

Pets

pet decision guide This interactive Q&A will help you decide whether you've got the vacuuming power for a Persian or the patience for an iguana.

petsforkids An interactive decision guide just for kids and their future pets.

petoweek Kids! Nominate your pet to be AOL's pet of the week!

Not Just for Foodies

You'll find a lot of information at **food+** the area of your concern, such as **food and wine**, **food talk**, **food allergies**, and so on. For some other ideas, try one of these on for size:

find recipes AOL's Recipe Finder lets you search for recipes by name, ingredient, by choosing a type of cuisine—or by finding everything you could make in the precious minutes you've allotted for dinner preparations.

egg The electronic Gourmet Guide knows that a cook can never have too many recipes.

everythingedible This area features recipes from real roadside diners as well as wonderful recipes for in-season fruits and vegetables.

comfort food Mmmm! Juicy meeeatloaf! Coco Cream Piiiie!

coupons Clip coupons for your local supermarket.

If you're having a culinary emergency of the more emotional kind, just dial **eating 911**.

Home

Find some interesting home-related stuff at **home+** such as **homebuilder**, **hometheater**, **homeopathy** (heh heh). Also check these out:

houses How are the interest rates? Looking for a rental? Selling? Everything you need is here at the AOL Personal Finance Real Estate area.

floor plans You too can use the home plans everyone else is using. Or you can use them as a starting point for your dream house—then calculate how much it's gonna take out of your pocket. Then again, there are always the home-improvement books...

seedlings Forget the house; with this seed-starting guide you can build walls of plants.

School

Dad forget his algebra already? Mom too busy to do your science project for you? Turn to **ko homework help** for solace and knowledge. If you're ready to move on, try one of these areas:

funschool School isn't usually much fun, but funschool is! Play interactive, educational games and show your parents that you can have fun while you learn!

college Prep for college with scholarship info, SAT help, and those essential guides to the best 4-year experience for you.

grad school There's a graduate or professional school for just about any inclination, whether it be work avoidance or work enhancement.

coursesonline No good classes in your area? Don't have time to deal with a reality- and interface-based classroom? Try virtual—I mean, *online*—learning.

Dictionaries and Reference Material

Sometimes Word-A-Day calendars just don't cut it when it comes to expanding your knowledge or studying for that English test. Here are some areas and sites to help you out.

dictionary All the entries in the Merriam-Webster Collegiate Dictionary at your beck and call.

children'sdictionary And for the wee ones, the Merriam-Webster Kids Dictionary is just as handy.

thesaurus The Merriam-Webster Thesaurus has those synonyms and antonyms you'll need to cease and desist repetition.

general reference Just when you thought you'd have to go to the library, more references appear!

foreigndictionary Search the language dictionary of your choice or try the computer's hand at translation.

refgeography Facts and fun about geography and maps.

refgovernment Legal issues, best-selling law books (oh boy!), and more.

lexis The Lexis-Nexis case law search engine is online, but not free.

refhistory History isn't just about dates anymore; it now includes such essential items as the paternity test for Thomas Jefferson.

refentertainment How much of a tip should you leave? Is that movie any good? What's the straight dope on that phrase your grandpa always used? Well, type the keyword in and find out already!

scoop Search newsgroups for your topic.

Health

For symptoms, causes, and treatments of what ails you, take an educated guess at what's going on in your body at **sick**. If you already know, try typing in the name of your condition or illness: from **acne** to **aids** to **fibromyalgia** to **std**, you can find most of them on AOL Health. And when you know what you need to fix it, mosey on over to the online **pharmacy**.

medical dictionary Merriam-Webster saves the day! Look up those medical terms your doctor bandies about.

medical reference And if Merriam-Webster doesn't have what you need, try these reference materials.

medline Abstracts of medical research going back to 1966, with the option to purchase full articles.

refhealth Info about your health and the well-being of those you love.

medscape Free to join, free to use, the latest news as well as all sorts of info on your meds.

epills Need aspirin? You got it. Want to know how that new medication is going to affect you? Step right up. HealthCentralRx .com has answers—and plenty of drugs.

smileworks Need a dentist? Ask around the office—or try this dentist-patient matching service.

feng shui A little energy flow never hurt anyone; at the very least you'll get some new redecorating ideas.

Don't fall into the trap of neglecting the mind while curing the body. Online Psych (at **olp**) features numerous useful areas: **olpexperts**, **olpmb** (the message boards), and **olp teen scene** among them.

Politics

Who's doing what in the world of politics? Find out at **politics**. But wait, there's more...

track votes Sign up to receive a weekly e-mail about the votes your congresspeople cast plus notification of what votes are coming up soon so you can tell your reps what you think.

politicsupdate If the daily rags aren't enough, how about hourly updates?

white house questions Each week the White House Democrats and Republicans write separate answers to the five most-asked questions.

elections Who's racing whom? Meet the candidates, read about the issues.

government Government services—such as shopping for surplus goods, the most-wanted list, applying for disaster relief, and NASA research—are all here.

dosomething Tired of this insular virtual world? Do Zine explores doing something in the real world about real issues.

Phew. Need a levity break yet? Take a gander at Mike Keefe's daily cartoon at **politicalcomic**.

HAVING FUN OFFLINE

Sometimes you just have to get away. Whether or not you bring your laptop is your business, but here are some keywords that will help you forget your troubles.

Travel

First, you gotta figure out where to go. Then you can move on to the best way to get there, then where to stay, how to get around, and, most importantly, what to do. Once all the practicalities have been dealt with through easy keywording, you'll be able to relax and do what you're supposed to do on vacation: have fun! Try these out:

destinations A groovy interactive decision-making guide.

exchange rates Converting your bucks to the currencies of the world has never been easier.

it trc Get the lowdown on trip essentials for the independent traveler, then check out **airdeals**.

ta Key into AOL Traveler's Advantage, a discount travel service.

fare aware When are you traveling and to where? Find out how much it'll cost ya. Need **car deals**? While you're at it, check out where you'll be checking in at **lodging**.

airfare Your personal flight booker from **Preview Travel**, where you can also take advantage of the **rentalcarfinder** and the **farefinder**.

insideflyer This may be the frequent flyer hub for you!

lp Tips, maps, and stories for your trip-planning pleasure at the Lonely Planet travel area.

amusement park Your guide to theme parks. If you're not into that kind of park, try **america's parks**.

hidden sf The Untourist guides you to hidden spots in the San Francisco Bay Area, a great find for travelers and locals alike!

If all else fails, try **travel**+ a related word, such as **travelreference** (for geography and maps), **travelers' opinions** (for messages and chat), and **travel bargains**.

Local Info

You can get information on your hometown or hometown-to-be right here. Just type in your city, like **boston**, and press Go. Or type your city's name + that which you seek, as in **sfrealestate**, or whatever. If you want something more general, try typing in your county name to see newspapers, latest news wire updates, travel tips, and more. And then check out everything **digital city** has to say about your town. Also take a look at these:

> **festivals** Grok Digital City's list of local festivals from Albany to Hampton Roads to Washington, DC.

> **localweather** Okay, so it brings you to the national weather area. From here you can get very, very local.

> **traffic** On a heavier note, get useful local traffic information for your morning and evening commute.

> **local twenty dollar** Party all weekend on $20? My first reaction was "Hah! What do I have to do, go *camping*?" But this site does have some interesting ideas and club/bar/movie house/museum recommendations. Don't overlook it.

Entertainment

For your daily R&R, turn to your computer and whip through the keywords below. Somewhere along the way, you'll begin to feel entertained.

Movies

Type in any recent movie name. In return, you get information about the movie, where it's playing, and who's in it. Exciting stuff! Here are some more:

> **movieshowtimes** Get local movie info.

> **indie films** Independent films get noticed.

> **IMAX** The IMAX official site, wherein you can not only buy merchandise but also read about IMAX films and find IMAX films and theaters near you.

> **entertainmentasylum** At Entertainment Asylum you can access new music, hot movies, info about your star crush, and more.

> **newonvideo** Get the scoop on videos.

If your perfect evening involves staying home and slouching in front of the tube, check out **tv+** (**tvchats**, **tvspoofs**, **tvguide**). For some real yucks, check out **tvfamilies** and discover which tv family is most like yours.

Music

It's time to kick it! Yeah! Check these out:

> **concerts** Get concert and tour info on your favorite bands or on all the bands coming to a favorite place near you.

> **music** AOL entertainment offers genre after genre of downloads, news, and featured artists.

> **musichot** What's everyone talking about this week? The message boards have it all.

> **musicweb** Add some new and cool music Web sites to your favorites.

> **musicforce** Before you knock Christian music, think about it: it may be the only way you can get your mother to let you crank rock and roll!

Art, the Arts, Graphic Arts, Whatever...

Expose yourself to a little culture at **theater**: CultureFinder will help you search for arts events near you. Try **rlart** for periodicals, books, and other resources, or look into one of these keywords:

> **artjam** This weekly electronic version of Exquisite Corpse (add your touch to an image and pass it on) is hosted.

> **fontdownloads** Download new fonts! Hot doggie!

> **web art** Spice up your Web page with these free web art items.

Books

Need a literary companion for your commute or vacation? New reading material abounds here:

book of the week Devoured the library? Turn to this area for weekly inspiration.

bookbag The Book Bag brings cool book news to teens.

reading Reading and writing resources for readers and writers—from book reports to research papers.

book reviews Read book reviews and more at this AOL entertainment area.

books to movies Which was better—the book or the movie? Plus lots of information about this often-controversial leap from imagination to reality.

bookworm Great bookish fun for kids!

The Sporting Life

You could type in something obvious, like **sports**—and you could even mistype it **sprots** and get the same results—but for something a little more unusual, here are a bunch of dedicated sprot—I mean *sport*—areas that'll serve up some different but still rather sporting action:

score AOL Sports scoreboards keep you up to date on the real thing.

extreme When football isn't doing it for you anymore, try Extreme Sports: inline skating, paintball, snowboarding...

gs+ Grandstand presents sports from **gscricket** to **gsbaton** (yes, Virginia, there is a Baton Twirling Forum!) as well as do-it-yourself get-involved information.

gsparks Learn about hiking America's Parks.

intl sports The International Sports Forum keeps you current with international sports events from fencing to sumo wrestling.

ntn+ (ntnfootball, etc.) NTN sports presents trivia games where you can test your knowledge of your favorite sport.

fantasy+ Join the fantasy sport team of your choosing—playing **fantasybasketball**, maybe?—and match your sporty know-how against other players.

skiweather Before getting in on some real action, first check the weather reports. Special golf lightning maps are also readily available.

NOTE

Thank you for joining this tour through AOL keywords; I hope you've found it fun and informative. Most of all, I hope you've found a keyword that amused you beyond your wildest dreams—or at least piqued your interest. Don't be afraid to go online and discover more terrific keywords!

Appendix B

HTML MASTER'S REFERENCE

Adapted from *Mastering HTML 4.0*, by Deborah S. Ray and Eric J. Ray

ISBN 0-7821-2102-0   1,040 pages $49.99

HTML Tags and Attributes

This section is a comprehensive reference guide to all HTML tags, including standard tags and those introduced by Netscape Navigator and Microsoft Internet Explorer. For each tag, we've provided sample code and indicated the following:

▶ The version of HTML with which the tag is associated

▶ Whether browsers widely support the tag

▶ Whether to pair the tag with a closing tag

For each tag's attributes, we've provided sample code and indicated the following:

▶ The version of HTML with which the attribute is associated

▶ Whether browsers widely support the attribute

If tags and attributes appear in the HTML 4 standard, in the HTML 3.2 standard, or in the HTML 2 standard, the version number appears next to Standard. We indicate tags or attributes that are specific to a browser, such as Internet Explorer. In general, a variety of browsers recognize technology-specific tags, such as those for frames, and other browsers rarely recognize browser-specific tags. HTML 2 was the first official HTML standard. The number of tags that this standard defined is small compared with what is in use today. HTML 2 did not support tables, client-side imagemaps, or frames. You can safely use all HTML 2 tags and attributes.

HTML 3.2 remains backward-compatible with HTML 2, but provides many new tags. Included in HTML 3.2 is support for tables, client-side imagemaps, embedded applets, and many new attributes that help control alignment of objects within documents. You can assume that most browsers support or soon will support all HTML 3.2 tags and attributes.

HTML 4 remains backward-compatible with other versions of HTML and expands the capabilities to better address multiple languages and browser technologies such as speech or Braille. Additionally, most formatting tags and attributes are deprecated (strongly discouraged) in HTML 4 in favor of style sheets.

Specifying that a tag or an attribute is Common means that approximately 75 to 80 percent of browsers in common use accommodate the tag. All recent versions of both Internet Explorer and Netscape Navigator recognize Common tags and attributes.

We indicate variables as follows:

Variable	What You Substitute
n	A number (such as a size)
URL	Some form of address (as in a hyperlink)
#RRGGBB	A color value or a color name
...	Some other value, such as a title or a name

!

`<!-- -->`

Inserts comments into a document. Browsers do not display comments, although comments are visible in the document source.

Standard: HTML 2
Common: Yes
Paired: Yes
Sample:

```
<!-- Here is the picture of Fido
-->
<IMG SRC="fidopic.jpg">
```

<!DOCTYPE>

Appears at the beginning of the document and indicates the HTML version of the document.

The HTML 2 standard is:

```
<!DOCTYPE HTML PUBLIC
"-//IETF//DTD HTML 2 //EN">
```

The HTML 3.2 standard is:

```
<!DOCTYPE HTML PUBLIC
"-//W3C//DTD/ HTML 3.2 Final//EN">
```

The HTML 4 standard is:

```
<!DOCTYPE HTML PUBLIC
"-//W3C//DTD/ HTML 4 Final//EN">
```

Standard: HTML 2
Common: Yes
Paired: No
Sample:

```
<!DOCTYPE HTML PUBLIC
"-//W3C//DTD/ HTML 4 Final//EN">
```

A

<A>

Also called the *anchor* tag, identifies a link or a location within a document. You commonly use this tag to create a hyperlink, using the

HREF= attribute. You can also use the <A> tag to identify sections within a document, using the NAME= attribute.

Standard: HTML 2
Common: Yes
Paired: Yes
Sample:

```
<A HREF="http://www.raycomm
.com/">Visit RayComm</a>
```

Attribute Information

ACCESSKEY="..."
Assigns a key sequence to the element.

Standard: HTML 4
Common: No
Sample:

```
<A HREF="help.html"
ACCESSKEY="H">HELP</a>
```

CHARSET="..."
Specifies character encoding of the data designated by the link. Use the name of a character set defined in RFC2045. The default value for this attribute, appropriate for all Western languages, is "ISO-8859-1".

Standard: HTML 4
Common: No
Sample:

```
<A HREF="help.html" CHARSET="ISO-
8859-1">HELP</a>
```

CLASS="..."
Indicates the style class to apply to the <A> element.

Standard: HTML 4
Common: No
Sample:

```
<A HREF="next.html"
CLASS="casual">Next</A>
```

COORDS="*x1, y1, x2, y2*"

Identifies the coordinates that define a click-able area. Measure coordinates, in pixels, from the top left corner of the image.

Standard: HTML 4

Common: No

Sample:

```
<A SHAPE="RECT"
COORDS="20,8,46,30"
HREF="food.html">
```

HREF="*URL*"

Specifies the relative or absolute location of a file to which you want to provide a hyperlink.

Standard: HTML 2

Common: Yes

Sample:

```
<A HREF="details.html">More
Info</a>
```

ID="..."

Assigns a unique ID selector to an instance of the <A> tag. When you then assign a style to that ID selector, it affects only that one instance of the <A> tag.

Standard: HTML 4

Common: No

Sample:

```
<A HREF="next.html"
ID="123">Next</A>
```

NAME="..."

Marks a location within the current docu-ment with a name. The browser can then quickly move to specific information within a document. You can link to existing named locations in a document by using a fragment URL, consisting of a pound sign (#) and the name (from within that document), or by using a more complete URL, including a pound sign and a name (from other docu-ments or sites).

Standard: HTML 2

Common: Yes

Sample:

```
<A HREF="#ingredients"
>Ingredients</A><BR><A
NAME="ingredients"><h1>
Ingredients</H1>
```

REL="..."

Specifies relationship hyperlinks.

Standard: HTML 3.2

Common: No

Sample:

```
<A REV="made"
HREF="mailto:bob@company.com">
```

REV="..."

Specifies reverse relationship hyperlinks.

Standard: HTML 3.2

Common: No

Sample:

```
<A REV="Previous" HREF="http://
www.raycomm.com/firstdoc.htm">
```

SHAPE="{RECT, CIRCLE, POLY}"

Specifies the type of shape used to represent the clickable area. SHAPE=RECT indicates that the shape is rectangular. SHAPE=CIR-CLE specifies that the shape is a circle. SHAPE=POLY indicates that the shape is a polygon represented by three or more points.

Standard: HTML 4

Common: No

Sample:

```
<A SHAPE="RECT"
COORDS="20,8,46,30"
HREF="food.html">
```

STYLE="..."

Specifies style sheet commands that apply to the contents within the <A> tags.

Standard: HTML 4

Common: No

Sample:

```
<A STYLE="background: red"
HREF="page2.html">Page 2</A>
```

TABINDEX="*n*"

Indicates where the element appears in the tabbing order of the document.

Standard: HTML 4

Common: No

Sample:

```
<A HREF="food.html"
TABINDEX="4">Food</A>
```

TARGET="..."

Indicates the name of a specific frame into which you load the linked document. You establish frame names within the <FRAME> tag. The value of this attribute can be any single word.

Standard: HTML 4

Common: Yes

Sample:

```
<A HREF="/frames/frame2.html"
TARGET="pages">Go to Page 2</a>
```

TITLE="..."

Specifies text assigned to the tag that you can use for context-sensitive help within the document. Browsers may use this to show tool tips over the hyperlink.

Standard: HTML 4

Common: Yes

Sample:

```
<A HREF="page2.html" TITLE="Go to
the next page">
```

Other Attributes

This tag also accepts the lang, dir, onClick, onDblClick, onMouseDown, onMouseUp, onMouseOver, onMouseMove, onMouseOut, onKeyPress, onKeyDown, and onKeyUp attributes. See the "Element-Independent Attributes" section of this reference for definitions and examples.

<ACRONYM>

Indicates an acronym in a document.

Standard: HTML 4

Common: No

Paired: Yes

Sample:

```
<P><ACRONYM>HTTP</ACRONYM> stands
for HyperText Transfer
Protocol</P>
```

Attribute Information

CLASS="..."

Indicates which style class applies to the <ACRONYM> element.

Standard: HTML 4

Common: No

Sample:

```
<P><ACRONYM
CLASS="casual">HTTP</ACRONYM>
stands for HyperText Transfer
Protocol</P>
```

ID="..."

Assigns a unique ID selector to an instance of the <ACRONYM> tag. When you then assign a style to that ID selector, it affects only that one instance of the <ACRONYM> tag.

Standard: HTML 4

Common: No

Sample:

```
<P><ACRONYM
ID="123">HTTP</ACRONYM> stands
for HyperText Transfer
Protocol</P>
```

STYLE="..."

Specifies style sheet commands that apply to the definition.

Standard: HTML 4

Common: No

Sample:

```
<P><ACRONYM STYLE="background:
blue; color: white">ESP</ACRONYM>
stands for extra-sensory
perception.</P>
```

TITLE="..."

Specifies text assigned to the tag. For the <ACRONYM> tag, use this to provide the expansion of the term. You might also use this attribute for context-sensitive help within the document. Browsers may use this to show tool tips over the text.

Standard: HTML 4

Common: No

Sample:

```
<P><ACRONYM TITLE="HyperText
Transfer Protocol">HTTP</ACRONYM>
stands for HyperText Transfer
Protocol</P>
```

Other Attributes

This tag also accepts the `lang`, `dir`, `onClick`, `onDblClick`, `onMouseDown`, `onMouseUp`, `onMouseOver`, `onMouseMove`, `onMouseOut`, `onKeyPress`, `onKeyDown`, and `onKeyUp` attributes. See the Element-Independent Attributes section of this reference for definitions and examples.

<ADDRESS>

In a document, distinguishes an address from normal document text.

Standard: HTML 2

Common: Yes

Paired: Yes

Sample:

```
I live at:
<ADDRESS>123 Nowhere Ave<BR>City,
State 12345</ADDRESS>
```

Attribute Information

ALIGN={LEFT, RIGHT, CENTER}

Indicates how the address text is aligned within the document. ALIGN=LEFT positions the address text flush with the left side of the document. ALIGN=RIGHT positions the address text flush with the right side of the document. ALIGN=CENTER centers the address text between the left and right edges of the document.

Standard: HTML 3.2; deprecated in favor of style sheets

Common: Yes

Sample:

```
<ADDRESS ALIGN="CENTER">123
Anywhere St.</ADDRESS>
```

CLASS="..."

Indicates the style class to apply to the <ADDRESS> element.

Standard: HTML 4

Common: No

Sample:

```
<ADDRESS CLASS="casual">123 First
Ave.</ADDRESS>
```

ID="..."

Assigns a unique ID selector to an instance of the <ADDRESS> tag. When you then assign a style to that ID selector, it affects only that one instance of the <ADDRESS> tag.

Standard: HTML 4

Common: No

Sample:

```
<ADDRESS ID="123">1600
Pennsylvania</ADDRESS>
```

STYLE="..."
Specifies style sheet commands that apply to the contents within the <ADDRESS> tags.

Standard: HTML 4

Common: Yes

Sample:

```
<ADDRESS STYLE="background: red">
```

TITLE="..."
Specifies text assigned to the tag. You might use this attribute for context-sensitive help within the document. Browsers may use this to show tool tips over the address text.

Standard: HTML 4

Common: No

Sample:

```
<ADDRESS TITLE="Address">
```

Other Attributes
This tag also accepts the lang, dir, onClick, onDblClick, onMouseDown, onMouseUp, onMouseOver, onMouseMove, onMouseOut, onKeyPress, onKeyDown, and onKeyUp attributes. See the Element-Independent Attributes section of this reference for definitions and examples.

<APPLET>

Embeds a Java applet object into an HTML document. Typically, items that appear inside the <APPLET> tags allow browsers that do not support Java applets to view alternative text. Browsers that do support Java ignore all information between the <APPLET> tags.

Standard HTML 3.2; deprecated in HTML 4 in favor of <OBJECT>

Common: Yes

Paired: Yes

Sample:

```
<APPLET CODE="game.class">It
appears your browser does not
support Java. You're missing out
on a whole world of neat
things!</APPLET>
```

Attribute Information

ALIGN={LEFT, CENTER, RIGHT}
Specifies the horizontal alignment of the Java applet displayed. For example, a value of CENTER tells the browser to place the applet evenly spaced between the left and right edges of the browser window.

Standard: HTML 3.2; deprecated in HTML 4 in favor of style sheets.

Common: No

Sample:

```
<APPLET ALIGN=CENTER
CODE=""http://www.raycomm.com/
checkers.class">You lose. Would
you like to play again? Hit the
RELOAD button.<BR></APPLET>
```

ALT="..."
Displays a textual description of a Java applet, if necessary.

Standard: HTML 3.2

Common: No

Sample:

```
<APPLET CODE=""http://www
.raycomm.com/checkers.class">ALT=
"A Game of checkers">We could
have had a relaxing game of
checkers if your browser sup-
ported Java applets. I'll gladly
play with you if you enable Java
applets or upgrade to a browser
that supports Java.</APPLET>
```

CODE="*URL*"

Specifies the relative or absolute location of the Java bytecode file on the server.

Standard: HTML 3.2

Common: No

Sample:

```
<APPLET CODE="http://www
.raycomm.com/checkers.class">
```

Dang! Your browser does not support Java applets. You may want to consider installing a newer web browser.

```
</APPLET>
```

CODEBASE="*URL*"

Specifies the directory where you can find all necessary Java class files on the WWW server. If you set this attribute, you need not use explicit URLs in other references to the class files. For example, you would not need an explicit reference in the CODE= attribute.

Standard: HTML 3.2

Common: No

Sample:

```
<APPLET CODEBASE="http://www
.raycomm.com/checkers.class"
CODE="checkers.html">
```

If your browser supported inline Java applets, you'd be looking at a very attractive checkerboard right now.

```
</APPLET>
```

HEIGHT="*n*"

Specifies the height (measured in pixels) of the Java applet object within the document.

Standard: HTML 3.2

Common: No

Sample:

```
<APPLET HEIGHT="200"
CODE="checkers.class">
```

Since your browser does not support inline Java applets, we won't be playing checkers today.

```
</APPLET>
```

HSPACE="*n*"

Specifies an amount of blank space (measured in pixels) to the left and right of the Java applet within the document.

Standard: HTML 3.2

Common: No

Sample:

```
<APPLET HSPACE="10"
CODE="/checkers.class">
```

Sorry. Due to the fact your browser does not support embedded Java applets, you'll have to play checkers the old way today.

```
</APPLET>
```

NAME="..."

Assigns the applet instance a name so that other applets can identify it within the document.

Standard: Internet Explorer

Common: No

Sample:

```
<APPLET SRC="/checkers.class"
NAME="Checkers">
```

```
</APPLET>
```

PARAM *NAME*="..."

Passes program parameters to the Java applet.

Standard: HTML 3.2

Common: No

Sample:

```
<APPLET CODE="/checkers.class"
PARAM COLOR="red">
```

Since your browser does not support inline Java applets, I win
this game of checkers by forfeit.

```
</APPLET>
```

TITLE="..."

Specifies text assigned to the tag. You might
use this attribute for context-
sensitive help within the document. Browsers
may use this to show tool tips over the
embedded applet.

Standard: HTML 4

Common: No

Sample:

```
<APPLET SRC="/java/thing.class"
TITLE="Thing">
```

VSPACE="n"

Specifies the amount of vertical space (measured in pixels) above and below the Java
applet.

Standard: HTML 3.2

Common: No

Sample:

```
<APPLET VSPACE="10"
CODE="/checkers.class">
```

If you had a Java-capable
browser, you could be playing
checkers!

```
</APPLET>
```

WIDTH="n"

Specifies the width (measured in pixels) of a
Java applet within a document.

Standard: HTML 3.2

Common: No

Sample:

```
<APPLET WIDTH="350"
CODE="/checkers.class">
```

Checkers can be a lot of fun, but
it's more fun if your browser
supports Java. Sorry.

```
</APPLET>
```

Other Attributes

This tag also accepts the lang, dir,
onClick, onDblClick, onMouseDown,
onMouseUp, onMouseOver, onMouseMove,
onMouseOut, onKeyPress, onKeyDown,
and onKeyUp attributes. See the Element-
Independent Attributes section of this reference for definitions and examples.

<AREA>

Defines an area within a client-side imagemap
definition (see the <MAP> tag). It indicates an
area where visitors can choose to link to
another document.

Standard: HTML 3.2

Common: Yes

Paired: No

Sample:

```
<AREA SHAPE=RECT
COORDS="20,8,46,30"
HREF="food.html">
```

Attribute Information

ALT="..."

Provides a textual description for visitors who
have text-only browsers.

Standard: HTML 4

Common: Yes

Sample:

```
<AREA ALT="This blue rectangle
links to blue.html"
HREF="blue.html">
```

CLASS="..."
Indicates the style class you want to apply to the <AREA> element.

Standard: HTML 4

Common: No

Sample:

```
<AREA CLASS="casual" SHAPE="RECT"
COORDS="20,8,46,30"
HREF="food.html">
```

COORDS="x1, y1, x2, y2"
Identifies the coordinates within an imagemap that define the imagemap area. Measure coordinates, in pixels, from the top left corner of the image.

Standard: HTML 3.2

Common: Yes

Sample:

```
<AREA SHAPE="RECT"
COORDS="20,8,46,30"
HREF="food.html">
```

HREF="URL"
Identifies the location of the document you want to load when the indicated imagemap area is selected.

Standard: HTML 3.2

Common: Yes

Sample:

```
<AREA SHAPE="RECT"
COORDS="20,8,46,30"
HREF="food.html">
```

ID="..."
Assigns a unique ID selector to an instance of the <AREA> tag. When you then assign a style to that ID selector, it affects this instance of the <AREA> tag.

Standard: HTML 4

Common: No

Sample:

```
<AREA ID="123">
```

NOHREF
Defines an imagemap area that does not link to another document.

Standard: HTML 3.2

Common: Yes

Sample:

```
<AREA SHAPE="RECT"
COORDS="20,8,46,30" NOHREF>
```

NOTAB
Excludes the imagemap area from the tab order.

Standard: Internet Explorer

Common: Yes

Sample:

```
<AREA SHAPE="RECT"
COORDS="20,8,46,30"
HREF="food.html" NOTAB>
```

SHAPE="{RECT, CIRCLE, POLY}"
Specifies the type of shape used to represent the imagemap area. SHAPE=RECT indicates that the shape of the imagemap area is rectangular. SHAPE=CIRCLE specifies that the shape of the imagemap area is a circle. SHAPE=POLY indicates that the shape of the imagemap area is a polygon represented by three or more points.

Standard: HTML 3.2

Common: Yes

Sample:

```
<AREA SHAPE="RECT"
COORDS="20,8,46,30"
HREF="food.html">
```

STYLE="..."
Specifies style sheet commands that apply to the imagemap area.

Standard: HTML 4

Common: No

Sample:

```
<AREA SHAPE="RECT"
COORDS="20,8,46,30"
HREF="food.html"
STYLE="background: red">
```

TABINDEX="*n*"

Indicates where the imagemap area appears in the tabbing order of the document.

Standard:	HTML 4
Common:	Yes

Sample:

```
<AREA SHAPE="RECT"
COORDS="20,8,46,30"
HREF="food.html" TABINDEX=4>
```

TARGET="..."

Identifies which named frame the linked document selected should load. For example, when visitors select an area within an imagemap, the linked document may load in the same frame or
in a different frame, specified by
TARGET="...".

Standard:	HTML 4
Common:	Yes

Sample:

```
<AREA SHAPE="RECT"
COORDS="20,8,46,30"
HREF="food.html"
TARGET="leftframe">
```

TITLE="..."

Specifies text assigned to the tag. You might use this attribute for context-
sensitive help within the document. Browsers may use this to show tool tips over the imagemap area.

Standard:	HTML 4
Common:	No

Sample:

```
<AREA SHAPE="RECT"
COORDS="20,8,46,30"
HREF="food.html" NAME="Food!">
```

Other Attributes

This tag also accepts the lang and dir attributes. See the Element-Independent Attributes section of this reference for definitions and examples.

B

<B>

Indicates text that should appear in boldface.

Standard:	HTML 2
Common:	Yes
Paired:	Yes

Sample:

```
The afternoon was <B>so</B> hot!
```

Attribute Information

CLASS="..."

Indicates which style class applies to the <B> element.

Standard:	HTML 4
Common:	No

Sample:

```
<B CLASS="casual">Boom!</B>
```

ID="..."

Assigns a unique ID selector to an instance of the <B> tag. When you assign a style to that ID selector, it affects only that one instance of the <B> tag.

Standard:	HTML 4
Common:	No

Sample:
```
I work for <B ID="123">Widgets
Inc.</B>
```

STYLE="..."
Specifies style sheet commands that apply to the contents within the <B> tags.

Standard: HTML 4
Common: No
Sample:
```
<B STYLE="background: red">
```

TITLE="..."
Specifies text assigned to the tag. You might use this attribute for context-sensitive help within the document. Browsers may use this to show tool tips over the bold-face

Standard: HTML 4
Common: No
Sample:
```
<B TITLE="Species">Dog
Species</B>
```

Other Attributes
This tag also accepts the lang, dir, onClick, onDblClick, onMouseDown, onMouseUp, onMouseOver, onMouseMove, onMouseOut, onKeyPress, onKeyDown, and onKeyUp attributes. See the Element-Independent Attributes section of this reference for definitions and examples.

<BASE>

Identifies the location where all relative URLs in your document originate.

Standard: HTML 2
Common: Yes
Paired: No

Sample:
```
<BASE HREF="http://www.raycomm
.com/info/">
```

Attribute Information

HREF="URL"
Indicates the relative or absolute location of the base document.

Standard: HTML 2
Common: Yes
Sample:
```
<BASE HREF="http://www.raycomm
.com/">
```

TARGET="..."
Identifies in which named frame you load a document (see the HREF= attribute).

Standard: HTML 4
Common: Yes
Sample:
```
<BASE HREF="http://www.raycomm
.com/frames/" TARGET="main">
```

<BASEFONT>

Provides a font setting for normal text within a document. Font settings (see the <FONT> tag) within the document are relative to settings specified with this tag. Use this tag in the document header (between the <HEAD> tags).

Standard: HTML 3.2; deprecated in HTML 4 in favor of style sheets
Common: Yes
Paired: No
Sample:
```
<BASEFONT SIZE="5">
```

Attribute Information

COLOR="#RRGGBB" or "..."

Sets the font color of normal text within a document. Color names may substitute for the explicit RGB hexadecimal values.

Standard:	HTML 3.2; deprecated in HTML 4 in favor of style sheets
Common:	Yes
Sample:	

```
<BASEFONT SIZE="2"
COLOR="#FF00CC">
```

FACE="...,..."

Specifies the font face of normal text within a document. You can set this attribute to a comma-separated list of font names. The browser selects the first name matching a font available.

Standard:	HTML 3.2; deprecated in HTML 4 in favor of style sheets
Common:	Yes
Sample:	

```
<BASEFONT FACE="Avant Guard,
Helvetica, Arial">
```

SIZE="n"

Specifies the font size of normal text within a document. Valid values are integer numbers in the range 1 to 7 with 3 being the default setting.

Standard:	HTML 3.2; deprecated in HTML 4 in favor of style sheets
Common:	Yes
Sample:	

```
<BASEFONT SIZE="5">
```

<BDO>

Indicates text that should appear with the direction (left to right or right to left) specified, overriding other language-specific settings.

Standard:	HTML 4
Common:	No
Paired:	Yes
Sample:	

```
<P LANG="IW" DIR="RTL">This
Hebrew text contains a number,
<BDO="LTR">29381</BDO>, that must
appear left to right.</P>
```

Attribute Information

This tag accepts the lang and dir attributes. See the Element-Independent Attributes section of this reference for definitions and examples.

<BGSOUND>

Embeds a background sound file within documents. Use in the document head of documents intended for visitors who use Internet Explorer.

Standard:	Internet Explorer
Common:	Yes
Paired:	No
Sample:	

```
<BGSOUND SRC="scream.wav">
```

Attribute Information

LOOP="{n, INFINITE}"

Specifies the number of times a background sound file repeats. The value INFINITE is the default.

Standard:	Internet Explorer
Common:	No

Sample:

```
<BGSOUND SRC="bugle.wav"
LOOP="2">
```

SRC="*URL*"

Indicates the explicit or relative location of
the sound file.

> **Standard**:   Internet Explorer
>
> **Common**:   No
>
> **Sample:**

```
<BGSOUND SRC="wah.wav">
```

<BIG>

Indicates that text display in a larger font.

> **Standard**:   HTML 3.2
>
> **Common**:   Yes
>
> **Paired**:   Yes
>
> **Sample:**

```
<BIG>Lunch</BIG>
<p>Lunch will be served at 2 p.m.
```

Attribute Information

CLASS="..."

Indicates which style class applies to the
<BIG> element.

> **Standard**:   HTML 4
>
> **Common**:   No
>
> **Sample:**

```
<BIG CLASS="casual">
Instructions</BIG>
```

ID="..."

Assigns a unique ID selector to an instance of
the <BIG> tag. When you then assign a style
to that ID selector, it affects only that one
instance of the <BIG> tag.

> **Standard**:   HTML 4
>
> **Common**:   No

Sample:

```
<BIG ID="123">REMINDER:</BIG>
Eat 5 servings of fruits and
vegetables every day!
```

STYLE="..."

Specifies style sheet commands that apply to
the contents within the
<BIG> tags.

> **Standard**:   HTML 4
>
> **Common**:   No
>
> **Sample:**

```
<BIG STYLE="background: red">
```

TITLE="..."

Specifies text assigned to the tag. You might
use this attribute for context-
sensitive help within the document. Browsers
may use this to show tool tips over the text
inside the <BIG> tags.

> **Standard**:   HTML 4
>
> **Common**:   No
>
> **Sample:**

```
<BIG TITLE="Bigger">
```

Other Attributes

This tag also accepts the lang, dir,
onClick, onDblClick, onMouseDown,
onMouseUp, onMouseOver, onMouseMove,
onMouseOut, onKeyPress, onKeyDown,
and onKeyUp attributes. See the Element-
Independent Attributes section of this reference for definitions and examples.

<BLINK>

A Netscape-specific tag that makes text blink
on and off.

> **Standard**:   Netscape Navigator; style
> sheets offer the same func-
> tionality in a more widely
> recognized syntax.

Common: No
Paired: Yes
Sample:

```
<P><BLINK>NEW INFO</BLINK>:
We moved!
```

Attribute Information

CLASS="..."
Indicates which style class applies to the
<BLINK> element.

Standard: HTML 4
Common: No
Sample:

```
<BLINK CLASS="casual">NEW
INFORMATION</BLINK>
```

ID="..."
Assigns a unique ID selector to an instance of
the <BLINK> tag. When you then assign a
style to that ID selector, it affects only that
one instance of the <BLINK> tag.

Standard: HTML 4
Common: No
Sample:

```
<BLINK ID="123">12 Hour
Sale!</BLINK>
```

STYLE="..."
Specifies style sheet commands that apply to
the contents within the <BLINK> tags.

Standard: HTML 4
Common: No
Sample:

```
<BLINK STYLE="background: red">
```

<BLOCKQUOTE>

Provides left and right indention of affected
text and is useful for quoting a direct source
within a document. Use for indention is dep-

recated. Use <BLOCKQUOTE> to signify only a
block quotation.

Standard: HTML 2
Common: Yes
Paired: Yes
Sample:

```
Dr. Henry's remarks are
below:<BLOCKQUOTE>I really like
the procedure.</BLOCKQUOTE>
```

Attribute Information

CITE="..."
Specifies a reference URL for the
quotation.

Standard: HTML 4
Common: No
Sample:

```
<BLOCKQUOTE CITE="http://www
.clement.moore.com/xmas.html">
```

```
Twas the night...</BLOCKQUOTE>
```

CLASS="..."
Indicates which style class applies to the
<BLOCKQUOTE> element.

Standard: HTML 4
Common: No
Sample:

```
<BLOCKQUOTE CLASS="casual">
```

```
Twas the night before
Christmas...</BLOCKQUOTE>
```

ID="..."
Assigns a unique ID selector to an instance of
the <BLOCKQUOTE> tag. When you then
assign a style to that ID selector, it affects
only that one instance of the <BLOCKQUOTE>
tag.

Standard: HTML 4
Common: No

Sample:

```
On July 12, John wrote a profound
sentence in his diary:

<BLOCKQUOTE ID="123">I woke up
this morning at nine and it was
raining.</BLOCKQUOTE>
```

STYLE="..."

Specifies style sheet commands that apply to the contents within the <BLOCKQUOTE> tags.

Standard: HTML 4

Common: No

Sample:

```
<BLOCKQUOTE STYLE="background:
red">
```

TITLE="..."

Specifies text assigned to the tag. You might use this attribute for context-sensitive help within the document. Browsers may use this to show tool tips over the quoted text.

Standard: HTML 4

Common: No

Sample:

```
<BLOCKQUOTE TITLE="Quotation">
```

Other Attributes

This tag also accepts the lang, dir, onClick, onDblClick, onMouseDown, onMouseUp, onMouseOver, onMouseMove, onMouseOut, onKeyPress, onKeyDown, and onKeyUp attributes. See the Element-Independent Attributes section of this reference for definitions and examples.

<BODY>

Acts as a container for the body of the document. It appears after the <HEAD> tag and is followed by the </HTML> tag. In HTML 3.2, the <BODY> tag also sets various color set-tings and background characteristics of the document; however, in HTML 4, those formatting attributes are deprecated in favor of style sheets.

Standard: HTML 2

Common: Yes

Paired: Yes

Sample:

```
<BODY>
<H1>HELLO!</H1>
</BODY>
```

Attribute Information

ALINK="#RRGGBB" or "..."

Indicates the color of hyperlink text while the text is selected. Color names can substitute for the RGB hexadecimal values.

Standard: HTML 3.2; deprecated in HTML 4 in favor of style sheets

Common: Yes

Sample:

```
<BODY BGCOLOR="#000ABC"
TEXT="#000000" LINK="#FFFFFF"
VLINK="#999999" ALINK="#FF0000">
```

BACKGROUND="URL"

Specifies the relative or absolute location of an image file that tiles across the document's background.

Standard: HTML 3.2; deprecated in HTML 4 in favor of style sheets

Common: Yes

Sample:

```
<BODY BACKGROUND=
"images/slimey.gif">
```

BGCOLOR="#RRGGBB" or "…"

Indicates the color of a document's background. Color names can substitute for the RGB hexadecimal values.

Standard:	HTML 3.2; deprecated in HTML 4 in favor of style sheets
Common:	Yes

Sample:

```
<BODY BGCOLOR="#000ABC"
TEXT="#000000" LINK="#FFFFFF"
VLINK="#999999" ALINK="#FF0000">
```

BGPROPERTIES="FIXED"

Specifies the behavior of the background image (see the BACKGROUND attribute.) BGPROPERTIES=FIXED indicates that the background image remains in place as you scroll the document, creating a watermark effect.

Standard:	Internet Explorer
Common:	No

Sample:

```
<BODY BACKGROUND="waves.jpg"
BGPROPERTIES="FIXED">
```

CLASS="…"

Indicates which style class applies to the <BODY> element.

Standard:	HTML 4
Common:	No

Sample:

```
<BODY CLASS="casual">
```

ID="n"

Assigns a unique ID selector to the <BODY> tag.

Standard:	HTML 4
Common:	No

Sample:

```
<BODY ID="123">
```

LEFTMARGIN="n"

Specifies the width (in pixels) of a margin of white space along the left edge of the entire document.

Standard:	Internet Explorer
Common:	No

Sample:

```
<BODY LEFTMARGIN="30">
```

LINK="#RRGGBB" or "…"

Indicates the color of hyperlink text within the document, which corresponds to documents not already visited by the browser. Color names can substitute for the RGB hexadecimal values.

Standard:	HTML 3.2; deprecated in HTML 4 in favor of style sheets
Common:	Yes

Sample:

```
<BODY BGCOLOR="#000ABC"
TEXT="#000000" LINK="#FFFFFF"
VLINK="#999999" ALINK="#FF0000">
```

SCROLL="{YES, NO}"

Indicates whether scrolling is possible within the document body.

Standard:	Internet Explorer 4
Common:	No

Sample:

```
<BODY BGCOLOR="silver"
SCROLL="NO">
```

STYLE="…"

Specifies style sheet commands that apply to the document body.

Standard:	HTML 4
Common:	No

Sample:

```
<BODY STYLE="background: red">
```

TEXT="#*RRGGBB*" or "..."

Indicates the color of normal text within the document. Color names can substitute for the RGB hexadecimal values.

>   Standard: HTML 3.2; deprecated in HTML 4 in favor of style sheets.
>
>   Common: Yes
>
>   Sample:

```
<BODY BGCOLOR="#000ABC"
TEXT="#000000" LINK="#FFFFFF"
VLINK="#999999" ALINK="#FF0000">
```

TITLE="..."

Specifies text assigned to the tag. You might use this attribute for context-sensitive help within the document. Browsers may use this to show tool tips.

>   Standard: HTML 4
>
>   Common: No
>
>   Sample:

```
<BODY TITLE="Document body">
```

TOPMARGIN="*n*"

Specifies the size (in pixels) of a margin of white space along the top edge of the entire document.

>   Standard: Internet Explorer
>
>   Common: No
>
>   Sample:

```
<BODY TOPMARGIN="10">
```

VLINK="#*RRGGBB*" or "..."

Indicates the color of hyperlink text within the document, which corresponds to documents already visited by the browser. Color names can substitute for the RGB hexadecimal values.

>   Standard: HTML 3.2; deprecated in HTML 4 in favor of style sheets

>   Common: Yes
>
>   Sample:

```
<BODY BGCOLOR="#000ABC"
TEXT="#000000" LINK="#FFFFFF"
VLINK="#999999" ALINK="#FF0000">
```

Other Attributes

This tag also accepts the `lang`, `dir`, `onload`, `onunload`, `onClick`, `onDblClick`, `onMouseDown`, `onMouseUp`, `onMouseOver`, `onMouseMove`, `onMouseOut`, `onKeyPress`, `onKeyDown`, and `onKeyUp` attributes. See the "Element-Independent Attributes" section of this reference for definitions and examples.

Breaks a line of continuous text and prevents text alignment around images.

>   Standard: HTML 2
>
>   Common: Yes
>
>   Paired: No
>
>   Sample:

```
I live at:<P>123 Nowhere
Ave<BR>New York, NY 12345
```

Attribute Information

CLASS="..."

Indicates which style class applies to the element.

>   Standard: HTML 4
>
>   Common: No
>
>   Sample:

```
<BR CLASS="casual">
```

CLEAR="{ALL, LEFT, RIGHT, NONE}"

Discontinues alignment of text to inline graphic images. The sample demonstrates how you can force the text to appear after the image and not alongside it.

Standard: HTML 3.2
Common: Yes
Sample:

```
<IMG SRC="portrait.jpg"
ALIGN="RIGHT"><BR CLEAR="ALL">
<P>The above photo was taken when
I was in Florida.
```

ID="..."

Assigns a unique ID selector to an instance of the <BR> tag. When you then assign a style to that ID selector, it affects only that one instance of the <BR> tag.

Standard: HTML 4
Common: No
Sample:

```
<BR ID="123">
```

STYLE="..."

Specifies style sheet commands that apply to the <BR> tag.

Standard: HTML 4
Common: No
Sample:

```
<BR STYLE="background: red">
```

TITLE="..."

Specifies text assigned to the tag. You might use this attribute for context-sensitive help within the document. Browsers may use this to show tool tips.

Standard: HTML 4
Common: No
Sample:

```
<BR CLEAR="ALL" TITLE="Stop
image wrap">
```

<BUTTON>

Sets up a button to submit or reset a form as well as to activate a script. Use the <IMG> tag between the opening and closing <BUTTON> tags to specify a graphical button.

Standard: HTML 4
Common: No
Paired: Yes
Sample:

```
<BUTTON TYPE="BUTTON" VALUE="Run
Program" onclick(doit)>Click
it</BUTTON>
```

Attribute Information

ACCESSKEY="..."

Associates a key sequence with the button.

Standard: HTML 4
Common: Yes
Sample:

```
<BUTTON ACCESSKEY="B">Click
Me!</BUTTON>
```

CLASS="..."

Indicates which style class applies to the <BUTTON> element.

Standard: HTML 4
Common: No
Sample:

```
<BUTTON CLASS="casual"
TYPE="SUBMIT" VALUE="Submit">
```

DISABLED

Denies access to the input method.

Standard: HTML 4
Common: No
Sample:

```
<BUTTON TYPE="SUBMIT" NAME="Pass"
DISABLED>
```

ID="*n*"

Assigns a unique ID selector to an instance of the <INPUT> tag. When you then assign a style to that ID selector, it affects only that one instance of the <INPUT> tag.

Standard: HTML 4

Common: No

Sample:

```
<BUTTON ID="123" TYPE="SUBMIT"
VALUE="Submit">
```

NAME="..."

Gives a name to the value you pass to the form processor.

Standard: HTML 4

Common: Yes

Sample:

```
<BUTTON TYPE="BUTTON" NAME="RUN-
PROG" VALUE="Click to Run">
```

STYLE="..."

Specifies style sheet commands that apply to the element.

Standard: HTML 4

Common: No

Sample:

```
<BUTTON STYLE="background: red"
TYPE="BUTTON" NAME="RUNPROG"
VALUE="Click to Run">
```

TABINDEX="*n*"

Specifies where the input method appears in the tab order. For example, TABINDEX=3 places the cursor at the button element after the visitor presses the Tab key three times.

Standard: HTML 4

Common: No

Sample:

```
<BUTTON TYPE="BUTTON" NAME=
"RUNPROG" VALUE="Click to Run"
TABINDEX="3">
```

TITLE="..."

Specifies text assigned to the tag. You might use this attribute for context-sensitive help within the document. Browsers may use this to show tool tips over the input method.

Standard: HTML 4

Common: No

Sample:

```
<BUTTON TYPE="SUBMIT" NAME="cc"
VALUE="visa" TITLE="Visa">
```

TYPE="..."

Indicates the kind of button to create. SUB-MIT produces a button that, when selected, submits all the name-value pairs to the form processor. RESET sets all the input methods to their empty or default settings. BUTTON creates a button with no specific behavior that can interact with scripts.

Standard: HTML 4

Common: Yes

Sample:

```
<BUTTON TYPE="BUTTON" VALUE="Send
Data..." onclick(verify())>
</FORM>
```

VALUE="..."

Sets the default value for the button face.

Standard: HTML 4

Common: No

Sample:

```
<BUTTON TYPE="BUTTON" NAME="id"
VALUE="Press Me">
```

Other Attributes

This tag also accepts the lang, dir, onfocus, onblur, onClick, onDblClick, onMouseDown, onMouseUp, onMouseOver, onMouseMove, onMouseOut, onKeyPress, onKeyDown, and onKeyUp attributes. See the Element-Independent Attributes section of this reference for definitions and examples.

C

<CAPTION>

Used inside <TABLE> tags to specify a description for a table.

Standard: HTML 3.2
Common: Yes
Paired: Yes
Sample:

```
<TABLE>
  <CAPTION VALIGN="TOP"
  ALIGN="CENTER">  Test Grades
  For COOKING 101  </CAPTION>
  <TR>

  <TH>Student</TH><TH>Grade</TH>
  </TR>
  <TR>
    <TD>B. Smith</TD><TD>88</TD>
  </TR>
  <TR>
    <TD>J. Doe</TD><TD>45</TD>
  </TR>
</TABLE>
```

Attribute Information

ALIGN="{TOP, BOTTOM, LEFT, RIGHT}"

Indicates whether the caption appears at the top, bottom, left, or right of the table.

Standard: HTML 3.2; LEFT and RIGHT added in HTML 4
Common: Yes

Sample:

```
<CAPTION ALIGN="TOP">Seattle
Staff Directory</CAPTION>
```

CLASS="..."

Indicates which style class applies to the <CAPTION> element.

Standard: HTML 4
Common: No
Sample:

```
<CAPTION CLASS="casual">Hydrogen
vs Oxygen</CAPTION>
```

ID="..."

Assigns a unique ID selector to an instance of the <CAPTION> tag. When you then assign a style to that ID selector, it affects only that one instance of the <CAPTION> tag.

Standard: HTML 4
Common: No
Sample:

```
<TABLE>
  <CAPTION ID="123">Great
  Painters</CAPTION>
```

STYLE="..."

Specifies style sheet commands that apply to the contents of the <CAPTION> tags.

Standard: HTML 4
Common: No
Sample:

```
<CAPTION STYLE="background: red">
```

TITLE="..."

Specifies text assigned to the tag. You might use this attribute for context-sensitive help within the document. Browsers may use this to show tool tips over the caption.

Standard:	HTML 4
Common:	Yes
Sample:	

```
<CAPTION TITLE="Table caption">
```

Other Attributes

This tag also accepts the lang, dir, onClick, onDblClick, onMouseDown, onMouseUp, onMouseOver, onMouseMove, onMouseOut, onKeyPress, onKeyDown, and onKeyUp attributes. See the Element-Independent Attributes section of this reference for definitions and examples.

<CENTER>

Positions text an equal distance between the left and right edges of the document. This tag, now officially replaced by the <DIV ALIGN="CENTER"> attribute, was included in HTML 3.2 only because of its widespread use.

Standard:	HTML 3.2; deprecated in HTML 4
Common:	Yes
Paired:	Yes
Sample:	

```
<CENTER><BLINK><H1>ONE-DAY
SALE!</H1></BLINK></CENTER>
```

<CITE>

Provides an in-text citation of a proper title such as the title of a book. Most browsers display the text inside the <CITE> tags in italics.

Standard:	HTML 2
Common:	Yes
Paired:	Yes

Sample:

```
I just finished reading
<CITE>Being Digital</CITE> by
Nicholas Negroponte.
```

Attribute Information

CLASS="..."

Indicates which style class applies to the <CITE> element.

Standard:	HTML 4
Common:	No
Sample:	

```
This came from <CITE
CLASS="casual">Thoreau's Walden
Pond</CITE>
```

ID="..."

Assigns a unique ID selector to an instance of the <CITE> tag. When you then assign a style to that ID selector, it affects only that one instance of the <CITE> tag.

Standard:	HTML 4
Common:	No
Sample:	

```
I read about this in
<CITE ID="123">
World Weekly News</CITE>
```

STYLE="..."

Specifies style sheet commands that apply to the contents within the <CITE> tags.

Standard:	HTML 4
Common:	No
Sample:	

```
<CITE STYLE="background: red">
```

TITLE="..."

Specifies text assigned to the tag. You might use this attribute for context-sensitive help within the document. Browsers may use this to show tool tips over the cited text.

Standard: HTML 4

Common: No

Sample:

```
<CITE TITLE="Citation">FDA
Vegetable Pamphlet</CITE>
```

Other Attributes

This tag also accepts the lang, dir, onClick, onDblClick, onMouseDown, onMouseUp, onMouseOver, onMouseMove, onMouseOut, onKeyPress, onKeyDown, and onKeyUp attributes. See the Element-Independent Attributes section of this reference for definitions and examples.

<CODE>

Embeds excerpts of program source code into your document text. This is useful if you want to show program source code inline within a paragraph of normal text. For showing formatted segments of source code longer than one line, use the <PRE> tag.

Standard: HTML 2

Common: Yes

Paired: Yes

Sample:

```
To display the value of the cost
variable use the
<CODE>printf("%0.2f\n", cost);
</CODE> function call.
```

Attribute Information

CLASS="..."

Indicates which style class applies to the <CODE> element.

Standard: HTML 4

Common: No

Sample:

```
<CODE CLASS="casual">x++;</CODE>
```

ID="..."

Assigns a unique ID selector to an instance of the <CODE> tag. When you then assign a style to that ID selector, it affects only that one instance of the <CODE> tag.

Standard: HTML 4

Common: No

Sample:

```
<CODE ID="123">while(x)
x-;</CODE>
```

STYLE="..."

Specifies style sheet commands that apply to the contents within the <CODE> tags.

Standard: HTML 4

Common: No

Sample:

```
<BODY STYLE="background: red">
```

TITLE="..."

Specifies text assigned to the tag. You might use this attribute for context-sensitive help within the document. Browsers may use this to show tool tips over the code text.

Standard: HTML 4

Common: No

Sample:

```
<CODE TITLE="C
Code">exit(1);</CODE>
```

Other Attributes

This tag also accepts the lang, dir, onClick, onDblClick, onMouseDown, onMouseUp, onMouseOver, onMouseMove, onMouseOut, onKeyPress, onKeyDown, and onKeyUp attributes. See the Element-

Independent Attributes section of this reference for definitions and examples.

<COL>

Specifies attributes for a table column.

Standard: HTML 4

Common: No

Paired: No

Sample:

```
<TABLE>
<COLGROUP>
  <COL ALIGN="RIGHT">
  <COL ALIGN="CENTER">
<TR>  <TD>This cell is aligned
right</TD>
  <TD>This cell is centered</TD>
</TR>
</TABLE>
```

Attribute Information

ALIGN="{LEFT, RIGHT, CENTER, JUSTIFY, CHAR}"

Specifies how text within the table columns will line up with the edges of the table cells, or if ALIGN=CHAR, on a specific character (the decimal point).

Standard: HTML 4

Common: No

Sample:

```
<COL ALIGN="CENTER">
```

CHAR="..."

Specifies the character on which cell contents will align, if ALIGN="CHAR". If you omit CHAR=, the default value is the decimal point in the specified language.

Standard: HTML 4

Common: No

Sample:

```
<COL ALIGN="CHAR" CHAR=",">
```

CHAROFF="*n*"

Specifies the number of characters from the left at which the alignment character appears.

Standard: HTML 4

Common: No

Sample:

```
<COL ALIGN="CHAR" CHAR=","
CHAROFF="7">
```

ID="..."

Assigns a unique ID selector to an instance of the <COL> tag. When you assign a style to that ID selector, it affects only that one instance of the <COL> tag.

Standard: HTML 4

Common: No

Sample:

```
<COL ID="123">
```

SPAN="*n*"

Indicates the number of columns in the group.

Standard: HTML 4

Common: No

Sample:

```
<COLGROUP>
  <COL ALIGN="RIGHT" SPAN="2">
```

STYLE="..."

Specifies style sheet commands that apply to the contents of the <COL> tags.

Standard: HTML 4

Common: No

Sample:

```
<COL STYLE="background: black">
```

TITLE="..."

Specifies text assigned to the tag. You might use this attribute for context-sensitive help within the document. Browsers may use this to show tool tips over the table column.

Standard: HTML 4

Common: No

Sample:

```
<COL TITLE="Table column">
```

WIDTH="*n*"

Specifies the horizontal dimension of a column (in pixels or as a percentage). Special values of "0*" force the column to the minimum required width, and "2*" requires that the column receive proportionately twice as much space as it otherwise would.

Standard: HTML 4

Common: No

Sample:

```
<COL WIDTH="100">
```

VALIGN="{TOP, BOTTOM, BASE-LINE, MIDDLE}"

Vertically positions the contents of the table column. VALIGN="TOP" positions the contents flush with the top of the column. VALIGN="BUTTON" positions the contents flush with the bottom. VALIGN="CENTER" positions the contents at the center of the column. VALIGN="BASELINE" aligns the contents with the baseline of the current text font.

Standard: HTML 4

Common: No

Sample:

```
<COL VALIGN="TOP">
```

Other Attributes

This tag also accepts the lang, dir, onClick, onDblClick, onMouseDown, onMouseUp, onMouseOver, onMouseMove, onMouseOut, onKeyPress, onKeyDown, and onKeyUp attributes. See the Element-Independent Attributes section of this reference for definitions and examples.

<COLGROUP>

Specifies characteristics for a group of table columns.

Standard: HTML 4

Common: No

Paired: Yes

Sample:

```
<TABLE>
<COLGROUP VALIGN="TOP">
  <COL ALIGN="RIGHT">
  <COL ALIGN="CENTER">
<TR>
  <TD>This cell is aligned top
  and right</TD>
  <TD>This cell is aligned top
  and centered</TD>
</TR>
</TABLE>
```

Attribute Information

ALIGN="{LEFT, RIGHT, CENTER, JUSTIFY, CHAR}"

Specifies how text within the table columns lines up with the edges of the table cells, or if ALIGN=CHAR, on a specific character (the decimal point).

Standard: HTML 4

Common: No

Sample:

```
<COLGROUP ALIGN="CENTER">
```

CHAR="..."

Specifies the character on which cell contents align, if ALIGN="CHAR". If you omit CHAR=, the default value is the decimal point in the specified language.

Standard: HTML 4

Common: No

Sample:

`<COLGROUP ALIGN="CHAR" CHAR=",">`

CHAROFF="n"

Specifies the number of characters from the left at which the alignment character appears.

Standard: HTML 4

Common: No

Sample:

`<COLGROUP ALIGN="CHAR" CHAR=","`
`CHAROFF="7">`

ID="..."

Assigns a unique ID selector to an instance of the tag. When you then assign a style to that ID selector, it affects only that one instance of the tag.

Standard: HTML 4

Common: No

Sample:

`<COLGROUP ID="123">`

SPAN="n"

Indicates how many consecutive columns exist in the column group and to which columns the specified attributes apply.

Standard: HTML 4

Common: No

Sample:

`<COLGROUP>`
`    <COL ALIGN="RIGHT" SPAN="2">`

STYLE="..."

Specifies style sheet commands that apply to the contents of the `<COLGROUP>` tags.

Standard: HTML 4

Common: No

Sample:

`<COLGROUP STYLE="color: red">`

TITLE="..."

Specifies text assigned to the tag. You might use this attribute for context-sensitive help within the document. Browsers may use this to show tool tips over the column group.

Standard: HTML 4

Common: No

Sample:

`<COLGROUP TITLE="Column Group">`

WIDTH="n"

Specifies the horizontal dimension of columns within the column group (in pixels or as a percentage). Special values of "0*" force the column to minimum required width, and "2*" requires that the column receive proportionately twice as much space as it otherwise would.

Standard: HTML 4

Common: No

Sample:

`<COLGROUP WIDTH=100>`
`    <COL ALIGN="RIGHT">`

VALIGN="{TOP, BOTTOM, BASELINE, MIDDLE}"

Vertically positions the contents of the table column. VALIGN="TOP" positions the contents flush with the top of the column. VALIGN="BOTTOM" positions the contents flush with the bottom. VALIGN="CENTER" positions the contents at the vertical center of the column. VALIGN="BASELINE" aligns the contents with the baseline of the current text font.

> **Standard**: HTML 4
> **Common**: No
> **Sample:**

<COLGROUP VALIGN="TOP">

Other Attributes

This tag also accepts the lang, dir, onClick, onDblClick, onMouseDown, onMouseUp, onMouseOver, onMouseMove, onMouseOut, onKeyPress, onKeyDown, and onKeyUp attributes. See the Element-Independent Attributes section of this reference for definitions and examples.

<COMMENT>

Indicates an author comment. Because these tags are Netscape-specific, we encourage you to use the <!--...--> tags instead.

> **Standard**: Netscape Navigator
> **Common**: Yes
> **Paired**: Yes
> **Sample:**

<COMMENT>This document was created September 19, 1997
</COMMENT>

D

<DD>

Contains a definition in a definition list. Use this tag inside <DL> tags. This tag can contain block-level elements.

> **Standard**: HTML 2
> **Common**: Yes

> **Paired**: Yes, optional
> **Sample:**

<DL><DT>Butter
<DD>Butter is a dairy product.
</DL>

Attribute Information

CLASS="..."

Indicates which style class applies to the <DD> element.

> **Standard**: HTML 4
> **Common**: No
> **Sample:**

<DL>
  <DT>HTML
  <DD CLASS="casual">Hypertext Markup Language
</DD>

ID="..."

Assigns a unique ID selector to an instance of the <DD> tag. When you then assign a style to that ID selector, it affects only that one instance of the <DD> tag.

> **Standard**: HTML 4
> **Common**: No
> **Sample:**

<DL>
  <DT>RS-232C
  <DD ID="123">A standard for serial communication between computers.
</DL>

STYLE="..."

Specifies style sheet commands that apply to the definition.

Standard: HTML 4

Common: No

Sample:

```
<DD STYLE="background: blue;
color: white">
```

TITLE="..."

Specifies text assigned to the tag. You might use this attribute for context-sensitive help within the document. Browsers may use this to show tool tips over the definition.

Standard: HTML 4

Common: No

Sample:

```
<DD TITLE="Definition">
```

Other Attributes

This tag also accepts the lang, dir, onClick, onDblClick, onMouseDown, onMouseUp, onMouseOver, onMouseMove, onMouseOut, onKeyPress, onKeyDown, and onKeyUp attributes. See the Element-Independent Attributes section of this reference for definitions and examples.

<DEL>

Indicates text marked for deletion in the document. May be either block-level or inline, as necessary.

Standard: HTML 4

Common: No

Paired: Yes

Sample:

```
<P>HTTP stands for HyperText
Transfer <DEL>Transport</DEL>
Protocol</P>
```

Attribute Information

CITE="url"

Indicates address of reference (definitive source, for example) for deletion.

Standard: HTML 4

Common: No

Sample:

```
<DEL CITE="http://www.w3.org/">
HTML 3.0 was used for 10
years.</DEL>
```

CLASS="..."

Indicates which style class applies to the <DEL> element.

Standard: HTML 4

Common: No

Sample:

```
<DEL CLASS="casual">POP stands
for Post Office Protocol</DEL>
```

DATETIME="..."

Indicates the date and time in precisely this format: YYYY-MM-DDThh:mm:ssTZD. For example, 1997-07-14T08:30:00-07:00 indicates July 14, 1997, at 8:30 AM, in U.S. Mountain Time (7 hours from Greenwich time). This time could also be presented as 1997-07-14T08:30:00Z.

Standard: HTML 4

Common: No

Sample:

```
<DEL DATETIME="1997-07-
14T08:30:00Z">POP stands for Post
Office Protocol</DEL>
```

ID="..."

Assigns a unique ID selector to an instance of the tag. When you then assign a style to that ID selector, it affects only that one instance of the <DEL> tag.

Standard: HTML 4

Common: No

Sample:

```
<DEL ID="123">WWW stands for
World Wide Web</DEL>
```

STYLE="..."

Specifies style sheet commands that apply to the deleted text.

Standard: HTML 4

Common: No

Sample:

```
<DEL STYLE="background: blue;
color: white">ESP stands for
extra-sensory perception.</DEL>
```

TITLE="..."

Specifies text assigned to the tag. You might use this attribute for context-sensitive help within the document. Browsers may use this to show tool tips over the text.

Standard: HTML 4

Common: No

Sample:

```
<DEL TITLE="Definition">More
deleted text.</DEL>
```

Other Attributes

This tag also accepts the lang, dir, onClick, onDblClick, onMouseDown, onMouseUp, onMouseOver, onMouseMove, onMouseOut, onKeyPress, onKeyDown, and onKeyUp attributes. See the Element-Independent Attributes section of this reference for definitions and examples.

<DFN>

Indicates the definition of a term in the document.

Standard: HTML 3.2

Common: No

Paired: Yes

Sample:

```
<DFN>HTTP stands for HyperText
Transfer Protocol</DFN>
```

Attribute Information

CLASS="..."

Indicates which style class applies to the <DFN> element.

Standard: HTML 4

Common: No

Sample:

```
<DFN CLASS="casual">POP stands
for Post Office Protocol</DFN>
```

ID="..."

Assigns a unique ID selector to an instance of the <DFN> tag. When you then assign a style to that ID selector, it affects only that one instance of the <DFN> tag.

Standard: HTML 4

Common: No

Sample:

```
<DFN ID="123">WWW stands for
World Wide Web</DFN>
```

STYLE="..."

Specifies style sheet commands that apply to the definition.

Standard: HTML 4

Common: No

Sample:

```
<DFN STYLE="background: blue;
color: white">ESP stands for
extra-sensory perception.</DFN>
```

TITLE="..."

Specifies text assigned to the tag. You might use this attribute for context-sensitive help within the document. Browsers may use this to show tool tips over the definition text.

Standard: HTML 4

Common: No

Sample:

```
<DFN TITLE="Definition">
```

Other Attributes

This tag also accepts the lang, dir, onClick, onDblClick, onMouseDown, onMouseUp, onMouseOver, onMouseMove, onMouseOut, onKeyPress, onKeyDown, and onKeyUp attributes. See the Element-Independent Attributes section of this reference for definitions and examples.

`<DIR>`

Contains a directory list. Use the `<LI>` tag to indicate list items within the list. Use `<UL>`, rather than this deprecated tag.

Standard: HTML 2; deprecated in HTML 4. Use `<UL>` instead.

Common: Yes

Paired: Yes

Sample:

```
Choose a music genre:<DIR>
   <LI><A HREF="rock/">Rock</A>
   <LI><A HREF="country/
   ">Country</A>
   <LI><A HREF="na/">New Age</A>
</DIR>
```

Attribute Information

CLASS="..."

Indicates which style class applies to the `<dir>` element.

Standard: HTML 4

Common: No

Sample:

```
<DIR CLASS="casual">
   <LI>Apples
   <LI>Kiwis
   <LI>Mangos
   <LI>Oranges
</DIR>
```

COMPACT

Causes the list to appear in a compact format. This attribute probably will not affect the appearance of the list as most browsers do not present lists in more than one format.

Standard: HTML 2; deprecated in HTML 4

Common: No

Sample:

```
<DIR COMPACT>...
</DIR>
```

ID="..."

Assigns a unique ID selector to an instance of the `<dir>` tag. When you then assign a style to that ID selector, it affects only that one instance of the `<dir>` tag.

Standard: HTML 4

Common: No

Sample:

```
<DIR ID="123">
   <LI>Thingie 1
   <LI>Thingie 2
</DIR>
```

STYLE="..."

Specifies style sheet commands that apply to the `<DIR>` element.

Standard: HTML 4

Common: No

Sample:

```
<DIR STYLE="background: blue;
color: white">
  <LI>Thingie 1
  <LI>Thingie 2
</DIR>
```

TITLE="..."

Specifies text assigned to the tag. You might use this attribute for context-sensitive help within the document. Browsers may use this to show tool tips over the directory list.

> **Standard**: HTML 4
>
> **Common**: No
>
> **Sample**:

```
<DIR TITLE="Directory List">
```

Other Attributes

This tag also accepts the lang, dir, onClick, onDblClick, onMouseDown, onMouseUp, onMouseOver, onMouseMove, onMouseOut, onKeyPress, onKeyDown, and onKeyUp attributes. See the Element-Independent Attributes section of this reference for definitions and examples.

<DIV>

Indicates logical divisions within a document. You can use these to apply alignment, line-wrapping, and particularly style sheet attributes to a section of your document. <DIV ALIGN=CENTER>
is the official replacement for the <CENTER> tag.

> **Standard**: HTML 3.2
>
> **Common**: No
>
> **Paired**: Yes

Sample:

```
<DIV ALIGN="CENTER"
STYLE="background: blue">
<FONT SIZE=+2>All About Formic
Acid</FONT>
</DIV>
```

Attribute Information

ALIGN="{LEFT, CENTER, RIGHT, JUSTIFY}"

Specifies whether the contents of the section align with the left or right margins (LEFT, RIGHT), are evenly spaced between them (CENTER), or if the text stretches between the left and right margins (JUSTIFY).

> **Standard**: HTML 3.2; deprecated in HTML 4 in favor of style sheets
>
> **Common**: No
>
> **Sample**:

```
<DIV ALIGN="RIGHT">
Look over here!</DIV>
<DIV ALIGN="LEFT">
Now, look over here!</DIV>
```

CLASS="..."

Indicates which style class applies to the <DIV> element.

> **Standard**: HTML 4
>
> **Common**: No
>
> **Sample**:

```
<DIV CLASS="casual">
```

DATAFLD="..."

Selects a column from a previously identified source of tabulated data (see the DATASRC= attribute).

> **Standard**: Internet Explorer 4
>
> **Common**: No

Sample:

```
<DIV DATASRC="#data_table">
<DIV DATAFLD="name"></DIV>
</DIV>
```

DATAFORMATAS="{TEXT, HTML, NONE}"

Indicates how tabulated data formats within the <DIV> element.

Standard: Internet Explorer 4

Common: No

Sample:

```
<DIV DATAFORMATAS="HTML"
DATASRC="#data_table">
```

DATASRC="..."

Specifies the source of data for data binding.

Standard: Internet Explorer 4

Common: No

Sample:

```
<DIV DATASRC="#data_table">
```

ID="..."

Assigns a unique ID selector to an instance of the <DIV> tag. When you then assign a style to that ID selector, it affects only that one instance of the <DIV> tag.

Standard: HTML 4

Common: No

Sample:

```
<DIV ID="123">
```

NOWRAP

Disables line-wrapping for the section.

Standard: Netscape Navigator

Common: No

Sample:

```
<HR>
<DIV ALIGN="LEFT" NOWRAP>
```

```
The contents of this section will
not automatically wrap as you
size the window.
</DIV><HR>
```

STYLE="..."

Specifies style sheet commands that apply to the contents within the <DIV> tags.

Standard: HTML 4

Common: No

Sample:

```
<DIV STYLE="background: red">
```

TITLE="..."

Specifies text assigned to the tag. You might use this attribute for context-sensitive help within the document. Browsers may use this to show tool tips over the contents of the <DIV> tags.

Standard: HTML 4

Common: No

Sample:

```
<DIV TITLE="Title"
CLASS="casual">
```

Other Attributes

This tag also accepts the lang, dir, onClick, onDblClick, onMouseDown, onMouseUp, onMouseOver, onMouseMove, onMouseOut, onKeyPress, onKeyDown, and onKeyUp attributes. See the Element-Independent Attributes section of this reference for definitions and examples.

<DL>

Contains the <DT> and <DD> tags that form the term and definition portions of a definition list.

Standard: HTML 2

Common: Yes

Paired: Yes

Sample:

```
<DL><DT>Hygiene
<DD>Always wash your hands before
preparing meat.</DL>
```

Attribute Information

CLASS="..."

Indicates which style class applies to the <DL> element.

> **Standard**:   HTML 4
>
> **Common**:   No
>
> **Sample**:

```
<DL CLASS="casual">
   <DT>RAM
   <DD>Random Access Memory
</DL>
```

COMPACT

Causes the definition list to appear in a compact format. This attribute probably will not affect the appearance of the list as most browsers do not present lists in more than one format.

> **Standard**:   HTML 2; deprecated in HTML 4
>
> **Common**:   No
>
> **Sample**:

```
<DL COMPACT>...
</DL>
```

ID="..."

Assigns a unique ID selector to an instance of the <DD> tag. When you then assign a style to that ID selector, it affects only that one instance of the <DD> tag.

> **Standard**:   HTML 4
>
> **Common**:   No

Sample:

```
<DL ID="123">
   <DT>Food
   <DD>We will be eating 3
   meals/day.
</DL>
```

STYLE="..."

Specifies style sheet commands that apply to contents within the <DL> tags.

> **Standard**:   HTML 4
>
> **Common**:   No
>
> **Sample**:

```
<DL STYLE="background: red">
```

TITLE="..."

Specifies text assigned to the tag. You might use this attribute for context-sensitive help within the document. Browsers may use this to show tool tips over the definition list.

> **Standard**:   HTML 4
>
> **Common**:   No
>
> **Sample**:

```
<DL TITLE="Definition List">
```

Other Attributes

This tag also accepts the lang, dir, onClick, onDblClick, onMouseDown, onMouseUp, onMouseOver, onMouseMove, onMouseOut, onKeyPress, onKeyDown, and onKeyUp attributes. See the Element-Independent Attributes section of this reference for definitions and examples.

<DT>

Contains the terms inside a definition list. Place the <DT> tags inside <DL> tags.

> **Standard**:   HTML 2
>
> **Common**:   Yes
>
> **Paired**:   Yes, optional

Sample:

`<DL><DT>Hygiene`

`<DD>Always wash your hands before preparing meat.</DL>`

Attribute Information

CLASS="..."

Indicates which style class applies to the `<DT>` element.

   Standard: HTML 4

   Common: No

   Sample:

`<DL>`

  `<DT CLASS="casual">CUL8R`

  `<DD>See You Later`

`</DL>`

ID="..."

Assigns a unique ID selector to an instance of the `<DT>` tag. When you then assign a style to that ID selector, it affects only that one instance of the `<DT>` tag.

   Standard: HTML 4

   Common: No

   Sample:

`<DL>`

  `<DT ID="123">Caffeine`

  `<DD>Avoid caffeine during the stress management course.`

`</DL>`

STYLE="..."

Specifies style sheet commands that apply to the contents within the `<DT>` tags.

   Standard: HTML 4

   Common: No

Sample:

`<DT STYLE="background: red">`

TITLE="..."

Specifies text assigned to the tag. You might use this attribute for context-sensitive help within the document. Browsers may use this to show tool tips over the definition term.

   Standard: HTML 4

   Common: No

   Sample:

`<DT TITLE="Term">Programmer</DT>`

`<DD>A method for converting coffee into applications.`

Other Attributes

This tag also accepts the `lang`, `dir`, `onClick`, `onDblClick`, `onMouseDown`, `onMouseUp`, `onMouseOver`, `onMouseMove`, `onMouseOut`, `onKeyPress`, `onKeyDown`, and `onKeyUp` attributes. See the Element-Independent Attributes section of this reference for definitions and examples.

E

`<EM>`

Makes the text stand out. Browsers usually do this with italic or boldface.

   Standard: HTML 2

   Common: Yes

   Paired: Yes

   Sample:

`It is <EM>very</EM> important to read the instructions before beginning.`

Attribute Information

CLASS="..."

Indicates which style class applies to the <EM> element.

> **Standard**: HTML 4
>
> **Common**: No
>
> **Sample**:

```
Did you say my house was on<EM
CLASS="casual">FIRE?!</EM>
```

ID="..."

Assigns a unique ID selector to an instance of the <EM> tag. When you
then assign a style to that ID selector,
it affects only that one instance of the <EM> tag.

> **Standard**: HTML 4
>
> **Common**: No
>
> **Sample**:

```
I have complained <EM
ID="123">ten</EM>times about the
leaking faucet.
```

STYLE="..."

Specifies style sheet commands that apply to the contents within the <EM> tags.

> **Standard**: HTML 4
>
> **Common**: No
>
> **Sample**:

```
<EM STYLE="background: red">
```

TITLE="..."

Specifies text assigned to the tag. You might use this attribute for context-
sensitive help within the document. Browsers may use this to show tool tips over the emphasized text.

> **Standard**: HTML 4
>
> **Common**: No
>
> **Sample**:

```
<EM TITLE="Emphasis">
```

Other Attributes

This tag also accepts the `lang`, `dir`, `onClick`, `onDblClick`, `onMouseDown`, `onMouseUp`, `onMouseOver`, `onMouseMove`, `onMouseOut`, `onKeyPress`, `onKeyDown`, and `onKeyUp` attributes. See the Element-Independent Attributes section of this reference for definitions and examples.

<EMBED>

Places an embedded object into a document. Examples of embedded objects include MIDI files and digital video files. Because the <EMBED> tag is not standard, we suggest you use the <OBJECT> tag instead. If the browser does not have built-in support for an object, visitors will need a plug-in to use the object within the document.

> **Standard**: Netscape Navigator, supported by Internet Explorer
>
> **Common**: No
>
> **Paired**: No
>
> **Sample**:

```
<EMBED SRC="fur_elise.midi">
```

Attribute Information

ACCESSKEY="..."

Specifies a key sequence that binds to the embedded object.

> **Standard**: Internet Explorer 4
>
> **Common**: No
>
> **Sample**:

```
<EMBED SRC="st.ocx"
ACCESSKEY="E">
```

ALIGN="{LEFT, RIGHT, CENTER, ABSBOTTOM, ABSMIDDLE, BASELINE, BOTTOM, TEXTTOP, TOP}"

Indicates how an embedded object is positioned relative to the document borders and surrounding contents. ALIGN="LEFT", ALIGN="RIGHT", or ALIGN="CENTER" makes the embedded object float between the edges of the frame either to the left, right, or evenly between. The behavior is similar to that of the ALIGN= attribute of the <IMG> tag.

ALIGN="TEXTTOP" or ALIGN="TOP" lines up the top of the embedded object with the top of the current text font.
ALIGN="ABSMIDDLE" lines up the middle of the embedded object with the middle of the current text font. ALIGN="ABSBOTTOM" lines up the bottom of the embedded object with the bottom of the current text font. ALIGN="BASELINE" or ALIGN="BOTTOM" lines up the bottom of the embedded object with the baseline of the current text font.

Standard: Internet Explorer 4
Common: No
Sample:

```
<EMBED SRC="song.mid" ALIGN="CEN-
TER">
```

HEIGHT="n"

Specifies the vertical dimension of the embedded object. (See the UNITS= attribute for how to measure dimensions.)

Standard: Netscape Navigator
Common: No
Sample:

```
<EMBED SRC="rocket.avi"
WIDTH="50" HEIGHT="40">
```

HIDDEN

Indicates that the embedded object should not be visible.

Standard: Internet Explorer 4
Common: No
Sample:

```
<EMBED SRC="song.mid" HIDDEN>
```

NAME="..."

Gives the object a name by which other objects can refer to it.

Standard: Netscape Navigator
Common: No
Sample:

```
<EMBED SRC="running.avi"
NAME="movie1">
```

OPTIONAL PARAM="..."

Indicates additional parameters. For example, AVI movies accept the AUTOSTART attribute.

Standard: Netscape Navigator
Common: No
Sample:

```
<EMBED SRC="explode.avi"
AUTOSTART="true">
```

PALETTE="#RRGGBB|#RRGGBB"

Indicates the foreground and background colors for the embedded object. You can specify colors with hexadecimal RGB values or with color names.

Standard: Netscape Navigator
Common: No
Sample:

```
<EMBED SRC="flying.avi"
PALETTE="Red|Black">
```

SRC="URL"

Indicates the relative or absolute location of the file containing the object you want to embed.

Standard: Netscape Navigator
Common: No

Sample:

```
<EMBED SRC="beethoven_9.midi">
```

TITLE="..."

Specifies text assigned to the tag. You might use this attribute for context-sensitive help within the document. Browsers may use this to show tool tips over the embedded object.

Standard: Internet Explorer 4

Common: No

Sample:

```
<EMBED SRC="explode.avi"
TITLE="movie">
```

UNITS="{PIXELS, EN}"

Modifies the behavior of the HEIGHT= and WIDTH= attributes. UNITS=PIXELS measures attributes in pixels. UNITS=EN measures dimensions in EN spaces.

Standard: Netscape Navigator

Common: No

Sample:

```
<EMBED SRC="rocket.avi"
WIDTH="50" HEIGHT="40">
```

WIDTH="n"

Indicates the horizontal dimension of the embedded object. (See the UNITS= attribute for how to measure dimensions.)

Standard: Netscape Navigator

Common: No

Sample:

```
<EMBED SRC="cartoon.avi"
WIDTH="50">
```

Other Attributes

This tag also accepts the lang, dir, onClick, onDblClick, onMouseDown, onMouseUp, onMouseOver, onMouseMove, onMouseOut, onKeyPress, onKeyDown,

and onKeyUp attributes. See the Element-Independent Attributes section of this reference for definitions and examples.

F

<FIELDSET>

Groups related form elements.

Standard: HTML 4

Common: No

Paired: Yes

Sample:

```
<FORM ...>
<FIELDSET>
...logically related field
elements...
</FIELDSET>
</FORM>
```

Attribute Information

CLASS="..."

Indicates which style class applies to the <FIELDSET> element.

Standard: HTML 4

Common: No

Sample:

```
<FIELDSET CLASS="casual">Group
Rates</FIELDSET>
```

ID="..."

Assigns a unique ID selector to an instance of the <FIELDSET> tag. When you then assign a style to that ID selector, it affects only that one instance of the <FIELDSET> tag.

Standard: HTML 4

Common: No

Sample:

```
<FIELDSET ID="123">now!</FIELD-
SET>
```

STYLE="..."

Specifies style sheet commands that apply to the contents within the <FIELDSET> tags.

Standard: HTML 4

Common: No

Sample:

```
<FIELDSET STYLE="background:
red">
```

TITLE="..."

Specifies text assigned to the tag. You might use this attribute for context-sensitive help within the document. Browsers may use this to show tool tips over the font text.

Standard: HTML 4

Common: No

Sample:

```
<FIELDSET TITLE="Personal data
fields">
```

Other Attributes

This tag also accepts the lang, dir, onClick, onDblClick, onMouseDown, onMouseUp, onMouseOver, onMouseMove, onMouseOut, onKeyPress, onKeyDown, and onKeyUp attributes. See the Element-Independent Attributes section of this reference for definitions and examples.

<FONT>

Alters or sets font characteristics of the font the browser uses to display text.

Standard: HTML 3.2; deprecated
             in HTML 4 in favor of style
             sheets

Common: Yes

Paired: Yes

Sample:

```
The cat was really <FONT
SIZE="+3">BIG!</FONT>
```

Attribute Information

COLOR="#RRGGBB" or "..."

Indicates the color the browser uses to display text. Color names can substitute for the RGB hexadecimal values.

Standard: HTML 3.2; deprecated
             in HTML 4 in favor of style
             sheets.

Common: Yes

Sample:

```
<FONT COLOR=#FF0000><H2>Win A
Trip!</H2></FONT> <FONT
COLOR="lightblue"><p>That's
right! A trip to Hawaii can be
yours if you scratch off the
right number!</FONT>
```

FACE="...,..."

Specifies a comma-separated list of font names the browser uses to render text. If the browser does not have access to the first named font, it tries the second, then the third, and so forth.

Standard: Netscape Navigator and
             Internet Explorer, not intro-
             duced in standard HTML in
             favor of style sheets.

Common: Yes

Sample:

```
<FONT SIZE=+1 FACE="Avant Guard,
Helvetica, Lucida Sans, Arial">
```

SIZE=n

Specifies the size of the text affected by the FONT tag. You can specify the size relative to the base font size (see the <BASEFONT> tag) which is normally 3. You can also specify the size as a digit in the range 1 through 7.

Standard: HTML 3.2; deprecated in HTML 4 in favor of style sheets.

Common: Yes

Sample:

```
<BASEFONT SIZE=4>

<FONT SIZE=+2>This is a font of
size 6</FONT> <FONT SIZE=1>This
is a font of size 1</FONT>
```

<FORM>

Sets up a container for a form tag. Within the <FORM> tags, you can place form input tags such as <FIELDSET>, <INPUT>, <SELECT>, and <TEXTAREA>.

Standard: HTML 2

Common: Yes

Paired: Yes

Sample:

```
<FORM METHOD=POST
ACTION="/cgi-bin/search.pl">

Search : <INPUT TYPE=TEXT
NAME="name" SIZE=20><BR>

<INPUT TYPE=SUBMIT VALUE="Start
Search"> </FORM>
```

Attribute Information

ACCEPT-CHARSET="..."

Specifies the character encodings for input data that the server processing the form must accept. The value is a list of character sets as defined in RFC2045, separated by commas.

Standard: HTML 4

Common: No

Sample:

```
<FORM METHOD=POST
ACCEPT-CHARSET="ISO-8859-1"
ACTION="/stat-collector.cgi">
```

ACCEPT="..."

Specifies a list of MIME types, separated by commas, that the server processing the form will handle correctly.

Standard: HTML 4

Common: No

Sample:

```
<FORM METHOD=POST
ACCEPT="image/gif, image/jpeg
"ACTION="/image-collector.cgi">
```

ACTION="*URL*"

Specifies the explicit or relative location of the form processing CGI application.

Standard: HTML 2

Common: Yes

Sample:

```
<FORM METHOD=POST
ACTION="/stat-collector.cgi">
```

CLASS="..."

Indicates which style class applies to the <FORM>.

Standard: HTML 4

Common: No

Sample:

```
<FORM METHOD=POST CLASS="casual
"ACTION="/stat-collector.cgi">
```

ENCTYPE="..."

Specifies the MIME type used to submit (post) the form to the server. The default value is "application/x-www-form-urlencoded". Use the value "multipart/form-data" when the returned document includes files.

Standard: HTML 4

Common: No

Sample:

```
<FORM METHOD=POST ENCTYPE=
"application/x-www-
form-urlencoded"ACTION=
"/stat-collector.cgi">
```

ID="..."

Assigns a unique ID selector to an instance of the <FORM> tag. When you then assign a style to that ID selector, it affects only that one instance of the <FORM> tag.

Standard: HTML 4

Common: No

Sample:

```
<FORM ACTION="/cgi-bin/ttt.pl"
METHOD=GET ID="123">
```

METHOD={POST,GET}

Changes how form data is transmitted to the form processor. When you use METHOD=GET, the form data is given to the form processor in the form of an environment variable (*QUERY_STRING*). When you use METHOD=POST, the form data is given to the form processor as the standard input to the program.

Standard: HTML 2

Common: Yes

Sample:

```
<FORM METHOD=POST
ACTION="/cgi-bin/www-search">
```

```
Enter search keywords:
<INPUT TYPE=TEXT NAME="query"
SIZE=20>
```

```
<INPUT TYPE=SUBMIT
VALUE="Search">
```

```
</FORM>
```

NAME="..."

Assigns the form a name accessible by bookmark, script, and applet resources.

Standard: Internet Explorer

Common: No

Sample:

```
<FORM METHOD=POST
ACTION="/cgi-bin/ff.pl"NAME="ff">
```

STYLE="..."

Specifies style sheet commands that apply to the contents within the <FORM> tags.

Standard: HTML 4

Common: No

Sample:

```
<FORM   STYLE="background: red">
```

TARGET="..."

Identifies in which previously named frame the output from the form processor should appear.

Standard: HTML 4

Common: Yes

Sample:

```
<FORM TARGET="output" METHOD=GET
ACTION="/cgi-bin/thingie.sh">
```

TITLE="..."

Specifies text assigned to the tag. You might use this attribute for context-sensitive help within the document. Browsers may use this to show tool tips over the fill-out form.

Standard: HTML 4

Common: No

Sample:

```
<FORM METHOD=POST ACTION="/cgi-
bin/ff.pl"TITLE="Fill-out form">
```

Other Attributes

This tag also accepts the `lang`, `dir`, `onsubmit`, `onreset`, `onClick`, `onDblClick`, `onMouseDown`, `onMouseUp`, `onMouseOver`, `onMouseMove`, `onMouseOut`, `onKeyPress`, `onKeyDown`, and `onKeyUp` attributes. See the Element-Independent Attributes section of this reference for definitions and examples.

<FRAME>

Defines a frame within a frameset (see the <FRAMESET> tag). The <FRAME> tag specifies the source file and visual characteristics of a frame.

Standard: HTML 4

Common: Yes

Paired: No

Sample:

```
<FRAMESET ROWS="*,70">
   <FRAME SRC="frames/body.html"
   NAME="body">
   <FRAME SRC="frames/buttons
   .html" NAME="buttons" SCROLLING
   =NO NORESIZE>
</FRAMESET>
```

Attribute Information

BORDER="*n*"

Specifies the thickness of the border (in pixels) around a frame. Use BORDER=0 to specify a frame with no border.

Standard: Netscape Navigator

Common: Yes

Sample:

```
<FRAME SRC="hits.html"
BORDER="2">
```

BORDERCOLOR="*#RRGGBB*" or "*...*"

Specifies the color of the border around the frame. Use the color's hexadecimal RGB values or the color name.

Standard: Internet Explorer, Netscape Navigator

Common: Yes

Sample:

```
<FRAME SRC="hits.html"
BORDERCOLOR="red">
```

FRAMEBORDER={1,0}

Indicates whether the frame's border is visible. A value of 1 indicates that the border is visible, and a value of 0 indicates that it is not visible.

Standard: HTML 4

Common: No

Sample:

```
<FRAME SRC="weather.html"
FRAMEBORDER=0>
```

MARGINHEIGHT="*n*"

Specifies the vertical dimension (in number of pixels) of the top and bottom margins in a frame.

Standard: HTML 4

Common: No

Sample:

```
<FRAME SRC="cats.html"
MARGINHEIGHT=10>
```

MARGINWIDTH="*n*"

Specifies the horizontal dimension (in pixels) of the left and right margins in a frame.

Standard: HTML 4

Common: No

Sample:

```
<FRAME SRC="dogs.html"
MARGINWIDTH=10>
```

NAME="..."

Gives the frame you are defining a name. You can use this name later to load new documents into the frame (see the TARGET= attribute) and within scripts to control attributes of the frame. Reserved names with special meaning include _blank, _parent, _self, and _top.

> **Standard:**   HTML 4
>
> **Common:**   Yes
>
> **Sample:**

```
<FRAME SRC="/cgi-bin/weather.cgi"
NAME="weather">
```

NORESIZE

Makes a frame's dimensions unchangeable. Otherwise, if a frame's borders are visible, visitors can resize the frame by selecting a border and moving it with the mouse.

> **Standard:**   HTML 4
>
> **Common:**   Yes
>
> **Sample:**

```
<FRAME SRC="bottom.html"
NAME="bottom" NORESIZE
SCROLLING=NO>
```

SCROLLING={YES, NO, AUTO}

Indicates whether a scrollbar is present within a frame when text dimensions exceed the dimensions of the frame. Set SCROLLING=NO when using a frame to display only an image.

> **Standard:**   HTML 4
>
> **Common:**   Yes
>
> **Sample:**

```
<FRAME NAME="titleimg"
SRC="title.html" SCROLLING=NO>
```

SRC="URL"

Specifies the relative or absolute location of a document that you want to load within the defined frame.

> **Standard:**   HTML 4
>
> **Common:**   Yes
>
> **Sample:**

```
<FRAME NAME="main"
SRC="intro.html">
```

<FRAMESET>

Contains frame definitions and specifies frame spacing, dimensions, and attributes. Place <FRAME> tags inside <FRAMESET> tags.

> **Standard:**   HTML 4
>
> **Common:**   Yes
>
> **Paired:**   Yes
>
> **Sample:**

```
<FRAMESET COLS="*,70">
    <FRAME SRC="frames/body.html"
    NAME="body">
    <FRAME SRC="frames/side.html"
    NAME="side">
</FRAMESET>
```

Attribute Information

BORDER="n"

Specifies the thickness of borders (in pixels) around frames defined within the frameset. You can also control border thickness with the <FRAME> tag.

> **Standard:**   Netscape Navigator
>
> **Common:**   No
>
> **Sample:**

```
<FRAMESET COLS="*,150" BORDER=5>
    <FRAME SRC="left.html"
    NAME="main">
    <FRAME SRC="side.html"
    NAME="side">
</FRAMESET>
```

BORDERCOLOR="#RRGGBB" or "..."

Sets the color of the frame borders. Color names can substitute for the hexadecimal RGB color values.

Standard: Netscape Navigator, Internet Explorer

Common: Yes

Sample:

```
<FRAMESET BORDERCOLOR="Red"
ROWS="100,*">

  <FRAME SRC="top.html"
  NAME="title">

  <FRAME SRC="story.html"
  NAME="Story">

</FRAMESET>
```

COLS="..."

Specifies the number and dimensions of the vertical frames within the current frameset.

Set COLS= to a comma-separated list of numbers or percentages to indicate the width of each frame. Use the asterisk (*) to represent a variable width. A frame of variable width fills the space left over after the browser formats space for the other frames (<FRAMESET COLS="100, 400,10% *">).

Setting COLS= with percentage values controls the ratio of frame horizontal space relative to the amount of space available within the browser (<FRAMESET COLS="10%,*">).

You cannot use COLS= and ROWS= in the same tag.

Standard: HTML 4

Common: Yes

Sample:

```
<FRAMESET COLS="*,100,*">

  <FRAME SRC="left.html"
  NAME="left">
```

```
  <FRAME SRC="middle.html"
  NAME="middle">

  <FRAMESET ROWS=2>

    <FRAME SRC="top.html"
    NAME="top">

    <FRAME SRC="bottom.html"
    NAME="bottom">

  </FRAMESET>

</FRAMESET>
```

FRAMESPACING="n"

Specifies the space (in pixels) between frames within the browser window.

Standard: Internet Explorer

Common: No

Sample:

```
<FRAMESET ROWS="*,100"
FRAMESPACING=10>

  <FRAME SRC="top.html"
  NAME="top">

  <FRAME SRC="middle.html"
  NAME="middle">

</FRAMESET>
```

ROWS="..."

Specifies the number and dimensions of the horizontal frames within the current frameset.

Set ROWS= to a comma-separated list of numbers or percentages to indicate the height of each frame. Use the asterisk (*) to represent a variable height. A frame of variable height fills the space remaining after the browser formats space for the other frames (<FRAMESET ROWS="100,400,*">).

Setting ROWS= to a comma-separated list of percentages allows you to control the ratio of frame vertical space relative to the space available within the browser (<FRAMESET ROWS="10%,*">).

You cannot use ROWS= and COLS= in the same tag.

> **Standard**:   HTML 4
>
> **Common**:   Yes
>
> **Sample**:

```
<FRAMESET ROWS="*,100,*">

  <FRAME SRC="top.html"
  NAME="top">

  <FRAME SRC="middle.html"
  NAME="middle">

  <FRAMESET COLS=2>

    <FRAME SRC="bottom1.html"
    NAME="left">

    <FRAME SRC="bottom2.html"
    NAME="right">

  </FRAMESET>

</FRAMESET>
```

Other Attributes

This tag also accepts the onload and onunload attributes. See the Element-Independent Attributes section of this reference for definitions and examples.

H

<Hn>

Specifies headings in a document. Headings are numbered 1–6, with <H1> representing the heading for the main heading in the document and <H3> representing a heading for a nested subtopic. Generally, text inside heading tags appears in boldface and may be larger than normal document text.

> **Standard**:   HTML 2
>
> **Common**:   Yes
>
> **Paired**:   Yes

> **Sample**:

```
<H1>Caring For Your Canary</H1>
```

This document explains how you should take care of a canary. With proper care, you and your new bird will have a lasting, happy relationship.

```
<H2>Feeding</H2>
```

Attribute Information

ALIGN={LEFT, CENTER, RIGHT}

Positions the heading in the left, right, or center of a document.

> **Standard**:   HTML 3.2; deprecated in HTML 4 in favor of style sheets
>
> **Common**:   Yes
>
> **Sample**:

```
<H3 ALIGN=RIGHT>History Of The
Platypus</H3>
```

CLASS="..."

Indicates which style class applies to the <Hn> element.

> **Standard**:   HTML 4
>
> **Common**:   No
>
> **Sample**:

```
<H1 CLASS="casual"
ALIGN=LEFT>River Tours</H1>
```

ID="..."

Assigns a unique ID selector to an instance of the <Hn> tag. When you then assign a style to that ID selector, it affects only that one instance of the <Hn> tag.

> **Standard**:   HTML 4
>
> **Common**:   No
>
> **Sample**:

```
<H2 ID="123">Paper Products</H2>
```

STYLE="..."
Specifies style sheet commands that apply to the heading.

    Standard: HTML 4

    Common: No

    Sample:

`<H1 STYLE="background: red">`

TITLE="..."
Specifies text assigned to the tag. You might use this attribute for context-sensitive help within the document. Browsers may use this to show tool tips over the heading.

    Standard: HTML 4

    Common: No

    Sample:

`<H1 TITLE="Headline">`

Other Attributes
This tag also accepts the lang, dir, onClick, onDblClick, onMouseDown, onMouseUp, onMouseOver, onMouseMove, onMouseOut, onKeyPress, onKeyDown, and onKeyUp attributes. See the Element-Independent Attributes section of this reference for definitions and examples.

<HEAD>

Contains document head information. You can place any of the following tags within the document head: <LINK>, <META>, <TITLE>, <SCRIPT>, <BASE>, and <STYLE>.

    Standard: HTML 2

    Common: Yes

    Paired: Yes

    Sample:

`<HTML>`

`<HEAD>`

`<TITLE>Making a Peanut-Butter and Jelly Sandwich</TITLE>`

`<LINK REL=Parent HREF="sandwiches.html">`

`</HEAD>`

Attribute Information

PROFILE="URL"
Specifies the address of data profiles. You might use this attribute to specify the location of, for example, <META> tag information.

    Standard: HTML 4

    Common: No

    Sample:

`<HEAD PROFILE="http://www.raycomm.com/general.html">`

`</HEAD<`

Other Attributes
This tag also accepts the lang and dir attributes. See the Element-Independent Attributes section of this reference for definitions and examples.

<HR>

Draws horizontal lines (rules) in your document. This is useful for visually separating document sections.

    Standard: HTML 2

    Common: Yes

    Paired: No

    Sample:

`<H2>Birthday Colors</H2>`

`<HR ALIGN=LEFT WIDTH="60%">`

`<P>Birthdays are usually joyous celebrations so we recommend bright colors.`

Attribute Information

ALIGN={LEFT, CENTER, RIGHT}

Positions the line flush left, flush right, or in the center of the document. These settings are irrelevant unless you use the WIDTH= attribute to make the line shorter than the width of the document.

    Standard: HTML 3.2; deprecated in HTML 4 in favor of style sheets

    Common: Yes

    Sample:

```
<H2 ALIGN=LEFT>Shopping List</H2>
<HR WIDTH="40%" ALIGN=LEFT>
<UL TYPE=SQUARE>
<LI>Eggs
<LI>Butter
<LI>Bread
<LI>Milk
</UL>
```

CLASS="…"

Indicates which style class applies to the <HR> element.

    Standard: HTML 4

    Common: No

    Sample:

```
<HR CLASS="casual" WIDTH="50%">
```

COLOR="#RRGGBB" or "…"

Specifies the color of the line. The color name can substitute for the hexadecimal RGB values.

    Standard: Internet Explorer. style sheets provide equivalent functionality.

    Common: No

    Sample:

```
<HR COLOR=#09334C>
```

ID="n"

Assigns a unique ID selector to an instance of the <HR> tag. When you then assign a style to that ID selector, it affects only that one instance of the <HR> tag.

    Standard: HTML 4

    Common: No

    Sample:

```
<HR ID="123">
```

NOSHADE

Specifies that the browser not shade the line.

    Standard: HTML 3.2

    Common: Yes

    Sample:

```
<HR NOSHADE ALIGN=CENTER
WIDTH="50%">
<IMG SRC="Bobby.jpg" ALIGN=CENTER
BORDER=0 ALT="Bobby">
<BR CLEAR=ALL>
<HR NOSHADE ALIGN=CENTER
WIDTH="50%">
```

SIZE="n"

Specifies the thickness of the line (in pixels).

    Standard: HTML 3.2; deprecated in HTML 4 in favor of style sheets

    Common: Yes

    Sample:

```
<HR SIZE=10>
```

STYLE="…"

Specifies style sheet commands that apply to the horizontal rule.

Standard: HTML 4
Common: No
Sample:
```
<HR WIDTH="50%" STYLE="color:
red">
```

TITLE="..."
Specifies text assigned to the tag. You might use this attribute for context-sensitive help within the document. Browsers may use this to show tool tips over the horizontal rule.

Standard: HTML 4
Common: No
Sample:
```
<HR TITLE="A line">
```

WIDTH="*n*"
Specifies the length of the line. You can specify the value with an absolute number of pixels or as a percentage to indicate how much of the total width available is used.

Standard: HTML 3.2; deprecated in HTML 4 in favor of style sheets
Common: Yes
Sample:
```
<H2 ALIGN=CENTER>The End!</H2>
<HR WIDTH="85%">
<P ALIGN=CENTER>
<A HREF="/index.html">Home</A> |
<A HREF="Story3.html">Next
Story</A> |
<A HREF="Story1.html">Prev
Story</A>
```

Other Attributes
This tag also accepts the onClick, onDbl-Click, onMouseDown, onMouseUp, onMouseOver, onMouseMove, onMouseOut, onKeyPress, onKeyDown, and onKeyUp attributes. See the Element-Independent Attributes section of this reference for definitions and examples.

<HTML>
Contains the entire document. Place these tags at the top and bottom of your HTML file.

Standard: HTML 2
Common: Yes
Paired: Yes
Sample:
```
<HTML>
<HEAD><TITLE>Test
Page</TITLE></HEAD>
<BODY>
    <H1>Is this working?</H1>
</BODY>
</HTML>
```

Attribute Information
This tag accepts the lang and dir attributes. See the Element-Independent Attributes section of this reference for definitions and examples.

I

<I>
Italicizes text.

Standard: HTML 2
Common: Yes
Paired: Yes
Sample:
```
After this, Tom told me to
read<I>Mastering HTML</I>. I had
no choice but to do so.
```

Attribute Information

CLASS="..."
Indicates which style class applies to the <I> element.

Standard: HTML 4
Common: No
Sample:

```
This mouse is
<I CLASS="casual">enhanced</I>
```

ID="..."
Assigns a unique ID selector to an instance of the <I> tag. When you then assign a style to that ID selector, it affects only that one instance of the <I> tag.

Standard: HTML 4
Common: No
Sample:

```
He called it a <I ID="123">Doo-
Dad</I>!
```

STYLE="..."
Specifies style sheet commands that apply to italicized text.

Standard: HTML 4
Common: No
Sample:

```
<I STYLE="color: green">
```

TITLE="..."
Specifies text assigned to the tag. You might use this attribute for context-sensitive help within the document. Browsers may use this to show tool tips over the italicized text.

Standard: HTML 4
Common: No
Sample:

```
<I TITLE="Italicized">
```

Other Attributes
This tag also accepts the lang, dir, onClick, onDblClick, onMouseDown, onMouseUp, onMouseOver, onMouseMove, onMouseOut, onKeyPress, onKeyDown, and onKeyUp attributes. See the Element-Independent Attributes section of this reference for definitions and examples.

<IFRAME>

Creates floating frames within a document. Floating frames differ from normal frames because they are independently manipulable elements within another HTML document.

Standard: HTML 4
Common: No
Paired: Yes
Sample:

```
<IFRAME NAME="new_win"
    SRC="http://www.raycomm.com">
</IFRAME>
```

Attribute Information

ALIGN={LEFT, CENTER, RIGHT}
Specifies how the floating frame lines up with respect to the left and right sides of the browser window.

Standard: HTML 4; deprecated usage. Use style sheets instead.
Common: No
Sample:

```
<IFRAME ALIGN=LEFT
SRC="goats.html"NAME="g1">
```

BORDER="n"
Indicates the thickness of a border around a floating frame (in pixels).

Standard: Internet Explorer 4
Common: No

Sample:

```
<IFRAME SRC="joe.html"
NAME="Joe"BORDER=5>
```

BORDERCOLOR="#RRGGBB" or "..."

Specifies (in hexadecimal RGB values or the color name) the color of the border around a floating frame.

Standard: Internet Explorer 4

Common: No

Sample:

```
<IFRAME SRC="joe.html"
NAME="Joe"BORDERCOLOR=#5A3F2E>
```

FRAMEBORDER={0,1}

Indicates whether the floating frame has visible borders. A value of 0 indicates no border, and a value of 1 indicates a visible border.

Standard: HTML 4

Common: No

Sample:

```
<IFRAME SRC="main.html"
NAME="main"FRAMEBORDER=0>
```

FRAMESPACING="n"

Indicates the space (in pixels) between adjacent floating frames.

Standard: Internet Explorer 4

Common: No

Sample:

```
<IFRAME SRC="joe.html" NAME="Joe"
FRAMESPACING=10>
```

HEIGHT="n"

Specifies the vertical dimension (in pixels) of the floating frame.

Standard: HTML 4

Common: No

Sample:

```
<IFRAME SRC="joe.html"
NAME="Joe"WIDTH=500 HEIGHT=200>
```

HSPACE="n"

Indicates the size (in pixels) of left and right margins within the floating frame.

Standard: Internet Explorer 4

Common: No

Sample:

```
<IFRAME SRC="joe.html"
NAME="Joe"HSPACE=10 VSPACE=10>
```

ID="..."

Assigns a unique ID selector to an instance of the <IFRAME> tag. When you then assign a style to that ID selector, it affects only that one instance of the <IFRAME> tag.

Standard: HTML 4

Common: No

Sample:

```
<IFRAME SRC="Joe.html" NAME="Joe"
ID="123">
```

MARGINHEIGHT="n"

Specifies the size of the top and bottom margins (in pixels) within the floating frame.

Standard: HTML 4

Common: No

Sample:

```
<IFRAME SRC="top.html"
NAME="topbar" MARGINHEIGHT=50>
```

MARGINWIDTH="n"

Specifies the size of the left and right margins (in pixels) within the floating frame.

Standard: HTML 4

Common: No

Sample:

```
<IFRAME SRC="body.html"
NAME="body"MARGINWIDTH=50>
```

NAME="..."

Assigns the frame a unique name. You can use this name within other frames to load new documents in the frame and to manipulate the attributes of the frame.

Standard: HTML 4

Common: No

Sample:

```
<IFRAME SRC="joe.html" NAME="Joe"
WIDTH=500 HEIGHT=200>
```

NORESIZE

Specifies that the floating frame cannot resize. Because the HTML 4 specification forbids resizable inline frames, this attribute is only relevant to Internet Explorer.

Standard: Internet Explorer

Common: No

Sample:

```
<IFRAME SRC="joe.html"
NAME="Joe"NORESIZE>
```

SCROLLING={YES, NO}

Indicates whether the floating frame has scrollbars.

Standard: HTML 4

Common: No

Sample:

```
<IFRAME SRC="top.html"
SCROLLING=NO>
```

SRC="*URL*"

Specifies the relative or absolute location of the document file to load in the floating frame.

Standard: HTML 4

Common: No

Sample:

```
<IFRAME NAME="pics" SRC="pics/">
```

STYLE="..."

Specifies style sheet commands that apply to the floating frame.

Standard: HTML 4

Common: No

Sample:

```
<IFRAME SRC="dots.html"
NAME="dots" STYLE="background:
red">
```

WIDTH=*"n"*

Specifies the horizontal dimension (in pixels) of the floating frame.

Standard: HTML 4

Common: No

Sample:

```
<IFRAME SRC="joe.html" NAME="Joe"
WIDTH=500 HEIGHT=200>
```

VSPACE=*"n"*

Indicates the size (in pixels) of top and bottom margins within the floating frame.

Standard: Internet Explorer 4

Common: No

Sample:

```
<IFRAME SRC="joe.html" NAME="Joe"
HSPACE=10 VSPACE=10>
```

Other Attributes

This tag also accepts the lang, dir, onClick, onDblClick, onMouseDown, onMouseUp, onMouseOver, onMouseMove, onMouseOut, onKeyPress, onKeyDown, and onKeyUp attributes. See the Element-Independent Attributes section of this reference for definitions and examples.

<IMG>

Places an inline image in a document. You can use the attributes ISMAP= and USEMAP= with the <IMG> tag to implement imagemaps.

Standard:	HTML 2
Common:	Yes
Paired:	No
Sample:	

```
<IMG SRC="images/left_arrow.gif"
ALT="<-">
```

Attribute Information

ALIGN={LEFT, RIGHT, TOP, MIDDLE, BOTTOM}

Specifies the appearance of text that is near an inline graphic image. For example, if you use RIGHT, the image appears flush to the right edge of the document, and the text appears to its left. Using LEFT produces the opposite effect.

HTML 2 mentions only attribute values of TOP, MIDDLE, and BOTTOM. TOP aligns the top of the first line of text after the <IMG> tag to the top of the image. BOTTOM (the default) aligns the bottom of the image to the baseline of the text. MIDDLE aligns the baseline of the first line of text with the middle of the image.

HTML 3.2 added LEFT and RIGHT to the list of attribute values.

You can use the <BR> tag to control specific points where text stops wrapping around an image and continues below the instance of the image.

Standard:	HTML 2; deprecated in HTML 4 in favor of style sheets
Common:	Yes
Sample:	

```
<IMG SRC="red_icon.gif"
ALIGN=LEFT>
```

```
It's about time for volunteers to
pitch in.<BR CLEAR=ALL>
```

ALT="..."

Provides a textual description of images, which is useful for visitors who have text-only browsers. Some browsers may also display the ALT= text as a floating message when the visitor places the mouse pointer over the image.

Standard:	HTML 2
Common:	Yes
Sample:	

```
<IMG SRC="smiley.gif" ALT=":-)">
```

BORDER="n"

Specifies the width (in pixels) of a border around an image. The default value is usually 0 (no border). The border color is the color of normal text within your document.

Standard:	HTML 3.2
Common:	Yes
Sample:	

```
<IMG SRC="portrait.jpg" BORDER=2>
```

CLASS="..."

Indicates which style class applies to the <IMG> element.

Standard:	HTML 4
Common:	No
Sample:	

```
<IMG CLASS="casual"
SRC="dots.gif">
```

CONTROLS

If the image is a video file, indicates the playback controls that appear below the image.

Standard:	Internet Explorer 2
Common:	No
Sample:	

```
<IMG DYNSRC="foo.avi" CONTROLS>
```

DATAFLD="..."
Indicates a column in previously identified tabular data.

Standard: Internet Explorer 4
Common: No
Sample:

```
<IMG SRC="thing.gif"
DATAFLD="color">
```

DATASRC="..."
Specifies the location of tabular data to be bound.

Standard: Internet Explorer 4
Common: No
Sample:

```
<IMG SRC="thing.gif"
DATASRC="#data_table">
```

DYNSRC="URL"
Specifies the relative or absolute location of a dynamic image (VRML, video file, and so on).

Standard: Internet Explorer 2
Common: No
Sample:

```
<IMG DYNSRC="foo.avi">
```

HEIGHT="n"
Specifies the vertical dimension of the image (in pixels). If you don't use this attribute, the image appears in the default height. Use this attribute, along with the WIDTH= attribute, to fit an image within a space. You can fit a large image into a smaller space, and you can spread a smaller image. Some Web designers use the WIDTH= and HEIGHT= attributes to spread a single pixel image over a large space to produce the effect of a larger solid-color image.

Standard: HTML 3.2
Common: Yes

Sample:

```
<IMG SRC="images/smiley.jpg"
WIDTH=50 HEIGHT=50>
```

HSPACE="n"
Establishes a margin of white space (in pixels) to the left and right of a graphic image. (See the VSPACE= attribute for how to control the top and bottom margins around an image.)

Standard: HTML 3.2
Common: Yes
Sample:

```
<IMG SRC="pics/pinetree.jpg"
HSPACE=20 VSPACE=15>
```

ID=n
Assigns a unique ID selector to an instance of the <IMG> tag. When you then assign a style to that ID selector, it affects only that one instance of the <IMG> tag.

Standard: HTML 4
Common: No
Sample:

```
<IMG SRC="grapes.jpg" ID="123">
```

ISMAP
Indicates that the graphic image functions as a clickable imagemap. The ISMAP= attribute instructs the browser to send the pixel coordinates to the server imagemap CGI application when a visitor selects the image with the mouse pointer. When HTML 2 established the ISMAP= attribute, imagemaps were implemented in a server-side fashion only. Now, client-side imagemaps are more popular (see the USEMAP= attribute).

Standard: HTML 2
Common: Yes

Sample:

```
<A HREF="/cgi-bin/
imagemap/mymap">

<IMG ISMAP
SRC="images/main.gif"></A>
```

LOWSRC="*URL*"

Indicates the absolute or relative location of a lower resolution version of an image.

Standard: Netscape Navigator

Common: No

Sample:

```
<IMG SRC="bigpic.jpg"
LOWSRC="lilpic.jpg">
```

LOOP={*n*, INFINITE}

Indicates the number of times a video file plays back.

Standard: Internet Explorer 2

Common: No

Sample:

```
<IMG DYNSRC="bar.avi"
LOOP=INFINITE>
```

NAME="..."

Specifies a name by which bookmarks, scripts, and applets can reference the image.

Standard: Internet Explorer 4

Common: No

Sample:

```
<IMG SRC="tweakie.jpg"
NAME="img_1">
```

SRC="*URL*"

Specifies the relative or absolute location of a file that contains the graphic image you want to embed in a document.

Standard: HTML 2

Common: Yes

Sample:

```
<IMG SRC="images/left_arrow.gif"
ALT="<-">
```

START={FILEOPEN, MOUSEOVER}

Specifies the event that triggers the playback of a dynamic image. START=FILEOPEN starts playback when the browser has completely downloaded the file. START=MOUSEOVER starts playback when a visitor places the mouse pointer over the image.

Standard: Internet Explorer 2

Common: No

Sample:

```
<IMG DYNSRC="ship.vrm"
START=MOUSEOVER>
```

STYLE="..."

Specifies style sheet commands that apply to the inline image.

Standard: HTML 4

Common: No

Sample:

```
<IMG SRC="dots.gif"
STYLE="background: red">
```

TITLE="..."

Specifies text assigned to the tag. You might use this attribute for context-sensitive help within the document. Browsers may use this to show tool tips over the image.

Standard: HTML 4

Common: No

Sample:

```
<IMG SRC="pics/jill.jpg"
TITLE="Image">
```

USEMAP="*URL*"

Specifies the location of the client-side imagemap data (see the <MAP> tag). Because the <MAP> tag gives the map data an anchor name, be sure to include the name with the URL of the document that contains the map data.

> **Standard**:   HTML 3.2
> **Common**:   Yes
> **Sample**:

```
<IMG ISMAP SRC="map1.gif"
USEMAP="maps.html#map1">
```

VRML="..."
Specifies the absolute or relative location of a VRML world to embed in a document.

> **Standard**:   Internet Explorer 4
> **Common**:   No
> **Sample**:

```
<IMG VRML="vr/myroom.vrml">
```

VSPACE="n"
Establishes a margin of white space (in pixels) above and below a graphic image. (See the HSPACE= attribute for how to control the left and right margins of an image.)

> **Standard**:   HTML 3.2
> **Common**:   Yes
> **Sample**:

```
<IMG SRC="pics/pinetree.jpg"
HSPACE=20 VSPACE=15>
```

WIDTH="n"
Specifies the horizontal dimension of the image (in pixels). If you don't use this attribute, the image appears in the default width. Use this attribute, along with the HEIGHT= attribute, to fit an image within a space. You can fit a large image into a smaller space, and you can spread a smaller image. Some Web designers use WIDTH= and HEIGHT= to spread a single pixel image over a large space to produce the effect of a larger solid-color image.

> **Standard**:   HTML 3.2
> **Common**:   Yes

> **Sample**:

```
<IMG SRC="images/smiley.jpg"
WIDTH=50 HEIGHT=50>
```

Other Attributes
This tag also accepts the lang, dir, onClick, onDblClick, onMouseDown, onMouseUp, onMouseOver, onMouseMove, onMouseOut, onKeyPress, onKeyDown, and onKeyUp attributes. See the Element-Independent Attributes section of this reference for definitions and examples.

<INPUT>

Identifies several input methods for forms. This tag must appear between the opening and closing <FORM> tags.

> **Standard**:   HTML 2
> **Common**:   Yes
> **Paired**:   No
> **Sample**:

```
<FORM ACTION="/cgi-bin/order/"
METHOD=POST>
<INPUT NAME="qty" TYPE="TEXT"
SIZE=5>
<INPUT TYPE="submit"
VALUE="Order">
</FORM>
```

Attribute Information

ACCEPT="..."
Specifies a list of acceptable MIME types for submitted files.

> **Standard**:   HTML 4
> **Common**:   No
> **Sample**:

```
<INPUT TYPE=FILE
ACCEPT="image/gif">
Please submit a GIF image.
```

ALIGN={LEFT, CENTER, RIGHT}

Lines up a graphical submit button
(TYPE=IMAGE). The behavior of this tag is
identical to that of the ALIGN= attribute of
the <IMG> tag.

Standard: HTML 3.2; deprecated
in HTML 4 in favor of style
sheets

Common: Yes

Sample:

```
<INPUT TYPE=IMAGE
SRC="picture.gif" ALIGN=RIGHT>
```

CHECKED

Use with TYPE=RADIO or TYPE=
CHECKBOX to set the default state of those
input methods to True.

Standard: HTML 2

Common: Yes

Sample:

```
<INPUT TYPE=CHECKBOX CHECKED
NAME="foo" VALUE="1"><BR>

2 <INPUT TYPE=CHECKBOX NAME="foo"
VALUE="2"><BR>
```

CLASS="..."

Indicates which style class applies to the
<INPUT> element.

Standard: HTML 4

Common: No

Sample:

```
<INPUT CLASS="casual" TYPE=TEXT
NAME="age">
```

DATAFLD="..."

Selects a column from previously identified
tabular data.

Standard: Internet Explorer 4

Common: No

Sample:

```
<DIV DATASRC="#data_table">

<INPUT TYPE=TEXT NAME="color"
DATAFLD="colorvals">
```

DATASRC="..."

Specifies the location of tabular data to be
bound.

Standard: Internet Explorer 4

Common: No

Sample:

```
<INPUT TYPE=TEXT
DATASRC="#data_table"
DATAFLD="dataval1">
```

DISABLED="..."

Disables an instance of the input method so
that data cannot be accepted or
submitted.

Standard: HTML 4

Common: No

Sample:

```
<INPUT TYPE=PASSWORD NAME="Pass"
DISABLED>
```

ID="*n*"

Assigns a unique ID selector to an instance of
the <INPUT> tag. When you then assign a
style to that ID selector, it affects only that
one instance of the <INPUT> tag.

Standard: HTML 4

Common: No

Sample:

```
Age:

<INPUT TYPE=TEXT NAME="age"
ID="123">
```

MAXLENGTH="*n*"

Indicates the number of characters you can
enter into a text input field and is only useful
to input methods of type TEXT or PASSWORD.

Contrary to the SIZE= attribute, MAXLENGTH= does not affect the size of the input field shown on the screen.

Standard: HTML 2

Common: Yes

Sample:

```
Phone: <INPUT TYPE=TEXT
NAME="phone" MAXLENGTH=11>
```

NAME="..."

Gives a name to the value you pass to the form processor. For example, if you collect a person's last name with an input method of type TEXT, you assign the NAME= attribute something like "lastname." This establishes a *name-value pair* for the form processor.

Standard: HTML 2

Common: Yes

Sample:

```
Enter your phone number: <INPUT
TYPE="text" NAME="phone" SIZE=10>
```

NOTAB

Removes the input element from the tab order.

Standard: Internet Explorer

Common: No

Sample:

```
Hair color:

<INPUT TYPE=TEXT NAME="hcolor"
NOTAB>
```

READONLY

Indicates that changes to the input method data cannot occur.

Standard: HTML 4

Common: No

Sample:

```
<INPUT TYPE=TEXT NAME="desc"
VALUE="1/4 inch flange assy"
READONLY>
```

SIZE="n"

Specifies the width of the input method (in characters). This applies only to input methods of type TEXT or PASSWORD. HTML 4 specifies size measurements in pixels for all other input methods, but pixel size specification is little supported.

Standard: HTML 2

Common: Yes

Sample:

```
Your Age: <INPUT TYPE="text"
NAME="Age" SIZE=5><BR>
```

SRC="URL"

Implements a graphic image for a submit button. For this to work, indicate TYPE=IMAGE.

Standard: HTML 3.2

Common: Yes

Sample:

```
<INPUT TYPE=IMAGE
SRC="/images/push-button.gif">
```

STYLE="..."

Specifies style sheet commands that apply to the input element.

Standard: HTML 4

Common: No

Sample:

```
<INPUT TYPE=RADIO NAME="food"
VALUE="1" STYLE="background:
red">
```

TABINDEX="n"

Specifies where the input method appears in the tab order. For example, TABINDEX=3 places the cursor at the input element after the visitor presses the Tab key three times.

Standard: Internet Explorer

Common: No

Sample:

Credit card number:

```
<INPUT TYPE=TEXT
NAME="ccard"TABINDEX=5>
```

TITLE="…"

Specifies text assigned to the tag. You might
use this attribute for context-
sensitive help within the document. Browsers
may use this to show tool tips over the input
method.

    Standard: HTML 4

    Common: No

    Sample:

```
<INPUT TYPE=RADIO NAME="cc"
VALUE="visa" TITLE="Visa">
```

TYPE="…"

Indicates the kind of input method to use.
Valid values are TEXT, PASSWORD, RADIO,
CHECKBOX, SUBMIT, RESET, IMAGE, FILE,
HIDDEN, and BUTTON.

TEXT produces a simple one-line text input
field that is useful for obtaining simple data
such as a person's name, a person's age, a dollar amount, and so on. To collect multiple
lines of text, use the <TEXTAREA> tag.

PASSWORD gives the visitor a simple one-line
text input field similar to the TEXT type.
When visitors enter data into the field, however, they do not see what
they type.

TYPE=RADIO produces a small radio button
that can be turned on and off. Use radio buttons when you want a visitor
to select only one of several items. For multi-
ple-value selections, see the CHECKBOX type
or the <SELECT> tag.

SUBMIT produces a button that, when
selected, submits all the name-value pairs to
the form processor.

RESET sets all the input methods to their
empty or default settings.

TYPE=IMAGE replaces the submit button
with an image. The behavior of this value is
identical to that of the submit button, except
that the x,y coordinates of the mouse position
over the image when selected are also sent to
the form
processor.

BUTTON creates a button with no specific
behavior that can interact with scripts.

    Standard: HTML 2

    Common: Yes

    Sample:

```
<FORM METHOD=POST ACTION="/cgi-
bin/thingie">
```

```
Name: <INPUT TYPE=TEXT
NAME="name"><BR>
```

```
Password: <INPUT TYPE=PASSWORD
NAME="pass"><BR>
```

```
Ice Cream:  Vanilla<INPUT
TYPE=RADIO VALUE="1" CHECKED
NAME="ice_cream"> Chocolate<INPUT
TYPE=RADIO VALUE="2"
NAME="ice_cream"><br>
```

```
<INPUT TYPE=SUBMIT VALUE="Send
Data...">
```

```
</FORM>
```

USEMAP="*URL*"

Indicates the relative or absolute location of a
client-side imagemap to use with
the form.

    Standard: HTML 4

    Common: No

    Sample:

```
<INPUT SRC="mapimage.gif"
USEMAP="maps.html#map1">
```

VALUE="..."

Sets the default input value method. Required when <INPUT> is set to TYPE=RADIO or CHECKBOX.

Standard: HTML 2

Common: Yes

Sample:

```
<INPUT TYPE=HIDDEN NAME="id"
VALUE="123">
```

Other Attributes

This tag also accepts the lang, dir, onfocus, onblur, onselect, onchange, onClick, onDblClick, onMouseDown, onMouseUp, onMouseOver, onMouseMove, onMouseOut, onKeyPress, onKeyDown, and onKeyUp attributes. See the Element-Independent Attributes section of this reference for definitions and examples.

<INS>

Indicates text to be inserted in the document. May be either block-level or inline, as necessary.

Standard: HTML 4

Common: No

Paired: Yes

Sample:

```
<P>HTTP stands for HyperText
<INS>Transfer</INS>Protocol</P>
```

Attribute Information

CITE="*URL*"

Indicates address of reference (definitive source, for example) for insertion.

Standard: HTML 4

Common: No

Sample:

```
<INS CITE="http://www.w3.org/">
HTML 2 was used for 2 years.
</INS>
```

CLASS="..."

Indicates which style class applies to the <INS> element.

Standard: HTML 4

Common: No

Sample:

```
<INS CLASS="joeadd">POP stands
for Post Office Protocol</INS>
```

DATETIME="..."

Indicates the date and time in precisely this format: YYYY-MM-DDThh:mm:ssTZD. For example, 1997-07-14T08:30:00-07:00 indicates July 14, 1997, at 8:30 AM, in U.S. Mountain Time (7 hours from Greenwich time). This time could also be presented as 1997-07-14T08:30:00Z.

Standard: HTML 4

Common: No

Sample:

```
<INS DATETIME="1997-07-
14T08:30:00Z">POP stands for Post
Office Protocol</INS>
```

ID="..."

Assigns a unique ID selector to an instance of the <INS> tag. When you then assign a style to that ID selector, it affects only that one instance of the <INS> tag.

Standard: HTML 4

Common: No

Sample:

```
<INS ID="123">WWW stands for
World Wide Web</INS>
```

STYLE="..."
Specifies style sheet commands that apply to the inserted text.

    Standard: HTML 4
    Common: No
    Sample:

```
<INS STYLE="background: blue;
color: white">ESP stands for
extra-sensory perception.</INS>
```

TITLE="..."
Specifies text assigned to the tag. You might use this attribute for context-sensitive help within the document. Browsers may use this to show tool tips over the inserted text.

    Standard: HTML 4
    Common: No
    Sample:

```
<INS TITLE="Definition">More
deleted text.</INS>
```

Other Attributes
This tag also accepts the lang, dir, onClick, onDblClick, onMouseDown, onMouseUp, onMouseOver, onMouseMove, onMouseOut, onKeyPress, onKeyDown, and onKeyUp attributes. See the Element-Independent Attributes section of this reference for definitions and examples.

<ISINDEX>

Inserts an input field into the document so that visitors can enter search queries. The queries then go to a CGI application indicated by the ACTION= attribute.

    Standard: HTML 2; deprecated in HTML 4 in favor of <FORM>
    Common: Yes
    Paired: No

    Sample:

```
<ISINDEX PROMPT="Keyword Search"
ACTION="/cgi-bin/search.cgi">
```

Attribute Information
ACTION="*URL*"
Specifies the URL of the application that processes the search query. If you don't include ACTION=, the query goes to a URL formed from the document base (see the <BASE> tag).

    Standard: HTML 2
    Common: Yes
    Sample:

```
<ISINDEX ACTION="/cgi-bin/index-
search">
```

PROMPT="..."
Changes the input prompt for keyword index searches. If you don't specify PROMPT=, the browser displays a default prompt.

    Standard: HTML 3.2
    Common: Yes
    Sample:

```
<ISINDEX PROMPT="Search for
something">
```

K

<KBD>

Specifies keyboard input within a document.

    Standard: HTML 2
    Common: Yes
    Paired: Yes
    Sample:

```
Press <KBD>CTRL+S</KBD> to save
your document.
```

Attribute Information

CLASS="..."

Indicates which style class applies to the
<KBD> element.

> **Standard**: HTML 4
>
> **Common**: No
>
> **Sample**:

```
Now press the <KBD
CLASS="casual">F4</KBD> key!
```

ID="..."

Assigns a unique ID selector to an instance of
the <KBD> tag. When you then assign a style
to that ID selector, it affects only that one
instance of the <KBD> tag.

> **Standard**: HTML 4
>
> **Common**: No
>
> **Sample**:

```
Press <KBD ID="123">F1</KBD> for
help.
```

STYLE="..."

Specifies style sheet commands that apply to
the text within the <KBD> tags.

> **Standard**: HTML 4
>
> **Common**: No
>
> **Sample**:

```
<KBD STYLE="background:
red">F10</KBD>
```

TITLE="..."

Specifies text assigned to the tag. You might
use this attribute for context-
sensitive help within the document. Browsers
may use this to show tool tips over the keyboard text.

> **Standard**: HTML 4
>
> **Common**: No
>
> **Sample**:

```
Now press the <KBD
TITLE="Keyboard stuff">F4</KBD>
key.
```

Other Attributes

This tag also accepts the lang, dir,
onClick, onDblClick, onMouseDown,
onMouseUp, onMouseOver, onMouseMove,
onMouseOut, onKeyPress, onKeyDown,
and onKeyUp attributes. See the Element-
Independent Attributes section of this reference for definitions and examples.

L

<LABEL>

Provides identifying text for a form
widget.

> **Standard**: HTML 4
>
> **Common**: No
>
> **Paired**: Yes
>
> **Sample**:

```
<LABEL FOR="idname">First
Name</LABEL>
<INPUT TYPE="TEXT" ID="idname">
```

Attribute Information

ACCESSKEY="..."

Assigns a keystroke to the element.

> **Standard**: HTML 4
>
> **Common**: No
>
> **Sample**:

```
<LABEL FOR="idname" ACCESSKEY=H>
```

CLASS="..."

Indicates which style class applies to the
<INPUT> element.

Standard: HTML 4

Common: No

Sample:

```
<LABEL FOR="idname"
CLASS="short">First Name</LABEL>
<INPUT TYPE="TEXT" ID="idname">
```

FOR="..."

Specifies the ID of the widget associated with the label.

Standard: HTML 4

Common: No

Sample:

```
<LABEL FOR="idname">First
Name</LABEL>
<INPUT TYPE="TEXT" ID="idname">
```

ID="n"

Assigns a unique ID selector to an instance of the <INPUT> tag. When you then assign a style to that ID selector, it affects only that one instance of the <INPUT> tag.

Standard: HTML 4

Common: No

Sample:

```
<LABEL FOR="idname"
ID="234">First Name</LABEL>
<INPUT TYPE="TEXT" ID="idname">
```

STYLE="..."

Specifies style sheet commands that apply to the input element.

Standard: HTML 4

Common: No

Sample:

```
<LABEL FOR="idname"
STYLE="background : red">
First Name</LABEL>
<INPUT TYPE="TEXT" ID="idname">
```

TABINDEX="n"

Specifies where the input method appears in the tab order. For example, TABINDEX=3 places the cursor at the input element after the visitor presses the Tab key three times.

Standard: HTML 4

Common: No

Sample:

```
Credit card number:
<INPUT TYPE=TEXT
NAME="ccard"TABINDEX=5>
```

TITLE="..."

Specifies text assigned to the tag. You might use this attribute for context-sensitive help within the document. Browsers may use this to show tool tips over the input method.

Standard: HTML 4

Common: No

Sample:

```
<INPUT TYPE=RADIO NAME="cc"
VALUE="visa" TITLE="Visa">
```

Other Attributes

This tag also accepts the lang, dir, onfocus, onblur, onselect, onchange, onClick, onDblClick, onMouseDown, onMouseUp, onMouseOver, onMouseMove, onMouseOut, onKeyPress, onKeyDown, and onKeyUp attributes. See the Element-Independent Attributes section of this reference for definitions and examples.

<LAYER>

Defines a layer within a document, which you can than manipulate with JavaScript. Specify the layer's contents by placing HTML between the <LAYER> tags or by using the SRC= attribute.

Standard: Netscape Navigator 4

Common: No

Paired: Yes

Sample:

```
<LAYER SRC="top.html" HEIGHT=100
WIDTH=100 Z-INDEX=4 NAME="top"
VISIBILITY=SHOW>
</LAYER>
```

Attribute Information

ABOVE="..."

Specifies the name of a layer above which the current layer should appear.

Standard: Netscape Navigator 4

Common: No

Sample:

```
<LAYER SRC="grass.gif" Z-INDEX=1
NAME="Grass" VISIBILITY=SHOW>
<LAYER SRC="dog.gif"
ABOVE="Grass"NAME="Dog">
```

BACKGROUND="URL"

Specifies the relative or absolute location of an image file that the browser tiles as the background of the layer.

Standard: Netscape Navigator 4

Common: No

Sample:

```
<LAYER Z-INDEX=5 NAME="info"
BACKGROUND="goo.gif">
<H1>Hi there</H1></LAYER>
```

BELOW="..."

Specifies the name of a layer below which the current layer should appear.

Standard: Netscape Navigator 4

Common: No

Sample:

```
<LAYER BACKGROUND="road.jpg"
NAME="Road" UNDER="Car">
</LAYER>
```

BGCOLOR="#RRGGBB" or "..."

Specifies the background color of the layer. Use either the hexadecimal RGB values or the color name.

Standard: Netscape Navigator 4

Common: No

Sample:

```
<LAYER BGCOLOR=#FF0011><DIV
ALIGN=CENTER>
  <H1><BLINK>EAT AT
  JOES!</BLINK></H1>
</DIV>
</LAYER>
```

CLIP="x1, y1, x2, y2"

Indicates the dimensions of a clipping rectangle that specifies which areas of the layer are visible. Areas outside this rectangle become transparent.

You can give the x and y coordinates in pixels or as percentages to indicate relative portions of the layer. You can omit *x1* and *y1* if you want to clip from the top left corner of the layer.

Standard: Netscape Navigator 4

Common: No

Sample:

```
<LAYER SRC="hawk.jpg"
CLIP="20%,20%">
</LAYER>
```

HEIGHT="n"

Specifies the vertical dimension of the layer (in pixels or as a percentage of the browser window height).

Standard: Netscape Navigator 4

Common: No

Sample:

```
<LAYER SRC="frame.gif"
ABOVE="bg"NAME="frame"
WIDTH=200 HEIGHT=200>
```

LEFT="*n*"

Specifies the layer's horizontal position (in pixels) relative to the left edge of the parent layer. Use the TOP= attribute for vertical positioning.

Standard: Netscape Navigator 4

Common: No

Sample:

```
<LAYER LEFT=100 TOP=150>This
layer is at {100,150}</LAYER>
```

NAME="..."

Gives the layer a name by which other layer definitions and JavaScript code can reference it.

Standard: Netscape Navigator 4

Common: No

Sample:

```
<LAYER SRC="car.gif"
NAME="CarPic"ABOVE="Road">
</LAYER>
```

SRC="*URL*"

Specifies the relative or absolute location of the file containing the contents of the layer.

Standard: Netscape Navigator 4

Common: No

Sample:

```
<LAYER SRC="ocean.jpg"></LAYER>
```

TOP="*n*"

Specifies the layer's vertical position (in pixels) relative to the top edge of the parent

layer. Use the LEFT= attribute for horizontal positioning.

Standard: Netscape Navigator 4

Common: No

Sample:

```
<LAYER LEFT=100 TOP=150>This
layer is at {100,150}</LAYER>
```

VISIBILITY={SHOW, HIDE, INHERIT}

Indicates whether the layer is initially visible. VISIBILITY=SHOW indicates the layer is initially visible. VISIBILITY =HIDE indicates the layer is not initially visible. VISIBILITY=INHERIT indicates the layer has the same initial visibility attribute as its parent layer.

Standard: Netscape Navigator 4

Common: No

Sample:

```
<LAYER SRC="grass.gif" Z-INDEX=1
NAME="Grass" VISIBILITY=SHOW>
```

WIDTH="*n*"

Specifies the horizontal dimension of the layer (in pixels or as a percentage of the browser window width).

Standard: Netscape Navigator 4

Common: No

Sample:

```
<LAYER SRC="frame.gif"
ABOVE="bg"NAME="frame"
WIDTH=200 HEIGHT=200>
```

Z-INDEX="*n*"

Specifies where the layer appears in the stack of layers. Higher values indicate a position closer to the top of the stack.

Standard: Netscape Navigator 4

Common: No

Sample:

```
<LAYER Z-INDEX=0 NAME="Bottom">
```

You may never see this text ifother layers are above it.

```
</LAYER>
```

<LEGEND>

Specifies a description for a fieldset. Use inside <FIELDSET> tags.

Standard:	HTML 4
Common:	No
Paired:	Yes
Sample:	

```
<FORM><FIELDSET>
  <LEGEND VALIGN=TOP
  ALIGN=CENTER>
  Test Grades For COOKING 101
  </LEGEND>...
</FORM>
```

Attribute Information

ALIGN={TOP, BOTTOM, LEFT, RIGHT}

Indicates whether the legend appears at the top, bottom, left, or right of the fieldset.

Standard:	HTML 4
Common:	No
Sample:	

```
<LEGEND ALIGN=TOP>
Seattle Staff Directory
</LEGEND>
```

CLASS="..."

Indicates which style class applies to the <LEGEND> element.

Standard:	HTML 4
Common:	No

Sample:

```
<LEGEND CLASS="casual">Hydrogen
vs Oxygen</LEGEND>
```

ID="..."

Assigns a unique ID selector to an instance of the <LEGEND> tag. When you then assign a style to that ID selector, it affects only that one instance of the <LEGEND> tag.

Standard:	HTML 4
Common:	No
Sample:	

```
<LEGEND ID="123">Great
Painters</LEGEND>
```

STYLE="..."

Specifies style sheet commands that apply to the contents of the <LEGEND> tags.

Standard:	HTML 4
Common:	No
Sample:	

```
<LEGEND STYLE="background: red">
```

TITLE="..."

Specifies text assigned to the tag. You might use this attribute for context-sensitive help within the document. Browsers may use this to show tool tips over the legend.

Standard:	HTML 4
Common:	Yes
Sample:	

```
<LEGEND TITLE="of Sleepy Hollow">
```

Other Attributes

This tag also accepts the lang, dir, onClick, onDblClick, onMouseDown, onMouseUp, onMouseOver, onMouseMove, onMouseOut, onKeyPress, onKeyDown, and onKeyUp attributes. See the Element-

Independent Attributes section of this reference for definitions and examples.

<LI>

Places items into ordered (see the <OL> tag), menu (see the <MENU> tag), directory (see the <dir> tag), and unordered (see the <UL> tag) lists.

> **Standard**:   HTML 2
> **Common**:   Yes
> **Paired**:   Yes, optional
> **Sample**:

```
My favorite foods are:<UL>
  <LI>Pepperoni Pizza
  <LI>Lasagna
  <LI>Taco Salad
  <LI>Bananas
</UL>
```

Attribute Information

CLASS="..."

Indicates which style class applies to the <LI> element.

> **Standard**:   HTML 4
> **Common**:   No
> **Sample**:

```
<LI CLASS="casual">Dogs
```

ID=n

Assigns a unique ID selector to an instance of the <LI> tag. When you then assign a style to that ID selector, it affects only that one instance of the <LI> tag.

> **Standard**:   HTML 4
> **Common**:   No
> **Sample**:

```
<LI ID="123">Bees</LI>
```

STYLE="..."

Specifies style sheet commands that apply to the list item.

> **Standard**:   HTML 4
> **Common**:   No
> **Sample**:

```
<LI STYLE="background: red">
```

TITLE="..."

Specifies text assigned to the tag. You might use this attribute for context-sensitive help within the document. Browsers may use this to show tool tips over the list item.

> **Standard**:   HTML 4
> **Common**:   No
> **Sample**:

```
<LI TITLE="List Item">Thingie
```

TYPE="..."

Specifies the bullets for each unordered list item (see the <UL> tag) or the numbering for each ordered list item (see the <OL> tag). If you omit the TYPE= attribute, the browser chooses a default type.

Valid TYPE values for unordered lists are DISC, SQUARE, and CIRCLE.

Valid TYPE values for ordered lists are 1 for Arabic numbers, a for lowercase letters, A for uppercase letters, i for lowercase Roman numerals, and I for uppercase Roman numerals.

> **Standard**:   HTML 3.2
> **Common**:   Yes
> **Sample**:

```
<UL>
  <LI TYPE=SQUARE>Food
  <OL>
    <LI TYPE=1>Spaghetti
```

```
   <LI TYPE=1>Tossed Salad
</OL>
</UL>
```

VALUE="..."

Sets a number in an ordered list. Use this attribute to continue a list after interrupting it with something else in your document. You can also set a number in an ordered list with the START= attribute of the <OL> tag.

Because unordered lists do not increment, the VALUE= attribute is meaningless when used with them.

Standard: HTML 3.2

Common: Yes

Sample:

```
<OL TYPE=1>
   <LI VALUE=5>Watch
   <LI>Compass
</OL>
```

Other Attributes

This tag also accepts the lang, dir, onClick, onDblClick, onMouseDown, onMouseUp, onMouseOver, onMouseMove, onMouseOut, onKeyPress, onKeyDown, and onKeyUp attributes. See the Element-Independent Attributes section of this reference for definitions and examples.

<LINK>

Establishes relationships between the current document and other documents. Use this tag within the <HEAD> section. For example, if you access the current document by choosing a hyperlink from the site's home page, you can establish a relationship between the current document and the site's home page (see the REL= attribute). At this time, however, most browsers don't use most of these relationships. You can place several <LINK> tags

within the <HEAD> section of your document to define multiple relationships.

With newer implementations of HTML, you can also use the <LINK> tag to establish information about Cascading Style Sheets. Some other relationships that the <LINK> tag defines include the following:

CONTENTS: A table of contents.

INDEX: An index.

GLOSSARY: A glossary of terms.

COPYRIGHT: A copyright notice.

NEXT: The next document in a series (use with REL=).

PREVIOUS: The previous document in a series (use with REV=).

START: The first document in a series.

HELP: A document offering help or more information.

BOOKMARK: A bookmark links to a important entry point within a longer document.

STYLESHEET: An external style sheet.

ALTERNATE: Different versions of the same document. When used with lang, ALTERNATE implies a translated document; when used with MEDIA, it implies a version for a different medium.

Standard: HTML 2

Common: Yes

Paired: No

Sample:

```
<HEAD>
<TITLE>Prices</TITLE>
<LINK REL=Top
HREF="http://www.raycomm.com/">
```

```
<LINK REL=Search
HREF="http://www.raycomm.com/
search.html">
</HEAD>
```

Attribute Information

HREF="*URL*"

Indicates the relative or absolute location of the resource you are establishing a relationship to/from.

> **Standard**: HTML 2
>
> **Common**: Yes
>
> **Sample**:

```
<LINK REL=Prev HREF="page1.html">
```

MEDIA="..."

Specifies the destination medium for style information. It may be a single type or a comma-separated list. Media types include the following:

> Screen—for online viewing (default setting)
>
> Print—for traditional printed material and for documents on-screen viewed in print preview mode
>
> Projection—for projectors
>
> Braille—for Braille tactile feedback devices
>
> Speech—for a speech synthesizer
>
> All—applies to all devices

> **Standard**: HTML 4
>
> **Common**: No
>
> **Sample**:

```
<LINK MEDIA=SCREEN
REL="STYLESHEET"
HREF="/global.css">
```

NAME="..."

Specifies a name by which bookmarks, scripts, and applets can reference the relationship.

> **Standard**: Internet Explorer 4
>
> **Common**: No
>
> **Sample**:

```
<LINK REL="Search"
HREF="/search.html"NAME="Search">
```

REL="..."

Defines the relationship you are establishing between the current document and another resource. The HTML 3.2 specification includes several standard values for the REL= attribute. REL=Top defines the site home page or the top of the site hierarchy. REL=Contents usually defines the location of a resource that lists the contents of the site. REL=Index provides a link to an index of the site. REL=Glossary indicates the location of a glossary resource. REL=Copyright indicates the location of a copyright statement. REL=Next and REL=Previous establish relationships between documents or resources in a series. REL=Help indicates the location of a help resource. REL=Search specifies the location of a search resource. REL=style sheet specifies information about style sheets.

> **Standard**: HTML 2
>
> **Common**: Yes
>
> **Sample**:

```
<LINK REL=Help
HREF="/Help/index.html">
<LINK REL=style sheet
HREF="sitehead.css">
</HEAD>
```

REV="..."

Establishes reverse relationships between the current document and other resources. One common use is REV="made", after which you can set the HREF= attribute to a mailto: URL to contact the author of the document.

Standard: HTML 2

Common: Yes

Sample:

```
<LINK REV=made
HREF="mailto:jdoe@somewhere.com">
```

TARGET="..."

Specifies the name of a frame in which the referenced link appears.

Standard: Internet Explorer 4

Common: No

Sample:

```
<LINK TARGET="_blank" REL="Home"
HREF="http://www.mememe.com/">
```

TITLE="..."

Specifies text assigned to the tag that can be used for context-sensitive help within the document. Browsers may use this to show tool tips.

Standard: HTML 4

Common: Yes

Sample:

```
<LINK REL=Top HREF="/index.html"
TITLE="Home Page">
```

TYPE="..."

Specifies the MIME type of a style sheet to import with the <LINK> tag.

Standard: HTML 4

Common: No

Sample:

```
<LINK REL=STYLESHEET
TYPE="text/css"HREF="/style/main
.css">
```

Other Attributes

This tag also accepts the lang, dir, onfocus, onblur, onchange, onselect, onClick, onDblClick, onMouseDown, onMouseUp, onMouseOver, onMouseMove, onMouseOut, onKeyPress, onKeyDown, and onKeyUp attributes. See the Element-Independent Attributes section of this reference for definitions and examples.

<LISTING>

Specifies preformatted text to include within a document. Unlike the <PRE> tags, the browser does not interpret HTML tags within the <LISTING>tags. HTML 3.2 declared this tag obsolete, so use <PRE> instead.

Standard: Obsolete

Common: Yes

Paired: Yes

Sample:

```
The output from these reports is
shown below.
<LISTING>
Company      Q1    Q2     Q3    Q4
---------    ---   ---    ---   ----
Widget Inc. 4.5m  4.6m   6.2m  4.5m
Acme Widget 5.9m  10.2m  7.3m  6.6m
West Widget 2.2m  1.3m   3.1m  6.1m
</LISTING>
```

M

<MAP>

Specifies a container for client-side imagemap data. Inside the <MAP> container, you place instances of the <AREA> tag.

Standard: HTML 3.2

Common: Yes

Paired: Yes

Sample:

```
<MAP NAME="mainmap"> <AREA
NOHREF ALT="Home" SHAPE=RECT
COORDS="0,0,100,100">

  <AREA HREF="yellow.html"
  ALT="Yellow" SHAPE=RECT
  COORDS="100,0,200,100">

  <AREA HREF="blue.html"
  ALT="Blue" SHAPE=RECT
  COORDS="0,100,100,200">

  <AREA HREF="red.html" ALT="Red"
  SHAPE=RECT
  COORDS="100,100,200,200">

</MAP>
```

Attribute Information

CLASS="..."

Indicates which style class applies to the element.

Standard: HTML 4

Common: No

Sample:

```
<MAP CLASS="casual" NAME="simba">
```

ID="..."

Indicates an identifier to associate with the map. You can also use this to apply styles to the object.

Standard: HTML 4

Common: No

Sample:

```
<MAP ID="123" NAME="simba">
```

NAME="..."

Establishes a name for the map information you can later reference by the USEMAP= attribute of the <IMG> tag.

Standard: HTML 3.2

Common: Yes

Sample:

```
<MAP NAME="housemap">
. . .
<IMG SRC="house.gif"
USEMAP="#housemap" BORDER=0
ALT="Map of House">
```

STYLE="..."

Specifies style sheet commands that apply to the contents within the
<MAP> tags.

Standard: HTML 4

Common: No

Sample:

```
<MAP STYLE="background: black">
```

TITLE="..."

Specifies text assigned to the tag. You might use this attribute for context-sensitive help within the document. Browsers may use this to show tool tips.

Standard: HTML 4

Common: No

Sample:

```
<MAP TITLE="imagemap spec">
```

<MARQUEE>

Displays a scrolling text message within a document. Only Internet Explorer recognizes this tag.

Standard: Internet Explorer

Common: No

Paired: Yes

Sample:

```
<MARQUEE DIRECTION=LEFT
BEHAVIOR=SCROLL SCROLLDELAY=250
SCROLLAMOUNT=10>Big sale today on
fuzzy wuzzy widgets!</MARQUEE>
```

Attribute Information

ALIGN={LEFT, CENTER, RIGHT, TOP, BOTTOM}

Specifies the alignment of text outside the marquee.

Standard: Internet Explorer

Common: No

Sample:

```
<MARQUEE WIDTH=200 HEIGHT=50
ALIGN=LEFT DIRECTION=LEFT>
How To Groom Your Dog</MARQUEE>
```

BEHAVIOR={SLIDE, SCROLL, ALTERNATE}

Indicates the type of scrolling. BEHAVIOR=SCROLL scrolls text from one side of the marquee, across, and off the opposite side. BEHAVIOR= SLIDE scrolls text from one side of the marquee, across, and stops when the text reaches the opposite side. BEHAVIOR=ALTERNATE bounces the marquee text from one side to the other.

Standard: Internet Explorer

Common: No

Sample:

```
<MARQUEE DIRECTION=LEFT
BEHAVIOR=ALTERNATE>GO BEARS! WIN
WIN WIN!</MARQUEE>
```

BGCOLOR="#*RRGGBB*" or "..."

Specifies the background color of the marquee. Use a hexadecimal RGB color value or a color name.

Standard: Internet Explorer

Common: No

Sample:

```
<MARQUEE BGCOLOR="red"
DIRECTION=LEFT>Order opera
tickets here!</MARQUEE>
```

DATAFLD="..."

Selects a column from a block of tabular data.

Standard: Internet Explorer 4

Common: No

Sample:

```
<MARQUEE DATASRC="#data_table"
DATAFLD="nitems">
```

DATAFORMATAS={TEXT, HTML, NONE}

Specifies how items selected from tabular data format within the document.

Standard: Internet Explorer 4

Common: No

Sample:

```
<MARQUEE DATASRC="#data_table"
DATAFLD="nitems"
DATAFORMATAS=HTML>
```

DATASRC="..."

Specifies the location of tabular data to be bound within the document.

Standard: Internet Explorer 4

Common: No

Sample:

```
<MARQUEE DATASRC="#data_table"
DATAFLD="nitems">
```

DIRECTION={LEFT, RIGHT}

Indicates the direction in which the marquee text scrolls.

Standard: Internet Explorer

Common: No

Sample:

```
<MARQUEE DIRECTION=LEFT>Order
opera tickets here!</MARQUEE>
```

HEIGHT="*n*"

Specifies the vertical dimension of the marquee (in pixels).

Standard: Internet Explorer

Common: No

Sample:

```
<MARQUEE WIDTH=300 HEIGHT=50>
GO BEARS!</MARQUEE>
```

HSPACE="*n*"

Specifies the size of the margins (in pixels) to the left and right of the marquee.

Standard: Internet Explorer

Common: No

Sample:

```
<MARQUEE DIRECTION=LEFT
HSPACE=25>Check out our detailed
product descriptions!</MARQUEE>
```

ID="..."

Assigns a unique ID selector to an instance of the <MARQUEE> tag. When you then assign a style to that ID selector, it affects only that one instance of the <MARQUEE> tag.

Standard: Internet Explorer 4

Common: No

Sample:

```
<MARQUEE ID="3d4">
```

LOOP={*n*, INFINITE}

Controls the appearance of the marquee text.

Standard: Internet Explorer

Common: No

Sample:

```
<MARQUEE LOOP=5>December 12 is
our big, all-day sale!</MARQUEE>
```

SCROLLAMOUNT="*n*"

Indicates how far (in pixels) the marquee text shifts between redraws. Decrease this value for a smoother (but slower) scroll; increase it for a faster (but bumpier) scroll.

Standard: Internet Explorer

Common: No

Sample:

```
<MARQUEE SCROLLAMOUNT=10
SCROLLDELAY=40>Plant a tree for
Arbor Day!
</MARQUEE>
```

SCROLLDELAY="*n*"

Indicates how often (in milliseconds) the marquee text redraws. Increase this value to slow the scrolling action; decrease it to speed the scrolling action.

Standard: Internet Explorer

Common: No

Sample:

```
<MARQUEE DIRECTION=RIGHT
SCROLLDELAY=30>Eat at
Joe's!</MARQUEE>
```

STYLE="..."

Specifies style sheet commands that apply to the text within the <MARQUEE> tags.

Standard: Internet Explorer 4

Common: No

Sample:

```
<MARQUEE STYLE="background: red">
```

TITLE="..."

Specifies text assigned to the tag. You might use this attribute for context-sensitive help within the document. Browsers may use this to show tool tips over the marquee.

Standard: Internet Explorer 4

Common: No

Sample:

```
<MARQUEE TITLE="Scrolling
Marquee">
```

VSPACE="*n*"

Specifies the size of the margins (in pixels) at the top and bottom of the marquee.

> **Standard**:   Internet Explorer
>
> **Common**:   No
>
> **Sample**:

```
<MARQUEE DIRECTION=LEFT
VSPACE=25>Check out our detailed
product descriptions!</MARQUEE>
```

WIDTH="*n*"

Specifies the horizontal dimension (in pixels) of the marquee.

> **Standard**:   Internet Explorer
>
> **Common**:   No
>
> **Sample**:

```
<MARQUEE WIDTH=300>
Go Bears!</MARQUEE>
```

<MENU>

Defines a menu list. Use the <LI> tag to indicate list items. Use <UL> instead of this deprecated element.

> **Standard**:   HTML 2; deprecated
>   in HTML 4
>
> **Common**:   No
>
> **Paired**:   Yes
>
> **Sample**:

```
Now you can:<MENU>
  <LI>Eat the sandwich
  <LI>Place the sandwich in the
fridge
  <LI>Feed the sandwich to the
dog
</MENU>
```

Attribute Information

CLASS="..."

Indicates which style class applies to the <MENU> element.

> **Standard**:   HTML 4
>
> **Common**:   No
>
> **Sample**:

```
<MENU CLASS="casual">
  <LI>Information
  <LI>Members
  <LI>Guests
</MENU>
```

COMPACT

Specifies that the menu list appear in a space-saving form.

> **Standard**:   HTML 2; deprecated
>   in HTML 4
>
> **Common**:   Yes
>
> **Sample**:

```
<H2>Drinks Available</H2>
<MENU COMPACT>
  <LI>Cola</LI>
  <LI>Fruit Drink</LI>
  <LI>Orange Juice</LI>
  <LI>Water</LI>
</MENU>
```

ID="..."

Assigns a unique ID selector to an instance of the <MENU> tag. When you then assign a style to that ID selector,
it affects only that one instance of the <MENU> tag.

> **Standard**:   HTML 4
>
> **Common**:   No

Sample:

```
You'll need the following:
<MENU ID="123">
  <LI>Extra socks
  <LI>Snack crackers
  <LI>Towel
</MENU>
```

STYLE="..."

Specifies style sheet commands that apply to the menu list.

Standard: HTML 4
Common: Yes
Sample:

```
<MENU STYLE="background: black;
color: white">
```

TITLE="..."

Specifies text assigned to the tag. You might use this attribute for context-sensitive help within the document. Browsers may use this to show tool tips over the menu list.

Standard: HTML 4
Common: No
Sample:

```
<MENU TITLE="Menu List">
```

Other Attributes

This tag also accepts the lang, dir, onClick, onDblClick, onMouseDown, onMouseUp, onMouseOver, onMouseMove, onMouseOut, onKeyPress, onKeyDown, and onKeyUp attributes. See the Element-Independent Attributes section of this reference for definitions and examples.

<MENU>

Specifies information about the document to browsers, applications, and search engines.

Place the <META> tag within the document head. For example, you can use the <META> tag to instruct the browser to load a new document after 10 seconds (client-pull), or you can specify keywords for search engines to associate with your document.

Standard: HTML 2
Common: Yes
Paired: No
Sample:

```
<HEAD>
<TITLE>Igneous Rocks In North
America</TITLE>
<META HTTP-EQUIV="Keywords"
CONTENT="Geology, Igneous,
Volcanos">
</HEAD>
```

Attribute Information

CONTENT="..."

Assigns values to the HTTP header field. When using the REFRESH HTTP header, assign a number along with a URL to the CONTENT= attribute; the browser then loads the specified URL after the specified number of seconds.

Standard: HTML 2
Common: Yes
Sample:

```
<META HTTP-EQUIV="Refresh" CON-
TENT="2; URL=nextpage.html">
```

HTTP-EQUIV="..."

Indicates the HTTP header value you want to define, such as Refresh, Expires, or Content-Language. Other header values are listed in RFC2068.

Standard: HTML 2
Common: Yes

Sample:

```
<META HTTP-EQUIV="Expires"
CONTENT="Tue, 04 Aug 1997
22:39:22 GMT">
```

NAME="..."

Specifies the name of the association you are defining, such as Keywords or Description.

Standard: HTML 2

Common: Yes

Sample:

```
<META NAME="Keywords"
CONTENT="travel,automobile">

<META NAME="Description"
CONTENT="The Nash Metro moves
fast and goes beep beep.">
```

Other Attributes

This tag also accepts the lang and dir attributes. See the Element-Independent Attributes section of this reference for definitions and examples.

<MULTICOL>

Formats text into newspaper-style columns.

Standard: Netscape Navigator 4

Common: No

Paired: Yes

Sample:

```
<MULTICOL COLS=2 GUTTER=10>
. . .
</MULTICOL>
```

Attribute Information

COLS="n"

Indicates the number of columns.

Standard: Netscape Navigator 4

Common: No

Sample:

```
<MULTICOL COLS=4>
```

GUTTER="n"

Indicates the width of the space (in pixels) between multiple columns.

Standard: Netscape Navigator 4

Common: No

Sample:

```
<MULTICOL COLS=3 GUTTER=15>
```

WIDTH="n"

Indicates the horizontal dimension (in pixels or as a percentage of the total width available) of each column.

Standard: Netscape Navigator 4

Common: No

Sample:

```
<MULTICOL COLS=2 WIDTH="30%">
```

N

<NOBR>

Disables line-wrapping for a section of text. To force a word break within a <NOBR> clause, use the <WBR> tag.

Standard: Netscape Navigator

Common: Yes

Paired: Yes

Sample:

```
<NOBR>This entire line of text
will remain on one single line in
the browser window until the
closing tag appears. That doesn't
happen until right now.</NOBR>
```

Attribute Information

CLASS="..."

Indicate which style class applies to the element.

> **Standard:** Netscape Navigator
>
> **Common:** No
>
> **Sample:**

```
<NOBR CLASS="casual">
```

ID="..."

Assigns a unique ID selector to an instance of the <NOBR> tag. When you then assign a style to that ID selector, it affects only that one instance of the <NOBR> tag.

> **Standard:** Netscape Navigator
>
> **Common:** No
>
> **Sample:**

```
You'll need the following:
<NOBR ID="123">
```

STYLE="..."

Specifies style sheet commands that apply to the nonbreaking text.

> **Standard:** Netscape Navigator
>
> **Common:** Yes
>
> **Sample:**

```
<NOBR STYLE="background: black">
```

<NOFRAMES>

Provides HTML content for browsers that do not support frames or are configured not to present frames. You can include a <BODY> tag within the <NOFRAMES> section to provide additional formatting and style sheet features.

> **Standard:** HTML 4
>
> **Common:** Yes
>
> **Paired:** Yes

> **Sample:**

```
<FRAMESET COLS="*,70">

 <FRAME SRC="frames/body.html"
 NAME="body">

 <FRAME SRC="frames/side.html"
 NAME="side">

</FRAMESET>
<NOFRAMES>

 <p>Your browser doesn't support
frames. Please follow the links
below for the rest of the story.

 <p><a href="Prices.html">
 Prices</a> | <a href="About.
html">About Us</a> | <a href
="Contact.html">Contact Us</a>

</NOFRAMES>
```

Attribute Information

TITLE="..."

Specifies text assigned to the tag. You might use this attribute for context-sensitive help within the document. Browsers may use this to show tool tips.

> **Standard:** HTML 4
>
> **Common:** No
>
> **Sample:**

```
<NOFRAMES TITLE="HTML for non-
framed browsers">
```

<NOSCRIPT>

Provides HTML content for browsers that do not support scripts. Use the <NOSCRIPT> tags inside a script definition.

> **Standard:** HTML 4
>
> **Common:** No
>
> **Paired:** Yes

Sample:

```
<NOSCRIPT>
```

```
Because you can see this, you can
tell that your browser will not
run (or is set not to run)
scripts. </NOSCRIPT>
```

O

<OBJECT>

Embeds a software object into a document. The object can be an ActiveX object, a Quick-Time movie, or any other objects or data that a browser supports.

Use the <PARAM> tag to supply parameters to the embedded object. You can place messages and other tags between the <OBJECT> tags for browsers that do not support embedded objects.

Standard:	HTML 4
Common:	No
Paired:	Yes
Sample:	

```
<OBJECT CLASSID="/thingie.py">
```

```
<PARAM NAME="thing" VALUE=1>
```

```
Sorry. Your browser does not
support embedded objects. If it
supported these objects you
would not see this message.
```

```
</OBJECT>
```

Attribute Information

ALIGN={LEFT, CENTER, RIGHT, TEXTTOP, MIDDLE, TEXTMIDDLE, BASELINE, TEXTBOTTOM, BASELINE}

Indicates how the embedded object lines up relative to the edges of the browser windows and/or other elements within the browser window.

Using ALIGN=LEFT, ALIGN=RIGHT, or ALIGN=CENTER will cause the embedded object to *float* between the edges of the window either to the left, right, or evenly between. The behavior is similar to that of the ALIGN= attribute of the <IMG> tag.

ALIGN=TEXTTOP aligns the top of the embedded object with the top of the surrounding text.

ALIGN=TEXTMIDDLE aligns the middle of the embedded object with the middle of the surrounding text.

ALIGN=TEXTBOTTOM aligns the bottom of the embedded object with the bottom of the surrounding text.

ALIGN=BASELINE aligns the bottom of the embedded object with the baseline of the surrounding text.

ALIGN=MIDDLE aligns the middle of the embedded object with the baseline of the surrounding text.

Standard:	HTML 4; deprecated in favor of style sheets
Common:	No
Sample:	

```
<OBJECT DATA="shocknew.dcr"
TYPE="application/director"
WIDTH=288 HEIGHT=200 ALIGN=RIGHT>
```

BORDER="*n*"

Indicates the width (in pixels) of a border around the embedded object. BORDER=0 indicates no border.

Standard:	HTML 4
Common:	No
Sample:	

```
<OBJECT DATA="shocknew.dcr"
TYPE="application/director"
WIDTH=288 HEIGHT=200 BORDER=10>
```

CODEBASE="..."

Specifies the absolute or relative location of the base directory in which the browser will look for data and other implementation files.

Standard: HTML 4

Common: No

Sample:

```
<OBJECT CODEBASE="/~fgm/code/">
</OBJECT>
```

CODETYPE="..."

Specifies the MIME type for the embedded object's code.

Standard: HTML 4

Common: No

Sample:

```
<OBJECT CODETYPE="application/
x-msword">
</OBJECT>
```

CLASS="..."

Indicates which style class applies to the element.

Standard: HTML 4

Common: No

Sample:

```
<OBJECT CLASS="casual"
CODETYPE="application/x-msword">
</OBJECT>
```

CLASSID="..."

Specifies the URL of an object resource.

Standard: HTML 4

Common: No

Sample:

```
<OBJECT CLASSID="http://www
.raycomm.com/bogus.class">
```

DATA="*URL*"

Specifies the absolute or relative location of the embedded object's data.

Standard: HTML 4

Common: No

Sample:

```
<OBJECT DATA="/~fgm/goo.AVI">
</OBJECT>
```

DATAFLD="..."

Selects a column from a block of tabular data.

Standard: Internet Explorer 4

Common: No

Sample:

```
<OBJECT DATA="dataview.ocx"
DATASRC="#data_table"
DATAFLD="datafld1">
```

DATASRC="..."

Specifies the location of tabular data to be bound within the document.

Standard: Internet Explorer 4

Common: No

Sample:

```
<OBJECT DATA="dataview.ocx"
DATASRC="#data_table">
```

DECLARE

Defines the embedded object without actually loading it into the document.

Standard: HTML 4

Common: No

Sample:

```
<OBJECT CLASSID="clsid:99B42120-
6EC7-11CF-A6C7-00AA00A47DD3"
DECLARE>
</OBJECT>
```

HEIGHT="*n*"

Specifies the vertical dimension (in pixels) of the embedded object.

Standard: HTML 4

Common: No

Sample:

```
<OBJECT DATA="shocknew.dcr"
TYPE="application/director"
WIDTH=288 HEIGHT=200 VSPACE=10
HSPACE=10>
```

HSPACE="*n*"

Specifies the size of the margins (in pixels) to the left and right of the embedded object.

Standard: HTML 4

Common: No

Sample:

```
<OBJECT DATA="shocknew.dcr"
TYPE="application/director"
WIDTH=288 HEIGHT=200 VSPACE=10
HSPACE=10>
```

ID="..."

Indicates an identifier to associate with the embedded object. You can also use this to apply styles to the object.

Standard: HTML 4

Common: No

Sample:

```
<OBJECT DATA="shocknew.dcr"
TYPE="application/director"
WIDTH=288 HEIGHT=200 VSPACE=10
HSPACE=10 ID="swave2">
```

NAME="..."

Specifies the name of the embedded object.

Standard: HTML 4

Common: No

Sample:

```
<OBJECT CLASSID="clsid:99B42120-
6EC7-11CF-A6C7-00AA00A47DD3"
NAME="Very Cool Thingie">

</OBJECT>
```

SHAPES

Indicates that the embedded object has shaped hyperlinks (that is, imagemaps).

Standard: HTML 4

Common: No

Sample:

```
<OBJECT DATA="navbar.gif" SHAPES>
```

STANDBY="..."

Specifies a message that the browser displays while the object is loading.

Standard: HTML 4

Common: No

Sample:

```
<OBJECT STANDBY="Please wait.
Movie loading." WIDTH=100
HEIGHT=250>

<PARAM NAME=SRC
VALUE="TheEarth.AVI">

<PARAM NAME=AUTOSTART VALUE=TRUE>

<PARAM NAME=PLAYBACK VALUE=FALSE>

</OBJECT>
```

TABINDEX="*n*"

Indicates the place of the embedded object in the tabbing order.

Standard: HTML 4

Common: No

Sample:

```
<OBJECT CLASSID="clsid:99B42120-
6EC7-11CF-A6C7-00AA00A47DD3"
TABINDEX=3>

</OBJECT>
```

TITLE="..."
Specifies text assigned to the tag. You might use this attribute for context-sensitive help within the document. Browsers may use this to show tool tips over the embedded object.

> **Standard:** HTML 4
> **Common:** No
> **Sample:**

```
<OBJECT TITLE="Earth Movie"
WIDTH=100 HEIGHT=250>
 <PARAM NAME=SRC
 VALUE="TheEarth.AVI">
 <PARAM NAME=AUTOSTART
 VALUE=TRUE>
 <PARAM NAME=PLAYBACK
 VALUE=FALSE>
</OBJECT>
```

TYPE="..."
Indicates the MIME type of the embedded object.

> **Standard:** HTML 4
> **Common:** No
> **Sample:**

```
<OBJECT DATA="shocknew.dcr"
TYPE="application/x-director"
WIDTH=288 HEIGHT=200
VSPACE=10 HSPACE=10>
```

USEMAP="URL"
Indicates the relative or absolute location of a client-side imagemap to use with the embedded object.

> **Standard:** HTML 4
> **Common:** No
> **Sample:**

```
<OBJECT USEMAP="maps.html#map1">
```

VSPACE="n"
Specifies the size of the margin (in pixels) at the top and bottom of the embedded object.

> **Standard:** HTML 4
> **Common:** No
> **Sample:**

```
<OBJECT DATA="shocknew.dcr"
TYPE="application/director"
WIDTH=288 HEIGHT=200 VSPACE=10
HSPACE=10>
</OBJECT>
```

WIDTH="n"
Indicates the horizontal dimension (in pixels) of the embedded object.

> **Standard:** HTML 4
> **Common:** No
> **Sample:**

```
<OBJECT DATA="shocknew.dcr"
TYPE="application/director"
WIDTH=288 HEIGHT=200 VSPACE=10
HSPACE=10>
```

Other Attributes
This tag also accepts the lang, dir, onClick, onDblClick, onMouseDown, onMouseUp, onMouseOver, onMouseMove, onMouseOut, onKeyPress, onKeyDown, and onKeyUp attributes. See the Element-Independent Attributes section of this reference for definitions and examples.

<OL>
Contains a numbered (ordered) list.

> **Standard:** HTML 2
> **Common:** Yes
> **Paired:** Yes
> **Sample:**

```
<OL TYPE=i>
 <LI>Introduction
 <LI>Part One
 <OL TYPE=A>
   <LI>Chapter 1
```

```
    <LI>Chapter 2
  </OL>
</OL>
```

Attribute Information

CLASS="..."

Indicates which style class applies to the <OL> element.

Standard: HTML 4

Common: No

Sample:

```
<OL CLASS="casual">
  <LI>Check engine oil
  <LI>Check tire pressures
  <LI>Fill with gasoline
<OL>
```

COMPACT

Indicates that the ordered list appears in a compact format. This attribute may not affect the appearance of the list as most browsers do not present lists in more than one format.

Standard: HTML 2, deprecated in HTML 4

Common: No

Sample:

```
<OL COMPACT>
```

ID="n"

Assigns a unique ID selector to an instance of the <OL> tag. When you then assign a style to that ID selector, it affects only that one instance of the <OL> tag.

Standard: HTML 4

Common: No

Sample:

```
Recommended bicycle accessories:
<OL ID="123">
```

```
  <LI>Water bottle
  <LI>Helmet
  <LI>Tire pump
</OL>
```

START="..."

Specifies the value at which the ordered list should start.

Standard: HTML 2

Common: Yes

Sample:

```
<OL TYPE=A START=F>
```

STYLE="..."

Specifies style sheet commands that apply to the ordered list.

Standard: HTML 4

Common: Yes

Sample:

```
<OL STYLE="background: black;
color: white">
```

TITLE="..."

Specifies text assigned to the tag. You might use this attribute for context-sensitive help within the document. Browsers may use this to show tool tips over the ordered list.

Standard: HTML 4

Common: No

Sample:

```
<OL TITLE="Ordered list">
```

TYPE="..."

Specifies the numbering style of the ordered list. Possible values are 1 for Arabic numbers, i for lower case Roman numerals, I for uppercase Roman numerals, a for lowercase letters, and A for uppercase letters.

```
Standard:   HTML 2
Common:     Yes
Sample:
<OL TYPE=a>
  <LI>Breakfast
  <LI>Mrs. Johnson will speak
  <LI>Demonstration
  <LI>Lunch
</OL>
```

Other Attributes
This tag also accepts the lang, dir, onClick, onDblClick, onMouseDown, onMouseUp, onMouseOver, onMouseMove, onMouseOut, onKeyPress, onKeyDown, and onKeyUp attributes. See the Element-Independent Attributes section of this reference for definitions and examples.

<OPTION>

Indicates items in a fill-out form selection list (see the <SELECT> tag).

```
Standard:   HTML 2
Common:     Yes
Paired:     No
Sample:
Select an artist from the
1970s:<SELECT NAME="artists">
  <OPTION>Boston
  <OPTION SELECTED>Pink Floyd
  <OPTION>Reo Speedwagon
</SELECT>
```

Attribute Information
CLASS="..."
Indicate which style class applies to the element.

```
Standard:   HTML 4
Common:     No
Sample:
<OPTION NAME="color"
CLASS="casual">
```

DISABLED="..."
Denies access to the input method.

```
Standard:   HTML 4
Common:     No
Sample:
<OPTION VALUE="Bogus"
DISABLED>Nothing here
```

ID="n"
Assigns a unique ID selector to an instance of the <OPTION> tag. When you then assign a style to that ID selector, it affects only that one instance of the <OPTION> tag.

```
Standard:   HTML 4
Common:     No
Sample:
<OPTION ID="123">Mastercard
```

SELECTED
Marks a selection list item as preselected.

```
Standard:   HTML 2
Common:     Yes
Sample:
<OPTION SELECTED VALUE=1>Ice
Cream</OPTION>
```

TITLE="..."
Specifies text assigned to the tag. You might use this attribute for context-sensitive help within the document. Browsers may use this to show tool tips over the selection list option.

```
Standard:   HTML 4
Common:     No
```

Sample:

```
<OPTION TITLE="Option">Thingie
```

VALUE="..."

Indicates which data is sent to the form processor if you choose the selection list item. If the VALUE= attribute is not present within the <OPTION> tag, the text between the <OPTION> tags is sent instead.

Standard: HTML 2

Common: Yes

Sample:

```
<OPTION
VALUE=2>Sandwiches</OPTION>
```

Other Attributes

This tag also accepts the lang, dir, onfocus, onblur, onchange, onselect, onClick, onDblClick, onMouseDown, onMouseUp, onMouseOver, onMouseMove, onMouseOut, onKeyPress, onKeyDown, and onKeyUp attributes. See the Element-Independent Attributes section of this reference for definitions and examples.

P

<P>

Indicates a paragraph in a document.

Standard: HTML 2

Common: Yes

Paired: Yes, optional

Sample:

```
<P >As soon as she left, the
phone began ringing. "Hello," I
said after lifting the
receiver.</P>
```

```
<P>"Is she gone yet?" said the
voice on the other end.</P>
```

Attribute Information

ALIGN={LEFT, CENTER, RIGHT}

Aligns paragraph text flush left, flush right, or in the center of the document.

Standard: HTML 3.2; deprecated in HTML 4 in favor of style sheets

Common: Yes

Sample:

```
<P ALIGN=CENTER>There will be fun
and games for everyone!
```

CLASS="..."

Indicates which style class applies to the <P> element.

Standard: HTML 4

Common: No

Sample:

```
<P CLASS="casual">Tom turned at
the next street and stopped.
```

ID="*n*"

Assigns a unique ID selector to an instance of the <P> tag. When you then assign a style to that ID selector, it affects only that one instance of the <P> tag.

Standard: HTML 4

Common: No

Sample:

```
<P ID="123">This paragraph is
yellow on black!
```

STYLE="..."

Specifies style sheet commands that apply to the contents of the paragraph.

Standard: HTML 4

Common: No

Sample:

```
<P STYLE="background: red; color:
white">
```

TITLE="..."

Specifies text assigned to the tag. You might use this attribute for context-sensitive help within the document. Browsers may use this to show tool tips over the paragraph.

> **Standard:** HTML 4
>
> **Common:** No
>
> **Sample:**

```
<P TITLE="Paragraph">
```

WIDTH="*n*"

Specifies the horizontal dimension of the paragraph (in pixels).

> **Standard:** Internet Explorer 4
>
> **Common:** No
>
> **Sample:**

```
<P WIDTH=250>
```

Other Attributes

This tag also accepts the lang, dir, onClick, onDblClick, onMouseDown, onMouseUp, onMouseOver, onMouseMove, onMouseOut, onKeyPress, onKeyDown, and onKeyUp attributes. See the Element-Independent Attributes section of this reference for definitions and examples.

<PARAM>

Specifies parameters passed to an embedded object. Use the <PARAM> tag within the <OBJECT> or <APPLET> tags.

> **Standard:** HTML 4
>
> **Common:** No
>
> **Paired:** No
>
> **Sample:**

```
<OBJECT CLASSID="/thingie.py">
 <PARAM NAME="thing" VALUE=1>
```

```
Sorry. Your browser does not
support embedded objects.
</OBJECT>
```

Attribute Information

DATAFLD="..."

Selects a column from a block of tabular data.

> **Standard:** Internet Explorer 4
>
> **Common:** No
>
> **Sample:**

```
<PARAM DATA="dataview.ocx"
DATASRC="#data_table"
DATAFLD="datafld1">
```

DATASRC="..."

Specifies the location of tabular data to be bound within the document.

> **Standard:** Internet Explorer 4
>
> **Common:** No
>
> **Sample:**

```
<PARAM DATA="dataview.ocx"
DATASRC="#data_table">
```

NAME="..."

Indicates the name of the parameter passed to the embedded object.

> **Standard:** HTML 4
>
> **Common:** No
>
> **Sample:**

```
<PARAM NAME="startyear"
VALUE="1920">
```

TITLE="..."

Specifies text assigned to the tag. You might use this attribute for context-sensitive help within the document. Browsers may use this to show tool tips.

> **Standard:** HTML 4
>
> **Common:** No

Sample:

```
<PARAM TITLE="Object parameter
"NAME="size" VALUE="0">
```

TYPE="..."

Specifies the MIME type of the data found at the specified URL. Use this attribute with the VALUETYPE=REF attribute.

Standard: HTML 4

Common: No

Sample:

```
<PARAM NAME="data"
VALUE="/data/sim1.zip"
VALUETYPE=REF
TYPE="application/
x-zip-compressed">
```

VALUE="..."

Specifies the value associated with the parameter passed to the embedded object.

Standard: HTML 4

Common: No

Sample:

```
<PARAM NAME="startyear"
VALUE="1920">
```

VALUETYPE={REF, OBJECT, DATA}

Indicates the kind of value passed to the embedded object. VALUETYPE=REF indicates a URL passed to the embedded object. VAL-UETYPE=OBJECT indicates that the VALUE attribute specifies the location of object data. VALUETYPE=DATA indicates that the VALUE= attribute is set to a plain text string. Use this for passing alphanumeric data to the embedded object.

Standard: Internet Explorer 3, HTML 4

Common: No

Sample:

```
<PARAM NAME="length" VALUE="9"
VALUETYPE=DATA>
```

<PLAINTEXT>

Specifies that text appears as preformatted. This tag is obsolete; the <PRE> tag has replaced it.

Standard: Obsolete

Common: No

Paired: Yes

Sample:

```
<PLAINTEXT>Now go to the store
and buy:
Wrapping paper
Tape
Markers
</PLAINTEXT>
```

<PRE>

Contains preformatted plain text. This is useful for including computer program output or source code within your document.

Standard: HTML 2

Common: Yes

Paired: Yes

Sample:

```
Here's the source code:
<PRE>
#include <stdio.h>
void main()
{
    printf("Hello World!\n");
}
</PRE>
```

Attribute Information

CLASS="..."

Indicates which style class applies to the <PRE> element.

Standard:	HTML 4
Common:	No
Sample:	

```
<PRE CLASS="casual">BBQ
INFO</PRE>
```

ID="..."

Assigns a unique ID selector to an instance of the <PRE> tag. When you then assign a style to that ID selector, it affects only that one instance of the <PRE> tag.

Standard:	HTML 4
Common:	No
Sample:	

```
An example of an emotion:
<PRE ID="123">
   :-)
</PRE>
```

STYLE="..."

Specifies style sheet commands that apply to the contents within the <PRE> tags.

Standard:	HTML 4
Common:	Yes
Sample:	

```
<PRE STYLE="background : red">
```

TITLE="..."

Specifies text assigned to the tag. You might use this attribute for context-sensitive help within the document. Browsers may use this to show tool tips over the preformatted text.

Standard:	HTML 4
Common:	No
Sample:	

```
<PRE TITLE="preformatted text">
```

WIDTH="*n*"

Specifies the horizontal dimension of the pre-formatted text (in pixels).

Standard:	HTML 4
Common:	No
Sample:	

```
<PRE WIDTH=80>
```

Other Attributes

This tag also accepts the lang, dir, onClick, onDblClick, onMouseDown, onMouseUp, onMouseOver, onMouseMove, onMouseOut, onKeyPress, onKeyDown, and onKeyUp attributes. See the Element-Independent Attributes section of this reference for definitions and examples.

Q

<Q>

Quotes a direct source within a paragraph. Use <BLOCKQUOTE> to signify only a longer or block quotation.

Standard:	HTML 4
Common:	No
Paired:	Yes
Sample:	

```
Dr. Henry remarked <Q>I really
like the procedure.</Q>
```

Attribute Information

CITE="..."

Specifies a reference URL for a quotation.

Standard:	HTML 4
Common:	No
Sample:	

```
<BLOCKQUOTE
CITE="http://www.clement.moore
.com/xmas.html">

Twas the night…"

</BLOCKQUOTE>
```

CLASS="..."

Indicates which style class applies to the
<BLOCKQUOTE> element.

> **Standard:**   HTML 4
> **Common:**   No
> **Sample:**

<BLOCKQUOTE CLASS="casual">

Twas the night before
Christmas...</BLOCKQUOTE>

ID="..."

Assigns a unique ID selector to an instance of
the <BLOCKQUOTE> tag. When you then
assign a style to that ID selector, it affects
only that one instance of the <BLOCKQUOTE>
tag.

> **Standard:**   HTML 4
> **Common:**   No
> **Sample:**

On July 12, John wrote a profound
sentence in his diary:

<BLOCKQUOTE ID="123">I woke up
this morning at nine and it was
raining.</BLOCKQUOTE>

STYLE="..."

Specifies style sheet commands that apply to
the contents within the <BLOCKQUOTE> tags.

> **Standard:**   HTML 4
> **Common:**   No
> **Sample:**

<BLOCKQUOTE STYLE="background:
red">

TITLE="..."

Specifies text assigned to the tag. You might
use this attribute for context-
sensitive help within the document. Browsers
may use this to show tool tips over the quoted
text.

> **Standard:**   HTML 4
> **Common:**   No

> **Sample:**

<BLOCKQUOTE TITLE="Quotation">

Other Attributes

This tag also accepts the lang, dir,
onClick, onDblClick, onMouseDown,
onMouseUp, onMouseOver, onMouseMove,
onMouseOut, onKeyPress, onKeyDown,
and onKeyUp attributes. See the Element-
Independent Attributes section of this reference for definitions and examples.

S

<SAMP>

Indicates a sequence of literal characters.

> **Standard:**   HTML 2
> **Common:**   Yes
> **Paired:**   Yes
> **Sample:**

An example of a palindrome is the
word <SAMP>TOOT</SAMP>.

Attribute Information

CLASS="..."

Indicates which style class applies to the
<SAMP> element.

> **Standard:**   HTML 4
> **Common:**   No
> **Sample:**

The PC screen read:

<SAMP CLASS="casual">Command Not
Found</SAMP>

ID="..."

Assigns a unique ID selector to an instance of
the <SAMP> tag. When you then assign a style
to that ID selector, it affects only that one
instance of the <SAMP> tag.

> **Standard:**   HTML 4

Common: No
Sample:

```
Just for fun, think of how many
words end with the letters
<SAMP ID="123">ing</SAMP>.
```

STYLE="..."
Specifies style sheet commands that apply to the contents within the <SAMP> tags.

Standard: HTML 4
Common: Yes
Sample:

```
<SAMP STYLE="background: red">
```

TITLE="..."
Specifies text assigned to the tag. You might use this attribute for context-sensitive help within the document. Browsers may use this to show tool tips.

Standard: HTML 4
Common: No
Sample:

```
<SAMP TITLE="Sample">
```

Other Attributes
This tag also accepts the lang, dir, onClick, onDblClick, onMouseDown, onMouseUp, onMouseOver, onMouseMove, onMouseOut, onKeyPress, onKeyDown, and onKeyUp attributes. See the Element-Independent Attributes section of this reference for definitions and examples.

<SCRIPT>

Contains browser script code. Examples include JavaScript and VBScript. It is a good idea to place the actual script code within the comment tags so that browsers that don't support the <SCRIPT> tag code can ignore it.

Standard: HTML 3.2
Common: Yes

Paired: Yes
Sample:

```
<SCRIPT LANGUAGE="JavaScript">
<!- . . . ->
</SCRIPT>
```

Attribute Information

LANGUAGE="..."
Indicates the type of script.

Standard: HTML 4,
                 Internet Explorer
Common: Yes
Sample:

```
<SCRIPT LANGUAGE="JavaScript">
```

SRC="*URL*"
Specifies the relative or absolute location of a script to include in the document.

Standard: HTML 4,
                 Internet Explorer
Common: Yes
Sample:

```
<SCRIPT type="text/javascript"
SRC="http://www.some.com/sc/
script.js">
</SCRIPT>
```

TYPE="..."
Indicates the MIME type of the script. This is an alternative to the LANGUAGE attribute for declaring the type of scripting.

Standard: HTML 3.2
Common: Yes
Sample:

```
<SCRIPT type="text/javascript">
 document.write
 ("<EM>Great!<\/EM>")
</SCRIPT>
```

<SELECT>

Specifies a selection list within a form. Use the <OPTION> tags to specify items in the selection list.

    Standard: HTML 2

    Common: Yes

    Paired: Yes

    Sample:

```
What do you use our product
for?<BR>
<SELECT MULTIPLE NAME="use">
  <OPTION VALUE=1>Pest control
  <OPTION VALUE=2>Automotive
  lubricant
  <OPTION VALUE=3>Preparing
  pastries
  <OPTION SELECTED VALUE=4>
  Personal hygiene
  <OPTION VALUE=5>Other
</SELECT>
```

Attribute Information

ACCESSKEY="..."

Indicates a keystroke sequence associated with the selection list.

    Standard: HTML 4

    Common: No

    Sample:

```
<SELECT NAME="size" ACCESSKEY=S>
```

CLASS="..."

Indicates which style class applies to the element.

    Standard: HTML 4

    Common: No

    Sample:

```
<SELECT NAME="color"
CLASS="casual">
```

DATAFLD="..."

Indicates a column from previously identified tabular data.

    Standard: Internet Explorer 4

    Common: No

    Sample:

```
<SELECT NAME="color"
DATASRC="#data_table"
DATAFLD="clr">
```

DISABLED

Denies access to the selection list.

    Standard: HTML 4

    Common: No

    Sample:

```
<SELECT NAME="color" DISABLED>
```

ID="..."

Assigns a unique ID selector to an instance of the <SELECT> tag. When you then assign a style to that ID selector, it affects only that one instance of the <SELECT> tag.

    Standard: Internet Explorer 4

    Common: No

    Sample:

```
<SELECT ID="123" NAME="salary">
```

MULTIPLE

Indicates that a visitor can select more than one selection list item at the same time.

    Standard: HTML 2

    Common: Yes

    Sample:

```
<SELECT MULTIPLE>
```

NAME="..."

Gives a name to the value you are passing to the form processor. This establishes a *name-value pair* with which the form processor application can work.

Standard:	HTML 2
Common:	Yes
Sample:	

```
What is your shoe size?
<SELECT SIZE=4 NAME="size">
  <OPTION>
  <OPTION>
  <OPTION>
  <OPTION>
  <OPTION>
  <OPTION>
</SELECT>
```

READONLY

Indicates that your visitor cannot modify values within the selection list.

Standard:	Internet Explorer 4
Common:	No
Sample:	

```
<SELECT NAME="color" READONLY>
```

SIZE="*n*"

Specifies the number of visible items in the selection list. If there are more items in the selection list than are visible, a scrollbar provides access to the other items.

Standard:	HTML 2
Common:	Yes
Sample:	

```
<SELECT SIZE=3>
```

STYLE="..."

Specifies style sheet commands that apply to the contents within the <SELECT> tags.

Standard:	HTML 4
Common:	Yes
Sample:	

```
<SELECT STYLE="background: red"
NAME="color">
```

TABINDEX="*n*"

Indicates where in the tabbing order the selection list is placed.

Standard:	HTML 4
Common:	No
Sample:	

```
<SELECT NAME="salary TABINDEX=3>
```

TITLE="..."

Specifies text assigned to the tag. You might use this attribute for context-sensitive help within the document. Browsers may use this to show tool tips over the selection list.

Standard:	HTML 4
Common:	No
Sample:	

```
<SELECT TITLE="Select List"
NAME="Car">
```

Other Attributes

This tag also accepts the lang, dir, onfocus, onblur, onchange, onselect, onClick, onDblClick, onMouseDown, onMouseUp, onMouseOver, onMouseMove, onMouseOut, onKeyPress, onKeyDown, and onKeyUp attributes. See the Element-Independent Attributes section of this reference for definitions and examples.

<SMALL>

Specifies text that should appear in a small font.

Standard:	HTML 3.2
Common:	Yes
Paired:	Yes
Sample:	

```
<P>Our lawyers said we need to
include some small print:

<P><SMALL>By reading this docu-
ment, you are breaking the rules
```

and will be assessed a $2000 fine.</SMALL>

Attribute Information

CLASS="..."
Indicates which style class applies to the <SMALL> element.

> **Standard:** HTML 4
> **Common:** No
> **Sample:**

```
<SMALL CLASS="casual">Void where
prohibited</SMALL>
```

ID="..."
Assigns a unique ID selector to an instance of the <SMALL> tag. When you then assign a style to that ID selector, it affects only that one instance of the <SMALL> tag.

> **Standard:** HTML 4
> **Common:** No
> **Sample:**

```
Most insects are <SMALL
ID="123">small</SMALL>.
```

STYLE="..."
Specifies style sheet commands that apply to the contents within the <SMALL> tags.

> **Standard:** HTML 4
> **Common:** Yes
> **Sample:**

```
<SMALL STYLE="background: red">
```

TITLE="..."
Specifies text assigned to the tag. You might use this attribute for context-sensitive help within the document. Browsers may use this to show tool tips over the text inside the <SMALL> tags.

> **Standard:** HTML 4
> **Common:** No

> **Sample:**

```
<SMALL TITLE="Legalese">Actually
doing any of this will subject
you to risk of criminal prosecu-
tion.</SMALL>
```

Other Attributes
This tag also accepts the lang, dir, onClick, onDblClick, onMouseDown, onMouseUp, onMouseOver, onMouseMove, onMouseOut, onKeyPress, onKeyDown, and onKeyUp attributes. See the Element-Independent Attributes section of this reference for definitions and examples.

<SPACER>

A Netscape-specific tag that specifies a blank space within the document. We recommend using style sheets or other formatting techniques unless you're developing documents exclusively for visitors using Netscape Navigator.

> **Standard:** Netscape Navigator 4
> **Common:** No
> **Paired:** No
> **Sample:**

```
<SPACER TYPE=HORIZONTAL SIZE=150>
Doctors Prefer MediWidget 4 to 1
```

Attribute Information

SIZE="n"
Specifies the dimension of the spacer (in pixels).

> **Standard:** Netscape Navigator 3
> **Common:** No
> **Sample:**

```
<SPACER TYPE=HORIZONTAL SIZE=50>
<IMG SRC="rosebush.jpg">
```

TYPE={HORIZONTAL, VERTICAL}

Indicates whether the spacer measures from left to right or from top to bottom.

Standard: Netscape Navigator 3

Common: No

Sample:

```
<P>After you've done this, take a
moment to review your work.
<SPACER TYPE=VERTICAL SIZE=400>
<P>Now, isn't that better?
```

<SPAN>

Defines an inline section of a document affected by style sheet attributes. Use <DIV> to apply styles at the block-element level.

Standard: HTML 4

Common: No

Paired: Yes

Sample:

```
<SPAN STYLE="background:
red">...</SPAN>
```

Attribute Information

CLASS="..."

Indicates which style class applies to the <SPAN> element.

Standard: HTML 4

Common: No

Sample:

```
<SPAN CLASS="casual">
```

DATAFLD="..."

Selects a column from a previously identified source of tabular data (see the DATASRC= attribute).

Standard: Internet Explorer 4

Common: No

Sample:

```
<SPAN DATASRC="#data_table">
  <SPAN DATAFLD="name"></SPAN>
</SPAN>
```

DATAFORMATAS={TEXT, HTML, NONE}

Indicates the format of tabular data within the <SPAN> element.

Standard: Internet Explorer 4

Common: No

Sample:

```
<SPAN DATAFORMATAS=HTML
DATASRC="#data_table">
```

DATASRC="..."

Specifies the source of data for data binding.

Standard: Internet Explorer 4

Common: No

Sample:

```
<SPAN DATASRC="#data_table">
```

ID="..."

Assigns a unique ID selector to an instance of the <SPAN> tag. When you then assign a style to that ID selector, it affects only that one instance of the <SPAN> tag.

Standard: HTML 4

Common: No

Sample:

```
<SPAN ID="123">
```

STYLE="..."

Specifies style sheet commands that apply to the contents within the <SPAN> tags.

Standard: HTML 4

Common: No

Sample:

```
<SPAN STYLE="background: red">
```

TITLE="..."

Specifies text assigned to the tag. You might use this attribute for context-sensitive help within the document. Browsers may use this to show tool tips.

Standard: HTML 4

Common: No

Sample:

```
<SPAN TITLE="Section"
STYLE="background: red">
```

Other Attributes

This tag also accepts the lang, dir, onClick, onDblClick, onMouseDown, onMouseUp, onMouseOver, onMouseMove, onMouseOut, onKeyPress, onKeyDown, and onKeyUp attributes. See the Element-Independent Attributes section of this reference for definitions and examples.

<STRIKE>, <S>

Indicate a strikethrough text style.

Standard: HTML 3.2; deprecated in HTML 4 in favor of style sheets

Common: Yes

Paired: Yes

Sample:

```
My junior high biology teacher
was <STRIKE>sorta</STRIKE> really
smart.
```

Attribute Information

CLASS="..."

Indicates which style class applies to the <STRIKE> element.

Standard: HTML 4

Common: No

Sample:

```
<STRIKE CLASS="casual">Truman
</STRIKE> lost.
```

ID="..."

Assigns a unique ID selector to an instance of the <STRIKE> tag. When you then assign a style to that ID selector, it affects only that one instance of the <STRIKE> tag.

Standard: HTML 4

Common: No

Sample:

```
Don <STRIKE ID="123">ain't
</STRIKE>isn't coming tonight.
```

STYLE="..."

Specifies style sheet commands that apply to the contents within the <STRIKE> tags.

Standard: HTML 4

Common: No

Sample:

```
<STRIKE STYLE="background: red">
```

TITLE="..."

Specifies text assigned to the tag. You might use this attribute for context-sensitive help within the document. Browsers may use this to show tool tips over the text.

Standard: HTML 4

Common: No

Sample:

```
He was <STRIKE TITLE="omit">
Ambitious</STRIKE>
<B>Enthusiastic</B>.
```

Other Attributes

This tag also accepts the lang, dir, onClick, onDblClick, onMouseDown, onMouseUp, onMouseOver, onMouseMove, onMouseOut, onKeyPress, onKeyDown, and onKeyUp attributes. See the Element-

Independent Attributes section of this reference for definitions and examples.

<STRONG>

Indicates strong emphasis. The browser will probably display the text in a boldface font.

Standard: HTML 2
Common: Yes
Paired: Yes
Sample:

If you see a poisonous spider in the room then <STRONG>Get out of there!</STRONG>

Attribute Information

CLASS="..."

Indicates which style class applies to the <STRONG> element.

Standard: HTML 4
Common: No
Sample:

Did you say my dog is
<STRONG CLASS="casual">DEAD?!</STRONG>

ID="..."

Assigns a unique ID selector to an instance of the <STRONG> tag. When you then assign a style to that ID selector, it affects only that one instance of the <STRONG> tag.

Standard: HTML 4
Common: No
Sample:

Sure, you can win at gambling. But it's more likely you will <STRONG ID="123">lose</STRONG>.

STYLE="..."

Specifies style sheet commands that apply to the contents within the <STRONG> tags.

Standard: HTML 4
Common: No
Sample:

<STRONG STYLE="background: red">

TITLE="..."

Specifies text assigned to the tag. You might use this attribute for context-sensitive help within the document. Browsers may use this to show tool tips over the emphasized text.

Standard: HTML 4
Common: No
Sample:

I mean it was <STRONG TITLE="emphasis">HOT!</STRONG>

Other Attributes

This tag also accepts the lang, dir, onClick, onDblClick, onMouseDown, onMouseUp, onMouseOver, onMouseMove, onMouseOut, onKeyPress, onKeyDown, and onKeyUp attributes. See the Element-Independent Attributes section of this reference for definitions and examples.

<STYLE>

Contains style sheet definitions and appears in the document head (see the <HEAD> tag). Place style sheet data within the comment tags (<!--... -->) to accommodate browsers that do not support the <STYLE> tag.

Standard: HTML 3.2
Common: No
Paired: Yes

Sample:

```
<HTML>
<HEAD>
<TITLE>Edible Socks: Good or
Bad?</TITLE>
<STYLE TYPE="text/css">
<!--
  @import url(http://www.raycomm
  .com/mhtml/styles.css)
  H1 { background: black; color:
yellow }
  LI DD { background: silver;
color: black }
-->
</STYLE>
</HEAD>
```

Attribute Information

MEDIA="..."

Specifies the destination medium for style information. It may be a single type or a comma-separated list. Media types include the following:

Screen—for online viewing (default setting)

Print—for traditional printed material and for documents on screen viewed in print preview mode

Projection—for projectors

Braille—for Braille tactile feedback device

Speech—for a speech synthesizer

All—applies to all devices

Standard:	HTML 4
Common:	No

Sample:

```
<HEAD>
<TITLE>Washington DC
Taverns</TITLE>
```

```
<STYLE TYPE="text/css"
MEDIA="all">
<!--
  @import url(Error! Bookmark not
defined.
  H1 { background: black; color:
white}
  LI DD { background: silver;
color: darkgreen }
-->
</STYLE>
</HEAD>
```

TITLE="..."

Specifies text assigned to the tag. You might use this attribute for context-sensitive help within the document. Browsers may use this to show tool tips.

Standard:	HTML 4
Common:	No

Sample:

```
<STYLE TITLE="Stylesheet 1"
TYPE="text/css">
<!-- H1 { background: black;
color: yellow }
  LI DD { background: silver;
color: black }
-->
</SCRIPT>
```

TYPE="..."

Specifies the MIME type of the style sheet specification standard used.

Standard:	HTML 4
Common:	No

Sample:

```
<HEAD>
<TITLE>Washington DC
Taverns</TITLE>
<STYLE TYPE="text/css">
<!--
```

```
@import url(Error! Bookmark not
defined.
  H1 { background: black; color:
white}
  LI DD { background: silver;
color: darkgreen }
-->
</STYLE>
</HEAD>
```

Other Attributes

This tag also accepts the lang and dir attributes. See the Element-Independent Attributes section of this reference for definitions and examples.

<SUB>

Indicates subscript text.

Standard:	HTML 3.2
Common:	Yes
Paired:	Yes
Sample:	

```
<P>Chemists refer to water as
H<SUB>2</SUB>O.
```

Attribute Information

CLASS="..."

Indicates which style class applies to the <SUB> element.

Standard:	HTML 4
Common:	No
Sample:	

```
<SUB CLASS="casual">2</SUB>
```

ID="..."

Assigns a unique ID selector to an instance of the <SUB> tag. When you then assign a style to that ID selector, it affects only that one instance of the <SUB> tag.

Standard:	HTML 4
Common:	No
Sample:	

```
. . . At the dentist I ask for
lots of
NO<SUB ID="123">2</SUB>.
```

STYLE="..."

Specifies style sheet commands that apply to the contents within the <SUB> tags.

Standard:	HTML 4
Common:	No
Sample:	

```
<SUB STYLE="background: red">
```

TITLE="..."

Specifies text assigned to the tag. You might use this attribute for context-sensitive help within the document. Browsers may use this to show tool tips over the subscripted text.

Standard:	HTML 4
Common:	No
Sample:	

```
Before he died, he uttered,
"Groovy."<SUB
TITLE="Footnote">2</SUB>
```

Other Attributes

This tag also accepts the lang, dir, onClick, onDblClick, onMouseDown, onMouseUp, onMouseOver, onMouseMove, onMouseOut, onKeyPress, onKeyDown, and onKeyUp attributes. See the Element-Independent Attributes section of this reference for definitions and examples.

<SUP>

Indicates superscript text.

Standard:	HTML 3.2
Common:	Yes

Paired: Yes

Sample:

```
<P>Einstein's most famous equa-
tion is probably E=mc<SUP>2</SUP>.
```

Attribute Information

CLASS="..."

Indicates which style class applies to the `<SUP>` element.

Standard: HTML 4

Common: No

Sample:

```
<STYLE>
<!--

  SUP.casual {background: black;
    color: yellow}

-->
</STYLE>

. . .

z<SUP CLASS="casual">2</SUP> =
x<SUP CLASS="casual">2</SUP> +
y<SUP CLASS="casual">2</SUP>
```

ID="..."

Assigns a unique ID selector to an instance of the `<PRE>` tag. When you then assign a style to that ID selector, it affects only that one instance of the `<SUP>` tag.

Standard: HTML 4

Common: No

Sample:

```
<STYLE>
<!--

  #123 {background: black;
    color: yellow}

-->
</STYLE>

. . . Pythagorean theorem says
```

```
z<SUP ID="123">2</SUP>=4+16.
```

STYLE="..."

Specifies style sheet commands that apply to the contents within the `<SUP>` tags.

Standard: HTML 4

Common: No

Sample:

```
<SUP STYLE="background: red">
```

TITLE="..."

Specifies text assigned to the tag. You might use this attribute for context-sensitive help within the document. Browsers may use this to show tool tips over the superscripted text.

Standard: HTML 4

Common: No

Sample:

```
x<SUP TITLE="Exponent">2</SUP>
```

Other Attributes

This tag also accepts the `lang`, `dir`, `onClick`, `onDblClick`, `onMouseDown`, `onMouseUp`, `onMouseOver`, `onMouseMove`, `onMouseOut`, `onKeyPress`, `onKeyDown`, and `onKeyUp` attributes. See the Element-Independent Attributes section of this reference for definitions and examples.

T

<TABLE>

Specifies a container for a table within your document. Inside these tags you can place `<TR>`, `<TD>`, `<TH>`, `<CAPTION>`, and other `<TABLE>` tags.

Standard: HTML 3.2

Common: Yes

Paired: Yes

Sample:

```
<TABLE BORDER=0>   <TR>

    <TD><IMG SRC="Pine.jpg"
BORDER=0 ALT="Pine"></TD>

    <TD VALIGN=MIDDLE><P>Pine
trees naturally grow at higher
elevations.

    They require less water and
do not shed leaves in the
fall.</TD>   </TR>
</TABLE>
```

Attribute Information

ALIGN={LEFT, CENTER, RIGHT}

Positions the table flush left, flush right, or in the center of the window.

Standard:	HTML 3.2
Common:	Yes
Sample:	

```
<TABLE ALIGN=CENTER>
```

BACKGROUND="*URL*"

Specifies the relative or absolute location of a graphic image file loaded as a background image for the entire table.

Standard:	Internet Explorer 3, Netscape Navigator 4
Common:	No
Sample:	

```
<TABLE BACKGROUND="paper.jpg">
```

BGCOLOR="*#RRGGBB*" or "..."

Specifies the background color within all table cells in the table. You can substitute color names for the hexadecimal RGB values.

Standard:	Deprecated in HTML 4 in favor of style sheets
Common:	No
Sample:	

```
<TABLE BGCOLOR="Peach">
```

BORDER="*n*"

Specifies the thickness (in pixels) of borders around each table cell. Use a value of 0 to produce a table with no visible borders.

Standard:	HTML 3.2
Common:	Yes
Sample:	

```
<TABLE BORDER=0>
```

BORDERCOLOR="*#RRGGBB*" or "..."

Specifies the color of the borders of all the table cells in the table. You can substitute color names for the hexadecimal RGB values.

Standard:	Internet Explorer 3.0
Common:	No
Sample:	

```
<TABLE BORDERCOLOR=#3F9A11>
```

BORDERCOLORDARK="*#RRGGBB*" or "..."

Specifies the darker color used to draw 3-D borders around the table cells. You can substitute color names for the hexadecimal RGB values.

Standard:	Internet Explorer 4
Common:	No
Sample:	

```
<TABLE BORDERCOLORDARK="silver">
```

BORDERCOLORLIGHT="*#RRGGBB*" or "..."

Specifies the lighter color used to draw 3-D borders around the table cells. You can substitute color names for the hexadecimal RGB values.

Standard:	Internet Explorer 4
Common:	No
Sample:	

```
<TABLE BORDERCOLORLIGHT="white">
```

CELLPADDING="*n*"

Specifies the space (in pixels) between the edges of table cells and their contents.

Standard: HTML 3.2

Common: Yes

Sample:

`<TABLE CELLPADDING=5>`

CELLSPACING="*n*"

Specifies the space (in pixels) between the borders of table cells and the borders of adjacent cells.

Standard: HTML 3.2

Common: Yes

Sample:

`<TABLE BORDER=2 CELLSPACING=5>`

CLASS="..."

Indicates which style class applies to the `<TABLE>` element.

Standard: HTML 4

Common: No

Sample:

`<TABLE CLASS="casual" BORDER=2>`

COLS="*n*"

Specifies the number of columns in the table.

Standard: HTML 4

Common: No

Sample:

`<TABLE BORDER=2 COLS=5>`

FRAME={VOID, BORDER, ABOVE, BELOW, HSIDES, LHS, RHS, VSIDES, BOX}

Specifies the external border lines around the table. For the FRAME= attribute to work, set the BORDER= attribute with a non-zero value.

FRAME=VOID indicates no border lines.

FRAME=BOX or FRAME=BORDER indicates border lines around the entire table. This is the default.

FRAME=ABOVE specifies a border line along the top edge.

FRAME=BELOW draws a border line along the bottom edge.

FRAME=HSIDES draws border lines along the top and bottom edges.

FRAME=LHS indicates a border line along the left side.

FRAME=RHS draws a border line along the right edge.

FRAME=VSIDES draws border lines along the left and right edges.

Standard: HTML 4

Common: No

Sample:

`<TABLE BORDER=2 RULES=ALL FRAME=VSIDES>`

ID="*n*"

Assigns a unique ID selector to an instance of the `<TABLE>` tag. When you then assign a style to that ID selector, it affects only that one instance of the `<TABLE>` tag.

Standard: HTML 4

Common: No

Sample:

`<TABLE ID="123">`

RULES={NONE, ROWS, COLS, GROUPS, ALL}

Specifies where rule lines appear inside the table. For the RULES= attribute to work, set the BORDER= attribute.

RULES=NONE indicates no rule lines.

RULES=ROWS indicates rule lines between rows.

RULES=COLS draws rule lines between columns.

RULES=ALL draws all possible rule lines.

RULES=GROUPS specifies rule lines between the groups defined by the <TFOOT>, <THEAD>, <TBODY>, and <COLGROUP> tags.

> **Standard:** HTML 4
>
> **Common:** No
>
> **Sample:**

`<TABLE BORDER=2 RULES=BASIC>`

STYLE="…"

Specifies style sheet commands that apply to the contents of cells in the table.

> **Standard:** HTML 4
>
> **Common:** No
>
> **Sample:**

`<TABLE STYLE="background: red">`

TITLE="…"

Specifies text assigned to the tag. You might use this attribute for context-sensitive help within the document. Browsers may use this to show tool tips over the table.

> **Standard:** HTML 4
>
> **Common:** No
>
> **Sample:**

`<TABLE TITLE="Table">`

WIDTH="n"

Specifies the width of the table. You can set this value to an absolute number of pixels or to a percentage amount so that the table is proportionally as wide as the available space.

> **Standard:** HTML 3.2
>
> **Common:** Yes
>
> **Sample:**

`<TABLE ALIGN=CENTER WIDTH="60%">`

Other Attributes

This tag also accepts the lang, dir, onClick, onDblClick, onMouseDown, onMouseUp, onMouseOver, onMouseMove, onMouseOut, onKeyPress, onKeyDown, and onKeyUp attributes. See the Element-Independent Attributes section of this reference for definitions and examples.

<TBODY>

Defines the table body within a table. This tag must *follow* the <TFOOT> tag.

> **Standard:** HTML 4
>
> **Common:** No
>
> **Paired:** Yes
>
> **Sample:**

`<TABLE>`
`<THEAD>…`
`</THEAD>`
`<TFOOT>…`
`</TFOOT>`
`<TBODY>…`
`</TBODY>`

Attribute Information

ALIGN="{LEFT, RIGHT, CENTER, JUSTIFY, CHAR}"

Specifies how text within the table footer will line up with the edges of the table cells, or if ALIGN=CHAR, on a specific character (the decimal point).

> **Standard:** HTML 4
>
> **Common:** Yes
>
> **Sample:**

`<TR>`
`<THEAD>`
`<TH><B>Television</B></TH>`

```
<TH> <IMG SRC="tv.gif" ALT="TV"
BORDER="0"> </TH>
</THEAD>
</TR>
```

CHAR="..."

Specifies the character on which cell contents
will align, if ALIGN="CHAR". If you omit
CHAR=, the default value is the decimal point
in the specified language.

    Standard: HTML 4

    Common: No

    Sample:

```
<THEAD ALIGN="CHAR" CHAR=",">
```

CHAROFF="n"

Specifies the number of characters from the
left at which the alignment character appears.

    Standard: HTML 4

    Common: No

    Sample:

```
<THEAD ALIGN="CHAR" CHAR=","
CHAROFF="7">
```

CLASS="..."

Indicates which style class applies to the
<TBODY> element.

    Standard: HTML 4

    Common: No

    Sample:

```
<TBODY CLASS="casual">
```

ID="n"

Assigns a unique ID selector to an instance of
the <TBODY> tag. When you then assign a
style to that ID selector, it affects only that
one instance of the <TBODY> tag.

    Standard: HTML 4

    Common: No

    Sample:

```
<TBODY ID="123">
```

STYLE="..."

Specifies style sheet commands that apply to
the contents between the <TBODY> tags.

    Standard: HTML 4

    Common: No

    Sample:

```
<TBODY STYLE="background: red">
```

TITLE="..."

Specifies text assigned to the tag.
You might use this attribute for
context-sensitive help within the document.
Browsers may use this to show tool tips over
the table body.

    Standard: HTML 4

    Common: No

    Sample:

```
<TBODY TITLE="Table Body">
```

VALIGN={TOP, BOTTOM, MIDDLE, BASELINE}

Specifies the vertical alignment of the contents of the table body.

    Standard: Internet Explorer 4

    Common: No

    Sample:

```
<TBODY VALIGN=MIDDLE>
```

Other Attributes

This tag also accepts the lang, dir,
onClick, onDblClick, onMouseDown,
onMouseUp, onMouseOver, onMouseMove,
onMouseOut, onKeyPress, onKeyDown,
and onKeyUp attributes. See the Element-
Independent Attributes section of this reference for definitions and examples.

<TD>

Contains a table cell. These tags go inside the
<TR> tags.

Standard:	HTML 3.2
Common:	Yes
Paired:	Yes
Sample:	

```
<TR>
<TD>Bob Jones</TD>
<TD>555-1212</TD>
<TD>Democrat</TD>
</TR>
```

Attribute Information

ALIGN={LEFT, RIGHT, CENTER, JUSTIFY, CHAR}

Specifies how text within the table header will line up with the edges of the table cells, or if ALIGN=CHAR, on a specific character (the decimal point).

Standard:	HTML 4
Common:	Yes
Sample:	

```
<TR>
<TD><B>Television</B></TD>
<TD> <IMG SRC="tv.gif" ALT="TV"
BORDER=0> </TD>
</TR>
```

AXIS="..."

Specifies an abbreviated cell name.

Standard:	HTML 4
Common:	No
Sample:	

```
<TD AXIS="TV"><B>Television</B>
</TD>
```

AXES="..."

Lists AXIS values that pertain to the cell.

Standard:	HTML 4
Common:	No
Sample:	

```
<TD AXES="TV,
Programs"><B>Television</B></TD>
```

BACKGROUND="URL"

Specifies the relative or absolute location of a graphic image file for the browser to load as a background graphic for the table cell.

Standard:	Internet Explorer, Netscape Navigator
Common:	No
Sample:	

```
<TD BACKGROUND="waves.gif">
```

BGCOLOR="#RRGGBB" or "..."

Specifies the background color inside a table cell. You can substitute the hexadecimal RGB values for the appropriate color names.

Standard:	Deprecated in HTML 4 in favor of style sheets
Common:	No
Sample:	

```
<TR><TD BGCOLOR="Pink">Course
Number</TD>
<TD BGCOLOR="Blue">Time
taught</TD></TR>
```

BORDERCOLOR="#RRGGBB" or "..."

Indicates the color of the border of the table cell. You can specify the color with hexadecimal RGB values or by the color name.

Standard:	Internet Explorer 2
Common:	No
Sample:	

```
<TR><TD BORDERCOLOR="Blue">
```

BORDERCOLORDARK="#RRGGBB" or "..."

Indicates the darker color used to form 3-D borders around the table cell. You can specify the color with its hexadecimal RGB values or with its color name.

Standard: Internet Explorer 4

Common: No

Sample:

```
<TD BORDERCOLORLIGHT=#FFFFFF
BORDERCOLORDARK=#88AA2C>
```

BORDERCOLORLIGHT="#RRGGBB" or "..."

Indicates the lighter color used to form 3-D borders around the table cell. You can specify the color with its hexadecimal RGB values or with its color name.

Standard: Internet Explorer 4

Common: No

Sample:

```
<TD BORDERCOLORLIGHT=#FFFFFF
BORDERCOLORDARK=#88AA2C>
```

CHAR="..."

Specifies the character on which cell contents will align, if ALIGN="CHAR". If you omit CHAR=, the default value is the decimal point in the specified language.

Standard: HTML 4

Common: No

Sample:

```
<TD ALIGN="CHAR" CHAR=",">
```

CHAROFF="n"

Specifies the number of characters from the left at which the alignment character appears.

Standard: HTML 4

Common: No

Sample:

```
<TD ALIGN="CHAR" CHAR=","
CHAROFF="7">
```

CLASS="..."

Indicates which style class applies to the <TD> element.

Standard: HTML 4

Common: No

Sample:

```
<TD CLASS="casual">Jobs
Produced</TD>
```

COLSPAN="n"

Specifies that a table cell occupy one column more than the default of one. This is useful when you have a category name that applies to more than one column of data.

Standard: HTML 3.2

Common: Yes

Sample:

```
<TR><TD COLSPAN=2>Students</TD>
</TR>
```
```
<TR><TD>Bob Smith</TDH><TD>John
Doe</TD></TR>
```

ID="n"

Assigns a unique ID selector to an instance of the <TD> tag. When you then assign a style to that ID selector, it affects only that one instance of the <TD> tag.

Standard: HTML 4

Common: No

Sample:

```
<TD ID="123">
```

NOWRAP

Disables the default word-wrapping within a table cell, thus maximizing the amount of the cell's horizontal space.

Standard: Deprecated in HTML 4 in favor of style sheets

Common: No

Sample:

```
<TD NOWRAP>The contents of this
cell will not wrap at all</TD>
```

ROWSPAN="*n*"

Specifies that a table cell occupy more rows than the default of 1. This is useful when several rows of information are related to one category.

Standard: HTML 3.2

Common: Yes

Sample:

```
<TR><TD VALIGN=MIDDLE ALIGN=RIGHT
ROWSPAN=3>Pie Entries</TD>
```

```
<TD>Banana Cream</TD>
<TD>Mrs. Robinson</TD></TR>
```

```
<TR><TD>Strawberry
Cheesecake</TD>
<TD>Mrs. Barton</TD></TR>
```

```
<TR><TD>German Chocolate</TD>
<TD>Mrs. Larson</TD></TR>
```

STYLE="..."

Specifies style sheet commands that apply to the contents of the table cell.

Standard: HTML 4

Common: No

Sample:

```
<TD STYLE="background: red">
```

TITLE="..."

Specifies text assigned to the tag. You might use this attribute for context-sensitive help within the document. Browsers may use this to show tool tips over the table header.

Standard: HTML 4

Common: No

Sample:

```
<TD TITLE="Table Cell Heading">
```

VALIGN={TOP, MIDDLE, BOTTOM, BASELINE}

Aligns the contents of a cell with the top, bottom, baseline, or middle of the cell.

Standard: HTML 3.2

Common: Yes

Sample:

```
<TD VALIGN=TOP>
<IMG SRC="images/bud.gif
BORDER=0></TD>
```

WIDTH="*n*"

Specifies the horizontal dimension of the cell in pixels or as a percentage of the table width.

Standard: HTML 3.2; not listed in HTML 4

Common: Yes

Sample:

```
<TD WIDTH=200
ALIGN=LEFT><H2>African
Species</H2></TD>
```

Other Attributes

This tag also accepts the lang, dir, onClick, onDblClick, onMouseDown, onMouseUp, onMouseOver, onMouseMove, onMouseOut, onKeyPress, onKeyDown, and onKeyUp attributes. See the Element-Independent Attributes section of this reference for definitions and examples.

<TEXTAREA>

Defines a multiple-line text input field within a form. Place the <TEXTAREA> tags inside the <FORM> tags. To specify a default value in a <TEXTAREA> field, place the text between the <TEXTAREA> tags.

Standard: HTML 2

Common: Yes

Paired: Yes

Sample:

```
Enter any comments here:
<TEXTAREA NAME="comments" COLS=40
ROWS=5>
No Comments.
</TEXTAREA>
```

Attribute Information

ACCESSKEY="..."

Assigns a keystroke sequence to the <TEXTAREA> element.

Standard: HTML 4
Common: No

Sample:

```
<TEXTAREA COLS=40 ROWS=10
NAME="Story"ACCESSKEY=S>
```

CLASS="..."

Indicates which style class applies to the <TEXTAREA> element.

Standard: HTML 4
Common: No

Sample:

```
<TEXTAREA CLASS="casual">
```

COLS="n"

Indicates the width (in character widths) of the text input field.

Standard: HTML 2
Common: Yes

Sample:

```
<TEXTAREA NAME="desc" COLS=50
ROWS=3></TEXTAREA>
```

DATAFLD="..."

Selects a column from a previously identified source of tabular data (see the DATASRC= attribute).

Standard: Internet Explorer 4
Common: No

Sample:

```
<TEXTAREA DATASRC="#data_table"
DATAFLD="name" NAME="st1">
```

DATASRC="..."

Specifies the source of data for data binding.

Standard: Internet Explorer 4
Common: No

Sample:

```
<TEXTAREA DATASRC="#data_table"
DATAFLD="name" NAME="st1">
```

DISABLED

Denies access to the text input field.

Standard: HTML 4
Common: No

Sample:

```
<TEXTAREA ROWS=10 COLS=10
NAME="Comments" DISABLED>
```

ID="n"

Assigns a unique ID selector to an instance of the <TEXTAREA> tag. When you then assign a style to that ID selector, it affects only that one instance of the <TEXTAREA> tag.

Standard: HTML 4
Common: No

Sample:

```
<TEXTAREA ID="123">
```

NAME="..."

Names the value you pass to the form processor. For example, if you collect personal feedback, assign the NAME= attribute something like "comments". This establishes a *name-value pair* with which the form processor can work.

Standard: HTML 2
Common: Yes

Sample:

```
<TEXTAREA COLS=30 ROWS=10
NAME="recipe"></TEXTAREA>
```

READONLY

Specifies that the visitor cannot change the contents of the text input field.

Standard: HTML 4

Common: No

Sample:

```
<TEXTAREA ROWS=10
COLS=10NAME="Notes" READONLY>
```

ROWS="*n*"

Indicates the height (in lines of text) of the text input field.

Standard: HTML 2

Common: Yes

Sample:

```
<TEXTAREA NAME="desc" COLS=50
ROWS=3></TEXTAREA>
```

STYLE="..."

Specifies style sheet commands that apply to the <TEXTAREA> tag.

Standard: HTML 4

Common: No

Sample:

```
<TEXTAREA STYLE="background:
red">
```

TABINDEX=*n*

Indicates where <TEXTAREA> appears in the tabbing order.

Standard: HTML 4

Common: No

Sample:

```
<TEXTAREA ROWS=5 COLS=40
NAME="story"TABINDEX=2>
```

TITLE="..."

Specifies text assigned to the tag. You might use this attribute for context-sensitive help within the document. Browsers may use this to show tool tips over the text entry input method.

Standard: HTML 4

Common: No

Sample:

```
<TEXTAREA COLS=10 ROWS=2
NAME="tt"TITLE="Text Entry Box">
```

Other Attributes

This tag also accepts the lang, dir, onfocus, onblur, onchange, onselect, onClick, onDblClick, onMouseDown, onMouseUp, onMouseOver, onMouseMove, onMouseOut, onKeyPress, onKeyDown, and onKeyUp attributes. See the Element-Independent Attributes section of this reference for definitions and examples.

<TFOOT>

Defines a table footer within a table. It must *precede* the <TBODY> tag.

Standard: HTML 4

Common: No

Paired: Yes

Sample:

```
<TFOOT>
<TR>
<TD>Totals</TD><TD>$100.25</TD>
</TR>
</TFOOT>
</TABLE>
```

Attribute Information

ALIGN={LEFT, RIGHT, CENTER, JUSTIFY, CHAR}

Specifies how text within the table footer will line up with the edges of the table cells, or if ALIGN=CHAR, on a specific character (the decimal point).

> Standard: HTML 4
> Common: Yes
> Sample:

```
<TR>
 <THEAD>
  <TH><B>Television</B></TH>
  <TH> <IMG SRC="tv.gif"
ALT="TV" BORDER=0>  </TH>
 </THEAD>
</TR>
```

CHAR="..."

Specifies the character on which cell contents will align, if ALIGN="CHAR". If you omit CHAR=, the default value is the decimal point in the specified language.

> Standard: HTML 4
> Common: No
> Sample:

```
<THEAD ALIGN="CHAR" CHAR=",">
```

CHAROFF="n"

Specifies the number of characters from the left at which the alignment character appears.

> Standard: HTML 4
> Common: No
> Sample:

```
<THEAD ALIGN="CHAR" CHAR=","
CHAROFF="7">
```

CLASS="..."

Indicates which style class applies to the <TFOOT> element.

> Standard: HTML 4
> Common: No
> Sample:

```
<TFOOT CLASS="casual">
```

ID="n"

Assigns a unique ID selector to an instance of the <TFOOT> tag. When you then assign a style to that ID selector, it affects only that one instance of the <TFOOT> tag.

> Standard: HTML 4
> Common: No
> Sample:

```
<TFOOT ID="123">
```

STYLE="..."

Specifies style sheet commands that apply to the contents between the <TFOOT> tags.

> Standard: HTML 4
> Common: No
> Sample:

```
<TFOOT STYLE="background: red">
```

TITLE="..."

Specifies text assigned to the tag. You might use this attribute for context-sensitive help within the document. Browsers may use this to show tool tips over the table footer.

> Standard: HTML 4
> Common: No
> Sample:

```
<TFOOT TITLE="Table Footer">
```

VALIGN={TOP, BOTTOM, MIDDLE, BASELINE}

Aligns the contents of the table footer with the top, bottom, or middle of the footer container.

> Standard: Internet Explorer 4
> Common: No

Sample:

```
<TFOOT ALIGN=CENTER VALIGN=TOP>
```

Other Attributes

This tag also accepts the lang, dir, onClick, onDblClick, onMouseDown, onMouseUp, onMouseOver, onMouseMove, onMouseOut, onKeyPress, onKeyDown, and onKeyUp attributes. See the Element-Independent Attributes section of this reference for definitions and examples.

<TH>

Contains table cell headings. The <TH> tags are identical to the <TD> tags except that text inside <TH> is usually emphasized with bold-face font and centered within the cell.

Standard:	HTML 3.2
Common:	Yes
Paired:	Yes, optional
Sample:	

```
<TABLE>
<TH>Name</TH><TH>Phone No</TH>
<TD>John Doe</TD>
<TD>555-1212</TD>
<TD>Bob Smith</TD>
<TD>555-2121</TD>
</TABLE>
```

Attribute Information

ALIGN={LEFT, RIGHT, CENTER, JUSTIFY, CHAR}

Specifies how text within the table header will line up with the edges of the table cells, or if ALIGN=CHAR, on a specific character (the decimal point).

Standard:	HTML 4
Common:	Yes
Sample:	

```
<TR>
```

```
<TH><B>Television</B></TH>
<TH> <IMG SRC="tv.gif"
ALT="TV" BORDER=0> </TH>
</TR>
```

AXIS="..."

Specifies an abbreviated cell name.

Standard:	HTML 4
Common:	No
Sample:	

```
<TH AXIS="TV">
<B>Television</B></TH>
```

AXES="..."

Lists AXIS values that pertain to the cell.

Standard:	HTML 4
Common:	No
Sample:	

```
<TH AXES="TV,
Programs"><B>Television</B></TH>
```

BACKGROUND="*URL*"

Specifies the relative or absolute location of a graphic image file for the browser to load as a background graphic for the table cell.

Standard:	Internet Explorer, Netscape Navigator
Common:	No
Sample:	

```
<TH BACKGROUND="waves.gif">
```

BGCOLOR="*#RRGGBB*" or "..."

Specifies the background color inside a table cell. You can substitute the hexadecimal RGB values for the appropriate color names.

Standard:	Deprecated in HTML 4 in favor of style sheets
Common:	No
Sample:	

```
<TR><TH BGCOLOR="Pink">Course
Number</TH>
```

```
<TH BGCOLOR="Blue">Time
taught</TH></TR>
```

BORDERCOLOR="#RRGGBB" or "..."

Indicates the color of the border of the table cell. You can specify the color with hexadecimal RGB values or by the color name.

Standard: Internet Explorer 2

Common: No

Sample:

```
<TR><TH BORDERCOLOR="Blue">
```

BORDERCOLORDARK="#RRGGBB" or "..."

Indicates the darker color used to form 3-D borders around the table cell. You can specify the color with its hexadecimal RGB values or with its color name.

Standard: Internet Explorer 4

Common: No

Sample:

```
<TH BORDERCOLORLIGHT=#FFFFFF-
BORDERCOLORDARK=#88AA2C>
```

BORDERCOLORLIGHT="#RRGGBB" or "..."

Indicates the lighter color used to form 3-D borders around the table cell. You can specify the color with its hexadecimal RGB values or with its color name.

Standard: Internet Explorer 4

Common: No

Sample:

```
<TH BORDERCOLORLIGHT=#FFFFFF
BORDERCOLORDARK=#88AA2C>
```

CHAR="..."

Specifies the character on which cell contents align, if ALIGN="CHAR". If you omit CHAR=, the default value is the decimal point in the specified language.

Standard: HTML 4

Common: No

Sample:

```
<TH ALIGN="CHAR" CHAR=",">
```

CHAROFF="n"

Specifies the number of characters from the left at which the alignment character appears.

Standard: HTML 4

Common: No

Sample:

```
<TH ALIGN="CHAR" CHAR=","
CHAROFF="7">
```

CLASS="..."

Indicates which style class applies to the <TH> element.

Standard: HTML 4

Common: No

Sample:

```
<TH CLASS="casual">Jobs
Produced</TH>
```

COLSPAN="n"

Specifies that a table cell occupy more columns than the default of one. This is useful if a category name applies to more than one column of data.

Standard: HTML 3.2

Common: Yes

Sample:

```
<TR><TH COLSPAN=2>
Students</TH></TR>

<TR><TD>Bob Smith</TDH>
<TD>John Doe</TD></TR>
```

ID="n"

Assigns a unique ID selector to an instance of the <TH> tag. When you then assign a style to that ID selector, it affects only that one instance of the <TH> tag.

Standard:	HTML 4
Common:	No
Sample:	

```
<TH ID="123">
```

NOWRAP

Disables default word-wrapping within a table cell, maximizing the the cell's horizontal space.

Standard:	Deprecated in HTML 4 in favor of style sheets
Common:	No
Sample:	

```
<TH NOWRAP>The contents of this
cell will not wrap at all</TH>
```

ROWSPAN="n"

Specifies that a table cell occupy more rows than the default of 1. This is useful if several rows of information relate to one category.

Standard:	HTML 3.2
Common:	Yes
Sample:	

```
<TR><TH VALIGN=MIDDLE ALIGN=RIGHT
ROWSPAN=3>Pie Entries</TH>

<TD>Banana Cream</TD>
<TD>Mrs. Robinson</TD></TR>

<TR><TD>Strawberry
Cheesecake</TD>
<TD>Mrs. Barton</TD></TR>

<TR><TD>German Chocolate</TD>
<TD>Mrs. Larson</TD></TR>
```

STYLE="..."

Specifies style sheet commands that apply to the contents of the table cell.

Standard:	HTML 4
Common:	No
Sample:	

```
<TH STYLE="background: red">
```

TITLE="..."

Specifies text assigned to the tag. You might use this attribute for context-sensitive help within the document. Browsers may use this to show tool tips over the table header.

Standard:	HTML 4
Common:	No
Sample:	

```
<TH TITLE="Table Cell Heading">
```

VALIGN={TOP, MIDDLE, BOTTOM, BASELINE}

Aligns the contents of a cell with the top, bottom, baseline, or middle of the cell.

Standard:	HTML 3.2
Common:	Yes
Sample:	

```
<TH VALIGN=TOP><IMG
SRC="images/bud.gif
BORDER=0></TH>
```

WIDTH="n"

Specifies the horizontal dimension of the cell in pixels or as a percentage of the table width.

Standard:	HTML 3.2; not listed in HTML 4
Common:	Yes
Sample:	

```
<TH WIDTH=200 ALIGN=LEFT>
<H2>African Species</H2></TH>
```

Other Attributes

This tag also accepts the lang, dir, onClick, onDblClick, onMouseDown, onMouseUp, onMouseOver, onMouseMove, onMouseOut, onKeyPress, onKeyDown, and onKeyUp attributes. See the Element-Independent Attributes section of this reference for definitions and examples.

<THEAD>

Defines a table header section. At least one table row must go within <THEAD>.

Standard: HTML 4
Common: No
Paired: Yes
Sample:

```
<TABLE RULES=ROWS>
 <THEAD>
 <TR><TD>Column 1
<TD>Column 2
 </THEAD>
```

Attribute Information

ALIGN={LEFT, RIGHT, CENTER, JUSTIFY, CHAR}

Specifies how text within the table header will line up with the edges of the table cells, or if ALIGN=CHAR, on a specific character (the decimal point).

Standard: HTML 4
Common: Yes
Sample:

```
<TR>
 <THEAD>
  <TH><B>Television</B></TH>
  <TH> <IMG SRC="tv.gif"
ALT="TV" BORDER=0> </TH>
 </THEAD>
</TR>
```

CHAR="..."

Specifies the character on which cell contents align, if ALIGN="CHAR". If you omit CHAR=, the default value is the decimal point in the specified language.

Standard: HTML 4
Common: No
Sample:

```
<THEAD ALIGN="CHAR" CHAR=",">
```

CHAROFF="n"

Specifies the number of characters from the left at which the alignment character appears.

Standard: HTML 4
Common: No
Sample:

```
<THEAD ALIGN="CHAR" CHAR=","
CHAROFF="7">
```

CLASS="..."

Indicates which style class applies to the <THEAD> element.

Standard: HTML 4
Common: No
Sample:

```
<THEAD CLASS="casual">
```

ID="n "

Assigns a unique ID selector to an instance of the <THEAD> tag. When you then assign a style to that ID selector, it affects only that one instance of the <THEAD> tag.

Standard: HTML 4
Common: No
Sample:

```
<THEAD ID="123">
```

STYLE="..."

Specifies style sheet commands that apply to the contents between the <THEAD> tags.

Standard: HTML 4
Common: No
Sample:

```
<THEAD STYLE="background: red">
```

TITLE="..."

Specifies text assigned to the tag. You might use this attribute for context-sensitive help within the document. Browsers may use this to show tool tips over the table head.

Standard: HTML 4
Common: No
Sample:

```
<THEAD TITLE="Table Heading">
```

VALIGN={TOP, MIDDLE, BOTTOM, BASELINE}

Aligns the contents of the table header with respect to the top and bottom edges of the header container.

Standard: HTML 4
Common: No
Sample:

```
<THEAD ALIGN=LEFT VALIGN=TOP>
```

Other Attributes

This tag also accepts the lang, dir, onClick, onDblClick, onMouseDown, onMouseUp, onMouseOver, onMouseMove, onMouseOut, onKeyPress, onKeyDown, and onKeyUp attributes. See the Element-Independent Attributes section of this reference for definitions and examples.

<TITLE>

Gives the document an official title. The <TITLE> tags appear inside the document header inside the <HEAD> tags.

Standard: HTML 2
Common: Yes
Paired: Yes
Sample:

```
<HTML>
<HEAD>
<TITLE>How To Build A
Go-Cart</TITLE>
</HEAD>
```

Attribute Information

This tag also accepts the lang and dir attributes. See the Element-Independent Attributes section of this reference for definitions and examples.

<TR>

Contains a row of cells in a table. You must place the <TR> tags inside the <TABLE> container, which can contain <TH> and <TD> tags.

Standard: HTML 3.2
Common: Yes
Paired: Yes, optional
Sample:

```
<TABLE>
<TR><TH COLSPAN=3>Test
Scores</TH></TR>
<TR>
    <TD>Bob Smith</TD>
    <TD>78</TD>
    <TD>85</TD>
</TR>
<TR>
    <TD>John Doe</TD>
    <TD>87</TD>
    <TD>85</TD>
</TR>
</TABLE>
```

Attribute Information

ALIGN={LEFT, RIGHT, CENTER, JUSTIFY, CHAR}

Specifies how text within the table row will line up with the edges of the table cells, or if ALIGN=CHAR, on a specific character (the decimal point).

Standard: HTML 4

Common: Yes

Sample:

```
<TR ALIGN=CENTER >
    <TD><B>Television</B></TD>
    <TD> <IMG SRC="tv.gif"
ALT="TV" BORDER=0> </TD>
</TR>
```

BGCOLOR="#RRGGBB" or "..."

Specifies the background color of table cells in the row. You can substitute the color names for the hexadecimal RGB values.

Standard: Deprecated in HTML 4 in favor of style sheets

Common: No

Sample:

```
<TR BGCOLOR="Yellow">
    <TD><IMG SRC="Bob.jpg"
ALT="Bob"    BORDER=0></TD>
    <TD ALIGN=LEFT VALIGN=MIDDLE>
Bob Smith sitting at his desk
on a July afternoon.</TD>
</TR>
```

BORDERCOLOR="#RRGGBB" or "..."

Specifies the color of cell borders within the row. Currently, only Internet Explorer accepts this attribute. You can substitute color names for the hexadecimal RGB values.

Standard: Internet Explorer 2

Common: No

Sample:

```
<TR BORDERCOLOR="#3F2A55">
    <TD ALIGN=RIGHT VALIGN=MIDDLE>
Computers</TD>
    <TD><IMG SRC="Computers.jpg">
</TD>
</TR>
```

BORDERCOLORDARK="#RRGGBB" or "..."

Indicates the darker color for the 3-D borders around the table row. You can specify the color with its hexadecimal RGB values or with its color name.

Standard: Internet Explorer 4

Common: No

Sample:

```
<TR BORDERCOLORLIGHT="silver"
BORDERCOLORDARK="black">
```

BORDERCOLORLIGHT="#RRGGBB" or "..."

Indicates the lighter color for 3-D borders around the table row. You can specify the color with its hexadecimal RGB values or with its color name.

Standard: Internet Explorer 4

Common: No

Sample:

```
<TR BORDERCOLORLIGHT="silver"
BORDERCOLORDARK="black">
```

CHAR="..."

Specifies the character on which cell contents align, if ALIGN="CHAR". If you omit CHAR=, the default value is the decimal point in the specified language.

Standard: HTML 4

Common: No

Sample:

```
<TR ALIGN="CHAR" CHAR=",">
```

CHAROFF="*n*"

Specifies the number of characters from the left at which the alignment character appears.

Standard: HTML 4

Common: No

Sample:

```
<TR ALIGN="CHAR" CHAR=","
CHAROFF="7">
```

CLASS="..."

Indicates which style class applies to the <TR> element.

Standard: HTML 4

Common: No

Sample:

```
<TR CLASS="casual">

   <TD>Uranium</TD>

   <TD>Plutonium</TD>

   <TD>Radon</TD>

</TR>
```

ID="*n*"

Assigns a unique ID selector to an instance of the <TR> tag. When you then assign a style to that ID selector, it affects only that one instance of the <TR> tag.

Standard: HTML 4

Common: No

Sample:

```
<TR ID="123">
```

NOWRAP

Indicates that text within table cells in the row not wrap. This may cause the table to expand beyond the horizontal dimensions of the current document.

Standard: Internet Explorer 3; depre-
            cated in HTML 4 in favor of
            style sheets

Common: No

Sample:

```
<TR NOWRAP>

   <TD>In this table cell I'm
   going to type a lot of
   stuff.</TD>

   <TD>In this table cell I'm
   going to  continue to type a
   lot of stuff.</TD>

</TR>
```

STYLE="..."

Specifies style sheet commands that apply to all cells in the table row.

Standard: HTML 4

Common: No

Sample:

```
<TR STYLE="background: red">
```

TITLE="..."

Specifies text assigned to the tag. You might use this attribute for context-sensitive help within the document. Browsers may use this to show tool tips.

Standard: HTML 4

Common: No

Sample:

```
<TR TITLE="Table Row">
```

VALIGN={TOP, MIDDLE, BOTTOM, BASELINE}

Specifies the vertical alignment of the contents of all cells within the row.

Standard: HTML 3.2

Common: Yes

Sample:

```
<TR VALIGN=TOP>

   <TD ALIGN=CENTER>John
   Smith</TD>

   <TD ALIGN=CENTER>Bob Doe</TD>

</TR>
```

Other Attributes

This tag also accepts the lang, dir, onClick, onDblClick, onMouseDown, onMouseUp, onMouseOver, onMouseMove, onMouseOut, onKeyPress, onKeyDown, and onKeyUp attributes. See the Element-Independent Attributes section of this reference for definitions and examples.

<TT>

Displays text in a monospace font.

Standard:	HTML 2
Common:	Yes
Paired:	Yes
Sample:	

After I typed in help, the words <TT>help: not found</TT> appeared on my screen.

Attribute Information

CLASS="..."

Indicates which style class applies to the <TT> element.

Standard:	HTML 4
Common:	No
Sample:	

I sat down and began to type. <P><TT CLASS="casual">It was a dark and stormy night.</TT>

ID="*n*"

Assigns a unique ID selector to an instance of the <TT> tag. When you then assign a style to that ID selector, it affects only that one instance of the <TT> tag.

Standard:	HTML 4
Common:	No
Sample:	

<TT ID="123">

STYLE="..."

Specifies style sheet commands that apply to the contents within the <TT> tags.

Standard:	HTML 4
Common:	No
Sample:	

<TT STYLE="background: red">

TITLE="..."

Specifies text assigned to the tag. You might use this attribute for context-sensitive help within the document. Browsers may use this to show tool tips over the text within the <TT> tags.

Standard:	HTML 4
Common:	No
Sample:	

Now, type <TT TITLE="User Typing">MAIL</TT> and hit the <KBD>ENTER</KBD> key.

Other Attributes

This tag also accepts the lang, dir, onClick, onDblClick, onMouseDown, onMouseUp, onMouseOver, onMouseMove, onMouseOut, onKeyPress, onKeyDown, and onKeyUp attributes. See the Element-Independent Attributes section of this reference for definitions and examples.

U

<U>

Underlines text in a document. Use this tag with moderation since underlined text can confuse visitors accustomed to seeing hyperlinks as underlined text.

Standard: HTML 2; deprecated
in HTML 4 in favor of style
sheets
Common: Yes
Paired: Yes
Sample:

After waterskiing, I was
<U>really</U> tired.

Attribute Information
CLASS="..."
Indicates which style class applies to the <U>
element.

Standard: HTML 4
Common: No
Sample:

Have you seen <U CLASS="casual">
True Lies</U> yet?

ID="*n*"
Assigns a unique ID selector to an instance of
the <U> tag. When you then assign a style to
that ID selector, it affects only that one
instance of the <U> tag.

Standard: HTML 4
Common: No
Sample:

<U ID="123">

STYLE="..."
Specifies style sheet commands that apply to
the contents within the
<U> tags.

Standard: HTML 4
Common: No
Sample:

<U STYLE="background: red">

TITLE="..."
Specifies text assigned to the tag. You might
use this attribute for context-
sensitive help within the document. Browsers
may use this to show tool tips over the underlined text.

Standard: HTML 4
Common: No
Sample:

Read the book <U
TITLE="BookTitle">Walden</U> and
you'll be enlightened.

Other Attributes
This tag also accepts the lang, dir,
onClick, onDblClick, onMouseDown,
onMouseUp, onMouseOver, onMouseMove,
onMouseOut, onKeyPress, onKeyDown,
and onKeyUp attributes. See the Element-
Independent Attributes section of this reference for definitions and examples.

<UL>

Contains a bulleted (unordered) list. You can
then use the <LI> (List Item) tag to add bulleted items to the list.

Standard: HTML 2
Common: Yes
Paired: Yes
Sample:

Before you can begin, you
need:<UL>
    <LI>Circular saw
    <LI>Drill with Phillips bit
    <LI>Wood screws
</UL>

Attribute Information

CLASS="..."

Indicates which style class applies to the
<UL> element.

    Standard: HTML 4

    Common: No

    Sample:

```
<UL CLASS="casual">
  <LI>Hexagon</LI>
  <LI>Pentagon</LI>
  <LI>Octagon</LI>
</UL>
```

COMPACT

Indicates that the unordered list appears in a
compact format. This attribute may not affect
the appearance of the list as most browsers
do not present lists in more than one format.

    Standard: HTML 2; deprecated
                     in HTML 4

    Common: No

    Sample:

```
<UL COMPACT>
  <LI>Flour
  <LI>Sugar
  <LI>Wheat
  <LI>Raisins
</UL>
```

ID="n"

Assigns a unique ID selector to an instance of
the <UL> tag. When you then assign a style to
that ID selector, it affects only that one
instance of the <UL> tag.

    Standard: HTML 4

    Common: No

    Sample:

```
<UL ID="123">
```

SRC="URL"

Specifies the relative or absolute location of
an image file to use for the bullets in the
unordered list. Style sheets provide a browser-
independent method that is equivalent to this
attribute.

    Standard: Internet Explorer 4

    Common: No

    Sample:

```
<UL SRC="blueball.gif">
```

STYLE="..."

Specifies style sheet commands that apply to
the contents of the unordered list.

    Standard: HTML 4

    Common: No

    Sample:

```
<UL STYLE="background: red">
```

TITLE="..."

Specifies text assigned to the tag. You might
use this attribute for context-
sensitive help within the document. Browsers
may use this to show tool tips over the
unordered list.

    Standard: HTML 4

    Common: No

    Sample:

```
<UL TITLE="Food List">
  <LI>Spaghetti
  <LI>Pizza
  <LI>Fettuccini Alfredo
</UL>
```

TYPE={SQUARE, CIRCLE, DISC}

Specifies the bullet type for each unordered list item. If you omit the TYPE= attribute, the browser chooses a default type.

>**Standard:** HTML 2
>
>**Common:** Yes
>
>**Sample:**

```
<UL TYPE=DISC>
  <LI>Spaghetti
  <UL TYPE=SQUARE>
    <LI>Noodles
    <LI>Sauce
    <LI>Cheese
  </UL>
</UL>
```

Other Attributes

This tag also accepts the lang, dir, onClick, onDblClick, onMouseDown, onMouseUp, onMouseOver, onMouseMove, onMouseOut, onKeyPress, onKeyDown, and onKeyUp attributes. See the Element-Independent Attributes section of this reference for definitions and examples.

V

<VAR>

Indicates a placeholder variable in document text. This is useful when describing commands for which the visitor must supply a parameter.

>**Standard:** HTML 2
>
>**Common:** Yes
>
>**Paired:** Yes
>
>**Sample:**

```
To copy a file in DOS type
<SAMP>COPY <VAR>file1</VAR>
```

```
<VAR>file2</VAR></SAMP> and press
the ENTER key.
```

Attribute Information

CLASS="..."

Indicates which style class applies to the <VAR> element.

>**Standard:** HTML 4
>
>**Common:** No
>
>**Sample:**

```
I, <VAR CLASS="casual">your
name</VAR>, solemnly swear to
tell the truth.
```

ID="n"

Assigns a unique ID selector to an instance of the <VAR> tag. When you then assign a style to that ID selector, it affects only that one instance of the <VAR> tag.

>**Standard:** HTML 4
>
>**Common:** No
>
>**Sample:**

```
<VAR ID="123">
```

STYLE="..."

Specifies style sheet commands that apply to the contents within the <VAR> tags.

>**Standard:** HTML 4
>
>**Common:** No
>
>**Sample:**

```
<VAR STYLE="background: red">
```

TITLE="..."

Specifies text assigned to the tag. You might use this attribute for context-sensitive help within the document. Browsers may use this to show tool tips over the text within the <VAR> tags.

>**Standard:** HTML 4
>
>**Common:** No

Sample:

```
Use a H<VAR TITLE="Heading Level
Number">n</VAR> tag.
```

Other Attributes

This tag also accepts the `lang`, `dir`, `onClick`, `onDblClick`, `onMouseDown`, `onMouseUp`, `onMouseOver`, `onMouseMove`, `onMouseOut`, `onKeyPress`, `onKeyDown`, and `onKeyUp` attributes. See the Element-Independent Attributes section of this reference for definitions and examples.

<WBR>

Forces a word break. This is useful in combination with the <NOBR> tag to permit line breaks where they could otherwise not occur.

Standard:	Netscape Navigator
Common:	No
Paired:	No

Sample:

```
<NOBR>
This line would go on forever,
except that I have this neat tag
called WBR that does <WBR>this!
</NOBR>
```

<XMP>

Includes preformatted text within a document. Unlike the <PRE> tag, the browser does not interpret HTML tags within the <XMP> tags. HTML 3.2 declared this tag obsolete; so use <PRE> instead.

Standard:	Obsolete
Common:	No
Paired:	Yes

Sample:

```
The output from these reports is
shown below.
<XMP>
Company    Q1    Q2    Q3    Q4
_____ ___   ___   ___   ___

Widget Inc  4.5m  4.6m  6.2m  4.5m
Acme Widget 5.9m 10.2m 7.3m  6.6m
West Widget 2.2m  1.3m 3.1m  6.1m
</XMP>
```

Element-Independent Attributes and Event Handlers

Many HTML elements accept the attributes and event handlers described in this section. See the cross-references from individual elements for specific support information.

Attributes

dir="{LTR, RTL}"

Specifies the direction (left to right or right to left) for the text used within the section. This attribute is used most often within documents to override site-wide language direction specifications.

Standard:	HTML 4
Common:	No

Sample:

```
<P>The following quote is in
Hebrew, therefore written right
to left, not left to right.
<Q LANG="IW" DIR="RTL">Hebrew
```

```
text goes here and is presented
right to left, not left to right.
</Q></P>
```

lang="..."

Specifies the language used within the section. This attribute is used most often within documents to override site-wide language specifications. Use standard codes for languages, such as DE for German, FR for French, IT for Italian, and IW for Hebrew. See ISO Specification 639 at `www.sil.org/sgml/iso639a.html` for more information about language codes.

Standard: HTML 4

Common: No

Sample:

```
<P>The following quote is in
German. <Q LANG="DE">Guten
Tag!</Q></P>
```

Event Handlers

Each of the following event handlers helps link visitor actions to scripts. See the JavaScript reference for a fuller explanation of their use.

onLoad="..."

Occurs when the browser finishes loading a window or all frames within a <FRAMESET>. This handler works with <BODY> and <FRAMESET> elements.

onUnload="..."

Occurs when the browser removes a document from a window or frame. This handler works with <BODY> and <FRAMESET> elements.

onClick="..."

Occurs when a visitor clicks the mouse over an element. This handler works with most elements.

onDblClick="..."

Occurs when a visitor double-clicks the mouse over an element. This handler works with most elements.

onMouseDown="..."

Occurs when a visitor presses the mouse button over an element. This handler works with most elements.

onMouseUp="..."

Occurs when a visitor releases the mouse button over an element. This handler works with most elements.

onMouseOver="..."

Occurs when a visitor moves the mouse over an element. This handler works with most elements.

onMouseMove="..."

Occurs when a visitor moves the mouse while still over an element. This handler works with most elements.

onMouseOut="..."

Occurs when a visitor moves the mouse away from an element. This handler works with most elements.

onFocus="..."

Occurs when a visitor moves the focus to an element either with the mouse or the tab key. This handler works with <LABEL>, <INPUT>, <SELECT>, <TEXTAREA>, and <BUTTON>.

onBlur="..."

Occurs when a visitor moves focus from an element either with the mouse or the tab key. This handler works with <LABEL>, <INPUT>, <SELECT>, <TEXTAREA>, and <BUTTON>.

onKeyPress="..."

Occurs when a visitor presses and releases a key over an element. This handler works with most elements.

onKeyDown="..."

Occurs when a visitor presses a key over an element. This handler works with most elements.

onKeyUp="..."

Occurs when a visitor releases a key over an element. This handler works with most elements.

onSubmit="..."

Occurs when a visitor submits a form. This handler works only with <FORM>.

onReset="..."

Occurs when a visitor resets a form. This handler works only with <FORM>.

onSelect="..."

Occurs when a visitor selects text in a text field. This handler works with the <INPUT> and <TEXTAREA> elements.

onChange="..."

Occurs when a visitor modifies a field and moves the input focus to a different control. This handler works with <INPUT>, <SELECT>, and <TEXTAREA>.

Appendix C
THE INTERNET DICTIONARY

&

Ampersand. In HTML (Web) documents, used with special codes to indicate special characters (the HTML code for an ampersand itself is *&*).

< >

Angle brackets, or *brokets*. 1. Used to surround address return paths in e-mail headers; 2. In IRC, MUDs, and some e-mail and Usenet posts, brackets surround descriptions of actions or expressions; for example, <looking over my left shoulder> or <groan>. Similarly, some use <grin> or <g>.

@

At. In Internet e-mail addresses, it separates the username from the domain.

****

Backslash, or *backslant*.
1. In DOS paths, it separates directories and subdirectories; 2. In UNIX, it precedes switches (command line arguments).

^

Caret, or *hat*. 1. Indicates an exponent (for example, x^2 means x^2— that is, x squared); 2. Sometimes used in e-mail and Usenet posts to underscore and emphasize text on the preceding line, as shown here:

```
pc-lover@online.com
wrote:
>DOS is a snap once you
figure out config.sys.
         ^^^^^^^^^^
```

But that's the problem with PC-compatibles in a nutshell!
They make you deal with such awkwardly named setup files.

^]

Caret/right bracket. This pair of characters sometimes represents Escape. If you see it, it means some application is misinterpreting something.

:

Colon. In URLs, a colon appears after the protocol name. In e-mail and Usenet posts, sometimes indicates included text.

,

Comma. In Usenet newsreaders, you can often cross-post your article to several newsgroups by simply listing them one after another, separated by commas. Likewise, in most mail programs, you may list several e-mail recipients the same way, separated by commas.

.

Dot. The separator character for domain names, newsgroup names, and other UNIX-oriented files.

..

Double dot. In UNIX (as in DOS), the abbreviation for a parent directory.

--

Double hyphen. Many mail programs and newsreaders automatically include a line containing just two hyphens before appending a signature. Many anonymous remailers strip off any part of a message following such a line to make sure that sig blocks are not included by mistake.

"

Double quotation mark. They surround URLs in Web HTML documents.

>>

Double right angle brackets. In UNIX, they append the redirected output of a command to the end of a file.

//

Double slash. In URLs, the separator between the protocol and the site name. For example, in the URL http://enterzone.berkeley.edu/ enterzone .html, *http* is the protocol, *enterzone.berkeley.edu* is the address of the Web server, and *enterzone.html* is the file name of the home page.

!

Exclamation point, or *bang.* 1. It precedes each site in a UUCP bang path; 2. In some UNIX programs, it enables the user to shell out; 3. Overuse of exclamation marks to punctuate Usenet posts is one of the hallmarks of a newbie or a B1FF.

#

Number sign, pound sign, hash, or *octo-thorp.* 1. In the UNIX ftp program, if the command hash is given, one hash mark appears on the screen for every kilobyte of data transferred; 2. In Web references, # indicates the start of an anchor within a specified HTML document.

%

Percent. In UNIX, job numbers are preceded by %.

|

Pipe, bar, or *vertical bar.* 1. In UNIX, used to redirect the output of one program into another. For example, the UNIX command *ls | more* creates a short listing of files in the current directory and displays them one screenful at a time (using the paging program *more*); 2. In e-mail and Usenet posts, sometimes indicates included text.

?

Question mark, or *query.* A wildcard character in UNIX (and hence in many Internet applications), it stands for any single character.

>

Right angle bracket. 1. In UNIX, it redirects the output of a command into a file; 2. In e-mail and Usenet posts, this character commonly indicates included (quoted) text.

;

Semicolon. In Web documents, special characters are preceded by an ampersand (&) and followed by a semicolon. For example, the less than sign is indicated by *<* (because the plain < indicates the beginning of a tag).

/

Slash, forward slash, solidus, or *virgule.* In UNIX (and hence in gopher addresses and URLs), the separator character between directory levels. For example, my home directory where I have my Internet account is /u39/xian.

*

Star. 1. A wildcard character in UNIX (and hence in many Internet applications), it stands for any number of characters; 2. In e-mail, and especially on Usenet, where plain ASCII text is the norm, writers place stars before and after words to emphasize them, like so: "That's what *you* think."

.

Star-dot-star. The DOS wildcard for any file name. In UNIX, just * will suffice.

~

Tilde, used in the UNIX mail program to issue commands (instead of inserting text).

_

Underscore, or *underline.* 1. Used to separate names in some e-mail addresses; 2. Used in place of spaces in the names of files transferred from Macintoshes to other platforms; 3. In e-mail and on Usenet, where plain ASCII text is the norm, writers place underscores before and after titles to suggest underlining or italics, like so: "The origin of fnord is explained in _Illuminati!_"

a

The command to add a bookmark in the UNIX programs gopher and lynx.

ABE

(rhymes with *babe*) A DOS binary-to-ASCII conversion program for sending files via e-mail.

ABEND

(*ab-end,* n) A computer crash (from the "abnormal end" error message).

abstract syntax

A syntax (a set of rules for properly formed commands) that is not limited to a single application or platform.

Abstract Syntax Notation One (ASN.1)

An OSI language used to encode Simple Network Management Protocol packets, part of the infrastructure of the Internet.

acceptable use

Internet service providers require that all their users agree to some guidelines of acceptable use of Internet and Usenet resources. Acceptable use policies vary from provider to provider.

access

(n) 1. A connection to the Internet; 2. A type of Internet connection (such as network access, dial-up access, etc.); 3. The degree of ability to perform certain activities or read privileged information.

(v) 1. To connect to the Internet; 2. To connect to a site; 3. To open a file.

Access Control List (ACL)

A site's table of services and hosts authorized to use those services.

access privileges

Authorization for a specific level of access.

access provider

An institution providing Internet access, such as a commercial service provider, university, or employer.

account

(n) A form of access to a computer or network for a specific username and password, usually with a home directory, an e-mail inbox, and a set of access privileges.

ACK

(rhymes with *pack*) 1. Acknowledgment from a computer that a packet of data has been received and verified; 2. The mnemonic for the ASCII character number 6.

active star

A network design (a way of arranging the devices themselves in a network) in which a central hub retransmits all network traffic.

ActiveX Controls

ActiveX Controls are part of a Microsoft technology that allows a compliant browser, namely Internet Explorer, to run a program within a Web page as if it were the program itself. In order for this to work, ActiveX must be enabled in your browser settings.

Add/Strip

A Macintosh shareware program that inserts or deletes carriage returns (ASCII 13) at the end of each line of a text file, for conversion between Macintosh and UNIX systems.

address

(n) 1. A unique identifier for a computer or site on the Internet—this can be a numerical IP address (logical address) or a textual domain-name address (physical address); 2. A fully specified e-mail address (of the form *username@host.domain*).

address book

In some programs, a list of abbreviations for e-mail addresses.

address command

A UUCP extension that provides additional routing and confirmation options to the basic file-copying transaction that underlies UUCP.

Address Mapping Table (AMT)

A table used to resolve physical addresses into logical addresses.

address mask

The portion of an IP address that identifies the network and subnet.

address resolution

Conversion of a physical address into a logical address.

Address Resolution Protocol (ARP)

A TCP/IP protocol for converting physical addresses to logical addresses.

ADJ

(rhymes with *badge*) A Boolean operator that means *adjacent to*. A text search with ADJ between two words matches only documents in which those words are adjacent.

admin

Administrator, as in *sysadmin*.

Administrative Domain (AD)

The portion of a net-work overseen by a single administrator.

administrator

1. A system administrator (someone who runs a network); 2. Someone who maintains the addresses and handles the administrative chores for a mailing list or other Internet discussion group.

Asynchronous Digital Subscriber Line (ADSL)

A new technology that uses existing copper wire telephone wiring (POTTs) and enables users to connect at anywhere from 640 kbps to 7 Mbps, and possibly faster in the not so distant future. ADSL users do not need to dial in to their Internet service provider, and can use a single line to access the Internet, send and receive faxes, and make voice phone calls—all at the same time.

Advanced Interactive Executive (AIX)

IBM's UNIX clone.

Advanced Program-to-Program Communications (APPC)

An IBM peer-to-peer network protocol.

Advanced Research Projects Agency (ARPA)

A U.S. Department of Defense agency that, along with universities and research facilities, created ARPAnet, the precursor of the Internet.

advTHANKSance

"Thanks in advance."

agent

1. The process in client/server communication that handles negotiation between the client and the server; 2. A Simple Network Management Protocol program that monitors network traffic; 3. A program that performs some action on the behalf of a user without the direct oversight of the user.

Agent

A newsreader for Windows made by Forté.

AIR NFS

A Windows version of NFS (Network File System).

alias

(n) 1. An abbreviation for an e-mail address stored in a mail program, allowing the user to type or select a shorter alias instead of the full address; 2. An alternate name for an Internet address.

ALL-IN-1

A VAX e-mail and conference program.

AltaVista

A search engine developed by Digital Equipment Corporation (at http://altavista.com).

alt.

A hierarchy of newsgroups in the Usenet mold but outside of Usenet proper, devoted to "alternative" top-

ics. It is easier to create alt. groups than to create standard Usenet groups, and it's effectively impossible to remove them.

alt.config

A newsgroup for the discussion of new newsgroup formation in the alternative newsgroups hierarchy. Although the alt. hierarchy was created in part to sidestep the consensus rules of Usenet, there are still a range of views about what new alt. newsgroups should be created, how they should be named, and whether or not they will be accepted and propagated by system administrators all over the Net.

alternative newsgroups hierarchy

1. Any hierarchy of newsgroups in the Usenet mold but not, strictly speaking, part of Usenet; 2. The alt. hierarchy in particular.

alt.fan group

A newsgroup devoted to a real-world or Net celebrity or villain.

American National Standards Institute (ANSI)

U.S. organization that develops and promotes voluntary standards in a wide range of academic and research fields.

Amiga

A line of desktop PCs, famous for their handling of graphics and the evangelical zeal of their users. Many

Amiga users include an ASCII graphic double check mark in their sig blocks.

ampersand (&)

In HTML (Web) documents, used with special codes to indicate special characters (the HTML code for an ampersand itself is &).

analog

(adj) Representing values as physical states and changes in values as changes in physical states. In a stereo, for example, a CD player converts the digital information encoded on the CD into an analog signal sent to the amplifier.

Anarchie

(anarchee) A Macintosh program that combines the functions of archie and FTP.

anchor

(n) An HTML tag that indicates a hypertext link or the destination of such a link.

AND

A Boolean operator meaning and. A text search with AND between two words matches only documents containing both words.

Andrew File System (AFS)

A set of network protocols that makes remote files accessible as if they were local (as contrasted with being available via FTP).

angle brackets

Paired brackets that surround return addresses in e-mail headers. In IRC channels, MUDs, and some e-mail and Usenet posts, angle brackets surround descriptions of actions or expressions: for example, <looking over my left shoulder> or <groan>. Similarly, some use <grin> or <g>.

In e-mail and Usenet posts, a right angle bracket (>) commonly precedes included (quoted) text.

In UNIX, a right angle bracket redirects the output of a command into a file. A double right angle bracket (>>) appends the redirected output of a command to the end of a file.

anonymous FTP

The most common use of FTP (file transfer protocol), such as that used by many Internet sites. FTP sites that allow anonymous FTP don't require a password for access—you simply log in as anonymous and enter your e-mail address as a password (for their records).

anonymous remailer

A service that provides anonymity to users on the Net who wish to send mail and Usenet posts without their actual e-mail address and real name attached. Instead of sending mail or posting articles directly, users send to the anonymous remailer, with special header lines indicating the ultimate destination and the pen name of the user (if any). The remailer strips off any identifying information and sends the message or post on its way.

ANSI

(*antsy* or *annzee*) American National Standards Institute, or various standards promulgated by them.

*.answers

Moderated Usenet newsgroups dedicated to the posting of FAQs (frequently asked questions) and their answers.

AOL

The standard abbreviation for America Online, from aol.com, the subdomain and domain for that online service.

app

Application program.

append

To attach a file to the end of another.

Apple

A computer company based in Cupertino, California, that makes the Macintosh computer.

Apple Attachment Unit Interface

Apple's Ethernet interface.

AppleLink

Apple's online service for employees, developers, and industry people, at www.applelink.apple.com; being phased out in favor of eWorld.

AppleTalk

Apple's built-in LAN software.

Applet

A small program. In the context of the Internet, the reference is to a Java Applet, which is a small program that is run from within the browser.

application

A computer program that performs a specific function for the user, as contrasted on one hand with a document (which is a file created by an application) and on the other with a shell, environment, or operating system (all of which handle communication between the user and the computer itself).

application layer

The top (seventh) layer of the OSI Model.

Application Programming Interface (API)

Software that controls communication between a program and a computer environment.

.arc

A DOS file extension that indicates a compressed archive file.

archie

A client/server application that gives users access to databases (also called *indexes*) that keep track of the contents of anonymous FTP *archives*—hence the name.

archie client

The archie program you run to get information from an archie server.

Archie for the Macintosh

A Macintosh archie client.

Archie for Nextstep

An archie client for the Nextstep operating system.

archie server

The archie program that houses a database listing the contents of anonymous FTP sites, in a searchable form, accessible to archie clients.

archie site

A computer with an archie server running on it.

archive file

A file that has been compressed or that contains a number of related files.

archive site

1. An FTP site, a computer on the Internet that stores files; 2. Any repository of information accessible via the Net.

argument

An additional statement (or subcommand) added to a command to modify how it works or what it works on. For example, to copy a file on most operating systems, you type a copy command, followed by several arguments—the name of the file to be copied and the name of the file to copy it to.

ARMM

Automated Retroactive Minimal Moderation, Dick Depew's Usenet robot that was intended to retroactively cancel anonymous posts and post follow-ups. It spun out of control instantly during its first run on March 31, 1993, posting follow-ups to its own follow-ups, spamming several newsgroups, and crashing systems all over the Net. For more on this, see the Net.Legends.FAQ at `gopher://dixie.aiss.uiuc.edu:6969/11/urban.legends/Net.Legends.FAQ`.

ARPAnet

(*are-puh-net*) The predecessor to the Internet, established in the 1970s by ARPA, which demonstrated the utility of the TCP/IP protocols. It no longer exists, having been superseded by the Internet.

article

A Usenet newsgroup post—that is, a message posted publicly and available for reading by every subscriber to the newsgroup(s) it's been posted to.

Artificial Intelligence (AI)

A field of computer science research aimed at understanding how the human mind thinks and creating intelligent machines that can learn from their experiences.

ASCII

(*askee*) *American standard code for information interchange.* ASCII is a standard character set that's been adopted by most computer systems around the world (usually extended for foreign alphabets and diacriticals).

ASCIIbetical order

A sorting order based on the ASCII character set that corresponds to English alphabetical order but sorts symbols and numbers before letters and uppercase letters before lowercase letters.

ASCII file

A file containing text only. ASCII files are easier and quicker to transfer than binary files.

ASCII file transfer

A method of file transfer by which an ASCII file is sent as a sequence of characters (letters, numbers, and symbols) instead of as a sequence of binary data (1s and 0s). When necessary, newline characters are changed by the file-transfer program.

ASCII font

A "font" created out of plain ASCII characters, usually found in sig blocks, often spelling out the writer's name.

ASCII graphic

A drawing composed of ASCII characters, such as an enormous medieval sword, an attempt to limn Bart Simpson, or a map of Australia.

AskERIC

An educational information service of the Educational Resources Information Center (ERIC), `askeric @ricir.syr.edu`.

aspect ratio

The proportion of height to width. Most computer displays have a 3 to 4 aspect ratio.

assigned numbers

Standard numbers for ports, sockets, and so on, established by the Internet Assigned Numbers Authority.

Association for Computing Machinery (ACM)

An association of computer researchers and developers that serves as both a source of technical information and an umbrella group for numerous SIGs (Special Interest Groups).

asynchronous

(adj) Not happening at the same time. The word is used both for data transmission and for human communication (e-mail is asynchronous, as opposed to IRC, which is synchronous).

Asynchronous Transfer Mode (ATM)

A standard for handling heavy network traffic at high speeds. Also called fast packet.

asynchronous transmission

A transmission method that uses start bits and stop bits to regulate the flow of data, as opposed to synchronous transmission, which uses a clock signal.

AT commands

Hayes-compatible modem commands, most of which begin with *AT* (for "attention"), such as *ATZ*, which resets a modem's factory initialization (the basic settings for the modem when it was created).

aTdHvAaNnKcSe

Thanks in advance.

atob

(*ay-to-bee*) A UNIX program that converts ASCII files to binary files.

attach

To send a document along with an e-mail message.

attached file

A file sent with an e-mail message; also called an *attachment*.

Attachment Unit Interface (AUI)

A universal Ethernet device that connects to a transceiver.

attribute

(n) A setting associated with a file that indicates who can read it and whether the file is a *system file* (a protected file created by the operating system and not to be tampered with), a *hidden file* (one that won't show up in normal file listings), or an *archive file* (one that has been grouped out of many and/or compressed).

attribution

The portion of a Usenet follow-up post that identifies the author of quoted text (from previous posts). Be very careful to attribute a quotation to the correct author, or you may face the ire of whomever you are misquoting. (When AOL first made Usenet available to its members, its newsreader software contained a bug that seemed to attribute the text of a follow-up to the author of the preceding post, which annoyed users to no end.)

authentication

Verification of the identity of the sender of a message.

automagically

(adv) Happening automatically and so smoothly that the process appears to be magic.

Autonomous System (AS)

A set of routers overseen by a common administrator, using the same protocol.

autoselect

(v) In Usenet kill files, to select automatically—the opposite of to kill (to mark as already having been read). A kill file comprises instructions to search for certain key words and then either kill or autoselect the articles containing those words.

A/UX

Apple's UNIX clone for the Macintosh.

awk

(rhymes with *gawk*) A UNIX-based programming language for manipulating text.

b

The shortcut for back in many UNIX programs.

back

The command in paging programs, gopher clients, and Web browsers to back up one screenful or return to the previous menu choice or link.

backbone

A large, fast network connecting other networks. The National Science Foundation maintains one of the largest backbones in the United States, NSFnet.

backbone cabal

A now-defunct group of large-site administrators who set in place most of the procedures for Usenet newsgroup creation and orchestrated the Great Renaming of the Usenet hierarchy.

back door

A security loophole that allows a programmer to evade restrictions and enter an otherwise secure system. If a back door remains after the software is released, it becomes a security risk.

background

In a multitasking computer environment, any processes that take place out of sight, or with lower priority than the main process, are said to take place in the background.

backslash

The \ character, often found just above the Enter key on keyboards. In DOS paths, it separates directories and subdirectories; in UNIX, it precedes switches (command-line arguments).

backspace

(v) To use the Backspace key to move a cursor to the left, and, in the process, delete characters on a computer screen.

Backspace key

A key found above the Enter key on most computer keyboards, often used to erase characters to the left of the cursor. (On some systems the Delete key plays this role.)

Use of the Backspace key in terminal emulations that don't support it sometimes leaves the original text onscreen, followed by one ^H character for every time Backspace is pressed. This results in the digital equivalent of an unzipped fly.

balanced line

A cable containing electrically equal wires, such as a twisted-pair cable.

balun

(*bal-un*, n) An impedance-matching device that connects a balanced line (containing electrically equal wires), such as a twisted-pair cable, to an unbalanced line (containing electrically unequal wires), such as a coaxial cable.

bandwidth

(n) Literally, the speed at which data can be transmitted across a medium. Also used colloquially throughout the Internet to refer to the speed or capacity of a network connection (which can be described as *low bandwidth* or *high bandwidth*) or network resources in general, something almost everyone at some time or another is accused of wasting.

If you post a uuencoded binary file containing a 9×12 24-bit image to a talk newsgroup, you're definitely wasting bandwidth. But even if you have a sig block of over four lines, if you include too much quoted text in your follow-up post, or if you continue a flame war, you too may be accused of wasting bandwidth.

bandwidth hog

A user or process that consumes more than his, her, or its fair share of bandwidth.

bang

(n) An exclamation point. It precedes each site in a UUCP mail path. In some UNIX programs, it enables the user to shell out.

bang path

A UUCP *mail path* that specifies every site along the way from the sender to the receiver. Although it is rarely necessary any longer to specify the route your mail will take (there are many interchangeable routes on the Internet), mail headers still often include the entire bang path back to the sender.

bar

A popular dummy variable used by programmers in place of specific terms, such as the dummy mail address foo@bar.baz.

barney

A dummy variable used by programmers in examples in combination with fred (alluding to characters from *The Flintstones* television show).

baseband

(adj) Signal transmission that uses the entire bandwidth of the medium, the method used by most LANs.

BASIC

Beginner's All-purpose Symbolic Instruction Code, a programming language invented at Dartmouth College in the 1960s as a teaching language. Many feel it teaches bad programming habits.

Basic Encoding Rules (BER)

A technique for encoding data (preparing data for transmission) defined in ASN.1 (Abstract Syntax Notation One).

Basic Rate Interface (BRI)

An ISDN (Integrated Services Digital Network) service that connects LANs (local area networks) via 64 kps data channels.

batch

(adj) 1. Noninteractive; handled without interaction, as in *batch mode*; 2. All at once, or in a bunch, as in *batch printing*.

baud

(*bawd*) Usually confused with bits per second (bps), baud is technically the number of times per second that your modem changes the signal it sends through the phone lines.

baz

A popular dummy variable used by programmers in examples in place of specific terms, such as the dummy mail address `foo@bar.baz`.

bboard

A BBS. Newbies often refer to Usenet newsgroups as bboards.

BBS

A *bulletin board system*, communications software that runs on a PC and enables users to log in via modem, check messages, communicate in topic groups, engage in real time chats, and (sometimes) access the Internet.

bcc:

Blind carbon copy. Borrowed from the world of paper memos, the blind carbon copy list is a list of additional recipients of an e-mail message whose names and addresses will not appear in the header. Not all e-mail systems support bcc, so it is not a perfectly safe way of keeping a recipient's identity secret.

Berkeley Internet Name Domain (BIND)

UNIX name server software developed and distributed by the University of California at Berkeley.

Berkeley Software Distribution (BSD)

A version of UNIX developed and distributed by the University of California at Berkeley.

beta

(*bay'-tuh*) Prerelease software made available to a small group of testers (often called *beta testers*) in the "real world" to put it through its paces and identify any bugs or design flaws that did not show up when it was tested by the developers before being shipped commercially.

Big Blue

Slang term for IBM (from the corporate logo).

B1FF

Also called *BIFF*. A prototypical newbie on Usenet, usually looking for "k00l warez" (*k00l* is B1FF-speak for *cool*; *warez*—pronounced *wares*, from *software*—means pirated game software). He posts in all caps, substitutes numbers for letters, uses exclamation marks liberally, and has a huge sig block—all of which are trademarks of the BBS culture of the 1980s, which was populated mainly by teenage boys.

Big Dummy's Guide to the Internet

The former name of the Electronic Frontier Foundation's excellent free Internet guide, now named *EFF's Guide to the Internet*.

big-endian

(adj) 1. A storage format in which the most significant byte has the lowest address, as opposed to little-endian; 2. The way Internet addresses are written in the United Kingdom, starting with domain, then sub-domain, then site (the opposite of the standard order used on the rest of the Internet).

big red switch

Sometimes abbreviated *BRS*, the on/off switch on a computer or any crucial toggle switch that, when switched off, will shut down the system.

big seven

The seven top-level Usenet hierarchies (also known as *traditional news-group hierarchies*): `comp.`, `misc.`, `news.`, `rec.`, `sci.`, `soc.`, and `talk`.

binaries newsgroup

A Usenet newsgroup dedicated to the posting of uuencoded binary files, often `.gif` or `.jpg` image files. Some sites won't carry binaries newsgroups because their uuencoded binaries consume so much bandwidth (and storage space on the news site computers).

binary

1. Base 2, a numerical system using only two digits: *0* and *1* (compare with *decimal*—base 10, a numerical system using 10 digits: *0* through *9*); 2. A binary file.

binary data

Computer information stored in the form of *0*s and *1*s (most program files and image files, as well as some documents, are stored as binary data).

binary file

A file that contains more than simple text, such as an image file, a sound file, or a program file (as opposed to an ASCII file, which contains text only). It must be copied literally, bit for bit, or it will be corrupted. Also called an *image file*.

Binary Synchronous Control (Bisync)

An IBM protocol for controlling communications in synchronous environments.

binary file transfer

A file transfer in which every bit of the file is copied exactly as is (as opposed to a text transfer, in which the text is transferred to whatever format the receiving machine prefers).

BinHex

A Macintosh program that converts binary files to ASCII files so that they may be transmitted via e-mail.

BIOSIS/FS

A database of biological and biomedical research available through the OCLC (Online Computer Learning Center).

Birds of a Feather (BOF)

An *ad hoc* discussion group on a conference program.

bis

In modem standards, an enhancement to the standard, but not a completely new standard. V.32bis is an improvement on V.32, for example.

bisynchronous

(adj) Communication in which the sending and receiving takes place at the same time.

bit

A binary digit, the smallest unit of computer information, transmitted as a single *on* or *off* pulse symbolized by *1* or *0*.

bit bucket

1. An imaginary place where extra bits land when they "fall off a register"—the computer equivalent of forgetting to "carry the 1" during addition; 2. The computer equivalent of the "circular file," or the place where all lost socks and pencils go.

bitnet.

A hierarchy in the Usenet mold populated by newsgroups gated to BITNET listserv mailing lists.

BITNET

Because It's Time Network, a huge network distinct from the Internet but fully connected to it, used largely for e-mail and listserv mailing lists.

bits per second (bps)

A measurement of the speed of a medium, meaning the number of bits that can pass through the medium in one second.

BIX

BYTE Information Exchange, an online service created by *BYTE* magazine. For information, contact TJL@mhis.bix.com, (800) 695-4775, or (617) 354-4137.

biz.

A hierarchy in the Usenet mold dedicated to commercial and business communication. Advertising is explicitly permitted in the biz. hierarchy.

block

(n) A standard unit of data (the size varies from system to system) measured in terms of storage or transmission.

board

(n) 1. A BBS; 2. A computer circuit board.

bogus

(adj) 1. Lame, stupid, false, useless; 2. Fake.

boink

(n) A party at which participants of a Usenet newgroup meet in person.

bomb

(v) To crash, to suffer from an unrecoverable error.

bookmark

In gopher clients and Web browsers, a reference to a menu or page to which you might want to return later. In gopher clients, bookmarks appear together on a gopher menu. In Web browsers, they appear on hotlists.

Boolean operator

One of several conjunctions used to limit or specify a search criterion (from George Boole, a nineteenth-century English mathematician). Boolean operators may be grouped with parentheses, if necessary, to clarify the order of application.

Boolean search

A method of searching a database or text in which Boolean operators are used to limit and specify the search criterion.

boot

(v) To start or restart a computer, or, technically, to load and start the operating system. The term comes from the expression "lifting oneself by one's bootstraps," because the computer kernel must write the remainder of the startup code itself each time that the computer is booted.

Bootstrap Protocol (BOOTP)

A protocol for booting diskless nodes on a network.

Border Gateway Protocol (BGP)

An exterior gateway protocol based on the External Gateway Protocol used by NSFnet.

'bot

A robotic entity on the Net that automatically performs some function that people usually do. Many IRC channels are kept open by semi-permanent 'bots that stay connected just as real users might. In the past, people have spammed Usenet by employing 'bots to automatically post (robopost) reams of redundant text.

bounce

(v) E-mail that fails to reach its destination and returns to the sender is said to have bounced.

bounce message

A message from a mailer daemon indicating that it cannot find the recipient of an e-mail message and is returning it to the sender.

Bourne shell

A common flavor of UNIX shells.

box

(n) A computer, as in a UNIX box.

bozo filter

A kill file. It allows you to filter out the bozos whose Usenet posts you don't wish to see.

brain dump

(n) An undifferentiated mass of information, often in response to a simple question (by analogy from core dump, screen dump, etc.).

brain-dead

(adj) 1. Completely broken or nonfunctional, usually said of hardware or software; 2. Ridiculously inappropriate, usually said of an approach to a problem.

branch

(n) 1. An intermediate part of a logical tree, somewhere between the root and a leaf; 2. A participant in a tape tree who receives copies of a tape from her parent and makes copies for her children (who may themselves be branches or leaves).

BRB

[I'll] *be right back* (written only).

bridge

A device that connects two network components (such as zones) that use the same protocols.

brief

(adj) An operating mode for some systems and applications in which the prompts and reports of activities are abbreviated or skipped altogether.

broadband

(adj) Signal transmission that can carry multiple signals at once, each on separate channels, each taking up a portion of the bandwidth.

broadcast

(n) A transmission sent to all hosts or clients at once, such as "System going down in 10 minutes. Please finish up."

broadcast storm

The confusion and possible network breakdown that occurs when a faulty packet is broadcast, generating multiple incorrect packets in response, ad infinitum.

broket

(*broe'-ket*) An angle bracket: < or >.

brouter

(*brow'-ter*) A device that combines the functions of a bridge and a router, controlling transmission from one network component to another (as a bridge) and from the network to the Internet (as a router).

browse

To skim an information resource on the Net, suchas Usenet, gopherspace, or the Web.

browser

A client program used to read the Web.

btoa

(*bee'-too-ay'*) A UNIX program that converts binary files to ASCII files.

btw

By the way (written only, also *BTW*).

BUAF

Big, ugly ASCII font. Character sets made from ASCII characters, often generated by special programs and often used to spell out names in sig blocks.

BUAG

Big, ugly ASCII graphic. Large, often crude drawing composed of ASCII characters, such as a map of Australia, a medieval sword, the *U.S.S. Enterprise* (from the TV show Star Trek), and so on, often appearing in a sig block.

buffer

(n) A memory location that stores a certain amount of data or text until it can be processed or displayed. A screen's *display buffer* is the amount of text you can scroll back to review. If your computer or connection freezes and you type repeatedly until each key press results in a beep, then you have overflowed your *keyboard buffer*.

bug

(n) A flaw in a program (from the expression "working the bugs out"). Also, jokingly defined as an undocumented feature.

buggy

(adj) Said of software; unstable, unreliable, full of bugs.

bundle

(v) To group packets of data into a single cell for transmission over a cell-switching network.

Bunyip

The company formed by the people who invented archie.

burble

(v) To flame at a very low level of competence or clarity.

bus

(n) An electronic pathway or connector.

bus topology

A network architecture in which all nodes are connected to a single cable.

buzz word

Also *stop word,* a word so common that it is useless to search for it (such as *and*, *address*, *record*, and so on). Most searchable databases have lists of buzz words and filter them out during searches.

by hand

(adv) Executed step-by-step by a human being, instead of automatically by a computer process.

byte

A binary "word" (unit of meaning), usually consisting of eight bits.

bzzzzt, wrong

A rejoinder to an incorrect Usenet post, alluding to radio and TV quiz shows in which a timer buzzes when a contestant answers incorrectly.

c

The "catch up" command in some UNIX newsreaders.

C

A programming language developed at Bell Labs that has become a standard for scientific and commercial applications. C++ is an object-oriented successor version of C.

cable

A sheathed length of wires used to transmit signals from device to device.

Cache

Rhymes with *stash.* The place where computer programs, including Web browsers, temporarily store information that may be reused during an ongoing session.

Call for Votes (CFV)

A stage in the Usenet newsgroup creation process, after the Request for Discussion (RFD).

Campus-Wide Information Server (CWIS)

The information system for a college or university, usually including schedules, announcements, job listings, bulletin boards, calendars, and so on.

cancel

On Usenet, to delete an article after you've posted it. It takes a while for the article to vanish everywhere, as the cancel message has to catch up with the propagating article.

canonical

1. Deriving from an official source. In *Star Trek* newsgroups, facts that come from any of the television series or movies is considered canonical; 2. Prototypical, to programmers. For instance,

10 GOTO 10

and

```
Do x=x+1 until x>x+1
```

are canonical infinite loops.

capture

(v) To save text or other data as it scrolls across the screen. Captured text can be read while offline.

card

A printed circuit board added to a computer to enable it to control an additional device.

caret

The ^ character. Indicates an exponent (for example, x^2 means x^2, that is, x *squared*).

The caret is also used in e-mail and Usenet posts to underscore and emphasize text on the preceding line, as shown in this example:

```
pc-lover@online.com
wrote:
>DOS is a snap once
you figure out
config.sys.
^^^^^^^^^^
But that's the prob-
lem with PC-compati-
bles in a nutshell!
They make you deal
with such awkwardly
named setup files.
```

careware

A form of shareware in which the creator of the software requests that payment be made to a charity.

carriage return

A character that moves the cursor back to the beginning of a line (ASCII 13), usually starting a new line in combination with a line feed character.

carrier

A signal constantly transmitted by a modem over a phone line as a reference for the modem on the other end of the line. When a line is disconnected, some modems will report "no carrier."

carrier detect

The notice that a modem has identified the carrier signal from another modem over a phone connection.

Carrier Sense Multiple Access (CSMA)

A protocol that enables multiple devices to transmit on the same channel, by "listening" for the sounds of other devices and only transmitting when the line is clear.

Carrier Sense Multiple Access with Collision Avoidance (CSMA/CA)

A version of CSMA in which devices can detect impending collisions and avoid them.

Carrier Sense Multiple Access with Collision Detection (CSMA/CD)

A version of CSMA in which devices can detect collisions as they occur and resend the corrupted signal.

cascade

A series of one-line follow-up posts, each a play on the previous one. Each post contains all of the previous ones leading up to the latest change, usually in ever-shortening lines, due to the rows of >'s (or sometimes other characters) automatically inserted by newsreader posting commands to indicate an inclusion from a previous post. For example:

```
>>>I'm tired and I'm
going to bed.
>>I'm wired and I'm
holding my head.
>>I've expired and
I'm lacking bread.
>I'm hired! I'm in
the red.
>Inspired, I'll
quickly wed.
I'm mired in this
boring thread.
```

case-insensitive

Not distinguishing between upper- and lowercase characters. In a case-insensitive search, *Internet*, *internet*, and *INTERNET* all match the same key word.

The DOS and Macintosh operating systems are case-insensitive, as are e-mail addresses. UNIX, on the other hand, is case-sensitive.

case-sensitive

Distinguishing between upper- and lowercase characters. To a case-sensitive program, *Peter*, *PETER*, *peter*, and *PeTeR* all mean different things. UNIX is case-sensitive; DOS and Macintoshes are not. E-mail addresses are not case-sensitive.

cat

A UNIX command (short for *'catenate*, from *concatenate*) that can pour the contents of one file into another or dump the contents onto the screen.

catch up

When reading news, to mark all the articles in a newsgroup as read, to clean the slate.

cc:

A list of additional recipients for an e-mail message in the header of the message (from *carbon copy*, a carryover from office-memo shorthand). Most e-mail programs enable the sender to add addresses to the cc: list.

CCITT

Comite Consultatif International de Telegraphique et Telephonique (International Telegraph and Telephone Consultative Committee), an international standards organization comprising telecommunications companies, part of the United Nations' International Telecommunications Union, creator of the X.25, X.400, and X.500 standards.

cd

A UNIX and DOS command meaning *change directory*.

CD-ROM

Compact Disc/Read-Only Memory, a format for storing data on compact discs. Some CD-ROMs contain vast amounts of shareware that can be downloaded for free from the Net.

cell

A packet with a fixed length (in bytes).

cell-switching

A variation on X.25 packet-switching protocol in which data is bundled into equal-sized cells.

Cello

An integrated Web browser and general Internet tool (gopher, WAIS, Usenet, mail) for Windows. Available by anonymous FTP from `ftp.law .cornell.edu`.

censorship

Restrictions placed on written or spoken material. The public spaces of the Internet (such as Usenet news-groups, IRC, and so on) are largely free from censorship, and can be noisy and childish at times. Online services, however, take more responsi-bility for the contents of their net-works and may therefore place some restrictions on what can be written in public or even in private.

central processing unit

See *CPU*.

Cerf, Vinton

Codesigner of the TCP/IP protocols.

CERN European Particle Physics Labo-ratory

(*surn*) The creators of the World Wide Web and the first (text-based) Web browser, www. (The acronym CERN comes from an earlier French title of the Lab: *Conseil Européen pour la Recherche Nucleaire.*) You can reach CERN on the Web at `www.cern.ch/`.

Chameleon NFS

Socket, TCP/IP, and Internet tools software for Windows, made by Net-Manage. Information is available on the Web at `www.netmanage.com`.

Chameleon Sampler

A free collection of socket, TCP/IP, and Internet tools available via FTP from `ftp.netmanage.com`, in the `/pub/demos/sampler` direc-tory, in a self-extracting archive file called `sampler.exe`.

channel

(n) 1. The path along which one device sends a signal to another, meaning a physical cable or wire or an assigned frequency of a physical chan-nel; 2. An IRC topic area.

channel hopping

On IRC, jumping around from channel (definition 2) to channel.

channel op

A privileged user of an IRC channel, able to kick antisocial participants.

character

A letter, number, space, punctuation mark, or symbol—any piece of information that can be stored in one byte.

character-based

(adj) Said of a computer, operating system, environment, or terminal emulation, displaying screens composed entirely of characters (as opposed to graphical images) and accepting input only in the form of characters (as opposed to mouse clicks).

character-based interface

A computer front end that displays only characters on the screen—no graphics, no icons, no mouse pointer, etc. Many dial-up Internet connections are to UNIX boxes with character-based interfaces.

character length

A terminal emulation setting that determines the number of bits in a character (usually seven or eight). ASCII characters require seven bits per byte (one byte per character); binary transfers may require eight bits per character.

character string

A string of characters that must be handled as text, not as numeric data.

charter

The founding document of a Usenet newsgroup or e-mail based discussion group, it defines what constitutes on-topic and off-topic discussion, and establishes whether the group is moderated or not.

chat

(n) 1. Synchronous (happening in real time, like a phone conversation, unlike an e-mail exchange), line-by-line communication with another user over a network; 2. The chat program itself, now largely superseded by the IRC program.

(v) To engage in a chat.

cheapernet

Slang for the "thin" Ethernet specification, generally used in offices.

checksum

An error-checking method in which the sending and receiving modems both sum up the bytes in a data packet and compare the totals.

child directory

A subdirectory.

chmod

(c-h-mode) The UNIX command for changing the read-write permissions of a file (from change mode).

cipher

(n) A code that involves character-for-character substitution (as contrasted with word-for-word substitution or other schemes), a simple example of which is rot13.

circuit

A channel carrying an electrical current between two devices.

circuit board

A computer card holding printed circuits.

circuit-switched network

A network arrangement in which each node is connected to the next via a dedicated line.

clari.

The Usenet-style newsgroup hierarchy dedicated to ClariNet news items.

ClariNet

An online news service analogous to newspaper wire services. If your service provider gets a ClariNet newsfeed, then the news is part of your overhead cost. Otherwise, you can get ClariNet news by direct subscription. For information, send e-mail to info@clarinet.com.

clear channel

A 64 kps channel with its entire bandwidth available for transmission.

Clearinghouse for Networked Information Discovery and Retrieval (CNIDR)

An organization supporting research and cooperation relating to information resources on the Internet (such as WAIS, gopher, archie, and the Web) and ways to search and retrieve information from them. They distribute free-WAIS, a free version of WAIS. CNIDR can be reached on the Web at http://cnidr.org/welcome.html.

client

An application or computer that communicates with and requests information from a server. In conventional networking, client usually refers to a computer; for Internet client/server applications, client usually refers to a program.

client/server

1. A method of distributing information or files in which a central server application archives (stores) the files and makes them available to requests from client applications; 2. A LAN architecture, in which files and other resources are kept on a central server computer and individuals interact with the network through client computers.

client/server application

A network application that functions with a central server as a repository of information and clients that communicate with the server and request information on behalf of individual users.

clip art

Generic pictures and icons, distributed as image files (or in the days before personal computers, in huge books).

Clipper Chip

A U.S. government-sponsored encryption standard that telecommunications industries will be encouraged to adopt when it becomes final, according to pending proposals. The Clipper Chip includes a back door that would allow government agencies to eavesdrop on communication encrypted with the chip. (The government would need a court order to use the decryption keys, otherwise kept in escrow.) Opponents of the Clipper Chip are suspicious of the government following its own rules and believe that any individual or company should have access to the best encryption technology available, not just government-approved encryption.

close

(v) To hang up a telnet, FTP, or other remote connection.

Coalition for Networked Information (CNI)

A coalition of libraries and research organizations dedicated to the sharing of information over computer networks.

coax

(co'-ax) Slang for coaxial cable.

coaxial cable

(co-ax'-ial) Cable containing two conductors, one inside the other, used for broadband and baseband networks, as well as for cable TV.

code

(n) Computer program contents.

(v) To write or edit a computer program.

cognitive dissident

The vocation, coined by Electronic Frontier Foundation cofounder John Barlow, for those who challenge the status quo in cyberspace.

cold boot

(v) To start a computer that's completely turned off.

collision

What happens when two devices try to use the same channel at the same time.

colon

In URLs, a colon (:) appears after the protocol name. In e-mail and Usenet posts, colons sometimes indicate included text.

Colorado Alliance of Research Libraries (CARL)

An alliance of seven libraries that contribute to a database containing abstracts of thousands of journals.

For more information, send e-mail to help@carl.org.

.com

The Internet domain dedicated to commercial entities, generally in the United States.

comm

Communications (sometimes spelled *com*), usually in the context of communications software, a communications port on a computer, and so on.

comma

In Usenet newsreaders, you can often cross-post your article to several newsgroups simply by listing them one after another, separated by commas (,). Likewise, in most mail programs, you may list several e-mail recipients the same way, separated by commas.

command line

A single line of text, with a prompt, often at the bottom of the screen, where the user may enter commands directly. DOS and UNIX are command-line operating systems; Macintosh, Windows, and X Window are graphical environments that do not automatically make a command line available.

command-line interface

A front end that allows or forces the user to memorize and type commands at a prompt, as opposed to one that allows or forces the user to click graphical elements and select commands from pull-down menus.

command mode

A program mode in which you can enter commands. In vi, the UNIX text editor, users start off in command mode and will be frustrated if they try to start typing text. First, they must switch to insert mode.

commercial access provider

A service provider that charges for access to the Internet, as opposed to employers, universities, and free-nets, which provide access for free.

Commercial Internet Exchange (CIE or CIX)

An organization of service providers that represents the interest in making commercial transactions acceptable and secure over the Internet. For more information, send e-mail to info@cix.org.

communications program

A program that operates a modem and provides terminal emulation so that the user can log in to and communicate with a remote computer.

Communications Terminal Protocol (CTERM)

Part of DECnet's virtual terminal service (protocols that allow a user to emulate a different terminal type) specifications.

Communications Toolbox (CTB)

A Macintosh tool that allows a communications program to take advantage of existing communications links.

comp.

A Usenet hierarchy devoted to computers.

Compact Pro

A Macintosh shareware compression program. Files compressed with Compact Pro have a *.cpt* extension.

COM port

The communications port on a computer. On PCs, it's a serial port.

compress

(v) To compact the size of a file in order to save disk storage space.

(n) A UNIX compression program.

compression

A method of compacting a file in order to save disk storage space or the amount of squishing.

CompuServe

An online service with partial Internet access, short for *CompuServe Information System* (CIS). CompuServe has a long-established presence and provides a large number of services to its nearly two million subscribers. Once only linked via e-mail to the Internet, CompuServe is now in the process of adding new Internet features, most recently Usenet newsgroup access. For information, contact postmaster@csi.compuserve.com, (800) 848-8990, or (614) 457-0802.

CompuServe Information Manager (CIM)

A program that provides a graphical interface (or front end) for CompuServe, available for both Macintosh and Windows.

Computer Emergency Response Team (CERT)

A network-security task force available round-the-clock to assist Internet users with security problems. For more information, send e-mail to cert@cert.org or call their 24-hour hotline at (412) 268-7090.

computer geek

Someone who enjoys messing around with a computer, not necessarily as a programmer or at the same level of sophistication as a hacker. This is not necessarily a derogatory term; it depends on the context and the company.

computer-mediated communication

Any form of communication aided and abetted by computers, including, but not limited to, e-mail, chat, and conferencing.

Computer Professionals for Social Responsibility (CPSR)

An organization of computer professionals concerned with the impacts computers might have on society. Originally formed to discuss the connections between computer research and the nuclear arms race, it now also addresses such issues as issues as privacy, the role of the computer in the workplace, and research priorities in the coming century.

Computer + Science Network (CSNET)

A computer-science research network that merged with BITNET to create the Corporation for Research and Educational Networking (CREN).

conductor

A particular type of wire, such as copper.

conferencing

(adj) Said of software that enables many users to engage in a more or less public, written conversation, either in real time (as on an IRC channel) or not (as in a Usenet newsgroup).

connection

A type, or level, of access to the Internet, ranging from a direct network connection (through SLIP or PPP dial-up access) to character-based shell-account dial-up access and simple e-mail gateways to the Net.

Connection closed by foreign host

A message during a telnet or other remote login session that tells you that the host you've logged in to has closed the connection.

Connection Control Language (CCL)

An AppleTalk scripting language for controlling modem functions.

connectionless communication

A form of communication between applications in which data can be requested and supplied during intermittent connections.

connection-oriented communication

A form of communication between applications in which all data is exchanged during a single connection.

connect time

The amount of time you spend connected to your service provider. Many providers charge a fee based on your connect time. Others are flat-rate providers.

Consortium for School Networking (CoSN)

A nonprofit organization that studies the uses of networking in K-12 schooling. For more information, send e-mail to cosn@bitnic.bitnet.

contention

The situation that occurs when two devices both try to use the same channel. Every network must have some protocol in place to deal with issues of contention.

control bus

The channel within a computer along which control signals (signals that control a device or routine) are carried.

control character

A special character, usually non-printing, that starts or stops a computer function.

Control key

The key marked *Ctrl* on most computer keyboards (including the Macintosh). In combination with other keys, the Control key can send control characters to the computer. It is sometimes symbolized by ^, so Control-C might be written ^C or Ctrl-C.

Conversational Monitor System (CMS)

The command-line interface of IBM's VM operating system.

cookie

1. A file containing identifying information about a user. Accepting a cookie means that you agree to share the information that is in that file with the parties that run the site from which the current request was submitted. 2. A fortune cookie program that spits out a different fortune every time you run it. Some systems run cookie as part of their startup or login procedure.

Coordinating Committee for Intercontinental Research Networks (CCIRN)

A committee that coordinates research networks in North America and Europe.

copyright

People debate how standing copyright law applies to articles posted to Usenet or to texts in general made available on the Internet. This is thus far not settled law. Some people attach copyright notices to their Usenet posts.

core

(n) 1. RAM, on UNIX and some IBM machines; 2. The name of a file that appears in your UNIX directory after a core dump. This file contains everything that was in memory at the time of the dump.

core dump

(n) 1. A copy of the contents of memory, dumped into a file when an unrecoverable error occurs; 2. A brain dump.

Corporation for Research and Educational Networking (CREN)

An organization formed by the merger of BITNET and CSNET. CREN can be reached via gopher at info.educom.edu.

corrupted

(adj) Said of a file, block of data, or other communication, damaged in transmission.

cp

The UNIX *copy file* command.

cpio

A UNIX command that makes whole directories into a single file, for easy transportation.

CP/M

A PC operating system that preceded DOS. If someone mentions CP/M, they're bragging about how long they've been working with microcomputers.

CPU

The heart of a computer, the part that does the "thinking."

cracker

One who breaks into computer systems. What many people in the real world call a hacker.

cracking

The act of breaking into a computer system or program.

crack root

(v) To break into the root account of a UNIX machine and, most likely, use the root privileges to break into other accounts.

crash

(n) An unrecoverable failure of a computer system, requiring rebooting as a minimum response.

(v) To suffer from a computer system failure.

crippleware

Shareware that lacks a useful or even crucial functionality, in order to entice you into registering as an owner to obtain the uncrippled version of the program.

crlf

A combination of two characters (carriage return and line feed) that on some computer systems constitutes a new line.

crosspost

(n) A Usenet article posted simultaneously to more than one newsgroup. Most newsreaders will show you crossposted articles only the first time you encounter them.

cross-post

(v) To post a Usenet article to several newsgroups at once. This takes up less disk space than posting it separately and repeatedly.

crosstalk

Interference between two wires in a cable.

CrossTalk

A communications and terminal emulation program for DOS and Windows.

cryptography

The study of codes, ciphers, and other security issues.

C shell

A common "flavor" of UNIX shells.

.cshrc

A startup file for the UNIX C shell.

CSLIP

Compressed Serial Line Internet Protocol, a faster version of SLIP in which Internet address information is compressed.

CSO

Computing Services Office, a system for searching campus telephone and address listings, reachable by gopher.

CSO name server

A searchable white pages listing of real names and associated e-mail addresses, usually reached via gopher.

The Cuckoo's Egg

A book by Clifford Stoll describing how he tracked East German crackers breaking into a system at Lawrence Berkeley Labs at the University of California at Berkeley.

CUSeeMe

(*see-you-see-me*) A new Internet protocol for synchronous video and sound communication.

c-ya

See you [later] (written only).

cyber-

A prefix overused to indicate a connection to computers, networks, technology, or futurism.

cybercafé

A coffeehouse that offers Internet access, often via coin-operated or free Internet terminals.

cyberdelics

1. Mind-altering effects brought about by computer technology (as opposed to hallucinogenic drugs); 2. Eye-bending screen savers.

cybernaut

A traveler in cyberspace, someone who uses their Internet connection to explore the furthest realms of cyberspace.

cyberpunk

(n) 1. A largely hype-driven category of popular culture at the crossroads of computer technology, science fiction, and youth culture; 2. A genre of science fiction that appeared in the mid-to-late '80s and combined a bleak, noirish view of the future with a fetishization of technology and human-computer interaction.

cyberspace

A term, coined by author William Gibson, for the shared imaginary reality of computer networks. Some people use cyberspace as a synonym for the Internet. Others hold out for the more complete physical-seeming consensual reality of Gibson's novels.

cycle power

(v) To turn a computer off and then on again.

cyclic redundancy check (CRC)

An error-detection technique used during file transfers and other forms of data transmission. Both the sending and receiving modems perform calculations on the data and then the two results are compared.

cypherpunk

(n) An activist interested in the political potentials of universal Internet access and cheap and foolproof privacy.

daemon

(*day'-mun* or *dee'-mun*) In UNIX and other operating systems, a program that runs all the time, in the background, waiting for things to do (from the mythological meaning, later rationalized as the acronym "Disk And Execution MONitor"). When you post an article to a *.test newsgroup, daemons all over the world send you e-mail confirmations when they receive your post.

daisy chain

A network architecture, also called bus topology, in which all nodes are connected to a single cable.

dark fiber

Unused cable in the fiber-optic network.

DARPA

Defense Advanced Research Projects Agency, the official name of ARPA during the 1980s and early 1990s.

data

Information of any type, usually information stored, transmitted, or processed by computers.

database

A repository of information stored on a computer and accessible to searches.

data bits

In asynchronous data transmission, the bits between a start bit (and sometimes a parity bit) and a stop bit, the only bits actually carrying data. There are usually seven or eight data bits, depending on the size of a character, or byte. *Data bits* is therefore one of the settings you have to specify on your modem to make a connection. Usually 7 or 8, it depends on the modem you're calling.

data block

A unit of data sent from one device to another.

data bus

The channel within a computer along which communication signals are carried.

data channel

Any channel over which data is sent in the form of a signal.

data communications equipment (DCE)

Devices such as modems that connect to a serial port and control data communications.

data encryption key (DEK)
> An element of key encryption that is used to encrypt and decrypt data.

data encryption standard (DES)
> A security protocol defined by the U.S. government.

data/fax modem
> A modem that can transmit raw data or a fax image.

datagram
> The basic unit of data transmission across a network, containing a header and the data itself. The header describes the data, its destination, and its relationship to other datagrams.

Datagram Delivery Protocol (DDP)
> An AppleTalk protocol that handles the routing of datagrams over an AppleTalk network.

data link
> 1. The device that enables data transmission; 2. An active connection for data transmission.

data link layer
> The second layer of the OSI Model that deals with transmission of data frames from node to node.

data stream
> A series of data blocks sent from one device to another.

data terminal equipment (DTE)
> A device at one end or the other of a data transmission. This usually means a PC or terminal.

.dd
> The extension of a file compressed with DiskDoubler on the Macintosh.

DEC
> (*deck*) See *Digital Equipment Corporation*.

DEChead
> (*deck'-head*) 1. An employee of Digital Equipment Corporation; 2. A Deadhead (Grateful Dead fan) employee of DEC.

DECnet
> (*deck'-net*) Network protocols designed for VAX and PDP-11 computers, used by Digital Equipment Corporation operating systems instead of TCP/IP.

DECnet/DNA
> DEC's implementation of DNA (Digital Network Architecture).

DECnet tunnel
> A protocol for packaging AppleTalk datagrams within DECnet packets.

decrypt
> (v) To remove the encryption from a file or e-mail message and make it readable.

decryption key

> In key encryption, a key used to decipher an encrypted message and make it readable.

dedicated

> (adj) Assigned to a single task or able to perform only a single task.

dedicated line

> A separate telephone line dedicated to the transmission of data.

deep hack

> The extreme state of concentration, bordering on a trance, that hackers enter after long hours of hacking.

default

> (n) A setting, state, instruction, or selection that a program uses unless you explicitly change it.

default route

> An entry in a routing table indicating where to route packets intended for destinations not otherwise listed in the table.

Defense Data Network (DDN)

> The network of networks used by the U.S. military, connecting with the Internet in some places and not in others.

Defense Data Network Network Information Center (DDN NIC)

> The Network Information Center for the DDN, a source of information as well as an administrative authority over the DDN.

Defense Information Systems Agency (DISA)

> The U.S. government agency that oversees the Defense Data Network.

delete

> (v) To erase a character, file, or directory.

Delete key

> A key used in most environments to erase the character under or just to the left of the cursor or insertion point. On some systems, Delete erases the character just typed or to the left of the cursor.

delimiter

> A character or symbol that indicates a break between two pieces of information, items in a table, or fields in a database.

delurk

> (*dee-lurk'*, v) To post to a list or newsgroup for the first time.

> (n) A first post to a newsgroup or list after the writer has lurked for a while.

Depew, Dick

> The inventor of ARMM, a roboposting utility designed to retroactively cancel off-topic Usenet posts. Depew's 'bot had a serious flaw and followed up its own posts, eventually bringing down part of the Internet, in "sorcerer's apprentice" style.

deprecated

(adj) Being phased out in favor of a new standard.

despew

(v) To robotically post reams of junk to the Net (from [Dick] Depew).

developer

A software publisher.

device

Any piece of computer equipment, though the term is often used to specify peripheral devices.

/dev/null

On UNIX boxes, the null device. Data piped to /dev/null disappears. People posting controversial articles to Usenet sometimes add the notice "flames to /dev/null."

dial up

(v) To use a modem to call up another computer or network and log in to it.

dial-up

(adj) Said of an Internet access that requires the user to connect via a modem.

dial-up account

An Internet account on a host machine that you must dial up with your modem to use.

DIALOG Information Retrieval Database

A commercial online database service with hundreds of databases and millions of records. To connect to DIALOG, telnet to dialog.com.

dictionary flame

A flame that focuses on someone's use of a particular word or their vocabulary; a weak sort of flame that indicates that the flamer really has nothing substantial to say against the flamee.

digest

(n) A collection of mailing list posts, sent out as one message.

digestified

(adj) Turned into a digest. Not all mailing lists are available in a digestified form.

digital

(adj) Representing values as discrete bits. CD is a digital medium because the sound or other information is *digitized* (converted into bits) and then stored. A CD player converts the digital information encoded on the CD into an analog signal sent to the amplifier.

Digital Data Communications Message Protocol (DDCMP)

A DECnet data link protocol that can handle both synchronous and asynchronous links.

Digital Equipment Corporation (DEC)

Manufacturer of VAX (and before that PDP-11) boxes and the VMS operating system.

Digital Network Architecture (DNA)

A set of protocols for network architecture.

DIP

Dual in-line package, the housing for an integrated circuit.

DIP switch

A switch used to select the operating mode of a device.

directed information

Information intended for a particular recipient, such as private e-mail.

directory

An organizing structure for files. In most operating systems, directories can themselves be organized hierarchically into a "tree" of parent and children directories.

Directory Access Protocol (DAP)

An X.500 protocol governing the communication between a Directory User Agent and a Directory System Agent.

directory listing

A summary list of available files, possibly including file sizes, attributes, date and time of creation or last changes, and the owner, where appropriate.

directory service

A database of sites and usernames that enables users to locate other users, hosts, and services.

Directory System Agent (DSA)

X.500 software that serves directory information to Directory User Agents.

Directory User Agent (DUA)

X.500 software that queries a Directory System Agent for directory information.

disable

(v) To temporarily disconnect or make nonfunctional (without necessarily shutting off).

discussion group

Any online group of likeminded people who may communicate using a mailing list, a newsgroup, an IRC channel, etc.

disk

A medium for storing computer data, either built into the computer (a hard disk) or removable (a floppy disk).

disk drive

The mechanism that spins, reads from, and writes to the disk itself.

diskette

A 51/4" or 31/2" removable floppy disk used for storing data.

disk server

A network program that enables a computer to use a disk drive on another computer (or a partition of such a disk drive) as though it were a local disk drive.

Distinct TCP/IP Tools

A set of Internet tools for Windows sold by Distinct Corporation.

distributed computing

An approach to computing that allows applications to run the same way across different types of networks.

Distributed Computing Environment (DCE)

A set of standards for servers, interfaces, and protocols promoted by the Open Software Foundation to enable distributed computing.

distributed database

A repository of information stored on various hosts and accessible to searches as if stored in a single location.

distributed server

Peer-to-peer network architecture, in which server functions are shared among the peer computers in the network, and disk drives, printers, and other devices are available to all.

distribution

The geographic range that a Usenet post is distributed to. By default, most newsreaders will give posts *World* distribution.

distribution list

A simple form of mailing list in which an alias is assigned to a list of e-mail addresses. Mail directed to the alias is sent to every address on the list.

disusered

(adj) Denied access to the Net; having an account canceled.

DIX

Digital, Intel, and Xerox, together the developers of the Ethernet protocol.

doc

Slang for *document*.

documentation

Paper or online manuals that describe the functions of a computer system, often in incomprehensible terms.

dogpile

(v) To quickly follow up a Usenet post with a large volume of critical replies.

domain

The main subdivision of Internet addresses; the last part of an Internet address after the final dot. In the United States, the standard domains are as follows:

DOMAIN
Meaning

.com
Commercial

`.edu`
Educational

`.gov`
Government

`.mil`
Military

`.org`
Non-profit organization

`.net`
Network

Outside the United States, the top-level domain is usually the country domain, such as *.ca* for Canada, *.de* for Germany (Deutschland), *.uk* for the United Kingdom, and so on.

domain name
A complete description of an Internet site including a host name, subdomain, and domain, all separated by dots.

domain name address
An Internet address expressed in terms of host, subdomain, and domain, as opposed to the numerical IP address. Also called a *fully qualified domain name*.

domain name resolution
The process of converting domain names to numerical IP addresses, by consulting domain name servers.

domain name server
An application that maintains a table of domain names and corresponding IP addresses in order to resolve the domain names of messages.

Domain Name System (DNS)
A collection of distributed databases (domain name servers) that maintain the correlations between domain name addresses and numerical IP addresses; for example, the domain name address `ruby.ora.com` gets resolved into the numeric Internet address `134.65.87.3`, and vice versa. DNS allows human beings to use the Internet without remembering long lists of numbers.

DOS
Disk Operating System, the operating system developed for IBM PCs.

dos2unix
A UNIX program that converts DOS text files to UNIX format (by stripping the carriage return character from the end of each line).

dot
The separator character for domain names, newsgroup names, and other UNIX-oriented files. Dots should only be used to separate hierarchical levels in newsgroup names, not to split compound names. So, for example, `alt.fan.dave.barry` would be improper, but `alt.fan.dave-barry` is fine.

dot address
A 32-bit numerical IP address of the form *number-dot-number-dot-number-dot-number* (such as

192.100.81.101). Each of the four numbers can range from 0 to 255.

dot com

Web-speak for a company or Web site. For example, one would say, "so and so company is a *dot com.*"

dot file

A UNIX file whose name begins with a dot, such as `.profile`, `.netrc`, `.cshrc`, and so on. Dot files will not show up in a normal directory listing.

doubled sig

A sig block that appears twice at the end the of an e-mail message or Usenet post, a sign that the writer is a newbie or that the software is hiccuping.

down

(adj) Said of a network or device that is not functioning.

download

(v) To transfer a file over a modem from a remote computer to your desktop computer. (Technically, to transfer a file from a larger computer to a smaller computer.)

downstream

Where your newsfeed goes after it has reached your host and your host has sent it along to other sites.

DRECnet

(*dreck'-net*) A derogatory name for DECnet.

driver

Software that controls peripheral devices such as monitors, printers, or keyboards.

drop-ins

Random characters that appear on the screen due to a faulty connection and/or line noise.

drop-outs

Characters that are missing from the screen or not passed on by the keyboard.

DS0

Digital Signal Level 0 is 64 Kbps, a standard level of digital transmission service (also called *fractional* T1).

DS1

Digital Signal Level 1 is 1.544 Mbps, a standard level of digital transmission service (also called T1).

DS2

Digital Signal Level 2 is 6.312 Mbps, a standard level of digital transmission service (also called T2).

DS3

Digital Signal Level 3 is 44.736 Mbps, a standard level of digital transmission service (also called T3).

DS4

Digital Signal Level 4 is 274.176 Mbps, a standard level of digital transmission service (also called T4).

dual in-line package

The housing for an integrated circuit.

dumb terminal

A keyboard-and-monitor device that sends keystrokes to a computer and displays output on the screen. If you dial up to a UNIX shell, then your PC is being used as a dumb terminal.

dump

(v) To send the contents of a file (or other data) to a device or to another file, in order to print, display, or store the data.

dup killer

(*doop killer*) FidoNet software that tries to detect and eliminate duplicate copies of the same message that may have arrived via different routes.

duplex

Transmission of signals in two directions at once.

dup loop

(*doop loop*) A series of nearly identical messages that have eluded the dup killer.

dynamic adaptive routing

A method of directing network traffic based on the current state of the network.

dynamic node addressing

A method of addressing used on AppleTalk networks in which nodes are assigned network addresses as needed, but do not have stable consistent network addresses, as in an IP network.

dynamic SLIP

A type of SLIP access to the Internet, in which the user is supplied with a new IP address, drawn from a pool of possibilities, every time they connect. This enables the service provider to assign fewer IP addresses to its SLIP customers, with the trade-off being that a user cannot function as a host without a consistent address.

EBCDIC

(*eb-sa-dic* or *eb-see-dic*) *Extended Binary Coded Decimal Interchange Code*, a proprietary IBM character set that is not entirely compatible with ASCII.

echo

(n) 1. A discussion group on FidoNet; 2. The method by which the characters you type are displayed on your screen, also known as *local echo*; 3. The method by which characters sent from a remote system are displayed on your screen, also known as *remote echo*.

EcoNet

(*ee'-coe-net*) A BBS dedicated to environmental issues. Its Internet domain name is igc.org.

ed

(rhymes with *bed*) A UNIX, line-at-a-time text editor.

EDGAR

Electronic Data Gathering Archiving and Retrieval, a database of corporate disclosure, transaction, and financial status data maintained by the United States Security Exchange Commission. For more information, see the Web page at `http://town.hall.org/edgar/edgar.html`.

editor

1. A text editor; a program used to edit simple text files; 2. Any program used to edit any type of file, such as a .WAV (Windows sound file) editor.

EDT

A text editor available on VMS machines and at Delphi Information Service.

.edu

The Internet domain dedicated to educational institutions, generally in the United States.

Educational Resources Information Center (ERIC)

A service for schools providing online bibliography and journal abstracts, via gopher at `ericir.syr.edu` and via e-mail at `askeric@ricir.syr.edu`.

EDUCOM

(*ed'-you-com*) An organization dedicated to facilitating the use of computers in educational institutions. It is a supporter of the National Research and Education Network (NREN).

Gopher: `educom.com`; e-mail: `inquiry@bitnic.educom.com`.

ee

(*ee-ee*) A UNIX text editor.

EFF's Guide to the Internet

The Electronic Frontier Foundation's excellent free Internet guide (formerly *Big Dummy's Guide to the Internet*), available via FTP, gopher, and the Web.

EIA/TIA-568

A document coauthored by the American National Standards Institute, the Electronics Industry Association, and the Telecommunications Industry Association that specifies a wiring standard for buildings suitable for both LANs and telecommunications systems.

8-bit clean

(adj) Said of a modem connection with 8 data bits and no corruption of the signal from line noise.

802.x

A set of communications standards (802.1 through 802.5) for physical and electrical connections in LANs, defined by the Institute of Electrical and Electronic Engineers.

80-character line length

The standard line length for an IBM or UNIX terminal, a recommended maximum line length for e-mail and Usenet posts (some prefer

75 characters to allow for quotation, since most e-mail and newsreader programs quote text by preceding it with a > or other character).

e-journal

An *electronic journal*; an academic journal that circulates via an e-mail mailing list. One advantage e-journals have over print journals is that they are searchable.

Electronic Frontier Foundation (EFF)

A lobbying and advocacy organization, founded by Mitch Kapor and John Barlow, working for the preservation of freedom on the cyberspace frontier.

Electronics Industries Association (EIA)

A standards organization for the electronics industry, the coauthor of EIA/TIA-568.

elm

(rhymes with *helm*) A full-screen UNIX e-mail program, easier to use than the basic, line-at-a-time mail but still more difficult than pine, which is much closer to modern word processors.

.elmrc

A setup file for elm.

emacs

(*ee-macs*) Also written *EMACS*, a UNIX text editor that doubles as an operating environment, mail program, and newsreader.

e-mail

(n) Messages carried electronically from computer to computer, short for *electronic mail*, one of the most popular features of networks, online services, and the Internet in general. The term *e-mail* (also *email*) is used both for the overall process and for the messages carried electronically from computer to computer.

(v) To send e-mail.

e-mail address

1. An Internet mail address of the form *username@host .domain*; 2. The username portion of a mail account on a network.

emoticon

A smiley or other sideways punctuation face such as these:

```
:-)   :-(   :-P   %^)
;-)   B-)   :D
```
Emoticons can convey some insight into the writer's emotional state.

emulation

For a computer, operating system, or application, the process of imitating the functions of another environment.

encapsulate

To embed a higher-level protocol within a lower-level protocol to create a single frame for transportation over a network.

Encapsulated PostScript (EPS)

A device-independent file format for PostScript files. EPS files are portable and can be printed with any PostScript printer.

encoding

The process of converting data to a coded format, generally to make it more easily transportable.

encrypt

To scramble the contents of a file or e-mail message so that only those with the key can unscramble and read them.

encryption

A process of rendering a file or e-mail message unreadable to anyone lacking the encryption key.

encryption key

A unique, secret data block used to encrypt e-mail.

end-to-end

(adj) Direct, said of a connection between two computers.

end-user

(n) From a programmer's perspective, the ultimate customer; the regular person using the program, operating system, or computer.

Enter key

A large key on the right side of most keyboards (sometimes called the *Return key*) used to submit commands or insert hard returns (newlines) into text.

enterprise computing

Corporate network computing, bridging a variety of platforms, operating systems, and networking protocols.

environment

A front end for an operating system, also called *operating environment*; a set of tools and a consistent look and feel that allow the user to interact with the computer. Windows is an environment that runs on top of the MS-DOS operating system.

EOF

An *end-of-file* marker.

.eps

The file extension for an Encapsulated PostScript file.

error

An unexpected action or result, or incorrectly transmitted data. Any process that causes results which a computer cannot properly interpret.

error control

Any method for verifying the correctness of transmitted data.

error message

A message from the operating system, alerting a user that something has gone wrong. Error messages can be as cryptic as a random number or as informative as a complete explanation of the problem.

escape character

1. ASCII 26; 2. Any character which, when preceded by an escape (usually ASCII 26, the character that is transmitted when the Escape key is pressed), sends a command to a device, such as a terminal or printer. They are often represented on the screen as capital letters preceded by carets, such as ^E, ^X, etc.

escape out

(v) 1. To substitute a special symbol for a character that would otherwise be misinterpreted (such as to escape out slash characters so they don't get interpreted as directory separators); 2. To run a temporary shell from within an application in order to send commands to the operating system (such as to escape out to UNIX to check your mail without exiting the newsreader).

escape sequence

A sequence of characters reserved for a special meaning by a computer's operating system; may be used to send commands (for example, to a printer).

e-text

Written works made available electronically.

Ethernet

A LAN network protocol and set of cabling specifications, originally developed by Digital, Intel, and Xerox, employing a bus topology and providing a transfer rate of up to 10 Mbps. Ethernet nodes may be connected with unshielded twisted-pair wiring or thick or thin coaxial cable. Ethernet uses CSMA/CD to prevent collisions, as opposed to token rings, which use token passing.

ETLA

(*ee-tee-ell-ay*) *Extended three-letter acronym* (in other words, a four-letter acronym). This acronym is a facetious comment on the proliferation of bewildering TLAs in the technical world. Too many TLAs and ETLAs thrown around make MEGO (my eyes glaze over).

.etx

File extension for a setext file.

Eudora

An e-mail program for Windows or the Macintosh that can use the Post Office Protocol and function as an offline mail reader. Available via anonymous FTP from `ftp.qualcomm.com`.

European Academic and Research Network (EARN)

A network of universities and research facilities in Europe that has e-mail and file-transfer connections to Bitnet.

even parity

A method of verifying the correctness of transmitted data by summing each byte, adding a parity bit of 1 if necessary to make the sum even before sending the data, and then repeating the summation on the receiving end.

exclamation mark (!)

1. A bang—it precedes each site in a bang path; 2. In some UNIX programs, an exclamation mark enables the user to shell out; 3. Overuse of exclamation marks to punctuate Usenet posts is one of the hallmarks of a newbie or a B1FF.

.exe

A DOS file extension used to indicate an executable file (such as a program or self-extracting archive file).

execute

To perform a command or run a program, something operating systems do.

exit

(v) To quit a program or leave a shell.

expansion slot

Inside a PC, a connector that gives an adapter access to the system bus, allowing the installation of additional peripheral devices.

expire

Applied to Usenet articles, to be removed after an expiration date to keep the newsfeed from growing too large.

export

(v) 1. To save a file in a different format (that of another program); 2. To send a product to a foreign country (whether physically or over the Internet).

Extended Binary Coded Decimal Interchange Code (EBCDIC)

A proprietary IBM character set that is not entirely compatible with ASCII.

extension

The portion of a filename after the last dot, often used to indicate the type of file. DOS extensions have a three-character maximum length.

External Gateway Protocol (EGP)

A routing protocol by which connected networks signal their availability to each other.

extranet

An enterprise's private intranet that relies on secure use of the public Internet to connect disparate locations.

e-zine

Also *ezine*, an electronically distributed fanzine or magazine. Many are sent as e-mail. Others are made available via gopher or the Web.

f

1. The forward command in many UNIX mail programs; 2. The follow up command in some UNIX newsreaders.

face time

(n) Time spent meeting with a person, as contrasted with time spent communicating via e-mail, voice mail, etc.

fair use

The legal doctrine that allows limited quotation of other people's work if the use of their work does not undercut its market value.

fall off

(v) Said of a portion of data that exceeds the size of a memory register and is lost.

fanzine

An underground, do-it-yourself magazine, often dedicated to a band, celebrity, or cult figure.

FAQ

(*fack*, n) 1. A *frequently asked question*; 2. A file containing frequently asked questions and their answers, sometimes called a FAQL (*frequently asked question list*). To find FAQs, look in the *.answers newsgroups or the FTP archive at

rtfm.mit.edu. Many mailing lists and Usenet newsgroups maintain FAQs so that participants won't have to spend lots of time answering the same set of questions.

FAQL

(*fackle*, n) *Frequently-asked-question list*, a file containing frequently asked questions and their answers, usually compiled and maintained by a newsgroup, mailing list, or Internet site.

FARNET (Federation of American Research Networks)

A nonprofit organization that works to promote the use of computer networks for research and education.

fast packet

A standard for high-speed, high-traffic, cell-switching networks. Also called *Asynchronous Transfer Mode (ATM)*.

fax

(n) 1. A *facsimile* of a document, digitized and transmitted over phone lines. While faxes are usually sent and received with a stand-alone fax machine, faxes may also be sent to and from computers using fax software and a fax modem; 2. A machine that can send and receive faxes.

(v) To send a fax.

fax modem

A modem that can fulfill some of the functions of a fax machine.

Federal Information Exchange (FIX)
A gateway linking U.S. government networks with the Internet.

Federal Information Processing Standards (FIPS)
A United States Department of Defense document specifying U.S. government networking plans.

Federal Networking Council (FNC)
An organization that coordinates the networking standards of U.S. government agencies.

FEDIX
An online information service linking educational institutions and the U.S. government. It offers the Minority On-Line Information Service (MOLIS).

fetch
(v) To transfer a file from a remote site on the Internet to your host computer.

(n) A Macintosh FTP program.

Fiber Distributed Data Interface (FDDI)
A backbone system for large networks, employing two rings of fiber-optic cabling with a signaling rate of 80 Mbps.

fiber-optic cable
Glass cabling designed to carry light pulses, often used for backbones; more dependable, lighter, and smaller than copper cable carrying electronic signals, but much more expensive and more difficult to repair.

FidoNet
A network of BBSs with Internet e-mail access.

Fiction Rag & Gossip
A Web site about writers maintained by the novelist Martha Conway (at www.syx.com/pilgrim/rag.html).

field
(n) A defined area containing a fixed number of characters, found in online forms and some databases.

56K
(adj) Said of a telephone circuit with a 64-Kbps bandwidth that uses 8K for signaling and the remaining 56K for traffic.

File Attach
A FidoNet procedure for attaching a file to an e-mail message to send it to another BBS.

file locking
Preventing all but the first user from making changes to a file that is opened by more than one user on a network.

File Request
A FidoNet procedure for transferring a file from one BBS to another.

file server

A computer that makes files available to other users on a network.

file transfer

The copying of a file over a network connection from a remote site to the local host.

filter

(n) 1. A program that converts one file format into another; 2. In e-mail, a program that allows certain messages to reach the user while eliminating other messages. On UNIX machines, it is easy to set up an e-mail filter to prevent unwanted mail from making it to your inbox.

(v) To ignore unwanted information by using a filter (definition 2).

finger

(v) To seek the identity of a user or the status of a network.

(n) The UNIX command that performs the finger function.

finn

(v) To pull rank on someone else in IRC by showing that you've been around a lot longer than the other person—demonstrating that they are a relative newbie, compared to you. (The IRC protocol was first used on servers in Finland, hence the term *finn*.)

firewall

(n) A security measure on the Internet, protecting information, preventing access, or ensuring that users cannot do any harm to underlying systems. Some networks are connected to the Internet via a firewall machine.

FirstSearch Catalog

A catalog maintained by the Online Computer Library Center that gives member libraries access to many databases of books and magazines in print.

flame

(n) An insulting e-mail or Usenet post. Flames are often ill-considered knee-jerk expressions of anger, but they can also be cruelly detailed and intended for the amusement of the general audience at the expense of the flamee.

(v) To post a flame.

flamebait

(n) A post to a mailing list or newsgroup designed to elicit flames. Flamebait can be recognized by the fact that it goes beyond the premises of the list or newsgroup. Nobody objects to provocative or even argumentative posts, but (for example) posts to the `alt.fan.frank-zappa` newsgroup saying "Zappa was a no-talent potty-mouthed dweeb" betray a lack of legitimate interest in the subject at hand.

flamefest

A flame war, particularly one involving many participants.

flame on

A comment in a post meaning
either "Here is where I start flaming"
or "I'm prepared to be flamed for the
following comment."

flamer

1. One who flames; 2. One who
flames habitually or incessantly.

flames to /dev/null

A tag line in posts to mailing lists
and newsgroups meaning "I'll ignore
(or delete) any flames," from the
UNIX name for the null device, a sort
of trash can.

flame war

Often written *flamewar*, a pro-
longed series of flames and counter-
flames, drowning out the on-topic
posts in a newsgroup or mailing list.
Traditionally, flame wars end when
Nazis are mentioned.

flavor

(n) A variety, as in "BSD is a flavor
of UNIX."

flood

(v) To spam an IRC channel, that
is, to type or paste in huge amounts
of text, effectively drowning out the
conversation.

floppy disk

A removable storage medium.

flow control

The method by which two devices,
generally modems, signal to each other
when to start and stop sending data.

fnord

(n) A nonsense word embedded in
posts or sig blocks, alluding to Robert
Anton Wilson's *Illuminati!* trilogy (in
which children are taught not to see
the fnords as part of their fnord con-
ditioning by fnord the state fnord).

FOAF

(n) A *friend of a friend* (written
only), the most common source or
attribution for urban legends, implying that the teller doesn't personally
know the participants, but knows
someone who does.

folder

1. A directory, either on a Macintosh or a Windows computer; 2.
An e-mail file containing related
messages.

follow up

(v) To respond to a post with a
replying post.

follow-up

(n) A post that replies to and possibly quotes an earlier post.

follow-up line

A line in the header of some
Usenet posts directing follow-ups to a
particular newsgroup or newsgroups.
Newbies who fail to heed the follow-

up line can be tricked into posting replies to inappropriate newsgroups (or worse, to `*.test` groups, resulting in thousands of automated replies stuffing their inbox).

foo

A dummy variable used by programmers as a stand-in for a real variable, often paired with bar.

footprint

The portion of a surface that a computer or peripheral device occupies.

foreground

In a multitasking computer environment, a process that takes place in full view or with higher priority than other running processes is said to take place in the foreground.

FORTRAN

An early computer programming language (the name comes from *FORmula TRANslator*).

fortune cookie

A program that spits out a different fortune every time you run it. Some systems run a fortune cookie program as part of their startup or login procedure.

forum

A discussion group on CompuServe and other online services and BBSs where users with similar interests may find valuable information, exchange ideas, and share files.

forward

(v) To send received e-mail along to another address, either manually or automatically.

forward slash

/, used to divide directories in a path in UNIX (and, hence, in many Internet applications).

FQA

Frequently questioned acronym.

frame

1. An area of the screen of some graphical Web browsers (such as Netscape and Microsoft Internet Explorer), which can be updated independently and may also scroll separately.

2. (n) A block of data encapsulated with a header and trailer for transmission over a network.

frame relay

A standard for transmission of frames over a packet-switching network, a variant of the X.25 standard.

fred

1. An easy-to-use X.500 interface;
2. A dummy variable used by programmers to stand for a real variable.

FrEdMail

(*fred-mail*) A network of BBSs for students and teachers.

free-net

A free public network providing Internet access to members of a community.

Free Software Foundation (FSF)

An organization dedicated to the production and distribution of free software, the creators of GNU, reachable via FTP at `prep.ai.mit.edu`.

free-WAIS

A free version of a WAIS server produced and distributed by CNIDR (Clearinghouse for Networked Information Discovery and Retrieval).

freeware

Software distributed for free (or for bragging rights) via the Net. The culture of the Internet encourages freeware.

frequency

A measurement of the number of cycles per second of an electronic signal, roughly a measurement of the speed of a process or device.

fringeware

Software of dubious stability, commercial value, or appeal, made available as freeware.

front end

The part of a computer process that the end-user interacts with. In client/server applications, the client acts as a front end for the server.

FSLIST

The *Forgotten Site List*. A list of Internet service providers available via anonymous FTP from `freedom.nmsu.edu` in the `/pub/docs/fslist/` directory.

ftp

The UNIX FTP program.

FTP

Internet *file transfer protocol*, the standard TCP/IP protocol for transferring files over the Internet, across any platforms.

FTPmail

A way to use FTP by e-mail if you don't have an FTP application. One address for an FTPmail server is `ftpmail@pa.dec.com`.

FTP server

An FTP file server, a computer serving files from an FTP archive.

FTP site

A host on the Internet containing archives and set up for FTP.

f2f

(adv or adj) Face-to-face, meeting in person (written only).

full duplex

Two-way communication in which the computers at either end of the transmission both send and receive at the same time.

full name

The real name associated with an e-mail address; can be an alias.

full-screen editor

A text editor that allows the user to move around the screen, editing an entire file.

fully qualified domain name (FQDN)

The complete domain name that identifies a specific computer (or host network, at the very least) on the Internet, including a host name, a subdomain name, and a domain name. Also called *domain name address*.

fwiw

For what it's worth (written only).

fyi

For your information.

FYI

(n) An Internet document that provides information about the Internet itself, but which does not define standards. Available via anonymous FTP from rtfm.mit.edu.

g

The *go* command in the UNIX programs gopher and lynx, used to go to a specific address.

G

Abbreviation for gigabyte (roughly one billion bytes).

<g>

Also *<grin>*, indicates that the author is grinning, similar to:

:-)

gate

(n) See *gateway*.

(v) To establish a gateway.

gated

(adj) Connected to another network or discussion group via a gateway.

gated newsgroup

A newsgroup whose posts are sent to a mailing list and which receives (or includes) posts from the mailing list.

gateway

Also called a *gate*; a computer providing a connection between two networks, two e-mail handling systems, or a Usenet newsgroup and a mailing list. A gateway reformats the data so that it will be acceptable to the system it is passing into.

geek

Someone who knows a lot about computers, networks, or the Internet and thinks they're interesting (not necessarily an insult).

geek code

A set of coded ratings in a sig block, describing the poster in humorous, geeky terms.

The code is maintained by Robert A. Hayden. For a complete key to all of the categories, finger hayden @vax1.mankato.msus.edu.

geek out

(v) 1. To get lost in the minutiae of a computer process; 2. To talk computers or networking in a social setting.

General Public License (GPL)

Also called *copyleft*, the license carried by Free Software Foundation software (such as GNU), granting reuse and reproduction rights to anyone and everyone.

get

(v) To copy a file from a remote source to your host computer, particularly via FTP.

(n) The FTP command to get a file.

.gif

The file extension for GIFs.

GIF! GIF! GIF!

A ritual follow-up to a post mentioning an image (such as a photograph), requesting that someone scan the image, save it a as a GIF, uuencode it, and post it to the newsgroup.

giga-

Prefix meaning one billion.

gigabyte

Roughly one billion bytes (actually 1,073,741,824 bytes), a large amount of storage.

GIGO

Garbage in, garbage out (written only); a longstanding computer truism meaning that the computer won't produce meaningful results if you feed it useless data.

gilley

(n) A unit of bogosity, specifically applied to bogus analogies.

glitch

An unexplainable small computer lapse, causing a faulty result.

global

(adj) Affecting an entire document or system (for example, a global search and replace is a search and replace operation performed on an entire document, rather than a small selection or a single item).

gnu.

A hierarchy in the Usenet mold devoted to the Free Software Foundation and to its free products, such as GNU and emacs.

GNU

(*noo*) A freely distributed set of applications and utilities intended as a replacement for UNIX. GNU is distributed by the Free Software Foundation. (Its name is a recursive acronym that stands for *GNU's not UNIX*.)

GNUMACS

A contracted form of GNU emacs.

Godwin's Rule

Usenet Rule #4, which states that a thread in which Nazis or Hitler have been invoked has reached irrelevancy and will end soon. For some (but not all) of the other Rules see the net.legends FAQ at www.ews .uiuc.edu/~tskirvin/faqs/ legends.html

gopher

A client/server application that allows you to browse huge amounts of information by performing FTP transfers, remote logins, archie searches, and so on, presenting everything to the end-user in the form of menus. This saves the user from having to know (or type in) the addresses of the Internet resources being tapped. Primarily obsolete.

Gopher Book for Windows

A gopher client for Windows, available via anonymous FTP from sunsite.unc.edu. Primarily obsolete.

gopher client

The gopher program that an end-user runs to get information from a gopher server. The gopher client retrieves the menus and documents and displays them for the user. Primarily obsolete.

gopher.micro.umn.edu

The site of the University of Minnesota Gopher, the original gopher server. Primarily obsolete.

Gopher for Nextstep

A gopher client for the Nextstep operating system, available via anony-

mous FTP from sonata.cc .purdue.edu. Primarily obsolete.

gopher server

An application that provides documents and menus to gopher clients, a starting point for a gopher search. Primarily obsolete.

gopher site

A computer with a gopher server running on it. Primarily obsolete.

gopherspace

A conceptual space encompassing all of the menus and documents that can be reached via the interconnected system of gopher servers on the Internet. Primarily obsolete.

gorets

(n) A generic noun that can have any meaning, especially as elaborated in the alt.gorets newsgroup.

go root

(v) To log in as root, a UNIX superuser or system administrator account, in order to exercise the extended privileges of that account.

GOSIP

See *Government OSI Profile*.

.gov

An Internet domain corresponding to U.S. government, including federal, state, and local governments.

Government OSI Profile (GOSIP)

A set of OSI standards that the U.S. government follows in the procurement of computers in order to preserve compatibility among various government computer networks.

graphical user interface (GUI)

A full-screen graphical interface (meaning not limited to just letters and numbers) that allows users to run programs, execute commands, and generally interact with the computer by using a pointing device such as a mouse to manipulate graphical screen elements, as opposed to typing commands at a prompt. Dial-up Internet users generally need SLIP or PPP access to be able to interact directly with Internet facilities within their GUI.

Graphics Interchange Format

1. An extremely popular compressed graphics (image) file format originated by CompuServe but readable in most platforms; 2. A file in the GIF format.

<gr&d>

(written only) *Grinning, running, and ducking* (what you post after you've tweaked someone). Also *<gd&r>*.

Great Renaming

A day in 1985 on which nonlocal Usenet newsgroup names were changed from the form *net.** to the hierarchy still in use today.

Great Worm

The 1988 worm that got out of control and crashed systems all over the Internet, throwing a scare into many.

grep

(rhymes with *prep*, v) To globally search a document, set of files, or newsfeed for a particular word or expression (from the UNIX grep command).

group

(n) Generally, a newsgroup, a Usenet or similar-style discussion group.

groupware

Software that gives multiple users access to the same information over a network, allowing collaboration on documents, scheduling of meetings, tracking of mission-critical projects, and so on.

grovel

1. To beg for something in a Usenet newsgroup; 2. For a programmer, to hunt through code looking for a problem.

guest

A special login account reserved for visitors checking out a BBS, online service, or service provider.

GUI

(*gooey*) See *graphical user interface*.

guiltware

Shareware that reminds you to register (and pay for) the product. See also *nagware*.

gunzip

(n) The UNIX uncompression program for gzipped files.

.gz

A file extension for files that have been compressed with gzip.

gzip

(n) A UNIX file compression program.

h

The help command in some UNIX applications. Also try *?* (question mark).

^H

The backspace character. Use of the Backspace key in terminal emulations that don't support it sometimes leaves the original text on-screen, followed by one ^H character for every time Backspace is pressed, as in "Let me be the first to call you a fool^H^H^H^Hfriend."

hack

(v) To write code, to work on a computer, to cleverly diagnose and fix a problem, or to dig beneath the surface of a computer process, reinventing things when necessary. (Outside of the Internet, the word *hack* suggests the action of breaking into computer networks. On the Internet, the word *crack* is used for that meaning.)

hack around

To figure a software program out for yourself, by trial and error, rather than by reading the manual.

hacker

Someone who is adept at and enjoys working with computers and testing the limits of systems; an enthusiastic or fast (or both) programmer. (Outside of the Internet, the popular media has perpetuated the idea that the word *hacker* has unsavory connotations, suggesting someone who breaks into computer networks and steals, creates and maliciously distributes viruses, or vandalizes information. To those in the know, such malevolent hackers are called *crackers*.)

hacker ethic

The philosophy, common among hackers, that information, technology, and clever tricks should be shared and disseminated rather than hoarded. It is this ideal that, when twisted by crackers who often think all information (both public and private, regardless of source) should be freely accessible to all (by legal means or not), causes uninformed persons to point to hackers as criminals. The hacker ethic relies on the hacker's simple ability to pass on what they know to others that do not. In other words, the hacker passes on for the benefit of others and the cracker passes on to the detriment of others.

Hacker's Dictionary

The New Hacker's Dictionary, Second Edition, compiled by Eric S. Raymond and published by MIT Press, or the paper book equivalent of the jargon file, an invaluable resource of hacker slang (much of which overlaps Internet slang and jargon).

half bridge

A device that connects a network to a communications link via a modem without passing routing information, which must be supplied by the network software.

half duplex

Two-way communication in which the computers at each end of the transmission take turns sending.

half router

A device that connects a network to a communications link via a modem, passing routing information along with data.

handle

A nickname or one-word name, such as a nick on IRC or a username. Network connections provided by employers often assign a strung-together version of a person's full name (using hyphens, underlines, dots, or capitalization to separate first and last name and sometimes even middle initials) as their username, instead of a handle.

handshaking

For two connected devices, the sending of signals to alert each other when they are ready to receive data.

hang

(v) Said of a computer, to stop working, to freeze, to become unresponsive, to wait for something that will never happen.

hard disk

A fixed computer storage medium.

hardware

Computer equipment—the actual pieces of metal and plastic, as opposed to the programs that run on computers (*software*).

hardware address

A specific physical address (as contrasted with a *virtual address*) assigned to a device.

hardware flow control

A form of flow control that is governed by devices themselves, instead of by communications software.

hash

1. A symbol (usually #) echoed at regular intervals to show that a process is still underway; 2. The FTP command that causes the hash symbols to be displayed.

hat

A common name for the caret character, ^ (ASCII 94), used to indicate exponents and to underscore text on the previous line in e-mail and Usenet posts.

Hayes-compatible

Said of a modem that understands the Hayes AT instruction set. (Hayes is a name-brand modem maker.) Most modems today are Hayes-compatible.

header

1. The rows of information at the top of an e-mail message that include who the message is from, who it's to, when it was sent, and what it's about; 2. Information preceding the data in a packet, specifying the addresses of the source and the destination as well as error-checking information.

help

A command that will bring up help information in some programs and in some operating systems. When you are stuck, it never hurts to type *help*, or *h*, or *?*, and press Enter to see what happens.

HEPnet

A network for physicists, not part of the Internet, but now called CERN WebServices and accessible via the Web at http://webservices.web.cern.ch/WebServices/

heterogeneous network

A network that includes various types of computers, operating systems, network cards, and so on, which therefore must be capable of different network protocols.

hexadecimal

(adj) Pertaining to a numerical system using base 16 (as opposed to our more common decimal system, which uses base 10, or the binary system, which uses base 2). Hexadecimal digits are represented by the numerals 0 through 9 and the letters A through F. Because 16 is a multiple of 2, it is easy to convert binary numbers into hexadecimal numbers, and some programs display data in hexadecimal form.

HGopher

A gopher client for Windows, available via anonymous FTP from ftp://lister.cc.ic.ac.uk/pub/wingopher.

hierarchical file system

1) A system of arranging files in directories and subdirectories in order to maintain hierarchical relationships between the files and make them easier to find and retrieve. 2) Referred to as HFS and HFS+ by Apple for use in the Macintosh computer line with MacOS.

hierarchical routing

A system of routing in which different parts of a large network are arranged in a hierarchical tree and each level takes care of routing information to subordinate levels.

The Internet maintains three different routing levels: backbone networks, mid-level networks, and stub networks.

hierarchy

1. In file storage, the arrangement of directories into a tree of parents and children; 2. In networks, the arrangement of levels for routing purposes; 3. In Usenet, the organization of newsgroups into general areas, topics, and subtopics, or the major groupings themselves.

High-Level Data Link Control (HDLC)

An ISO protocol for the data link layer of X.25 and OSI networks. It specifies that data is sent in frames that may vary in length.

High Performance Parallel Interface (HPPI)

An ANSI standard for connecting supercomputers to other devices, such as routers and other computers.

hing

(n) A hint (originally from a typo) on IRC, used in initgame.

history

1. A list of a user's recent actions or commands; 2. A list of the gopher menus a user has passed through; 3. A list of the hypertext links a Web browser has followed.

hit

1. A connection made to a Web server; 2. A successful match in a database search (in some searches, you can specify a maximum number of hits).

holy war

An never-ending argument between intractable sides, such as over gun control, abortion, or IBM vs. Mac. There are usually special `talk.*` newsgroups set up for the people who can't resist arguing with their opposites, and it's considered bad form to bring up a holy war topic in an inappropriate forum. (Newsgroups and mailing lists often have their own local holy wars.)

$HOME

In UNIX, a variable that serves as an abbreviation for the path of your home directory.

home directory

The directory allotted to your specific account, where you start off when you log into your UNIX account, and where you store your files.

home page

On the Web, a starting page with links to other related pages. Many people have personal home pages with biographical information and a hotlist of favorite Web destinations.

homogeneous network

A network that includes only one type of computer, operating system, network card, and so on, and therefore a single network protocol.

hop

(n) Each short individual trip that packets (or e-mail messages) make many times over, from router to router, on their way to their destinations.

hop count

The number of hops it will take for a packet to make it from a source to a destination.

host

(n) A computer on a network that allows many users access at once. If you connect to the Internet by dialing up a provider via a modem, then the computer you log into is your local host. If you connect via FTP to an archive site, then the computer you're getting the files from is a remote host.

host address

A numerical IP address of the form *number-dot-number-dot-number-dot-number* (such as 192.100.81.101).

host name

Also *hostname*, the leftmost portion of a fully qualified domain name, uniquely identifying a specific computer (host) on a network in a subdomain in a domain.

hotlist

A list of frequent destinations, or sites, arranged on a menu, such as a list of Web pages.

HotJava

A Web browser made by Sun Microsystems to demonstrate the use of Java.

HP-UX

Hewlett-Packard's version of UNIX.

.hqx

A file extension that indicates the file has been compressed with the Macintosh BinHex compression.

HTML

Hypertext markup language, the hypertext language used in Web pages. It consists of regular text and tags that tell the browser how to "render" or draw the page and what to do when a link is activated, among many other things. It is a subset of SGML, a preexisting markup language that allows users to define the appearance of a page and the function of its elements.

HTTP

Hypertext transport protocol, the Internet protocol that defines how a Web server responds to requests for files, made via anchors and URLs.

hub

In networks arranged with star topology, the central connecting device, a device that allows a network to add workstations by extending the transmission signal.

hung

(adj) Said of a computer, unresponsive, frozen, and possibly stuck in an infinite loop.

HyperCard

The Macintosh hypermedia program that features cards that may contain text, pictures, sounds, movies, and so on, with clickable links to other cards.

hyperlink

See *hypertext link* or *hypermedia link*.

hypermedia

An extension of the concept of hypertext to include pictures, sounds, movies, and so on, along with text and links to other documents.

hypermedia link

A link from one document to another, from an anchor to a named location, or from an anchor to another form of media entirely, such as a picture, sound, or movie.

Hypernews

An experimental Web news format, in some ways analogous to Usenet, found at www
.hypernews.org.

hypertext

Text that contains links to other text documents, allowing the reader to skip around and read the documents in various order.

hypertext link

A link from one text document to another or from a text anchor to a named location.

HyperWais

A WAIS client for HyperCard (for the Macintosh), available via anonymous FTP from sunsite.oit
.unc.edu.

hyperzine

An electronic hypermedia magazine or 'zine.

hyphen

On computer keyboards, the - character, used also to indicate a dash. Compound portions of newsgroup names are hyphenated, as in alt.fan.dave-barry (alt.fan
.dave.barry would be incorrect), as are some usernames.

Hytelnet

A telnet shell that runs in UNIX; it helps you find the telnet site you want and then runs the telnet session for you. It contains a huge list of university and public library catalogs, as well as gopher servers, WAIS servers, BBSs, and so on.

Hytelnet for DOS

A version of Hytelnet that runs in MS-DOS on a PC, available via anonymous FTP from access.usask.ca.

IEEE

See *Institute of Electrical and Electronic Engineering*.

image file

Another name for a binary file.

IMAP

Internet Message Access Protocol, a protocol for the storage and retrieval of e-mail, not yet a widespread standard.

impression

(n) A Web server's record of a browser's visit to a single page of a Web site. (The word is used to distinguish from a hit, in that a single impression may register as several hits—one on the HTML document, one for each graphic on the page, and so on.)

inbox

A file in which a mail program stores incoming e-mail messages (also *in box* or *in-box*).

include

To copy some or all of the message to which you are responding. Most e-mail programs and newsreaders will add a character such as > before each line of included text.

#include <disclaimer.h>

A C joke that appears in sig blocks, meaning that a standard disclaimer should be understood to have been included there.

include war

(n) A flame war in which so many previous posts have been included that it's impossible to follow the argument amidst all the >'s.

index

(n) 1. A file in a directory at a site that describes the contents of the directory; 2. An archie database; 3. A default Web page that a Web server provides when no file is specified.

INET

An annual conference put on by the Internet Society; 2. An abbreviation for Internet.

infinite loop

A computer process that repeats forever due to a programming error, causing the computer to hang. The instructions on the back of many a shampoo bottle—lather, rinse, repeat—would cause an infinite loop in a computer.

info

A common username for a mailbot (`info@host.subdomain.domain`) providing information about a network, service provider, or information service.

Infobahn

A euphemism for Internet that conjures up images of elevated freeways through a Bauhaus cyberscape.

Info-Mac archives

A huge collection of Macintosh software at the `sumex-aim` `.stanford.edu` FTP site, in the `/info-mac` directory. It's also mirrored at `wuarchive.wustl.edu` in the `/mirrors/info-mac` directory.

information agent

A program that searches databases for information without requiring that the user know where the information is stored.

info-server

An e-mail address that triggers a mail server, responding to messages that contain key words by sending stored information.

initialization string

A string of seemingly nonsense characters (really AT commands) sent to a modem to get it ready to make a connection.

inline graphic

An illustration on a Web page (as opposed to a linked graphic).

insert mode

In text editors such as vi, a special mode the user has to switch into (from command mode) to insert text.

Institute of Electrical and Electronic Engineering (IEEE)

A professional organization that, among other things, has defined a number of networking standards, such as the 802.x protocols.

integrated circuit

A computer chip—a tiny circuit housing many electronic components.

intelligent agent

A (mostly theoretical so far) type of computer program that can handle a user's mail, database searches, file transfers, and so on over the Internet without the user having to oversee the process directly or even remain connected to the Net.

interactive

(adj) Said of programs or environments, able to respond and give feedback to a user and to take instruction from user commands.

Interagency Interim National Research and Education Network (IINREN)

A set of network and operating system protocols under development for the National Research and Education Network.

INTERCAL

A mock programming language designed to be written only (INTERCAL is said to stand for *Compiler Language with No Pronounceable Acronym*) that is the subject of the `alt.lang.intercal` newsgroup.

interface

The "face" presented to a user by a computer operating system or application that allows the user to interact with the system or application; the set of rules governing how information is displayed and how users may enter commands.

Interior Gateway Protocol (IGP)

A protocol that defines how routing information is distributed among routers in a network.

Intermediate System (IS)

An OSI system that moves packets across a network.

Intermediate System to Intermediate System Protocol (IS-IS)

An OSI Interior Gateway Protocol that can route both OSI and IP packets.

internal modem

A modem chip mounted on a board installed inside a computer.

International Organization for Standardization (ISO)

An international standards organization attempting to foster international cooperation in science, engineering, and technology. Creator of the OSI Model.

internet

Any network that uses the TCP/IP protocol suite. (Now most often referred to as an intranet).

Internet

An international network of well over ten thousand networks linked using the TCP/IP protocols. Also used more loosely to mean either the worldwide information net or the conglomeration of all computers and networks that can be reached via an Internet e-mail address.

Internet Adapter, The (TIA)

A UNIX program that enables a dial-up shell account to emulate a SLIP connection, allowing the user to run Internet software native to his or her desktop environment without the full costs (or full functionality, either) of real SLIP. TIA is available from Cyberspace Development at http://marketplace.com/.

Internet Architecture Board (IAB)

A group that oversees the maintenance of TCP/IP protocols and promulgates other Internet standards.

Internet Assigned Numbers Authority (IANA)

A group that assigns the standard numbers used for ports, sockets, and so on. Assigned numbers can be found in the Internet document called STD2 (one of the RFCs).

Internet Control Message Protocol (ICMP)

An Internet protocol that defines error messages and governs how test packets and the ping command function.

Internet-Draft (I-D)

> Draft documents written by the Internet Engineering Task Force dealing with potential problems and networking developments. They are archived at the `rtfm.mit.edu` anonymous FTP site.

Internet Engineering Steering Group (IESG)

> A group that manages the Internet Engineering Task Force and reviews Internet standards.

Internet Engineering Task Force (IETF)

> A voluntary group made up of researchers that studies technical problems and proposes solutions to the Internet Architecture Board.

Internet Experiment Note (IEN)

> A now-obsolete series of reports on the development of the Internet, parallel to the RFCs.

Internet Explorer

> Microsoft's Web browser, which is rapidly morphing, version to version, into the basic Windows desktop interface. (Download it from www `.microsoft.com/ie/`.)

Internet Hunt

> A monthly contest consisting of ten questions whose answers must be dug up on the Internet. The contest is reachable by gopher via `gopher.cic .net` in the hunt directory. Here's a sample question from the October,

1994 hunt (question designed by Dan Marmion):

> > `"Surrey with the Fringe on Top."` How many stars did Down Beat magazine give that album?

Internet Monthly Report (IMR)

> A monthly publication about the Internet, produced for the Internet Research Task Force.

Internet Protocol (IP)

> The protocol that handles routing of datagrams from one Internet host to another. It works along with the Transmission Control Protocol (TCP) to ensure that data is transmitted accurately across the Internet.

Internet Research Steering Group (IRSG)

> A group that manages the Internet Research Task Force.

Internet Research Task Force (IRTF)

> A voluntary group that projects long-term issues and problems for the Internet and proposes solutions and new directions, reporting to the Internet Architecture Board.

Internet service provider (ISP)

> A company or enterprise that provides Internet access.

Internet Services List

> An exhaustive list of Internet services, maintained by Scott Yanoff and

available via anonymous FTP from `csd4.csd.uwm.edu`, in the `/pub` directory, with the file name `inet.services.txt`.

Internet Society (ISOC)

A nonprofit organization that promotes the use of the Internet in academic and research communities and supports networking research, publishing the *Internet Society News* and putting on the INET conference every year.

Internet Talk Radio (ITR)

A set of audio programs, similar to radio broadcasts, distributed over the Internet via the MBONE. For more information, send e-mail to `info @radio.com`.

Internet tools

A set of utility programs that can use various Internet facilities and that have interoperability.

Internet Underground Music Archive (IUMA)

A database of (mostly unsigned) bands, including sound clips, video clips, information, and many other music-related links, available via the Web at `www.iuma.com`.

Internetwork Packet Exchange (IPX)

Novell's NetWare network-layer protocol that specifies addressing, routing, and switching packets between a server and workstations and across interconnected LANs.

Encapsulated IPX packets can be carried by Ethernet packets and token ring frames.

InterNIC

Short for the Internet Network Information Center, a service of the National Science Foundation. It provides information about the Internet and registers domain names, available via e-mail at `info@internic .net` or on the Web at www `.internic.net/`.

interoperability

The ability of devices made by different manufacturers or as part of different computer systems to communicate and share information over a network.

InterSLIP

Macintosh SLIP software, developed by InterCon Systems Corporation and available as freeware via anonymous FTP from `ftp.intercon.com`.

InterText

An online fiction magazine distributed via the Web from www `.etext.org/Zines/InterText/`.

intranet

A private network that uses the standard Internet protocols.

IP

Internet Protocol, the protocol that handles routing of datagrams from one Internet host to another. It works along with the Transmission Control Protocol (TCP) to ensure that data is transmitted accurately across the Internet.

IP address

Also called a *dotted quad*, the numerical Internet Protocol address that uniquely identifies each computer on the Internet, made up of four numbers separated by three dots.

irc

UNIX client software for IRC.

IRC

Internet Relay Chat, a protocol for client/server programs that allows you to chat with people in real time (synchronously) all over the Internet in channels devoted to different topics.

Ircle

Macintosh client software for Internet Relay Chat, available via anonymous FTP from `mac.archive.umich.edu`.

ISDN

Integrated Services Digital Network, a digital circuit-switched network that can carry both voice and data communication over a single cable. ISDN standards have been specified by the CCITT. (Some people joke that ISDN stands for *It Still Does Nothing*.)

ISO

See *International Organization for Standardization*.

ISO Development Environment (ISODE)

Software that enables networks using OSI standards to communicate with TCP/IP networks.

jack in

To log onto the Internet (from a cyberpunk term popularized by William Gibson).

Janet

The major United Kingdom backbone network.

jargon file

A list of hacker jargon and slang—compiled and maintained collectively since the 1960s—with excellent definitions, great humor, and lots of interesting anecdotes, available via the Web at `www.ccil.org/jargon/jargon.html` and as a printed book from MIT Press under the name *The New Hacker's Dictionary, Second Edition* (buy the book!).

Java

A programming language for making software that can be run on any type of computer over an Internet connection.

JavaScript

A scripting language developed by Netscape to add dynamic (interactive) capabilities to Web pages.

joe

A UNIX text editor.

Joint Photographic Experts Group

An ISO committee that proposed the JPEG image compression standard.

JPEG

A compressed file format for images that is more efficient than GIF (but newer and therefore not so widespread).

.jpg

A file extension that indicates JPEG compression.

Jughead

An index of high-level gopher menus. (After the creation of Archie, other Internet tool developers have not been able to resist naming their applications after other Archie Comics characters. Besides Jughead, there is also Veronica. What's next, Big Moose?)

jupiter

(v) To kill an IRC 'bot or kick a user and then keep the 'bot or user from reconnecting by adopting its nick. (Jupiter is the handle of the first user to use this tactic.)

k

1. An abbreviation for kilobit; 2. The kill command in many UNIX newsreaders.

K

An abbreviation for kilobyte.

KA9Q

An adaptation of TCP/IP protocols for radio systems.

Kb

An abbreviation for kilobit.

KB

An abbreviation for kilobyte.

Kbps

An abbreviation for kilobits per second, a measurement of transmission speed (such as modem speed or network speed).

Kbyte

An abbreviation for kilobyte.

ken

Ken Thompson, the primary inventor of UNIX, a net.god (to some) who appears in the jargon file.

Kermit

A very common, but now relatively slow, protocol for downloading and uploading via a modem.

kevork

(v) To abort a process or reboot a computer (from Dr. Jack Kevorkian, a.k.a. Dr. Death, a Michigan physician who routinely assists terminally ill patients in committing suicide).

key

1. In encryption, a phrase or string that allows you to decrypt encrypted text. In public-key encryption, there are two kinds of keys, public keys and private keys; 2. A key word.

key encryption

A form of encryption that relies upon keys for the encrypting and decrypting of messages or files.

keyword

(Also *key word*.) 1. In a database search, a word to search for in target documents—hits (successful matches) must include the keyword; 2. In online services, a word used to jump directly to a topic area.

kgbvax

One of the machines on the bang path of the famous April Fool's kremvax post.

Kibo

The username of James F. Parry, acclaimed by some as the first deity of the Internet. Also known as "he who greps," Kibo reportedly notes every mention of his name on Usenet and follows up worthy posts. He is also the founder of HappyNet. Students of kibology can read more on the subject in the `alt.religion.kibology` newsgroup.

kibology

The religion (or is it a science?) of Kibo. Its main doctrine is You're Allowed. Only Spot, Kibo's dog, is Not Allowed. For more adept instruction in the ways of kibology, try to follow the `alt.religion.kibology` newsgroup or wait for the kibologists to start cross-posting their metaposts into your favorite newsgroup. Beware of trolls.

kick

(v) To eject a participant from an IRC conversation and prevent the user from rejoining (done by the channel op).

kill

(v) 1. To delete a post (mark it as having been read); 2. To delete posts automatically, using a kill file; 3. To stop a process; 4. To erase a file.

kill file

Also a *killfile*, a file containing search instructions for automatically killing or autoselecting Usenet posts. Sometimes called a bozo filter, a kill file can be used to screen out annoying posters and avoid uninteresting threads.

kilobit

(Abbreviated *k* or *Kb*.) Roughly one thousand (actually 1,024) bits. Kilobits per second (kps or Kbps) is a common measurement of transmission speed (such as modem speed or network speed).

kilobits per second

(Abbreviated *kps* or *Kbps*.) A measurement of the speed of a medium, meaning the number of kilobits that can pass through the medium in one second.

kilobyte

(Abbreviated *K*, *KB*, or *Kbyte*.)
Roughly one thousand (actually
1,024) bytes, usually a measurement
of memory or storage capacity.

kludge

(*klooj*, n) The more common
spelling of *kluge*, a clumsily assembled
program or feature of a program that
functions well enough but is not ele-
gant, similar to the non-computer
expression *jury-rigged*.

kluge

See *kludge*.

Knowbot Information Services (KIS)

An experimental information service on the Net, intended to function
as a robotic librarian that can search
databases and, among other things,
help find e-mail addresses. To access
the Knowbot, telnet to nri.reston
.va.us. For more information, send
e-mail to kis@nri.reston.va.us.

Korn shell

A common flavor of UNIX shells.

kps

An abbreviation for kilobits per
second, a measurement of transmission speed (such as modem speed or
network speed).

k12.

An alternative newsgroup hierarchy in the Usenet mold, dedicated to
elementary and secondary school

(kindergarten through 12th grade)
education.

l

The UNIX *directory list* command,
producing full information about the
files (except dot files) in the working
directory.

LAN

(n) *Local area network*, a computer
network, usually confined to a single
office or building, that allows for the
sharing of files and other resources
(such as printers) among several users
and makes interoperability among various systems possible.

LAN adapter

Also called a *network interface
card* or *network interface controller*, a
card installed into a PC to attach it to
a LAN.

LAN Workplace

Novell's TCP/IP client software
for Macintosh and DOS computers.

lcd

The UNIX FTP command to
change the local directory (as
opposed to the working directory at
the ftp host site).

leaf

1. In network architecture, a computer that receives a signal from a
more central computer but does not
pass a signal along to a more remote
computer; 2. In (audio cassette) tape

trees, a participant who receives a copy of the tape being distributed but does not make copies of the tape for anyone else.

leaf site

A Usenet computer that receives a newsfeed from another site but does not distribute news to any other computers.

League for Programming Freedom

A group that opposes software patents and copyrights; information available via anonymous FTP at `prep.ai.mit.edu` in the `pub/lpf` directory or by e-mail at `league @prep.ai.mit.edu`.

leased line

A telephone line leased from the telephone company to provide a permanent connection from a LAN to an Internet service provider or to a WAN.

letterbomb

An e-mail message containing either escape characters that can lock up certain types of terminals, or harmful commands to be interpreted by the user's shell.

Lexis/Nexis

A proprietary system of searchable databases of legal briefs (Lexis) and newspaper and magazine articles (Nexis).

lharc

A file compression program for DOS.

.lhz

A file extension that indicates lharc compression.

library catalogs

Most university and public library catalogs are available via telnet (and some via gopher). Hytelnet has an excellent index of library catalogs.

Library of Congress

The main repository of information of the U.S. government, available by telnet at `locis.loc.gov` or on the Web at `www.loc.gov/`.

line eater

A bug in older versions of Usenet newsreader software for UNIX that caused certain lines at the beginning of posts to vanish. To appease the line eater, posters would include lines of spurious text to be sacrificed instead of the actual contents of the message.

line feed

Also *linefeed*, a character that moves the cursor down one line (ASCII 10), usually starting a new line in combination with a carriage return character.

line length

The number of characters that fit on a line—fixed on some systems, settable on others. The standard line length on the Internet is 80 characters; e-mail or Usenet posts produced with software using longer line lengths will wrap irregularly and appear awkward to users with 80-character lines.

line noise

Static or interference on a wire that corrupts the signal. On a character-based modem connection, for example, line noise might result in random gibberish and escape characters interpolated with the intended text.

line-oriented

(adj) Said of applications and interfaces that display text one line at a time, rather than making an entire screenful of text available at once.

link

(n) 1. In UNIX, a reference to a directory or file contained elsewhere that appears in directory listings just as if the remote directory or file were in the current directory (also called a *symbolic link*); 2. On Web pages, a hypertext connection, a button or highlighted bit of text that, when selected, jumps the reader to another page.

Link Access Protocol (LAP)

A data link layer protocol for AppleTalk that specifies the interface to network hardware.

Linux

(*line-ux*) An implementation of UNIX for IBM PC-compatibles. It has been developed as a collaborative effort by widespread Internet users and is distributed for free.

LISP

The acronym for *List Processor*, a popular Artificial Intelligence programming language.

list

(v) 1. To view the names of files in a directory; 2. To display the contents of a file.

(n) An Internet or BITNET mailing list.

listserv

A type of automated mailing list software that runs on IBM mainframes and originated on the BITNET network.

little-endian

(adj) A storage format in which the most significant byte has the highest address, as opposed to big-endian.

liveware

People (as opposed to hardware or software); also known as *wetware*.

local

(adj) Said of a computer to which a user is connected directly or of a device (such as a printer) or process under the user's direct control, as contrasted with remote hosts, devices, and processes.

Local Area Transport (LAT)

Digital (DEC) architecture for connecting terminal servers on Ethernet networks to host computers.

local echo

1. A copy of the data being sent (usually typed) over a communications device (such as a modem) displayed in a terminal window so that the sender can monitor the process; 2. A terminal mode in some communications programs, specifying half duplex transmission, in which the communications program displays the user's input on the screen, instead of relaying an echo from the host.

Local host

(n) Also *localhost*; the host computer a user is currently logged in to. The *loopback address* of any user's current local host is always 127.0.0.1.

local node

The computer on a network to which a user is directly connected.

LocalTalk

Shielded, twisted-pair wiring and connectors for using the Macintosh's built-in AppleTalk network hardware.

locative domain name

A two-letter geographical domain name, such as *.us* for the United States, *.uk* for the United Kingdom, *.de* for Germany (Deutschland), and so on.

LOCIS

The *Library of Congress Information Service*, available by telnet at `locis.loc.gov` or on the Web at `www.loc.gov/`.

lock up

(v) To freeze, as when certain sequences of characters lock up a keyboard, preventing the user from typing.

logical

(adj) Said of a computer address or device, identified by a numerical reference, which may or may not correspond to a physical address or device.

logical conjunction

A word that joins two or more key words by specifying a logical relationship between them.

Logical Link Control (LLC)

1. The Institute of Electrical and Electronic Engineering 802 standard that specifies a uniform user interface; 2. A data link layer defined in IEEE 802.2.

logical tree

Any logical arrangement of devices, files, data, and so on in which all relationships stem from a root; child branches are subordinate to parent branches, and an element without any children is called a leaf.

Logical Unit

Software that communicates with an IBM SNA network.

log in

(v) To connect to a network or computer, identify oneself as a user, supply a password, and start a session.

login

(n) 1. A username or *handle* that a user logs in with, corresponding to an account; 2. An instance of logging in.

login script

A prerecorded sequence of login steps that can play back automatically to connect a user to a computer or network. Login scripts can breach security if they automate the process of supplying a password, thereby allowing anyone who runs the script to log in.

log out

(v) To end a session and disconnect from a computer or network.

LOL

Laughing out loud (written only, also *lol*).

loopback

(n) A test in which a signal is sent from a source to an intermediate point and then back to the original source to evaluate the accuracy of the transmission.

loopback address

The Internet address (127.0.0.1) that always points back to the local host.

low-bandwidth

(adj) 1. Said of a connection that can only manage a slow connect speed or of a resource on the Internet that a user with a slow connection

will still find useful; 2. Colloquially, containing little useful information.

ls

The UNIX "short directory list" (list short) command.

lurk

To read a mailing list or newsgroup without posting to it. Every new user should lurk for a while before posting to get a feel for what the group is all about and how others in the group behave.

lurker

One who lurks. On any mailing list or in any newsgroup, there are usually many times more lurkers than regular contributors.

lynx

An excellent, text-based, UNIX browser for the Web that was created at the University of Kansas. To try out lynx (if it's not installed on your system), telnet to ukanaix.cc.ukans.edu and log in as www.

m

The mark as unread command in some UNIX newsreaders.

M

Abbreviation for megabyte.

^M

One way that the carriage return character (ASCII 13) can appear. Some computers use a carriage return to indicate a new line, some use a line-feed, and some use both. If an ASCII file is transferred from a computer that uses carriage returns to one that doesn't, and a binary file transfer rather than an ASCII file transfer is used, ^M may appear at the end of each line.

MaasInfo Package

A set of documents written by Robert E. Maas explaining how to use various Internet resources, available via anonymous FTP from `aarnet.edu.au` in the `pub/doc` subdirectory.

MAC address

The address that identifies a particular piece of hardware out of several connected to shared media.

MacBinary

A Macintosh file transfer protocol that specifies how files should be transmitted over modems.

Macintosh

A line of personal computers made by Apple.

Macintosh archive

The largest source of Macintosh shareware and files is the Macintosh archive at Stanford University. Connect via anonymous FTP to `sumex-aim.stanford.edu` and look in the `info-mac` directory. This site is also mirrored at the `wuarchive.wustl.edu` FTP site in the `/mirrors/infomac` directory.

MacPPP

PPP (Point-to-Point Protocol) software for the Macintosh, developed by Merit Computer Network and available as freeware via anonymous FTP from `ftp.merit.edu` in the `internet.tools/ppp/mac` directory.

macro

A shortcut consisting of a sequence of memorized keystrokes or a more elaborate set of scripting commands used to automate repetitive tasks, similar to a rudimentary program.

MacSLIP

SLIP (Serial Line Internet Protocol) software for the Macintosh, developed by Hyde Park Software.

MacTCP

TCP/IP protocol software for the Macintosh, built into versions 7.5 through 7.5.2 of the Macintosh operating system. For more information, send e-mail to `apda@applelink.apple.com`.

MacWeb

A Web browser for the Macintosh, created by EINET and available via anonymous FTP from `ftp.einet.net` in the `/einet/mac/macweb` directory.

mail

(n) 1. On the Internet, synonymous with e-mail, that is, *electronic mail*, messages carried electronically from computer to computer; 2. The name of a simple UNIX mail program.

(v) To send an e-mail message.

mail address

1. An Internet e-mail address of the form *username@host .domain*; 2. The *username* portion of a mail account on a network.

mailbomb

(n) A huge number of messages or an enormous chunk of data, such as a core dump, sent to an e-mail address as a prank or attack on the recipient, in hopes that the bomb will overload or even crash the user's mailer program.

(v) To send or encourage others to send a huge number of messages or an enormous chunk of data.

mailbot

A *mail server*, a program that automatically responds to mail by sending information or performing functions specified in the incoming mail.

mailbox

A file, directory, or area of hard disk space used to store e-mail messages.

mail bridge

A device that connects networks and filters mail between them, passing only messages that meet certain criteria.

mail-enabled application

A program that, in addition to its normal capabilities, can also handle the sending and receiving of mail.

Mail Exchange Record

A record type in the Domain Name System that identifies the mail-serving host for a given domain.

mail exploder

A program that forwards an e-mail message to all the addresses on a mailing list.

mail gateway

A computer that passes e-mail from one network to another, from a network to the Internet, or vice versa, reformatting the headers as necessary.

mailing list

A discussion group, commonly referred to on the Internet simply as a *list*, consisting of people with a common interest, all of whom receive all the mail sent, or posted, to the list. Mailing lists are often more specialized than Usenet newsgroups. Lists can be moderated or unmoderated.

mail path

Also bang path, a list of sites an e-mail message must pass through on the way from the sender to the receiver. Although it is rarely necessary any longer to specify the route your mail will take, mail headers still often include the entire mail path back to the sender.

mail program

Also *mail reader*, the program a user reads, replies to, forwards, and saves mail with. Common UNIX mail programs include mail, elm, and pine. Eudora is a popular mail program for PCs and Macs.

.mailrc

A setup file for UNIX mail programs (other than elm).

mail reflector

A mail address that automatically forwards any mail it receives to a list of other addresses.

mail server

A *mailbot*, a program that automatically distributes files or information in response to e-mail requests.

mainframe

(n) A large, fast, multiuser computer (larger than a minicomputer or microcomputer), capable of handling large quantities of data and complicated tasks, generally designed for batch (as opposed to interactive) use, and most often used by large corporations, universities, and military organizations.

majordomo

A type of automated mailing list management software, similar to listserv.

MAKE.MONEY.FAST

A chain letter still making its rounds on the Net after many years. A classic Ponzi/pyramid scheme. As someone replied last time I saw this garbage reposted, "Don't make your first Federal crime one that includes your name and address at the top!"

man

The UNIX command that displays the man pages, online documentation for UNIX programs and commands.

MAN

A Metropolitan Area Network, a high-speed (100 Mbps) public network, capable of voice and data transmission over long distances (but smaller than a WAN), connecting LANs across a city or campus.

Management Information Base (MIB)

A database on a host, router, or bridge that stores information about a network's configuration and performance.

Management Information System (MIS)

A computer-organized system of synthesizing information from various departments in a corporation in order to provide information, assessments, and recommendations to management; a corporate computer center.

Manchester encoding

A method of data-transmission that enables network interface cards to transmit digital signals using direct current, encoding data, and timing signals in the same data stream, as opposed to non-return to zero (NRZ) encoding, which employs two voltage levels—negative and positive—to represent 0 and 1.

man pages

The *manual pages*—online documentation for UNIX commands and programs.

Marble Teleconnect

SLIP (Serial Line Internet Protocol) software for the Nextstep operating system, developed by Marble Associates.

mark as unread

To save a newsgroup article as if it were still unread.

Martian

(adj) Said of a packet that arrives with an incorrect or impossible source address.

Mass ACK

A message sent to a mailing list requesting a response, in order to test the currency of the addresses on the list.

massage

(v) To edit, extract information from, or format a file, as in "I'll have to massage this data some to figure out what it means."

match

(n) In a search, a record or document that meets the specified criteria, also called a hit.

Matrix News

A newsletter of the Matrix Information and Directory Services, on the subject of networks, available via WAIS at `matrix_news.src`.

Maximum Transmission Unit (MTU)

The greatest datagram length allowed on a particular network.

Maxwell's Demon

Nineteenth-century Scottish philosopher James Clerk Maxwell postulated that temperature could be regulated in a room by posting a demon at the entrance who would allow only air molecules moving at a certain speed or higher to enter. Some believe that this theory is the probable source for the computer terms *daemon* and *demon*.

Mb

Abbreviation for megabit.

MB

Abbreviation for megabyte.

MBONE

The *multicast backbone*, an experimental, high-speed virtual network that can send packets simultaneously to a large number of Internet sites, suitable for audio and visual transmission. In 1994, a Rolling Stones concert was multicast to workstations around the world via the MBONE.

Mbps

Abbreviation for megabits per second.

Media Access Control (MAC)

The lower component of the data link layer, which defines how computers on a LAN share access to a transmission medium, used in CSMA/CD (Carrier Sense Multiple Access with Collision Detection) and token ring LANs.

media filter

A device that converts the signal from a token ring adapter board for a particular type of wiring.

medium

Any substance that conveys a signal from a sender to a receiver, such as copper or other wire, coaxial cable, optical fiber, and so on.

megabit

Roughly one million (actually 1,048,576) bits.

megabits per second

A measurement of transmission speed (such as modem speed or network speed).

megabyte

Roughly one million (actually 1,048,576) bytes, usually a measurement of memory (RAM) or storage (HD).

meltdown

What happens when a network is so overloaded that it crashes.

meme

(n, rhymes with *seem*) A self-replicating and self-perpetuating idea, concept, saying, pun, or way of thinking. For example, how many times have you heard "The Eskimo language has a thousand words for *snow*" or words to that effect? It doesn't matter that it's not actually true; it is such an infectious or useful metaphor that it sticks in the mind and circulates from person to person perpetually.

The word *meme* was coined as an analogy to *gene* (in the sense of the "selfish" gene that propagates itself, using people as a medium) as well as *phoneme* and *morpheme* (in the sense of a "unit" of thought). The study of memes is called *memetics*. When a powerful set of memes is unleashed on the Internet (such as a religious philosophy), it is called a *meme plague*.

MemeWatch

A Web site (at http://syx.com/MemeWatch/) that tracks prevalent memes on the Net and off.

memory

Generally synonymous with RAM (random access memory), a location where files and processes a computer is currently working on are stored. The operating system reads applications and documents into memory and also writes (saves) the results back to the disk (or other storage medium).

menu

A list of options available to a user. Options can usually be selected with a mouse or other pointing device, or by typing the number of the desired menu item and pressing Enter.

menu-driven program

A program whose commands are accessible via menus, relieving the user of the need to memorize commands.

message

1. An e-mail letter; 2. A comment sent to a specific person on IRC and not to the entire channel; 3. A packet.

message cancel

A feature of some mail programs that allows the user to catch a message and "unsend" it (for only a short while after sending).

message handling service (MHS)

A popular e-mail protocol for storage, management, and exchange, especially in corporate offices, licensed by Novell.

message handling system

The CCITT X.400 protocol for store-and-forward messaging.

message switching

Also called packet switching, a store-and-forward method for routing messages in which each message is passed from a source through intermediate nodes to a destination address.

metanetwork

A network made up of other networks. The Internet is one.

metapost

A Usenet post, such as troll, the actual purpose of which is different from its literal content.

metasyntactic variable

A dummy variable, a stand-in variable used in an example to clarify a point of syntax.

mget

The command in the UNIX ftp program for *multiple get*, to get a number of files at once.

Microcom Networking Protocol (MNP)

An error-checking feature built into many modems. MNP organizes data into frames, then transmits the frames, sometimes compressing the data as well.

microcomputer

A small computer with a single-chip processor, smaller than a mini-computer or a mainframe, though currently as powerful as either of these earlier computer types once were. Scorned at first by the mainframe establishment, PCs (personal computers) ushered in the microcomputer revolution, bringing computing power into the hands of lay people for the first time. Microcomputers can range in size from desktops to portables to laptops to notebooks.

Microphone

A communications program for the Macintosh.

microprocessor

A CPU (central processing unit) housed on a single integrated circuit, as in a microcomputer. The processor is the part of the computer that communicates with RAM, the storage medium (hard disk), the keyboard, the printer, and any other devices; performs arithmetic and logical comparisons; and controls the operations of the computer. The Pentium, PowerPC, 680x0 series, 80x86 series, and 80x8 series are all microprocessors.

MicroSerf

An employee of Microsoft.

Microsloth Windows

A derogatory term for Microsoft Windows.

Microsoft

A computer company founded in 1975 that sells MS-DOS (the operating system for IBM PCs and compatibles), the Microsoft Windows operating environment, and a host of applications for PCs and Macintoshes. Some groups, like the U.S.

Department of Justice, believe it to exert hegemony over the PC market.

Microsoft Network

An online service from Microsoft, access to which comes built-in with Windows and is only available to Windows users.

Microsoft Windows

A multitasking operating environment that runs on top of MS-DOS and provides IBM PCs and compatibles with a GUI (graphical user interface) not unlike that of the Macintosh, including icons, dialog boxes, menus, and a mouse pointer.

mid-level network

A regional network, a vague Internet level category between backbone and rib levels.

.mil

An Internet domain corresponding to U.S. military organizations.

Military Network (MILNET)

A network of U.S. military sites (it was part of the original ARPAnet) that carries nonclassified military communication.

MIME

Multipurpose Internet Mail Extensions, a protocol that allows e-mail to contain simple text plus color pictures, video, sound, and binary data. Both the sender and the receiver need MIME-aware mail programs to use it.

minicomputer

A medium-sized computer (larger than a microcomputer but smaller than a mainframe), such as DEC's VAX, which can handle multitasking and over one hundred users (compared with over one thousand for mainframes).

Minority On-Line Information Service (MOLIS)

A service maintained by the U.S. government offering educational and other information, as part of Fedix, available via telnet at fedix.fie.com (log in as *fedix*).

MIPS

Millions of instructions per second, a measurement of chip (CPU) processing speed. Also, humorously, *meaningless indication of processor speed*.

mIRC

A windows IRC program.

mirror

(v) To store an exact copy of files at another archive site (in order to minimize the load at the original site or provide an archive site geographically closer to some users).

mirror site

An archive site (generally FTP) containing an exact copy of the files at another site.

misc.

A Usenet hierarchy devoted to whatever doesn't fit in the other hierarchies.

mkdir

The UNIX command to make a directory.

mnemonic

(*ne-mon-ic*, n) A word that helps one remember a command or shortcut. For example, in WordStar (an archaic word processing language), the *cut text* command is Ctrl+Y; the mnemonic to help remember this is *yank* (because you're yanking the text out of the document). By association, the term has also taken on the meaning of the shortcut or command itself; thus, in the WordStar example, *Ctrl+Y* can also be called the mnemonic for *cut*.

mode

One of several possible states a program can be in. The most common example of this is the requirement some older text editors such as vi have that the user must first enter insert mode before typing anything.

modeless editor

A text editor that does not require the user to execute a special command to enter insert mode in order to begin typing. Most new text editors are modeless. On UNIX systems, pico is a modeless editor and vi is not.

modem

(n) Short for *modulator/demodulator*, a device that connects your computer to a phone jack and, through the phone lines, to another modem and computer, transmitting data by converting the computer's digital signal into the telephone's analog carrier signal, and vice versa.

The standard 33600 bps modem is 112 times faster than the 300 bps modems of 15 years ago.

modem bank

A set of shelved modems connected to a host or BBS to allow many callers to log in.

moderate

(v) To review articles submitted to a list or newsgroup and post only those which meet certain criteria (minimally, they must be on topic).

moderated

(adj) Said of lists and newsgroups whose posts must pass muster with a moderator before appearing.

moderator

The volunteer who decides which submissions to a moderated list or newsgroup will be posted.

monospace font

A font in which all the characters are the same width (as opposed to a proportional-width font, in which the letters *w* and *i*, for instance, vary greatly in width).

```
This text is written
in a monospace font.
```
For e-mail and newsgroup posts, the 80-character line length standard presupposes a monospace font (as do ASCII graphics and many people's sig blocks).

more

A common UNIX paging program. Type

```
more filename
```
to see *filename* displayed one screenful at a time.

MorF

Short for *Male or Female* (written only), asking another user's sex.

Morning Star PPP

PPP (Point-to-Point Protocol) software for Nextstep, developed by Morning Star Technologies.

Mosaic

The first graphical Web browser, developed by National Center for Supercomputing Applications, which greatly popularized the Web in its first few years, and by extension the Internet, as it made the multimedia capabilities of the Net accessible via mouse clicks. Mosaic exists in freeware and shareware versions for the Macintosh, Windows, and X Window systems and is available via anonymous FTP at ftp.ncsa.uiuc.edu.

motto!

A follow-up post on a newsgroup, proposing the previous post as a motto for the group or for Usenet as a whole, perhaps facetiously.

mouse potato

A human being who spends inordinate chunks of his or her waking life glued to a computer screen, mouse in hand.

Mozilla

1) A slang name for the Netscape Web browser. 2) The name of the Open Source project started by Netscape to allow public development of Netscape 6. 3) The name of the browser produced by the Mozilla project that is remarkably similar to Netscape 6.

MPEG

A compressed file format for movies (audiovideo files).

.mpg

A file extension that indicates MPEG compression.

mput

The command in the UNIX ftp program for *multiple put*, to send a number of files at once.

MS-DOS

An operating system for IBM PCs and compatibles, made by Microsoft.

MU*

An abbreviation for any one of a series of acronyms for *m*ultiuser role-playing game environments.

mud

(v) To explore a MUD.

MUD

A *multiuser domain/dimension /dungeon*. A role-playing game environment that allows people all over the Net to play together in something like interactive text adventures. Other names for MUDs include *MOO*, *MUSE, Muck, Mush, Fugue, TinyFugue,* and *TinyMUD*.

multicast

(v) To send a packet simultaneously to multiple sites.

(adj) Said of a packet intended to be received by a number of hosts.

Multics

A late '60s predecessor to UNIX.

multimedia

A form of communication combining text with graphics, page layout, motion pictures, animation, sounds, and so on.

Multiple Virtual Storage (MVS)

IBM's standard mainframe operating system, similar to VM (Virtual Machine).

multiplex

(adj) Using a single transmission medium to transmit over multiple logical channels at once, such as when an Internet site maintains HTTP, FTP, SMTP, telnet, and other channels.

multitasking

(n) The simultaneous execution of two or more programs by a single computer.

MUSE

A *multiuser simulation environment* (for role-playing games).

n

The "next article" command in many UNIX newsreaders.

nagware

Shareware that reminds the user, automatically and frequently, to register the software and pay for it. See also *guiltware*.

NAK

(rhymes with *pack*) A *negative acknowledgment* from a computer that a packet of data has not been received successfully, i.e., the check-sum figure does not match that of the sent packet (ASCII 21).

Name Binding Protocol (NBP)

AppleTalk's transport layer proto-col. It resolves numeric AppleTalk addresses into names and vice versa.

name server

1. Also *domain name server*, an application that maintains a table of domain names and corresponding IP addresses in order to resolve the domain names of messages; 2. Also *CSO name server*, a searchable white pages listing of real names and associ-ated e-mail addresses, usually reached via gopher.

NAND

(rhymes with *hand*) A Boolean operator meaning *Not and*. A text search with NAND between two words will match any documents that fail to contain both words.

nastygram

1. An e-mail chastisement from a net.god for violating netiquette; 2. A particularly vicious flame; 3. A letterbomb.

National Center for Supercomputing Applications (NCSA)

Part of the National Science Foun-dation and the creator of NCSA telnet and Mosaic.

National Information Infrastructure (NII)

The U.S. government's name for the Internet and other public net-works. More information about the government's plans for the NII is available via anonymous FTP from ftp.ntia.doc.gov in the / pub directory in a file called NIIAGENDA.ASC.

National Information Standards Organization (NISO)

A U.S. organization for standards in information, technology, and computing, most specifically as related to the Internet and WAIS, author of the revised WAIS standard.

National Institute for Standards and Technology (NIST)

A U.S. government organization that promotes national standards of measurement, technology, computing, and networking (formerly the National Bureau of Standards).

National Public Telecommunications Network (NPTN)

A nonprofit network that promotes free-nets and public networking in general.

National Research and Education Network (NREN)

The network established by the High-Performance Computing Act of 1991, intended to link government agencies, research organizations, and schools.

National Science Foundation (NSF)

The U.S. government agency that funds and runs NSFnet, and consequently many university links to the Internet. Besides its involvement with the Net, NSF promotes science and research.

natural language

The way real human beings communicate, as contrasted with computer languages, which are generally much more logical, literal, and inflexible.

natural language query

A query written in natural language (for example, plain English) seeking information from a database.

navigate

A computer jargon term meaning to get around a program, find commands, move through a document, or hunt around the Internet.

Navigator

CompuServe's graphical software for browsing its online service.

ncftp

A sophisticated UNIX ftp program (a cut above FTP) that helps to automate and streamline ftp operations.

NCSA telnet

A free telnet client for Macintosh or Windows, available via anonymous FTP from ftp.ncsa.uiuc.edu.

net.

1. The original Usenet hierarchical distinction, superseded by the big seven hierarchies (`comp.`, `news.`, `misc.`, `rec.`, `sci.`, `soc.`, and `talk.`) in the Great Renaming; 2. A prefix added to a lot of common words to suggest their counterparts on the Internet (such as `net.cop`, `net.god`, and so on).

.net

An Internet domain, corresponding to constituent networks.

Net

Also *net* and *'net*, often used as an abbreviation for the Internet or for Usenet, really a more general term for the lump sum of interconnected computers on the planet.

net address

An Internet address.

netcasting

A method for distributing information over the Web (also called *push* or *Webcasting*), wherein, after initial setup or subscription by the user, Web sites are automatically checked for updates and displayed in a window or on the desktop, automatically.

net.celebrity

Someone famous on the Net.

net.citizen

A responsible member of an online community.

Netcom

A large ISP; for information, contact info@netcom.com.

NetComplete

An all-in-one software tool for connecting to Netcom.

net.cop

A derogatory term for someone who tries to censor or control the posts of others on Usenet.

NetCruiser

Netcom's old connection software, now superseded by NetComplete.

netdead

(adj) Said of someone who has signed off IRC and can no longer be reached.

Netfind

An Internet resource for finding e-mail addresses, reachable by telnet (the exact address depends on where you are).

nethead

1. A Deadhead (fan of the Grateful Dead) who participates in the rec.music.gdead newsgroup (which is gated to the dead-flames mailing list) or any of the many Dead discussion groups on online services; 2. Any obsessed Internet user (a more recent definition of the term).

net.heavies

People who know a lot about how the Internet and Usenet work and whose opinions carry a lot of weight.

netiquette

Accepted proper behavior on the Net, especially in regard to e-mail and Usenet. Violate netiquette at your peril. Although the Internet and Usenet are effectively anarchies, they still have strong social cultures, and most of the rules and regulations of the Net are enforced by peer pressure.

netizen

A net.citizen.

net.kook

Any frequent Usenet poster whose posts reveal a strange and possibly obsessive personality. For more information, see the newsgroup `alt.usenet.kooks`.

netlag

An excessive delay on IRC that causes messages to bunch up.

net.legend

A net.celebrity, net.kook, or other famous Internet/Usenet figure, many of whom are discussed in the `Net.Legends` FAQ.

Net.Legends FAQ

A FAQ document that praises and excoriates various net.legends, available via gopher from `dixie.aiss.uiuc.edu` port 6969 (choose `urban.legends`, then `Net.Legends FAQ and other assorted FAQs`, then `Net.Legends.FAQ` or any of the other related FAQs).

NetManage Chameleon

TCP/IP software for Windows and DOS.

netnews

Also *net news*, another name for Usenet.

net.personality

A somewhat well-known person on the Net.

.netrc

A setup file for the UNIX ftp and ncftp programs.

Netscape

1. A popular Web browser. The current version is a suite of programs called Netscape Communicator. The Web browser portion of the suite is called Netscape Navigator, but most people refer to the program generically as Netscape; 2. The company that makes Netscape Communicator and other software for the Internet.

netter

Someone who explores the Net.

network

A group of computers or other devices connected by a communications channel, to enable the sharing of files and resources among users. Networks typically provide for the sharing of printers and distribution of e-mail.

network address

1. The unique name of a node on a network; 2. An e-mail address.

Network File System (NFS)

Not to be confused with *NSF* (the National Science Foundation), a UNIX presentation layer protocol developed by Sun Microsystems that makes it possible for a user to access files elsewhere on the network just as if they were on the user's own computer.

Network Information Center (NIC)

An organization that provides information and help to users of a network, as the InterNIC does for the Internet.

network interface card

Also called a *LAN adapter*, a card installed into a PC to attach it to a LAN.

network layer

The third layer of the OSI Model. (IP governs the network layer in the TCP/IP protocol suite.)

network news

A synonym for *Usenet*.

Network News Transfer Protocol (NNTP)

The protocol used to distribute Usenet newsgroups.

network operating system (NOS)

A set of programs that enables networked computers to share files and devices.

Network Operations Center (NOC)

An organization that oversees a network, monitoring its traffic and solving problems.

network peripheral

A device, such as a printer, that is directly connected to a network and not to one of the computers or workstations.

Network Time Protocol (NTP)

A protocol that synchronizes time information on the Internet.

newgroup

A special kind of control message that creates a new newsgroup.

newgroup wars

Competing newgroup and rmgroup messages repeatedly posted by people who alternately want and don't want a new newsgroup to be propagated.

The New Hacker's Dictionary

The printed-book version of the jargon file, published by MIT Press and well worth owning in book form. The contents of the jargon file are also available via the Web at www.ccil.org/jargon/jargon.html.

newline

Any character or group of characters used to indicate the start of a new line in an ASCII text file. The newline characters vary from system to system. An ASCII file that is mistakenly transmitted as a binary file to an incompatible system can end with garbage characters such as ^M at the end of each line.

news

Usenet articles, posted to newsgroups.

newsfeed

The packet of news articles passed along from one computer to the next on Usenet.

newsgroup

A Usenet discussion group.

newsgroup creation

In the big seven Usenet newsgroup hierarchies, new newsgroups can be created only after a formal RFD (Request for Discussion) and a subsequent CFV (Call for Votes).

In the alternative newsgroup hierarchies, it is much easier to create a new newsgroup, which accounts for the proliferation of abandoned silly groups.

newsgroup name

The hierarchical name of a Usenet newsgroup, starting with the first-level hierarchical distinction, followed by a dot, then one or more further qualifying names, none of which may be longer than 15 characters, each of which is separated by a dot.

In proper newsgroup naming, hyphens or underscores rather than dots should be used to break up com-

pound words. For example, alt.fan .jimi.hendrix is incorrect (and implies other jimis besides hendrix with their own fans), but alt.fan .jimi-hendrix is correct.

.newsrc

A setup file for newsreaders on UNIX systems that keeps track of which Usenet newsgroups the user is subscribed to and which articles have been read.

newsreader

A program used to read Usenet articles, and usually also to save, respond to, and post follow-ups to articles, as well as to post new articles.

news server

A program or computer that supplies a newsfeed.

NewsWatcher

A newsreader for the Macintosh, available via anonymous FTP from sumex-aim.stanford.edu.

newsweeding

A pun on *newsreading*, meaning the process of killing or ignoring uninteresting threads and zeroing in on the worthwhile content of a high-volume newsgroup.

News Xpress

A newsreader for Windows.

Nexis

An information service of Mead Data giving access to a searchable database of news and magazine articles and abstracts.

Nextstep

An operating environment for UNIX that offers a graphical user interface.

NeXT-WAIStation

Nextstep software that functions as both a WAIS server and as a client.

nibble

Half a byte (generally four bits).

nick

A nickname used on IRC, not necessarily the same as your username.

nickname

An alias or address book entry in some e-mail programs (such as Eudora).

nixpub

A list of Internet service providers, posted regularly to `comp.bbs.misc` and `alt.bbs`.

nn

A UNIX newsreader (it stands for *no news*, as it tries to hide everything you don't want to see).

nntpd

A UNIX news server program.

NO CARRIER

The message a modem displays when it detects no carrier signal from the phone line.

Nodal Switching System (NSS)

The routing method of the NSFnet backbone.

node

1. In a network, any computer or other device (such as a printer); 2. Any computer on the Internet, a host.

nodename

The unique name of a device attached to a network.

noninteractive

Automated, taking place all at once, without input from a user.

non-return to zero (NRZ) encoding

A data-transmission method that employs two voltage levels—negative and positive—to represent 0 and 1, as opposed to Manchester encoding, which enables network interface cards to transmit digital signals using direct current, encoding data, and timing signals in the same data stream.

NOT

A Boolean operator meaning *Not*. Used to reverse the logical relationship to one of the search elements. A text search for x AND NOT y will match only documents that contain x and do not contain y.

NRIE

No reply is expected (written only); appended to e-mail messages that do not require a courtesy reply.

NSA line eater

A (probably) mythical National Security Agency program that would sift through the entire Usenet newsfeed (and perhaps all e-mail traffic as well) looking for telltale words (such as *glock*, *Uzi*, *TNT*, and so on) that would incriminate terrorists and anarchists. Some people deliberately put such words in their sig blocks to confuse the NSA line eater.

NSFnet

A major Internet backbone, operated by the National Science Foundation.

nuke

To kill a file or a process.

null device

A logical device that corresponds to no actual physical device, functioning as a sort of wastebasket.

numeric string

Any sequence of numbers taken as text rather than as a numeral.

Nuntius

A newsreader for the Macintosh, available via anonymous FTP from `sumex-aim.stanford.edu`.

NUPop

A newsreader for Windows, available via anonymous FTP from `ftp.acns.nwu.edu`.

o

The *options* command (for setting user preferences) in many UNIX console programs.

oak.oakland.edu

A huge FTP archive at Oakland University.

Ob-

A prefix for an obligatory addendum to an off-topic Usenet or list post. Say you get into a political debate in the `rec.music.dylan` newsgroup. To keep your post technically relevant to the group, you might add:

```
ObDylan: Ah, but I
was so much older
then/I'm younger than
that now.
```

object-oriented

Said of an operating system, programming language, or application that makes use of self-contained *objects* that can contain both programming code and data, and which function as modular program pieces.

obligatory * content

Something added to a mailing list or Usenet post to make it relevant to the charter of the list or newsgroup (replacing the * with the subject of the group, as in *obligatory Amiga content* or *obligatory cat content*, and so on).

octet

Eight bits, especially on a system in which eight bits do not equal a byte.

octothorpe

A number sign (#).

odd parity

A method of verifying the correctness of transmitted data by summing each byte, adding a parity bit of 1 if necessary to make the sum odd, before sending the data, and then repeating the summation on the receiving end.

offline

(adj) 1. Not currently connected to the Net; 2. Not responding to network requests; 3. Said of a person no longer involved in a chat.

offline mail reader

A program that connects to the Net, downloads your e-mail, and then disconnects, allowing you to read, reply to, and send mail without being charged for connect time.

offline newsreader

A newsreader that connects to the Net, downloads all unread articles in all subscribed newsgroups, and then disconnects, allowing you to read, reply to, and post articles without being charged for connect time.

Oldie

A text editor available in the Delphi Information Service.

127.0.0.1

The Internet *loopback address*, it is always the address of your local host, the computer you are currently logged in to.

online

(adj) 1. Currently connected to the Net; 2. Available for network requests; 3. Said of a person, participating in a chat.

Online Book Initiative (OBI)

An organization that publishes uncopyrighted (or no longer copyrighted) books via the Internet, reachable via anonymous FTP at ftp.std .com/obi.

Online Career Center

A nonprofit organization that maintains a searchable database of employment information. It offers free access to job listings and résumés to both employers and job-seekers. For more information, gopher to gopher.msen.com or send e-mail to occ@msen.com.

online community

Also *virtual community*, a group of people with shared interests who meet, communicate, and interact via a network, BBS, Internet discussion group, or any other form of electronic common space. Online communities have many of the properties of real-world communities.

Online Computer Library Center (OCLC)

A nonprofit organization providing computer services (such as cataloging and interlibrary loans) for over ten thousand libraries and educational institutions. OCLC maintains the FirstSearch Catalog. For more information, send mail to listserv@oclc.org.

online service

A company that maintains a proprietary network and provides e-mail, forums, chats, games, databases of information, downloadable files, and information services (stocks, airlines, and so on), such as America Online, CompuServe, Delphi, eWorld, GEnie, Prodigy, Microsoft Network, and so on.

Most online services have e-mail connections to the Internet (though some charge extra for that e-mail). More and more are adding other Internet facilities, such as FTP, gopher, and the Web, blurring the distinction further between online services and Internet service providers.

open

(adj) Said of a protocol, using algorithms and technologies available to anyone (as contrasted with proprietary).

(v) To make a connection to a remote host.

open protocol

A protocol that may be utilized by a variety of developers, not just the organization that formulated the protocol.

Open Software Foundation (OSF)

An alliance of DEC, IBM, and Hewlett-Packard.

Open Systems Interconnection (OSI)

An international organization sponsored by the ISO with a mission to create international computer communications standards, such as the OSI Model, specifically to facilitate internetworking among incompatible systems.

operating environment

A front end for an operating system, a set of tools and a consistent look and feel that allow the user to interact with the computer. For instance, Microsoft Windows (versions 1.0 through 3.x) was an operating environment that ran on top of the MS-DOS operating system.

operating system

The software that governs all communication with and use of a computer's system resources, such as memory, disk space, the attention of the processor, and peripheral devices (monitor, keyboard, mouse, printer, modem, and so on). It also mediates between applications and system resources. The operating system starts running before any other software and stays in memory the whole time a computer is on.

Popular operating systems include Windows, MacOS, OS/2, Linux, UNIX, and VMS.

option

A command or selection available on a menu or list.

OR

A Boolean operator meaning *Or*. A text search with OR between two words matches any documents containing either word.

.org

An Internet domain corresponding to (nonprofit) organizations.

OS/2

An IBM operating system for PCs and compatibles.

OSF/1

A port of UNIX that runs on VAXen.

OSI

Open Systems Interconnection, an international organization sponsored by the ISO with a mission to create international computer communications standards, such as the OSI Model, specifically to facilitate internetworking among incompatible systems.

OSI Model

The seven-layer networking reference model (sometimes called the *seven-layer cake*) defined by the ISO's OSI to facilitate the internetworking of incompatible computers and networks. The organization of the seven layers, together known as a protocol stack, represents the dependence of each layer on the next lower layer in the stack.

Open Transport (OT)

Apple's Open Transport technology is a comprehensive collection of Networking and Internet connectivity protocols, which was introduced with System 7.5.3, and is included with each subsequent Operating System upgrade.

Outernet

A collective name for all the networks, BBSs, and online services that have e-mail gateways with the Internet but no full connection.

overhead

(n) The accumulation of protocol information wrapped around data transmitted over networks.

packet

Any unit of data (the size varies) sent across a network. Besides the data, a packet also includes the addresses of the sender and the recipient, as well as error-control information. On the Internet, a packet is the same thing as a datagram. A large piece of data will be split into several packets, each of which may take an independent route to the destination, where they will be reassembled.

Packetized Ensemble Protocol (PEP)

A proprietary feature of Telebit brand modems that allows two modems to be connected directly.

packet sniffer

1. A person who tries to "listen in" on Internet traffic in search of information to steal; 2. The program that such a person employs to "sniff out" interesting packets.

packet-switched network

A network made up of interconnected circuits that route packets over a variety of alternative paths, as opposed to a circuit-switched network, in which packets are routed over dedicated lines.

packet switching

A method of transmitting data in which packets for many unconnected operations are routed simultaneously over a communications channel (often a telephone line) to make best use of the line. Related packets are reassembled at the destination.

packet switch node (PSN)

The computer that handles the routing of packets in a packet-switched network.

page

(v) To display a document one screenful at a time in a character-based interface.

(n) A document published on the Web.

paging program

A program (sometimes called a *pager*) that displays documents one screenful at a time, such as the UNIX utility more.

paper-net

The U.S. Postal Service.

parallel

(adj) Said of a connection in which bits are transmitted simultaneously.

parallel port

A port in the back of a PC that can connect via a cable to a parallel device.

paren

(n) A parenthesis.

parent directory

1. In a hierarchical file system, the directory for which the current directory is a subdirectory, symbolized in UNIX, DOS, and OS/2 by a two dots (..); 2. Any directory which contains other directories.

parity

An error-checking method in data transmission in which an extra bit is added to each byte (between the data bit and the stop bit) to round off bit-total values to even or odd numbers. The parity bit must match at both ends of the transmission.

Parity is therefore one of the settings you have to specify on your modem to make a connection. It's usually set to None or Even, but it depends on the modem you're calling.

parity bit

A redundant bit added to a byte in data transmission as part of an error-checking technique.

parity error

An error caused by mismatched parity bits in a byte of transmitted data.

parse

(v) To interpret an instruction by breaking it down and analyzing its parts.

Pascal

A beginner's programming language, often used as a stepping stone to C.

passive star

A network design with a central hub that connects all the branches but does not retransmit signals that pass through it.

password

A secret code used to restrict access to an account, channel, file, and so on, only to authorized users who know the password.

A bad password is one that is a real word or is otherwise easily guessable (a birth date, a pet's name, and so on). A good password contains upper- and lowercase letters and numerals, and the longer it is, the better.

passwd

The UNIX command to change an account's password.

patch

(n) A quick-and-dirty correction that fixes a bug, or at least works around it.

(v) To fix a problem with a temporary work-around or kludge.

path

1. A bang path, the route an e-mail message takes between its sender and receiver; 2. The channel through which a signal passes; 3. A completely specified location of a directory or file, starting from the root directory.

PC

A *personal computer*, generally a microcomputer, usually either an IBM PC or compatible, a Macintosh, or perhaps an Amiga.

PC-compatible

Said of a computer that emulates the functionality of an IBM PC.

PC Eudora

A Windows mail program (a port of Eudora for the Macintosh) that uses Post Office Protocol (POP) and can function as an offline mail reader. It is available via anonymous FTP from `ftp.qualcomm.com/Eudora`.

PC Pursuit

A SprintNet service that allows users to connect directly to another computer (as opposed to an online service).

PC/TCP Plus for DOS

DOS software that enables an IBM PC or compatible to connect via modem to a computer connected to the Internet for FTP and telnet.

PC-Xware

Windows software that includes TCP/IP, NFS, FTP, and server access for X Window applications, developed by Network Computing Devices, Inc.

PDP-11

A series of DEC computers now largely superseded by VAXen. PDP stands for *programmed data processor*. The PDP-11 series was preceded by PDP-10, according to hacker lore the first real timesharing machine.

PeaceNet

A BBS for nonprofits, religious organizations, and people concerned with peace and justice. For more information, anonymous FTP to igc.org in the /pub directory.

peer

A network device that communicates directly with other devices on the network.

peer-to-peer

(adj) A network architecture in which each computer on the network can communicate directly with other nodes and function as both a client and a server.

Pegasus Mail

Also known as *p-mail*, a freeware e-mail program for IBM PCs and compatibles and Macintoshes, available via FTP from risc.ua.edu.

PENpages

A database and information service covering every imaginable aspect of rural life in general and agriculture in particular, administrated by Pennsylvania State University. It is updated daily and the latest additions are always available on the main menu. To connect, telnet to psupen.psu.edu and log in as your two-letter state abbreviation (no password).

Pentium

A 64-bit microprocessor, Intel's successor to the 80486 chip (named Pentium after the courts decided that Intel could not defend as a trademark the number 586 or 80586).

The discovery of an error in the much-vaunted chip has spun off a long series of jokes about rounding errors (for example, "Q: How many Pentiums does it take to screw in a light bulb? A: 1.9999998657586.").

peripheral

(adj) Said of a device that is not essential to the computer or physically a part of it (as opposed to the processor or hard-disk drive), such as a printer or modem.

(n) A peripheral device.

Perl

A programming language (it stands for *practical extraction and report language*) distributed over Usenet, favored by UNIX system administrators.

permissions

Settings associated with an account on a network or multiuser system that define a level of access (to certain system resources) permitted to the user of the account.

PGP

A shareware public-key encryption program (it stands for *pretty good privacy*), developed by Phillip Zimmerman. For more information see the Web page at www.mantis.co.uk/pgp/pgp.html.

phage

(n) A program that modifies other programs or databases in unauthorized ways.

phreak

(v) To crack (break into) a network or phone system.

(n) One who enjoys cracking secure networks or phone systems.

physical

(adj) Said of hardware and mechanical connections, as opposed to logical.

physical layer

Layer 1 (the bottom layer) of the OSI Model; it defines protocols for connecting cables and other hardware.

pico

A full-screen, modeless text editor for UNIX machines based on the built-in editor in the pine e-mail program.

pile-on

(n) A flame war in which many participants take turns attacking a single victim, creating long posts of polymorphous abuse.

pine

A UNIX e-mail program whose name is a recursive acronym (pine stands for *pine is not elm*). Pine has a built-in full-screen modeless editor, MIME support, and the ability to attach files.

ping

(v) 1. To check the presence of a host with PING; 2. To send e-mail to an entire mailing list, requesting a response, in order to check which addresses are still valid.

(n) The UNIX command that uses the PING protocol.

PING

Said to stand for *Packet Internet Groper*, a protocol for sending a signal to see whether another network host or other device is online and responding. (It's probably actually named for the sound made by submarine sonar/depth equipment.)

pipe

(v) To send the output of a process or dump the contents of a file to a device (such as a printer), program (such as one that will process the data), or another file.

(n) The | character (also called a *vertical bar*), used in the piping process.

.pit

The file extension for Macintosh PackIt files. (PackIt has largely been superseded as a Macintosh compression standard by StuffIt.)

pixel

A single dot on a monitor or in a bit-mapped image (from *picture element*).

.pkg

The file extension for an AppleLink Package file.

pkunzip

The uncompression program for pkzipped files.

pkzip

A DOS file compression program.

plain ASCII

(adj) Said of an ASCII text file (a document with no word-processor formatting).

.plan

(*dot plan*) A text file that is displayed when your username is fingered. Originally intended to alert people to your whereabouts or immediate plans, .plan files have evolved into personalized files sometimes filled with information or absurdities. Here's my old .plan:

```
Released December 1:
Enterzone, a quar-
terly hyperzine on
the World Wide Web
<http://enterzone
.berkeley.edu/
enterzone.html>
Current Project:
Internet Dictionary
(Sybex)
Available Now:
A Guided Tour of the
Internet (Sybex)
WordPerfect 6 Roadmap
(Sybex)
Word for Windows
Quick & Easy (Sybex)
Last Story:
No Bird but An
Invisible Thing
(hypertext version)
<http://enterzone.ber
keley.edu/homies/
nobird/nobird.html>
```

platform

A computer or operating system type.

plonk

A follow-up post that means "I just put you in my kill file." (It's supposed to be the sound of the bozo falling into the kill file.)

p-mail

1. Pegasus Mail; 2. Physical mail, as opposed to e-mail.

point at

To start a client program, such as a Web browser, by supplying it with an address, as in "Point your Web browser to `http://ezone.org/ez` to see the latest episode of Enterzone."

point of presence (POP)

A local phone number connected to a modem connected to the network of a service provider, to enable users to log in to the network without paying long distance charges.

Point-to-Point Protocol (PPP)

A TCP/IP protocol, similar to SLIP, for transmitting IP datagrams over serial lines such as phone lines. With PPP, PC users can connect to the Internet and still function in their native environment (instead of having to deal with a character-based UNIX environment).

poll

(v) 1. To check a port to see whether a device is connected and available for network or communications activity; 2. To connect to another system to check for new mail or news.

port

(n) 1. A socket on the back of a computer for connecting cables and hence modems, printers, etc.; 2. On Internet hosts, a channel dedicated to a specific program, so that a multiplexing host can run telnet sessions on one port, FTP connections on another, logins on another, etc.; 3. The interface between a router and a network; 4. A version of a program that was originally designed for a different platform.

(v) To translate software designed for one platform so that it will run on another.

post

(v) 1. To send a message to a mailing list or an article to a newsgroup; 2. To publish information in any medium on the Internet. (The word *post* comes from the bulletin-board metaphor, in which scraps of paper are posted to the board to be read by anyone who comes by, as opposed to the British usage, which means to send mail.)

(n) A message sent to a mailing list or newsgroup.

postcardware

Shareware that's almost free, except the programmer requests that satisfied users send a postcard (so she can see how far the software has spread).

poster

One who posts.

postmaster

A person who oversees a network's e-mail connection to the Internet. Questions about users at a host or problems with e-mail to or from that host can often be addressed to postmaster@*hostname.domain*.

Post Office Protocol (POP)

A protocol that specifies how a personal computer can connect to a mail server on the Internet and download e-mail.

PostScript

A proprietary "page-description" computer language developed by Adobe Systems. It describes pages (text, graphics, layout) in mathematical terms. PostScript files generally have a .ps or .eps extension.

pour

(v) To pipe the output from a process or file to a device or other file.

power cycling

Turning the hardware off, waiting, and then turning it on again.

PPP

Point-to-Point Protocol, a TCP/IP protocol similar to SLIP for transmitting IP datagrams over serial lines such as phone lines. With PPP, users connect to the Internet and still function in their native environment (instead of having to deal with a character-based UNIX environment).

presentation layer

Layer 6 of the OSI Model, it defines how data is formatted, encoded, converted, and presented.

prime time

The period of heaviest usage of a network, usually 9 a.m. to 5 p.m. during the work week.

printed circuit

A computer chip with microcircuits literally printed (via a photographic process) onto it.

Printer Access Protocol (PAP)

The AppleTalk protocol that defines how a workstation and a printer communicate.

privacy-enhanced mail (PEM)

E-mail handling systems that incorporate encryption techniques to secure privacy and verification of message integrity.

private key

In public-key encryption, the secret key the user reveals to no one and uses to sign outgoing messages and to decrypt incoming messages that were encrypted with the public key.

private virtual circuit (PVC)

Software circuits that maintain a private line between hosts.

privatization

On the Internet, generally refers to the U.S. government's process of placing maintenance of backbone networks in the hands of private organizations. So far this has not significantly changed the pricing structure for individual users.

privileges

Also called *access privileges*, a set of system resource and directory actions that a user is permitted to perform.

process

A program or part of a program being executed in a multitasking operating system. More generally, one task of many that a computer is doing.

ProComm Plus

A popular communications package for IBM PCs and compatibles, sold by Symantec, Inc.

.profile

A startup file in some flavors of UNIX.

programmer

A person who writes computer programs.

programming

The process of writing programs.

.project

(*dot project*) On some systems, a file similar to a .plan that is displayed when a user is fingered, intended to discuss the project the user is currently working on.

prompt

(n) Also *command-line prompt*, a string of text that a character-based operating system displays on the screen to tell a user that it is ready to accept input (such as a command or the name of a program to run).

propagation

The process of dissemination for packets in general, and Usenet newsfeeds in particular, as they are passed from computer to computer. Propagation delays are responsible for the confusing situation that sometimes occurs when you read a follow-up to a post that hasn't yet appeared at your site.

proprietary

(adj) Said of a technology, architecture, or set of protocols whose design is the property of the company that developed it.

protocol

An agreed-upon set of rules that allows otherwise incompatible machines or software to communicate. Protocols can govern a wide range of the aspects of communications, from the order in which bits are transmitted to the rules for opening and maintaining a connection to the format of an electronic mail message.

protocol layer

One portion of a set of protocols that handles one aspect of the transmission of data.

protocol stack

A set of protocol layers that work together to provide reliable communication between a computer and a network or another computer, also called a *protocol family* or *protocol suite*. The TCP/IP protocol stack includes such protocols as TCP, IP, FTP, SMTP, telnet, and so on.

proxy server

A security measure that enables users behind a firewall to browse the Web (visited resources are actually downloaded by the intervening proxy server and then viewed internally from there) without exposing the contents of the intranet to public scrutiny. A proxy server may render some Web services inaccessible to the user.

.ps

The file extension for PostScript files.

pseudo

(n) A new identity assumed on Usenet in order that the user might act (provocatively or otherwise) without those actions being associated with the user's real (or better-known) name.

/pub

A UNIX directory often found on FTP hosts, where public information is stored and made available.

public data network (PDN)

A type of commercial packet-switched network offering wide-area services to customers, with sophisticated error-checking, buffering, and handling of protocols. Tymnet, SprintNet, and the CompuServe Packet Network are all PDNs.

Public Dial-Up Internet Access List (PDIAL)

Peter Kaminski's excellent list of Internet service providers, complete with cost information, posted regularly to alt.internet.access .wanted and alt.bbs.lists, and available via anonymous FTP from rtfm.mit.edu in the /pub/ usenet/news.answers directory, with the file name pdial.

public domain

(adj) Available for free to the public, uncopyrighted, as are much of the information, system software, and applications available on the Internet.

public key

In public-key encryption, the key a user distributes freely and which correspondents use to encrypt messages to the user and decrypt the user's signature (encrypted with the user's private key) on messages from the user.

public-key encryption

A form of key encryption which uses two keys, a public key (for encrypting messages) and a private key (for decrypting messages) to enable users to verify each other's messages without having to securely exchange secret keys.

publishing

Posting on the Net (to newsgroups, the Web, gopher, etc.) is considered equivalent to publishing, though the paradigm is different—the reader comes to you and you do not distribute the information.

push

(n) A method of distributing information over the Web, by which updates are (scheduled and then) automatically sent to the user's screen or window, as if the content were being "broadcast" to a receiver (hence the synonymous terms netcast and Webcast).

(v) To distribute content over the Web via netcasting.

put

(v) To copy a file from your host computer to a remote site, particularly via FTP.

(n) The FTP command to put a file.

pwd

The UNIX command (short for *print working directory*) that displays the current working directory (the directory the user is "in").

q

The quit command in many UNIX programs. (Often a capital *Q* will mean *quick quit* and will allow you to quit without any questions.)

qotd

Quotation of the day (written only). Some systems display a quotation when you log in. Some Usenet posters change the quotations in their sig block daily (or more often).

query

(n) 1. A search request submitted to a database to find a particular record (piece of information) or all records that meet certain criteria, such as an archie query; 2. A question mark.

question mark

? 1. a wildcard character in UNIX (and hence in many Internet applications), it stands for any single character; 2. A help command in some character-based applications.

questionnaires

Usenet newsgroups are often bombarded by purveyors of questionnaires, hoping to exploit a ready-made audience. That the responders are self-selecting doesn't seem to bother the questioners, but to regular readers of the newsgroups, these posts and the ubiquitous surveys get tiresome awfully fast.

queue

(*cue*, n) A list of items (such as print jobs or messages) waiting to be sent from one device to another.

QuickTime

A collection of Apple technologies that compress, store, translate, and play back files combining text, sound, animation, and video, on both the Windows and Macintosh platforms. QuickTime clips are distributed via the Internet and the Web.

quit

To stop running an application.

quoting

Including a relevant portion of a preceding article when posting a follow-up. Most newsreaders precede quoted text with a symbol, such as >, and try to indicate who said what, though multiple embedded quotations often require that the latest author untangle the attributions.

It is bad netiquette to quote no text (unless the follow-up makes it absolutely clear what it is responding to), and it's both bad netiquette and an unmistakable marker of a clueless newbie to quote an entire article merely to add "I agree" or "Right on, d00d!!" at the end.

QWERTY

(n) The standard typewriter and computer-keyboard layout, so named for the first six characters of the first alphabetical row.

r

The reply command in many UNIX mail programs; 2. The *reply by e-mail* command in many UNIX newsreaders.

RAM

Random access memory, memory that any application or process can

read or write to. It's frequently confused with storage, because both resources are often measured in megabytes.

ranking

The order in which a WAIS program displays the results of a database search—from most likely to least likely.

rb

The Ymodem command for receiving (uploading) a file.

rc file

A UNIX text file with a file name of the form .*rc, containing command line instructions or other startup information for an application or for the operating system itself. Examples include .newsrc, .pinerc, and so on.

rcp

The UNIX *remote copy* command.

read

To copy data from a disk into memory.

README file

An information file describing the contents of an FTP directory or the files associated with an application.

readme.txt

Typical name for a README file.

read notification

A feature of some e-mail programs that lets you know when the recipient of your e-mail has received and opened the message.

read-only

(adj) Said of a file that can be read but not altered.

read-write

(adj) Said of a file that can be both read and written to (altered).

RealAudio

Progressive Networks' original streaming audio format. The latest version is called RealPlayer.

RealPlayer

Progressive Networks' format for streaming audio and movies.

real life

The offline world, as in the question "What do you do in real life?"

real name

A user's full name as it appears on e-mail messages and Usenet posts (also called a *full name*), as opposed to their username (the real name can also be a pseudonym). On UNIX systems, the user's real name is a variable that can be set with the `chfn` command. Many Windows and Macintosh Internet applications allow the user to enter or change a real name on the fly.

real time

Also *realtime*, the time used for synchronous communication, in which both participants must be available (as in a telephone conversation). Also, taking place at the present time, live, not delayed or recorded.

reboot

To restart a crashed operating system, either through a designated key combination (a warm boot), or by turning it off and on again (power cycling).

receipt notification

A proof-of-delivery feature provided by some e-mail programs (similar to the idea of registered mail in the real world).

record

(n) A set of related data from a database.

recursive acronym

An acronym that contains the acronym itself in its spelled out form, such as GNU, which stands for *GNU's not UNIX*, and pine, which stands for *pine is not elm*.

redirection

Sending output from one device or file to another device or file.

redundant path

A secondary path that a router can assign to a packet when the normal route is not available.

refresh

To redraw the screen, usually either to reflect changes to the data or to restore the screen when something has marred its intended appearance.

register

(v) To sign up and pay for shareware.

(n) A designated area of memory.

registered jack (RJ)

Any of a series of specialized jacks used for connecting wires, such as RJ-11 and RJ-45.

rehi

Hi again, typed on IRC when you rejoin a channel.

relevance feedback

A system used by WAIS applications to rank documents retrieved in a search in order of relevance to the search criteria. Documents are ranked based on the number of times that key words from the query appear in them.

reliable

Said of networks with dedicated connections.

remailer

A program that receives e-mail and then resends it, with different information attached. Often used by persons that believe all network communications should be kept anonymous.

remote

Said of a host or other network resource that is located on a computer or network elsewhere, as opposed to a local host or resource.

remote access

The process of accessing another computer's resources, such as files or printers. Dial-up accounts and telnet are both forms of remote access.

remote login

To connect to a remote computer over a network, usually done on the Internet with telnet or rlogin.

rename

To change the name (or path) of a file or directory.

repeater

A device that connects two stretches of cable and boosts the power of the signal it passes, to reduce line noise and the risk of errors.

reply

(v) To respond to an e-mail message or Usenet post.

(n) 1. A message sent in response to a previous message or post; 2. An e-mail command that takes the return path from the current message and makes that address the recipient of a new message, possibly quoting the previous message as well.

repost

(n) An article posted again in full. (Many newsgroups expect that reposts be labeled as such in their subject lines.)

(v) To post the same information again.

Request for Discussion (RFD)

The first stage in the formal process of Usenet newsgroup creation.

-request

A suffix appended to the username of a human-administered mailing list to form the username of the administrative address for the list. (So a human-administered mailing list called atoz@netcom.com would have an administrative address called atoz-request@netcom.com associated with it.) It is a Bad Thing to post administrative requests (generally to subscribe or unsubscribe) to the actual mailing list rather than to the -request address.

Research Libraries Information Network (RLIN)

An online catalog of catalogs with information from most major research libraries in the United States, reachable by telnet at rlg.stanford.edu (it's not free). For information, send e-mail to bl.ric@rlg.standord.edu or call (800) 537-RLIN.

Reseaux Associés pour la Recherche Européenne (RARE)

A European group of research networks. For more information, connect via anonymous FTP to ftp.rare.nl.

Reseaux IP Européenne (RIPE)

A group of European TCP/IP networks.

resolution

1. Conversion of a physical address into a logical address (*address resolution*); 2. The degree of detail, sharpness, or fineness of an image.

resolve

(v) To convert a physical address to a logical address or vice versa.

return path

An address in the header of an e-mail program that tells the recipient's mail program where to send a reply message.

Reverse Address Resolution Protocol (RARP)

A TCP/IP protocol for converting logical addresses to physical addresses.

RFC

Request for Comments, one of a set of documents that contain Internet protocols, standards, and information, and together more or less define the Internet, in an open way. The standards contained in them are followed carefully by software developers (both commercial and freeware). The name Request for Comments can be confusing, since the contents are settled, but they arrived from free and open discussion on the Net.

RFCs can be found via anonymous FTP at the `ftp.internic.net` site, among others.

rib site

A computer with a high-speed link to a backbone site that distributes traffic to smaller networks.

rights

Another name for privileges.

ring topology

A network architecture in which the nodes are arranged in a circle.

RINGO

An experimental service at MIT that that allows you to rate a list of musicians and bands and receive back some suggestions about other music you might like. To participate, send e-mail to `ringo@media.mit.edu`.

RJ

A registered jack.

RJ-11

A typical phone jack.

RJ-45

A modular jack that can hold up to four pairs of wires, used most often to connect unshielded twisted-pair wiring in LANs. An RJ-45 looks like a phone jack (RJ-11) except bigger.

rlogin

A protocol (and program) for remote login from one UNIX machine to another. It automatically supplies the username and password given when the user first logged in.

rm

The UNIX *remove* command, for deleting a file. (Note: Be very careful not to type *rm* * and press Enter by mistake—there's no "undelete" function in UNIX!)

rmdir

The UNIX *remove directory* command, for deleting a directory.

rmgroup

A special kind of control message that removes a newsgroup.

rn

The most common UNIX newsreader. It's not a threaded newsreader.

robocancel

(v) To automatically cancel articles. A controversial (because it's a form of censorship) method for dealing with spammers and roboposters.

robopost

(v) To post automatically, usually done by a 'bot that is programmed to post reams of articles and responses to Usenet.

roboposter

1. A 'bot that automatically posts and reposts huge numbers of articles to Usenet; 2. The programmer behind the roboposting 'bot. A reputed roboposter using the name of Serdar Argic single-handedly rendered `soc.history` (and a number of other newsgroups) unreadable without a kill file to screen him out. His howling through the wires (ranting holocaust revisionism about the Turks and the "x-Soviet" Armenians) came to an unexpected but welcome halt in the spring of 1994.

robot

A user on IRC or in a MUD (or, less commonly, on Usenet) that is actually a program. Some perform useful functions while others are merely annoying.

robust

(adj) Said of software that doesn't crash often and recovers well when it does.

rofl

Rolling on the floor laughing (written only, also *ROFL*).

role-playing game

A game or activity, such as a MUD, in which participants take on fictional identities and strive to remain in character.

ROM

Read-only memory. Fixed memory that can't be altered.

root

1. In a hierarchical file system, the first directory, to which all other directories are subdirectories; 2. On UNIX machines, a superuser account with unlimited permissions.

ROT13

(*rot-thirteen*) A simple cipher in which each letter is replaced with the one 13 letters away from it in the alphabet, traditionally used to hide spoilers and off-color jokes from sensitive eyes. (Because the alphabet has 26 letters, the same rotation will both encode and decode.)

rotfl

Rolling on the floor laughing (written only, also *ROTFL*).

route

(n) The path a packet takes from sender to destination.

(v) To send a packet along a path.

router

A device that physically connects two networks or a network to the Internet, converting addresses and sending on only the messages that need to pass to the other network.

routing information protocol (RIP)

A TCP/IP protocol that specifies how routers exchange information.

routing table

A list used by a router to determine the best route for a packet.

RS-232C

> A 25-pin connector, such as the one used to connect a computer to an external modem.

rtfm.mit.edu

> A huge FTP archive, with FAQs from many Usenet newsgroups, RFCs, FYIs, and more.

rx

> The Xmodem command for receiving (uploading) a file.

rz

> The Zmodem command for receiving (uploading) a file.

s

> The save command in many UNIX applications.

samizdat

> (*sam-is-dot*) Also *samizdata*, from the Russian word for self-published underground pamphlets, a word used to describe the flow of unofficial information on the Internet, particularly e-zines.

save

> Literally, to copy a file or some data from memory (RAM) to a disk (or other storage medium). More loosely, to preserve the work you're doing by storing it on a disk.

sb

> The Ymodem command for sending (downloading) a file.

sci.

> A Usenet hierarchy devoted to science.

screen dump

> A copy of the contents of a screen, saved to a file or sent to a printer.

screen name

> An America Online term for a user's real name or one of several allowable pseudonyms.

screen-oriented

> (adj) Said of applications that permit the user to move the cursor around the screen.

script

> A sequence of commands to be executed by an application or operating system, often saved as a text file.

scroll

> (v) To browse through a document, moving the text up the screen as if on a continuous parchment. Usually suggests being able to move as little as a line at a time, as opposed to the display of a paging program, which always moves through a document one screenful at a time.

scroll-back

> The ability to scroll to an earlier part of a document, which in a terminal-emulation program requires that it be saved in a buffer.

SCSI

(*scuzzy*) *Small Computer Systems Interface*, a standard for connecting personal computers to certain peripheral devices, including CD-ROM drives and external hard drives.

.sea

A file extension that indicates a Macintosh self-extracting archive.

search

(v) To seek information from a database, document, or other source, usually by specifying key words to match.

(n) The process of seeking specific information from a source.

(adj) Said of programs, interfaces, or tools that facilitate the process of seeking specific information.

searchable

(adj) Said of indexes, databases, and documents that are formatted to facilitate searches by standard Internet search tools, such as WAIS, gopher, and Web clients.

search criterion

A set of keywords separated by Boolean operators (such as AND, OR, and NOT) specified in a query in order to find matching documents or entries in a database, such as an archie or WAIS server.

search engine

Database software, usually fronted by a Web site for searching the Internet, the Web, or some other computer domain, such as AltaVista (at `http://altavista.digital.com`). Most search engines feature, at minimum, a text box for typing key words and a Search (or Go, or Do it Now!, or whatever) button.

secondary service provider

An organization that provides a direct Internet connection to a regional set of networks.

security

The Internet is not inherently secure. For example, e-mail messages are in some ways more like postcards than like letters sealed in envelopes. Your mail generally passes through many sites on the way to its destination, and postmasters and other superusers can read your mail if they want, although it would be unethical for them to do so.

If you are interested in making your e-mail more private or secure, look into encryption software, such as PGP. New Web products are exploring methods of making private transactions over the Internet as well.

seed

In a tape tree, the original master tape from which the first set of copies is made.

segment

(n) 1. A length of cable in a network; 2. A unit of data packaged by TCP for IP.

self-extracting archive

An executable file, containing one or more compressed files, that will extract the files it contains when run.

sequenced packet exchange (SPX)

A Novell NetWare transport layer protocol that coordinates messages between workstations.

serial

Said of a connection, such as a phone line, in which bits are transmitted one at a time.

Serial Line Internet Protocol (SLIP)

A TCP/IP protocol for transmitting IP datagrams over serial lines, such as phone lines. With SLIP, personal computer users can connect to the Internet and still function in their native environment (instead of having to deal with a character-based UNIX environment).

serial port

A port in the back of a PC that can connect via a cable to a serial device, such as a modem or printer.

server

A network application or computer that supplies information or other resources to client applications that connect to it. In conventional networking, server usually refers to a computer; for Internet client/server applications, server usually refers to a program.

Many Internet features are provided by servers: file servers, mail servers, WAIS servers, Web servers, FTP servers, archie servers, name servers, finger servers, and so on.

service provider

A company that provides direct access to the Internet.

session

A period of connection and exchange of communications between hosts.

session layer

Layer 5 of the OSI Model, it specifies how computers make and maintain connections.

setext

A sophisticated text-formatting program for UNIX.

shareware

Software available for a free trial that must be registered and paid for if you decide to use it. Payment may also buy you manuals, support, and updates. Much shareware is distributed via the Internet. A large FTP archive for Macintosh software can be found at sumex.aim .stanford.edu; another large FTP site for IBM PC and compatible software can be found at wuarchive.wustl.edu in the /systems/ibmpc directory.

shar file

Also called a *sharchive*, a UNIX archive file that contains one or more compressed files. It can be uncompressed in a UNIX shell without any special software.

shell

1. An operating environment; that is, a program through which a user communicates with the operating system. There are many flavors of UNIX shells, such as Bourne, Korn, Bourne again (bash), C shell, and so on; 2. A command in many applications that allows you to enter shell commands without quitting the program.

shell account

An Internet account that provides access to a UNIX shell, usually via a modem and a terminal-emulation program.

shell command

An operating-system command entered at a command-line prompt or from within an application.

shell out

(v) To temporarily escape an application and get access to a shell without quitting the program.

shielded cable

A cable protected from electromagnetic interference by wire mesh and plastic, such as a coaxial cable. Shielded cable will not interfere with other electronic devices and is secure from wire tapping.

shielded twisted-pair (STP)

A cable shielded with foil and a copper braid surrounding the wire in twisted pairs, suitable for high-speed transmission over long distances, often used in token ring networks.

Shub-Internet

A mythical god or demon thought to be responsible for all slowdowns on the Net. It lives under the Pentagon and is worshipped by some MUD people. Its name is spoken aloud at great peril.

sig block

Also *sig, .sig, signature, .signature*, or *signature block, or signature file*, a text file containing a user's name and, optionally, e-mail address, other identifying information, aphorisms, ASCII graphics, etc., automatically attached to the ends of e-mail messages and Usenet posts. A UNIX sig block is a file called `.signature` in the user's home directory.

It is generally considered a breach of netiquette to have a sig block over four lines long. Sig blocks are the bumper stickers of the information highway.

signal

(n) An electronic impulse passing over a medium such as a wire, carrying data from one device to another; 2. More loosely, any useful information.

signal-to-noise ratio

1. Literally, an electrical engineering measurement of the quality of a

communication medium; 2. On the Internet, colloquially used as a metaphor for the proportion of useful information to junk on a list or in a newsgroup.

sig quote

A quotation contained in a sig block, not unlike yearbook quotations and frequently about as interesting.

silicon

The mineral that computer chips (and sand) are made from.

silly group

A newsgroup created simply for the sake of amusement, either because the name itself is silly or because the topic to be discussed in it is silly, many of which can be found in the `alt .silly-group.*` hierarchy. Some silly groups have a *gag.gag.gag* ending, for instance, `alt.tv.dinosaurs .barney.die.die.die`.

Simple Mail Transfer Protocol (SMTP)

The TCP/IP protocol that specifies how computers exchange electronic mail. It works with Post Office Protocol, and is one of the reasons that Internet e-mail functions so well.

Simple Network Management Protocol (SNMP)

A TCP/IP protocol that specifies how nodes are managed on a network, using agents to monitor network traffic and maintain a management information base.

Simple Wide Area Information Server (SWAIS)

A WAIS interface for VT100 terminals that shows sources in numbered lists.

simplex

Transmission of a signal in one direction at a time.

.sit

The file extension of a Macintosh StuffIt file.

site

An Internet host that allows some kind of remote access, such as FTP, telnet, gopher, and so on.

site name

Also *sitename*, the portion of an Internet address that precedes the (subdomain, if any, and the) domain. In the address `mang@garnet .blob .com`, *garnet* is the site name.

64K line

A 64 kps telephone circuit, also called a DS0 line. A 64K line is called a clear channel when its entire 64 kps bandwidth is available for transmission.

slack

(n) 1. Unused storage space on a disk; 2. According to the teachings of the Church of the SubGenius, the prerequisite of all human happiness. For more information, see the newsgroup `alt.slack`.

slash

/, in UNIX (and hence in gopher addresses and URLs), the separator character between directory levels.

SLIP

Serial Line Internet Protocol, a TCP/IP protocol for transmitting IP datagrams over serial lines, such as phone lines. With SLIP, personal computer users can connect to the Internet and still function in their native environment (instead of having to deal with a character-based UNIX environment).

SLIP emulator

A UNIX program, such as TIA, that runs in a shell account and mimics the behavior of a SLIP connection, enabling a shell user to run Internet applications on a personal computer.

SlipKnot

A program made by MicroMind that provides graphical access to the Web for people with character-based Unix accounts.

slot

A rack inside a computer where an expansion card can be put.

smart terminal

A terminal that can handle some of the display processing, taking some of the load off the computer it's connected to (an obsolete term in the PC world).

smiley

A sideways smiley face, also called an emoticon, used to indicate an emotion. Here some examples of smileys:

: -)
;)
%^$

snail

(n) A snail mail address, especially labeled as such in a sig block.

(v) To send snail mail.

snail mail

Internet slang for U.S. Postal Service mail, so called for its relative slowness, compared to electronic mail.

snarf

(v) To fetch a set of files across a network, as with FTP.

sneakernet

The kind of network in which you copy the file to a diskette, walk the diskette over to another computer (that's the sneaker part), and then copy the file onto the new computer. The lowest-tech LAN.

'Snooze

A derogatory term for Usenet News, commenting on the low signal-to-noise ratio.

soc.

The Usenet hierarchy devoted to society (and usually sectarian groups in it).

socket

A subdivision of a network node reserved for a single application or process.

socket client

An application or process that reserves a socket for a specific purpose.

socket number

A unique number assigned to a socket by a network.

soda remailer

An anonymous remailer. For information, send mail to `remailer @soda.csua.berkeley.edu` with `remailer-info` as your subject.

soft boot

(v) To reboot only part of a system without restarting the whole thing.

software

1. A program—either an application or operating system—that a computer can execute, as opposed to hardware (the computer itself); 2. A suite of related programs.

software description database (SDD)

A list of file names and directories accessible via archie.

solidus

A slash (/).

source

A remote database storing files available to WAIS searches.

source code

The original, uncompiled program instructions that make up a piece of software.

spam

(v) To post (or robopost) huge amounts of material to Usenet, or to post one article to huge numbers of inappropriate groups. (The term comes from the commercial meat product Spam and the Monty Python routine in which rowdy Vikings in a diner chant "Spam, Spam, Spam, Spam Spam, Spam, Spam, Spam, wonderful Spam, marvelous Spam," and so on, *ad nauseam*.)

Crossposting, even to an inappropriately large number of groups, is not the same thing as spamming, because any decent newsreader will ignore the same crossposted article after it has displayed it once, no matter in what newsgroup it appears.

Special Interest Group (SIG)

1. An e-mail discussion group; 2. One of several technical discussion groups sponsored by ACM (the Association for Computing Machinery).

spew

To post excessively.

spoiler

A post that reveals a plot twist or the solution to a puzzle or riddle. It is good netiquette to label such a post with the word *spoiler* in the subject line and/or to encode the post with rot13.

SprintNet

A global public data network providing local dial-up access from six hundred locations. SprintNet is a packet-switched network using X.25 protocols. It used to be called *Telenet* (not to be confused with telnet).

squick

(v) To exceed someone's threshold for violent or tasteless imagery.

standard

(n) A description of the expected performance of a device or system.

standard disclaimer

A disclaimer attached to the end of a Usenet or mailing list post, usually to the effect that the user is not speaking in an official capacity for the user's employer or access provider.

standard generalized markup language (SGML)

A set of formatting tags designed to show the logical relationships between text elements. The language of Web documents, HTML (hypertext markup language), is a subset of SGML.

star

* 1. A wildcard character in UNIX (and hence in many Internet applications), it stands for any number of characters; 2. In e-mail and especially on Usenet, where plain ASCII text is the norm, writers place a * before and after words to emphasize them: "I'm *really* sorry about posting your phone number."

star-dot-star

., the DOS wildcard for any file name. (In UNIX, just * will suffice.)

start bit

A bit, set to 0, preceding the transmission of a byte, to tell the receiving computer that the following bits are a character.

star topology

A network architecture in which all the nodes are connected to a central hub computer and not to each other.

startup

(adj) Said of a process or set of instructions that take place when a system or application is started up, usually in order to set user preferences.

STD

An RFC that has been adopted as an Internet standard. (*STD* stands for *standard*.) STDs are numbered consecutively.

stop bit

A bit, set to 1, following the transmission of a byte, to tell the receiving computer that the character is complete. Also, the number of stop bits is one of the things you have to set to use your modem (usually 1 or 2; it depends on the modem you're calling).

stop word

A word so common that it is useless to search for it (such as *and*, *address*, *record*, and so on). Most searchable databases have lists of stop words and filter them out during searches. (Also called *buzz words*.)

store-and-forward

(n) 1. A method of transmitting messages in which they reside at intermediate nodes before being sent to their eventual destination in order to wait for a more cost-effective transmission time or to wait until the receiving network is available; 2. The usual method of e-mail distribution, in which e-mail is stored on a server until the user connects to check her mail, at which point it is forwarded to the user.

streaming

(adj) Said of a media format that enables a player program to begin playing back or displaying the media content quite soon after the data starts flowing (in a *stream*) from the server (as opposed to formats that require that the browser download an entire, possibly huge, file before playing anything).

string

A sequence of characters (letters, numbers, or symbols) to be input or output as data.

stroke

A slash (/).

Structured Query Language (SQL)

An ANSI and ISO standard language used to search relational databases.

stub network

A network that transmits data only among local hosts.

StuffIt

An extremely popular Macintosh compression program that was originally distributed as shareware. It is now a commercial product, but StuffIt Expander, which can uncompress StuffIt and other compressed files, is freeware, available from the `sumex-aim.stanford.edu` FTP site.

subdirectory

In a hierarchical file system, a directory that is the child of another directory.

subdomain

A named portion of an Internet domain, usually a network, university, or company. In `editor @enterzone.berkeley.edu`, `berkeley` is the subdomain.

subnet

A subdivision of a network.

subnet address

The portion of an IP address that identifies a subnet.

subscribe

To join a mailing list or start reading a newsgroup.

substring search

An archie option that specifies that the text to be searched for may be contained within a longer file name and need not match the file name exactly.

suite

1. A group of related protocols; 2. A group of related programs that make up a software package.

summarize

To collect the results of a survey or voting process via e-mail and then post the results to a newsgroup to prevent all the votes or opinions from being posted individually to the Net.

Sun Microsystems

A computer company that makes workstations.

SunOS

(*sun-oss* or *sun-o-s*) A flavor of UNIX for Sun Microsystems workstations.

supercomputer

The most powerful type of computer. Supercomputers cost tens of millions of dollars and are used for very complex calculations and modeling.

SuperTCP/NFS for Windows

Windows TCP/IP software, developed by Frontier Technologies Corp.

superuser

A special user account with unlimited permissions.

surf

(v) To browse, following tangents (trendy slang). You can surf Usenet or gopherspace, but the Web is best suited for surfing, since hypertext links allow you to follow digressions more or less infinitely.

switch

(n) A command-line instruction that modifies a command, often preceded by a slash in UNIX and DOS.

(v) To send packets along whatever route is best without attempting to send related packets via the same routes.

switched access

A network connection that disappears when not needed, such as the type used for SLIP or PPP connections.

Switched Multimegabit Data Service (SMDS)

A new high-speed technology for data networks, developed by Bell Labs.

sx

The Xmodem command for sending (downloading) a file.

synchronous

(adj) Said of communication that happens for both participants at the same time. IRC is a synchronous form of communication, while e-mail is asynchronous.

Synchronous Data Link Control (SDLC)

A data link layer protocol used on IBM SNA networks.

synchronous transmission

A transmission method that uses a clock signal to synchronize the sending and receiving computers in order to regulate the data flow, instead of using start bits and stop bits, as in asynchronous transmission. Data is then sent at a fixed rate.

syntax

Rules for properly formed commands.

system

1. A program that supervises a computer and coordinates all its functions, also called an operating system; 2. An entire computer taken together with all its devices; 3. A large program.

system administrator

Someone who runs or maintains a network.

system file

A file reserved for use by the system and not ordinarily killable by a user (at least not without a warning).

system operator

Someone who runs or maintains a BBS.

Systems Application Architecture (SAA)

A set of standards that specify interfaces (user interface, programming interface, and communications) for IBM software.

Systems Network Architecture (SNA)

A set of communications protocols for networks running on IBM mainframe computers, incompatible with the OSI Model.

sz

The Ymodem command for sending (downloading) a file.

table of services

A service provider's internal list of Internet services (such as FTP, finger, IRC, and so on) offered to users.

talk

(n) 1. One-to-one synchronous chatting over the Net; 2. The UNIX command for initiating or accepting a talk request (the form of the command is talk *username@address*).

talk.

A Usenet hierarchy devoted to discussion, argument, and debate.

talk mode

A UNIX feature in which two or more users can participate in an online conversation.

The Internet Dictionary 935

tape tree

A distributing mechanism for audio cassette tapes employed in some of the music-related newsgroups and mailing lists (see the `rec.music.*` Usenet hierarchy), in which a seed tape is copied by a root participant for a number of branches. Each branch, in turn, dubs copies for their children on the tree, until copies of the tapes reach leaf participants, who have parents but no children in the tree structure.

tar

(n) A UNIX program (*tape archiver*) that concatenates a number of files into a single file (without compressing them).

(v) To create an archive file with the tar program.

.tar

A file extension indicating that the file is a tarred file, an *archive* consisting of several concatenated files.

tar file

A file containing several files, concatenated with the UNIX tar program.

.tar.Z

A file extension indicating that the file is tarred *and* compressed with the UNIX compress program.

T-carrier

A series of long-distance, digital, point-to-point communications circuits numbered T1, T2, T3, T4.

TCP

Transmission Control Protocol, part of the TCP/IP stack. It functions on the transport layer (layer 4) of the OSI Model, establishing and verifying the data connection.

TCP Connect/II

A suite of Macintosh software comprising Internet tools such as e-mail, a Usenet newsreader, FTP, and telnet, developed by InterCon Systems Incorporated.

TCP/IP

A protocol stack, designed to connect different networks, on which the Internet is based. The suite includes protocols for remote login (telnet), file transfer (FTP), e-mail (SMTP), and so on. TCP/IP can work with any hardware or operating system.

TCP/IP was developed by DARPA in the late 1970s as a set of robust internetworking protocols that could survive the partial destruction of constituent networks (as might occur in a nuclear war).

TECO

A once-popular text editor with a powerful built-in programming language, now largely supplanted by emacs.

Telenet

The original name of SprintNet (often confused with *telnet*).

telex

An international communications system made up of linked terminals that can send and receive data. Some online services offer telex access.

telnet

(n) 1. A terminal-emulation protocol (defined in RFC 854) for remote login over the Internet, part of the TCP/IP suite; 2. The UNIX program that uses that protocol.

(v) To log in to a remote computer via the telnet protocol.

10BaseF

The Ethernet specification (802.3 standard) for fiber-optic cable (*10* for the 10 Mbps bandwidth, *base* for baseband, and *F* for fiber-optic).

10Base5

The Ethernet specification (802.3 standard) using "thick" coaxial cable, also known as *thicknet*. (*10* for 10 Mbps bandwidth, *base* for baseband, and *5* for 500-meter-long cable segments.)

10BaseT

The Ethernet specification (802.3 standard) using two pairs of unshielded twisted-pair (UTP) wire. (*10* for 10 Mbps bandwidth, *base* for baseband, and *T* for twisted-pair cable.)

10Base2

The Ethernet specification (802.3 standard) using "thin" coaxial cable (~FB3/8~FE~"), also known as *thin-net*, or *cheapernet*. (*10* for 10 Mbps bandwidth, *base* for baseband, and *2* for 200-meter long cable segments.)

term

A DOS program that enables a personal computer to function as a UNIX terminal-emulation program over a dial-up connection.

terminal

A keyboard-and-monitor combination, one of many, connected to a computer. The terminal passes the user input from the keyboard to the computer and displays the computer's output on the monitor (screen). Large, multiuser computers such as mainframes have traditionally been accessed via terminals, as have UNIX machines.

Terminal Access Controller (TAC)

A device that provides and maintains a dial-up terminal connection to the Internet.

terminal emulation

Behaving like a specific type of terminal (such as a DEC VT100 or VT52 or an IBM 3270), passing keyboard input to a computer and displaying computer output on the screen (possibly in a window).

terminal-emulation program

Software a personal computer uses to imitate a specific type of terminal (such as a VT100, ANSI, or TTY terminal) and connect to a host.

terminal/host computing

The model of computing used by dumb terminals and host computers, in which the terminal is only a messenger and the host does all of the processing.

terminal server

A device that enables several modems (usually assembled on a modem bank) or terminals to connect to a host on one channel by sending a combined signal.

terminal window

A window in a graphical user interface in which a terminal-emulation program displays an emulated terminal screen connected by network to a remote computer.

terminator

A device connected to the end of a LAN cable to prevent signals from being transmitted.

*.test

Any of the newsgroups with names such as misc.test, alt.test, rec.test, and so on, designated for test posts. If you post to a *.test newsgroup, daemons all over the Internet send you e-mail acknowledgments when your post reaches their site. It is a breach of netiquette to post test messages to any newsgroup other than *.test newsgroups.

One trap often set for newbies is a post with its follow-up line set to a *.test newsgroup. Anyone who responds to the post without noticing and removing the *.test group will suffer a mailbox flooded by well-meaning daemons.

test post

A post with no meaningful content, posted to a newsgroup (preferably a *.test newsgroup) so that users can determine whether their newsreader software and Internet connection are working properly.

text editor

An application for editing text files, usually less fully featured than a word processor. The Notepad accessory in Windows is a text editor, as are the UNIX programs vi, pico, emacs, ee, and joe, among others.

text file

Also *ASCII file* or *ASCII text file*, a file containing only ASCII characters. This means no formatting—no bold or italics, no headers, footers, margin adjustments, nonbreaking hyphens, and so on.

text file transfer

A form of file transfer, both with FTP and with uploading/ downloading programs (kermit, zmodem, etc.) used to transfer files containing only ASCII characters. (Newline characters are automatically converted for the operating system being transferred to.)

text transfer

1. A text file transfer; 2. A transfer of text directly from a local file to a remote computer, as if typed directly from the keyboard, or from the output of a remote program running on a remote host computer to the terminal window and/or to a text file on the local computer.

T4

A long-distance, digital, point-to-point communications circuit developed by AT&T that transmits a signal at 274.176 Mbps, with up to 168 T1 channels (4,032 channels of 64 Kbps), handling both voice and data.

TFTP

Trivial File Transfer Protocol, a simplified version of FTP that does not include password protection.

thanks in advance

Often abbreviated *TIA* or more whimsically as *aTdHvAaNnKcSe*, a common sign-off for requests made in Usenet or elsewhere on the Internet.

The Internet Adapter (TIA)

A UNIX program that enables a dial-up shell account to emulate a SLIP connection, allowing the user to run Internet software native to his desktop environment without the full costs (or full functionality, either) of real SLIP. TIA is available from Cyberspace Development at http://marketplace.com/.

thread

(n) 1. A series of messages related to the same topic in a discussion group, such as an original post and related follow-ups. It is appropriate to read an entire thread before contributing to it to avoid repeating something that may already have been contributed one or more times; 2. A process that is part of a larger process or program.

threaded newsreader

A newsreader that organizes posts according to thread and allows you to read your way up or down a thread, such as trn, tin, and Newswatcher.

3270

An IBM terminal type.

throughput

A measure of the rate of data transmitted, expressed as bits per second.

TIA

1. An abbreviation for *thanks in advance*; 2. The Internet Adapter, a SLIP-emulation program for UNIX.

TidBITS

A weekly newsletter about the Internet and Macintosh computers, distributed via e-mail by Adam Engst. For more information, contact info@tidbits.com.

tilde

The ~ character, used to issue commands in the UNIX mail program.

tilde escape

A command in the UNIX mail program that starts with a tilde character (~) and performs a function, rather than inserting text into the mail.

Time to Live (TTL)

An IP packet header field that tells how long the packet should be held before it's purged.

time out

(v) To fail, as a network process, because the remote server or computer has not responded in time, to close a connection after waiting too long for acknowledgment.

timeout

(n) The occasion when a remote computer times out.

tin

A threaded newsreader for UNIX.

tn3270

A program similar to telnet that emulates a 3270 terminal connected to an IBM mainframe.

toggle

(n) A logical or physical switch (or even a single bit) that can be set to two positions, usually on and off. A light switch is a toggle.

(v) To change a switch or bit from one state to the other (from 0 to 1 or back again).

token ring

A (typically IBM) type of network architecture in which nodes are connected in a closed circle. The nodes continually pass a token (a special message) around the circle. To transmit data, a node has to wait until it's "it." Then the data rides along with the token and gets off at the right stop.

TokenTalk

An Apple product that enables AppleTalk protocols to work on a token ring network.

T1

A long-distance, digital, point-to-point communications circuit, developed by AT&T, that transmits a DS1 signal at 1.544 Mbps, with 24 (voice) channels of 64 Kbps. If the circuit uses fewer than 24 channels, it's called *FT1* or *fractional T1*. T1 is also called *High-Cap*, *T-span*, and *T-carrier*.

tool

A utility program, a useful program that performs a set function.

topic drift

As threads wear on in discussion groups, they frequently stray from the original topic, as listed in the Subject header. Some posters take the initiative of changing the Subject line to spawn new threads.

This same phenomenon is noticed in e-mail conversations, in which the original header, perhaps preceded by *Re: Re: Re:* outlasts its relevance.

topic group

Any electronic common space for people who share an interest.

topology

Any type of physical network layout, organizing the devices and the cables connecting them. Most LANs have bus topology, star topology, or ring topology.

traditional newsgroup hierarchy

The seven newsgroup hierarchies in Usenet news proper: comp., misc., news., rec., sci., soc., and talk. New newsgroups in any of the traditional hierarchies can only be created after a formal process, including a request for discussion and a call for votes.

traffic

1. Mailing list or newsgroup posts, taken as a whole; 2. Network activity, measured in bits per second, kilobits per second, or megabits per second.

trailer

Information following the data in a packet, signifying the end of the data and possibly including error-checking information.

transceiver

A device that both transmits and receives signals, exchanging frames between a node and a network.

Transmission Control Protocol (TCP)

Part of the TCP/IP stack. It functions on the transport layer (layer 4) of the OSI Model, establishing and verifying the data connection.

transmit network

A network that communicates with at least two other networks and transmits data among networks as well as among local nodes.

transport layer

Layer 4 of the OSI Model, controlling delivery and verification of messages.

tree administrator

In a tape tree, the person who designs the tree and administers the process, not necessarily the person who provides the seed (usually not, in fact).

trn

A threaded newsreader for UNIX, based on rn.

troff

A UNIX text processor that can produce output for typesetting equipment, superseded largely by TEX.

Trojan horse

An attack program, hidden inside a seemingly benign program, that enables the program's creator to gain access to the user's system.

troll

(v) 1. To deliberately post egregiously false information to a newsgroup in hopes of tricking dense know-it-alls into correcting you; 2. From the fishing term, to explore information sources or communication methods on the Net, looking for something specific, as in the *New Yorker* cartoon in which a boss tells his employee: "I hear you've been trolling for babes on the Internet."

(n) A deliberately false post.

TrueSound

Microsoft's own streaming sound format.

Trumpet newsreader

Windows newsreader software that works with NNTP, available by anonymous FTP from `biochemistry.cwru.edu`.

Trumpet for Windows

Windows Internet software featuring a newsreader and a mail program, available by anonymous FTP from `biochemistry.cwru.edu`. Also referred to as Trumpet WinSock.

T3

A long-distance, digital, point-to-point communications circuit, developed by AT&T, that transmits a signal at 44.746 Mbps, with up to 28 T1 channels (762 voice channels of 64

Kbps), running over a leased line, usually fiber-optic cable.

T2

A long-distance, digital, point-to-point communications circuit, developed by AT&T, that transmits a signal at 6.3 Mbps, with up to four T1 channels (92 channels of 64 Kbps). T2 is used within telephone company networks, not commercially.

tunafish test

A series of posts in 1994 to a `*.test` newsgroup via the `anon.penet.fi` anonymous remailer service that may have compromised the identities of some of the remailer's users.

tunneling

Encapsulating a datagram of one protocol within that of a different protocol to transport the enclosed data across an intervening backbone that does not support the former protocol.

tuple

(*toople*) A pair of related values in a routing table (the network number and the number of hops to that network).

TurboGopher

1. A gopher client for the Macintosh, available via anonymous FTP from `sumex-aim.stanford.edu`; 2. An improved version of the original gopher software developed at the University of Minnesota.

Tweak

1. To make small changes in order to get something just exactly perfect; 2. To tease someone in a minor way.

twilight zone

An imaginary place where only IRC channel ops may go.

twisted-pair cable

Cable comprising four or more copper wires, twisted in pairs (one grounded, one carrying a signal) to reduce interference, usually one pair for sending, one for receiving. There are two types of twisted-pair cable: shielded twisted-pair (STP) and unshielded twisted-pair (UTP).

.txt

A file extension indicating a text file.

Tymnet

A global public data network, offering local dial-up access in one hundred countries, including access to some online services and Internet service providers.

Ultrix

A port of UNIX that runs on VAXen.

UN*X

A generic term for the various flavors and ports of UNIX, used also to refer to UNIX without including the ~TM notice erroneously thought to be required by AT&T.

unbalanced line

A cable containing electrically unequal wires, such as a coaxial cable.

uncompress

(v) To uncompact a compressed file.

(n) A UNIX uncompression program.

uncompression

A method of uncompacting a compressed file.

UnCover

A search service provided by CARL with access to over ten thousand journals.

undelete

To restore a deleted file. This is not possible on UNIX systems.

undernet

A network of IRC servers formed as an alternative to EFnet, the "mainstream" IRC net. Undernet IRC servers always have domain names of the form *city.state*.undernet.org or *city.country*.undernet.org.

underscore

In e-mail and Usenet posts, only plain text may appear, so to suggest underlining and italics, users often precede and follow text with the underscore character (_), like so: "The origin of fnord is explained in _Illuminati!_"

undirected information

Information intended for the public at large, such as Usenet or mailing list posts.

Unicode

A standard 16-bit character code (as compared with ASCII, which is a 7-bit character code) with 65,536 possible characters, as well as the ability to encode color and graphics. A possible eventual successor to ASCII.

uniform resource locator (URL)

A Web address (also *universal resource locator*). It consists of a protocol, a host name, a port (optional), a directory (optional), and a file name (optional). In the URL `http://ezone.org/ez`, the protocol is HTTP, the host name is `ezone.org`, and the file name is `ez`. URLs can be used to address other Internet resources besides Web pages, such as FTP sites, gopher servers, telnet addresses, and so on.

Universal Asynchronous Receiver/Transmitter (UART)

A device that combines the transmitting and receiving functions of asynchronous communications over a serial line.

Universal Time Coordinate (UTC)

Greenwich mean time, used to synchronize computers on the Internet.

University of Maryland Info Database

A huge information resource intended to demonstrate the breadth of potential information on the Net. Telnet to `info.umd.edu` and log in as *info*.

UNIX

(*you-nix*) An 32-bit, multiuser, multitasking operating system common to workstations and dominant (but getting gradually less so) on the Internet. It was originally developed at Bell Labs in 1969 by Ken Thompson, and is now owned by Novell, although it has spawned many ports and clones.

Dealing with UNIX is a frustrating barrier to most Internet newbies, what with its arbitrary command abbreviations, rigorous syntax, case-sensitivity, lack of an undelete feature, and so on. Fortunately, alternative routes to the Internet that require no knowledge of UNIX (or very little) are sprouting up every day.

UNIX box

A computer running the UNIX operating system.

unix2dos

A program that converts UNIX text files to DOS format, by changing the line breaks.

UNIX wizard

A helpful UNIX expert, such as those who answer questions in the `comp.unix.wizards` newsgroup.

unmoderated

(adj) Said of lists and newsgroups whose posts are not vetted by a moderator.

unselect articles

(v) To remove the selection tag from Usenet articles selected for reading.

unshielded cable

Cable that's not protected from electromagnetic or radio-frequency interference by a foil shield.

unshielded twisted-pair (UTP)

A cable containing unshielded wire in twisted pairs.

unsubscribe

1. To remove one's name from a mailing list. 2. To remove the name of a newsgroup from the list of subscribed groups.

untar

(v) To separate a tarred file into its component parts.

upload

To transfer a file over a modem from a desktop computer to a remote computer.

upstream

(adv) Where your newsfeed comes from.

URL

See *uniform resource locator*.

Usenet

1. From *User's Network* and often written *USENET*, the collection of computers and networks that share news articles. Usenet is *not* the Internet (though it overlaps pretty well). It's sometimes called the world's largest electronic bulletin board. 2. The newsgroups in the traditional newsgroup hierarchies.

Usenet cabal

A imaginary set of net.gods who establish the policy for Usenet.

Usenet News

The traffic of posted articles in the Usenet newsgroups.

Usenet newsgroup

A newsgroup in one of the seven traditional newsgroup hierarchies. Newsgroup names go from the general to the specific: `rec.music .makers.bass` is the newsgroup for musicians who play the bass.

Usenet Oracle

A cooperative project of mostly humorous questions and oracular responses. Anyone can submit questions or answers. To find out more about the Oracle, send mail to `oracle@cs.indiana.edu` with the word *help* in the Subject line, or read the `rec.humor.oracle` newsgroup.

user

Anyone logged on to a computer system or network.

user agent

One way to refer to a mail program.

User Datagram Protocol (UDP)

A connectionless transport protocol in the TCP/IP suite. UDP is used for Simple Network Management Protocol, database lookups, and other functions instead of TCP, because it does not add overhead to the transmission.

username

A login, the name a user logs in with. Also, the first part of an Internet e-mail address (up to the @). Choose your username well. In many ways it is more important (on the Net) than your real name. It's the name people see most often.

/usr

A directory on many UNIX machines containing users' home directories.

utility

A program that performs some useful function, often something that helps monitor or tweak an operating system.

.uu

A file extension that indicates a uuencoded file.

UUCP

From *Unix to Unix Copy Program*, a protocol and a program for copying files, news, and mail from one UNIX box to another during intermittent dial-up connections.

.uud

A file extension that indicates a uuencoded file.

uudecode

(*you-you-decode*, n) A UNIX program that converts uuencoded files back into their binary form.

(v) To turn a uuencoded file back into its normal form.

.uue

A file extension that indicates a uuencoded file.

uuencode

(*you-you-encode*, n) A UNIX program that converts binary files into an ASCII format suitable for inclusion in an e-mail message (and one-third again as long as the original).

(v) To convert a binary file into a text form that can be sent as part of an e-mail message.

uupc

A Macintosh program that can transfer files using the UUCP protocol.

vaporware

Software that a developer has been promising for a long time (possibly as a marketing strategy), but which is nowhere in sight.

VAX

A DEC minicomputer (the name comes from *Virtual Address Extension*) with 32-bit architecture, a successor to the PDP-11 series, favored by hackers. Mythological source of Microsoft's Windows NT. The truth is simpler; two engineers from the VAX team worked on the Windows NT team.

verbose

(adj) A mode of certain programs, such as FTP, in which they return as much information as possible and narrate their processes for the user's benefit.

Veronica

An searchable index of gopher menus (it supposedly stands for *Very Easy Rodent-Oriented Netwide Index to Computerized Archives*, but more likely is named after the Archie Comics character Veronica (note the other applications Archie and Jughead). The results are themselves presented to you as a gopher menu.

v.42

A modem standard defined by CCITT, describing error control.

v.42bis

A modem standard defined by CCITT, describing data compression.

vi

A common but difficult to learn UNIX text editor with two modes, edit and insert. (To start inserting text, press *i*; to stop inserting, quit, and save, press Escape, then *ZZ*.)

viewer

1. An application used to view image files, such as GIFs and JPEGs; 2. By extension, any auxiliary application that enables the user to open, see, or play a file in a special format.

vine

A variation on the tape tree concept used for digital tapes (for which there is no generational loss of quality from one copy to the next), in which the source tape is passed along to each participant in the vine, copied, and then passed again.

Viola

Also called *ViolaWWW*, a Web browser for the X Window operating environment.

virtual

(adj) Said of something that exists only in software, not physically.

virtual address

A memory location accessed by an application program in a system with virtual memory such that intervening hardware and/or software maps the virtual address to real (physical) memory. During the course of execution of an application, the same virtual address may be mapped to many different hardware addresses as data and programs are paged out and paged in to other locations. Contrast with *hardware address*.

virtual circuit

A technology used in packet-switched networks, in which users share communication paths that appear to each as a dedicated end-to-end connection.

virtual community

Also *online community*, an electronic community of people who share some discussion groups or chat rooms and behave socially much like people in a small village who know all their neighbors. The Well is often cited as a virtual community.

virtual reality

An overused term for computer-simulated three-dimensional environments with which the user can interact, often by wearing equipment such as gloves and goggles. By analogy, role-playing environments such as MUDs are sometimes considered examples of virtual reality.

virus

A program that deliberately does damage to the computer it's on, often hidden inside an apparently benign program.

VM

An IBM mainframe operating system (it stands for *Virtual Machine*), similar to MVS.

VMS

A operating system used on VAXen (it stands for *Virtual Memory System*).

vmsnet.

An alternative hierarchy in the Usenet mold dedicated to discussion of the VMS operating system.

vn

A now rare UNIX newsreader (it stands for *visual newsreader*), on which the Windows newsreader WinVN is loosely based.

.voc

The audio format for the Sound-Blaster sound card.

voice-net

A facetious name for the telephone system, as often cited with phone numbers in sig blocks.

volume

A generic name for a storage medium or portion thereof, such as a disk, diskette, or network file server.

Vote ACK

Also called a *Mass ACK*, a Usenet post listing the e-mail address of each person who votes for and against a proposed newsgroup.

VRML

Virtual Reality Modeling Language; VRML files usually have a .wrl extension.

VT52

A DEC terminal type, less commonly emulated than the VT100.

v.32

A modem standard defined by CCITT, describing 9600-bps modems.

v.32bis

A modem standard defined by CCITT, describing 14400-bps modems.

VT100

A terminal type, originally designed by DEC for VAXen, that has become the standard terminal. If you dial up a UNIX shell, then your communications program probably emulates a VT100.

WAIS-for-Mac

Macintosh WAIS client software made by WAIS Incorporated, available via anonymous FTP from `ftp.wais.com`.

WAIS Manager for Windows

Windows WAIS client software available via anonymous FTP from `sunsite.unc.edu`.

WAN

Wide area network, a long-distance computer network using dedicated phone lines and/or satellites to interconnect LANs across large geographical distances up to thousands of miles apart.

warm boot

(v) To reboot a computer without turning it off.

Washington University Services

A gateway to many Internet services, libraries, and other information resources. To use it, telnet to `wugate.wustl.edu` and log in as `services`.

.WAV

(*wave*) A sound file format from Microsoft, perhaps the most widespread sound format used on the Internet.

Web

See *World Wide Web*.

Web address

A URL, consisting of a protocol, a host name, a path, and a file name. In the address of my home page, `http://ezone.org:1080/homies/xian.html`, the protocol is HTTP, the host name is `ezone.org`, the port number is 1080, the path is `/homies/` and the file name is `xian.html`.

Web browser

Client software for the World Wide Web, such as Lynx, Netscape, or Internet Explorer. A Web browser displays HTML and other documents, and allows the user to follow hypertext links.

Webcasting

Also called *netcasting* or *push*, a method of distributing information on the Web by pre-arranged downloading and scheduled updates. It gives the impression of information being broadcast from a Web server to your desktop.

Web page

An HTML document on the World Wide Web, usually containing hypertext links to other documents on the Web, often on other Web servers entirely. Surfing the Web consists of following links from page to page.

Web server

An application that stores Web pages and associated files, databases, and scripts, and serves up the pages to Web browsers, using HTTP.

Web site

A site on the Internet that hosts a Web server.

well-connected

(adj) Said of a network with dependable e-mail links and a relatively full newsfeed.

wetware

Also *liveware*, slang for human beings, seen as part of a greater computer system including software and hardware.

whatis

An Archie command that looks for key words in a software-description database containing file names and associated descriptions, used to find key words to search for.

wheel

(n) A privileged user, someone with unrestricted access to some particular system resource.

white pages

Informal name for databases of Internet e-mail addresses or other information. For example, telnet to wp.psi.net and log in as fred.

whois

1. One of many online databases of Internet e-mail addresses and other identifying information about users, admins, domains, and so on; 2. The UNIX command that draws on the whois resource.

WIBNI

Wouldn't it be nice if (written only; also *wibni*).

wildcard

A special character used to represent either any single character or any number of characters. Usual wildcard characters are ? (for single characters) and * (for any number of characters).

WIMP

(adj) From *Window, Icon, Menu, Pointing device*, said of a graphical user interface such as Macintosh, Windows, or X Window).

WinCIM

CompuServe Information Manager for Windows.

Windows

Short for *Microsoft Windows*, a
multitasking operating environment
that runs on top of MS-DOS and provides IBM PCs and compatibles with
a GUI (graphical user interface) not
unlike that of the Macintosh, including icons, dialog boxes, menus, and a
mouse pointer.

Windows 95

The current version of Windows.

Windows NT

A 32-bit operating system based on
the Windows operating environment
with built-in networking capabilities
and no remaining traces of DOS.

Windows socket

The conventional method of configuring the Windows operating environment for TCP/IP networking.

Windows for Workgroups

A version of Windows with built-in
peer-to-peer networking capabilities.

WinGopher

A gopher client for Windows.

winkey

A winking smiley:

;-)

Winqvt/Net

Combined mail, news, telnet, and
FTP software for Windows. Available
via anonymous FTP from wuarchive
.wustl.edu.

Winsock

A type of Windows application
that sets up a socket and works with
TCP/IP protocols to establish an
Internet connection.

WinVN

A newsreader for Windows based
on the UNIX vn newsreader that communicates with Network News Transfer Protocol-based news servers,
available via anonymous FTP from
titan.ksc.nasa.gov.

WinWAIS

A Windows WAIS client program,
available via anonymous FTP from
ridgisd.er.usgs.gov.

WinZip

A Windows compression file that
can handle pkzip and other compression formats.

wizard

Someone who really understands
how a piece of hardware or software
works and is willing to help newbies

workaround

A temporary patch for a bug that
avoids but does not fix the underlying
problem.

workgroup

A group of users, often on a LAN,
working on the same project.

working directory

The current directory, the directory you're "in" right now.

workstation

A computer on a network, usually of a type somewhere in the range between microcomputers and minicomputers.

world

The default distribution choice for newsgroup posts. Post distribution can also be limited to geographical areas (by their two-letter abbreviations) or to *local*.

World Wide Web

Also called the *Web, WWW, W3*, and *w3*; an interlinked collection of hypertext documents (Web pages) residing on Web servers and other documents, menus, and databases, available via URLs (uniform resource locators). Web documents are marked for formatting and linking with HTML (hypertext markup language), and Web servers use HTTP (hypertext transport protocol) to deliver Web pages. The Web was invented as an online documentation resource by physicists at the CERN European Particle Physics Laboratory in Switzerland.

worm

A program that duplicates itself repeatedly, potentially worming its way through an entire network.

:wq

The *save and quit* command in vi, often seen at the end of newbies' posts when they fail to switch back from insert mode to edit mode before typing the command.

write

To save, to copy the contents of memory onto a storage medium such as a disk.

wrt

With respect to (written only; also *WRT*).

WS_FTP

A Windows FTP client program made by John A. Junod, available via anoymous FTP from `129.29.64.246` in the `/pub/msdos` directory.

WSArchie

A Windows Archie client.

WSGopher

A Windows gopher client.

WSIRC

A Windows IRC client.

w3

See *World Wide Web*.

wustl archives

A huge FTP archive at `wuarchive.wustl.edu`.

www

The original text-based UNIX Web browser, developed at CERN European Particle Physics Laboratory. To try out www (if it's not installed on your system), telnet to `info.cern.ch`.

WWW

See *World Wide Web*.

WWW Browser for the Macintosh

A Macintosh Web browser available via anonymous FTP from `info.cern.ch`.

WYSIWYG

(*wizzy-wig*) *What you see is what you get*, a description of display technology (as in GUIs) that closely matches printed output on the screen, or at least claims to.

x

The exit command in many UNIX programs.

.x

The extension for SuperDisk self-extracting archive files and More DiskSpace compressed files.

X Consortium

A group of hardware developers that oversees the X Window standard.

Xerox Network System (XNS)

A suite of communications protocols, similar to TCP/IP, developed by Xerox Corporation and later used by Novell and other network developers.

Xerox PARC

Xerox's legendary Palo Alto Research Center, where the modern GUI (which combines the use of a mouse, windows, and icons) was invented, not to mention laser printers and LANs.

X.500

A CCITT- and ISO-recommended standard for electronic directory services, using a distributed database of X.400 information, including usernames, postal addresses, telephone numbers, fax numbers, and so on.

X.400

A CCITT and ISO standard for international e-mail handling. X.400 is different from Internet e-mail standards, but mail can be transferred from one system to the other via gateways.

XGopher

X Window gopher client software, available via anonymous FTP from `boombox.micro.umn.edu`.

Xibo

The evil anti-Kibo. This unfortunate devil has many fewer adherents than his nemesis.

XLibrary for the Macintosh

Macintosh software for designing SLIP front ends to network services, available via anonymous FTP from `sumexaim.stanford.edu`.

Xmodem

A file-transfer protocol supported by just about every communications program. Xmodem sends 128-byte blocks and is used for uploading and downloading to and from dial-up Internet accounts and BBSs.

Xmodem-CRC

An extension of Xmodem using more stringent error-checking (called a *cyclical redundancy check*).

XOFF

Ctrl+S (ASCII 19), a character that pauses data transmission.

XON

Ctrl+Q (ASCII 17), a character that resumes data transmission.

XON/XOFF

A form of flow control, using ASCII characters 17 and 19 to control the flow of data over an asynchronous connection, usually one of the choices for configuring a modem to connect to a dial-up service.

XOR

A Boolean operator meaning *exclusive or*. A text search with XOR between two words matches any documents containing one word or the other, but not both.

XRemote

X Window software for connecting to a network over phone lines.

X.25

A CCITT-recommended standard for connecting computers to public packet-switched networks that specifies transmission and error-correction protocols, now largely superseded by frame relay.

XWAIS

X Window WAIS client software available via anonymous FTP from `sunsite.unc.edu`.

X Window

Also called *X*, an open, nonproprietary graphical user interface often used with UNIX. It was developed at MIT and is independent of the hardware or operating system it runs on. It's easy to find Internet client software for X Window. There are implementations of X called Motif and OpenLook.

YAFIYGI

(*yaffy-yiggy*, also written *yafiygi*) *You asked for it, you got it*, applied to certain forms of word-processing and desktop publishing applications in which the user gets no preview of the eventual appearance of the document (the opposite of WYSIWYG).

yellow pages

1. An informal name for the database of machine names and addresses of the InterNIC Registration Service; 2. An informal name for the security and file-access database of a UNIX system.

Ymodem

Also called *Xmodem 1K*, a file-transfer protocol supported by many communications programs. Ymodem sends 1024-byte blocks, is faster than Xmodem, and can send multiple files.

.z

A file extension indicating a file that has been compressed with GNU Zip.

.Z

A file extension indicating a file that has been compressed with the UNIX compress program.

'zine

Also *zine*, a fanzine or other underground publication, possibly produced on company time or using office equipment. Most 'zines are still produced on paper and mailed to subscribers, but many are archived on the Internet, and there are also some e-zines, electronic 'zines distributed by e-mail, by gopher, or on the Web.

zip

(v) To compress a file with pkzip or another program.

(n) A compression program.

.zip

A file extension indicating the file has been compressed with the programs pkzip, zip, or WinZip.

zip codes

U.S. postal zip codes as of 1991 can be found via anonymous FTP from oes.orst.edu in the /pub/almanac/misc directory with the file name zicode.txt.Z.

zip file

A compressed file.

zip up

(v) To compress a file with pkzip or with another program.

Zmodem

A batch file-transfer protocol supported by some communications programs. Zmodem is faster than Ymodem and Xmodem and recovers from disconnections more gracefully.

zone

(n) A logical (as opposed to physical) group of users on a LAN, such as an AppleTalk network, within a larger group of interconnected networks.

Zone Information Protocol (ZIP)

The protocol AppleTalk routers use to exchange zone names and network numbers.

Zone Information Table (ZIT)

A list of zone names and corresponding network numbers used by AppleTalk routers.

zone list

A list of AppleTalk zones in the Chooser.

zone name

1. The text name of a zone, corresponding to a network number; 2. The name of an AppleTalk network zone.

.zoo

A file extension indicating a file compressed with the zoo210 program.

zoo210

A UNIX file compression program.

Zterm

A Macintosh communications and terminal emulation application.

Z39.50

The ANSI information-retrieval service definition and protocol specification for library applications, a format by which all Internet database information could potentially be made available.

ZZ

A *quit and save* command in vi.

INDEX

Note to Reader: In this index, **boldfaced** page numbers refer to primary discussions of the topic; *italics* page numbers refer to figures.

Symbols & Numbers

<!-- --> tag (HTML), **690–691**

!WorldVillage Games, 536

" (quotation marks)

    for HTML attributes, 554–555

    in Internet searches, 185

+ (plus sign) in Internet searches, 185

< and > (angle brackets) for HTML tags, 552

@ sign in e-mail address, 26

_private folder, 604

1 Cool Button, 638

2 Minute Trivia, 530

3Space Assistant, 269

5 Alarm Trivia, 530

A

A/S/L, 247

<A> tag (HTML), **691–693**

a2b format, **451**

Abalone, 517

Ability.org, 535

About Internet Explorer, 135

absolute font size, 598

Absolute Zero, 516

accessibility issues in Web page design, **659–660**

Accommodation Search Engine, 397

Accor hotels, 396

acoustic coupler, 393

Acrobat (Adobe), 268

<ACRONYM> tag (HTML), **693–694**

Acrophobia, 531

action games, **516–517**

active links, color of, 596, 597

Active Names Email Tracker, **108–109**

active page

    in FrontPage, 610

    spell checker for, **620–621**

active web, 602

ActiveX controls, 150, 269

activity indicator, in Netscape Navigator, 180

add-on. *See* helper programs

Add Songs To Music Library dialog box, 508, *508*

B

<B> tag (HTML), 589, **699–700**

Back button, in Internet Explorer toolbar, 125, 138

Backgammon, 517

background color, **594–595**

Baker Street Assistant, 363

bandwidth

and multimedia, 257

Web page design issues, **658–659**

Barnes & Noble, 356

<BASE> tag (HTML), **700**

<BASEFONT> tag (HTML), 597, **700–701**

basic rate interface (BRI), 465

Basketball, 527

BBEdit Lite, 629

<BDO> tag (HTML), **701**

Best of the Web, 140

Best Western hotels, 395

Better Business Bureau Online, 437

Better Web Business Bureau, 437

Beyerdynamic DT831 headphones, 460

<BGSOUND> tag (HTML), **701–702**

bibliofind.com, 357

bidding, winning strategies, 419–420

<BIG> tag (HTML), **702**

billing date, for America Online, 280

Bingo, 518

BinHex, 58

bios, including in tag information, 505

bitmap, including in tag information, 505

Blackjack, 520

Blender, 524

<BLINK> tag (HTML), 589, **702–703**

blocking e-mail in Hotmail, 94

<BLOCKQUOTE> tag (HTML), 576, **703–704**

BlueTooth, 390

board games, **517–519**

body of newsgroup messages, 228

<BODY> tag (HTML), **704–706**

attributes, 595, 596

bombing, 110

BookFinder.com, 357

Bookmark Properties dialog box, *174*

bookmarks, 568

in Netscape Navigator, 169, **171–175**

creating and opening, **171–175**

deleting, **175**

folder creation, **173–174**

moving, **175**

in Winamp, *485*, **485–486**

F

X

Y

Z

ABOUT THE CONTRIBUTORS

Some of the best—and best-selling—Sybex authors have contributed chapters from their current books to *Internet Complete, Second Edition*.

Christian Crumlish   contributed material from *The Internet: No experience required* as well as material written specifically for *Internet Complete, Second Edition*.

Mr. Crumslish is a writer, painter, and citizen of the Net. He has been writing and editing computer books for many years and is the publisher of *Enterzone*, a hypermedia magazine on the World Wide Web.

Richard A. Sherman   contributed material from *Mr. Modem's Internet Guide for Seniors*.

"Mr. Modem", a.k.a. Richard A. Sherman, is a nationally recognized seniors advocate and syndicated columnist. His "Ask Mr. Modem" column appears in 50 regional publications across the U.S. and reaches more than 2.5 million households each month. President of Get-the-Net, Inc., an Internet consulting firm, Richard is a highly acclaimed, entertaining, and technologically motivating speaker specializing in Internet and online communications.

Alan R. Neibauer   contributed material from *Internet! I Didn't Know You Could Do That...*

Mr. Neibauer is an experienced author and computer consultant who has written dozens of best-selling computer books. A graduate of the Wharton School, University of Pennsylvania, he has helped numerous companies and institutions make their presence known on the Internet.

Alan Simpson   contributed material from *Internet To Go*.

Mr. Simpson is a software consultant, best-selling author, and teacher who has been active in the computer industry for over two decades. His books include dozens of popularly, critically, and technically acclaimed titles.

Bob LeVitus   contributed material from *iMac! (and iBook) I Didn't Know You Could Do That...*

Mr. Levitus ("Doctor Mac") has written and co-written 32 popular computer books (strongly focused on the Mac), which have sold over a million copies worldwide. He is a columnist for the *Houston Chronicle*, *Current Technology*, and *MacHome Journal*. Bob writes a weekly question and answer column for MacCentral (www.maccentral.com) and has been published, all told, in more than a dozen computer magazines.

Guy Hart-Davis and Rhonda Holmes   contributed material from *MP3! I Didn't Know You Could Do That...*

Mr. Hart-Davis is the author of a dozen computer books, including *Word 2000 Developer's Handbook and Mastering VBA 6*. Ms. Holmes has ten years of experience in computer books. Rhonda plays guitar, and Guy tries to play the drums.

Gene Weisskopf   contributed material from *Microsoft Frontpage 2000: No experience required* and *Mastering Internet Explorer 4* (coauthored with Pat Coleman).

Mr. Weisskopf is a software applications developer whose articles are frequently published in computer magazines. He has written several books for Sybex, including *ABCs of FrontPage 97*, *ABCs of Excel 97*, and *FrontPage 98: No experience required*. He has also taught spreadsheet and introductory computer courses for many years.

E.Stephen Mack and Janan Platt Saylor   contributed material from *HTML 4.0: No experience required*.

Mr. Mack is a Web designer, software trainer, and computer consultant. He has worked with several major companies over the last 10 years, written computer articles, and co-created two best-selling computer books. Ms. Platt Saylor has 15 years experience as a controller and consultant teaching people to use computers. She publishes multimedia poetry, often from her online poetry workshop, Alien Flowers.

Gayle Ehrenman and Michael Zulich   contributed material from *Mastering Palm Organizers*.

Ms. Ehrenman is a high-tech reporter and editor with InternetWeek. She has ten years of experience working for computer publications and Internet services. Mr. Zulich is an IT consultant and writer with twenty-three years of high-tech experience.

Pat Coleman   contributed material from *PC Complete* and *Mastering Internet Explorer 4* (coauthored with Gene Weisskopf).

Mr. Coleman writes about the Internet, Windows, and Windows applications and is the co-author of *Mastering Intranets* and *Mastering Internet Explorer 4*, both from Sybex.

Laura Arendal   contributed material written specifically for *Internet Complete, Second Edition*.

Ms. Arendal has long labored behind the scenes at Sybex—editing, re-writing, even ghost writing—to produce books of the highest quality. *America Online Amazing Secrets* is the first book to bear her name—and only one of many to have benefited from her knowledge and abilities.

Chris Collins   contributed material written specifically for *Internet Complete, Second Edition*.

Mr. Collins had worked in advertising and computer book publishing most of his adult life, until he discovered that he was actually supposed to be some kind of political scientist. He's recently gotten his Master's in social work, and has worked with people regarding civil liberties issues and juvenile justice intiatives. He currently lives in Indianapolis.

Deborah S. Ray and Eric J. Ray   contributed material from *Mastering HTML 4.0, Second Edition*.

Mr. and Ms. Ray are owners of RayComm, Inc., a technical communications consulting firm that specializes in cutting-edge Internet and computing technologies. Together they have coauthored more than 10 computer books, including the first edition of *Mastering HTML 4* from Sybex. They also write a syndicated computer column, which is available in newspapers across North America.

SYBEX BOOKS ON THE WEB

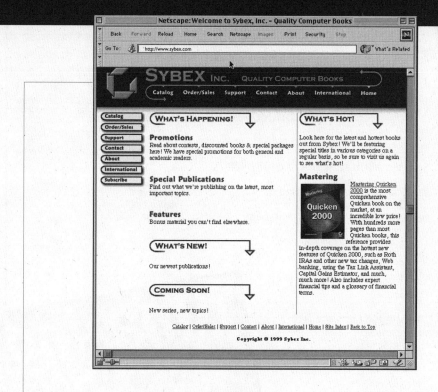

At the dynamic and informative Sybex Web site, you can:

- view our complete online catalog
- preview a book you're interested in
- access special book content
- order books online at special discount prices
- learn about Sybex

www.sybex.com

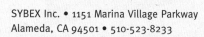

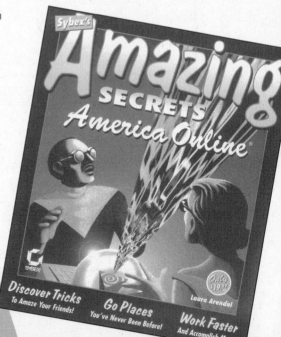